Supply Chain Management Strategies and Risk Assessment in Retail Environments

Akhilesh Kumar
Indian Institute of Technology Kharagpur, India

Swapnil Saurav
JDA Software, India

A volume in the Advances in Logistics, Operations, and Management Science (ALOMS) Book Series

IGI Global
DISSEMINATOR OF KNOWLEDGE

Published in the United States of America by
IGI Global
Business Science Reference (an imprint of IGI Global)
701 E. Chocolate Avenue
Hershey PA, USA 17033
Tel: 717-533-8845
Fax: 717-533-8661
E-mail: cust@igi-global.com
Web site: http://www.igi-global.com

Library of Congress Cataloging-in-Publication Data

Names: Kumar, Akhilesh, 1982- editor. | Saurav, Swapnil, editor.
Title: Supply chain management strategies and risk assessment in retail environments / Akhilesh Kumar and Swapnil Saurav, editors.
Description: Hershey, PA : Business Science Reference, [2018]
Identifiers: LCCN 2017013426| ISBN 9781522530565 (hardcover) | ISBN 9781522530572 (ebook)
Subjects: LCSH: Business logistics--Management. | Retail trade--Management.
Classification: LCC HD38.5 .S896134 2018 | DDC 658.8/700687--dc23 LC record available at https://lccn.loc.gov/2017013426

This book is published in the IGI Global book series Advances in Logistics, Operations, and Management Science (ALOMS) (ISSN: 2327-350X; eISSN: 2327-3518)

British Cataloguing in Publication Data
A Cataloguing in Publication record for this book is available from the British Library.

For electronic access to this publication, please contact: eresources@igi-global.com.

Advances in Logistics, Operations, and Management Science (ALOMS) Book Series

John Wang
Montclair State University, USA

ISSN:2327-350X
EISSN:2327-3518

Mission

Operations research and management science continue to influence business processes, administration, and management information systems, particularly in covering the application methods for decision-making processes. New case studies and applications on management science, operations management, social sciences, and other behavioral sciences have been incorporated into business and organizations real-world objectives.

The **Advances in Logistics, Operations, and Management Science** (ALOMS) Book Series provides a collection of reference publications on the current trends, applications, theories, and practices in the management science field. Providing relevant and current research, this series and its individual publications would be useful for academics, researchers, scholars, and practitioners interested in improving decision making models and business functions.

Coverage

- Production management
- Networks
- Computing and information technologies
- Decision analysis and decision support
- Operations management
- Finance
- Political science
- Information management
- Marketing engineering
- Risk Management

IGI Global is currently accepting manuscripts for publication within this series. To submit a proposal for a volume in this series, please contact our Acquisition Editors at Acquisitions@igi-global.com or visit: http://www.igi-global.com/publish/.

The Advances in Logistics, Operations, and Management Science (ALOMS) Book Series (ISSN 2327-350X) is published by IGI Global, 701 E. Chocolate Avenue, Hershey, PA 17033-1240, USA, www.igi-global.com. This series is composed of titles available for purchase individually; each title is edited to be contextually exclusive from any other title within the series. For pricing and ordering information please visit http://www.igi-global.com/book-series/advances-logistics-operations-management-science/37170. Postmaster: Send all address changes to above address.

Titles in this Series

For a list of additional titles in this series, please visit: www.igi-global.com/book-series

Motivationally Intelligent Leadership Emerging Research and Opportunities
Michael A. Brown Sr. (Florida International University, USA)
Business Science Reference • copyright 2018 • 139pp • H/C (ISBN: 9781522537465) • US $155.00 (our price)

Novel Six Sigma Approaches to Risk Assessment and Management
Vojo Bubevski (Independent Researcher, UK)
Business Science Reference • copyright 2018 • 251pp • H/C (ISBN: 9781522527039) • US $200.00 (our price)

Enterprise Resiliency in the Continuum of Change Emerging Research and Opportunities
Raj Kumar Bhattarai (Tribhuvan University, Nepal)
Business Science Reference • copyright 2018 • 186pp • H/C (ISBN: 9781522526278) • US $150.00 (our price)

Examining Cultural Influences on Leadership Styles and Learning From Chinese Approaches to Management Emerging Research and Opportunities
Valerie Zhu (Xi'an University of Science and Technology, China)
Business Science Reference • copyright 2017 • 207pp • H/C (ISBN: 9781522522775) • US $125.00 (our price)

Globalization and the Ethical Responsibilities of Multinational Corporations Emerging Research and Opportunities
Tarnue Johnson (Argosy University - Chicago, USA)
Business Science Reference • copyright 2017 • 110pp • H/C (ISBN: 9781522525349) • US $125.00 (our price)

Multi-Criteria Decision Making for the Management of Complex Systems
Albert Voronin (National Aviation University of Ukraine, Ukraine)
Business Science Reference • copyright 2017 • 201pp • H/C (ISBN: 9781522525097) • US $175.00 (our price)

Handbook of Research on Manufacturing Process Modeling and Optimization Strategies
Raja Das (VIT University, India) and Mohan Pradhan (Maulana Azad National Institute of Technology, Bhopal, India)
Business Science Reference • copyright 2017 • 530pp • H/C (ISBN: 9781522524403) • US $285.00 (our price)

Managerial Strategies and Green Solutions for Project Sustainability
Gilman C.K. Tam (Independent Researcher, China)
Business Science Reference • copyright 2017 • 255pp • H/C (ISBN: 9781522523710) • US $180.00 (our price)

Optimal Management Strategies in Small and Medium Enterprises
Milan B. Vemić (Higher School of Academic Studies "DOSITEJ", Serbia)
Business Science Reference • copyright 2017 • 437pp • H/C (ISBN: 9781522519492) • US $225.00 (our price)

IGI Global
DISSEMINATOR OF KNOWLEDGE

701 East Chocolate Avenue, Hershey, PA 17033, USA
Tel: 717-533-8845 x100 • Fax: 717-533-8661
E-Mail: cust@igi-global.com • www.igi-global.com

Editorial Advisory Board

Table of Contents

Detailed Table of Contents

Global retail business has become diverse and latest Information Technology (IT) advancements have created new possibilities for the management of the deluge of data generated by world-wide business operations of its supply chain. In this business, external data from social media and supplier networks provide a huge influx to augment existing data. This is combined with data from sensors and intelligent machines, commonly known as Internet of Things (IoT) data. This data, originating from the global retail supply chain, is simply known as Big Data - because of its enormous volume, the velocity with which it arrives in the global retail business environment, its veracity to quality related issues, and values it generates for the global supply chain. Many retail products manufacturing companies are trying to find ways to enhance their quality of operational performance while reducing business support costs. They do this primarily by improving defect tracking and better forecasting. These manufacturing and operational improvements along with a favorable customer experience remain crucil to thriving in global competition. In recent years, Big Data and its associated technologies are attracting huge research interest with academics, industry practitioners, and government agencies. Big Data-based software applications are widely used within retail supply chain management - in recommendation, prediction, and decision support systems. The spectacular growth of these software systems has enormous potential for improving the daily performance of retail product and service companies. However, there are increasingly data quality problems resulting in erroneous tesing costs in retail Supply Chain Management (SCM). The heavy investment made in Big Data-based software applications puts increasing pressure on management to justify the quality assurance in these software systems. This chapter discusses about data quality and the dimensions of data quality for Big Data applications. It also examines some of the challenges presented by managing the quality and governance of Big Data, and how those can be balanced with the need of delivery usable Big Data-based software systems. Finally, the chapter highlights the importance of data governance; and it also includes some of the Big Data managerial practice related issues and their justifications for achieving application software quality assurance.

In this book chapter, the authors highlight the potential of big data analytics for improving the forecasting capabilities to support the after-sales customer service supply chain for a global manufacturing organization. The forecasting function in customer service drives the downstream resource planning processes to provide the best customer experience at optimal costs. For a mature, global organization, its existing systems and processes have evolved over time and become complex. These complexities result in informational silos that result in sub-optimal use of data thereby creating inaccurate forecasts that adversely affect the planning process in supporting the customer service function. For addressing this problem, the authors argue for the use of frameworks that are best suited for a big data ecosystem. Drawing from existing literature, the concept of data lakes and data value chain have been used as theoretical approaches to devise a road map to implement a better data architecture to improve the forecasting capabilities in the given organizational scenario.

Recent technologies in the market trends have demanded the significant need for the possible solutions to intelligent video cameras that are nothing but intelligent video analytics. Today in the retail industry, intelligent video analytics has gone beyond the tradition of the domain of security and loss prevention by providing retailers insightful business intelligence such as store traffic statistics and queue data. This provides accurate and reliable information by monitoring continuously through a large number of video cameras events that human operators or employees can overlook. This paper gives an overview study of applications of intelligent video analytics in retail management as well as the state-of-the-art computer vision techniques behind them to analyze the data. It clearly demonstrates that the importance of the role that intelligent video systems and analytics play can be found in a variety of applications of intelligent video Analytics in the field of Retail Management.

Few industries are changing more rapidly than today's retail sector. A still-turbulent economy, new selling channels, advanced digital technologies, and increasingly demanding consumers all challenge retailers to find new ways of remaining relevant and competitive. The purchasing decision journey for consumers

Foreword

It gives me immense pleasure to write this foreword for the book *Supply Chain Management Strategies and Risk Assessment in Retail Environments* by Akhilesh Kumar and Swapnil Saurav. Retailing business is a major part of economy of every country in the world. Until recently, every company viewed Supply Chain as necessary evil and had only one focus - how to reduce cost. Now with business becoming more global in nature and shelf life of products decreasing, supply chain is playing a role of competitive weapon for these companies. Retailers are not only looking to control the expenses but also look up to supply chain to give top-line revenue growth. To achieve the competitive advantage, the retailers need to have a responsive supply chain and best in class customer service. I am happy to see that the book has focused on such issues.

The wide range of topics covered by this book are very relevant for today's competitive times. As competition in the retailing industry is getting developed immensely, the customers are now demanding more, better and customized services. The papers which has been selected as part of this book will serve well for all the students and practitioners of Retail industry.

Book covers topics like Big Data, Retail Analytics, Green Supply chain along with traditional topics makes this book must to have for everyone interested to understand the Retail world and how supply chain can provide a competitive edge to the Retailers.

Manoj K. Tiwari
IIT Kharagpur, India

Preface

Dear reader, we would like to thank you for showing interest in our book. Visiting this page or taking up this book in your hand implies you have an interest in Supply chain or in retail management or in both. We believe in sharing of knowledge and if you choose to read through this book, we are sure that you will enjoy and learn as much as we have enjoyed and learnt editing through this book.

HOW THE IDEA OF WRITING THIS BOOK WAS BORN?

Indian Institute of Technology, Kharagpur is India's premium institute which encourages and promotes research activities in various areas including Supply Chain Management. Institute also promote engagement with industry. JDA Software, as a company, constantly promotes industry and academia interaction. JDA actively participates in events like SCPC and organizes OPTSUM event. A daylong event, the SCPC aims to bring together the leading supply chain practitioners from across industries to showcase achievements and share best practices, while building a community which can influence policy making.

During one such industry-academia interactions the two editors met and the idea of editing a book on Retail Supply Chain was born. The editors felt that there is a disconnect between industry and academia especially in India. We firmly believe that industry and academia should work and exchange ideas for the betterment of the supply chain community. This book is a small effort from our side aiming to bridge the gap.

ABOUT THE TITLE OF THE BOOK

Supply Chain Management (SCM) is critical to business operations and success. Many well-known authors have said that these days, competition is between the supply chains of the companies hence SCM has become increasingly importance for the organizations and at the same time it is getting more challenging for the practitioners. e-Commerce, omnichannel experience, pricing and globalization has led to lengthening supply chains by involving more partners which has only made the SCM more volatile and complex. SCM is the design, maintenance, and operation of supply chain processes for satisfaction of end user needs. In the light of cut throat competition in the market, organizations have to focus on continuous improvement of the extended supply chain processes. The battleground becomes supply chain versus supply chain. The coordination of materials, information, and financial flows among suppliers, manufacturers, distributors, and retailers of products and services enables higher supply chain efficiency, quicker delivery, and higher customer service at substantially lower cost. Retailers and their suppliers are under tremendous pressure to deliver goods to more destinations faster and at the same time be cost efficient. In the book, we cover issues that occur in current dynamic environment and how the practitioners can deal with complex issues.

With the advancement in technology, Retail management field has become exciting and is flourishing with new and bigger opportunities. Experts in the Retail Management field are constantly looking for new innovative ways to buy, develop, and sell products, and to enhance customer experience leading to higher sales. At the same time, the industry is also facing the challenge of meeting the demands where the requirements of customers are ever changing. We are also witnessing a renewed interest in topics like Cold Chain Logistics and Green Supply Chain. Emergence of online shopping and the need for Omni Channel experience requires retail management professionals to think outside the box along with excellent decision-making skills. One needs strong problem-solving skills with sole focus on providing excellent customer service. With the emergence of social media, the power has shifted to customers. Starved of time, consumers seek both convenience and good customer service. They demand product availability, expect regular promotions and price reductions, and have an infinite range of nutritional, lifestyle, and fashion preferences. Smart shoppers also want consistent pricing across various channels and stay more informed through the information available via social media. SCM has played, and continues to play, a strategic role in retail organizations throughout the recession and remains a key driver of business success and competitive advantage in today's challenging market.

OBJECTIVE

Supply chain experts are always on lookout for tips for tracking and expediting inventory in today's 'I-want-it-now,' multi-channel retail world. So, what steps can, and should, retailers take to make sure their supply chain operations are running smoothly? Over the past few decades, companies have embraced supply chain management as a vital area of emphasis for companies. Many companies have risen to the top of their respective industries by forging effective supply chain management techniques into strategic weapons. In short, supply chain management means effectively handling the relationships between one's suppliers and buyers. But in practice, the field covers a wide range of issues, including supplier selection, purchasing, risk management, logistics, distribution, pricing, demand and supply management, and channel coordination.

This comprehensive and timely publication aims to be an essential reference source, building on the available literature in the field of supply chain management focusing on aspects of retail, analytics, and risk management. It explores the risks, challenges, and opportunities in the SCM space. Our aim is to discuss the latest developments in the field of retail management and provide insights into this dynamic industry. It is our hope that this book will provide the necessary resources for policy makers, technology developers, and managers to adopt and implement supply chain best practices.

The book is aimed to discuss supply chain issues in the changing business paradigms. The book will bring together research topics from various practicing professionals whose main interests are in dealing with the challenges in the Supply Chain Management (SCM) landscape, and discuss the issues of contemporary importance from academic and practitioners' perspectives.

Objective and value:

1. New insights on how supply chain management can be aligned to achieve competitive advantage.
2. An increased understanding of the impact of supply chain management on costs and financial performance.
3. Appreciation of approaches and frameworks that can be applied to different market segments.
4. Reviews of the latest thinking on supply chain strategy, planning and execution.
5. Ability to address the management of supply chain risks.
6. Understanding of the impact of enhanced supply chain performance on the overall profitability of the organization.

TOPICS THAT HAVE BEEN COVERED

We are very pleased with the response we received for our call for paper. We received over 35 abstracts. After the strict review criteria that we had set for the book, we shortlisted 16 chapters. These chapters include the following topics relating to Retail, analytics, e-commerce, and risk in the area of supply chain management:

- Retail Management
- Supply Chain Planning and Inventory Management
- Omni Channel Retail
- Supply Chain Analytics/Big Data in SCM
- Perishable Goods Supply Chain Management
- Coordination and Collaboration in Supply Chain Networks
- Supply Chain Visibility and Risk Management
- Green Supply Chain
- E-Commerce Supply Chain
- Customer Loyalty
- Innovation in Retail Management

This book has been designed to provide a variety of interesting supply chain risks, challenges, and opportunities. Overall, the 16 chapters in the book touch upon many of the important supply chain issues facing modern retail organizations. Each chapter contains real-time challenges for the management of retail organization or those supporting the retailers' business, leaving enough room for the reader to ponder, analyze, and practice the next best steps. Most of the chapters are primarily based on qualitative research, while couple of chapters are based on the authors' experience and presented as case studies and quantitative analysis. The book is truly the "strategic supply chain for retailers" where the topics cover almost all aspects of retail supply chain.

One of the most attractive features of this book is that we have equal contribution of information from both industry experts and academic world. Not only are many supply chains' discussions global in nature, but the chapters also discuss the challenges faced by the industry and the areas where researchers are putting their effort to solve the same. Even though the coordination between the academic world and industry experts could be improved, we are glad to find that there is no disconnect between them. This book also serves this purpose. We have put in our best effort to bring both the industry experts and researchers on the same page.

INTRODUCTION TO BOOK CHAPTERS

We present brief introduction about each of the chapter here.

Chapter 1: Building High Quality Big Data-Based Applications in Supply Chains

Global retail business has become diverse and latest Information Technology advancements have created new possibilities for the management of world-wide business operations. This is combined with data from sensors and intelligent machines, commonly known as Internet of Things data. This data, originating from the global supply chain, is simply known as Big Data – because of its enormous volume, the velocity with which it arrives in the global retail business environment, its veracity to quality related issues, and values it generates for the global supply chain. In recent years, Big Data and its associated technologies are attracting huge research interest with academics, industry practitioners, and government agencies. Big Data-based software applications are widely used within retail supply chain management – in recommendation, prediction, and decision support systems. he chapter highlights the importance of data governance; and it also includes some of the Big Data managerial practice related issues and their justifications for achieving application software quality assurance.

Chapter 2: Improving Forecasting for Customer Service Supply Chain Using Big Data Analytics

In this book chapter, the authors highlight the potential of big data analytics for improving the forecasting capabilities to support the after-sales customer service supply chain for a global manufacturing organization. The forecasting function in customer service drives the downstream resource planning processes to provide the best customer experience at optimal costs. For a mature, global organization, its existing systems and processes have evolved over time and become complex. These complexities result in informational silos that result in sub-optimal use of data thereby creating inaccurate forecasts that adversely affect the planning process in supporting the customer service function. For addressing this problem, the authors argue for the use of frameworks that are best suited for a big data ecosystem. Drawing from existing literature, the concept of data lakes and data value chain have been used as theoretical approaches to devise a road map to implement a better data architecture to improve the forecasting capabilities in the given organizational scenario.

Chapter 3: Applications of Intelligent Video Analytics in the Field of Retail Management – A Study

Recent technologies in the market trends have demanded the significant need for the possible solutions to intelligent video cameras that are nothing but intelligent video analytics. Today in the retail industry, intelligent video analytics has gone beyond the tradition of the domain of security and loss prevention by providing retailers insightful business intelligence such as store traffic statistics and queue data. This provides accurate and reliable information by monitoring continuously through a large number of video cameras events that human operators or employees can overlook. This paper gives an overview study of applications of intelligent video analytics in retail management as well as the state-of-the-art computer vision techniques behind them to analyze the data. It clearly demonstrates that the importance of the role that intelligent video systems and analytics play can be found in a variety of applications of intelligent video Analytics in the field of Retail Management.

Chapter 4: Realizing the Potential of Retail Analytics

Few industries are changing more rapidly than today's retail sector. A still-turbulent economy, new selling channels, advanced digital technologies, and increasingly demanding consumers all challenge retailers to find new ways of remaining relevant and competitive. The purchasing decision journey for consumers involves multiple steps, many of which are now being captured, digitized, and transformed into metrics and data. As this data becomes an implied derivative of essential retail and consumer technologies, the focus is shifting from how to acquire the data to how to extract insights from it— insights that can be turned into differentiation and competitive advantage for the retailer and a better shopper experience for the consumer.

Chapter 5: Technologies Enabling Omni-Channel: Understanding Key Success Factors for IT Framework

The retail industry has been scaling up by better co-ordination among channel partners, improving shipment delivery time at a lower possible cost over last few years. Looking at the Indian scenario, large logistics companies such as Bluedart, FedEx, Gati, etc. have launched dedicated services for online retailers. However, entrance and elevation of e-commerce focused logistic companies such as Chhotu, Mudita, Unicommerce and Delhivery seem to be promising and can be the real game changer. These companies offer solutions that address the various pain-points pertaining to the supply chain of e-commerce companies, which traditional and big supply chain & logistic providers so far failed to do. This is a global phenomenon. Despite considerable improvement in recent past, many logistics providers still struggle to cope up with inadequate infrastructure leading to operational inefficiencies to support their services. Some of such operational concerns, but not limited to, are wrong delivery, unaccepted shipment pick-ups, product unavailability leading to promise to deliver.

Chapter 6: Omni-Channel Retailing – The Risks, Challenges, and Opportunities

Technological developments, changes in consumer behavior and intense competition are the most important threats of today, affecting many sectors as well as the retail industry. Innovative retailers, in the face of with these threats, have embraced and implemented the omni-channel retailing approach, which is the next step in multi-channel. However, other players in the retail industry lag behind this change. The aim of this chapter is to establish the experiences of innovative retailers that have adopted omni-channel retailing in the context of risks, challenges and opportunities. The research data were obtained using questionnaire method from the retailers in Turkey, one of the developing countries. As a result of the study, it was found that retailers who would adopt the omni-channel retailing would have the opportunities to be able to dominate all channels, provide better services to the customers, increase customer satisfaction and loyalty, keep in constant contact with the customers, get better customer recognition and increase sales volume.

Chapter 7: Designing Distribution Centres for Omni-Channel Fulfilment – In Indian Context

The E-Commerce market is thriving and poised for robust growth in Asia. The success of eCommerce players depend on their understanding of the market and offering various types of features. This paper gives an overview of the future of E-Commerce in India and discusses the future growth segments in India's E-Commerce. Also find out various factors that would essential for future growth of Indian E-commerce. And represent the various opportunities for retailers, wholesalers, producers and for people. In this paper we found that the Overall E-Commerce will increase exponentially in coming years in the emerging market of India. A review of the literature revealed that, to date, no research has been conducted on the supply chain that is needed to support the growth of eCommerce business in a developing country such as India. This study aim at studying - why will e-commerce have an impact on supply chain" and "where will e-commerce affect the supply chain in future.

Chapter 8: Retail Management and Electronic Retailing

This chapter explains the overview of retail management; retail management and technology; the aspects of Electronic Retailing (e-tailing); e-tailing and Electronic Commerce (e-commerce); the perspectives on online consumer behavior; and the advanced issues of e-tailing in retail environments. Retail management focuses on the processes that go into ensuring consumers can obtain the products they want from their chosen retail store. Effective retail management helps company distributes the finished products created by the business to consumers in order to determine and satisfy what buyers want and require. E-tailing is a powerful marketing technique for the right product with the right message to the right person. The chapter argues that effective retail management and e-retailing applications generate business revenue, build brand awareness, and pave the way for broader distribution in retail environments.

Chapter 9: Enhancing Closed-Loop Supply Chain in Global Supply Chain

This chapter explains the overview of Closed-Loop Supply Chain (CLSC); CLSC activities and reverse logistics outsourcing in global supply chain; and the applications of CLSC in global supply chain. CLSC, the integration of the forward and reverse supply chains, is an emerging area of interest as firms seek to reduce the costs of product returns, increase profits through value recovery, and meet more rigorous environmental standards. In CLSC, the original manufacturer will take the used product and remake it. CLSC deals with the uncertainty in the timing, location, quantity, and quality of returned products. CLSC integrates the returns of end-of-life products from end-users to retailers, manufacturers, and suppliers for refurbishment, remanufacturing, and recycling. The chapter argues that enhancing CLSC has the potential to reach strategic goals toward sustainability in global supply chain.

Chapter 10: Predicting Online Returns

The E-commerce industry is growing year on year in double digits. But customers today are not only buying more through their computers, they are also returning more. The volume of these returns is such that it just can't be ignored. E-tailers today are following many practices to handle these returns but the 'predictability' factor is still missing from their approaches. This paper tries to fulfill that void. The framework suggested in this paper will help the E-tailers to predict the probability of a particular item being returned by a particular shopper. The idea is that if the E-tailer will know the probability of return during any transaction he/she would certainly be better equipped to handle the situation.

Chapter 11: Building an Effective Customer Loyalty Program

Customer loyalty schemes is a practice, employed by retailers, to reward their loyal customers. It entails giving incentives such as loyalty cards, reward points, etc. These also serve as a repository of information about a customer which helps in targeted marketing. This chapter analyses some of the successful customer loyalty programs by companies, discusses some of the reasons of failures of such program and looks at what industry experts have to say in this regard. We then collate all these information to suggests a process to identify and choose the right customer loyalty programs for a company.

Chapter 12: Classification Essay of SCRM Research

This article investigates the current developments in research and practices in the domain of Supply Chain Risk Management (SCRM) through a systematic and typological approach in order to improve the understanding of SCRM field. This field has created a strong scientific and professional polemic, resulting in an exponential growth of published research work, reports and article. However, it has been discussed that SCRM lacks of typological approach by several authors underlining this fact through their frameworks. In response, this review examines various perceptions, notions, definitions, drivers and sources of Supply Chain Risk (SCR), in order to identify major SCRM frameworks. This analysis is required in order to identify the main issues that needed to be addressed in the field of SCRM. Thus, the objective of this paper is to classify these frameworks so as to identify news issues, opportunities and directions for further study and researches

Chapter 13: Perishable Goods Supply Cold Chain Management in India

India has seen a phenomenal growth and occupies the top three positions in production from last decades in production of horticulture produce, dairy and meat products over the last decade. But at present, India's share in global farm trade is still very small even with such large production volumes. This is mainly caused due to lack of cold chain infrastructure which includes both storage and transportation facilities. The cold chain industry in India is still at a nascent stage and despite large production of perishables, the cold chain potential still remain untapped due to high share of single commodity cold storage, high initial investment (for refrigerator units and land), lack of enabling infrastructure like power and roads, lack of awareness for handling perishable produce and lapse of service either by the storage provider or the transporter leading to poor quality produce. Cold chain systems are crucial to the growth of global trade in perishable products and to the worldwide availability of food and health supplies.

Chapter 14: Wastage and Cold Chain Infrastructure Relationship in Indian Food Supply Chain – A Study From Farm to Retail

India, the world's second-largest producer and one of the centers of origin of Fruits and Vegetables is also one of the biggest food wasters in the world. The challenge of feeding India's billion plus people is not really about agriculture and food production but getting the quality food to the concerned people in a right time. The biggest contributors to this waste are lack of temperature controlled transport and inadequate quality of cold storage facilities for both Farmers and Food sellers i.e. retailers. What India lacks, and needs, is a well-developed, world-class cold chain infrastructure. Without it, India's problems are vast and likely to grow. In this chapter, the authors tries to outlines the extent of Fruits and Vegetables waste in India (at various stages from farm to retail) and its ramifications on food production and safety. Authors also highlighted the challenges faced by cold chain sector in India and a roadmap for improvements. As Indian economy is based on agriculture, development of Cold Chain infrastructure from farm to retail points will play a crucial role.

Chapter 15: Supply Chain Management in Pharmaceutical Industry – Opportunities and Challenges for Retailers

In this research paper, author has studied top pharmaceutical companies around the globe and their relationship with pharmacies. Based on the analysis author has identified current challenges their supply chain is facing and how IT can help them to make their supply chain more responsive and reliable. IT framework which can address the supply chain challenges has also been proposed here. Second part of the paper deals with how retailers can help the industry to overcome these challenges. Pharma companies need to partner with pharmacies for a win-win situation and this partnership can address most of the challenges being faced by the industry. This partnership will help in various ways like getting accurate information across the entire chain at any point and at any location, Instant access to real-time demand by the end user, visibility of all handovers in the supply chain and helps in setting-up seamless collaboration between all parties.

Chapter 16: Developing Sustainable Retail Food Value Chain for India – A Challenge for the Next Century

Ever increasing population, rising prosperity supported by ongoing urbanization has accelerated the demand for food in India. At the same time, area under agriculture is decreasing and food production is coming under pressure owing to limitations on resources and other environmental considerations. In the coming decades, doing more with less will be a key priority for all those involved in food production. In this chapter, we will also look at the challenges and opportunities available for the food supply chain management. This chapter sets out the premise that the food industry, throughout the value chain, has a tremendous opportunity, as well as an obligation, to meet the needs of new, more sophisticated and more demanding consumers while satisfying shareholders' demands for returns—and in doing so creating a sustainable food supply for the new millennium.

TARGET AUDIENCE

This book has been designed to appeal to policy makers, academicians, researchers, advanced-level students, technology developers, and government officials. University instructors will find useful information that can be used for their curriculum. We also expect that supply chain managers and business professionals in general will find the book to be of great interest. The chapters are full of ideas for addressing sticky supply chain issues. Plus, it always helps to consider how to address challenges before being faced with them.

Although some topics are vast and lengthy, many of the chapters in this book are intentionally designed to be relatively short and focused, allowing the reader to delve directly into the issues at hand. We hope that you will find this book useful in extending your research exposure to pertinent topics in retail supply chain management and assisting in furthering research efforts in this field.

CONCLUSION

We have compiled various chapters in this book that discusses and addresses the risks, challenges, and opportunities in the retail space of supply chain management. We have shortlisted chapters that address different aspects of merchandizing, assortment, fulfillment, distribution, store operations, and related topics. The authors of the chapters have explored the current trends and evaluated the industry best practices. It is a handbook for both researchers and practitioners, and provides the current state of the art on recent trending topics. Looking ahead, the study also cites several key issues that should be on the radar of SCM executives moving forward, including sustainability, fluctuating fuel costs, government regulations, streamlining multi-channel supply chain operations, and utilizing the latest technological advancements. We hope you will find the information useful.

Thank you for your time.

Acknowledgment

We would like to express our immense gratitude to all those who saw us through this book; to all those who provided support, talked things over, read, wrote, offered comments, allowed us to quote their remarks, and assisted in the editing, proofreading, and designing this book.

We would like to thank each author for taking time out of their schedules and making their contribution to this book. We greatly value your contribution without which this book would not have been in our hands.

We would also like to thank the members of the editorial advisory board for helping us in the process of reviewing, selecting, and editing each chapter. Thanks to Maria Rohde and other members from IGI for staying with us till the end and encouraging us at every step.

Last but not the least, a big thank you to our family members, who supported and encouraged us in spite of all the time it took us away from them.

Akhilesh Kumar
Indian Institute of Technology Kharagpur, India

Swapnil Saurav
JDA Software, India

Section 1
Data Analytics Applications in Retail

Chapter 1
Building High Quality Big Data-Based Applications in Supply Chains

Kamalendu Pal
City, University of London, UK

ABSTRACT

Global retail business has become diverse and latest Information Technology (IT) advancements have created new possibilities for the management of the deluge of data generated by world-wide business operations of its supply chain. In this business, external data from social media and supplier networks provide a huge influx to augment existing data. This is combined with data from sensors and intelligent machines, commonly known as Internet of Things (IoT) data. This data, originating from the global retail supply chain, is simply known as Big Data - because of its enormous volume, the velocity with which it arrives in the global retail business environment, its veracity to quality related issues, and values it generates for the global supply chain. Many retail products manufacturing companies are trying to find ways to enhance their quality of operational performance while reducing business support costs. They do this primarily by improving defect tracking and better forecasting. These manufacturing and operational improvements along with a favorable customer experience remain crucil to thriving in global competition. In recent years, Big Data and its associated technologies are attracting huge research interest with academics, industry practitioners, and government agencies. Big Data-based software applications are widely used within retail supply chain management - in recommendation, prediction, and decision support systems. The spectacular growth of these software systems has enormous potential for improving the daily performance of retail product and service companies. However, there are increasingly data quality problems resulting in erroneous tesing costs in retail Supply Chain Management (SCM). The heavy investment made in Big Data-based software applications puts increasing pressure on management to justify the quality assurance in these software systems. This chapter discusses about data quality and the dimensions of data quality for Big Data applications. It also examines some of the challenges presented by managing the quality and governance of Big Data, and how those can be balanced with the need of delivery usable Big Data-based software systems. Finally, the chapter highlights the importance of data governance; and it also includes some of the Big Data managerial practice related issues and their justifications for achieving application software quality assurance.

DOI: 10.4018/978-1-5225-3056-5.ch001

INTRODUCTION

The retail business world is grappling with major changes of new retail channels, increasing global customers, and growing complexity of supply chain operations. Customers are increasingly influencing how retail businesses design and set out their supply chain operations. These demanding customers can now do their shopping *anywhere* and *anytime*, and expect a more fulfilling experience from retailers. However, many retail businesses are dealing with how to find an innovative approach to sourcing, replenishment and distribution strategies to address these changes. Retail businesses are starting to consider seriously how best to optimize their supply chain operations to face fast-changing customer demand, while minimizing corporate expenditure and achieving healthy growth.

A retail supply chain consists of interconnected activities, and their associated business processes together to provide value-added service to its customers. Customer-engaged retail companies, from *automobile dealers* to highly attractive summer *beachwear makers*, always need different stakeholders' information for their supply chains. An entire network of manufacturers and distributors, transportation and logistics agencies, financial institutions, warehouses and freight-forwarders work together to make sure that the right goods and services are available at the right price, where and when the customers want them. Having supplied value-added services (e.g. products and associated customer services), the supply chain does not terminate. The retail supply chain is comprised of several steps from the front end, through the customer request, supply chain order processing initiation, quality assurance assessment for products and services, relevant training processes for staffs, customer support facilities, to maintenance and replacement facilities. Retailers are investing in *state-of-the-art* operational practices to optimize both cost and efficiency of their supply chain.

In a typical retail supply chain, raw materials are purchased from suppliers and products are manufactured at one or more manufacturing plants. Then they are transported to intermediate storage (e.g. warehouse, distribution center) for packaging and shipping to retailers or customers. The path from supplier to customer can include several intermediaries such as wholesalers, warehouse, and retailers, depending on the products and markets. In this way, supply chain management relates to business activities such as inbound and outbound transportation, warehousing, and inventory control. Importantly, it also embodies the information systems necessary to monitor these business activities. Figure 1 presents a simple diagrammatic representation of a retail supply chain, which consists of two separate legal entities, a retailer and a manufacturer. The retailer owns the first two nodes on the left-hand-side of the diagram,

Figure 1. A schematic diagram of retail supply chain

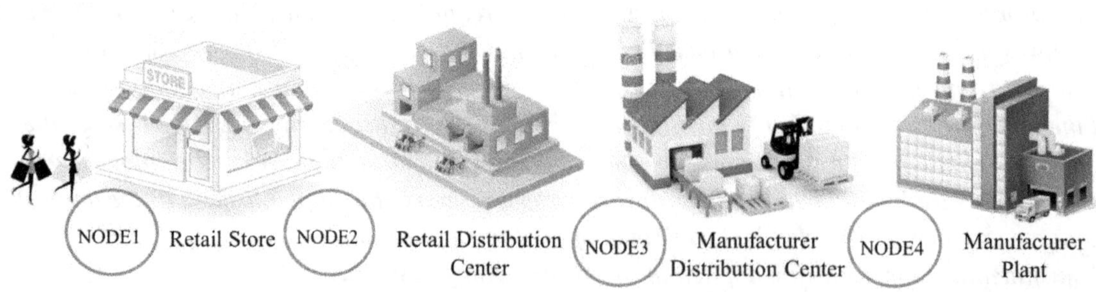

which consists of the retail store and the retail distribution center; and the manufacturer owns the last two nodes, the manufacturing distribution center and the plant.

Increased internationalization of retail industries is changing the operational practices of global retail supply chains, and many retailers have adopted new business models, either by outsourcing or by establishing business-alliances in other countries. Globalization has also led to changes in operational practices, where products are designed and manufactured in one part of the world and sold in another. The retail supply chain has become more global in its geographical scope; the international market is getting more competitive and customer demand oriented. Customers are looking for more variety as well as better *quality assured* products and services.

This evolution of many retail supply chain networks means that their members are working across different time zones, and bringing together many culturally diverse workforces. These teams are often quickly brought together and coordinated in nearly real-time to provide retail deliverables within short time spans and limited resources. In this way, collaboration and coordination among these teams plays a key role in delivering the ultimate customer experience; and it is also more information intensive. Under this working environment, nearly real-time collaboration between mobile and geographically distributed retail supply chain members is a very difficult task. It highlights the need for an efficient communication infrastructure that provides reliable on-demand access to supply process information accurately (Pal, 2016).

Information Systems (IS) play a significant role in coordination and decision-making for global retail supply chains. Recent development in IS, such as Enterprise Resource Planning (ERP), Material Requirement Planning (MRP), Customer Relationship Management (CRM), Vendor Managed Inventory Systems (VMIS), Warehouse Management Systems (WMS), Transportation Management Systems (TMS), marketing and collaborative planning, forecasting and procurement systems, help to make global retail supply chains more efficient. The generation of large volumes of supply chain data by these systems has provided an impetus for global retail supply chains to extract information from raw data to improve business performance.

More and more business activities are digitized and computerized; new sources of information and machineries with global retail supply chains bring new types of information. The amount of digital information pertaining to a specific retail supply chain fluctuates in real-time on different business topics, such as price, weight, packaging dimension, *carbon foot print* for consignments, weather forecast for consignments supply and delivery routes. Business practitioners get excited about 'Big Data' – the term *du jour* that describes the expanding universe of available data outside of that traditionally circulating in a retail company's CRM, ERP, or MRP systems stored for analysis. These new data sources originate in cyber-physical computing environments of global retail supply chains. For example, with every online survey from customers, Global Positioning System (GPS) signals from trucks or trains, tweets from the head of marketing, and every Radio-Frequency Identification Device (RFID) tagged package speeding off to the shrink-wrap station, retailers have more data than they know what to do with. Retail supply chain operations are hotbeds of data-inputs sought, captured, and reported. Some of this data produced within the global retail chain is unstructured and unwieldy – not suitable for applications based on standard relational database management systems. There is, however, a huge amount of unwanted noise in generated data simply waiting to be released into the operational environment. Intelligent business analysis brings rigorous data manipulating techniques with special purpose software, the *business analytic* platform, for timely decision making.

Retail supply chain mangers are increasingly seeking to '*win with data*'. They are reliant upon data to gain visibility into expenditure, looking for trends in corporate operational cost and related performance, and support process control, inventory monitoring, production optimization, and process improvement efforts. In fact, many retail businesses are awash in data, with many seeking to capture data analysis as a means for gaining a competitive advantage. In this way, appropriate data capture, data cleaning, and different data analysis techniques are each thought to be part of an emerging competitive area that will transform the way in which retail supply chains are designed and managed. In addition, due to the huge volume of generated data, the fast velocity of arriving data, and the large variety of heterogeneous data, the Big Data-based applications bring new challenges. It is a hard job to test the correctness of a Big Data-based software system due to its enormous size and timeliness. This is an important concern for Big Data-based software system practitioners who are motivated to come up with innovative ways of thinking about how data is produced, organized, and analyzed. Thus, Big Data-based systems quality assurance plays a crucial role.

The main objective of this chapter is to provide some perspectives on Big Data-based decision-making software applications and their quality related issues. The reminder of this chapter is organized as follows. Section 2 discusses basic concepts of Big Data and importance of business analytics; and the advantages of their use are highlighted in the context of retail supply chain management. Section 3 introduces a brief review of research in Big Data-based supply chain applications; and in particular it examines the influence of intelligent business software applications to modern supply chain management. Section 4 provides the fundamentals of data, data quality, and dimensions of data quality related issues. Section 5 highlights scope and process of data quality management. It also includes role of business teams in corporate data governance, and main advantages of seamless data governance. Section 6 examines some of the data quality monitoring facts. Finally, concluding remarks have been put forward in Section 7.

DATA EXPLOSION IN RETAIL SUPPLY CHAIN

In recent years due to increased automation of business activity planning and execution using a new generation of information systems (e.g. ERP, SCM, CRM), retail supply chains experience a deluge of data. Additional data is received by many sources, such as mobile devices, Radio Frequency Identification Device (RFID) sensors, robotic devices, and different online portal for global supply chain management. Such a '*data explosion*' has created issues on how to effectively and optimally manage copious amounts of data. There are also issues around how to identify innovative ways to analyses huge volumes of data to unlock information from it. Doing so would lead subsequently to crucial knowledge used to manage the retail supply chain.

As Big Data is one of the most '*hyped*' terms in the business information systems world now-a-days, there is no consensus as to how to define it. The term is often used synonymously with related concepts – such as Business Intelligence (BI) and data mining. This creates an interesting question about how these technical terms (i.e. Big Data, Business Intelligence, and Data Mining) are related. In a simplistic sense, all these terms are involved in analyzing data and may perform *advanced analytics*. However, Big Data is different from the two other concepts when data volumes, number of transactions and the number of data sources are so *huge* and *complex* that that they need *dedicated techniques* and *technical infrastructures* to produce meaningful outcomes out of it.

Figure 2. The typical types of Big Data application systems

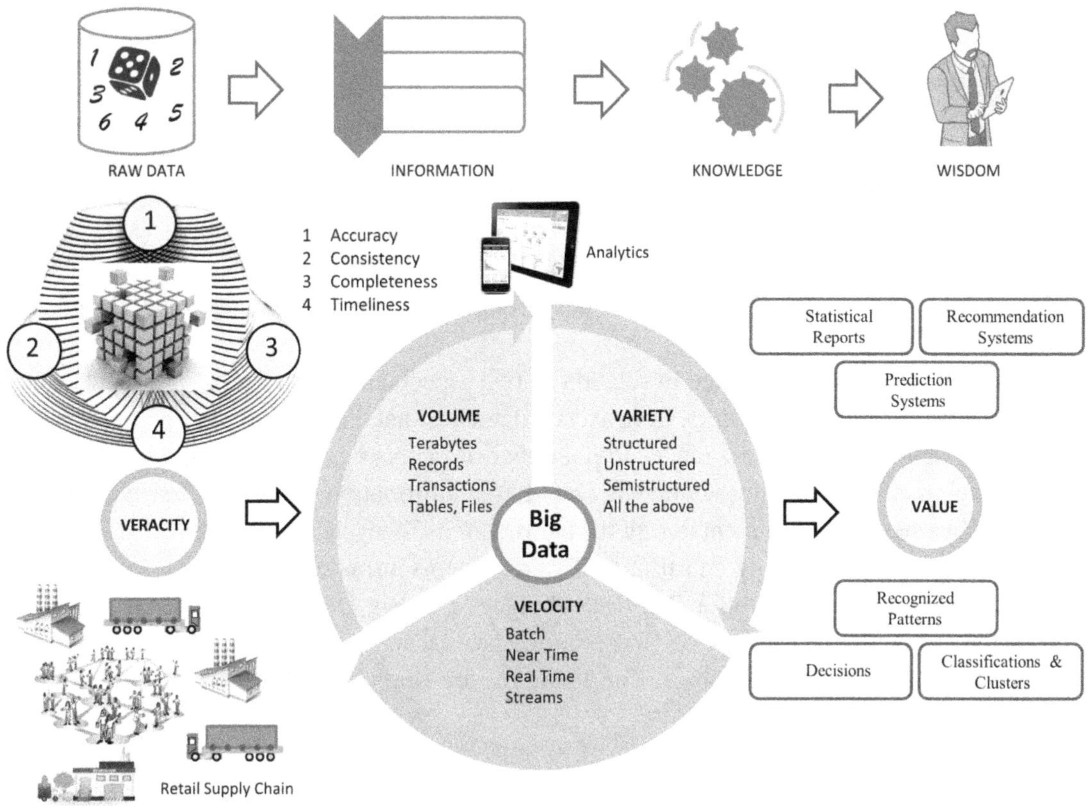

This also forms the basis for the most used definition of Big Data, the five V's: Volume, Velocity, Variety, Veracity, and Values as shown in Figure 2.

1. **Volume:** The sheer size of the data set (e.g. petabytes, exabytes or larger) in a transactional applications environment, of course, is a major challenge, and is the one that is most easily recognized. A petabyte is one quadrillion bytes, or the equivalent of about 20 million filing cabinets' worth of text. An extrabyte is 1,000 times that amount. However, availability of fine-grained raw data is not sufficient unless appropriate analyzing techniques are used for abstracting them in meaningful ways that are actionable. This characteristic, volume, bears demand on Big Data-based software application infrastructures.
2. **Velocity:** The velocity, with which data flows into the retail supply chain environment, or the expected response time to the data, is the second V-feature of Big Data. In several retail business applications, data continuously arrives at possible very high frequencies, resulting in continuous high-speed data streams. It is very important that the time needed to act on such data be very short. In this way, there is a huge shift in the data processing operation from batch processing to real time streaming. Big Data streams may arrive quickly in (near) real-time, requiring a timely response from the computing infrastructure to avoid data loss. Additionally, real-time or nearly real-time information makes it possible for a retail business to be much more *agile* than its competitors.

3. **Variety:** Data comes from different data sources. In other words, this characteristic refers to the fact that data comes in many formats: from structured data, organized according to some structures like the data record, to unstructured data, like image, sound, email text, social media (e.g. Facebook, Twitter) messages, which are much more difficult to search and analyses. Data streams can come from both internal and external sources within global retail businesses. Big Data may have diverse structures and forms, not conforming to the rigid relational structure of SQL (Standard Query Language) databases. In this way, Big Data-based software applications are using NoSQL database systems, which are useful for storing unstructured data such as sensor data, HTML documents, web pages, text, and e-mail message streams from data storage hardware and environment sensors, GPS (Global Positioning, System) data, click stream from web queries, social media updates, and so on).
4. **Veracity:** This feature is defined in relation to two aspects in a business environment: *data consistency* and *data trustworthiness*. Consistency demands that the data set must be statistically reliable; and data trustworthiness relates to a number of factors e.g. data origin, data collection and processing methods, facilities within Big Data-based information systems infrastructure. The data must be in a secure environment during the entirety of its lifecycle: beginning with collection from trusted sources to processing on trusted software systems infrastructure.
5. **Value:** The fourth V-feature for Big Data is value. The Big Data Value dimension denotes the potential value of Big Data which first requires processing, in order to make it useful for retail business decision making purposes. The Value feature bears special importance for retail supply chain design and management.

Big Data is changing the way resources are used within retail business environments. The managerial challenges are acknowledged within academic and practitioner circles; it is also highlighted that senior decision makers must embrace evidence-based decision-making. Detailed analysis and interpretation from Big Data can help those in global retail businesses make judicious decisions. In addition, it can help deepen customer engagement, optimize retail operational costs, enable business operational risks related warnings, facilitate resource management appropriately and capitalize on new sources of revenue. This extra demand on Big Data-based software applications for clear insights needs an innovative approach. An approach to find out meaningful value from Big Data-based software processing power as well as abilities to analyses the data (analytics) as well as appropriate skills.

In this way, data manipulation mechanisms transform data into information. Knowledge workers equipped with analytical tools identify patterns in the information and create rules and models, to be used to develop global retail business strategies. Retail enterprises gain wisdom by reviewing the impact of their strategies and repeating the cycle, as shown in Figure 3.

Value resides in Big Data, and the insights derived from the data can be leveraged for improved operational competitive advantage. Researchers and practitioners define analytics by three categories:

1. **Descriptive Analytics:** These types of analytics prepare and analyses historical data; they identify patterns from samples for reporting trends.
2. **Predictive Analytics:** These types of analytics predict future probabilities and trends; they find relationships in data that may not be clear with descriptive analysis.
3. **Prescriptive Analytics:** These types of analytics evaluate and use innovative ways to operate, consider business operational objectives, and try to mitigate all business constraints.

Figure 3. A diagrammatic representation of enterprise data transformation cycle

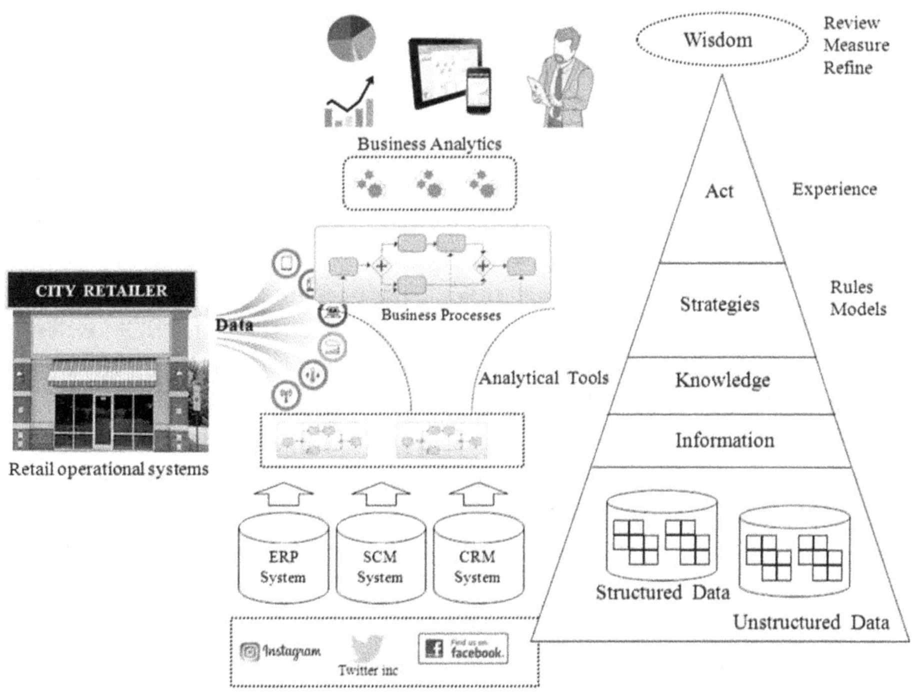

In addition, International Business Machines (IBM) Corporation provides the definition of Social Media Analytics and Entity Analytics. Social media analytics try to analyses data based on patterns embedded in it; and they use data classification and clustering mechanisms. The main characteristic of social media analytics is that data does not originate from within an enterprise; these are simply considered transactional data. Entity Analytics focus on sorting and grouping data belonging to the same entity. Modern computing power permits the analysis of data much more quickly, in a much more detailed fashion than ever before.

In a broad range of functional areas within the retail supply chain, data is being collected on an unprecedented scale. Decisions that previously were based on guesswork, or on painstakingly constructed models of reality, can now be made based on the data itself. Such Big Data analysis now drives nearly every aspect of global retail business. The promise of Big Data-driven decision-making is now being recognized broadly, and there is growing enthusiasm for this research challenges among academics and practitioners. While the potential advantages of Big Data are real and significant, and some initial successes have already been achieved, there remain many technical challenges that must be addressed to fully realize this potential.

RESEARCH IN BIG DATA-BASED SUPPLY CHAIN APPLICATIONS

In recent years Big Data and Business Analytics have attracted burgeoning interest among researchers due their potential in the business community (Waller & Fawcett, 2013). Particularly, research conducted by IBM Institute for Business Value in collaboration with MIT Sloan Review revealed the importance of Big Data to business managers (LaValle et al, 2011). The subject has been embraced in special journals including Harvard Business Review (HBR, 2012), and some articles in MIT Sloan Management Review (LaValle et al, 2011) (Wixom & Ross, 2017). However, despite increasing contributions, Big Data-based software applications in supply chain management (SCM) are still in their infancy.

J R Stock (Stock, 2013) discusses Big Data driven supply chain management related issues in one of his recent publications. He also proposes that Big Data-based analytics for SCM will allow decision makers to make faster decisions. In an industry survey conducted by Mitsubishi Heavy Industries and consulting company Deloitte (Deloitte & MHI, 2014) supply chain executives were questioned about innovations that drive supply chains. The main objective was to get the views of business executives on emerging technology trends that could dramatically impact supply chains of the future. The survey also identified areas for analytics-based SCM. The Council for Supply Chain Management Consultants published a report on Big Data in SCM, based on interviews with supply chain managers. One of the objectives of this research was to find out best practices in using Big Data for better SCM performance. Many commercial Big Data applications related to SCM have attracted the attention of academics and practitioners (Watson et al, 2014) (Davenport, 2006) (Davenport & Harris, 2007) (McAfee & Brynjolfsson, 2012) (Deloitte & MHI, 2016). For example, some research work in corporate marketing management shows tremendous opportunity in Big Data-based business analytics (Svilar et al, 2013). The number of publications on supply chain network design using Big Data-based business analytics is also growing ceaselessly (Baesens, 2014) (Dietrich et al, 2014) (Sathi, 2012) (Siegel, 2013) (Watson et al, 2013).

It is evident from reviewing research literature that the critically important organizational functions of SCM will evolve and adapt to Big Data analytics. A particular industry report (Deloitte & MHI, 2016) expressed a view about the potential of supply chains to deliver massive economic and environmental rewards for society. However, to fulfill this potential, the report suggests technological innovation will need to play a crucial role. Big Data analytics can provide step-change improvements in supply chain visibility, cost savings, and customer service. The key is to not only generate insightful data analysis, but to share it between business partners along retail supply chain so that they can act on it.

To solve a problem, Big Data-based application used intelligent reasoning in automated software environment that helps users apply analytical and scientific methods to business decision making. The software applications that focus on the retail supply chain domain are referred to as retail decision support systems, providing Big Data-based tools to support a user for global supply chain related reasoning processes to come up with a solution to a problem. This type of reasoning can be considered an intellectual process by which retail managers use diverse types of artificial intelligence-based inference mechanisms (e.g. rule-based reasoning, case-based reasoning, model-based reasoning, and neutral network-based reasoning) to solve day-to-day operational problems.

Each of these approaches focuses on enriching some aspect of the traditional retail intelligent decision support systems. In addition, these automated software systems regularly make use of models that are expected to be reasonably accurate reflections of real-world work practices. In the term, *reasonably accurate*, one discovers the need of evaluation. The way these models are obtained and deployed across decision-making entities (i.e. *human* and *machine*) can introduce inconsistencies, incompleteness, redundancies, as well as problems in coordination. Consequently, there is a clear need for the evaluation of Big Data-based systems that are intended for serious business use.

Moreover, considering both the proliferation of Big Data-based analytics use for global retail business management and the fact that the data upon which these software applications (i.e. analytics) functions rely are often error-prone, there is an important need to assess the *data quality* as it pertains to the field of global retail management. As such, poor data quality can have a direct impact on retail supply chain operational decisions, and this will promote several tangible and intangible losses for global business. Retail operational managers are seeing the problems and impacts attributed to poor *data quality* growing in importance.

DATA QUALITY AND ITS RAMIFICATION TO BUSINESS ANALYTICS

In simple, pieces of data describe characteristics of retail supply chain day-to-day operations. Data is a formalized representation of the characteristics of business objects suitable for communication, interpretation, and processing. For example, the numeric value of price (e.g. 10 pounds sterling) and weight (e.g. 450 grams) of a commodity in a retail business represent some meaningful information. In this way, data are the building blocks of business information systems. When data is used within a context or when data is being processed, it turns into information. The value of data as an economic good depends on its quality. It is worth to note that poor data quality would impact setting strategy, its execution, ability to derive value from data, and ability to lead a retail business. It would also affect decision-making capability, trust between business partners, customer satisfaction, and employee morale.

Data quality is defined as a context dependent, multidimensional concept. Context dependency means that data quality is in the "eye of the beholder" (i.e. the user). Multidimensionality refers to the fact that there is no single criterion by which data quality can be fully ascertained. Therefore, data quality is often described as *"fitness for use"*.

The term 'quality' is derived from the Latin (*qualitas*) and means characteristic, property, or condition. There are many definitions but the most commonly accepted definition of quality is *"The degree to which a set of inherent characteristics fulfills a requirement"*. Quite simply, quality must be *defined* and *measured* if improvement is to be achieved. But one of the main problems in quality practice in the business world and its management is that quality is ambiguously defined such that it is commonly misunderstood. This confusion may be due to many reasons. First, quality is not a *single idea* but rather a *multidimensional* concept. The dimensions of quality include the *object of interest*, the viewpoint on that object, and the *quality attributes* of that object. Secondly, there are various levels of abstraction for any concept and when people discuss quality; one group could be referring to it in its broadest sense, whereas another group might be referring to its specific meaning. Thirdly, the term quality is used by ordinary people in their day-to-day communication. The popular views of the term may be totally and utterly different from its use in professions in which it is approached from the *manufacturing, or logistics management* perspective.

Popular Views of Quality

A 'popular view' of quality is that it is an *intangible trait*; it can be discussed, felt, and judged, but cannot be weighted or measured. For example, an important view of quality is based in luxury, class-based societies, and its testimony. Costly, big, and more complex items are regarded as offering a *higher level* of quality than their poor siblings. In this way, an Aston Martin is a quality car, but a Ford Fiesta is not, regardless of their actual reliability and logbook records (e.g. number of previous owners, accident history). In this view, quality is restricted to a small group of expensive products with supplicated functionality and items that have a brand name for *privileged groups*.

Professional Views of Quality

The misconceptions and vagueness of the popular views do not help the quality improvement effort in the commercial world. To that end, quality must be described and prescribed in a workable way. Several individuals made significant contributions to the professional world of quality, its measurement, and control. Edward Deming (Deming, 2000) defines quality as – "to create constancy of purpose for improvement of product and service"; Philip B Crosby (Crosby, 1995) presents quality as "conformance to requirements"; and Joseph M Juan and his colleague (Juan & Godfrey, 1999) define it as "fitness for use". These two definitions are interrelated and consistent with each other. These definitions of quality have been adopted and used among quality professionals (e.g. qualified industrial engineers, certified business engineers). These three definitions are interrelated and consistent with each other. These definitions of quality have been adopted and used among quality professionals.

"Conformance to requirements" implies that requirements must be clearly stated such that they cannot be misunderstood. Then in the development and production process, measurements are taken in pre-defined intervals to determine conformance to those requirements. The nonconformances are then regarded as defects – the absence of quality. For example, if an Aston Martin conforms to all the requirements of an Aston Martin, then it is a quality car. If a Ford Fiesta conforms to all the requirements of a Ford Fiesta, then it is also a quality car. The two cars may be very different in style, performance, and economy. But if both measure up to the standards set for them, then both are quality cars.

The 'fitness for use' definition considers customers' expectations and needs into account. Customers' expectations and needs involve where the products or services fit their uses. Since different customers may use the products in diverse ways, it means that products must possess multiple elements of fitness for use. According to quality management guru J. M. Juan (Juan, 1970), each of these elements is a quality characteristic and they can be classified into categories known as parameters for fitness for use. The two most important parameters are 'quality of design' and 'quality of conformance'.

Quality of design in popular terminology is known as grades or models, which are related to the spectrum of purchasing power. The differences between grades are the result of intended or designed differences. Using the example of cars again, all automobiles provide to the user the service of transportation. However, models differ in size, comfort, performance, style, economy, and status conferred. In contrast, quality of conformance is the extent to which the product conforms to the intent of the design. In other words, quality of design can be regarded as the determination of requirements and specifications and quality of conformance is conformance to requirements.

Figure 4. Analogical comparison between engineering production and big data production

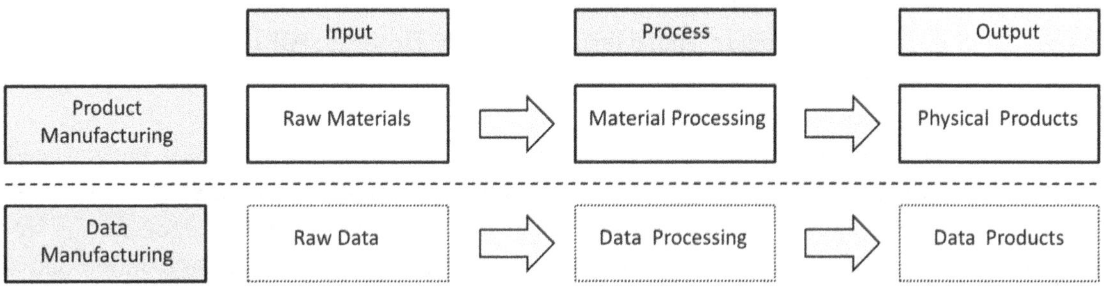

The two definitions of quality (conformance to requirements and fitness for use), therefore, are essentially similar. The difference is that the fitness for use concept implies a more significant role for customers' requirements and expectations.

To increase overall customer satisfaction as well as satisfaction towards various quality attributes, the quality attributes must be considered in the planning and design of the software. However, these quality attributes are not always congruous with each other. For example, the higher the functional complexity of the software, the harder it becomes to achieve maintainability. Depending on the type of software and customers, different weighting factors are needed for different quality attributes.

In view of these discussions, the updated definition of quality (i.e. conformance to customers' requirements), is specifically relevant to the software industry. It is not surprising that requirements errors constitute one of the major problem categories in software development. Particularly, Big Data-based application systems quality assurance is heavily dependent on data quality. To understand the data quality, one needs to appreciate the overview of data production process and related data quality issues.

Data Manufacturing Processes

Quality assurance has its roots in assuring the quality of a manufactured physical product; this is achieved by inspecting the product and evaluating its quality near its completion or at various stages of production. Data however is not as tangible as products that are more physical. Typically, a data product is its functionality and not its use. There is no physical data product to evaluate. This complex nature of data adds to the complications of assessing its quality.

To understand data and its quality assurance related issues in Big Data-based software applications, one needs to pay a closer attention to data production processes in global retail supply chains. Various researchers and practitioners have tried to compare the similarities between engineering, product manufacturing, and data manufacturing processes (Emery, 1996; Arnold, 1992; Ballou et al, 1998; Huh et al, 1990; March & Heiner, 2007; Roner & Spiegler, 1991; Wang & Kong, 1993; Wang et al, 1995). Particularly, Wang and his fellow researchers (Wang et al, 1995) introduced a framework, as shown diagrammatically in Figure 4, to present the analogical similarities between these two manufacturing processes.

Moreover, Richard Wang (Wang, 1998) extended the previous analogical comparison between data and manufacturing processes by proposing data quality be addressed via a Total Data Quality Management (TDQM) cycle, which calls for continuously defining, measuring, analyzing, and improving data quality. This approach resembles Edward Deming's Total Quality Management cycle (Plan, Do, Check, and Act) and is analogous to the Define, Measure, Analyze, Improve, Control (DMAIC) cycle, as ascribed by Six Sigma (Smith, 1993), for data manufacturing processes. However, Allison Jones-Farmer and her colleagues (Jones-Farmer et al, 2013) pointed out that unlike the DMAIC cycle from Six Sigma, there is no control stage recommended in the TDQM cycle.

The analogy of data production process to a manufacturing process is, perhaps, one of the most widely accepted views in the business world. However, practitioners are putting forward some differentiating points, too. It is worth mentioning two of the most significant differences. In the manufacturing world, raw ingredients are input into engineering fabrication processes, and in the end the required output is produced. The raw ingredients are generally depleted as the items of interest are produced. However, in data production processes, the data represents the input into the data production process, and a transformed data product is the output of the production process. The data is generally not depleted through production. A bad batch of data in the data production process will remain until it is purposefully cleaned up. Perhaps the most pertinent, yet challenging, difference between a manufacturing and data production process relates to the difficulty in measuring the quality of intangible data. A very common phrase, of the quality controlling world, is "*you cannot improve that which you cannot measure*". Therefore, intentional attempts need to be made for defining and measuring data quality in Big Data-based applications. In order to do this, one needs to figure out the dimensions of data quality in a manufacturing supply chain.

Dimension of Data Quality

Dimensions of data quality are fundamental to understanding how to improve data. Data quality can be defined as "data that is fit for use by data consumers"; and *data quality dimension* can be defined as "a set of data quality attributes that represent a single aspect or construct of data quality". In this way, dimensions of data quality are already an active research area for quality assurance purposes. Practitioners and researchers suggest that data quality is comprised of several dimensions (Ballou & Pazer, 1985; Ballou et al, 1998; Pipino et al, 2002; Redman, 1996; Wand & Wang, 1996; Wang & Strong, 1996). Specifically, two research groups (Wang & Strong, 1996; Lee et al, 2002) categorized data quality dimensions into two distinct categories: *intrinsic* and *contextual.* Intrinsic data quality denotes that data has quality; understood largely as the extent to which data values are in conformance with the actual or true values. Intrinsically, useful data is accurate, correct, and objective, and comes from a reputable source. Dimensions include: *accuracy objectivity*, *believability*, and *reputation.* Contextual data quality points to the requirement that data quality must be considered within the context of the task at hand, understood largely as the extent to which data is applicable to the task of the data user. The focus of contextual data quality is the data consumer's task, not the context of representation itself. In this process - contextual dimensions consist of *relevancy*, *value-added*, *quality* (Wang & Strong, 1996), *believability*, *accessibility*, and *reputation of the data* (Lee et al, 2002; Lee et al, 2004). Identification and measurement of these dimensions have mainly been based on self-report surveys and user questionnaires, as they rely on subjective and contextual judgments of decision-markers' for quantification. But contextual dimensions of data quality put forward are inclined towards *information* as opposed to *data.* These dimensions are put forward by using data within a specific situation (Batini et al, 2009; Davenport & Prusak, 2000; Watts et al, 2009). The main consideration in this chapter is the quality of data, and concept of information creation out of raw data is irrelevant. The discussion is mainly focused to the intrinsic data and measurement of its quality related issues.

Intrinsic data quality has been consistently categorized along four dimensions: *accuracy*, *timeliness*, *consistency*, and *completeness* (Ballou & Pazer, 1985; Batini et al, 2009; Haug & Arlbjorn, 2011; Blake & Mangiamli, 2011; Haugh et al, 2009; Kahn et al, 2002; Lee et al, 2002; Passion, 2006; Canopies & Cataract, 2002; Wang & Strong, 1996; Zeithaml et al, 1990). The main concepts of these four dimensions are discussed below:

1. **Accuracy:** Accuracy indicates how close a measurement is to the accepted value. In the case of Big Data, the term "accuracy" means the degree to which the 'data' correctly presents the phenomena it was designed to measure. For example, a data record in a retailer's Supplier Relationship Management (SRM) system, where the postal address for a supplier in the system matches the street address where the supplier is currently located. In this case, correctness of the street address value in the system could be assessed by validating the shipping address on the most recent material order. In this validation process, no problem context or value-judgment of the data is needed; it is either correct or incorrect.
2. **Timeliness:** Timeliness refers the temporal correctness of data values. Data values can be correctly inserted in a Big Data-based system, but is incorrect (out-of-date) if there is a change in the status of the object being represented between the times the data is inserted and when it is used. For some data, the concept of currency (the degree to which data value is up-to-date) is very important. For other data (which has got low volatility or representing '*permanent*' values), the concept of currency is not very crucial. For example, a floor manager in a retail business wants to keep track of inventory levels in real-time for effective operation management.
3. **Consistency:** This dimension of *data quality* refers to the extent to which data is presented in the same format. Consistency problems appear when datasets overlap and represent the same or similar concepts in a different manner, or when their specific content does not correspond. For example, in a retail supply chain information system's application all required delivery dates are entered in a DD/MM/YY (where DD is the day of the month between 01 and 31, MM is the month of the year between 01 [January] and 12 [December], and YY is the last two digits of the year in standard calendar) format to maintain system consistency.
4. **Completeness:** Completeness refers to the population of data fields. Incompleteness of any given field can have different effects on the quality of data. In other words, completeness refers to the degree to which data is full and complete in content, with no missing data. For example, if a supplier's address includes a name and high street address, but no county (or district), city, and postal code, then that record is considered incomplete. The minimum amount of data needed for a correct address is not present. A simple ratio of complete versus incomplete record can then form a potential measure of completeness.

Once data quality measures are understood, these quality measures can be monitored for improvement or adherence to standards. For example, data can be tagged as either accurate or not. Once tagged, there should be a method in place to monitor the long-term accuracy of the data. Combined with the measuring and monitoring the other three data quality dimensions, this helps to ensure that the records in the dataset are as accurate, timely, complete, and consistent.

Many of the issues in Big Data-based retail supply chain applications may not be new, but there is an evolving positive view of business analytics that is resulting in significant business transformations. The use of the term business analytics is now becoming standard to communicate the full life cycle of enhanced data-driven business decision making. Big data is the key ingredient in the computation of many analytical models in different areas of retail supply chain operations (e.g. demand forecasting, risk management, inventory planning).

In addition, the scale and scope of value that Big Data can bring is coming to an inflection point, set to expand greatly as the availability of Big Data converges with the ability to affordably harness it. Hidden in the immense volume, variety and velocity of data that is produced today is new information – facts, relationships, indicators and pointers that either could not be practically discovered in the past, or simply did not exist before. This new information, effectively captured, managed, and analyzed, has the power to change the retail supply chain management.

So, it is simple to become so focused on the anticipated business advantages of huge-scale data analytics that enterprises lose sight of the intricacy associated with data acquisition, preparation and quality assurance. In some ways, the clamoring demand for large-scale analysis only heightens the need for data governance and data quality assurance. And while there are some emerging challenges associated with managing Big Data quality, reviewing good data management practices will help to maximize data usability.

SCOPE AND PROCESS OF DATA QUALITY MANAGEMENT

The traditional prudence among conventional data quality professionals has evolved in recent years to advocate the application of manufacturing quality practices to Big Data management and its governance. With inferior quality data, a retail supply chain management system will fail to enhance its decision making. In general, Big Data-based application quality assurance refers to the study and use of different assurance processes, methods, standards, criteria, and systems to make sure the quality of Big Data-based systems in terms of a set of quality assessment criteria. The expectation of controlling the quality of Big Data must be viewed in reference to two aspects that increase the complexity of what one might call "*Big Data Quality*", namely:

1. **Widespread Repurposing:** One of the crucial properties of Big Data is the desire to use a wide collection of data sets, both *structured* and *unstructured*, for different user-group analyses. In the lack of proper data governance on reusing data sets means that each retail supply chain application must structure its data use in reference to the expected outcome. The result is that the same data sets are perceived to have different meanings in different references, creating technical questions about data *validity* and *consistency*.
2. **Data Restoration:** The assurance of being able to handle huge data sets creates the possibility of prolonging the lifetime of historical data that previously might have been demoted to near-line archival storage. The ability to access these older data sets and align them with data sets of more recent vintage implies the capability for enhancing *validation* and *governance* by controlling the information moves across the data life cycle into the Big Data-base retail business application systems.

These technical issues make Big Data quality assurance much more complex. The conjectural struggle posed when data sets are brought in from uncontrolled external sources is quickly being subsumed by the demand to make sure Big Data usability for the retail supply chain information consumers. The traditional method of attempting to govern the process of data creation and preventing errors is taking a back seat to pinpointing inconsistencies, standardizing data, and introducing improvements. In this way, realistic data quality techniques – including data profiling, data cleansing, entity recognition and identity resolution – are very important to assure the success of any Big Data-based system initiative.

The growing practice of Big Data, particularly about *business analytics*, pays much more attention to the aggregate outputs resulting from the accumulation and analysis of huge-size data sets, holding a variety of artifacts that are both structured and unstructured. This data variety, in conjunction with the fact that that data sets are likely to originate outside the retail business enterprise as opposed to inside, complicates data governance and data quality assurance for many reasons. A summary of the problems and the corresponding description is presented in Table 1.

There is an expectation that to include data, originating from various sources (e.g. including emails, electronic documents, blog posts, text messages in social media and tweets) beyond retail business corporate boundaries needs guarantee *consistency* and *usability*. Big data quality managers generally try to inoculate the whole end-to-end data production flow against the introduction of data incorrectness, about design and development of Big Data-based analytics for supply chain management. Analytics developing software engineers are looking for trustworthy results, which can be achieved by using appropriate *data governance*.

In simple, governance is the means to infuse order, thereby mitigating conflict and realizing mutual gains (Williamson, 1996). Data governance is a framework of decision-making rights and responsibilities regarding the management and use of data, aiming at maximizing the value of data. Data governance is a crucial facet of delivering quality for business related analytical and corporate data integration projects. In doing this, data governance identifies the *relevant area* of business, *ownership* and meaning of information with efficient *procedures* and *corporate policies*. It also identifies *data infrastructure* and *processing capability* to meet demands of self-service data and accessibility while supporting compliance for *risk* and *security* requirements.

Retail organizations need to determine who should manage corporate Big Data resources. Data scientist roles have emerged to capitalize on the analytical opportunities of Big Data, but placing these specialists in retail operational business units without leadership at the organizational level might be insufficient to harness the full potential of Big Data and its software applications. To address the challenges and opportunities of Big Data, leading organizations have established a new breed of management role, the

Table 1. Some of the issues of data governance

Criteria	Description
Data Diagnosis	The hereditary meaning associated with data values that are originated from outside the retail enterprise may be slightly (or totally) different from the meaning of the internal business data.
Data Volume	The volumes of retail enterprise data may swamp the capability of existing data manipulation approaches (e.g. SQL queries or flat-file edits) to make sure there is conformance with anticipations.
Affirmative Management	There is very limited capability to manage the consistency of data sets that are produced outside retail business's administrative boundaries. For example, it would be very hard to try to make sure that Twitter feeds be free of spelling mistakes.
Keeping Consistency	In some cases, it is unwise to cleanse values in a procured source if the corrections would make the data inconsistent with the original source. This type of inconsistency can disallow traceability of application processes, and likely asking question about application outcomes.

Chief Data Officer (CDO). One can describe the position of CDO as a *main data strategist* and this particular role will be responsible for business data management, data governance, use of data for corporate information systems (e.g. data warehousing, business intelligence, and business analytics), data quality assurance practices, metadata management related polices, and enterprise data management strategy formulation. In this way, to create appropriate collaborative data governance with business partners, it is important for CDOs to engage the proper teams within Data Governance Organization in order to align *corporate data governance* and *business objectives*. These teams are crucial to formulate strategic vision, identify data and their sources to be governed help the deployment of data governance policies, while proactively taking part in change management where it is necessary; and most importantly support the monitoring activities. Information and communication technology (ICT) teams are responsible for the management of data and measurement of data quality, and at the same time these teams collect and manage the overall business processes of *metadata* and *master data*. These teams also provide tools and technical provisions for data governance. Role of these business teams in a simple data governance environment is shown in Figure 5.

Under the right circumstances, applying proactive data quality monitoring, maintain Big Data-based software applications correctness, business users empowerment, and appropriate management of data and metadata can provide a motivating data governance environment.

Figure 5. Role of business teams in data governance

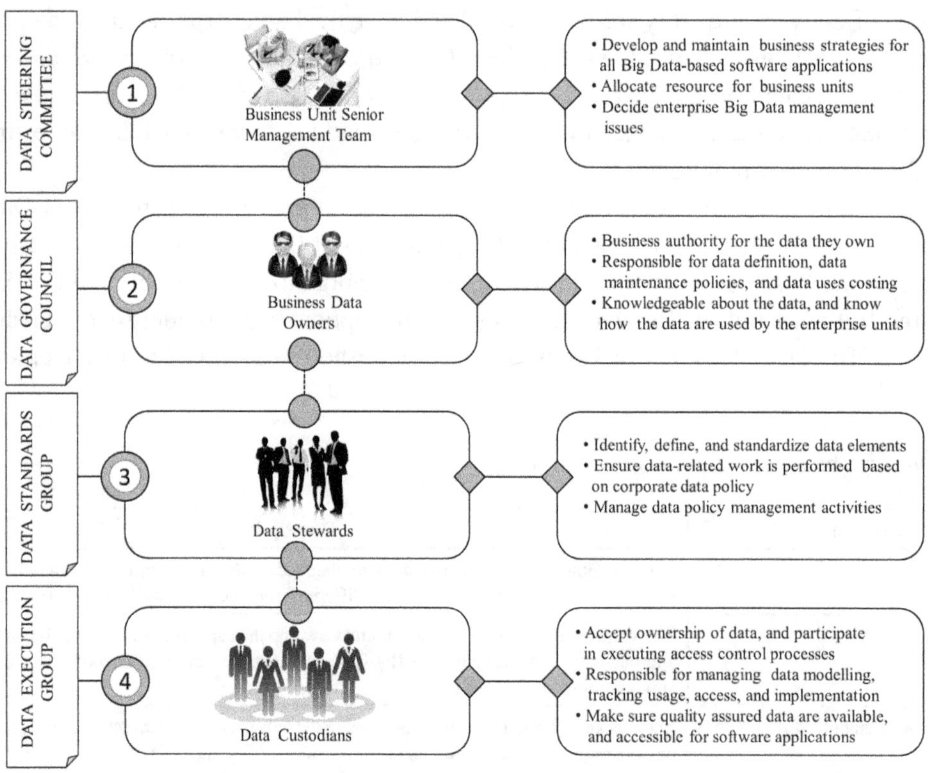

Benefits of Seamless Data Governance Initiatives

Seamless data governance initiatives need to keep al the business partners engaged and makes sure pro-active participation. It is also important to articulate the value created by data governance practices by using the correct enterprise data metrics. Business intelligence application software with proper graphical user interface facilities and relevant data metrics can be an appropriate tool to facilitate the impact of retail data governance initiatives. It can enhance business data quality parameters, and the capability to harmonize enterprise metrics to data definition standardization; and such software tools play crucial role in monitoring and managing the enterprise data governance policies.

The data governance plan consists of business operational rules for data quality management, corporate information systems master data management, metadata management, as well as the control the data access, use, and movement of data deemed sensitive by external regulations (e.g. HIPAA, and Basel II) or internal measures (e.g. the enterprise privacy policy). The deployment of each and every aspects of enterprise policies usher the intended advantages, as shown in Figure 6. However, enterprise data governance strategies and deployments, which enhance common objectives and integrate outcomes across these areas, enjoy advantages like improved reliability, traceability, and appropriate security of enterprise data. This will also create an appropriate communication platform for all the global business partners.

Figure 6. Main advantages of seamless data governance

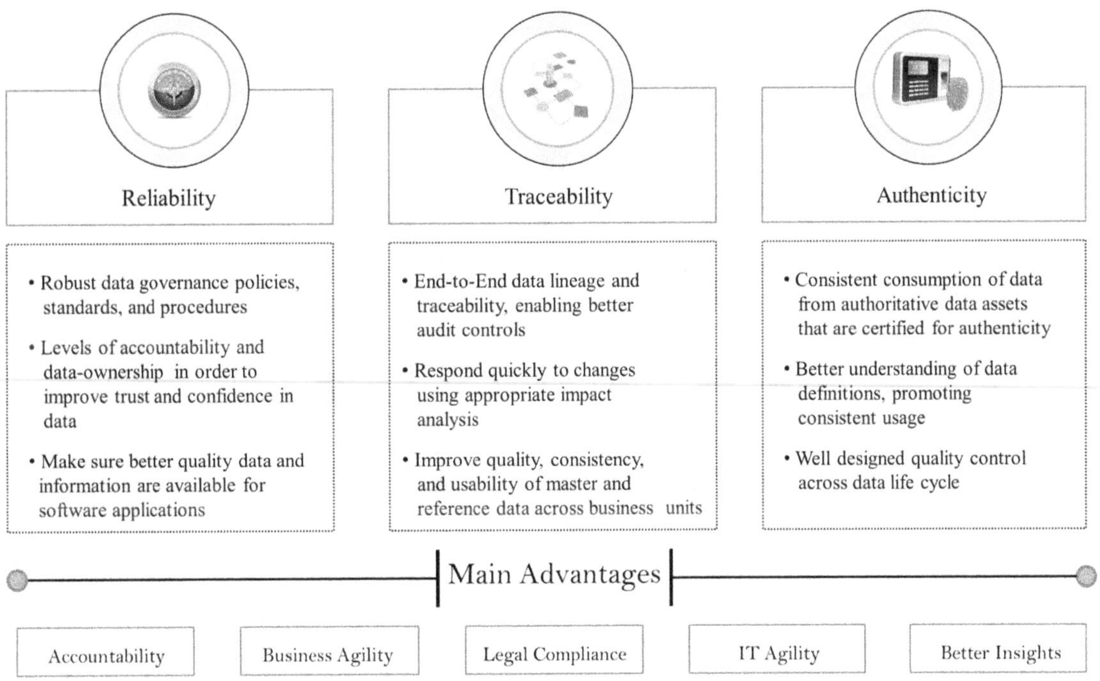

BIG DATA QUALITY MONITORING FACTORS

Digital technologies have a dual role – empowering, liberating, and transparent, yet also intrusive, restricting, and opaque. Big Data, as the embodiment of the latest advances in digital technologies, represents this dual character in a rigorous way, creating the tensions and dilemmas of modern technology savvy business world. Dilemmas, of course, do not easily lend themselves to solutions or resources. Nonetheless, they should not be understood as impediments to action. To go beyond dilemma, one needs to understand their conceptual origins, the dynamics of their development, the drivers of the dynamics, and the alternative motivating factors that they present. This tactic helps to trace out motivating factors for big data quality.

That suggests that under the right circumstances, applying proactive data quality methods such as profiling, standardization, cleansing, and record matching and linking can positively contribute to the ultimate business objectives. Introducing these techniques as part of a Big Data program is motivated by many key improvement factors, as shown in Figure 7, which will ultimately shape how those data quality management techniques need to be applied.

Figure 7. Big data quality motivating factors

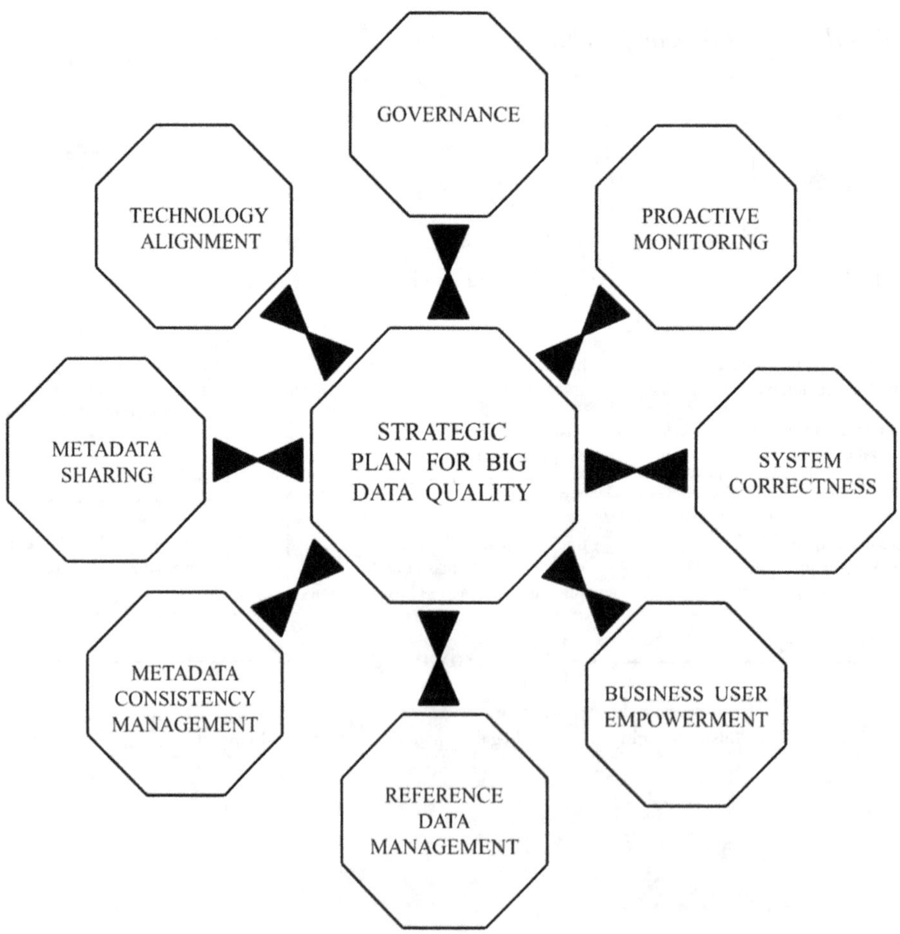

- **Proactive Monitoring:** The first step to proactive monitoring is to know the source of the data and how the data will be used. Data source is particularly important with inter / intra-enterprise monitoring as data formats are more likely to differ from source to source. Because a poor-quality data source will require more time and resources to resolve data issues, creating and using an excellent quality source should be the primary goal. When data errors are found to be contained with the data source, it is generally recommended that corrections be made to the data source. Proactive monitoring of most of important data quality dimensions can be used to signal data quality managers when data is not achieving expectations thus activating necessary business policy.
- **Business User Empowerment:** The incapability to impose management over the production of collected data sets is a naked truth that cannot be neglected. This conveys that the only policy for data quality assurance is given out from the end-user group. Requesting data confidences from the users will structure the analysis and finally the assurance of data quality and usability. In addition, given the big data skills deficiency, reveling data quality processes to business users can serve to unburden IT and straightway engage relevant business users in the data quality process.
- **System Correctness:** Knowing the primary source of data and what happens to it as it moves through different systems across the enterprise is basic to enact confidence in the completeness and correctness of that data. Data validation and traceability is a crucial factor in business regulations (e.g. Sarbanes-Oxley Act, international customs and excise related regulations). These regulatory and compliance rules help to verify the accuracy, history and origin of the information. Global retail supply chains' data stewards promote this holistic system correctness culture within their business communities.
- **Reference Data Management:** Reference data is a special type of data. It is essentially code whose basic job is to turn other data into meaningful business information and to provide an informational context for the wider world in which the retail business functions. Even with a high numbers of data source, it is credible to put-together standards for commonly used reference data domains, particularly if those domains are to be used for monitoring data consistency and validity. Moreover, more data about individuals means that the need for entity recognition and record linkage will increase; similarity-assessment depends on good reference information for similarity scoring and linkage.
- **Metadata Consistency Management:** The data management office shall keep a data dictionary of key business terms. Data stewards shall be responsible for ensuring the correctness of data definitions within their subject areas. This makes sure appropriate reference data is a prelude to developing more general metadata standards. While the need may seem obvious for a variety of structured sets, consider that metadata definition is integral to any kind of examination of unstructured content, where it refers to the information about various images, graphics, videos or audio artifacts, or contributes to parsing content from freeform text documents.
- **Metadata Sharing:** Data stewards shall focus on customer, product, and vendor data as core subject areas. The data stewards for customer, product, and vendor areas will report into the sales, research and development, and supply chain groups, respectively. The data stewards will be responsible for ensuring the quality of the data within their respective subject areas. In this way, a different byproduct of the absence of source data semantics is the need for reinterpretation of meaning. The quality of data will reference how that information is used, and when data sets are used in diverse ways. There will be a requirement to collaborate on business terms that appear

with frequency and what different users believe those terms to mean. Creating a participative view of metadata that urges collaboration and sharing will minimize the potential of sever inappropriate assessments.

- **Technology Alignment:** Data quality and data governance should not be counterproductive for the big data platform's performance. In this way, IT operational managers need to make sure that their data quality tools are adapted to execute within the Big Data environment appropriately.
- **Data Governance:** Data governance plays a crucial role in retail supply chain businesses. A well-defined catalog of information is required to align business and compliance requirements within enterprise and reference architectures. It is important to urge a standardized mechanism for information governance to lay structure and understanding within any retail business about data integration. This improves the value of information and empowers its usage.

CONCLUSION

One of the valuable assets within a retail company is its business-critical data regarding corporate partners, staff, products, financial information, and customers. Despite its importance, data is often replicated and scattered across business processes, systems, and applications throughout the company. Managing data effectively is a continuous activity, whereby retailers define the principles, policies, processes, business rules and matrices for fulfilling corporate strategic goals, by managing the quality of their data.

This chapter highlights the growing importance of Big Data-based trends that have the potential of changing and impacting the retail supply chain industry. Some of the sources of Big Data within retail business have been identified and discussed briefly. There are numerous examples of supply chain operations applying big data solutions which demonstrate the abundance of process improvement opportunities available through the effective use of data. The development of Big Data-based software applications has been proven useful in a diverse area of application for solving problems in global retail industry, for example – raw material procurement planning, marketing strategy formulation, logistics planning, and so on. The retail enterprises are leveraging the power of analytics in formulating business strategy in every facet of their operations to mitigate a healthy corporate growth. Nevertheless, there are increasing quality problems resulting in erroneous data costs in retail enterprises. This chapter provides informative discussions on Big Data-based systems; quality assurance related issues, including discussion about dimensions of data quality for Big Data, justify the reasons for approaches to proactive monitoring. It also discusses managing reference data and metadata, and sharing knowledge about interpreting data sets.

REFERENCES

Arnold, S. E. (1992). Information manufacturing: The road to database quality. *Database, 15*(5), 32–39.

Baesens, A. (2014). *Analytics in a big data world: The essential guide to data science and its applications*. Hoboken, NJ: John Wiley & Sons.

Ballou, D. P., & Pazer, H. L. (1985). Modeling data and process quality in multi-input, multi-output information systems. *Management Science, 31*(2), 150–162. doi:10.1287/mnsc.31.2.150

Ballou, D. P., Wang, R., & Pacer, H. (1998). Modeling information manufacturing systems to determine information product quality. *Management Science*, *44*(4), 462–484. doi:10.1287/mnsc.44.4.462

Battani, C., Cappelli, C., Francians, C., & Maurino, A. (2009). Methodologies for data quality assessment and improvement. *Association for Computing Machinery Computing Surveys*, *41*(3), 1–52.

Blake, R., & Mangiameli, P. (2011). The effects and interactions of data quality and problem complexity on classification. *Association for Computing Machinery Journal of Data and Information Quality*, *2*(2), 1–28. doi:10.1145/1891879.1891881

Cooke, J. A. (2013). Three trends to watch in 2013, Perspective. *Supply Chain Quarterly*, *1*, 11.

Crosby, P. (1995). *Philip Crosby's Reflections on Quality*. McGraw-Hill.

Davenport, T. H., Harris, J. G., & Morison, R. (2010). *Analytics at work – smart decisions, better results*. Boston: Harvard Business Press.

Davenport, T. H., & Prusiks, L. (2000). *Working knowledge: how organizations manage what they know*. Boston: Harvard Business Press.

Deloitte & MHI. (2014). *The 2014 MHI Annual Industry Report – Innovation the driven supply chain*. Charlotte, NC: MHI.

Deloitte & MHI. (2016). *The 2016 MHI Annual Industry Report – Accelerating change: How innovation is driving digital, always-on Supply Chains*. MHI.

Deming, W. E. (2000). The New Economics for Industry, Government, Education (2nd ed.). MIT Press.

Dietrich, B., Plachy, E. C., & Norton, M. F. (2014). *Analytics across the enterprise: How IBM realize business value from big data and analytics*. Boston: IBM Press Books.

Emery, J. C. (1969). *Organizational planning and control systems: Theory and management*. New York: Macmillan.

Haug, A., & Arlbjorn, J. S. (2011). Barriers to master data quality. *Journal of Enterprise Information Management*, *24*(3), 288–303. doi:10.1108/17410391111122862

Hauge, A., Arlbjorn, J. S., & Pedersen, A. (2009). A classification model of ERP system data quality. *Industrial Management & Data Systems*, *109*(8), 1053–1068. doi:10.1108/02635570910991292

HBR. (2012, Oct.). Getting Control of Big Data. *Harvard Business Review*.

Huh, Y. U., Keller, F. R., Redman, T. C., & Watkins, A. R. (1990). Data quality. *Information and Software Technology*, *32*(8), 559–565. doi:10.1016/0950-5849(90)90146-I

Immonen, A., Paakkonen, P., & Ovaska, E. (2015, October 16). paracone, P., & vasa, E (2015). Evaluating the quality of social media data in big data architecture. *IEEE Access*, *3*, 2028–2043. doi:10.1109/ACCESS.2015.2490723

Jones-Farmer, L. A., Ezell, J. D., & Hazen, B. T. (2013). *Applying control chart methods to enhance data quality*. Technimetrics.

Juran, J. M., & Godfrey, A. B. (1999). *Juran's Quality Handbook* (5th ed.). McGraw-Hill.

Kahan, B. K., Strong, D. M., & Wang, R. Y. (2002). Information quality benchmarks: Product and service performance. *Communications of the ACM*, *45*(4), 184–192. doi:10.1145/505248.506007

Lee, Y. W., Pipino, L., Strong, D. M., & Wang, R. Y. (2004). Process-embedded data integrity. *Journal of Database Management*, *15*(1), 87–103. doi:10.4018/jdm.2004010104

Lee, Y. W., Strong, D. M., Kahn, B. K., & Wang, R. Y. (2002). AIMQ: A methodology for information quality assessment. *Information & Management*, *40*(2), 133–146. doi:10.1016/S0378-7206(02)00043-5

March, S. T., & Hevner, A. R. (2007). Integrated decision support systems: A data warehousing perspective. *Decision Support Systems*, *43*(3), 1031–1043. doi:10.1016/j.dss.2005.05.029

McAfee, A., & Brynjolfsson, E. (2012). Big data: The management revolution. *Harvard Business Review*, *90*(10), 61–68. PMID:23074865

Murphy, C., Kaiser, G., Hu, L., & Wu, L. (2008). Properties of machine learning applications for use in metamorphic testing, *Proceeding of the 20th Internal Conference on Software Engineering and Knowledge Engineering (SEKE)*, 867-872.

Pal, K. (2016). *Supply Chain Coordination Based on Web Service, Supply Chain Management in the Big Data Era*. IGI Global.

Parssian, A. (2006). Managerial decision support with knowledge of accuracy and completeness of the relational aggregate functions. *Decision Support Systems*, *42*(3), 1494–1502. doi:10.1016/j.dss.2005.12.005

Pipino, L. L., Lee, Y. W., & Wang, R. Y. (2002). Data quality assessment. *Communications of the ACM*, *45*(4), 211–218. doi:10.1145/505248.506010

Sathi, A. (2012). Big data analytics: Disruptive technologies for changing the game. MC Press Online, LLC.

Scannapieco, M., & Catarci, T. (2002). Data quality under a computer science perspective. *Archivi and Computer*, 21-15.

Siegel, E. (2013). *Predictive analytics: The power to predict who will click, buy, lie or die*. Hoboken, NJ: John Wiley & Sons Inc.

Stock, J. R. (2013). Supply chain management: A look back, a look ahead. *Supply Chain Quarterly*, *2*, 22–26.

Svilvar, M., Charkraborty, A. & Kenora, A. (2013, Oct.). Big data analytics in marketing. *OR/MS Today*, 22-25.

Wang, R. Y., & Kon, H. B. (1993). Towards total data quality management (TDQM). In R. Y. Wanf (Ed.), *Information technology in action: Trends and perspectives*. Englewood Cliffs, NJ: Prentice-Hall.

Wang, R. Y., Storey, V. C., & Firth, C. P. (1995). A framework for analysis of data quality research. *IEEE Transactions on Knowledge and Data Engineering*, *7*(4), 623–640. doi:10.1109/69.404034

Wang, R. Y., & Strong, D. M. (1996). Beyond Accuracy: What data quality means to data consumers. *Journal of Management Information Systems, 12*(4), 5–33. doi:10.1080/07421222.1996.11518099

Watson, M., Lewis, S., Cacioppi, P., & Jayaraman, J. (2013). *Supply chain network design – applying optimization and analytics to the global supply chain*. FT Press.

Watts, S., Shankaranarayanan, G., & Even, A. (2009). Data quality assessment in context: A cognitive perspective. *Decision Support Systems, 48*(1), 202–211. doi:10.1016/j.dss.2009.07.012

Williamson, O. (1996). *The Mechanisms of Governance*. New York: Oxford University Press.

Wixom, B. H., & Ross, J. W. (2017). How to Monetize Your Data, MIT Sloan Management Review. *Spring Issue, 58*(3), 10–13.

Zeithaml, V. A., Berry, L. L., & Parasuraman, A. (1990). *Delivering quality service: Balancing customer perceptions and expectations*. New York: Free Press.

KEY TERMS AND DEFINITIONS

Big Data Analytics: Analytics is the discovery, interpretation, and visualization of meaningful patterns in Big Data. To do this, analytics use data classification and clustering mechanisms.

Data Governance: Data governance is a crucial fact of delivering quality for business related analytical and corporate data integration projects. Simply put, data governance refers to the overall management of the availability, usability, integrity, and security of the data employed in an enterprise. A proper data governance strategy consists of a governing council, a defined set of policies (or procedures), and a plan to execute those procedures.

Decision Making Systems: A decision support system (DSS) is a computer-based information system that supports business or organizational decision-making activities, typically resulting in ranking, sorting, or choosing from among alternatives. DSSs serve the management, operations, and planning levels of an organization (usually mid and higher management) and help people make decisions about problems that may be rapidly changing and not easily specified in advance - i.e. unstructured and semi-structured decision problems. Decision support systems can be either fully computerized, human-powered or a combination of both.

Internet of Things: The Internet of things (IoT) is the inter-networking of physical devices, vehicles (also referred to as "connected devices" and "smart devices"), buildings, and other items; embedded with electronics, software, sensors, actuators, and network connectivity that enable these objects to collect and exchange data.

Neural Network: Neural network is an information processing paradigm that is inspired by the way biological nervous systems, such as brain, process information. It uses a classification mechanism that is modelled after the brain and operates by modifying the input through use of weights to determine what it should output.

Quality Assurance: Quality Assurance (QA) is a way of preventing mistakes or defects in manufactured products and avoiding problems when delivering solutions or services to customers; which ISO 9000 defines as "part of quality management focused on providing confidence that quality requirements will be fulfilled". This defect prevention in quality assurance differs subtly from defect detection and rejection in quality control.

Radio Frequency Identification (RFID): This is a wireless technology used to identify tagged objects in certain vicinities. Generally, it has three main components: a tag, a reader and a back-end. A tag uses the open air to transmit data via radio frequency (RF) signal. It is also weak in computational capability. RFID automates information collection regarding an individual object's location and actions.

Supply Chain Management: A supply chain consists of a network of key business processes and facilities, involving end users and suppliers that provide products, services and information. In this chain management, improving the efficiency of the overall chain is an influential factor; and it needs at least four important strategic issues to be considered: supply chain network design, capacity planning, risk assessment and management, and performances monitoring and measurement. Moreover, the details break down of these issues need to consider in the level of individual business processes and sub-processes; and the combined performance of this chain. The coordination of these huge business processes and their performance are of immense importance.

Chapter 2
Improving Forecasting for Customer Service Supply Chain Using Big Data Analytics

Kedareshwaran Subramanian
T. A. Pai Management Institute, India

Kedar Pandurang Joshi
T. A. Pai Management Institute, India

Sourabh Deshmukh
H. P. Inc., India

ABSTRACT

In this book chapter, the authors highlight the potential of big data analytics for improving the forecasting capabilities to support the after-sales customer service supply chain for a global manufacturing organization. The forecasting function in customer service drives the downstream resource planning processes to provide the best customer experience at optimal costs. For a mature, global organization, its existing systems and processes have evolved over time and become complex. These complexities result in informational silos that result in sub-optimal use of data thereby creating inaccurate forecasts that adversely affect the planning process in supporting the customer service function. For addressing this problem, the authors argue for the use of frameworks that are best suited for a big data ecosystem. Drawing from existing literature, the concept of data lakes and data value chain have been used as theoretical approaches to devise a road map to implement a better data architecture to improve the forecasting capabilities in the given organizational scenario.

INTRODUCTION

In any global manufacturing organization, as highlighted by Waller and Fawcett (2013), forecasting is an important dimension of interest from a big data analytics standpoint. From a business process perspective, forecasting using big data analytics can be applied to solve issues related to inventory management,

DOI: 10.4018/978-1-5225-3056-5.ch002

transportation management & customer and supplier relationship management. A sample research question in the area of customer and supplier relationship management as cited in the paper by Waller and Fawcett (2013) include - How can more granular sales data from a wide variety of sources that exist be used to improve visibility and trust between trading partners?

The research question which the authors attempt to address in this book chapter is as follows:

How can a global manufacturing organization unlock the value hidden in its big data ecosystem to build better forecasting capabilities for its after-sales customer service supply chain?

This question is of great relevance to any global manufacturing organization which services customers across different parts of the world. From a business process perspective, the post-sales customer service function can be broadly sub-divided into the following operations:

1. Customer support contact center (over different channels – phone, web & service centers).
2. Spares management.
3. Field service technician organization.

In such global manufacturing organizations, more often than not, each of these three operations are managed as a separate entity with each operation creating its own set of planning processes and internal IT systems. Part of the reason being that global organizations are serving customers across different geographies - North & South Americas (NSA); Europe, Middle-East & Africa (EMEA) & Asia Pacific (APAC). Each geography would have its own strategic business units (SBU's) which have its localized operations and thereby creating its own systems to handle the post-sales customer support function. This eventually leads to having a fragmented view of the customer support function and poor forecasting capabilities for this customer service function as a whole.

From a technology standpoint as well, as discussed by Kumar and Deshmukh (2005), companies which followed the data mart bus architecture began by creating dependent data marts organized for each function such as customer service, procurement, finance, planning and quality.

As a result, today in most global organizations, every region and function has their own dedicated resources to extract the relevant data from their respective source systems and feed it into their forecasting models. Each of these teams is using their own set of tools and models creating many opportunities for data duplication and redundancy.

However, in reality, in order to service a post-sales customer need, query or issue, each of the three post-sales customer operations - namely customer support contact center, spares management & field service technician organization are inter-related and inter-dependent on each other. As pointed by Davenport (1998), fragmentation of information systems lead to a fragmented way of doing business. This argument is equally applicable in the current context. Fragmentation of SBU's and their information processing systems leads to sub-optimal forecasting capabilities with each region and operation creating its own independent forecast engine. This problem gets further compounded as these forecasts are built at different levels of granularity – forecast type (call –phone/web, spares, spares, field technicians); location (NSA/EMEA/APAC). Ultimately, these have a bearing on the quality of the post-sales customer support provided by the organization.

One of the significant recent developments in IT has been in area of 'Big data analytics'. Earlier, most global organizations developed Business Intelligence (BI) systems primarily relying on structured data residing in their internal systems. These BI applications have addressed managerial analytical queries by sifting through large data warehouses or data marts and presenting the results using interactive dashboards and visualizations.

A lot has changed with the arrival of big data. Today, organizations realize that much of the goldmine of information is present in semi-structured and unstructured data formats which can be used by different functions. In this book chapter, the authors illustrate the potential of big data analytics in developing more robust predictive forecasting models for the customer service supply chain. Waller and Fawcett (2013) characterize this form of analytics as 'SCM Predictive analytics'. However, one challenge is to identify the right source of data for a particular forecast type. Given the sheer size, diversity and complexity of data strewn across multiple data sources in structured, semi-structured and unstructured formats, there is a possibility that some of these data fields get duplicated in these different databases given that these databases are managed by different teams spread across different regions working within their own 'silos'.

It is also possible that some of these data fields may get completely ignored. This is mainly attributed to the cumbersome process of extracting the relevant data from the many databases and feeding it into the forecasting models. Both these problems of data duplication and data exclusion limit the reliability and accuracy of the forecasts and thereby limit its overall utility to the organization. Data governance challenges include maintaining completeness of data, accuracy of the source and target data systems and timely refresh rates to ensure reliable and relevant information to the various stakeholders involved in the customer service function.

This work attempts to do the following:

1. Examine the potential of big data in improving the forecasting models for the customer support function in the context of a global, manufacturing organization.
2. Address the data governance challenges inherent in any big data analytics project by adopting a research framework which help organizations manage their data better.

BACKGROUND: BIG DATA AND SERVICE SUPPLY CHAIN

This section describes two main strands of literature namely big data and service supply chain.

Big Data

Here, the various definitions of 'Big data' and its related terminology are reviewed to help define and differentiate big data from 'normal' data. This is followed by indicating the role of big data in a global manufacturing company context and reviewing the architectures and frameworks which can be applied in big data analytics applications.

'Big Data' when compared to 'normal' data has been often described by the 3 V's – Volume, Velocity and Variety. The earliest discussion on these 3-V's has been mentioned by Laney (2001) in his research note in a Gartner blog. The 3 V's were used by him in the context of the e-commerce industry. However, the general applicability of the 3 V's has been used to provide a generalized understanding of what characterizes a big data ecosystem.

Attempts have been made by several industry practitioners and researchers to provide a more detailed definition of big data. In the article by Adrian (2011), big data has been defined (and differentiated from 'normal' data) from an IT infrastructure standpoint, "Big data exceeds the reach of commonly used hardware environments and software tools to capture, manage and process it within a tolerable elapsed time for its user population." On similar lines, Madden (2012) prefers to define big data by qualifying it as too big or too fast or too hard for existing tools to process.

Another 'V'–'Veracity' of data is added in the info-graphic provided by IBM (2015) as depicted in Figure 1. Over time, sources of data have expanded beyond the traditional corporate data warehouses and data marts to include semi-structured and unstructured data sources such as social media content, sensors and so on. However, these new sources have their own set of challenges. The biggest being the issue of veracity or authenticity of the data given that most of this data is user generated on social media platforms. As a result, the data can be messy; yet it remains an important source of customer insight which is of importance to the organization.

Waller and Fawcett (2013) argue that it is even more important in today's big data environment to pay a lot more attention to theory so that one does not end up making spurious connections based on unreliable (big) data. They state that theory is particularly important for preventing false positives[1]. Big data leads to an explosion of new variables and therefore there are far too many false positives generated when testing models on big data. These concerns are further supported by boyd and Crawford (2012) who argue that bigger data are not always better data. Cases of breach of privacy raise ethical concerns of the usefulness of big data analytics. These concerns again reinforce the importance of veracity of the data and results generated in a big data ecosystem.

Figure 1. IBM Infographic
Source: http://www.ibmbigdatahub.com/infographic/four-vs-big-data

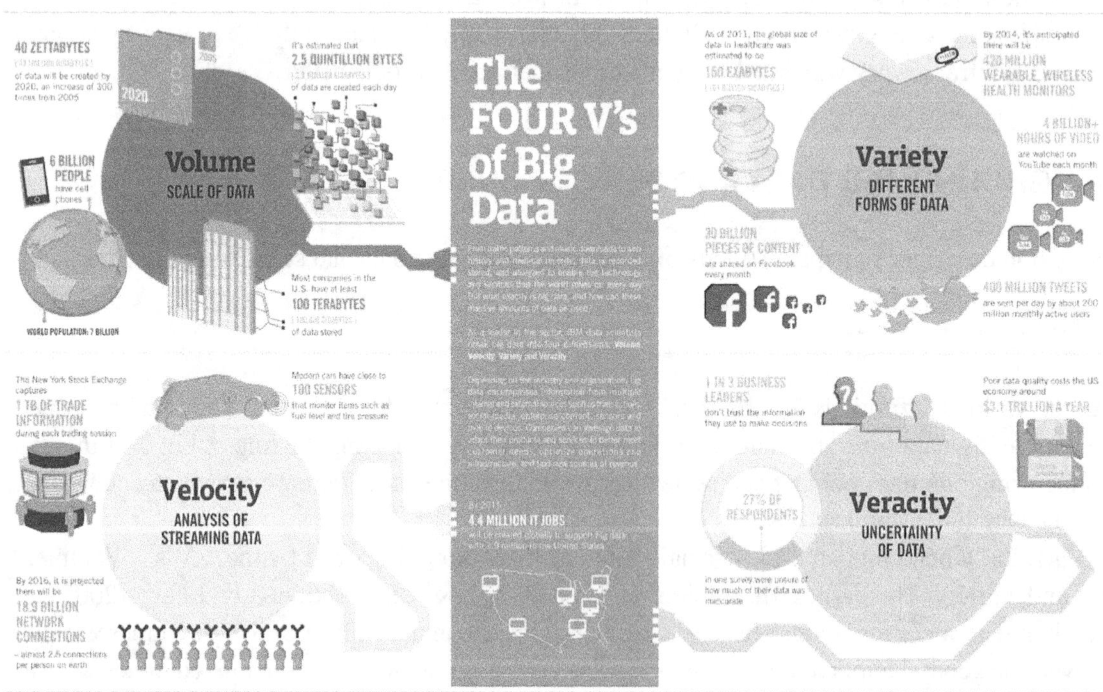

In this literature review on how big data is understood today, the authors also come across one more 'V'–'Value'. Beulke (2011) argues that besides the other four V's (Volume, Velocity, Variety, Verifiability or Veracity), it is also extremely important for organizations to be able to assess the extent to which the four V's of data help you find more value or insights from the data. Otherwise, it is simply not worth the effort. Hence, this has also been added to make up a total of '5 V's' which are used to define big data and also differentiate it from normal data. The authors explore the different V's in the context of a global, manufacturing organization.

The variety of data comes from structured, semi-structured and unstructured data fields from different source systems. The description of the various data fields which are relevant for the forecasting model is shown in Table 1.

This data is generated with high velocity by the respective source systems at different points in time. Telemetry data is created from millions of machines round the clock (24/7). Social media updates are also created round the clock. Table 2 provides a description of the frequency with which the various data fields relevant to the customer service function are updated.

High variety and velocity leads to high volume of data. There are millions of units of install base with about a billion service interactions over web, call center and field staff. These lead to thousands of engineering change notifications all resulting in terabytes of data generated every day. Table 3 shows the number of transactions generated in the system and the volume of data generated in supporting the customer service function in the organization.

However, as pointed in the introduction, there are challenges in identifying the 'right' sources of data suitable for a particular forecast function. The sheer size, diversity and complexity of data strewn across multiple data sources in structured, semi-structured and unstructured formats raises serious concerns regarding data quality and veracity. As pointed in Table 2, there are different velocities with which data

Table 1. Variety of data

Sr. No.	Data Field	Data Type	Data Format	Data Description
1	Install base	Structured, User-generated	RDBMS Tables	Contains the sales information of customers divided based on geography, type of customer (retail/corporate), what product they own, which location is product kept.
2	Service Bill of Material (SBOM)	Structured, User-generated	RDBMS Tables	Contains details of the components and kits that is used to repair the product. The supply chain stores and moves these components in SBOM.
3	Telemetry data	Semi-structured, machine generated	Machine specific	Generated by machines in form of logs and alerts that can be used to diagnose a problem and/or preempt it.
4	Spares demand	Structured	Excel	Users creating excel based forecasting models on a standalone basis to forecast spares demand.
5	Shipments forecast	Semi-structured	Excel	Users creating excel based forecasting models on a standalone basis to forecast shipments requirement.
6	Call logs	Unstructured	Text	Notes from interaction with customer support staff at call center to address customer queries.
7	Social media feedback	Unstructured	Web pages	Posts by customers regarding company's products on any of the widely used social media channels such as Twitter, Facebook or specific customer complaint forums/blogs.

Table 2. Velocity of data

Sr. No.	Data Field	Frequency
1	Social media feedback	Continuous, 24/7
2	Service Bill of Material (BOM)	Monthly refresh
3	Telemetry data	Continuous, 24/7
4	Spares demand	Daily updates
5	Shipments forecast	Monthly
6	Call logs	Continuous, 24/7
7	Social media feedback	Continuous, 24/7

Table 3. Volume of data

Sr. No.	Data Field	Volume Description
1	Install base	Millions of units globally with refresh in location, contracts
3	Telemetry data	Millions of Logs and alerts annually
4	Repair events	Millions of repair events annually
5	Shipments forecast	A few thousand line items refreshed monthly. Since this is forecast latest data replaces the previous data every month
6	Service interactions (web, call, field)	Billions of lines of data from calls, social media, web

is generated in the organization and ensuring that it is synchronized to ensure completeness and accuracy of data is a big challenge.

These data challenges impact operational decision making as well. Managers are never fully certain if their operational dashboards are showing the 'right' status of operations. These lead to misleading insights from the data affecting the overall customer service quality.

Service Supply Chain

This section describes the literature related to the service supply chain and its various aspects. Service supply chain refers to those supply chain system which does not include physical products rather "products" as pure services. For example, in many well-established service industries such as healthcare sector, financial consultancy, after sales service, etc. the respective supply chains are service supply chains. After-sales activities are recognized as a significant source of revenue as well as gaining competitive advantage in most manufacturing businesses (Ellram, Tate, & Billington, 2004; Saccani, Johansson, & Perona, 2007). In case of new products especially the after-sales service market is up to four or five times larger than the market. In their work, Saccani et al. (2007) addresses development of after-sales service supply chain through a case study approach of seven different firms. With special emphasis on durable consumer goods, and on three configuration choices: vertical integration, centralization, and decoupling of activities the study has been carried out. Three main after sales activities are compared across those seven firms viz. field technical assistance, spare parts distribution and customer care. The empirical evidence suggests that no one best way exists in configuring the after-sales supply chain.

Most service organizations understand that, in order to grow an efficient and effective service supply chain, service supply chain management needs to be measured for its performance. de Waart and Kemper (2004) envisage a roadmap toward gaining excellence in service supply chain management where five steps details highlights performance measurement is an important process. Cho, Lee, Ahn, and Hwang (2012) explore the performance measurement of service supply chains. A framework emphasizes on performance measures such as demand management, customer relationship management, supplier relationship management, capacity and resource management, service performance, information and technology management and service supply chain finance.

Recently, He, Xie, Wu, Hu, and Dai (2016) present a review of operational models in the context of service supply chain. The basic definition of service supply chain with specific examples also provided. Service Only Supply Chain (SOSC) is different than Product Service Supply Chain (PSSC). PSSC handles both the physical product as well as services while SOSC handles products (non-physical) and pure services. In reality, SOSCs are seen in industries such as financial services, travel & tourism, internet based services, mobile apps, and telecommunication.

Furthering in their study, He et al. (2016) present a model for an automobile Logistics Service Supply Chain (LSSC) which integrates Functional Logistics Service Provider (FLSP). Such integration brings challenges like forecasting spare parts because the data handled at both levels is of different nature. During this era the volume of data produced and transferred over the Internet is considerably growing. It also generates challenges for the organizations that would like to gain the profits from analyzing this immense advent of big data. Demand planning, is a crucial activity which analyzes various customer segments in terms of brands and product, down to the SKU level and develops models used to predict demand and generate revenue plans. This is the most fundamental step for collaborative planning and forecasting (CPFR) with major supply chain partners.

Syntetos, Babai, Boylan, Kolassa, and Nikolopoulos (2016) review forecasting aspect in supply chain with the emphasis on difficulty in extrapolating demand requirements at one echelon. This involves complex issues such as supply chain coordination and involvement of multiple stakeholders for information sharing. In a typical forecasting process, initial step is to identify the outputs to be forecast. The aggregated forecasts are better from minimizing error point of view. Therefore the aggregation level must be specified. In turn, three dimensions requires identifying the: Product: e.g. Stock keeping unit (SKU), item, family, etc.; Market / Location: customer, Point of Sale (POS), region, country, business area, etc.; Time: hour, day, week, month, year, etc. There is an emergence of studies related to frameworks related to service supply chain management.

Ramish, Azhar, and Rasheed (2017) build a comprehensive supply chain framework for service industry that includes engagement in purchasing of services, make of services and delivery the services, through the comparative analysis of models and conceptual frameworks in the earlier literature. This work offers basic understanding as to how service business can grow their performance systems to be converted into more effective service supply chains by focusing on newer dimensions. Their comparative analysis and theoretical framework would document the finding of the problems that surround result assessment within and transversely single supply chains. They also expand existing knowledge in the performance measurement in the service supply chain.

There is an interesting work by Sepúlveda-Rojas, Rojas, Valdés-González, and San Martín (2015), about forecasting in supply chain of Chilean companies. Their work presents an alternative methodology to assess the best-forecast model without the requisite to estimate all the forecast models or complement with any visual technique. Many studies are published with focus on forecasting in supply chain (Ali, Babai, Boylan, & Syntetos, 2017; van der Laan, van Dalen, Rohrmoser, & Simpson, 2016). Big data and forecasting is first compiled into a review work by Hassani and Silva (2015), in which challenges for forecasting with big data is detailed on various aspects like skills, noise, hardware, statistical significance and architecture of algorithms. In their work various applications like economics, finance, population dynamics, crime, energy, biomedical science and media has been covered. The authors of this book chapter have not come across prior studies where specific big data frameworks and architectures have been applied to improve the forecasting function in a global manufacturing company context. All these studies emphasize on various frameworks related to service supply chain and aspects like demand planning, forecasting without reference to big data environment. Therefore it is worth to research further to explore such issues in big data environment.

NEED FOR BIG DATA ANALYTICS

Big data analytics is deployed in several sectors of the economy. As per the seminal study conducted by Manyika et al. (2011) from the McKinsey Global Institute (MGI), big data can generate significant financial savings across different sectors such as healthcare, public sector, manufacturing, retail. In the manufacturing sector, they expect the benefits of big data analytics to decrease the cost of product development and assembly by half and reduction in working capital by up to seven percent. In their report, they develop two indices – 'Value potential index (VPI)' and 'Ease of capture index (ECI)' and different sectors have been evaluated based on these two indices. VPI refers to the extent to which the sector stands to gain by deploying big data analytics. The variables used to construct the value potential index include the amount of data per firm, firm relative performance, customer and supplier intensity, transaction intensity and sector turbulence. The ECI refers to possible constraints or barriers which may act as limitations to deploying big data analytics. These include talent pool, intensity/dependence on IT, data-driven mindset and data availability of data.

Data Lake and Big Data Architecture

Large manufacturing companies such as General Electric (GE) have been able to sell services to its customers based on a detailed analysis of data streaming from its equipment and the ability to predict failures and other key events as per Fitzgerald (2015). In the interview given by GE's CIO, Mr. Vince Campisi, he describes how they have used a '*data lake*' as the platform to develop their big data analytics applications. They ingest data from 25 airlines, 3.4 million flights into a data lake – a storage system to hold enormous amounts of raw data in its native format for future use.

The data is stored in raw format because they are not fully sure of what variables would be necessary to build their analytics application. Hence they prefer to collect the data first and then as they develop their analytical models, they extract the relevant data for the model. Since this is done in an iterative manner, more data is extracted from the data lake as they become clearer with the outcomes they are trying to arrive at.

This approach is diametrically opposite in its world-view as compared to the concept of data warehouses and data marts. In the latter, there is a predetermined set of data fields which need to be cleaned and loaded in a predetermined data format in order to enter into the data warehouse (or mart). The idea of a data lake is to collect all the data before it is potentially lost as per Watson (2015). This approach is more suited to a big data ecosystem where there is far more complexity attached with the dataset as compared to the traditional business intelligence system for which data warehouses or marts are a necessary precondition.

However, Violino (2015) argues that the concept of data lake is quite new. Like data warehouses, data lakes are a concept, not a technology. At its core, a data lake is a data storage strategy. The data lake does not require a predetermined schema. Data can be simply ingested and the schema gets created and applied when the data is read. The data lakes are not a replacement for existing analytical platforms or infrastructure. Instead, they complement existing efforts and supports the discovery of new (analytical) questions. Once these questions are solved, the insights can now be operationalized by shifting the data analytics solution from the data lake into the data marts or data warehouses.

Big data has not only brought new ways of storing data but also new frameworks and architectures. In the paper by Tekiner and Keane (2013), they attempt at defining a framework that captures all the stages of a Big data application with a strategic point of view. The framework consists of seven layers – systems layer, data layer, data collection layer, processing layer, modelling layer, access layer and visualization layer (Tekiner & Keane, 2013, pp. 1497). There are different tools being used to handle the operations in each of these layers.

For example, MapReduce developed by Google is being used to process and store large datasets on commodity hardware. Its main advantage is a programming paradigm which allows useable and manageable distribution of many computationally intensive tasks. Map-Reduce involves two main parts, a map operation where a simple function is used to emit key/value pairs in parallel similar to using primary keys in a relational database. Once the data to be processed is mapped into a key/value groups, then a reduce operation is used to apply the core processing logic to produce results in a timely manner as per McCreadie, Macdonald, and Ounis (2012). This simple concept of Map-Reduce removes many traditional challenges in High Performance Computing (HPC) to achieve fault tolerance and availability. Therefore, it paves the way for development of highly parallel, highly reliable and distributed applications on large datasets.

In the paper by Miller and Mork (2013), an alternative big data framework has been conceptualized. Based on Porter (1980) seminal book of industry value chain, the authors have developed a 'Data value chain'. This value chain consists of three stages – data discovery, data integration and data exploitation. Each of these stages have their own set of activities associated with it starting from creating an inventory of data sources to taking decisions based on which results are more appropriate and relevant within a given data analytics context (Miller & Mork, 2013, pp. 58).

The three key objectives to address using this data value chain approach is as follows:

1. Manage and coordinate data across the service continuum;
2. Form collaborative partnerships between the various data stakeholders to enable positive outcomes; and lastly
3. Establish a portfolio management approach to invest in people, process and technology that enhance the organization's performance by improved operations and lower costs.

In their article, Davenport, Barth, and Bean (2012) provide three recommendations which differentiate how organizations should undertake their big data analytics (as compared to their traditional business intelligence and data analysis environments). The first suggestion is to pay more attention to data flows as opposed to stocks. The second is to rely on data scientists and product and process developers rather than data analysts. Lastly, to move analytics away from the IT function into the core business functions. Storing data in its native format aids in shifting the attention from data stocks to flows.

In fact, Dutta and Bose (2015) follow a similar approach in developing a new framework for a big data analytics application. They integrate the widely adopted Cross Industry Standard Process for Data Mining (CRISP-DM)[2] with typical IT project management and create a new framework. They divide the lifecycle of any big data analytics project into three phases – strategic groundwork, data analytics and implementation. However, there are two limitations in applying this new framework to the current context. The first and primary limitation in the paper by Dutta and Bose (2015) is their claim that the Ramco Cements case study is an 'analytics' project.

As per the criteria given by Hardoon and Shmueli (2013), the case fits the description of a business intelligence project rather than an analytics project. They also raise concerns regarding the general lack of consensus of what differentiates a business intelligence project from an analytics project. As per their classification, projects can be treated as analytics project only if there is a machine-generated intelligence created based on some statistical or machine learning algorithm. Business Intelligence reports can at best provide intuitive aggregated data presented in an easy to understand graphical manner. But there is no native intelligence generated by the system. Hence, by applying this criteria, the case of Ramco Cements on which the big data framework is applied is not a good comparison to the big data context described here. The second limitation is that the framework follows a sequential process where one phase leads to another from business problem definition to training people in their framework for implementation of big data projects in firms (Dutta & Bose, 2015, pp. 295). However, in reality most analytics projects like any scientific experiment move back and forth between the various phases such as business understanding, data understanding and so on. This has been rightly shown in the original CRISP-DM model (Figure 2). In this framework, there are inter-relationships between each and every phase of the data analytics project. Starting with business understanding till evaluation, it is quite natural to find that even after defining the problem and modeling the data, if the results of the model are not in agreement with the business users, it can lead to redefining the problem again after exploring the results obtained from the data model and what business sense can be made from them.

Ultimately, the model can be deployed only after there is a happy marriage between the business users and data scientists in ensuring that requirements in terms of analytical queries from business side as well as model robustness in terms of reliability and validity are satisfied. Hence the authors believe that the model proposed by Dutta and Bose (2015) which makes an assumption of a linear approach appears unrealistic in terms of applicability to the given big data analytics case study and in general to most typical big data analytics projects.

Hence, based on the literature review, the authors conclude that the big data framework proposed by Miller and Mork (2013) is the most appropriate and hence is applied in the current case study. The authors have not come across any prior studies applying this framework to a big data analytics project and hence this is one of the key contributions of this book chapter. The following section describes the application of the data value chain framework in the customer service supply chain function in a global manufacturing organization.

Figure 2. CRISP-DM framework
Source: Shearer (2000), pp. 14.

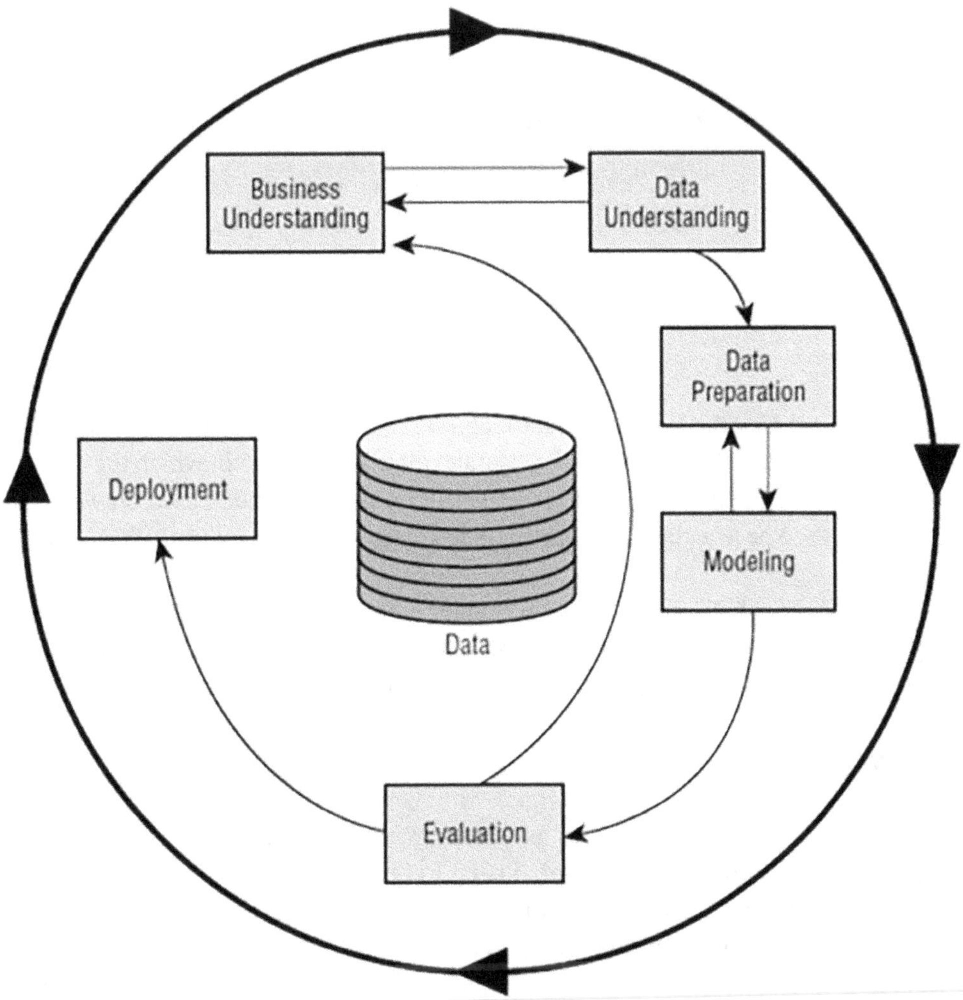

APPLICATION OF DATA VALUE FRAMEWORK

Miller and Mork (2013) develop data value chain (Figure 3) specifically for big data analytics scenarios. Drawing inspiration from the seminal work of Porter (1980) which developed the concept of industry value chain, the authors have drawn parallels in the big data ecosystem. As per their framework, the value chain in a big data ecosystem consists of three parts – data discovery, data integration and data exploitation.

Data discovery primarily addresses the stages involved prior to model building and essentially examine the various aspects involved in deciding what data entities are required, the source of data and necessary pre-processing or data cleaning which is required in order to make it ready to be used in the analytical model. In specific terms, the tasks highlighted in their framework include – 'Collect and annotate', 'Prepare (the data)' and 'Organize (the data)'.

Figure 3. Big data value chain
Source: Miller and Mork (2013), pp. 58.

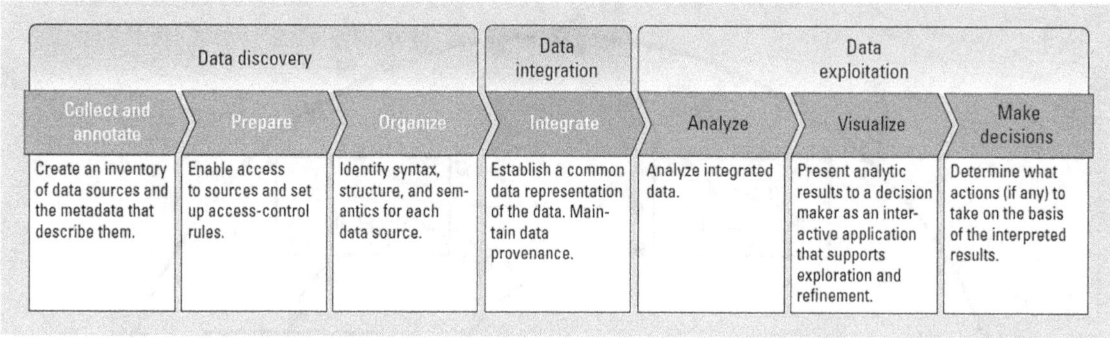

This stage is followed by the stage of 'Data integration' which addresses all issues related to data governance and access. This is followed by the 'Data exploitation' phase in which the analytical model is built using the data provided in the previous stages and results obtained based on which the analytical decisions are made. Specifically this stage includes tasks such as 'Analyze', 'Visualize and 'Make decisions'.

One of the central contributions of this book chapter is the application of the data value framework developed by Miller and Mork (2013) in the context of improving the forecasting capabilities in the service supply chain for a global manufacturing organization.

Data Discovery

This phase aims at addressing the challenges associated with disparate, dispersed & non-standard data granularity. Data across multiple systems which need to be used are identified. This data needs to be standardized and scalable across different regions and functions by creating a global meta-dictionary of forecasting variables with their definitions and nomenclature.

These variables need to be (a) flexible to "plug and play" for other downstream systems and with service providers (suppliers) as needed (b) accurate with right rate of refresh and (c) consistent in granularity and which enables availability of data at the right time.

To create such a solution will require working with the Subject Matter Experts (SME) across regions and global teams who run the process to gather their requirements and understand the current operations. The first step is to onboard the regional and functional teams in the project and initiate an assessment of their data requirements and current leading practices across. This provides key insights into creating a "best in class" data management process to ensure a level playing field for all.

In parallel, the project core team led by big-data architects initiate assessment of data sourcing options and big-data solution exploration to identify the right extraction point(s) and big data technology that aligns with the organization's IT strategy. Once all the SMEs align on the data management and provisioning process, extraction points are determined. Then big data solution architecture is defined and the solution development process is initiated.

The solution development includes creating Extract, Transform, Load (ETL) data capabilities, developing data structures in big data environment (linking data elements coming from diverse data sources at right level of granularity), and enabling data provision vehicles (reports, system feeds, Electronic Data Interchange(EDI)). One of the most critical activity after the solution development process is User Acceptance Testing (UAT), where the SMEs and users validate the availability of data per their requirements.

Data Integration

At the organizational level, in order to enable any changes to IT infrastructure and business processes the authors propose the idea of creating Centers of Excellence (COE) for achieving integrated planning and forecasting across the various organizational verticals. This organizational restructuring is necessary to ensure that there is uniformity in the process of planning and forecasting and also enables collaboration across different functions and regions.

As part of stages of organizational restructuring, first the COEs is created for each function (such as spares forecasting across regions) separately. Subsequently, an integrated COE is created to cover all functions and all regions enabling integrated cascading forecast across functions. This COE definitely needs to work closely with the regional supply chain stakeholders to fine-tune forecasts based on business context and market conditions. It is critical because every demand driver cannot be included in the forecast models and the 'tribal' knowledge of local business planners and stakeholders is crucial to ensure the forecast variable and values are appropriate for any given market.

Data Exploitation

This phase focuses on developing advanced forecasting models and enhancing the current processes & downstream interlocks to leverage the richer data (more demand drivers) that is now available for planners. Usually the legacy forecasting models that are usually being used are rudimentary such as moving averages or at best univariate (mostly hindsight based) forecasting models. With richer data, the project core team, led by analytics & modelling professionals, work with the planners and create multivariate data models to enhance the forecast accuracy.

Multiple forecasting models need to be developed to cater to regional nuances, business context across demand drivers, and also the lifecycle of the product. This is an iterative process and requires expertise in modeling and data science.

The accuracy of forecasts of multivariate models can be further improved by incorporating business variables like promotions working with the business SMEs. Once the new models are created it is important to incorporate them in forecasting and planning process, establish a governance to review forecast numbers and fine tune them in collaboration with regions and functions to ensure most current business context is considered and forecast numbers are realistic.

In parallel a team of automation experts should work on automating the activities and handoffs between sources of data, data mart, forecast generation tools (modeling tools) and their output into planning systems. This requires the project team working closely with the business and IT organizations and is a critical component in this big data analytics solution and the change management inherent in such an implementation.

FUTURE RESEARCH DIRECTIONS

This work is based on a single global manufacturing organization's customer support function. Hence there may be limitations in terms of generalizability in this approach and findings with other such comparable organizations. Industry specific contexts and prior data technology investments may also limit the applicability of this work to other organizational contexts. The authors provide below some considerations for such transformations as well as opportunities to further enhance the forecasting ecosystem.

The focus is first on creating a foundational capability to enable single source for forecasting data needs. In '*Data exploitation*' section, forecasting models have been developed based on unique '*demand drivers*' as variables. Identifying the right demand drivers and creating a forecasting model requires advanced use of analytics and very close integration with business and operations teams. Data lakes have made enhanced data available for analysis and modeling at one place. However the key challenge lies in making the best use of the data in improving business outcomes. It is an iterative process and should lead to significant improvements in accuracy of the forecast as well as downstream supply planning.

The technology and logic used to create the data lake depends on an organization's IT strategy. Incompatible technologies can lead to silos, gaps in data and significant costs. During such transformations, IT architects play a critical role in defining the solution that is aligned with current system constraints as well as long term IT strategy. Much of the big data analytics literature review includes newer ways of storing data (such as data lake) and processing data (using Hadoop). Further research may be undertaken to find the applicability of these new technologies in such organizational scenarios.

Further, every industry has its own unique industry constraints and characteristics. For example in the Food & Beverages (F&B) sector, the challenge is on managing the low shelf life of its products. Similarly, in the Computer Electronics industry, high rates of technological obsolescence makes its R&D operations and innovation its top priority. The authors view the role of foundational capabilities in building and managing data lakes in every industry to be critical. But the downstream application of the data and the nature of usage of data will vary depending on the industry requirements. Further studies may be undertaken to explore industry specific case studies which highlight the role of developing big data analytics solution to enhance business outcomes in those specific contexts.

In a globalized economy, any value chain consists of multiple organizations working in tandem. Partnerships between them is critical to ensure effective operations in areas such as design, manufacturing, distribution & customer support to the company's products and services. Sharing business signals through information across partnerships enable the value chains to work in the most optimal manner. In this book chapter, the authors have explored the aspects related to sharing information outside organizational boundaries to manage the service supply chain for a multinational enterprise. Further research may be conducted to explore aspects related to the service operations and supporting Information and Communication Technology (ICT) infrastructure to delve deeper into the process and technology. It may help tackle business concerns needed to answer questions such as "what to share" and "when to share" and "how to share". Specific areas of concern related to security and access management of data stored in data lakes have sufficient scope for further research.

CONCLUSION

In this book chapter, the authors begin by examining the V's of big data – volume, velocity, variety and veracity in the context of managing the post-sales customer support function in a global manufacturing organization. Using detailed descriptions, the authors argue how this scenario fits the description of a big data ecosystem. This is followed by examining the issues involved in the process of generating forecasting models which are currently being followed.

The authors find that there are significant limitations in terms of the reliability and accuracy of the current forecasting models which are hampering managerial decision making. The key reason for these limitations are the fragmented ways in which the forecasting function is being currently carried out. Using a big data value chain as the research framework, the authors propose a reorganization of the process followed in generating these forecasts. The value chain combines people, process and technology aspects in ensuring that there is a coordinated and standardized process followed in building these forecasts to ensure that there is a better data governance mechanism in place to support the global manufacturing organization in building its forecasting capabilities for handling its post-sales customer service support function.

REFERENCES

Adrian, M. (2011, January). Big Data: It's going mainstream, and it's your next opportunity. *Teradata Magazine*, *Q1*(5), 38–42.

Ali, M. M., Babai, M. Z., Boylan, J. E., & Syntetos, A. A. (2017). Supply chain forecasting when information is not shared. *European Journal of Operational Research*, *260*(3), 984–994. doi:10.1016/j.ejor.2016.11.046

Beulke, D. (2011). *Big Data Impacts Data Management: The 5 Vs of Big Data*. Retrieved from http://davebeulke.com/big-data-impacts-data-management-the-five-vs-of-big-data/

boyd, d., & Crawford, K. (2012). Critical questions for big data. *Information, Communication & Society*, *15*(5), 662-679. doi:10.1080/1369118X.2012.678878

Cho, D. W., Lee, Y. H., Ahn, S. H., & Hwang, M. K. (2012). A framework for measuring the performance of service supply chain management. *Computers & Industrial Engineering*, *62*(3), 801–818. doi:10.1016/j.cie.2011.11.014

Davenport, T. H. (1998). Putting the enterprise into the enterprise system. *Harvard Business Review*, *76*(4). PMID:10181586

Davenport, T. H., Barth, P., & Bean, R. (2012). How 'Big Data' Is Different. *MIT Sloan Management Review*, *54*(1), 43–46.

de Waart, D., & Kemper, S. (2004). 5 steps to service supply chain excellence. *Supply Chain Management Review*, *8*(1), 28–35.

Dutta, D., & Bose, I. (2015). Managing a Big Data project: The case of Ramco Cements Limited. *International Journal of Production Economics, 165*, 293–306. doi:10.1016/j.ijpe.2014.12.032

Ellram, L. M., Tate, W. L., & Billington, C. (2004). Understanding and Managing the Services Supply Chain. *Journal of Supply Chain Management, 40*(4), 17–32. doi:10.1111/j.1745-493X.2004.tb00176.x

Fitzgerald, M. (2015). Gone fishing -- for data. *MIT Sloan Management Review, 56*(3), 7–7.

Hardoon, D. R., & Shmueli, G. (2013). *Getting started with business analytics: insightful decision-making*. CRC Press.

Hassani, H., & Silva, E. S. (2015). Forecasting with big data: A review. *Annals of Data Science, 2*(1), 5–19. doi:10.1007/s40745-015-0029-9

He, M., Xie, J., Wu, X., Hu, Q., & Dai, Y. (2016). Capability Coordination in Automobile Logistics Service Supply Chain Based on Reliability. *Procedia Engineering, 137*, 325–333. doi:10.1016/j.proeng.2016.01.265

IBM. (2015). *The Four V's of Big Data.* Retrieved from http://www.ibmbigdatahub.com/infographic/four-vs-big-data

Kumar, S., & Deshmukh, S. (2005). *Business intelligence: delivering business value through supply chain analytics.* Infosys White Paper. Retrieved from http://www.bcubeglobal.com/wp-content/uploads/supply-chain-analytics.pdf

Laney, D. (2001). *3D data management: controlling data volume, velocity, and variety*. Retrieved from http://www.blogs.gartner.com/doug-laney/files/2012/01/ad949-3D-Data-Management-Controlling-Data-Volume-Velocityand-Variety.pdf

Madden, S. (2012). From databases to big data. *IEEE Internet Computing, 16*(3), 4–6. doi:10.1109/MIC.2012.50

Manyika, J., Chui, M., Brown, B., Bughin, J., Dobbs, R., Roxburgh, C., & Byers, A. H. (2011). *Big data: The next frontier for innovation, competition, and productivity*. Retrieved from http://www.mckinsey.com/business-functions/business-technology/our-insights/big-data-the-next-frontier-for-innovation

McCreadie, R., Macdonald, C., & Ounis, I. (2012). MapReduce indexing strategies: Studying scalability and efficiency. *Information Processing & Management, 48*(5), 873–888. doi:10.1016/j.ipm.2010.12.003

Miller, H. G., & Mork, P. (2013). From Data to Decisions: A Value Chain for Big Data. *IT Professional, 15*(1), 57–59. doi:10.1109/MITP.2013.11

Porter, M. E. (1980). *Competitive strategy: technique for analyzing industries and competitors.* New York: Free Press.

Ramish, A., Azhar, T. M., & Rasheed, H. (2017). Building a comprehensive service supply chain conceptual framework: A step ahead, based on comparative analysis of previous frameworks. *International Journal of Services and Operations Management, 26*(1), 97–121. doi:10.1504/IJSOM.2017.080679

Saccani, N., Johansson, P., & Perona, M. (2007). Configuring the after-sales service supply chain: A multiple case study. *International Journal of Production Economics, 110*(1–2), 52–69. doi:10.1016/j.ijpe.2007.02.009

Sepúlveda-Rojas, J. P., Rojas, F., Valdés-González, H., & San Martín, M. (2015). Forecasting Models Selection Mechanism for Supply Chain Demand Estimation. *Procedia Computer Science, 55*, 1060–1068. doi:10.1016/j.procs.2015.07.068

Shearer, C. (2000). The CRISP-DM model: The new blueprint for data mining. *Journal of Data Warehousing, 5*(4), 13–22.

Syntetos, A. A., Babai, Z., Boylan, J. E., Kolassa, S., & Nikolopoulos, K. (2016). Supply chain forecasting: Theory, practice, their gap and the future. *European Journal of Operational Research, 252*(1), 1–26. doi:10.1016/j.ejor.2015.11.010

Tekiner, F., & Keane, J. A. (2013). *Big Data Framework.* Paper presented at the 2013 IEEE International Conference on Systems, Man, and Cybernetics, Manchester, UK. doi:10.1109/SMC.2013.258

van der Laan, E., van Dalen, J., Rohrmoser, M., & Simpson, R. (2016). Demand forecasting and order planning for humanitarian logistics: An empirical assessment. *Journal of Operations Management, 45*, 114–122. doi:10.1016/j.jom.2016.05.004

Violino, B. (2015, July 31). 5 Things You Need to Know about data lakes. *CIO, 28*(10), 17–17.

Waller, M. A., & Fawcett, S. E. (2013). Data Science, Predictive Analytics, and Big Data: A Revolution That Will Transform Supply Chain Design and Management. *Journal of Business Logistics, 34*(2), 77–84. doi:10.1111/jbl.12010

Watson, H. J. (2015). Data Lakes, Data Labs, and Sandboxes. *Business Intelligence Journal, 20*(1), 4–7.

ENDNOTES

1. A false positive is a result that indicates a given condition has been fulfilled, when it actually has not.
2. The CRISP-DM framework was conceived in 1996 and was elaborated by Shearer (2000). Till date, it remains the leading methodology used by industry for analytics, data mining or data science projects as per polls conducted by KDNuggets.

Chapter 3
Applications of Intelligent Video Analytics in the Field of Retail Management: A Study

Harkirat Singh
ICFAI University, India & IBS Hyderabad, India

ABSTRACT

Recent technologies in the market trends have demanded the significant need for the possible solutions to intelligent video cameras that are nothing but intelligent video analytics. Today in the retail industry, intelligent video analytics has gone beyond the tradition of the domain of security and loss prevention by providing retailers insightful business intelligence such as store traffic statistics and queue data. This provides accurate and reliable information by monitoring continuously through a large number of video cameras events that human operators or employees can overlook. This paper gives an overview study of applications of intelligent video analytics in retail management as well as the state-of-the-art computer vision techniques behind them to analyze the data. It clearly demonstrates that the importance of the role that intelligent video systems and analytics play can be found in a variety of applications of intelligent video Analytics in the field of Retail Management.

INTRODUCTION

Recent technology trends in the market have created a significant need for intelligent videos and cameras, which in turn has given rise to need for intelligent video analytics. This white paper attempts to provide a comprehensive account of study and application of intelligent video analytics in the field of retail management. Today in the retail industry, intelligent video analytics has gone beyond the traditional domain of product security and loss prevention, and has drifted into the field of Datascience, by providing the retailers with business intelligence, such as store traffic statistics and queue data. The analytics

DOI: 10.4018/978-1-5225-3056-5.ch003

utilizes the video system architecture employed, to enhance the utility of security and other available surveillance solutions. This architecture involves: automatically monitoring the video of people, vehicle and other objects, and tracking their behavior within the field of view of the camera. Intelligent video analytics continuously monitor the data provided by these cameras thus ensuring extremely high levels of security and efficiency all around the clock. This level of minute monitoring, 24X7, and without virtually any data outages, involves keeping a track of huge amount of data, which would otherwise have been humanly impossible to do. The event of overlooking a tiny but important detail due to human error by oversight, fatigue or slow processing of information, is completely eliminated. We can with mounting certainty claim that the way the intelligent video analytics is currently developing; that it will improve the efficiency of the overall retail processes and help to secure retail industry. Thus, this will lead to prevention of shrinkages, better-merchandising management and optimized facility utilisation.

This paper gives an overview of the study of applications of intelligent video analytics in retail management as well as the study of the state-of-the-art computer vision techniques utilized behind the scenes to analyze the data. It clearly demonstrates that the importance of the role that intelligent video systems and analytics play can be found in a variety of applications of intelligent video Analytics in the field of Retail Management.

BACKGROUND

Few years ago, when big data was in its nascent state it had constricted utilization, even though there were technological products available which could capture data at the magnitude at which Big Data is really capable of working with. The major reason for this paucity was the limited tools available at the disposal of the organizations to understand and explore the information that lay underneath this heap of data. That is to say people knew they had a lot of information under this abundance of data, they knew the importance of Bigdata, they were ready to discover facts; however, they did not know how to extract these facts from the available mound (Adams 2007). This obviously was the most important task at hand for the organization. Even now with the advancement in Bigdata analytics, there is yet a lot of potential learning which is still hidden in plain sight. So, when did the companies steer towards understanding their own, easily available but for long forgotten or unused data? Well! That was right after the recent economic recession (Adams 2010). The week economy forced deep changes into almost every industry and across the globe, the burden of change was heavier on those businesses which were customer facing and especially those that were dependent on bulk purchasing (Spindler 2008). These later group of companies needed to know the expected trends in purchases of their customer segments, to make any changes or decisions on what to do and how to transform their businesses in future, if at all. Using advanced analysis techniques, they can now do exactly this. The study of big data helps them understand the industry trends, and current and future expected states of their businesses and customer expectations (by looking at customer behavior trends). If one wants to know what exactly is happening or going to happen to their business, their customer their industry, one needs large volumes of highly detailed data, and advanced analytics to extract meaning out of the data (Adams 2012).

Some of these untapped data seems foreign to most business till they are shown how useful it can be to them. Most of often than not it is not the lack of data that a company suffers from, but from a lack of analytical tool to tell them what this data really means. Though it is the size of the data stored that determines whether we consider the dataset as big data or not, however, this size itself is not firmly defined but based on convention, which itself keeps continuously changing over time. Currently most analysts working this area use the term big data for datasets of the order of terabytes to multiple petabytes (Annesley 2007).

The difficulty in working with big data is primarily caused by the unstructured storage. The points of generation of the data points are usually more than one, e.g. it could be from different devices, it could be from different technological platforms which may not always be compatible with each other, or they could just be in different formats like textual, numerical, photograph, etc.

Textual Structured data is generally created by various sources such as E-mail, documents such as M.S Word, spreadsheets such as M.S Excel, instant messaging apps, relational databases or conventional business applications, such as Enterprise Resource Planning (ERP) or Customer Relationship Management (CRM). And the non-textual unstructured data is generated by (a) media files like video outputs (), or images (mpg, jpeg etc), (b) from sensors which are embedded in web login, or from sensors installed in heavy machinery, vehicles etc, (c) from the Internet search engines (Google, Bing), social networks (Facebook, Instagram, Twitter) (d) from devices such as portable computers, smart phones and other mobile devices (e) GPS devices and call center records (f) video data from the video cameras/CCTV itself which also contains valuable information. With advancement in technology data is also generated from the Internet of Things (IOT). Big data has the potential to help various different companies achieve their organizational goals and improve their operations by making faster and more intelligent decisions. This data is captured, cleaned, formatted, transformed, stored and analyzed through various techniques. It can help a company gain useful insight to increase revenues, increase sales, lower costs, get new or retain existing customers. Nowadays big data utilization has become a point of comparison between companies. There is a competition of sorts within various organizations and industries that support new waves of productivity growth, innovation, and consumer surplus. Some Big data sources continuously generate data unceasingly in real time. Put all together, and we can conclude that big in 'big data' is not just about giant or extraordinary data volumes, but it's also about an exceptionally diverse data types, delivered at different speeds and frequencies (Helbing 1995). In most cases, in order to efficiently utilize big data, the data from all these sources have to be combined, and then two technical entities of businesses have to merge to perform one single task: first, big data for the massive amount of information available and second advanced analytics, which helps to fetch out the information from this data. These advanced analytics is actually a collection of different tool types, and intelligence including those based on predictive analytics, data mining, statistics etc (Bazzani 2012). The combination of these into one to perform a single task is called big data analytics or the new practice in Business Intelligence (BI).

Characteristics of Big Data Analytics (Volume, Variety, Velocty)

Most definitions of big data focus on the size of the data in storage. Size matters but there are other attributes of big data, namely data variety and data velocity that is significant too. The three V's of big data (volume, variety, and velocity) constitute a comprehensive definition and they bust the myth that big data is only about data volume. In addition, each of these three V's has its own branch of analytics. Let us look at each in detail in the following section.

Volume of Data Type

It's painfully obvious that data is the primary component of big data. With that in mind, most people define big data in terms of huge sizes (terabytes, petabytes) or volumes of data gathered by a company (Berger 2007). Statistic shows that 500+terabytes of new data gets ingested into the database of the social media site Facebook, every day. This data is mainly generated in form of media, that is in the form of photo and video uploads, message exchanges, published comments etc (Hempel 2004). Now Facebook uses this data for their internal customer behavior analytics. Now, big data can also be quantified by counting records, transactions tables or files (Shitrit 2007). In the old days, all the data generated in a company, was internal by the paid employees.

The Scope of Big Data

The scope of big data affects its quantification too. For example, in many of the organizations, the data collected for general data warehousing differs from data collected specifically for analytics. Different form of analytics may have different data sets (Cezar 2010). Some analytics practices can also lead a business analyst or similar user to create ad hoc analytic data sets per analytics project.

Variety of Data Type

One of the things that make big data really big is that the input is coming from a great variety of sources than ever before. With the modern technological advancements, the data generated by all these technologies are in the different form and variety. Many of the newer sources of generation are web sources: including logs, click streams and social media (Dufaux 2008). The website/page host organization has been collecting these for years. Some of the other similar sources of untapped big data collected and gathered are: RFID information from supply chain applications, text data from call center applications, and semi-structured data from various business to business processes. Big data itself isn't new but the effective analytical leveraging of big data is. The recent tapping of these sources for analytics has led to the need for consolidating these different varieties of data. This data may be structured, unstructured and semi-structured. Big data could be of any type, including structured and unstructured data such as text, sensor data, audio, video, click streams, log files and so on. The analysis of this consolidated data types brings new problems and situations, e.g. monitoring hundreds of live video feeds from surveillance cameras of targets or points of interest (Evans 2012). Multidimensional data can also be drawn from a data warehouse to add historic context to big data. There's far more diverse mix of data types today than analytics has ever seen.

Velocity of Data Type

Big data can also be described by the time it takes to access and process them or the time we can afford to spend on processing them. In short velocity can be measure in terms of the frequency of data generation or the frequency of data delivery (Goold 2002). Some activities are very important and need an immediate response, and hence require fast processing with high efficiency levels. For example, data coming off any kind of device or sensors, thermometers sensing temperature, microscope listening for movement in a secure area, or video cameras scan for a specific face in a crowd (Dee 2004). Every modern car has more than 100 sensors that monitor items such as fuel level, temperature inside the car and tire pressure (Dee 2006). The collection of big data in real time isn't new; many firms have been collecting click stream data from websites for years, by using streaming data, to make purchase recommendations to the web visitor. What is even more challenging is the analytics that goes with the streaming data has to make sense of the data and possibly take action—all in real time (Dee 2008).

Categories of 'Big Data'

Big data is found in two forms:

- **Structured Data:** Structured data is that which can be stored, accessed and processed in permanent formats. Over the span of time advancement in the computer industry and science have achieved greater success in developing techniques to work with such kind of data (where the format is well known in advance). The values that can be derived from these data form are immense. This includes data contained in relational databases and spreadsheets (Donald 2005).
- **Unstructured Data:** Unstructured data refers to that type of data that doesn't have any predefined structure or form. Unstructured is a generic label for describing data that is typically text-heavy and descriptive. Unstructured data can be divided into two categories textual unstructured data or non-textual unstructured data. Textual unstructured data is generated by E-mail, PowerPoint presentations, M.s word documents, M.S excel documents, the collaboration of various software and instant messages. Non-textual unstructured data is generated by mediums like JPEG images, Flash video files, MP3 audio files.
- **Semi Structured:** Semi-structured data is that data which is neither raw data nor typed data in a conventional database system. The line between unstructured data and semi-structured is little fuzzy. It is structured data, but it is not organized in a relational model like a table or an object based graph. Or in other words the structured data which doesn't conform to the formal structure of data models in the context of relationships is semi-structured data. A lot of data found on the web can be described as semi-structured. Data integration especially makes use of these semi-structured data, e.g. XML, JSON, some NOSQL Databases like MongoDB which store the data natively in JSON, etc.

Intelligent Video Analytics

The application of computer vision techniques in retail dates back to more than a decade. The more recent ones are due to advancement in computer vision, machine learning, and data analysis, retail video. This analytics can provide retailers with much more insightful business intelligence. Thus it provides much higher business value, far beyond the traditional domain of security, authentication and loss prevention. Examples include analysis of store traffic, shopper's behaviors, and purchase decision-making, among others. The retail environment, with its own unique business and technical challenges, is also considered a practical test bed for novel computer vision approaches. For these reasons, retail video analytics and its various applications have become a great interest to both retailers as well as the computer vision community.

Figure 1. Example of output returned by google search

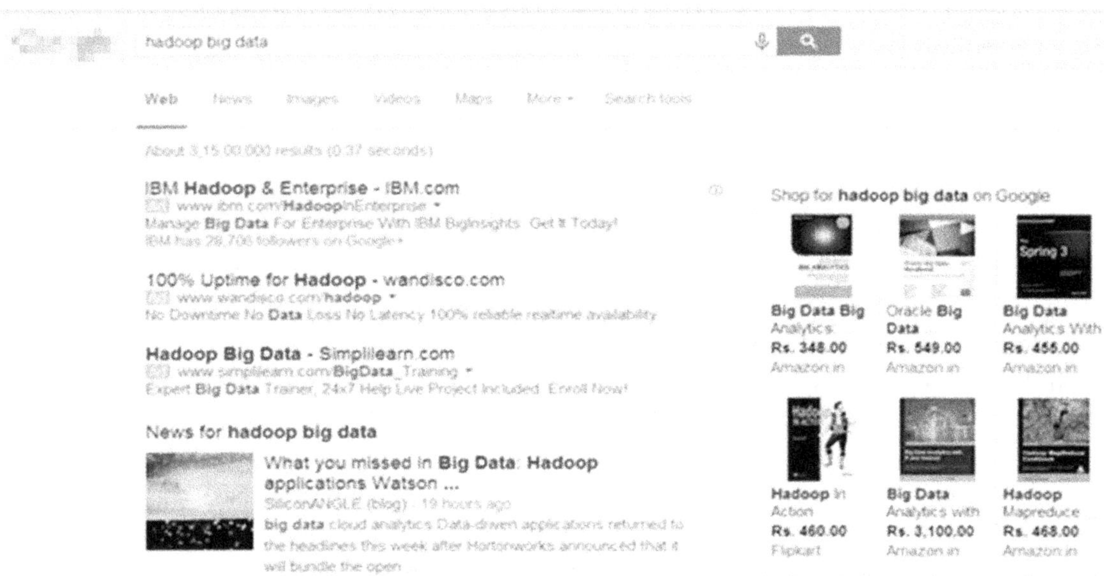

Table 1. Example of employee table in a database

Employee_ID	Employee_Name	Gender	Department	Salary_In_lacs
2365	Harkirat Singh	Male	Finance	6,50,000
3398	Sukhwinder kaur	Female	Admin	6,50,000
7465	Harvinder Singh	Male	Admin	5,00,000
7500	Kiranbir Kaur	Female	Finance	5,00,000

As with many other video surveillance systems, retail video analytics faces many technical challenges coming from a real world scenario, which include but are not limited to changeable and uncontrollable lighting conditions, high level complex human and crowd activities, cluttered backgrounds, crowded scenes, occlusion, odd viewing angles, low resolution cameras, limited contrast and low object discriminability. A retail analytics system also has to be designed to handle an extremely diverse group of employees, customers, merchandise, scenes and target objects, and each with rich appearance models. Scalability is another issue that needs to be taken into careful consideration in system design i.e. the ability to handle a realistic number of cameras without extravagant computational resources and systems need to be robust and reconfigurable, and able to operate at different types of store layout while requiring minimal or no return and modification. Finally, for retail, it is widely agreed that it is nontrivial to define meaningful metrics or even a plausible methodology for rigorous evaluation.

Existing Technology

Loss Prevention (LP) Systems

While generic video surveillances security features (e.g. abandoned bag detection) are equally applicable to stores scenarios retail in unique in terms of its focus on loss prevention. Loss prevention systems can be broadly classified into three categories by their location within the store. Store floor Surveillance systems what h for shoplifting by shoppers or theft involving floor staff either during regular operations or after hours. The cameras used are almost exclusively ceiling mounted cameras.

Back of store surveillance systems watch the shipping/receiving/loading dock and warehouse areas of any suspicious a questionable behavior such as removal instead of delivery of goods.

Store front surveillance systems deals with cashier and self-checkout systems, which are again of diverse types and forms. The cameras at these stores are either ceiling mounted or wall mounted and analytics involves in recognition of images of objects and of events/actions/interactions. It is further classified into subcategories based on their intended functionality. First cart basket assesses whether the shoppers/cashiers have presented all the acquired items at the checkout. Second, non –scan systems determine whether all the shopped items have effectively been registered at the point of scale system and the shoppers are appropriately charged. Next, ticket switching systems look for any discrepancy between the appearance of the shopping item and the identity printed on the receipt. Depending upon whether the item is bar coded or a produce, the technical approach involves different visual analytics. Finally, cashier fraud systems attempt to detect any explicit mismanagement of the cash by the cashiers. There are also systems in place for returned goods, which involves tracking the shoppers from the store entrance to the returns desk, which is often located near the entrance. The idea is to make sure the customer arrived with an item rather than simply picking it up off the sales floor.

- **People Counting:** Provides the number of visitors to a store at any given time or during some time period. When combined with sales data it can be used to calculate the store conversion rate, i.e the percentage of visitors converted to buyers. The conversation rate is an indicator of high importance to retailers since it tells how well a store is performing. The traffic statistics can also be used by store managers to make merchandising or staff planning decisions.
- Total population counting is usually achieved by installing cameras monitoring the entrance and exit of the store.
- To obtain customer counts in particular areas, the problem is often addressed using background subtraction and blob tracking. A given blob can be covered to a person count(since groups often merge together) by comparing the area of the blob to the area typically occupied by a single person. The parameter can either be set empirically or learned from sample data . in more crowded spaces estimation based on foreground pixel area does not work as well since it assumes homogeneous crowd density. Alternatively, as proposed in people counting can be approached more directly by tracking each individual based on head and shoulder detection.

Hot zone and dwell time analysis involves knowing where customers go and stay within a store and are often as important as counting them. Trajectory analysis based on tracking people can pinpoint spots with the greatest traffic activity and reveal where customers spend their time in the store managers to optimize store layout for better product placements. In addition, this data can be used to evaluate or enhance the effectiveness of sale or advertising displays. Hot zone and dwell time analysis are relatively straightforward if the trajectories of customers in a store can be obtained. Numerous approaches have been proposed for visual object tracking. While some work has reported promising results using real store data, robust in-store tracking of people using cameras still remains a big challenge, especially under heavy occlusions (Coudert 2011).

Customer behavior analysis is less statistical in nature and provides finer grained information regarding how customers interact with products and how they make buying decisions. Gaze analysis offers a way to discover customers' interest in merchandise by tracking their attention on a store display. Shopper group clustering, on the other hand, detects in store dynamic group activities or queuing activities at checkout lines (Coetzer 2011).

More recently there has been an increasing focus on shopping behavior analysis via activity recognition. For example, some approaches detect customers' interest in products by recognizing actions like reaching or grabbing products. Propose an approach to further recognize buying events, namely detecting when customers fetch products and place them into their shopping carts or carry them in their hands.

CHALLENGES

Shoplifting

Shoplifting comprises many of the most important concerns in today's retail industry and also it remains the most serious threats to profitability and store safety. Each year, the retail industry suffers huge losses due to shoplifting alone. Therefore, all types of shoplifting affect retail profitability, but most damaging is the professional shoplifters or boosters. These career criminals steal large quantities of valuable materials and convert it to cash via fences, flea markets, online auctions and street vendors. Boosters are often well aware of stores security systems and will use a variety of plans to avoid or counter these protective efforts. While there is no typical shoplifter and different types of shoplifting varies just as widely, one fact remains discouraging constant-as anti-shoplifting strategies evolve, so too do the shoplifters.

Employee Theft and Abuse

Nowadays, in every retail sector employee theft and fraud, is common in retail stores most of are related to retail threats, accounts for several billion in store cash, inventory, and supply losses every year. For many retailers, internal theft can be destructive. Every Employee who is working in the retail sector often has insider knowledge of in and out and access to both products and the other important procedures. They know where cash is stashed, and they are often able to require passwords alarm codes and combinations (Tickner 1975). They may even have copies of store keys. Store associates are intimately aware of security procedures and systems, and therefore believe they are able to accurately weigh their risk of being caught if they steal (Welsh 2009).

Considerably, most of the employees are able to accurately assess the attentiveness of coworkers. They know when to alert, caring managers and colleagues are staffed, as well as when native or indifferent associates are in charge of shoplifting, types of employee deviation range considerably, some of which include “sweet hearting (passing on low prices to friends, family), trading goods with other businesses employees, under-ringing items at the register to pass along a lower price, removing goods from the store in all manner of ways(hidden in the bags or clothing), cash theft from registers or safes, manipulations of returns or receipts to obtain cash or store credit).

To minimize employee theft and deviation in retail sector it is important to thoroughly screen applicants, create a workplace atmosphere that promotes honesty, also take proper detection systems which help to identify employees who are dishonest towards their work and encourage and reward good behavior while not be tolerated (Valera 2011). It is also important to develop a program that employees acknowledge as being thorough, accurate and well-monitored. if dishonest employees perceive a store’s security systems as weak or spotty, they will take advantage of the situation. Control procedures, article control, and detection technologies signal employees their productivity is appreciated and reinforce that dishonesty will be quickly detected and punished (Tweed 2008). Like all commercial threats, employee deviance should also be addressed with integrated policies and technologies.

MOVING BEYOND BASIC SECURITY TECHNOLOGY

Detection Systems

In the retail industry, there are several types of alarmed detection systems that are directing helping the security professionals to reduce theft and loss interruption detection systems sense; also it helps to record all the entries of the people and employee, break-ins.

Therefore, theft detection systems handle removal of the dishonest merchandise during operating hours in the retail industry and also it helps fraud detection systems handle fraudulent receipts, and internal theft.

Intrusion detection systems send an alert for any authorized, unauthorized or forced entries which are happening inside the store. These detection systems can be attached to various places that are in Comprised of door, window and motion detectors, therefore these systems are further tied into an alarm that notifies both local officials of a security breach.

Another disadvantage of traditional burglar alarm is response time seasoned thieves are unafraid by an alarm system if they know it will take a certain amount of item, for authorities to react. Hence, traditional alarm systems also provide very little assistance to retailers in carrying through with criminal prosecution. so unless a witness happens to see the break- in, the incident goes largely unrecorded.

In theory, store employees will react to the alarm sound and either resolve a faulty tag with a receipt or apprehend a shoplifter. Unfortunately, the reality is that most of the alarm activations are not theft related and are either live tags generally not deactivated by the employees or that came into the store from retail stores. To successfully respond to a break-in and more ideally, to put off it, retailers should implement more intelligent alarm systems to catch the offenders Access control systems can limit the theft and violence in workplaces by keeping everyone but current employees out of restricted areas.

Video Surveillance and Analytics

Recent years we have witnessed that enormous advancement is done in the field of video surveillance so much so that a new subcategory has emerged within it video analytics which is followed by most of the big organizations (Norris 1999). Today, cameras are able to not only film activity, but automatically track suspicious individuals, distinguish between genuine and non-genuine consumer behaviors and predict paths of exit once a crime has been committed (Lee 2006). Also, the ability for cameras to interact with and send alerts to the object control devices and intrusion detection systems and video surveillance emerges as one of the most powerful tools a retailer can employ to his store so that it can able to identify and intercept store losses (Moussaid 2010).

FINDINGS

Intelligent Video Analytics

Video surveillance is a booming business and installations which are becoming larger and larger day by day. At the same time, several studies have been highlighted that show the hit and miss nature of human intervention to spot the change in a surrounding environment, and these challenge becomes larger as systems expand. To add on to the woes, a massive amount of video is being recorded, but never watched or reviewed, due to lack of time or lack of interest, or just lack of knowledge on what can be learnt from them.

As a result, events and activities are missed and suspicious behavior, other activities is not noticed in time to prevent incidents. This has led to the development of intelligent video analytics which is about reducing the vast amount of information contained in the video itself which helps in making it more manageable for systems and reliable for the persons. Intelligent video analytics can also extract the data from real-time video and from the past data itself which help to streams and integrate that information with other applications that automatically do the required analysis part and provide the required information from the video data., such as in retail sector it helps to access control systems, create new benefits and opening up new business possibilities. This is where intelligent Video Analytics can play a very crucial role. Therefore, the basic function of the intelligent video analytics is security and surveillance.

Video Analytics is simultaneously being used to extract various customer-centric information, this helps to improve footfalls and minimize the challenges faced in day-to-day operations in the retail industry. Through the results coming from the intelligent video analytics that become the key to driving customer satisfaction and improving trace. The retail trends can be different depending on the geographical location and they continuously keep changing and updating. Hence we can analyze that our purchasing patterns have changed and our behavior towards the product which is kept on the shelf of the retail store also changes with time. Also, there is one more important factor that is changing demographics which including age, gender and income etc. Therefore this also govern the buying patterns in different geographic locations Building this sort of analysis of the data which is being generated from the video cameras creates a reliable and adaptable video surveillance system which radically reduces workload for the staff and provide accurate information from the real time data.

In addition to this, intelligent video allows the operator to use the video surveillance system more pro-actively by giving early warning about the situations which help to avoid potential risk scenario.

The application performing these analyses are referred to as video content analytics or video analytics which helps to fetch out the data from the video itself and intelligent video analytics also have inbuilt predefined algorithms. Video analytics range from video motion detection and audio detection to more advanced systems including improve customer service, reduce shrinkage, increase public safety, measure performance and also measure traffic flow patterns by aisle, display, or other areas.

Why It Is an Important Development in Retail

Intelligent video allows video cameras to be used in such a way that it becomes host for the new applications which ensures that every video camera become smarter, more accurate and cost-effective. In summary intelligent video automatically analyzes the data from the video itself that is basically analysis is done from the past data and tags surveillance video in real-time, Detects suspicious activities, Initiates video recording, alarms or other actions, Alerts operators or employees who are working in the retail store. It enables users to be proactive which help in preventing crime rather than reacting or analyzing after the fact. Intelligent video also creates a platform for a more pro-active approach to video surveillance. By configuring intelligent video analytics in retail, helps us get instant alerts when pre-set parameters have been breached or violated, thus delivering early warnings to staff.

The retail practice has identified a strategic shift in the retail market from the goods. Retailers sell towards the customers who buy them. In short, retailers are looking to be more customer-focused. From the few years the retail industry has been moving away from being product centric all about the merchandise to increasingly customer-centric. To fully achieve this customer focus, it has been observed that greater organizational alignment and collaboration is needed in retail businesses in order to effortlessly satisfy customer needs. Therefore, tight cross-functional collaboration between Loss Prevention, Merchandising and Sales/Service is necessary to deliver the desired customer experience.

Further, new customer metrics must be used along with traditional metrics to manage performance and guide incentives. Intelligent video analytics is playing an important role in the retail sector by taking various initiatives which are not going to avoid loss prevention but also help in achieving broader organization goals. In short, intelligent video analytics can assist retail organizations' initiatives to create superior customer experiences by:

- **Increasing Public Safety:** Increasing the effectiveness and avoiding the loss prevention is done by providing actionable real-time alerts as well as significantly improving the process of video review, which help in notify to reduces shrinkage, increases store safety, provides new training opportunities, and reduces delays in incident response.
- **Measuring Business Performance:** Providing retail companies a new performance measures to help enhance store layout, warning, and product organization.
- **Improving Customer Service:** Customer service can be improved by Accelerate checkout and reduce customer service wait times through real-time notification which can be done if queues exceed a certain time period set by the user.

Different retail areas where it can be applied (knowing customer patterns, path etc)

- **Retail Shrink:** Intelligent video analytics can detect people who evade payment by pass point of sales location and it can also help in raising the Real-time alarms upon identification and classification of a person loitering running from a scene, etc by alarming from potential high loss actions such as people exiting via indoors.
- **Restricted Zone Detection:** Intelligent video analytics trespass alarms at storeroom entry points and detection of entry and exit of people or vehicles from protected zone including high-value targets such as pallet storage on warehouse floors. And it can also detect vents and behaviors that precede theft such as people loitering or meeting based on duration, time and other factors.
- **Real-Time Alert of Item Removal and Warehouse Theft:** Intelligent video analytics detect in real-time the removal of an item off the store shelf. This is especially valuable when applied to common theft items, such as iPods. It can distinguish between a customer who removes a single item from a shelf (normal shopping behavior) from a customer to removes five items from a shelf in a short period of time (suspicious shopping behavior). Also, it quantifies the impact of stopping the theft of iPods DVD Box sets and other music systems, baby products, vacuums, disposable razors, cosmetics and more in various store risk categories. Also, it will detect the activity of people and vehicles at loading docks and in the warehouse. Hence, Real-time alarms also been established for the employees who exit from an unauthorized door while doing their work, detection of vehicles parked in violation of established rules, monitoring inappropriate traffic flow in warehouses which create many problems, tracking of employees leaving and going to their cars, meeting with family, and friends and also collaborating with truck drivers, etc.
- **Public Safety and Traffic Flow Rate:** While personal safety is priceless, there is a cost to providing a safe store environment for staff and customers. It can also watch for potentially troublesome individuals/ groups, vandals, movement in alarm zones, and loitering without putting store personnel at undue risk during the monitoring process. At the same time, it can permanently record and index for easy retrieval, any incidents which may need real-time or forensic review. It can also help in a number of people or vehicles flowing through gates, doors or waiting in line at point-of-sale terminals. By enabling staffing adjustments in real time to increase customer service which can be done by provides the comparison of traffic patterns against different store layouts from different time periods. Therefore, it can help in optimization display effectiveness and the potential for charging premiums for prime display locations, based on flow and purchasing data.
- **Analyzing Marketing Efforts:** Retail stores are required to map the effectiveness of the advertisements. With the help of intelligent video analytics, the marketing efforts and the advertisements can be managed proactively. It can help in gaining insights on the ads in different aisles and change them boost the advertising depending on the customer's response when he/she is standing to see a particular advertisement flashing on the board. So this becomes a major player in analyzing the ad revenues and thus concentrating efforts in the right areas inside the store.
- **Compliance:** Intelligent video analytics can also identify variant behavior from store compliance rules. For instance, the can generate an alert when people exit the store and trigger Electronic Article Surveillance alarms, thus ensuring that store staff inspects the customer's receipt before leaving the store. Activity after business hours can be flagged and often upon review and store personnel can be observed not following protocol. Alerts such as these yield valuable information and data regarding staff adherence to corporate and individual store protocols. Are receipt checks being properly done? Is there merchandise being lost due to lack of diligence by staff? Are there internal theft issues?

- **Proactive Customer Service:** The traditional methods of customer service have evolved to an era of greater personalization. Most customers seek personalized attention while they shop so that shopping becomes convenient. Most stores are innovating customer service in order to provide their customers with a unique shopping experience. Analytics like queue management helps in identifying the wait time in queues and alternatively open other counters for quick and speedy service. Such proactive actions and understanding customer behavior can raise loyalty towards the store. Most consumers not only like to shop but also talk about their experience. Proactive and personalized customer service can help increase brand loyalty which ultimately leads to more revenue, popularity and more customers.
- **Staff Optimization:** Intelligent Video Analytics also helps in monitoring and optimizing your staff. It allows you to detect any fraudulent activities that are carried out and can help capture any suspicious activities and appropriate steps can be taken to prevent it. Queue management also allows for measuring the performance of the store clerks during peak hours. If a customer requires any assistance, you can also send alerts to your store staff and inform them to assist the customer. You can identify the high traffic areas inside your store and position your staff in such a way so that the customers visiting your store can be served properly. So, it allows you to effectively manage your workforce and also allows you to identify flaws in your system and address them immediately
- **Designing Optimal Store Layouts:** With a past video data and the real time data set around shopper traffic, directional analysis, in-store movement patterns, hot spots and dwell times, retailers are able to use that information to improve store layout and overall design. If a certain department is rarely visited, the store layout can be modified in order to help drive shoppers to the area By reviewing people count, in-store traffic patterns and dwell times around specific areas and products, retailers can use this data to modify their promotion, design or product placement in the retail store.

FUTURE RESEARCH DIRECTIONS

Study done in this paper can be extended to other futuristic areas. Some of the areas where one can do more research are mentioned below.

Ethical Gazing

We are seeing increasing capabilities of CCTV surveillance as the quality and the features/application that can be deployed along with CCTV are also improving which gives more power to the user. There will be applications developed to work with CCTV cameras which can perform ethical gazing and will employ the power of predictive analytics to better manage security resulting in lower losses for the businesses.

Tracking, Privacy, and Oppression

Tracking and identification of individuals and objects within a surveillance area has many uses, both legitimate and illegitimate. Off course if the technology is used in the legitimate and ethical ways, it will be very useful. Research can be done into the areas of legitimate and ethical ways of tracking for the larger good of the society.

Cognitive Inference

The inference by automated systems of the state of mind of an individual, their likely intentions or even their previous behavior, based upon external clues of posture, small scale body movements (hands touching the face, for example) or large scale movements (the pattern of movement within a surveillance area) has similar possibilities for overreaction by security and law enforcement personnel. There will be multiple uses of cognitive inference applications.

CONCLUSION

This paper has summarized the recent development of video surveillance, which has led to the development of intelligent video analytics. Typical contributions are addressed for a variety of application. Representative works are listed for readers to have a general overview of the state-of-the-art technology in the field. In conclusion, these early video systems might not be as good as what people expect at the moment, however as the applications of this technology grows rapidly, so will their utilization spread. Thousands of companies have emerged in the past decade those are especially developing products of intelligent video analytics. One of the reasons for this is the pull by the demands of retail sector. Intelligent Video analytics surely makes managing stores very convenient and helps in improving footfalls and steadily increasing their profits by stopping stealing from the retail store. Though the primary focus has always been on improving security and surveillance, Intelligent Video Analytics adds more by playing a great role in improving customer experience and managing in-store operations seamlessly. Since Intelligent video analytics are constantly evolving, going further, smarter and complex analytical features can be expected to improve business processes. Customer experience is a key factor for any retail store. A unique shopping experience encourages customers to not only comeback but also be loyal to the business. Intelligent video analytics can help you proactively serve your customers and improve the quality of your service. It is expected that the intelligent video analytics would be maturely applied rapidly in this decade.

Video analytics provide us countless opportunities and problems are waiting to be solved using video analytics. Benefits will continue to be seen across multiple sectors as the computing power of IP cameras continues to improve. Video analytics will continue to solve more complex problems like aiding intelligence agencies to local retail outlets. We will see few hurdles, on the way as video analytics gain popularity in benefits but ultimately various organizations - government, intelligence agencies, business houses and technologists will have to come together to remove these hurdles.

Technology is evolving at a rapid pace and in the distant future there may be fully predictive surveillance systems available to us. Advancement in the field of IoT (Internet of things) has given a new term for the video analytics world - the Internet of Recognition (IoR), meaning computer image processing that can recognise, through a single frame to many frames of video, capture and analyse any object and intelligently analyse what it is and what it does. Without doubt, video analytics will be one of the most exciting areas to watch and one of the most explosive areas of growth to keep a look out for.

REFERENCES

Adams, A. A. (2007). Regulating CCTV. In *Ethicomp 2007: Proceedings of the Ninth International Conference*. Tokyo: Meiji University.

Adams, A. A., Murata, K., & Orito, Y. (2010). The Development of Japanese Data Protection. *Policy and Internet, 2*(2), 95–126.

Adams, A. A., Murata, K., & Orito, Y. (2012). Tender Electronic Eyes. *Case Studies on CCTV Deployment in Japan.*

Annesley, J., Colombo, A., Orwell, J., & Velastin, S. A. 2007. A Profile of MPEG-7 for Visual Surveillance. *Proceedings Fourth IEEE Advanced Video and Signal-Based Surveillance (AVSS)*, 482-487. doi:10.1109/AVSS.2007.4425358

BBC. (2003). *Pensioner Freed After FBI Bungle.* Retrieved from news.bbc.co.uk/2/hi/uk_news/england/2799791.stm

Bazzani, L., Cristani, M., Perina, M., & Murino, V. (2012). Multiple-Shot Person ReIdentification by Chromatic and Epitomic Analyses. *Pattern Recognition Letters, 33*(7), 898–903. doi:10.1016/j.patrec.2011.11.016

Ben Shitrit, H., Berclaz, J., Fleuret, F., & Fua, P. (2011). Tracking Multiple People under Global Appearance Constraints. *Computer Vision (ICCV), 2011 IEEE International Conference on*, 137-144.

Berger, A. M. (2000). *Privacy Mode for Acquisition Cameras and Camcorders.* U.S. Patent 6,067,399.

Cezar, J., Jacques, S., & Musse, S. R. (2010). Crowd Analysis Using Computer Vision Techniques. *IEEE Signal Processing Magazine, 27*, 66–77.

Coetzer, B., van der Merwe, J., & Josephs, B. (2011). *Information Management and Video Analytics: The Future of Intelligent Video Surveillance.* InTech. Retrieved from http://tinyurl.com/78flxuy

Coudert, F., Gemo, M., Beslay, L., & Andritsos, F. (2011). Pervasive Monitoring: Appreciating Citizen's Surveillance as Digital Evidence in Legal Proceedings. *Imaging for Crime Detection and Prevention 2011 (ICDP 2011), 4th International Conference on*, 1-6.

Dee, H., & Hogg, D. (2004). Detecting Inexplicable Behaviour. In *Proceedings of the British Machine Vision Conference*. The British Machine Vision Association.

Dee, H., & Hogg, D. (2006). Navigational Strategies and Surveillance. In *Proceedings of the IEEE International Workshop on Visual Surveillance (ECCV-VS)*. IEEE Computer Society Press.

Dee, H. M., & Velastin, S. A. (2008). How Close Are We To Solving the Problem of Automated Visual Surveillance? A Review of Real-World Surveillance, Scientific Progress and Evaluative Mechanisms. *Machine Vision and Applications, 19*(5-6), 329–343. doi:10.1007/s00138-007-0077-z

Dick, A. R., & Brooks, M. J. (2003). Issues in Automated Visual Surveillance. Academic Press.

Dollár, P., Wojek, C., Schiele, B., & Perona, P. (2012). *Pedestrian Detection: An Evaluation of the State of the Art. Pattern Analysis and Machine Intelligence, 34*(4), 743–761.

Donald, C. (2005). How Many Monitors Should a CCTV Operator View? In *CCTV Image* (p. 355). London: STL Publishing.

Dufaux, F., & Ebrahimi, T. (2008). Scrambling for Privacy Protection in Video Surveillance Systems. *IEEE Transactions on Circuits and Systems for Video Technology, 18*(8), 1168–1174. doi:10.1109/TCSVT.2008.928225

Evans, M., Boyle, J. N., & Ferryman, J. (2012). Vehicle Classification using Evolutionary Forests. *Proceedings International Conference on Pattern Recognition Applications and Methods*, 387-393.

Gong, S., Loy, C. C., & Xiang, T. (2011). *Security and Surveillance*. Springer. doi:10.1007/978-0-85729-997-0_23

Goold, B. J. (2002). Privacy Rights and Public Spaces: CCTV and the Problem of the Unobservable Observer. *Criminal Justice Ethics, 21*(1), 21–27. doi:10.1080/0731129X.2002.9992113

Helbing, D., & Molnar, P. (1995). Social Force Model for Pedestrian Dynamics. *Physical Review E: Statistical Physics, Plasmas, Fluids, and Related Interdisciplinary Topics*, 51. PMID:9963139

Hempel, L., & Töpfer, E. (2004). *CCTV in Europe* (Final Report). Tech. rept. Urban Eye Project: HPSE-CT2001-00094.

Hu, W., Tan, T., Wang, L., & Maybank, S. (2004). A Survey on Visual Surveillance of Object Motions and Behaviour. *IEEE Transactions on Systems, Man, and Cybernetics, 34*(3), 334–252. doi:10.1109/TSMCC.2004.829274 PMID:15369076

Independent Police Complaints Commission (UK). (2007). *Stockwell One: Investigation into the shooting of Jean Charles de Menezes at Stockwell underground station on 22 July 2005*. Author.

Introna, L. D., & Wood, D. (2004). Picturing Algorithmic Surveillance: The Politics of Facial Recognition Systems. *Surveillance & Society*, 2(2/3), 177–198.

Jia, K., & Gong, S. (2008). Generalized Face Super-Resolution. *IEEE Transactions on Image Processing, 17*(6), 873–886. doi:10.1109/TIP.2008.922421 PMID:18482883

Ko, T. (2011). *Video Surveillance*. InTech. Retrieved from http://tinyurl.com/8hlveuk

Lee, S.-W., Park, J., & Lee, S.-W. (2006). Low Resolution Face Recognition Based on Support Vector Data Description. *Pattern Recognition, 39*(9), 1809–1812. doi:10.1016/j.patcog.2006.04.033

MarketResearch.com. (2011). *Global Video Surveillance Market, Applications and Management Services Forecasts (2010-2015)*. Retrieved from www.marketresearch.com/MarketsandMarkets-v3719/GlobalVideo-Surveillance-Applications-Management-6083117/

Moussaid, M., Perozo, N., Garnier, S., Helbing, D., & Theraulaz, G. (2010). The Walking Behaviour of Pedestrian Social Groups and Its Impact on Crowd Dynamics. *PLoS ONE*, *5*(4), e10047. doi:10.1371/journal.pone.0010047 PMID:20383280

Norris, C., & Armstrong, G. (1999). *The Maximum Surveillance Society: The Rise of CCTV*. Oxford, UK: Berg.

Orrite, C., Martinez, F., Herrero, E., Ragheb, H., & Velastin, S. (2008). Independent Viewpoint Silhouette-based Human Action Modelling and Recognition. *Proc. 1st International Workshop on Machine Learning for Vision-based Motion Analysis in conjunction with the European Conference on Computer Vision (ECCV)*.

Park, J.-S., & Lee, S.-W. (2008). An Example-Based Face Hallucination Method for SingleFrame, Low-Resolution Facial Images. *IEEE Transactions on Image Processing*, *17*(10), 1806–1816. doi:10.1109/TIP.2008.2001394 PMID:18784029

Patino, L., Bremond, F., Evans, M., Shahrokni, A., & Ferryman, J. (2010). Video Activity and Reporting with Incremental Unsupervised Learning. *Proceedings Seventh IEEE Advanced Video and Signal-Based Surveillance (AVSS)*, 511-518. doi:10.1109/AVSS.2010.74

Ragheb, H., Velastin, S., Remagnino, P., & Ellis, T. (2008). ViHASi: Virtual Human Action Silhouette Data for the Evaluation of Silhouette-Based Action Recognition Methods. *Proceedings Computer Vision and Pattern Recognition (CVPR'07)*, 1-8.

Reeves, B., & Nass, C. (2002). *The Media Equation* (2nd ed.). Stanford, CA: CSLI.

Senior, A., Pankanti, A., Brown, L., Ying-Li, T., Ekin, A., Connell, J., & Lu, M. et al. (2005). Enabling Privacy through Computer Vision. *IEEE Security and Privacy*, *3*(3), 50–57. doi:10.1109/MSP.2005.65

Spindler, T., Wartmann, C., Hovestadt, L., Roth, D., Van Gool, L., & Steffen, A. (2008). Privacy in Video Surveilled Spaces. *Computers & Security*, *16*(2), 199–222. doi:10.3233/JCS-2008-16205

C. Sun, H. Talbot, S. Ourselin, & T. Adriaansen (Eds.). (2003). *Proceedings of the Seventh International Conference on Digital Image Computing: Techniques and Applications, DICTA 2003*. Sydney, Australia: CSIRO Publishing.

Tickner, A. H., & Poulton, E. C. (1973). Monitoring up to 16 Synthetic Television Pictures Showing a Great Deal of Movement. *Ergonomics*, *16*(4), 381–401. doi:10.1080/00140137308924529 PMID:28086276

Tweed, D., & Ferryman, J. (2008). Enhancing Change Detection in Low-Quality Surveillance Video with Markov Random Fields. *Proc. 1st ACM International Workshop on Vision Networks for Behaviour Analysis (VNBA'08)*.

Valera, M., Velastin, S., Ellis, A.-L., & Ferryman, J. (2011). Communication Mechanisms and Middleware for Distributed Video Surveillance. *IEEE Transactions on Circuits and Systems for Video Technology*, *21*(12), 1795–1809. doi:10.1109/TCSVT.2011.2133850

Welsh, B. P., & Farrington, D. P. (2009). Public Area CCTV and Crime Prevention: An Update Systematic Review and Meta-Analysis. *Justice Quarterly*, *26*(4), 716–745. doi:10.1080/07418820802506206

Yilmaz, A., Javed, O., & Shah, M. (2006). Object Tracking: A Survey. *ACM Computing Surveys*, *38*(4), 13, es. doi:10.1145/1177352.1177355

Zaidenberg, S., Boulay, B., & Bremond, F. (2012). A Generic Framework for Video Understanding Applied to Group Behaviour Recognition. *Proceedings of the IEEE Ninth International Conference on Advanced Video and Signal-Based Surveillance (AVSS 2012)*, 126-142.

Zhan, B., Monekosso, D. N., Remagnino, P., Velastin, S. A., & Xu, L. Q. (2008). Crowd Analysis: A Survey. *Machine Vision and Applications*, *19*(5-6), 345–357. doi:10.1007/s00138-008-0132-4

KEY TERMS AND DEFINITIONS

Administrator Client: A web-based interface for configuring and managing Video Analytics.

Alarm: A video display that is initiated by an alert.

Analytic Profile: A profile that determines the set of analytic algorithms and associated configuration that the Smart Surveillance Engine (SSE) uses to process the incoming video stream to produce event or alert metadata.

Camera Definition: The set of parameters that enable the software to communicate with the VMS to analyze the data from the camera. The camera definition can also include camera location information, such as latitude and longitude coordinates.

Channel: A defined view of a camera, or an input from a related device, that is identified by a uniquely assigned channel ID.

Channel Group: A collection of channels, typically created for geographic areas, such as floors of a building, sections of a city, or sections of a region. Groups can be used to limit or filter the channels that can be accessed in the Intelligent Video Analytics operator client.

Channel Group: A collection of channels, typically created for geographic areas, such as floors of a building, sections of a city, or sections of a region. Groups can be used to limit or filter the channels that can be accessed in the Intelligent Video Analytics operator client.

Image Map: A customized graphical image that is plotted with cameras or links to other maps.

Key Frame: A static image from a camera that is usually smaller than the actual video size. A key frame might contain more visual information about an event or alert such as a bounding box, or a track of motion.

Person Model: A graphic that is superimposed on a snapshot of a scene image. The person model supplies analytics information on the height (in pixels) of an average person at a particular location in the scene. This height varies across the scene because of camera perspective. The height distribution of person models across the scene image is used to improve the accuracy of analytics and the speed of processing.

Smart Surveillance Engine (SSE): A component of Intelligent Video Analytics, which receives and analyzes video streams from a VMS and generates video metadata.

Video Management System (VMS): A third-party software application for managing video surveillance systems that provide the video stream source for Intelligent Video Analytics.

Chapter 4
Realizing the Potential of Retail Analytics

Swapnil Saurav
JDA Software, India

ABSTRACT

Few industries are changing more rapidly than today's retail sector. A still-turbulent economy, new selling channels, advanced digital technologies, and increasingly demanding consumers all challenge retailers to find new ways of remaining relevant and competitive. The purchasing decision journey for consumers involves multiple steps, many of which are now being captured, digitized, and transformed into metrics and data. As this data becomes an implied derivative of essential retail and consumer technologies, the focus is shifting from how to acquire the data to how to extract insights from it— insights that can be turned into differentiation and competitive advantage for the retailer and a better shopper experience for the consumer.

INTRODUCTION

Retailing today is changing at a much faster pace than any other industry. Retailing industry is trying to be competitive by changing rapidly. A still-turbulent economy, with new and innovative selling channels, advanced digital technologies, and increasingly demanding consumers all challenge retailers to find new ways of remaining relevant and competitive. Looking at the purchasing decision journey of consumers which involves multiple steps, almost of these are now being captured, digitized, and transformed into metrics and data. This data which are captured have become an implied derivative of essential retail and consumer technologies, and are the source of retail analytics which is how to acquire the data to how to extract insights from it. Retailers look to turn these insights into differentiation and competitive advantage for the them and at the same time provide better shopper experience for the end consumer.

DOI: 10.4018/978-1-5225-3056-5.ch004

But the main challenge of big data is just that—it's not only big but also unstructured most of the times. Massive amounts of structured and unstructured information are piling up in retailer and supplier data warehouses, stores (both physical and online) and at the manufacturing location as well. Unstructured data holds the key insight as customer metrics derived from video and other sensors, social media and mobile devices have the power to provide unprecedented insight into the purchase decision process.

Retailing industry are among the first industries that recognized the benefits of using predictive analytics and started to employ it mostly to stay ahead of competition and putting understanding of the customer as a first-priority goal. Today's competitive business environment understanding of your customer requirement and offering the right products at right time is the key of any successful business. Due to high growth of internet, online shopping is becoming most interesting and popular activities for the consumers. Online shopping is providing a variety of products for consumers and is increasing the sales challenges for e-commerce players.

Offline or the brick and mortar and the pure play online retailers are evaluating its performance in terms of point of sale (POS) transactions and working to address questions like how much the customer bought, the size of the purchase, impact of marketing, how to leverage online visitors' data to improve the customer experience and the driving factors of online shoppers' behaviors. Predictive analytics is used to identify an untapped sales opportunity for new items shoppers' online behavior.

Using statistical analytical techniques like A/B/multivariate testing, visitor engagement, behavioral targeting can lead toward high propensity of a prospect's willingness to buy a product. In this chapter, authors provide insights on how the online data can support customized targeting, resulting in incremental increases in e-commerce revenues by advanced predictive modeling on visitors' behavior.

Almost all of ecommerce retailers want to understand their customer behavior and need to maximize customer satisfaction in order to maximize their sales. As retailers look to build an optimum marketing strategy to deliver the targeted advertising, promotions and product offers, their expectations from these strategies is to motivate the prospects to buy more. Still it's a challenge for most of the retailers to digest all of the data, technology, and analytics that are available to them.

Retail Business Analytics in Context

There are millions of products on offer by the retailers around the world but not everything interests the consumer. How to retailers know what their customers want to buy? Well, analytics is the answer and by using business intelligence and business analytic methods retailers would be able to find it. Key is to use right methodology.

The main purpose for companies to use business analytics is to gain a competitive advantage. By using different tools, models and skills this can be done in a number of ways. Below, we briefly present some commonly known business issues within retail today and what potential benefits and insights could be gained from business analytics to help address those issues.

One of the major challenge in using business analytics is to know how to get started. Retailers do not often know what data to collect, how to collect, how to analyze and how to derive the insights that will help drive growth and improve profitability. So these retailers collect enormous amounts of data every hour to make sense from it later. Retailers are able to make basic analysis but when it comes to making spectacular insights that really make a difference, retailers more often fail to do so as they may not which data to take into consideration.

Analytics works best when business objective is defined and relevant data needed for the analysis are identified and captured. Data can come from a number of different sources and some of them may not look important at the first time, such as:

- Average cleaning time of a store.
- Time and place of shopliftings.
- Average number of faulty products in a delivery.
- Number of lights per square meter in a store.
- Open floor area as a percentage of the total floor area of a store.
- Each week's number of products advertised in the weekly flyer …and much more.

In the Table 1 below, presented are the business issues and the potential benefits that retailers can derive from it.

Retailers need to understand how to identify what data to collect and which data to consider for their business problem to get the most out of business analytics. Once the data source is identified and have the relevant data then the retailers' possibilities to gain extreme insights from business analytics are significantly increased.

BACKGROUND

How Can Retailers Get Started With Analytics?

Defining a far-reaching analytics strategy to find extreme insight starts with the basics step: defining the business objective. Defining the decisions that need to be made and mapping the right data to inform them has to be part of designing the retail analytics strategy (Chen 2012). Once the data requirements are defined for the identified business objective, the data sources are then selected.

Let's look at some of the examples to understand it better.

Table 1. Business issues and potential benefits from the retail analytics

Business Issues	Potential Benefits From Business Analytics
Enhance assortment and shelf space management	Know what products to sell in the store
Out of stock	Improve stock levels to never run out or tie-up unnecessary capital
Planning new stores and their marketing	Match the store design with surrounding preferences from its given location to improve profit
Know your customers when marketing	Understand customer behaviors and needs by developing a closer relationship with them
Improve the market mix	Understand what motivates customers to make a purchase and use advertisement, promotions and offerings to trigger their willingness to buy
Price Optimization	Increase profit by charging the exact price a customer is willing to pay for a product at a certain moment
Forecasting	Anticipate customers' demands for the future and plan ahead to increase profit

Case 1: A Retail Store at a Shopping Mall Wants to Increase Average Sales per Customer

A retail store at a shopping mall wants to improve its average shopping bucket size per consumer. Store has identified that the conversion rate can be higher when more customers enter into the store. Hence, store wants to increase volume of traffic entering the store. The focus of the store owner/manager would be to acquire and analyze data on traffic passing by versus actual shoppers entering their store.

Store managers would like to examine the traffic conversion – the percent of shoppers passing by who also enter the store) over time based on the various strategies they would be adopting like changing window displays, introduce incentives, and leverage promotions to shoppers who are nearby, also using social media. Store managers are also interested in mobile metrics such as unique and repeat visits and associated and unassociated devices. The store will benefit from monitoring Twitter, posting on Facebook and photo postings on social media platforms to ensure the right products are being featured which increases the chances of customers coming to the store. Understanding what works best for getting the mall visitors to enter the store, measuring it, and analyzing it allows the retailers to use the right data to be competitive in their business.

Case 2: A Winning Situation for a Multi-Department Retailer for Launch of Its New Back-To-School Product Line

In this example two, we will take up a case of multi-department retailer which wants to win the market share from its competitors with a new back-to-school product line. Focus of the retailer is to raise customer awareness with a seasonal display featured at the front of the store. Business objective identified here is to get shoppers to stop and notice the display at the front of the store so as to increase the probability of people buying these products. Objective is to expose the entire back-to-school product line, and the effectiveness of this display becomes critical to achieving the endgame.

For such business objective, the retailer is best served by measuring the percentage of store traffic reaching the fixture, those stopping there, and those who reach the aisle location of the product line. The metrics needed here are times and traffic counts, with analysis that correlates them. The stats can be derived from a combination of mobile- and video-based analytics which will track the customers' movement through out the day.

Measuring conversion at the aisle and at the fixture locations will help the analyst identify the locations where the shoppers are mostly likely to purchase and which products will be purchased and when. Key metrics need to be captured to understand whether shoppers need to actually spend time at the fixture to convert or just enough to become aware and continue to the home aisle location.

If the time spent by the shoppers at the aisle or the product line are shorter, indicating less engagement, but at the same time, associated with higher conversion, then the assortment on the fixture may not needed to provide visibility to additional or related products in this high-priority location. However, if the time spent at these locations are high (showing interest and engagement) but conversion is low, indicate that the display may not be aligned with the shoppers' needs and the assortment need to be reconfigured to be more effective at driving shoppers to the aisle.

Analysis can run more accurately and efficiently through video and mobile analytics and also provide better scalability than ever before to the analyst. Such analysis will also require fewer stores and less investment to attain large sample sizes than regular and traditional methods. Analysis help retailers to compare and evaluate the effectiveness of variables taken into consideration such as display features, location, assortments, and adjacencies. Apart from being more effective, results also more accurate resulting in better decision process than traditional methods like shopper interviews.

Combining the results from in-store observations with social media information will help in building a connection to what customers truly think and feel (Brown 2007). This will provide a strong differentiator for competitive advantage as with such valuable data in hand, will focus at making the right decisions. Retailers can know sooner, act faster, and decide smarter about the data they need for their business objective. This leads to better decisions that can save the retailer up to millions of dollars in costs while gaining additional millions of dollars in sales lift across the enterprise. The key is knowing what it takes to win and lining up the decisions, data, and analytics to support and execute for success (Myers 2002). Data analysis process can be facilitated with experienced retail analytics experts who helps with defining data requirements for projects and mapping data sources to the project.

Table 2. Advanced analytical application in ecommerce

Example	Description	Business Value
Customer Segmentation	Groups customers together statistically based on similar characteristics, helping to identify smaller, yet similar, groups perfect for targeting marketing opportunities (Cuzzocrea 2011).	> Use segment profile information to drive offers, advertising, and direct marketing (Bhattacherjee 2012) > Track continually changing customer preferences and expectations (Braun 2006) > Link segments to CRM and business intelligence environments (Yadav 2015)
Basket Segmentation	Provides information about customers through the contents of each transaction, even when it cant be identify (Camm 2014).	> Classify each basket into segments based on apparent mission of the customer while coming to store (Davenport 2013) > Behavioral segmentation is "the voice of the customer" in that it utilizes variables that the customer directly controls (Agrawal 2011). > Identify key customer behaviors and adjust marketing merchandising and operations plans to address specific, desirable behaviors (Fisher 2012).
Affinity and Purchase Path Analysis	Identifies those products that sell in conjunction with each other on an everyday, promotional, an seasonal basis, as well as the links between purchases over time.	> Use results for cross-product promotions, selling strategies, and overall product merchandising. > Identify which products are purchased in addition to promoted products (Devlin 2012) > Identify products that drive the purchase of primary items (Ularu 2012).
Marketing Mix Modelling	Provides customer promotion campaign response models, product propensity models, and attrition models that predict customer behavior (Delen 2013).	> Devise communication strategies that match appropriate and relevant marketing messages to the right targeted customers (Fan 2013) > Predict the likelihood of a customer's response to an offer based on the product appeal, offer receptivity, and frequency of use > Predict ROI on each marketing campaign by media type and expenditures – category, region and time

From Business Intelligence to Business Analytics

There are 4 key trends that is reshaping retail, including an explosion of consumer and enterprise data that dwarfs anything that the industry has ever dealt with before. The biggest challenge facing retailers isn't managing the volume or variety of data but it's the ability to identify what business outcomes they can impact through the integration and analysis of big data (Chen 2014).

As seen in the couple of examples above, retailers can use the data analytics at different levels of maturity and in the process achieve varying degrees of success. Leading retailers such as Best Buy, CVS, Amazon, Target and Wal-Mart are leveraging analytics to achieve cost efficiency and as well as increase sales through improved customer satisfaction. Some of the examples of how analytics is being used are:

- Gain a deeper understanding of shoppers' behaviors, their needs and preferences to build a more personal relationship with their customers.
- Improve marketing effectiveness through social media marketing and micro-targeting, personalization and delivery of context. Channel sensitive promotions and offers that increase the likelihood of purchase are also identified and executed well for greater benefits.
- Optimized supply chain to ensure the most profitable outcome in terms of demand fulfillment balanced against cost of carrying excess inventory.
- Determine pricing, including bundle and basket pricing, based on the value customers attach to their needs at any given time.
- Spot flash trends, such as a celebrity sighting in a particular pair of jeans, that have an impact on demand to be able to turn them into revenue capturing opportunities.

Even as such industry leaders evolve their business structures, strategies, tools and resources in an effort to embed analytics into their organization, most retailers, by their own assessment are still struggling with wide ranging issues that prevent them from leveraging analytics strategically.

They are overwhelmed by a data tsunami from various sources like POS systems, enterprise transactional data, machine logs, loyalty data, unstructured and semi-structured data from emails and machine logs, social media data. Retailer are unable to build a data management and integration strategy best aligned with their format and business objectives (Kaisler 2013).

Beyond Big Data

Analytics are driving the move from merchant-driven business models—where the product is the differentiator—to digital models, where every decision is informed by the analysis of the data (Cooper 2012). Brand engagements are becoming more closely aligned with individual shopper preferences, creating a brand relationship that is shifting from a "nice to have," time-sensitive offer-based relationship to a "must have" digital companionship based on deep insights and understanding of the consumer, where each individual customer takes center stage. Its no longer about the group of shoppers but its about what each individual customer wants. Its about providing personalized offerings to the shoppers (Davenport 2012). To achieve this critical differentiation, retailers are depending less on increasingly shorter product cycles and more on the enduring differentiators of relationship and customer experience created through strategic use of data and analytics based on each shopper's past data (Kwon 2014).

Retailers are increasingly able to understand that their ability to compete is tied to their ability to create and harness value from right set of data, and are seeking new ways to look at big data. More than half of retailers worldwide have big data initiatives, and across all industries companies will spend an average of $10 million on big data initiatives in one year alone (Jacobs 2009). Digital transformation is the next big thing and retailers will be using insights from data analytics initiatives to its digital transformation strategy (Davenport 2012).

Retailers regularly utilize web analytics for site maintenance, management, and marketing. These companies now look forward to utilize advanced analytics in the physical store too. Physical stores are not going to go away. Physical stores provide great opportunities for the retailers to meet, greet and interact with their customers. Shopper insights in the physical store have historically been gained through highly manual processes lacking objectivity and scale. According to Tony Costa in the Harvard Business Review, "most companies are flying blind when it comes to understanding their customers in the analog world."

In fact, Cisco research shows that retail has a significantly high potential value to be gained by using IoE to gather store metrics—up to 11 percent, or up to $1.584 trillion in additional net profits. This value is driven by specific use cases: For example, it might encompass guiding and influencing the customer journey, improving workforce productivity, creating connected inventory views, or reinventing investment models for marketing, promotion management, and advertising.

Retailers need good data; but more importantly, they need the right data to gain the insights that can transform their businesses (Madsen 2013). Value comes from analyzing new data types in the context of specific business knowledge, such as transaction log (T-log) and loyalty information, campaign results, and pricing actions. Every shopper engagement, inventory movement, and promotion leaves a data trail providing opportunities for new capabilities, both from historical data and real-time information, to support decisions across the business (Manyika 2011).

Operationalizing new metric is described in Figure 1 below.

Figure 1. Operationalizing metrics

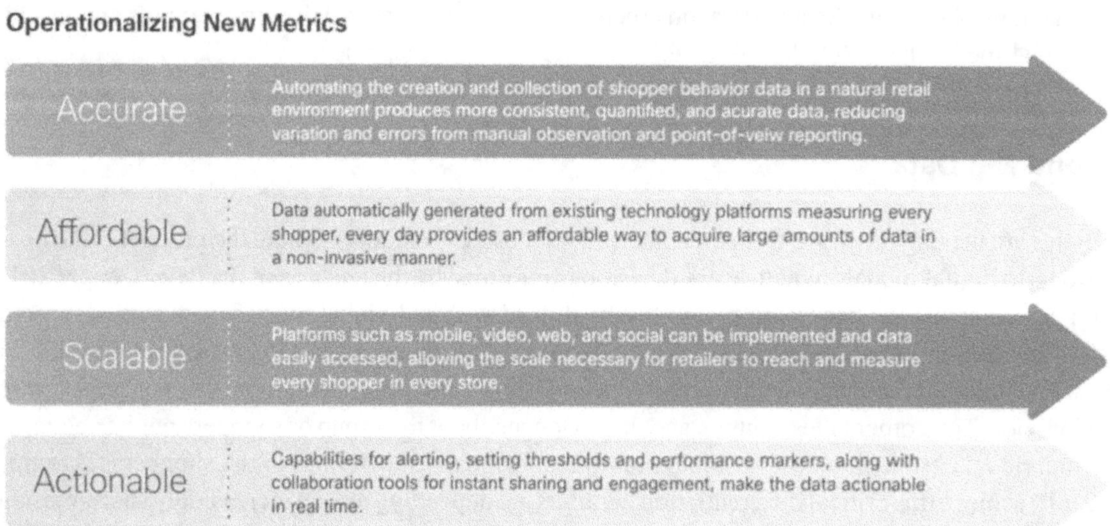

RESEARCH METHODOLOGY

Author has performed qualitative and descriptive research based on secondary sources and extensive literature review. The retail analytics deployed by various companies are studied. The present study undertakes a thorough review of basic and contemporary literature available and identified the issues which are affecting the retail analytics.

Author has collected Literature, including research papers from peer-reviewed journals, conference proceedings, white papers and presentations from the industry. Papers were collected applying a structured search, using phrases such as "Retail analytics", "ecommerce strategy". The author has referred various International Journals like Supply Chain Management: An International Journal, International Journal of Operations and Production Management, International Journal of Physical Distribution & Logistics Management, Journal of Agribusiness in Developing and Emerging Economies, International Food and Agribusiness Management Review, IUP Journal of Supply Chain Management etc. The literature has been divided into various themes according to the delivery models and further investigation has been attempted to identify various factors affecting the supply chain.

Figure 2 below shows the break-up of the companies which were studied as part of writing this chapter.

FINDINGS

Retailers rate, by far, improving customer insight as their #1 objective that they are looking from analytics initiatives. Interestingly, retailers rate themselves much higher than competition in terms of their use of customer analytics. Close to 50% of these retailers consider themselves lagging behind competition, while 40% state they are at par with their competitors. It can be interpreted as most of the retailers consider themselves leaders in this space are few and far between.

Analyzing the maturity level in the industry, retailers' analytics maturity varies by function, and Customer Insights ranks low, with 2 in 3 retailers able to conduct "basic" analytics at best. Authors borrowed an Analytics Maturity Assessment Framework from various secondary source for detailed descriptions of the levels of analytics maturity. This model is in basic design stage and authors are planning to launch the assessment framework soon for carrying out similar research in future.

The last wave of analytics investments in retail is centered on operational efficiency and transparency leading to cost reduction and better operation management. The top 3 functions in terms of analytics maturity - supply chain, merchandising and finance - are all operationally focused for efficiency and visibility. Improving customer insight will help the for retailers to leverage analytics more strategically,

and to be able to create competitive differentiation and improve its top line as well. To achieve this, they will need to move up the analytics maturity curve quickly, which in turn will require investments in redefining processes, skill-development, resourcing and upgrading of tools. That's where the big opportunities exist for service providers.

Retail has always been a data-intensive industry focused on customer buying habit. As the tools available to store, manage and analyze this data evolved, so did the role the analysis of data played in retail decision-making. Their role has expanded from visibility and control, to transparency, to efficiency, to customer engagement. Efficiency makes the analysis cheaper, faster and easier today to store and process

Figure 2. Description of the retailers that were considered for this study

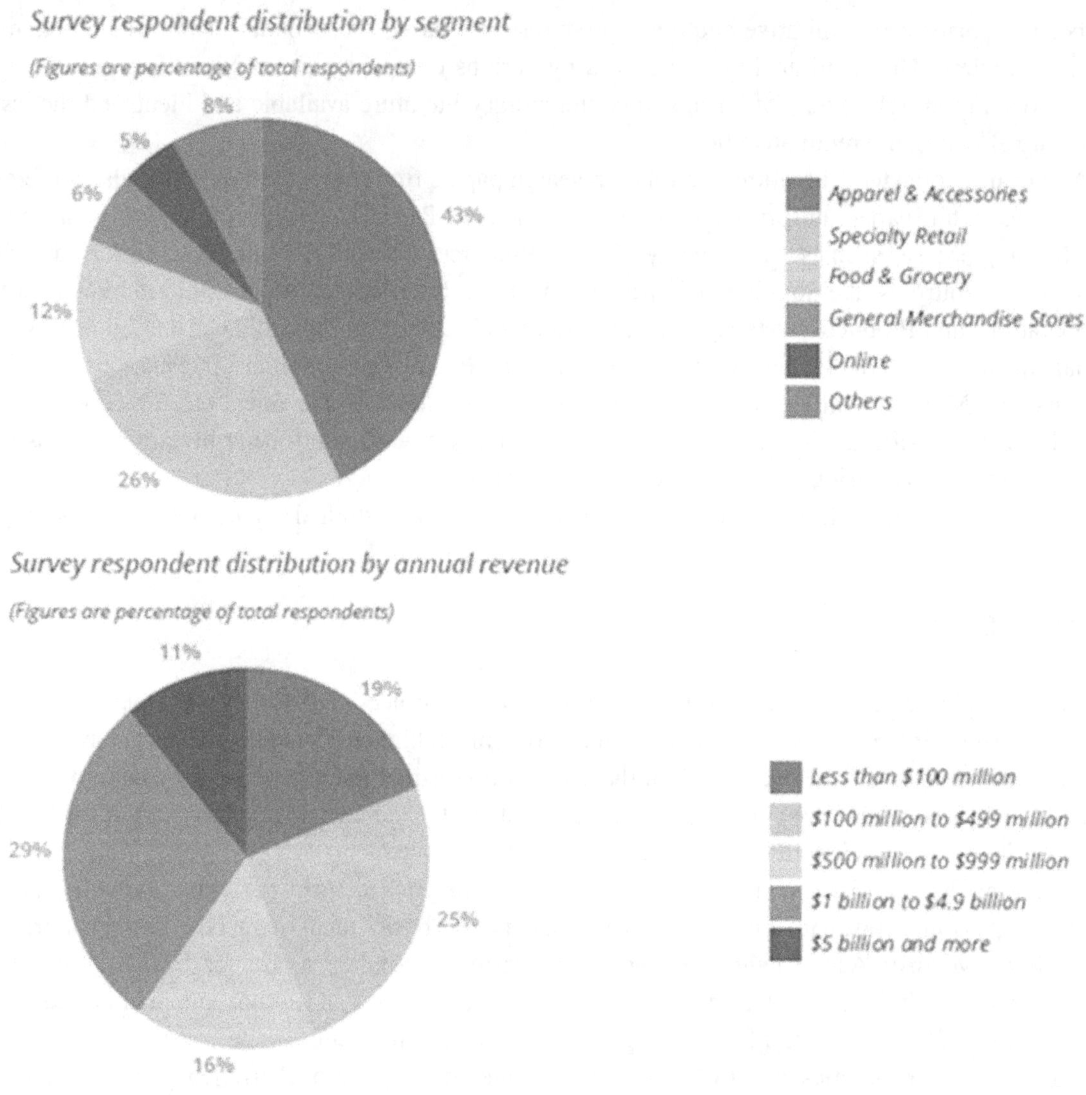

more data than ever before. Retailers have gotten better at data management. Question management is looking for is, how well are they able to leverage insights from this analysis to drive strategic decisions?

In a laser thing marking retail environment where consumer spending is stunted and competition from newer, digital channels is eroding store sales, the route for brick and mortar retailers to earn a larger share of wallet of the customer is through deeper, Omni-channel customer engagement. Effective customer engagement is only as important as how well you know the customer and how well you are equipped to act on that insight across your channels.

Other findings from the study are:

- **Retailers' Analytics Maturity Is Low:** 2 in 5 retailers state they lag behind their competitors in terms of their analytics maturity and a further 2 in 5 suggest they are at par. The "analytical retailer" is thus the exception rather than the rule.
- Data management and integration will be a key area of investment in an effort to increase analytical maturity. Retailers are looking to integrate a variety of data sources over the next 2 years, however public and open data remains a relatively under-explored opportunity.
- Retailers find their current analytics organizational setup sub-optimal. Only 1 out of 5 currently have a shared services model for analytics in place whereas approximately 60% would like to move towards such a model.
- Retailers will invest in contextual, visual and mobile-friendly delivery of insights to combat the biggest challenge that prevents them from leveraging analytics strategically – delivery of insights to the right resource at the right time.
- Retailers' eCommerce or Omni-channel function emerges as the business function with the highest potential opportunity for analytics impact, the highest rate of data growth and the highest planned technology investment. However, it is also currently the function with the lowest analytics maturity.
- Usability is the most important feature retailers will look for when choosing analytics solutions in 2013. Even with the delivery of insights being their biggest challenge, mobile or tablet access ranks relatively low.

PREDICTIVE ANALYTICS SOLUTION FRAMEWORK

Figure 3 depicts the detailed step by step process to perform the online buyers' behavior analysis.

Behavior analysis process is a 3-step process which starts from collecting the data. In the second step, data is analyzed for pattern and finally in the third step, insights are presented to the user.

The Power of Understanding Conversion

Conversion is an important metric to track in the traditional retail too as conversion rate is used as one of the important tool for comparative performance measurement. Conversion rate is a foundational metric—the first of the predictive analytics building blocks and a requirement for creating high-performance retailing. Conversion rate normalizes sales performance against the variable opportunity associated with each store, aisle, and category. There are different definitions of conversion, but the true basic calculation is quite simple: Conversion is the measure of transactions generated by a population of shoppers. For example, if 1,000 shoppers generate 800 transactions, the result is an 80% conversion rate.

Some retailers, particularly in fast-moving consumer products (FMCG) segments, use the number of transactions as a proxy for conversion, assuming that all shoppers generate at least one transaction. This is fundamentally incorrect and can cause businesses to overlook key problem areas. Of course, in grocery and other areas where conversion is usually very high, some of the most valuable conversion comparisons actually come from aisle-, category- and display-level analysis. Here the same calculation applies, only the traffic count, or opportunity, is the number of shoppers reaching the aisle, category, or display. In the past, T-log data has been used to measure store performance, with comparisons being

Figure 3. Step by step process to perform the online buyers' behavior analysis

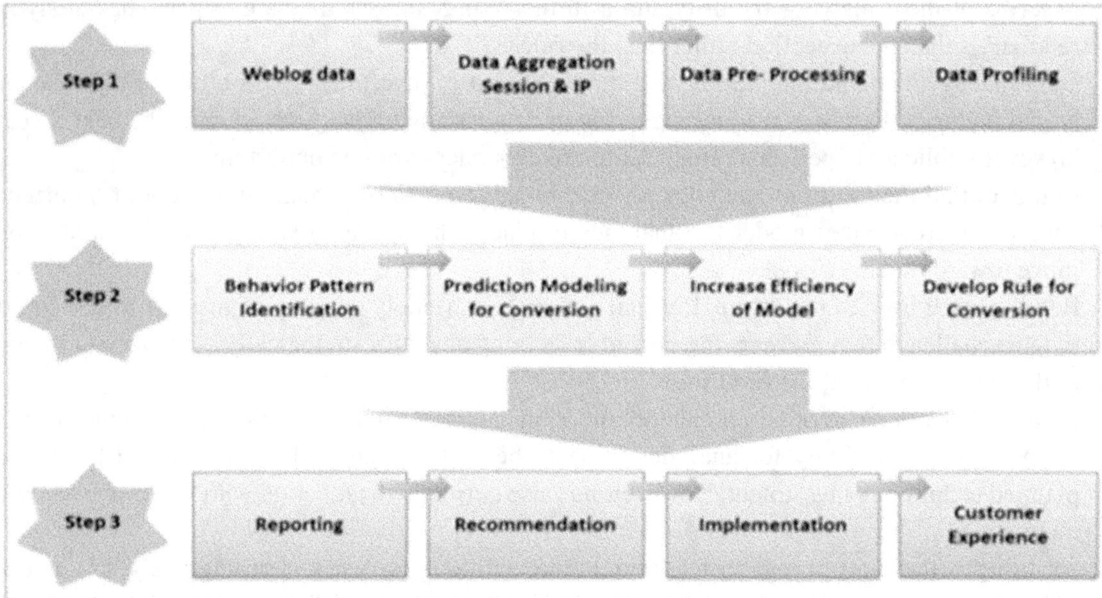

made between stores, prior years, and seasons based on sales revenues. The issue is that store managers and financial officers often assess such numbers and then offer anecdotal insights to caveat the numbers, such as "Traffic was down that week," or "The weather was especially bad this week and fewer people were shopping." These insights can in fact contribute to performance variations. But because they are collected subjectively and not consistently reported, their important contributions to learnings are often discounted or even disqualified from the analysis.

Let's examine a typical store-to-store comparison using sales revenue and transaction count. If Store A reports POS revenue of $1000 and 6 transactions, and Store B reports $2,000 and 10 transactions, the conclusion might be that Store B is the better performer. However, once shopper traffic is taken into consideration, we may find that Store A had 10 shoppers that week and Store B had 20. We now must consider the performance results in the context of one very important variable: opportunity. What opportunity did each store have that week to generate sales? Let's look at the population of shoppers. Using this definition of the opportunity variable, we see that Store A actually converted 60% of its opportunity, while Store B only converted 50%. The sales numbers are of course better in Store B, but over time they can create a false sense that the business is healthy, when in fact more shoppers may be leaving without purchasing. If Store B could actually convert at the rate of Store A (60%) and keep its average transaction value ($20/transaction) the same, it would contribute $400 more each week, even without any improvement in traffic. That would be an additional $146,000 per year from a single store!

Above example illustrates how lack of visibility into store metrics can unintentionally give wrong picture and put the business at risk. Its important that the retailers who don't measure traffic to get a true conversion calculation may find themselves confronting the "silent killer".

However, the good news is that today's automated analytics provide powerful ways to detect, track, and measure these critical factors and bring symptoms to the surface early, before they do too much damage. With these and other analytical capabilities, not only can retailers accurately measure store-level traffic, scaling up to the largest of retail enterprises, but they can also measure traffic at more granular levels down to departments, aisles, fixtures, and individual products and focus on its business objectives accurately.

FUTURE RESEARCH DIRECTION

A fundamental shift in organizational structure, skills and culture is required. Retailers need to shed some of the art and embrace some of the science. This study can be extended to understand the impact of the Retail analytics on the organization from change management perspective. How can organization train their employees and make them ready to embrace the change? Focus should also be to create an organization structure to handle the retail analytics. Analytics process and capability maturity framework needs to be developed to measure the current level of maturity for the retailers. Which can not be measured can not be improved so maturity framework will help to measure and benchmark analytics maturity level of these retailers.

CONCLUSION

The above solution framework shown in the Figure 1 can be customized with the specific requirement with each client. Due to technology agnostic nature of this it can be integrated with any existing database platform without modifying the present process and infrastructure significantly. The data can further be sliced and diced using our proprietary data mining algorithms and methods which will lead to the customers towards optimizing their strategy, improve significantly on the ROI and increase consumer satisfaction.

Millions of consumers visit e-commerce sites, but only few thousands visitors may buy the products. The E-retailer wants to improve the customer experience and would like to improve the conversion rate. The objective of the study is to identify the potential buyers based on their demographics, historical transaction pattern, clicks pattern, browsing pattern in different pages etc. Data analysis revealed the buyers' buying behaviors which are highly dependent on their activities like number of clicks, session duration, previous session, purchase session, clicks rate per session etc. Using the solution framework (Figure 1) and applying data mining and predictive analytics methods, the propensity to conversion scores of each visitor has been derived. This leads to multiple benefits of the e-retailer to offer right & targeted product for the customers at right time, increase conversion rate and improve customer satisfaction. Based on this analysis retailer can optimize the marketing strategy based on identified hidden factors of conversion and understand the purchase funnel of customers.

REFERENCES

Agrawal, D., Bernstein, P., & Bertino, E. (2011). Challenges and Opportunities with big data 2011-1. *Proceedings of the VLDB Endowment* (pp. 1–16). Retrieved from http://dl.acm.org/citation.cfm?id=2367572

Bhattacherjee, A. (2012). Social Science Research: principles, methods, and practices. Open Access Textbooks.

Braun, V., & Clarke, V. (2006). Using thematic analysis in psychology. *Qualitative Research in Psychology, 3*(2), 77–101. doi:10.1191/1478088706qp063oa

Brown, I., & Russell, J. (2007). Radio frequency identification technology: An exploratory study on adoption in the South African retail sector. *Inter. J.Informat.Manage., 27*(4), 250–265. doi:10.1016/j.ijinfomgt.2007.02.007

Camm, J., Cochran, J., Fry, M., Ohlmann, J., & Anderson, D. (2014). A Categorization of Analytical Methods and Models. In *Essentials of Business Analytics* (pp. 5–7). Cengage Learning.

Charman, A. J., Petersen, L. M., Piper, L. E., Liedeman, R., & Legg, T. (2015). Small area census approach to measure the township informal economy in South Africa. *Journal of Mixed Methods Research*, 1–23.

Chen, C. L., & Zhang, C. Y. (2014). Data-intensive applications, challenges, techniques and technologies: A survey on big data. *Information Sciences*, 1–34. doi:10.1016/j.ins.2014.01.015

Chen, H., Chiang, R., & Storey, V. (2012). Business Intelligence and analytics: From big data to Big Impact. *Management Information Systems Quarterly, 36*(4), 1165–1188.

Cooper, A. (2012). What is Analytics? Definition and Essential Characteristics. *CETIS Analytics Series, 1*(5), 1–10.

Cuzzocrea, A., Song, I., & Davis, K. (2011). Analytics over large-scale multidimensional data: the big data revolution! In *Proceedings of the ACM 14th international workshop on Data Warehousing and OLAP* (pp. 101–103). New York: ACM. doi:10.1145/2064676.2064695

Davenport, T. (2013). Analytics 3.0. *Harvard Business Review, 91*(12), 64–72.

Davenport, T., Barth, P., & Bean, R. (2012). How “big data” is different. *MIT Sloan Management Review, 54*(1), 22–24.

Davenport, T., & Dyche, J. (2013). *Big data in Big Companies* (White paper). Retrieved from http://swqlab.fov.unimb.si/moodle/pluginfile.php/9774/course/section/534/Big-Data-in-BigCompanies.pdf

Davenport, T., & Patil, D. (2012). Data Scientist: The sexiest job of the 21 st century. *Harvard Business Review, 90*(10), 70–76. PMID:23074866

Delen, D., & Demirkan, H. (2013). Data, information and analytics as services. *Decision Support Systems, 55*(1), 359–363. doi:10.1016/j.dss.2012.05.044

Devlin, B., Rogers, S., & Myers, J. (2012). *Big data comes of age* (whitepaper). Retrieved from http://www-03.ibm.com/systems/hu/resources/big_data_comes_of_age.pdf

Fan, W., & Bifet, A. (2013). Mining big data: Current status, and forecast to the future. *ACM SIGKDD Explorations Newsletter*, *14*(2), 1–5. doi:10.1145/2481244.2481246

Fisher, D., DeLine, R., Czerwinski, M., & Drucker, S. (2012). Interactions with big data analytics. *Interaction*, *19*(3), 50–59. doi:10.1145/2168931.2168943

Jacobs, A. (2009). The pathologies of big data. *Communications of the ACM*, *52*(8), 36–44. doi:10.1145/1536616.1536632

Kaisler, S., Armour, F., Espinosa, J. A., & Money, W. (2013). Big data: Issues and Challenges Moving Forward. In *2013 46th Hawaii International Conference on System Sciences* (pp. 995–1004). Maui, HI: IEEE. doi:10.1109/HICSS.2013.645

Kwon, O., Lee, N., & Shin, B. (2014). Data quality management, data usage experience and acquisition intention of big data analytics. *Inter. J. Informat. Manage.*, *34*(3), 387–394. doi:10.1016/j.ijinfomgt.2014.02.002

Madsen, M. (2013). *The Challenges of big data & Approaches to Data Quality (White paper)*. Rogue River. Retrieved from http://fm.sap.com/data/UPLOAD/files/The_Challenges_of_Big_Data_&_Approaches_to_Data_Quality.pdf

Manyika, J., Chui, M., Brown, B., Bughin, J., Dobbs, R., Roxburgh, C., & Byers, A. (2011). Big data: The next frontier for innovation, competition, and productivity. Academic Press.

McAfee, A., & Brynjolfsson, E. (2012). Big data: The management revolution. *Harvard Business Review*, *90*(10), 1–9. PMID:23074865

Michael, K., & Miller, K. (2013). Big data: New opportunities and new challenges. *Computer*, *46*(6), 22–24. doi:10.1109/MC.2013.196

Mohamed, S., Ismail, O., & Hogan, O. (2012). *Data equity Unlocking the value of big data*. London: Whitepaper.

Mohanty, S., Jagadeesh, M., & Srivatsa, H. (2013). *Big data Imperatives: Enterprise "big data" Warehouse," BI'Implementations and Analytics*. Apress. doi:10.1007/978-1-4302-4873-6

Myers, M., & Avison, D. (2002). An introduction to qualitative research in Information Systems. In *Qualitative Research in Information Systems* (pp. 3–12). London: Sage Publications. doi:10.4135/9781849209687.n1

Rajakumar, M., & Sushma, M. (2013). Challenges and Opportunities of big data Analytics in Business Applications. *Inter. J.Electro. Communicat.Computer Engineer.*, *4*(6), 6–9.

Retail Trade Sales. (2013). Retrieved from http://www.statssa.gov.za/publications/P62421/P62421March2013.pdf

Russom, P. (2011). *Big data analytics*. TDWI Best Practices Report, Fourth Quarter.

Saunders, M., Lewis, P., & Thornhill, A. (2009). Research methods for business students (5th ed.). London: Pearson Education Limited.

Sawant, N., & Shah, H. (2013). *Big data Application Architecture. Big data Application Architecture Q & A*. Apress. doi:10.1007/978-1-4302-6293-0

Shmueli, G., & Koppius, O. (2011). Predictive Analytics in Information Systems Research. *Management Information Systems Quarterly*, *35*(3), 553–572.

Singh, S., & Singh, N. (2012). Big data analytics. *2012 International Conference on Communication, Information & Computing Technology (ICCICT)*, 1–4.

Spiess, J., TJoens, Y., Dragnea, R., Spencer, P., & Philippart, L. (2014). Using big data to improve customer experience and business performance. *Bell Labs Technical J.*, *18*(4), 3–17. doi:10.1002/bltj.21642

Strydom, J. (2015). David Against Goliath: Predicting The Survival Of Formal Small Businesses In Soweto. *Inter.Busin. Econ.Res. J.*, *14*(3), 463–476.

Ularu, E., Puican, F., Apostu, A., & Velicanu, M. (2012). Perspectives on big data and big data Analytics. *Database Syst. J.*, *3*(4), 3–15.

Yadav, R., & Kumar, T. (2015). Usage of Big Data Analytics for Customer Relationship Management. *Inter. J. Adva. Res. Computer Sci.*, *6*(2).

KEY TERMS AND DEFINITIONS

Affiliate: A publisher or site owner that forwards qualified web traffic to an online merchant on a pay-for-performance basis is called an affiliate in the context of online marketing.

Affiliate Links: A universal (uniform) resource locator (URL) that includes an affiliate's identification number and additional information that makes it easier for merchants to track affiliate activity is an affiliate link.

Amazon: In the retail context, Amazon is a multi-national online retailer with a market capitalization in excess of $128 billion U.S. as of January 2013. Amazon also hosts a marketplace wherein other Internet purveyors may display and sell products, and offers several software-as-a-service and infrastructure-as-a-service solutions for business.

Application Programming Interface: (API): An API is a protocol created to allow separate software solutions to communicate over a relatively simple interface. Developers will often use APIs to connect or integrate systems and services.

Authorization: A payment card transaction performed specifically to determine if the payment account has sufficient funds to complete a given transaction.

Bing: Microsoft's search engine, Bing, displays results in response to a user's search query. The site uses a complex and secret algorithm to select which sites to display in response to a particular search. Bing also offers a pay-per-click advertising platform, and allows merchants to offer a discount to shoppers.

Blog: A blog is an online journal or publication that includes relatively short, discrete articles, called posts, that are typically organized by date with the most recent posts first. Frequently, blogs allow readers to add comments to posts. The term blog is a combination of "web" and "log." At first, blogs tended to be personal journals or opinion sites, but the term has come to include an array of different types of publications. In the ecommerce context, blogs are frequently used as a marketing tool, and may be included in a merchant's social media or content marketing campaigns.

Bootstrapping: In business, bootstrapping is the concept of self-funding a new company, meaning that a business pays its operating expenses either with profits or from its founder's own investments, rather than accepting external capital.

Bounce Rate: An Internet marketing term used to describe the percentage of site visitors that arrive at a single page on a given website, and then leave (bounce) from that same page without visiting any other page on the site.

Brick and Click: This term refers to retailers that integrate their brick and mortar store with their ecommerce site. These retailers bring the best of both worlds into their business. Most brick and click companies even offer seamless web-to-store services such as in-store pick ups and returns.

Call-to-Action: A phrase, button, link or other site element that specifically asks a visitor to take some action, including purchasing a product, registering, subscribing or similar.

Canonicalization: The practice of selecting preferred URLs for a specific set of content. Many modern sites allow content to be accessed from a number of URLs, including URLs that may contain session or query information. Canonicalization helps to manage which of those URLs search engines index and credit.

Cash Flow: The movement of money in and out of a business and the resulting availability of cash.

Category Killer: A large retail chain store that is dominant in its product category. This type of store generally offers an extensive selection of merchandise at prices so low that smaller stores cannot compete.

Click and Collect: This is a service in which retailers enable shoppers to buy items online and pick them up in their physical stores. Modern consumers love stores that offer click-and-collect because it makes their life a lot easier. They can buy something from the comfort of their home, and just pick up the item whenever it's convenient for them, instead of paying for shipping or waiting for the mail to arrive.

Ecommerce: Buying and selling products over electronic networks, including the Internet or mobile applications. The term may apply specifically to electronic transactions or more generally to the online retailing and online business.

Exporting: The practice of selling items to wholesale or retail customers in another country.

Fraud: Intentional deception for the purpose of gain.

Fulfillment: In ecommerce, fulfillment is the process of completing an order. The term may also be applied to third-party companies that inventory products and ship orders on behalf of an online store.

Last Mile Delivery: Last mile is a term used in supply chain management and transportation planning to describe the movement of people and goods from a transportation hub to a final destination in the area. The term "last mile" was originally used in the telecommunications field but has since been applied to supply chain management. Transporting goods via freight rail networks and container ships is often the most efficient and cost-effective manner of shipping. However, when goods arrive at a high-capacity freight station or port, they must then be transported to their final destination. This last leg of the supply chain is often less efficient, comprising up to 28% of the total cost to move goods. This has become known as the "last mile problem."

Logistics: The management of products or other resources as they travel between a point of origin and a destination. In ecommerce, logistics might describe the process of transporting inventory to a merchant or the act of shipping orders to customers.

Long Tail: Posited in the October 2004 issue of Wired Magazine, the Long Tail is Chris Anderson's idea that markets and marketplaces, especially online, are moving away from mainstream, broad-appeal products toward niche products. In ecommerce, new retailers may find it easier and more cost effective to focus on niche products.

Long-Tail Variations: In search engine optimization and pay-per-click advertising, Long-Tail variations are keywords similar in meaning or root to other high-volume keywords, but less competitive. Long-Tail variations are often employed when a business is just starting out and cannot gain traction or afford to bid on top performing keywords.

Omni-Channel Retailing: Omni-channel means establishing a presence on several channels and platforms (i.e. brick-and-mortar, mobile, online, catalog etc) and enabling customers to transact, interact, and engage across these channels simultaneously or even interchangeably. It's important to note that omni-channel goes beyond simply being on multiple channels or platforms. Just because you have a website, a mobile app, and a physical store doesn't necessarily mean that you're an omni-channel retailer. In order to truly be one, you must fuse all those channels together so they give customers a seamless experience.

Pay Per Click (PPC): An online advertising model wherein advertisers pay only when a prospect clicks on an advertisement and is directed to the advertiser's website. Google's AdWords platform is an example of pay-per-click promotion.

Per-Order Fee: When a manufacturer or distributor drop ships an order directly to a customer on a retailers behave that manufacturer or distributor may change a per-order fee for processing.

Search Engine Marketing (SEM): Online marketing aimed at increasing a given website's visibility on a search engine results page (SERP) by both optimizing the website for indexing and purchasing ads or paid inclusions.

Search Engine Optimization (SEO): The process of making a website easier for search engine bots to index and categorize.

Search Engine Results Page (SERP): A search engine web page displaying the list of responses to a particular search query.

Social Commerce: S-Commerce refers to retail models or ecommerce practices that incorporate social media, user-generated content, or social interaction. Do note that the role of social networks like Facebook or Twitter in S-Commerce isn't necessarily to serve as platforms for buying and selling; rather, they're meant to assist the process and help drive sales.

Trade Show: An exhibition created so that manufacturers and distributors may show or demonstrate new products or services.

Traffic: In Internet marketing, traffic represents the number of visitors a particular page or site receives.

Section 2
Omni-Channel Retailing

Chapter 5
Technologies Enabling Omni-Channel:
Understanding Key Success Factors for IT Framework

Rohit Das
MET Institute of Management, India

ABSTRACT

The retail industry has been scaling up by better co-ordination among channel partners, improving shipment delivery time at a lower possible cost over last few years. Looking at the Indian scenario, large logistics companies such as Bluedart, FedEx, Gati, etc. have launched dedicated services for online retailers. However, entrance and elevation of e-commerce focused logistic companies such as Chhotu, Mudita, Unicommerce and Delhivery seem to be promising and can be the real game changer. These companies offer solutions that address the various pain-points pertaining to the supply chain of e-commerce companies, which traditional and big supply chain & logistic providers so far failed to do. This is a global phenomenon. Despite considerable improvement in recent past, many logistics providers still struggle to cope up with inadequate infrastructure leading to operational inefficiencies to support their services. Some of such operational concerns, but not limited to, are wrong delivery, unaccepted shipment pick-ups, product unavailability leading to promise to deliver.

INTRODUCTION

One of the intentions of retail supply chain was to fulfil stores. Supply chain faces many challenges: increasing sense among retailers that they aren't just missing out on some demand but they are missing out on a lot of demand, escalating pressure on inventory turns and margins, lack of visibility of inventory. Annual growth rate of sales by E-commerce is 20%. Sales through online medium are surging rapidly which is making the retailers to not only grow but to increase customer loyalty. Due to mass shifting of global customers towards E-commerce is forcing the retail and logistics industries to change how they

DOI: 10.4018/978-1-5225-3056-5.ch005

operate. All aspects of the retail industry such as strategic location and total real estate footprints are getting influenced by this trend.

Evolution of retail sales to more robust Omni-channel environment has been in the mind of executives of supply chain for more than a decade (Brown and Reid, 1955). As in many of the cases, companies don't want to lose a single sale will without any serious consideration open up new channels to take new orders. Hence fulfilling these orders becomes a challenge. The order size arising from customer directly is very small and often a single unit. Hence, these types of orders are delivered directly to customers rather that shipping it in bulk to stores. So there is decline in bulk shipping rates such as truckload carries which are cheap in comparison to the emerging parcel shippers. These ongoing changes should be addressed in supply chain; otherwise the resulting new business would be less profitable (Cullen, 1990).

As with any new concept Omni-channel retailing strategy also consists of leaders and laggards. With the help of technology even laggards have an opportunity to become successful in this field. Omni-channel retailing problems can be solved with the help of technology. In the following sections we attempt to take a closer look at the trends in omni-channel retailing, the key challenges that it presents to supply chain operations and how technology can ensure that profitability is maintained as new sales channels are pursued. There is also an attempt to present an IT framework (Gillett, 1973). The analysis presented focuses on the challenges in supporting omni-channel and how Information Technology can help to integrate Customer Order Management and the different stores (Kline, 1994).

Many retailers struggle to break silos that are built around their IT and Marketing departments, between their IT and operations departments. Typically, we see that, when the CIO went off and focused on big, enterprise-level technologies rooted in multi-year analysis, road mapping and complex implementations, the CMO would go about his or her business of building brand with a keen focus on creative, messaging and media (Forrester Consulting, 2014). Each department has their own goals and objectives and go about doing own things. Marketing and Operations departments should break the silos and work with IT department to make use of the technologies available (Balfour et. al., 1998).

As companies grow and needs change, they'll often switch platforms. But IT needs for Omni-channel is much more than just about the platforms. But clarity is required for who owns the digital strategy. IT leading technology roadmaps that aren't tied to eCommerce and marketing strategies. For Omni-channel, IT is just an enabler but has a big role to play. Marketing and the Operations teams must be talking to the IT team and creating their plans (Donthu et al., 1999). Omni Channel strategy just wont with silos and working with processes of yesterday.

To thrive in today's always-on, always-with-you digital environment and to stay one step ahead of the competition retailers need to be more nimble and responsive. The retailers need to be faster at driving innovative new ideas and no longer have "3-year IT Roadmap". This means the IT strategy is more flexible and demand for innovative technologies that can power customer experiences across today and tomorrow's growing touchpoints (Baroudi and Orlikowski, 1988). The IT Strategy is to provide a means to collect and harness data to drive decisions across the retail enterprise.

Breaking Silos

One important way how retailers are breaking silos is by being innovative in team formation, setting up innovation centres realigning internal processes, etc. Let's understand some of these ideas by the retailers in this section.

Hybrid Teams formation: Some of the retailers are breaking the functional silos by making smaller teams with associates from various departments. The smaller, independent project teams are formed representing multiple functions like Operations, Finance, Marketing, Sales and IT. These teams are autonomous and empowered to take their own decisions (Burke, 1997).

Emergence of Centers of Excellence (CoEs): Another successful way of breaking silos is by creating digital or eCommerce "Centers of Excellence". These CoEs consist of key cross functional resources who work to share best practices, streamline processes and better leverage investments to take retailers to Omni-channel path (Janardhan, 2008).

Setting Up Innovation Centers: Big retailers who have operations in multiple countries are setting up stand-alone units bringing together techies, innovators, creative brains, marketers, and analysts with lean startup methodologies to rapidly develop and test newer, cutting edge solutions unhindered by the traditional corporate road blockers (Lim et al., 2010). These centers are given the responsibilities to run Omni channel operations as close communication is required between different departments (Bellenger et al, 1980).

Re-alignment of Internal Processes: Apart from re-alignment of teams and organizational restructuring, retailers also need to realign the internal processes to better bridge business and technical discussions and resources. Information Technology should be at the forefront of business strategy discussions for developing a successful Omni channel strategy (Taleb, 2007). Retailers should be integrating technology into its road mapping initiatives to make sure that valuable resources and budgets are realigned (Johnston, 1995).

Hiring business/technology hybrids: Omni channel way of retailing is forcing the retailers to accelerate the convergence between digital and traditional shopping and media channels. This means that IT should understand the business, and at the same time business and marketing teams should now need to have a deeper understanding of technology (Morris, 2012). IT teams and the technologists need to be educated and trained on being more connected to the business drivers and priorities for running a successful Omni channel business. CMOs with no digital or eCommerce backgrounds, or CIOs who do not think like business people, are not going to help the retailers in current scenario (Baker, et. al., 1994).

With the rise of Omni channel business requirements, breaking down these silos has never been more critical and has become "must have" strategy.

STUDY RATIONALE

With increase in broadband internet connection and 3G penetrations coupled with changing socio-economic status - going online is a new way of shopping for urban population in the developing countries. Developing countries like India and China are the new growth engines. Just in India, retail market is witnessing a lot of momentum with a $600 Million business in 2011; it is expected to touch $9 Billion by end of 2016 and $70 Billion by 2020 at an estimated CAGR of 61% (Wikipedia). This opens up a new era for distribution channel, as for any retail ecommerce business "logistics" is paramount, with enormous opportunities and challenges. The existing players in this business are yet to make any profit (or ROI: please check as profit is normally termed as operational profit), currently, they are focusing on improving quality of service, earning customer's trust and increasing customer base etc. while attracting investor owing to huge growth potential. Moreover, the lack of proper infrastructure discourages smaller players to enter or survive in this business. Clearly at this juncture, Indian marketplace lacks the technological and logistic infrastructure for high-rising e-commerce transactional volume. One of the important factors that are aiding ecommerce growth is logistics.

Since it is easy for us to study Indian retail industry, most of our studies, assumptions and analysis are based on studying Indian retail landscape. Indian online retail industry has been scaling up by better co-ordination among channel partners, improving shipment delivery time at lower possible cost over last few years. Still there are issues of wrong delivery, unaccepted shipment pick-ups, product unavailability leading to promise to deliver, etc. (Tang, 2012). To overcome logistical issues, retailers and brands selling online have started working with multiple service providers, according to a report by Forrester. The report, titled "Trends in Indian ecommerce market" released during August 2012 says that serving all parts of the country effectively can be quite daunting for e-tailers and hence they work with multiple partners. Following the lead from Flipkart, ecommerce players as well as start ups are realizing the need to reduce logistics spend and at the same time increase customer delight. However, the increase in volumes of e-tail shipments has made all logistics companies sit up and take notice of this opportunity.

Following questions were raised in our research:

- Changing face of ecommerce business.
- Challenges faced by e-tailers in India and the world.
- IT Strategies for ecommerce business.

Although a wide variety of literatures has developed, addressing each of the challenging areas but the majority of studies discussed problems they faced arising from their own inefficiency. Little was found in reference to IT strategy and IT framework to address the challenges. This is our focus in this research paper.

METHODOLOGY

We performed qualitative and descriptive research based on secondary sources and case studies available in the public domain. The method used to analyse the gathered information was "BOOT" method. It identified the following aspects:

- **Business Challenges:** Retailers of all shapes and sizes face significant external challenges. These issues provide a business context for the subject being discussed and drive decision-making across the enterprise.
- **Opportunities:** Every challenge brings with it a set of opportunities, or ways to change and overcome that challenge. The ways retailers turn business challenges into opportunities often define the difference between Winners and "also-rans". Within the BOOT, we can also identify opportunities missed- and describe leading edge models we believe drive success.
- **Organizational Inhibitors:** Even as enterprises find opportunities to overcome their external challenges, they find internal organisational inhibitors that keep them from executing on their vision. Opportunities can be found to overcome these inhibitors as well. Leaders understand their organization inhibitors and find creative, effective ways to overcome them.

- **Technology Enablers:** If a company can overcome its organizational inhibitors it can use technology as an enabler to take advantage of the opportunities it identifies. Retail winners are most adept at judiciously and effectively using these enablers, often far than their peers.

The steps adopted to study and analyse the findings are listed in Table 1.

FINDINGS AND DISCUSSIONS

We present our study in the below sub-sections.

Challenges Faced by Retailers in Implementing Omni-Channel Strategy

While logistics is the aiding factor in growth of multi-channel business, it is the differentiation factor too (both in terms of cost and service). There are many challenges faced by ecommerce retailers today. It is evolving field with no well known strategy to manage the ecommerce business. Companies are making their own way through this (Lucas, 2013). Unlike warehouse shipments, where logistics partners have to deal with large Pallets, the ecommerce logistics partners need to look at smaller shipments and be able to provide door to door delivery.

Three main challenges faced by e-commerce logistic partners are shown in figure 1:

- **Speed:** Ecommerce players have to be agile and flexible to deliver goods from point to point. Speed can help them to command better price than its peers in the market. Customers prefer to get the items delivered at its door steps in minimum possible time. This impacts the inventory policy, channel co-ordination, shipment mode etc.
- **Maintain Accuracy:** Maintain accuracy is one of the major challenges of the e-tailers. It's important to know the inventory accuracy, its can damage companies reputation if they deliver something which is not available in the warehouse. Traceability of the product in the entire supply chain-warehouse, inbound and outbound shipments, is another factor which e-tailers are concerned. E-tailers wants to reach a perfect level where they can track each item from point of origin to final destination.

Table 1. Analytical steps

Step 1	Identify largest retailers by revenue and operating multi-channels.
Step 2	Identify the challenges faced by them by reading articles and other materials available in public domain.
Step 3	Once challenges identified, look for how companies are addressing those challenges.
Step 4	Talk to industry experts from companies like- BigBasket.com, Flipkart. Talk to industry experts from JDA who work with clients on solving their problems
Step 5	Read the journal articles where omnichannel challenges are discussed and solved. Identify different approaches adopted by the companies
Step 6	Map the various approaches to the challenges
Step 7	Study IT strategy to address each of the challenges and then present a combined picture.
Step 8	Present the study

Figure 1. Challenges for e-Commerce logistics partners

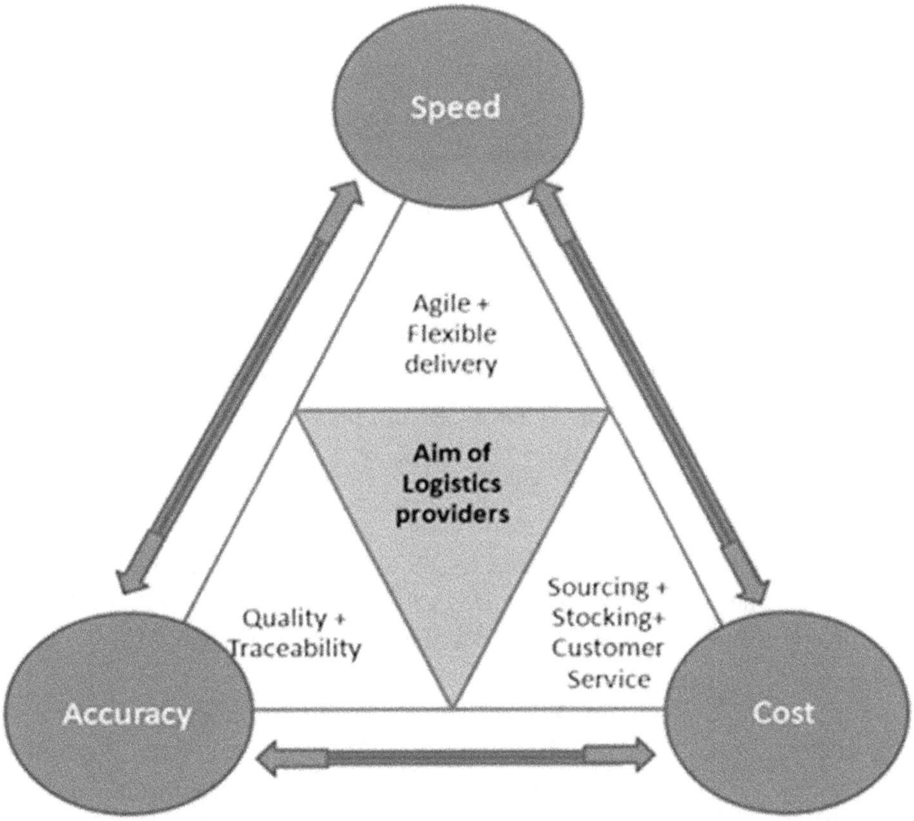

- **Reduce Cost:** E-tailers want to achieve the entire things we discussed above but at reduced cost. In ecommerce business costs of goods is a major competitive factor and at the same time provide better customer service. Companies are looking to for sourcing and stocking decisions that will help to reduce cost and increase customer service.

Question today is how do keep cost effective while maintain volume and deliver at incredible speed. In this paper, our focus is global Retail ecommerce enterprises.

Top 3 Challenges in Point to Point Delivery

- Speed at which goods need to be delivered point to point
- Maintain volume as well as accuracy, and
- Reduce cost

Top 3 challenges in Distribution

- Accurate Information flow
- Inventory accuracy
- Ship the product quickly

Retailer's Perspective

- Ecommerce Retailers look at city-wise and state-wise to see if it makes sense in terms of volume-wise and cost-wise to enter into the market.
- Then retailers would want to meet their own commitment like-same day shipping,
- Have minimal touch-point in the system
- Avoid loss, damage to the product

Changing Face of Ecommerce Business

As indicated in Table 2, multi-channel companies are looking to provide products at lowest cost and increase the availability of the products. Keys factors that define the service factors of e-tailers are: Order Fulfilment time, Home Delivery, Cash on Delivery, Return policy and Reverse Logistics.

IT Strategies for Ecommerce Business

Shown in the Figure 1, are the pillars of functionality, required by the retailer operating in multi-channel scenario. An Omni-channel IT solution is expected to be based these four pillars: Distributed Order Management, Customer Service, Store Fulfilment and Enterprise Inventory.

1. **Distributed Order Management:** Regardless of whether an order originates online, in-store, through the call centre or catalogue, Distributed Order Management solution is designed to provide a global, real-time view of inventory, order status and location (Birchall and Rigby, 2008). Omni-channel retailers and consumer goods manufacturers have the capabilities to manage, monitor and optimize cross-channel order management.
2. **Customer Service:** Customers can shop from any channel of their choice like voice, email, SMS/text, web, mobile or social media but they expect to receive similar services irrespective of the channel chosen. Retailers have begun to provide service on all of these channels – but too often, those channels may exist in silos. This multi-channel service can be taken to the next level with an omni-channel solution that integrates channels to provide a consistent customer experience.
3. **Store Fulfilment:** Handling of complexities associated with enabling store-level fulfilment of orders from any retail channel
4. **Enterprise Inventory:** This includes managing high inventory storage costs, inability to fill orders on time and visibility to inventory levels across channels.

Table 2. Key performance indicator

Product Range	Service	Cost
Price Availability	Order fulfil time Home delivery Cash on delivery Returns policy, Reverse Logistics	Manage the cost

Figure 2. Omni Channel pillars of functionality

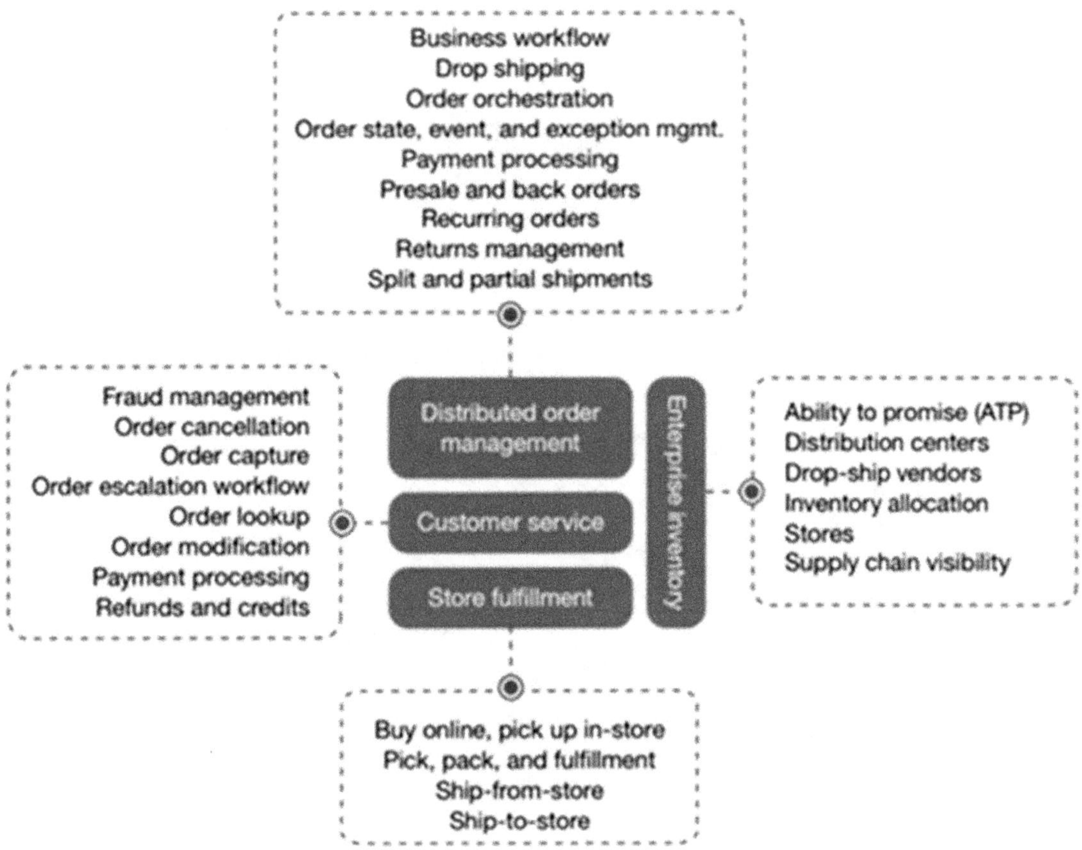

In Figure 3, we present the challenges that can address by IT strategy for a successful Omni-Channel operation.

Figure 4 shows a typical IT system landscape. Channel here is to use combine the above IT System Landscape with the pillars of functionality and address the challenges mentioned in the Figure 3. Based on the study, essential aspects of the IT framework is listed in the Figure 5.

Every company has different business model and their distribution centres work according to the company's' business model but there is a common process and the methodology based on which best in class fulfilment strategies work. Best in class omni-channel distribution strategies are formed based on below four strategies:

1. Identify and evaluate common features across different channels.
2. Identify, evaluate and execute operating models for the channels.
3. Invest in best in class practices and technologies at every step of the fulfilment model.
4. Define and evaluate optimal delivery method supported by right set of tools.

The system is depicted in the Figure 6. The system required is described under 4 main headers which impacts the 4 pillars of functionality.

Figure 3. Challenges addressed by IT strategy

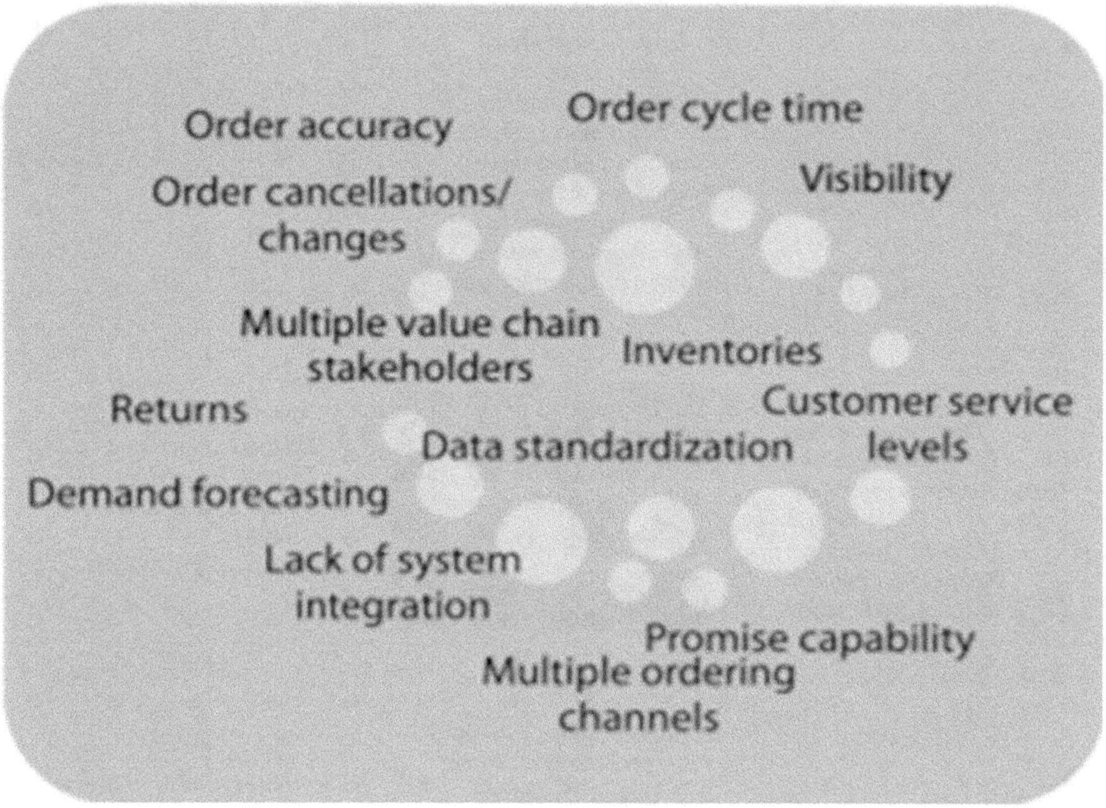

Making Information Technology Work

Retailers starting new or been running a successful retail business for years, eventually will move to Omni-channel retailing because that's the future. Top ecommerce retailers like Amazon, are too, looking for other channels to sell their products because the rewards for going Omni channel are significant.

Based on the analysis, authors have come up with following strategies for the retailers who are planning to go Omni-channel way.

Be Clear About Your Business Model

Omni channel is the way to go and this paper is focused on that but from business perspective, we need to focus on the core segment. Whether its an established brick-and-mortar shop looking to start selling online, a new venture ready to launch a web-based business from scratch, or an online business looking to expand their distribution channel, the retailer need to deal with the business side as their first priority.

Many retailers put their immediate focus on the website itself. The companies that have done well selling online most successfully already have a clear vision of their current business model. This includes a deep knowledge of the industry and the types of products they offer, managing the competition,

Figure 4. A typical IT system landscape

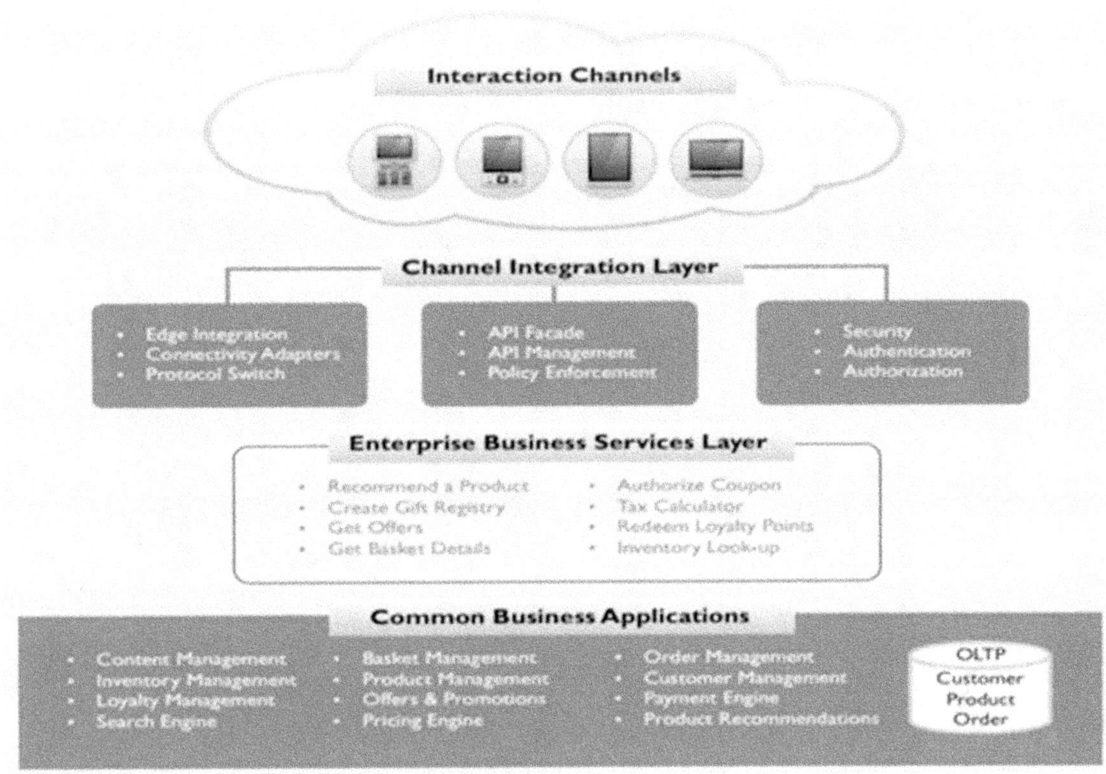

Figure 5. Essentials of IT framework for omni channel retailing

Figure 6. IT framework for omni channel retailing

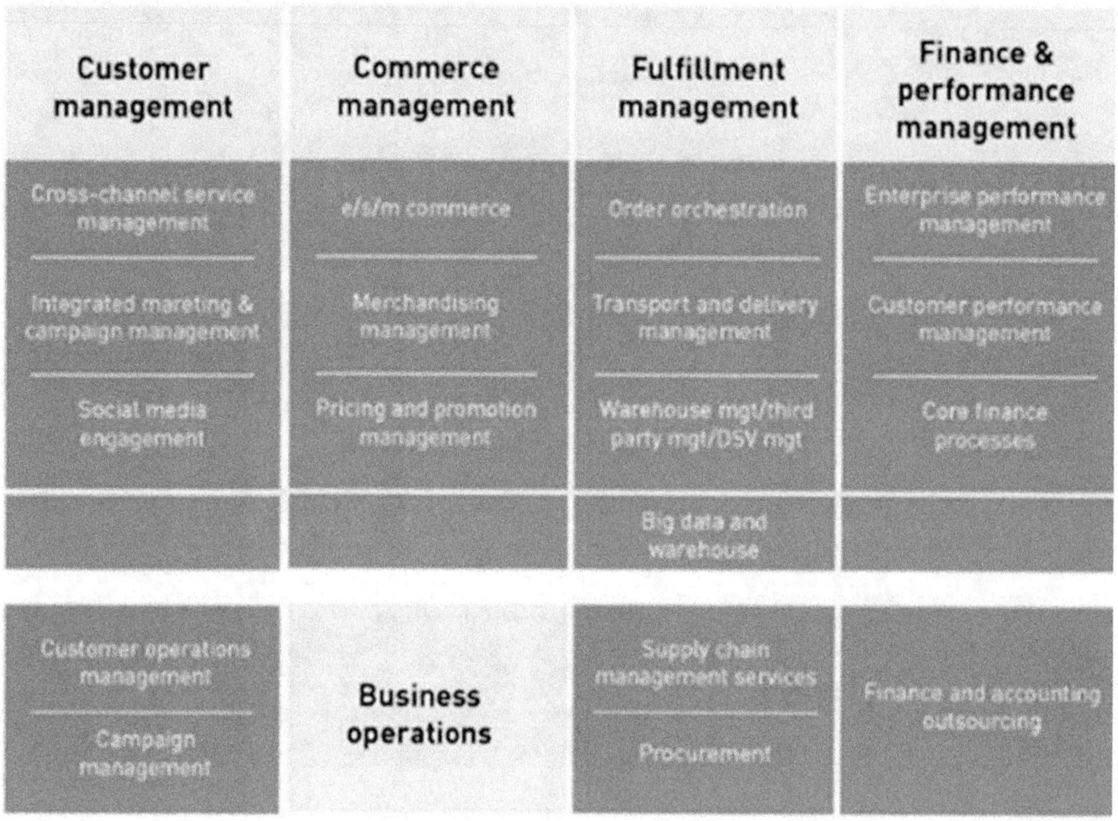

understands about their ideal customers, how to attract them, and have a compelling marketing message without worrying too much about the technology. After all the technology behind the business is just a tool to get the job done.

Sketch Your Product Path

Second step would be to sketch out the path of the products – from the production to how would it be fulfilled. We would be asking following questions:

- Where is it manufactured?
- Where is inventory stored?
- How will sales be handled?
- What is the payment structure?
- Who handles customer service?
- How are rush orders fulfilled?

There is a need to focus on customer experience and providing personalized service to each one of them. Selling online provides the benefit of measuring every metric. Investment in SEO (Search Engine

Optimisation), taking advantage of free Google Analytics, which shows audience demographics and top sources of traffic, such as results returned from online searches, clicks from your Facebook page, or users who typed in your website name directly are some of the examples where the investment is required from the retailers.

Choose Your Technology

Last step would be about the technology. There are three options for retailers and it can be chosen based on the given situation.

- **Do It Yourself (DIY):** For companies that are beginning their e-commerce venture and are comfortable digging into the technology, do-it-yourself is a possibility. There are many websites which provide services for free or with reasonable fees.
- **Sell With the Big Retailers:** One easy way to get started is to set up your store with websites like Amazon or eBay. The sellers can integrate their websites with additional capabilities such as payment methods, account login and shopping carts. These retailers provide online training for the sellers which will provide all the information required.
- **Get Custom Solution:** The third option is to hire a website development team to create a custom ecommerce solution. This option gives retailers more options and provide high level of customization, such as integrating sites like Salesforce.com for customer relationship management (CRM) or specific design considerations. Costs will vary widely, but its much higher than the other two options.

FUTURE RESEARCH

Since internet has made an unprecedented opportunity of business for e- essential meaning to research on satisfaction of customers with its services. We will be extending our research to see how analytics can be implemented as part of the IT strategy and which all areas will be impacted by analytics.

CONCLUSION

Though e-Commerce has been there for long time but it's still a mystery for most of the retailers. Retailers are still experimenting with techniques to integrate e-commerce business models with their fulfilment strategies with logistics being one of the important aspects. There are many challenges faced by ecommerce retailers today. It is evolving field with no well-known strategy to manage the ecommerce business. Companies are making their own way through this. Unlike warehouse shipments, where logistics partners have to deal with large Pallets, the ecommerce logistics partners need to look at smaller shipments and be able to provide door-to-door delivery.

Setting up IT strategy for next generation Omni-channel operations can provide both retailers and manufacturers with distinct competitive edge by:

1. Connect the order management process directly with the users. This will be achieved by leveraging mobility and Web 2.0 technologies.
2. Engage customers actively be engaged throughout the process
3. Next generation systems to provide ability to track an order in real-time, and provide a mobile app for both B2B and B2C stakeholders.
4. All the stakeholders from Manufacturers to Retailers, will be connected and will be flexible and agile enough to respond to any disruptions in the market place.
5. Omni-channel will be much more than just selling a product. It will provide a total customer experience.
6. Tight integration of order management with the Sales and Operations Planning (S&OP) process will be possible.

REFERENCES

Chopra & Sodhi. (2004). *Managing Risk to Avoid Supply-Chain Breakdown.* Retrieved from www.sloanreview.mit.edu

Tang, C.S. (2012). Robust Strategies for Mitigating Supply Chain Disruptions. *International Journal of Logistics Research and Applications, 9*(1), 33-45.

Lim, M., Bassamboo, A., Chopra, S., & Daskin, M. S. (2010). *Flexibility and Fragility: Use of Chaining Strategies in the Presence of Disruption Risks.* Northwestern University research report.

Birchall, J., & Rigby, E. (2008). Oil Costs Force P&G to Rethink Supply Network. *Financial Times.*

Lucas, L. (2013). Diageo Overhauls Its Supply Chain. *Financial Times.*

Sodhi, M. S., & Tang, C. S. (2012). *Managing Supply Chain Risk.* Springer. doi:10.1007/978-1-4614-3238-8

Taleb, N. N. (2007). *The Black Swan: The Impact of the Highly Improbable.* New York: Random House.

Nandita. (2014). *E-tailers growth ensnared in India's logistics jungle.* Reuters.com.

Janardhan, S. (2008). *Unified View of Customer: It's All About Customer Experience.* TCS.com.

Morris. (2012). *Online supply models: Who's doing what?* IGD Supply Chain Analysis.

Forrester Consulting. (2014). *Customer Desires Vs. Retailer Capabilities: Minding The Omni-Channel Commerce Gap.* Author.

Lewis. (2014). *Greatest challenge – The omni channel customer experience.* ijgolding.com.

Bimschleger. (2014). *How to Compete with Amazon in an Omnichannel World.* RIS News: Business/Technology Insights for Retail, Supermarket Executives.

The omni-channel opportunity for retailers: What's the story?. (n.d.). *The Guardian.*

Omnichannel Retail 2014 - Intelligence report. (2014, July). L2 Research.

Schaeffer. (n.d.). *How to Succeed in Omni-Channel Retailing.* crmsearch.com.

Banker. (n.d.). *ARC's WMS global market research study.* Forbes.com.

Kearns. (2013). *Supply chain 2.0.* Academic Press.

Gera. (n.d.). *The Six Key Pillars for Building An Everyday Bank.* Accenture.com.

Bellenger, D. N., & Korgaonkar, P. (1980). Profiling the Recreational Shopper. *Journal of Retailing, 56*(3), 77–92.

Brown, S., & Reid, R. (1955). Psychological Aspects of Shopping: A Supplement to the New Consumer. *Chicago Tribune.*

Cullen, C. W. (1990). *Shopping as Entertainment: Implications for the Shopping Centre Manager.* University of Stirling: Institute for Retail Studies.

Donthu, N., & Garcia, A. (1999, May). The Internet Shopper. *Journal of Advertising Research*, 52–58.

Gillett, P. L. (1973, July). A Profile of In-home Shoppers. *Journal of Marketing, 34*, 40–45.

Kline, B., & Wagner, J. (1994). Information Sources and Retail Buyer Decision-Making: The Effect of Product Specific Buying Experience. *Journal of Retailing, 70*(1), 75–88. doi:10.1016/0022-4359(94)90030-2

Moschis, G. P. (1976). Shopping Orientations and Consumer Uses of Information. *Journal of Retailing, 52*(2), 61–70, 93.

Balfour, A., Farquhar, B., & Langmann, G. (1998). The consumer needs in global electronic commerce. *Electronic Markets, 8*(2), 9–12. doi:10.1080/10196789800000017

Baroudi, J. J., & Orlikowski, W. J. (1988). A short-form measure of user information satisfaction: A psychometric evaluation and notes on use. *Journal of Management Information Systems, 4*(4), 44–59. doi:10.1080/07421222.1988.11517807

Burke, R. R. (1997). Do you see what I see? The future of virtual shopping. *Journal of the Academy of Marketing Science, 25*(4), 352–360. doi:10.1177/0092070397254007

Carman, J. M. (1990). Consumer perceptions of service quality: An assessment of the SERVQUAL dimensions. *Journal of Retailing, 66*(1), 33–35.

Cox, J., & Dale, B. G. (2001). Service quality and e-commerce: An exploratory analysis. *Managing Service Quality, 11*(2), 121–131. doi:10.1108/09604520110387257

Doll, W. J., & Torkzadeh, G. (1988). The measurement of end-user computing satisfaction. *Management Information Systems Quarterly, 12*(June), 259–274. doi:10.2307/248851

Duffy, J. A. M., & Ketchand, A. A. (1998). Examining the role of service quality in overall service satisfaction. *Journal of Managerial Issues, 10*(2), 240–255.

Gray, R. (2000, March 2). E-tail must deliver on Web promises. *Marketing*, 37-8.

Griff, D. A., & Palmer, J. (1999, Jan.). Leveraging the Web for corporate success. *Business Horizons*, *42*, 3–10. doi:10.1016/S0007-6813(99)80043-3

Griffith, D. A., & Krampf, R. A. (1998). An examination of the Web-based strategies of the top 100 US retailers. *Journal of Marketing Theory and Practice*, *6*(3), 12–23. doi:10.1080/10696679.1998.11501801

Johnston, R. (1995). The determinants of service quality: Satisfiers and dissatisfiers. *International Journal of Service Industry Management*, *8*(5), 53–71. doi:10.1108/09564239510101536

Luedi, A. F. (1997). Personalize or perish. *Electronic Markets*, *7*(3), 22–25. doi:10.1080/10196789700000032

Storbacka, K., Strandvik, T., & Gro¨nroos, C. (1994). Managing customer relationships for profit: The dynamics of relationship quality. *International Journal of Service Industry Management*, *5*(5), 21–38. doi:10.1108/09564239410074358

Zeithaml, V. A., Berry, L. L., & Parasuraman, A. (1993). The nature and determinants of customer expectations of service. *Journal of the Academy of Marketing Science*, *21*(1), 1–12. doi:10.1177/0092070393211001

Gol, A. (2008). Issues and challenges of retail business. *Journal of Retail Management*, *6*, 23.

Ram, M. (2013). To identify the factors impacting customer satisfaction in food retail supermarkets. *International Journal of Research and Development - A Management Review*, *2*, 2319–5479.

Ian, P. H. L., & Grace, L. B. (2011). *Customer satisfaction towards retailers*. ICA, ICA NÄRA and Coop Forum.

Gauri, D. K., Talukdar, D., & Ratchford, B. (2008). *Empirical Investigation of the Impact of Loss Leader Promotion on Store and Category Performance in Grocery Industry*. Syracuse University.

Brown, J. R., & Dant, R. P. (2008). Scientific Method and Retailing Research: A Retrospective. *Journal of Retailing*, *84*(1), 1–13. doi:10.1016/j.jretai.2008.03.001

Baker, Grewal, & Parasuraman. (1994). The Influence of Store Environment on Quality Inferences and Store Image. *Journal of Academy of Marketing Science, 22*(4), 328-39.

Bitner, M. J. (1992, April). Servicescapes: The Impact of Physical Surroundings on Customer and Employees. *Journal of Marketing*, *56*, 57–71. doi:10.2307/1252042

Chebat, J.-C., Gelinas-Chebat, C., & Filiatrault, P. (1993). Interactive Effects of Musical and Visual Cues on Time Perception: An Application to Waiting Lines in Banks. *Perceptual and Motor Skills*, *77*(3), 995–1020. doi:10.2466/pms.1993.77.3.995 PMID:8284188

Darden, W. R., & Babin, B. J. (1994, Feb.). Exploring the Concept of Affective Quality: Expanding the Concept of Retail Personality. *Journal of Business Research*, *29*, 101–110. doi:10.1016/0148-2963(94)90014-0

Donovan, R. J., Rossiter, J. R., Marcoolyn, G., & Nesdale, A. (1994). Store Atmosphere and Purchasing Behavior. *Journal of Retailing*, *70*(3), 283–294. doi:10.1016/0022-4359(94)90037-X

Eroglu, S., & Harrell, G. D. (1986). Retail Crowding: Theoretical and Strategic Implications. *Journal of Retailing*, *62*(4), 346–363.

Foxall, G. R., & Greenley, G. E. (1999). Consumers Emotional Responses to Service Environments. *Journal of Business Research*, *46*(2), 149–158. doi:10.1016/S0148-2963(98)00018-6

Gardner, M. P., & Siomkos, G. J. (1985). Toward a Methodology for Assessing the Effects of In-Store Atmospherics. In R. Lutz (Ed.), *Advances in Consumer Research*. Chicago, IL: Association for Consumer Research.

Gentry, J. W., & Burns, A. C. (1977-78). How 'Important' Are Evaluative Criteria in Shopping Center Patronage. *Journal of Retailing*, *4*(Winter), 73–85.

Grewal, D., & Baker, J. (1994). Do Retail Environmental Factors Affect Consumers Price Acceptability? An Empirical Examination. *International Journal of Research in Marketing*, *11*(2), 107–115. doi:10.1016/0167-8116(94)90022-1

Griffitt, W. (1970). Environmental Effects on Interpersonal Affective Behavior: Ambient Temperature and Attraction. *Journal of Personality and Social Psychology*, *15*(3), 240–244. doi:10.1037/h0029432 PMID:5485416

Grossbart, S., Hampton, R., Rammohan, B., & Lapidus, R. S. (1990). Environmental Dispositions and Customer Response to Store Atmospherics. *Journal of Business Research*, *21*(3), 225–241. doi:10.1016/0148-2963(90)90030-H

Hui, M. K., & Bateson, J. E. G. (1991, Sept.). Perceived Control and the Effects of Crowding and Consumer Choice on the Service Experiences. *The Journal of Consumer Research*, *25*, 175–186.

Hui, M. K. (1997). The Impact of Music on Consumers Reactions to Waiting for Services. *Journal of Retailing*, *73*(1), 87–104. doi:10.1016/S0022-4359(97)90016-6

Hult, G., Neese, W. T., & Bashaw, R. E. (1997). Faculty Perceptions of Marketing Journals. *Journal of Marketing Education*, *19*(1), 37–52. doi:10.1177/027347539701900105

Levy, M., & Weitz, B. A. (1998). *Retailing Management* (3rd ed.). Chicago: Irwin McGraw-Hill.

Malhotra, N. K. (1983). A Threshold Model of Store Choice. *Journal of Retailing*, *59*(2), 3–21.

Milliman, R. E. (1982). Using Background Music to Affect the Behavior of Supermarket Shoppers. *Journal of Marketing*, *46*(2), 86–91. doi:10.2307/1251706

Milliman, R. E. (1986, Sept.). The Influence of Background Music on the Behavior of Restaurant Patrons. *The Journal of Consumer Research*, *13*, 286–289. doi:10.1086/209068

Mitchell, D. J., Kahn, B. E., & Knasko, S. C. (1995, Sept.). Theres Something in the Air: Effects of Ambient Odor on Consumer Decision Making. *The Journal of Consumer Research*, *22*, 229–238. doi:10.1086/209447

Smith & Curnow. (1966, June). 'Arousal Hypothesis' and the Effects of Music on Purchasing Behavior. *Journal of Applied Psychology, 50*, 255-56.

Spangenberg, E. R., Crowley, A. E., & Henderson, P. W. (1996, April). Improving the Store Environment: Do Olfactory Cues Affect Evaluations and Behaviors. *Journal of Marketing*, *60*, 67–80. doi:10.2307/1251931

Oracle. (n.d.). *The Store: The Intersection Of All Channels.* Retail TouchPoints E-Book.

Carroll & Guzmán. (n.d.). *The New Omni-Channel Approach to Serving Customers.* accenture.com.

Bardwell. (n.d.). Redefining the Shopper Experience With Omnichannel Retailing. *IDC Retail Insights.*

KEY TERMS AND DEFINITIONS

5G: is the coming fifth-generation wireless broadband technology based on the IEEE 802.11ac standard. 5G will provide better speeds and coverage than the current 4G. 5G operates with a 5Ghz signal and is set to offer speeds of up to 1 Gb/s for tens of connections or tens of Mb/s for tens of thousands of connections.

Action Alley: The sales area of a store located immediately after entering.

Ad Slick: Ad slicks refer to the final, camera-ready advertisement. It gets its name from the glossy paper on which it is printed.

Anchor Store: A major retail store used to drive business to smaller retailers that physically surround it. These larger department stores or grocery stores are generally part of a retail chain and are the prominent business in a shopping mall.

Assortment: Assortment is the number of SKUs within a category. It is also called depth.

Backup stock: Backup stock is the buffer stock or the safety stock which retailer holds to guard against stockouts, when there is a mismatch between supply and demand.

Big Box Stores: Large stand-alone store with varying market niches.

Cash Flow: The movement of money in and out of a business and the resulting availability of cash.

Category: The category is the basic unit of analysis for making merchandising decision.

Category Captain: Category Captain is the retailer preferred vendor, who advises the retailer on a certain category of merchandise offered by them.

Category Killer: A large retail chain store that is dominant in its product category. This type of store generally offers an extensive selection of merchandise at prices so low that smaller stores cannot compete.

Chain Store: One of a number of retail stores under the same ownership and dealing in the same merchandise.

Comp Sales: Comparable-store sales are a measurement of productivity in revenue used to compare sales of retail stores that have been open for a year or more. Historical sales data allows retailers to compare this year's sales in their store to the same period last year.

CO-OP: An advertising allowance offered by a vendor, payable upon proof of an ad having been run.

Fad Merchandise: Fad merchandise is the merchandise items that generate a high level of sale for a short period of time.

Footfall: Footfall is the count of shoppers entering in to a retail store on a given day.

Gross Margin: A way to measure gross profit calculated as the difference between selling price and cost price.

Gross Margin Return on Floor (GMROF): Gross margin or profit returned per floor space usually measure in gross margin per square foot.

Gross Margin Return on Inventory Investment (GMROII): Gross Margin $ returned for every $ invested in inventory (and inventory costs).

Hypermarket: According to the Webster dictionary (1993) a hyper market is a superstore which combines a supermarket and a department store (where usually are sold products like apparel, furniture, appliances, electronics, and additionally select other lines of products such as paint, hardware, toiletries, cosmetics, photographic equipment, jewellery, toys, and sporting goods), being the result a very large retail facility which carries an enormous range of products under one roof, including full lines of groceries and general merchandise.

Impulse Buying: Any unplanned buying is called as Impulse Buying. An individual might not require a particular product but picks it up out of mere emotions and feelings.

Markdown: The difference between the original retail price and the reduced price.

Markup: The amount of money added to the wholesale price to obtain the retail price.

Millennials: (also known as the Millennial Generation or Generation Y) are the demographic cohort following Generation X. There are no precise dates when the generation starts and ends. Researchers and commentators use birth years ranging from the early 1980s to the early 2000s.

On Shelf Availability: One of important metric every retailer's performance is measured is using On Shelf Availability (OSA). OSA is defined as availability of product for sale to a shopper, in the place he expects it and at the time he wants to buy it. It is impacted by a host of different factors, all along the supply chain.

Out Of Stock (OOS): Also known as Stockout. It is a situation where the retailer does not physically possess a particular product category, on its shelf, to sell to the customer. It can be estimated from store inventory data.

Point of Purchase (POP): POP refers to all materials and physical setup in a retailer, in and around where the product is displayed.

Point of Sale (POS): POS refers to materials, brochures, signs at point of sale, or can refer to point of sale or cash register.

Point of Sale Activation (POSA): POSA is a process by which software becomes activated, useable, at the point of purchase.

Private Label: Private Label brands are the retailers store brands which are developed by retailers and available for sale at only that specific retailer.

Softlines: Softlines is the retail store department or the product line which primarily consists of merchandise such as clothing, footwear, jewelry, linens and towels.

Space Management: Management of selling space, based on consumer demand and shopping habit in order to achieve enhanced business results.

Stock Keeping Unit: A stock keeping unit (SKU) is the smallest unit available for keeping inventory control. In soft goods retailer, for instance, a SKU usually means size, color, and style. For example, a pair of boys' size 10, navy blue color, boot-cut Levis is one SKU. In some cases, a buyer is responsible for several classifications.

Supermarket: According to the Webster International dictionary (1993), a Supermarket is a self-service store or independent retail market offering a wide variety of food and household merchandise, organized into departments. It is larger in size and has a wider selection than a traditional grocery store and it is smaller than a hypermarket or superstore.

Variety: Variety is the number of different merchandising categories within a store or department. It is also called breadth.

Visual Merchandising: Visual merchandising is the art of implementing effective design ideas to increase in-store traffic and sales volume.

Working Capital: Liquid assets available to build and grow a retail business. It is measured by current assets minus current liabilities. A positive working capital is needed until the retailer can produce a profit.

Chapter 6
Omni-Channel Retailing:
The Risks, Challenges, and Opportunities

Erkan Özdemir
Uludag University, Turkey

Mine Yılmaz
Uludag University, Turkey

ABSTRACT

Technological developments, changes in consumer behavior and intense competition are the most important threats of today, affecting many sectors as well as the retail industry. Innovative retailers, in the face of with these threats, have embraced and implemented the omni-channel retailing approach, which is the next step in multi-channel. However, other players in the retail industry lag behind this change. The aim of this chapter is to establish the experiences of innovative retailers that have adopted omni-channel retailing in the context of risks, challenges and opportunities. The research data were obtained using questionnaire method from the retailers in Turkey, one of the developing countries. As a result of the study, it was found that retailers who would adopt the omni-channel retailing would have the opportunities to be able to dominate all channels, provide better services to the customers, increase customer satisfaction and loyalty, keep in constant contact with the customers, get better customer recognition and increase sales volume.

INTRODUCTION

The rapid developments in the technological field have affected the field of retailing considerably, as well as many other fields. In the face of the increasing changes in the consumer behavior towards the use of digital technologies, retailers have had to reconsider the purchasing process of the consumers. It is because customers of today have begun to increasingly combine real life and digital activities (Lazaris & Vrechopoulos, 2014). Factors such as assessing many different product options, having products and/or services in a shorter period of time, lower price and convenience have shaped today's consumer behaviors. Moreover, the fact that the new generation begins to use digital technologies at an earlier age

DOI: 10.4018/978-1-5225-3056-5.ch006

and do not mind using these technologies in comparison to the previous generations, in other words the lower risk perception for digital technologies, creates both a threat and an opportunity for the retailers. At this point, the retailers that can redesign the management of their retail processes according to the needs of their consumer will take advantage of this opportunity. However, the retailers that fail to redesign their processes or miss this opportunity will fall behind in this competition battle.

With the development of the internet, the fact that consumers use both the digital channels and stores in real life has led the retailers to use the multi-channel. Multi-channel formed by the addition of different digital media over time with the aim of facilitating and accelerating the purchasing process of consumers, is utilized by many retailers today. Multi-channel retailing has become a standard business model in which almost all big companies today have developed online operations to complement their existing stores (Dorman, 2013). However, this model ignores the fact that the consumers do not prefer a single channel to buy products and/or services. Indeed, the consumers of today do not limit themselves to a single purchasing channel in the purchasing process- even if the retailers fail to develop a system-, but use different channels simultaneously in the purchasing process. This consumer behavior has led to the emergence of the concept of omni-channel retailing.

Omni-channel retailing is a retail medium that brings together both online and offline channels in an attempt to improve customer services and provide brand experience to the customers (Gulnaz & Gokulakannan, 2016, p. 245). The omni-channel model assumes that consumers can contact a company through many different channels before making the purchase. This current situation is different from the traditional multi-channel concept. It is because there is no channel A and channel B customer here. Instead, there is a large consumer base that gets in touch with the retailers through all possible channels (Dorman, 2013). Another important difference in the *omni-channel retailing* is that the barriers regarding the consumers' geographical distances and consumer ignorance is eliminated (Verhoef, Kannan & Inman, 2015). Therefore, it is now a necessity for the retailers to redesign the retailing process and competitive strategies.

Omni-channel retail sales in the world amounted to $ 1.8 trillion in 2016. This trend is expected to grow rapidly and reach $ 7 trillion by 2025. In order for them to be profitable in this competition, these businesses will need to make sure that they have factors such as variety, suitability, price, low cost, flexible delivery options and achieve it in one piece product delivery. While the developed countries compete to integrate the stores and online channels, the developing countries, on the other hand, work for financial and logistical infrastructure. In this case, adoption of the omni-channel structure will be important for retailers (Kumar & Hu, 2015, p. 76).

Successful application examples of the omni-channel retailing as a new concept and application have started to emerge over time. At this point, many companies in the omni-channel retailing process face different risks and challenges as well as opportunities. The aim of this chapter, after reviewing the literature on omni-channel, is to investigate the experience of retailers in the process of implementing omni-channel retailing in the Turkish sample, one of the emerging countries. In addition to the contribution it will make to the creation and management of the omni-channel retailing, this chapter will also make significant contributions to the avoidance of the potential risks to be faced by the retailers wishing to implement these processes in their organizations and to take advantage of the opportunities.

The remainder of the chapter is structured as follows: Firstly, the relevant literature on multi-channel and omni-channel will be addressed in the background section and the obstacles and risks that retailers will face in the omni-channel retailing process will be revealed. Next, the methodology used in the research to identify the omni-channel applications of innovative retailers will be described. The findings of the research are then presented. In the conclusion section of the chapter, recommendations will be made for the retailers that will implement the omni-channel retailing and for researchers who will conduct research on these issues in the future.

BACKGROUND

Multi-Channel Retailing

With the rise of e-commerce, the number of different channels where consumers can buy their products has been rapidly increasing, and the shopping journey has many new ways and possibilities (Barnes, 2016, p. 60). Over time, together with both in technology and in changes in consumer behavior, businesses are now able to reach potential or existing customers not only through physical channels, but through different channels such as online, mobile and catalog. At this point, it has become more important for retailers to understand the factors that drive consumers to shop online (Ha & Stoel, 2012).

Customers can purchase products or services using traditional channels such as mobile devices and online stores as well as the traditional stores (Govindarajan, Sinha, & Uichanco, 2017). The convenience offered by the online shopping at this point is one of the main motivations for consumers to buy online (Jiang, Yang & Jun, 2013). Online shopping provides consumers time and effort savings, low transaction costs, value suitability, low return cost, ease of ordering and benchmarking across many retailers (Akroush & Al-Debei, 2015). Online shopping also leads the online shoppers to make better quality decisions. It is because online stores offer consumers a lot of product choices, interactive videos, animations, short films, three dimensional visuals and live online support. Moreover, since the price is important because of the large number of online retailers, it is much easier for consumers to research the best price (Punj, 2012).

With the development of the internet, retailers have begun to debate the issue of multi-channel retailing. Multi-channel involves targeting customers through different channels (store, website, mobile, catalog, etc.), each of which has its own specific purpose. The multi-channel strategy allows the businesses to create robust customer relationships by providing information, products, services and support at the same time to the existing and potential customers via two or more channels (Lima, 2015). Since today's customers use more digital tools in evaluating the search of the relevant retailers, placing orders and delivery options, retailers also need to meet the extremely dynamic needs and expectations of consumers. Retailers who are capable of doing this will be able to differentiate themselves from their competitors (Belu & Marinoiu, 2014). At this point, the multi-channel approach where more than one channel is used to reach consumers (Lima, 2015), made a difference for retailers. The use of multi-channel has improved in many sectors, with businesses continually adding new channel alternatives to their systems (Beck & Rygl, 2015). A well-integrated multi-channel format offers the opportunity to examine consumer products from one channel, purchase from the other one, and receive from a third channel (Berman & Thelen, 2004).

Many concepts such as strategy, pricing, consumer decision making process, establishing a presence in the channel availability, service quality, customer loyalty, customer satisfaction, multi-channel quality, channel merging optimization, channel exchange, customer experience, coordination, integration, synergy and reverse synergy were addressed as issues related to the multi-channel literature. The last seven of these are the most suitable for the omni-channel concept. In fact, omni-channel is built on a multi-channel retail infrastructure (Lazaris & Vrechopoulos, 2014). In order to be successful in a multi-channel medium, retailers need to promote the brands, identify the customers, use advertising, fulfill their promises and monitor their costs (Schoenbachler & Gordon, 2002). At this point, there are five main challenges in multi-channel management. These challenges are compiled as data integration, understanding the consumer behavior, channel assessment, allocation of resources acres channels and coordination of channel strategies (Neslin et al., 2006). Managers should develop innovative channels that improve the way the company operates and interacts with the customers, while providing a consistent service (Wilson & Daniel, 2007).

Omni-Channel Retailing

As the technology began to blur the advantages between the physical and online retailing, retailers and supply chain partners needed to rethink their competitive strategies (Brynjolfsson, Hu & Rahman, 2013). Digital technology is one of the most significant changes that have impacted the retail industry over the past 50 years. Today, when online shopping, mobile devices and social networks are in place, retailers' managements change radically in response to consumers' shopping behavior, anticipations and this consumer behavior (Rigby, Kris, Josh & Suzanne, 2012). In addition to creating a significant threat to the traditional retailers, technology offers great opportunities for retailers as well (Rigby, 2011a).

Technological advances have also changed the consumer behavior. Many consumers have begun to use multi-channels simultaneously where businesses reach them. In the early days, consumers implemented this process by making use of the digital media to search for product information and/or compare product prices before and/or during their shopping (Lazaris &Vrechopoulos, 2014). However, this is no longer enough now. Presently, the omni-channel structure, which expresses the integration of multi-channels instead of reaching customers through multi-channels, has emerged as a new concept. Omni-channel, derived from the Latin word "omni" meaning "all", "universal" (Lazaris & Vrechopoulos, 2014, p. 1) refers to the integration of all physical and digital channels to provide an innovative and unified customer experience. The customers in this integrated structure are able to integrate physical stores and / or online purchases (websites, mobile applications and other digital channels) (Belu & Marinoiu, 2014, p. 123). Consumers, for instance, can complete their online shopping at the physical store by continuing where they have left off with an ID number they take. Or they can continue the purchasing process started at the store on the internet or mobile with an ID number. In fact, in daily life, some customers see products in the store, browse the digital media of the store or other stores where they access the internet via their smartphones without leaving the store, and buy their products or services from stores or online media based on their own liking. Today, however, the vast majority of retailers still try to reach customers through the multi-channel structure; in other words, through physical or online stores and separate channels. However, combining these different channels will increase retailers' customer satisfaction and customer retention.

Omni-channel applications are also the game changers in the retail industry. While omni-channel provides more information and power to consumers, it also forces retailers to be innovative and offer value propositions (Rigby, 2011a). The popularity of the omni-channel model has begun to increase with the decline in the profitability of most retailers' physical stores (Dorman, 2013). Today's consumers are now able to access much more online and physical stores more easily and quickly, and make the process of researching information with mobile devices much easier and faster. This means that it is possible for consumers to find a lot of suitable product choices and/or prices. This is seen in the selection of the webrooming purchasing decision-making process, which is the opposite of showrooming, where consumers search for information online and shop offline (Verhoef, Kannan & Inman, 2015).

The presence of omni-channel consumers is seen as one of the most important forces shaping the future of e-commerce as well as physical store retailing. The omni-channel structure is designed to meet demand, wherever and whenever it is needed. The omni-channel consumer expects everything to be ready on their finger tips and the overall brand experience to be within the same reach. With the omni-channel model, online shopping have come to contribute to physical retail stores as well (Fairchild, 2014).

Omni-channel combines the advantages of physical stores with a rich online shopping experience and offers its customers an integrated purchasing experience. Moreover, as natural borders between the channels begin to disappear, nowadays different channels become blurred and each channel is redesigned to maximize its current potential. Customers can now order from anywhere (phone line, website, store, catalogs, mobile and social media) and at any time from different channels (e-commerce, outlet locations, B & M stores, retail DCs, Pop up stores, kiosk etc.) has the opportunity to complete their shopping (Lima, 2015). Today, retailers develop an appropriate (stable) omni-channel physical distribution process where the stores play a greater role in order taking and delivery (Ishfaq, Defee, Gibson & Raja, 2016)

A successful omni-channel structure may occur by integrating different areas. In their study, Staflund & Kersmark (2015, p. 10) collected the areas where the omni-channel structure was integrated under five headings. These include shipping services (click-and-collect, online orders to be picked up at the store, free delivery of goods in store), logistics (integrated inventory systems, using online returns as inventory, click-and-collect orders to be packed at the store), promoting the use of unified channels (providing financial incentives for combining the channels, consistency in pricing, store locator in website, availability of online information in store, QRcode and/or app to view product information at the store), omni-channel measurements (being able to track additional sales from click-and-collect).

When compared to multi-channel, omni-channel has more channels. One of the important contributions of the omni-channel is the disappearance of the natural boundaries between the channels. In this sense, the difference between the channels becomes blurred. In terms of channel management, the multi-channel method and the omni-channel management comparison are illustrated in Table 1 (Verhoef, Kannan & Inman, 2015, p. 176).

The Risks and Challenges in the Omni-Channel Retailing

With the increase in diversity in the channel types, the transition from single channel to multi-channels and then to omni-channel marketing has also changed the purchasing process of consumers. While this provides more affordable purchases for consumers, it creates a more difficult process for marketing managers to manage, from the highest level of the production chain to the lowest level of distribution (Ailawadi & Farris, 2017).

In the omni-channel retailing process, retailers will face a variety of risks and challenges. These risks and challenges can arise from the retailer itself, its partners and customers. For instance, factors such as the awareness and willingness of the top management of the retailer regarding the adoption and use of omni-channel applications, the current technological infrastructure of the retailer, the cost of the necessary technological investments, and the adaptation of employees to changes are the important factors. Furthermore, the partners of retailers, such as suppliers, logistics providers and advertising agencies will also be effective in the adoption and implementation of the omni-channel process. Even if all these obstacles and challenges are overcome, perhaps the most important risk is that customers will not be

Table 1. Omni-channel - multi-channel comparison

	Multi-Channel Management	Omni-Channel Management
Channel focus	Only the interactive channels	Interactive and mass-communication channels
Channel scope	Retail channels: store, web site, and direct marketing (catalog)	Retail channels: store, web site, direct marketing, mobile channels (smartphones, tablets, apps), social media, consumer touchpoints (including TV, radio, print, C2C channels).
Separation of channels	Separate channels that do not overlap	Integrated channels enabling seamless retail experience
Customer relationship center channel against the brand	Customer-retail channel focus	Customer - retail channel - brand focus
Channel management	Each channel	Cross-channel
Objectives	The individual goals of each channel (such as sales per channel, experience per channel)	Cross-channel objectives (overall retail customer experience, total sales of channels)

Resource: Verhoef, Kannan & Inman, 2015, p. 176.

able to adopt and use the omni-channel applications. Finally, it is essential for a business to consider and overcome all these factors for the success of omni-channel applications.

Today, most traditional retailers are still not fully aware of the technology. There are only a few innovative retailers in learning and implementing new technologies (Rigby, 2011a). The fact that retailers follow the technology and have high level of awareness will be an important factor in the spread of the omni-channel retailer. However, this awareness is not enough. The top management must also be willing to adopt the technological innovations and that risk taking skills must be at a high level.

It is also important that the current technological infrastructure of the retailer is applicable for the transition to omni-channel. At this point, the retailers with multi-channel infrastructure are more advantageous than those without one. It is because the multi-channel infrastructure can be used for omni-channel applications. However, the integration between channels and each additional channel will require the retailer to make new technological investments. At this point, the cost of these technological investments and return of these investments will be important in the decision of top management to switch to omni-channel. In addition, the conflicts between the channels may also arise as a significant risk to be resolved by the top management.

The determination of the top management and the technological investments made will become significant with the employees' adoption and use of omni-channel applications. Therefore, the training and motivation of the employees will be as an important obstacle to be resolved before the top management.

The partners such as suppliers, logistics providers and advertising agencies also have a critical stake in omni-channel retailing. At this point, the challenges that the omni-channel retailer will face are; How much logistics partner is needed, what kind of values these partners will provide, how delivery and refund options will be met (Fairchild, 2014; Hübner, Holzapfel, & Kuhn, 2016).

In order to ensure full channel integration, customers should be offered the opportunity to return their purchased products through an appropriate sales channel. Being able to cope with refund management is seen as one of the most important challenges that the retailers face. The source of this challenge is the increasing amount of refunds that comes from online ordering. Completed omni-channel integration requires all stores to accept such refunds (Staflund & Kersmark, 2015).

Consumers' purchasing decisions can be shaped according to the information and strategies followed by store, store website, mobile applications or social media. At this point, other intermediary firms and advertising agencies working for the retailers should be more data driven and analytically managed (Brynjolfsson, Hu & Rahman, 2013).

Today, consumers use their smartphones as an important device of shopping. Mobile channels are, therefore, an important channel option for reaching the consumers. At this point, it is important to understand which channels the consumers use and how they use them in order to be able to understand the mobility between different channels and eventually develop appropriate strategies (Falk, 2014). The increased use of smartphones allows the omni-channel retailers to reach consumers with much more information than is necessary during their purchase decision process. When combined with other channels, the astonishing accumulation of information in the retailers' power will give the retailers an advantage in identifying and implementing marketing strategies, while management of that information, on the other hand, can be a major problem.

Technological developments make omni-channel retailing unavoidable. Technology reduces the adverse effects of geographic expansion and provides competitive advantages to the retailers thanks to data collected and analyzed through technology. Omni-channel retailing allows businesses to reach the market more easily and reach even more consumers. With omni-channel retailing, competition will increase considerably. At this point, early adoption of omni-channel by the retailers and supply chain partners will gain competitive advantage omni-channel (Brynjolfsson, Hu & Rahman, 2013).

METHODOLOGY

The purpose of the study is to reveal the risks and challenges in the practice of innovative retailing in the case of developing country, which is the pioneering practice of omni-channel retailing, a rapidly developing concept today from the theoretical and practical point of view. The information that will be obtained as a result of the study will help the early adopters (the visionaries) who will be the next adopters of omni-channel which is in the development trend and the early majority (practitioners) to be proactive and be ahead in the competition.

The research was out in the case of Turkey, one of the developing countries. The present study used an open-ended questionnaire method. The study was conducted via e-mail because the respondents were located in different cities and even in different countries depending on their professions. Some criteria were taken into consideration in determining who would participate in the study. Firstly, people who had LinkedIn accounts and who identified themselves as omni-channel managers in their job titles were selected to participate in the study. Secondly, the selected people were involved in the retail sector. Only one questionnaire form was sent to one of the omni-channel managers working at the same company. Friendship request was sent to the people who meet the above criteria via the Linkedin and 30 people who accepted the invitation request were sent the questionnaire form by e-mail. The study was conducted between March 1-31, 2017. The number of people who responded to e-mails sent was 12. Therefore, it is possible to say that the return rate of the study was 40%.

FINDINGS

All the omni-channel managers who responded to the study questions worked in the retail sector. Respondents participating in the study and the information about the retailing sector they worked in are illustrated in Table 2.

The retail companies in the study are the leading large companies in Turkey both in terms of number of employees and volume of transactions. When the web pages of the retail companies that the participating respondents worked with during the survey period and *the about us* link at the linkedin accounts are examined, it is clearly seen that almost all of these retail companies have a large number of branches both domestically and abroad. All of these retail companies with the size of an international company present to the globally well-known domestic and foreign brands to their customers. Consequently, it is possible to say that innovative retailers that embrace omni-channel retailing are large-scale companies. Twelve open-ended questions in the questionnaire form were asked to the participants. The information obtained from the survey of participants from twelve different companies was evaluated below;

Question 1: *Which channels do you use to reach your customers? which of these channels were integrated in accordance with the operation of omni-channel?*

Table 2. Information regarding the respondents participating in the study and the sector they worked in

Participant	Age	Gender	Total work experience	Position	Sector	Number of Employees*
A	36	Male	13 years	E-commerce manager	Technology retailing	1001-5000
B	32	Male	10 years	E-Commerce project manager	Fashion and luxury retailing	1001-5000
C	33	Male	10 years	Omni-channel business development/ programs manager	Technology retailing	10.001+
D	38	Male	16 years	Digital channel and omni-channel manager	Home improvement retailing	1001-5000
E	30	Female	12 years	Omni-channel project manager	Large food and non-electronic retail group	10.001+
F	27	Female	8 years	E-commerce omni-channel and operation specialist	Ready-to-wear and fashion retailing	10.001+
G	39	Male	17 years	Digital marketing manager	Fast consumption - baby feeding	10.001+
H	36	Female	9 years	Digital platforms portfolio planning manager	E-commerce	501-1000
I	34	Male	7 years	E-commerce manager	Retailing (Beds, furniture, home textiles and accessories)	1001-5000
J	35	Male	8 years	E-commerce manager	Retailing, non-food products	10.001+
K	40	Male	19 years	E-commerce coordinator	Retailing, food	1001-5000
L	42	Male	15 years	E-commerce director	Apparel retailer	10.001+

* Information available in the company profile at Linkedin. Access Date: April 4, 2017

Table 3 shows the channels used by the retailers to reach customers.

When Table 3 was examined, it was found that retailers often used the channels of stores (11 participants), websites (11 participants) and mobile & application (10 participants) to reach their customers. In general, the participants stated that they had just started their omni-channel practice (participants D, I and J). Therefore, it was expressed that since the system requirements/transitions could not be completed, the transition from offline to online or from offline to offline could not be followed appropriately (Participant J). Most of the participants stated that they integrated the channels of store, website and mobile/apps. There was also a retailer (participant D) with the omni-channel application where the store and its websites were no longer integrated but the product order could be made through the kiosks in the stores. Some retailers (participants F, G, K, L), on the other hand, stated that all channels were integrated because of the compatibility of the technology used in the infrastructure of the channels.

Question 2: *What are your reasons of integrating sales channels?*

Table 4 lists the reasons of retailers' omni-channel implementation. This listing was organized according to the answers given by the respondents.

When Table 4 is examined, it is seen that the main reason for the omni-channel implementation of all retailers is to "offering the experience of multi-channel and uninterrupted service to the customers". When the other reasons are examined, it is seen that minimizing the service (participants A, D and L) and knowledge (participants A and K) differences between the channels was an important reason. Offering the customers a smooth digital experience was another important reason (participants C and J).

Question 3: *How do you define your company's omni-channel strategy?*

Table 5 illustrates the omni-channel strategies of retailers according to respondents' responses.

When Table 5 is examined, it is seen that retailers' strategies for omni-channel applications were reflected in retailers' strategies as well. In other words, it seems that retailers adopted the basic logic of

Table 3. The channels used to reach the customers

No	The Channels Used to Reach the Customers	Number of Participants
1	Store	11
2	Web site	11
3	Mobile&Apps	10
4	Call centers	3
5	E-market places (Amazon, Lazada etc.)	2
6	Kiosk	2
7	Other digital platforms	2
8	Insert and catalogs	1
9	In-store custom tablet implementation	1
10	Telesales	1

Table 4. The reasons of retailers' omni-channel implementation

No	The Reasons of Retailers' Omni-Channel Implementation	Number of Participants
1	Providing our customers with multi-channel and uninterrupted service experience	12
2	Minimizing the service gap between channels.	3
3	Minimize the information difference between channels.	2
4	Giving customers a smooth digital experience	2
5	Creating / enhancing customer loyalty	1
6	Leading customers to make basket average high spending	1
7	Making the supply chain faster	1
8	Offering channel-specific opportunities	1
9	Research online purchase offline	1
10	Providing flexibility to the customer in processes	1
11	Combining the advantages of online and offline channels (offering the opportunity to make product modification from e-commerce within the store)	1
12	Offering the customers easier and happier experiences with applications such as 'home delivery with one click', 'pay at the door', 'single basket', 'fast delivery'.	1

Table 5. Omni-channel strategies of the participating retailers

Participant	Omni-Channel Strategies of the Retailers / Explanation
A	Our omni-channel strategy is one of the four main strategies of our company
B	To be able to access the customers from every channel and make the supply process faster
C	Regardless of the channel, getting the customers to feel that they have made a purchase from our company
D	"100% integrated, single customer, multi and accurate channel" in the medium term
E	Offering smooth and personalized shopping experience to our customers
F	Offering an easy and accessible shopping experience
G	Cooperation of the each business unit from marketing to the supply chain that has contact the customer together with the brand and the agencies.
H	All-line access to customers from all channels
I	Offering a shopping experience equipped with up-to-date technology that will enable our customers to complete and purchase the desired product whenever and wherever they wish.
J	(Unspecified)
K	Implementing logistics and digital service design so that our customers can access the products easily and with minimum costs by placing the customer in the center.
L	Understanding and interpreting the customer's transition between all channels and devices by providing the mobilization of all the stocks in the company's network

the omni-channel as a strategy which expressed that "reaching customers from all channels and being able to interact with other partners in a way that will increase the customer satisfaction".

Question 4: *What are the benefits that the omni-channel strategy offers to you?*

Table 6 illustrates the responses given by participants regarding the benefits that omni-channel strategies provide.

When Table 6 is examined, a significant part of the participants stated that being able to dominate all sales channels (participants C, F, G, H, K) and providing better service to customers (participants A, E, C, D, H, L) were the benefits of omni-channel strategies to the retailers. Other expected benefits included "increasing customer satisfaction and loyalty" (participants A, E, L), "continuous communication with the customers" (participants C and K), "knowing/listening to the customer better" (participants A and C), "increase in the sales volumes" (participants B and I), "providing accurate campaigns to the right channel (participants D and E) to increase the value of the customers", and "the sales channels feed each other" (participants E and I) respectively. Other benefits were listed in Table 6 as the expressions of a single participant.

Question 5: *What are the obstacles before the use the omni-channel structure?*

Table 7 illustrates the responses given by participants regarding the obstacles before the use of omni-channel.

When Table 7 is examined, a significant part of the participants stated that "the costs of technological integration investments" (participants A, C, D, J and L), "integration of the existing technological infrastructure" (participants C, F, I, J and L) and "introducing omni-channel to employees and making them use the system" (participants A, D, F, I and L) were the obstacles before the use of the omni-channel. The other obstacles were "employees embrace the system" (participants A, I and L), "customers adopt the system" (participants A and I), "omni-channel requires different competencies" (participants E and G) and "dependence on other chains when there is no physical store in online-offline integration"

Table 6. Benefits of the omni-channel strategy to the retailers

No	Benefits	Number of Participants
1	Better service to customers dominate all the sales channels	5
2	Better service to customers	5
3	Increasing customer satisfaction and loyalty	3
4	Being in constant contact with the customers	2
5	Knowing / listening to our customers better	2
6	Increase in the sales volume	2
7	Providing accurate campaigns to customers that will increase the customer value	2
8	Sales channels feed each other	2
9	Improvement in stock consumption rates	1
10	Being able to make analyzes to optimize the processes	1
11	Integrating the closed customer groups into the system	1
12	Access to single customer data via the multiple channels	1
13	Providing a versatile solutions	1
14	Being the first brand remembered by the customers	1
15	Removing the physical obstacles	1

Table 7. The obstacles before the use of omni-channel structure

No	The Obstacles Before the Use of Omni-Channel	Number of Participants
1	Cost of technological integration investments	5
2	The existing technological infrastructure and the integration of this infrastructure	5
3	Introducing omni-channel to employees and making them use the system	5
4	Employees embrace the system	3
5	Customers adopt the system	2
6	Omni-channel requires different competencies	2
7	Dependence on other chains when there is no physical store in online-offline integration	2
8	Directing customer perception towards purchasing without touching the products	1
9	Traditional sales approaches	1
10	Regulatory and legal reasons	1
11	Adaptation in logistics and field practices	1
12	Perception of the e-commerce as a competitor of stores	1
13	Employees resist to integrate with other channels in order to maintain sales targets in the physical store channel	1
14	Low online shopping penetration	1

(participants C and H) respectively. The other obstacles were illustrated in Table 7 as the expression of a single participant.

Question 6: *What are the reactions of your customers to your use the omni-channel structure?*

Table 8 illustrates the responses provided by the participants with regard to the responses given by customers using the omni-channel structure.

When Table 8 is examined, a significant proportion of participants (participants A, E, F, G, H, I, and L) reported that customers using Omni-channel had a high level of satisfaction. Moreover, participants expressed that they felt comfort, security and relaxation in the purchases of consumers (participants D

Table 8. Reactions of customers using the omni-channel structure

No	Customer Feedback	Number of Participants
1	High level of satisfaction as a result of interviews and surveys	7
2	Consumers feel comfort, security and relaxation in shopping	2
3	Meeting the needs of the consumers and solving their problems	2
4	Requests for improvement	1
5	Satisfaction with the delivery speed	1
6	The overall satisfaction that customers have in being able to communicate with each and every channel	1
7	Satisfaction with time, price and diversity	1

and K), and that their needs were met and their problems were solved (participants E and L). The other answers were expressed individually by each participant. When the statements of the participants are examined, it is seen that consumers were generally pleased with the use of omni-channel.

Question 7: *Is there any difference in usage levels in terms of customer segments? If so, what are they? Which customer segments use this structure more or have the potential to use them?*

Table 9 illustrates participants' responses to the omni-channel customer segments and characteristics. When Table 9 is examined, it is seen that the omni-channel customer segment was generally composed of consumers under the age of 40, who had jobs and with high digital penetration and were consumers in groups B and C1 in terms of Socioeconomic Status (SES). However, it should be emphasized that this segment was made on the sample of Turkey which was one of the developing countries.

Question 8: *Could you give us information about your infrastructure that you use for the omni-channel?*

Table 10 illustrates participants' responses to the technology that retailers use for omni-channel. When Table 10 is examined, it is seen that retailers developed different solutions according to the needs of the sector according to the responses given by the participants. While some retailers use their own software, others use a variety of software. Besides, it is seen that there are various procedures that guide retailers with their practices.

Table 9. Participants' responses to the omni-channel customer segments and characteristics

Participant	Participants' Responses to the Omni-Channel Customer Segments and Characteristics
A	There is a mass of people over time that is customized to use this structure and consumes more.
B	As age decreases and education level increases, the use of omni-channel rate also increases.
C	Consumer segment is mainly composed of consumers aged between 15-30; this segment is more relevant and sensitive to omni-channel.
D	Customer segments differ from sector to sector. However, the consumers who use credit cards with high internet usage and are aged between 18-40 are potential segments of omni-channel.
E	(Unspecified)
F	It is possible to mention a multi-mass based change rather than a segment-based change.
G	Customers with more digital penetration are more likely to be involved in this system.
H	People who are mostly white-collar workers constitute the potential customer segment. It is because they want packages from the store as they will not be at home at the time of delivery. They try them out in the cabins there. If they do not like the product, they return it immediately.
I	In terms of location, the customers in the first three major cities of Turkey make up about 40% of customers using omni-channel. In terms of socio-economic status, they are the groups B and C1, respectively.
J	Customers / users aged 25-34 who are prone to use Mobile App and Mobile site are more suitable for this structure.
K	High income groups adapt more easily.
L	The younger the client base, the greater the response to this application. Other prominent characteristics are the level of education and working status of consumers. The working customer segment uses them with much higher percentage.

Table 10. Technological infrastructure used for omni-channel

Participant	Participants' Explanations Regarding the Technological Infrastructure Retailers Used for Omni-Channel
A	There is software that we have ourselves developed.
B	We have no special technology.
C	We use very different SaaS (software as a service) products.
D	An integrated single system and a full organization working subsidiary to it are quite sufficient. It is very important that the product and all the information related to the product are the same in every channel.
E	We have developed an application for our customers who come to the store and add to their basket for products that are not then available at the store to be sent later on.
F	We have a special infrastructure and procedures available.
G	A good CRM system and Customer Experience approach is the core of omni-channel.
H	We have software enabling to take online orders from the stores. We also have various procedures for this.
I	We use mostly tablet applications etc. in our offline channels and personalization technologies in the online channels.
J	Unspecified.
K	We use SAP / Hybris installed with the Content and Commerce modules.
L	Technological infrastructure is developed in-house. Each application is put into practice together with the company procedures.

Question 9: *What are the fundamental changes resulting from the omni-channel application?*

Table 11 illustrates the main changes according to participants that retailers experienced with the transition to the omni-channel application.

When Table 11 is examined, retailers' ability to combine the different channels with omni-channel applications led to increased flexibility and increased organizational productivity among the channels. As a result of all these, number of customers of the retailers, volume of sales and hence their revenues

Table 11. The changes achieved via the omni-channel

No	The Changes Achieved via the Omni-Channel	Number of Participants
1	Increase in data volume	3
2	Increase in revenues	3
3	Increase in the level of services offered to customers	3
4	Increase in sales volume	2
5	Progress in customer analysis	2
6	Increase in the numbers of customer	1
7	Access to customers in an integrated way from multiple channels	1
8	Flexibility between the channels	1
9	Increase in organizational productivity	1
10	Combining the different channels	1
11	Increase in the use of the website	1

increased. It is also seen that together with the increase in the amount of data, more advanced customer analyses could be made.

Another question that is asked in connection with the question nine is related with retailers' marketing performance, acquiring new customer, level of customer loyalty, and the level and status of stock activity. Almost all of the participants stated that with the use of omni-channel, they were positive progression in all these criteria.

Question 10: *Five years from now, what do you think, are the changes in retailing and channel strategies going to be like?*

Table 12 illustrates the summary of the interesting responses of each participant to the question of how changes in the retail sector and channel strategies to be followed in the next five years were going to be like.

Table 12. Participants' predictions regarding the change and the channel strategies to be followed in the retail sector after five years

Participant	The Predictions of the Participants
A	Consumer trends will determine how channel strategies will be followed in the retailing sector in the next five years. There is no doubt that the potential on the online side is quite strong. Digital channels are the showcases of brands and they will always maintain and boost their importance. They will continue to grow as well. Nevertheless, I anticipate that the equation of multi-channel experience in the long-term will be shaped by consumers' preferences.
B	I predict that while those with the store channel go to full cycle omni-channel, those in e-commerce trade will use compatibility with the mobile apps.
C	For the next five years, I predict an omni-channel structure in which all the stock visibility (company + marketplaces + retailer + brick and mortar) can be viewed from one screen, all the CRM data is collected in one tool and personalization is performed based on this data. I do not think that the companies that insist on the single channel strategy will be able to survive. Those companies that are able to implement each channel in a compatible and integrated manner will be one step ahead. At the same time, the companies that maintain the brand image constant and consistent in these channels will be even more prominent.
D	I envisage that there will be different store formats in the future in which the companies that are concentrated in the physical market will turn to digital, and in which some other companies which are only present in digital will turn into physical shops (Argos store model (UK)). It is because serious store costs and customer expectations lead retailers to systems that are more effectively managed.
E	We are at a time period when omni-channel has become an obligation, not an option. I predict that personalization, localization and experience will gain importance when the conscious and technological development of the customers is taken into account. The penetration of the mobile channel has not yet reached saturation and has shown an increase.
F	I anticipate that omni-channel applications will become more common in the sector and will be implemented by many retailers.
G	In the future, I envisage that we will see more of neuro-marketing applications. Messages on all channels will be optimized for brain chemistry.
H	There will be strategies that include artificial intelligence. Technology is moving. Deliveries using drone will be made. Fast delivery will be the retail new channel strategies. I also anticipate that the security levels associated with payments will increase and the use of e-wallets will accelerate.
I	I anticipate that there will be increasingly more digital and online channels in place, but that offline channels will not be over and become customer experience centers.
J	In five years' time, I predict that the strategies will continue to be as offline and online (like today). Five years from now is still an early time for Turkey for omni-channel strategies since the necessary investments, infrastructure, human resources, education and other elements are subjects that need to be completed.
K	I imagine that the strategy of the leading company will be imitated because there is intense competition.
L	I anticipate that there will be no online-offline distinction, and that the stores will be replaced by existing buildings with 95% stores, 5% stocking areas, which will have a much higher stocking area and more showrooms in the future.

Question 11: *What are the trends you expect your business to influence the selection of the omni-channel structure?*

Table 13 illustrates the trends that participants expect the retailers to influence the choice of the omni-channel structure.

When Table 13 is examined, it is seen that respondents who participated in the study in the sample of Turkey stated as important trends that mobile life level would continue to increase, secure payment methods would become more widespread, smart phone and 4,5G penetration would increase, children born into the mobile world would be consumers in the medium term and effect of the social media would continue.

Question 12: *Finally, what are the parties, what kind of duties should they take for the adoption of omni-channel in retailing or for their accommodation in the sector? What are your suggestions?*

Table 14 illustrates participants' responses to what kind of duties the relevant parties involved should take for the adoption or accommodation of omni-channel in the retailing sector.

When Table 14 is examined, the respondents who participated in the survey in the Turkish sample indicated that the top managers and employees of the company, logistics and delivery companies, IT departments, online and offline store channel management should take on important tasks for the adoption of omni-channel in retailing or for its settlement in the sector.

Table 13. The Trends to be influenced by omni-channel selection of retailers according to the participants

No	Trends	Number of Participants
1	Mobile lifestyle continues to rise	5
2	Spread of secure payment methods	4
3	Increase in smartphone numbers and 4.5G penetration	3
4	Children born into the mobile world and young people become consumers in the medium term	3
5	Impact of social media	3
6	Personalization applications	2
7	Algorithms	1
8	Increase in importance of influencers in the social media	1
9	Creative shopping experience with augmented reality (both online and offline)	1
10	3D printers	1
11	Click–connect applications	1
12	Customer loyalty applications	1
13	Increasing desire to create video content for consumers	1
14	A consistent brand experience (a brand experience similar experience on each channel)	1

Table 14. The duties the relevant parties should take for the adoption/accommodation of omni-channel in the retailing sector

Participant	The Participants' Responses
A	Our customer interaction is very high since we are a leading company in the multi-channel model in the relevant sector. This interaction, thus, shows the way ahead for our company. As the number of experienced people increases and becomes widespread, it will grow with new demands.
B	IT departments have great responsibilities. Retailer must be intertwined to act together with App and Web application teams.
C	Companies here should have all the responsibility. Brands should make the customers the focus of everything and try to become distinct through the initiatives that are innovative, make the journey of buying easy, fast and more based on the demands from the customers.
D	It is necessary to encourage digital buying experience, provide tax advantages if necessary, focus on investments and R&D, rather than focusing on profitability for a certain period, listen to customers, and take customer pulses with A/B tests.
E	It is up to top management to undertake the task of supporting change and appoint the teams and leaders who will form the culture of this task. It is the task of those teams to adapt to change and to omni-channel.
F	The development of the operation and technical infrastructure of the companies is very important in terms of the healthy operation of the process.
G	It is necessary for companies to complete their digital conversions, invest in these subjects, attach importance to data-related issues, and build on forward-looking digital-data.
H	All e-commerce companies, delivery companies have to work on this issue. It is important that physical stores, which also have an online store, prioritize the subject.
I	For a good omni-channel structure, especially the delivery, logistics infrastructure should be perfect. Payment management companies (Fintech) quickly develop themselves. Related institutions should support such initiatives in various ways.
J	Offline and online channels should identify strategies accurately and simultaneous participation of each sales department should be ensured. All parties involved in the process should agree on this issue and the analysis steps must be taken carefully before moving on to the technology part of the task.
K	Omni-channel is a big data management application. Therefore, it is absolutely necessary to be able to convert into action at the end of data processing.
L	Unspecified.

CONCLUSION

Technological advances, changes in consumer behavior and intense competition are the most important threats of today, affecting many sectors as well as the retail industry. In the face of these threats, innovative retailers try to attract new customers with innovative and personalized presentations (Pollamarasetty & Potti, 2016) and increase the loyalty of existing customers. The fact that services such as selection, packaging and delivery are attractive and appealing to the consumers today (Rowell, 2015), push retailers to different pursuits. As a result of these pursuits, omni-channel retailing has developed as the next step within the existing multi-channel retailing. With the omni-channel retailing system, the retailers can reach their customers through integrated channels instead of reaching their customers with multi-channels. In this way, purchasing journey of the customers is ensured uninterruptedly.

In the present study, the omni-channel applications of innovative retailers, which are pioneers of omni-channel retailing, have been investigated on the companies with omni-channel applications in Turkey. As a result of the study, the obstacles, challenges and opportunities encountered by the retailers with omni-channel practices have been established. With the information obtained as a result of the present study, it was aimed to help other retailers who would adopt the omni-channel retailing in an uninterrupted manner. The present study, conducted with the help of omni-channel experts, provided valuable insights into the risks, challenges and opportunities that the omni-channel retailers faced.

The study concluded that retailers' reasons for implementing omni-channel strategies were to provide uninterrupted service experience with the integrated channels, minimize the service and information gap between the channels, provide customers with a streamlined digital experience, and establish and increase the customer loyalty. The benefits that retailers have achieved as a result of omni-channel applications, on the other hand, can be stated as being able to dominate all the channels, provide better service to the customers, improve customer satisfaction and loyalty, keep in touch with the customers, recognize the customers better, and increase the sales volume.

There are many obstacles for retailers to adopt omni-channel applications. The cost of technological integration investments, the integration of the necessary omni-channel infrastructure with the existing technological infrastructure, the omni-channel employees' embracing of this system, the adoption of customers are the main obstacles. The failure to overcome these obstacles proves that the omni-channel system of the operator is unsuccessful. At this point, the top management of the retail companies and their employees should adopt the omni-channel.

To overcome the obstacles faced in omni-channel process, companies need to make necessary changes and updates in their marketing strategies and logistics processes (Carvalho & Campomar, 2014). Expanding the delivery methods, increasing the delivery speed and service levels are critical issues for the success of omni-channel (Hübner, Holzapfel & Kuhn, 2016). As the present study also concluded, there are important tasks and responsibilities falling to logistics and delivery companies, the retailer's IT department, online and offline store channel management.

The online channels should be developed in a way that is compatible with the retailers' omni-channel strategies. Otherwise, online channels can damage brick & mortar shopping channels of retailers (Kemperman, Delft & Borgers, 2015). In addition, since the retailers deal with very large amounts of data during the process of omni-channel retailing, businesses are required to create omni-channel retail information systems within the company and optimize their operations at the channel level. Otherwise, inadequate customer service delivery and/or operational deficiencies will occur in different channels (Tambo, 2015: 875).

Another important factor in the success of omni-channel retailing is whether the consumers will adopt omni-channel retailing. If customers do not adopt omni-channel retailing, all the investments, time and efforts exerted until that time will be wasted. At this point, before switching to omni-channel retailing, retailers should investigate whether the target customers will adopt the omni-channel. The literature on this subject is also new. In one of these studies Juaneda-Ayensa et al. (2016) investigated the adoption of omni-channel retailing by the consumers in Spain regarding clothing retailers. As a result of their study, it was found that personal innovativeness, effort expectanct, and performance expectanct were important determinants on consumers' intention to purchase over omni-channel. However, such studies should be made not only in academic terms, but also in the countries and sub-sectors in which retailers are located for the success of your omni-channel retailing.

As it is the case many studies, this study, too, has some limitations. During the period when omni-channel has begun to be implemented, the number of omni-channel retailers and experts in developing countries such as Turkey is quite low. This has influenced choice of the method for the study. Therefore, it is not possible to generalize the results obtained from this study. The novelty of the research subject has led to the research being carried out only on those who are experts in e-commerce with omni-channel knowledge. Another limitation of the study is its cost. Since the participants were in very different cities and even abroad, this caused questionnaire method to be used online.

Similar studies in future research can be done in different countries. The differences in the level of development of countries can also lead to different outcomes from those studies. Studies can also be conducted on different samples regarding the adoption of omni-channel retailing. For instance, employees' acceptance and use of omni-channel practices, consumer's adoption of omni-channel, supply chain partners' adoption and use of the omni-channel can be investigated.

REFERENCES

Ailawadi, K. L., & Farris, P. W. (2017). Managing multi- and omni-channel distribution: Metrics and research directions. *Journal of Retailing*, *93*(1), 120–135. doi:10.1016/j.jretai.2016.12.003

Akroush, M. N., & Al-Debei, M. M. (2015). An integrated model of factors affecting consumer attitudes towards online shopping. *Business Process Management Journal*, *21*(6), 1353–1376. doi:10.1108/BPMJ-02-2015-0022

Barnes, C. (2016). Omni-channel retail-challenges and opportunities for packaging innovation. In P. Burgess (Ed.), Integrating the packaging and product experience in food and beverages: a road-map to consumer satisfaction. Duxford: Woodhead Publishing. doi:10.1016/B978-0-08-100356-5.00004-8

Beck, N., & Rygl, D. (2015). Categorization of multiple channel retailing in multi-, cross-, and omni-channel retailing for retailers and retailing. *Journal of Retailing and Consumer Services*, *27*, 170–178. doi:10.1016/j.jretconser.2015.08.001

Belu, M. G., & Marinoiu, A. M. (2014). A new distribution strategy: The omnichannel strategy. *The Romanian Economic Journal*, *17*(52), 117–133.

Berman, B., & Thelen, S. (2004). A guide to developing and managing a well-integrated multi-channel retail strategy. *International Journal of Retail & Distribution Management*, *32*(3), 147–156. doi:10.1108/09590550410524939

Brynjolfsson, E., Hu, Y. J., & Rahman, M. S. (2013). Competing in the age of omnichannel retailing. *MIT Sloan Management Review*, *54*(4), 22–29.

De Carvalho, J., & Campomar, M. C. (2014). Multichannel at retail and omni-channel: Challenges for marketing and logistics. *Business & Management Review*, *4*(3), 103–113.

Dorman, A. J. (2013). *Omni-channel retail and the new age consumer: an empirical analysis of direct-to- consumer channel interaction in the retail industry*. CMC Senior Theses. Paper 590. Retrieved March 29, 2017, from http://scholarship.claremont.edu/cmc_theses/590

Fairchild, A. M. (2014). Extending the network: Defining product delivery partnering preferences for omni-channel commerce. *Procedia Technology*, *16*, 447–451. doi:10.1016/j.protcy.2014.10.111

Falk, J. (2014). *Physical mobile interaction in omni-channel retailing using the customers' smartphone to interact with smart objects in a store* (Student paper). Linköpings universitet. Retrieved March 30, 2017, from http://www.diva-portal.org/smash/get/diva2:728289/FULLTEXT01.pdf

Govindarajan, A., Sinha, A., & Uichanco, J. (2017). *Inventory optimization for fulfillment integration in omnichannel retailing*. Ross School of Business Working Paper, Working Paper No. 1341, February 2017. Retrieved March 30, 2017, from https://deepblue.lib.umich.edu/bitstream/handle/2027.42/136157/1341_Govindarajan.pdf?sequence=1&isAllowed=y

Gulnaz, B. P., & Gokulakannan, P. (2016). Omnichannel retailing. In S. Dixit & A. Sinha (Eds.), *E-Retailing Challenges and Opportunities in the Global Marketplace* (pp. 244–255). Hershey, PA: IGI Global.

Ha, S., & Stoel, L. (2012). Online apparel retailing: Roles of e-shopping quality and experiential e-shopping motives. *Journal of Service Management, 23*(2), 197–215. doi:10.1108/09564231211226114

Hübner, A., Holzapfel, A., & Kuhn, H. (2016). Distribution systems in omni-channel retailing. *Business Research, 9*(2), 255–296. doi:10.1007/s40685-016-0034-7

Ishfaq, R., Defee, C. C., Gibson, B. J., & Raja, U. (2016). Realignment of the physical distribution process in omni-channel fulfillment. *International Journal of Physical Distribution & Logistics Management, 46*(6/7), 543–561. doi:10.1108/IJPDLM-02-2015-0032

Jiang, L. A., Yang, Z., & Jun, M. (2013). Measuring consumer perceptions of online shopping convenience. *Journal of Service Management, 24*(2), 191–214. doi:10.1108/09564231311323962

Juaneda-Ayensa, E., Mosquera, A., & Murillo, Y. S. (2016). Omnichannel customer behavior: Key drivers of technology acceptance and use and their effects on purchase intention. *Frontiers in Psychology, 7*, 1–11. doi:10.3389/fpsyg.2016.01117 PMID:27516749

Kemperman, A., van Delft, L., & Borgers, A. (2015). Omni-channel fashion shopping. In E. Pantano (Ed.), *Successful Technological Integration for Competitive Advantage in Retail Settings* (pp. 144–167). Hershey, PA: IGI Global. doi:10.4018/978-1-4666-8297-9.ch007

Kumar, R., & Hu, M. (2015, Sept.). Is your supply chain ready for the omni-channel revolution? *Supply Chain Management Review,* 76-78. Retrieved March 29, 2017, from https://www.atkearney.com/documents/10192/6464222/SCMR1509_OpAdvantage2.pdf/705bfa25-814b-4991-9853-66cf7648d0b2

Lazaris, C., & Vrechopoulos, A. (2014). From multi-channel to "omnichannel" retailing: review of the literature and calls for research. *2nd International Conference on Contemporary Marketing Issues,* 1-6.

Lima, A. F. S. (2015). *Omni-channel retail strategies: an outlook to portuguese business transformation*. Dissertation Proposal Master in Management. Retrieved March 10, 2017, from https://repositorio-aberto.up.pt/bitstream/10216/79958/2/36198.pdf

Neslin, S. A., Grewal, D., Leghorn, R., Shankar, V., Teerling, M. L., Thomas, J. S., & Verhoef, P. C. (2006). Challenges and opportunities in multichannel customer management. *Journal of Service Research, 9*(2), 95–112. doi:10.1177/1094670506293559

Pollamarasetty, S., & Potti, R. (2016). Omni-channel retailing: enriching customers' shopping experience. In N. Kamath & S. Saurav (Eds.), *Handbook of Research on Strategic Supply Chain Management in the Retail Industry* (pp. 233–249). Hershey, PA: IGI Global. doi:10.4018/978-1-4666-9894-9.ch013

Punj, G. (2012). Consumer decision making on the web: A theoritical analysis and research guidelines. *Psychology and Marketing*, *29*(10), 791–803. doi:10.1002/mar.20564

Rigby, D. (2011a). The future of shopping. *Harvard Business Review*, *89*(12), 65–76.

Rigby, D. (2011b, Dec. 7). Omnichannel retail delivering on customer expectations. *Harvard Business Review,* 1-4.

Rigby, D., Kris, M., Josh, C., & Suzanne, T. (2012). Omnichannel retailing: digital disruption and retailer opportunities. *Bain Retail Holiday Newsletter.* Retrieved March 29, 2017, from http://goo. gl/47MwZX

Rowell, J. (2015). Omni-channel retailing: The changing battleground. *Romanian Distribution Committee Magazine*, *6*(4), 10–17.

Schoenbachler, D. D., & Gordon, G. L. (2002). Multi-channel shopping: Understanding what drives channel choice. *Journal of Consumer Marketing*, *19*(1), 42–53. doi:10.1108/07363760210414943

Staflund, L., & Kersmark, M. (2015). *Omni-channel retailing: Blurring the lines between online and offline* (Dissertation). Retrieved March 29, 2017, from http://urn.kb.se/resolve?urn=urn:nbn:se:hj:diva-27392

Tambo, T. (2015). Omni-channel retail information systems. In *Encyclopedia of Information Science and Technology* (3rd ed.; pp. 874–882). IGI Global. doi:10.4018/978-1-4666-5888-2.ch083

Verhoef, P. C., Kannan, P. K., & Inman, J. J. (2015). From multi-channel retailing to omni-channel retailing introduction to the special issue on multi-channel retailing. *Journal of Retailing*, *91*(2), 174–181. doi:10.1016/j.jretai.2015.02.005

Wilson, H., & Daniel, E. (2007). The multi-channel challenge: A dynamic capability approach. *Industrial Marketing Management*, *36*(1), 10–20. doi:10.1016/j.indmarman.2006.06.015

KEY TERMS AND DEFINITIONS

Customer Loyalty: It is conversion of the consumer's positive attitude towards a product/service or business into intent to re-purchase the same product/service.

Multi-Channel: It is the channel structure that retailers use to access different channels individually and physically and/or online to reach their goals. In multi-channel, the channel structure is chosen according to the characteristics of target market. Each channel is managed separately.

Omni-Channel: Together with the developing technology, omni-channel brings together the physical and online shopping experiences of the consumers, thus removing the differences between the channels and providing a single channel shopping system to the consumers.

Online Customer: Online customers are the customers who make online purchases as a result of the development and possibilities provided by the internet and other technologies.

Retailer: Retailers who are between producers and consumers are intermediaries that carry out marketing activities related to the sale of products or services directly to the final consumer.

Retailing: A distribution channel function that involves purchasing products from suppliers or manufactures for profit, then selling these products to consumers.

Technology: It is the innovations or inventions for the discovery and development of new management methods in the process of new product or service development resulting from research and development activities.

Turkey: Turkey is a developing country with a democratic, secular, unitary, parliamentary republic and various cultural heritage in Eurasia.

Chapter 7
Designing Distribution Centres for Omni-Channel Fulfilment:
In Indian Context

Navneet Kumar Singh
Amazon, India

ABSTRACT

The E-Commerce market is thriving and poised for robust growth in Asia. The success of E-Commerce players depends on their understanding of the market and offering various types of features. This paper gives an overview of the future of E-Commerce in India and discusses the future growth segments in India's E-Commerce. Also find out various factors that would essential for future growth of Indian E-commerce. And represent the various opportunities for retailers, wholesalers, producers and for people. In this paper, we found that the Overall E-Commerce will increase exponentially in coming years in the emerging market of India. A review of the literature revealed that, to date, no research has been conducted on the supply chain that is needed to support the growth of E-Commerce business in a developing country such as India. This study aim at studying - why will e-commerce have an impact on supply chain" and "where will e-commerce affect the supply chain in future.

INTRODUCTION

The E-commerce Industry in India has come a long way since its early days. The market has matured and new players have entered the market space. In the present dynamic scenario, E-Commerce market in the B2C space is growing in demand as well as in the array of services. The transition to online purchasing from traditional purchasing is taking a long time in the Indian market. E commerce includes not only buying and selling goods over Internet, but also various business processes within individual organizations that support the goal. As with E-Commerce, e-business (electronic business) also has a number of different definitions and is used in a number of different contexts.

India's E-Commerce market, if not in infancy, is at an early stage barely adequate logistic and technological infrastructure in place leading to operational inefficiencies makes high-volume e-commerce

DOI: 10.4018/978-1-5225-3056-5.ch007

business very challenging (Subramanian, 2012). Given the complexities and challenges of E-Commerce, it is inevitable to have a framework that account for logistics costs and capabilities while evaluating the opportunity to expand the service to larger population and hence increase profit margin. Traditionally, practice has been to manufacture at economically favoring locations or source from vendors with lowest cost. This trend, however, is often offset by increased logistics costs and delivery times.

The complexities of managing logistics in Indian market locations finally add to the total landed costs of the associated goods. Therefore, the process of redesigning supply chain operations to establish logistics management capabilities in India is a fundamental dimension for a long-term business strategy for online players. Design of such strategy should include a focus on end-to-end integrated operations and sound process discipline that will help e-tailers achieve flexibility, responsiveness and resiliency to enable more effective competition in today's dynamic business environment. As the E-Commerce business landscape continues to evolve, so do its challenges. New competitors are entering the market. Product life cycles are getting shorter. Customers are more demanding, and their expectations now extend beyond cost and service to include ethical, environmental, and sustainability concerns (Hui et. al., 1991). This complex and fast changing environment puts new demands on supply chains, as companies seek ways not just to manage the change, but also to use their supply chains as a source of competitive advantage. Those that succeed are thinking far beyond their organizational boundaries. They are optimizing their supply chains from end to end, and are finding new ways to collaborate with both suppliers and customers. The innovations, lessons in practice and new technological solutions in managing retail supply chains are not just important in retailing but crucial in the ultimate effective management of the complete supply chain (Ronald, 2012).

In this research, we evaluated the current state of Indian E-Commerce and the challenges faced by them. Thereafter, we have proposed a framework that caters needs of SMEs in E-Commerce business to achieve supply chain operational efficiencies. The framework builds upon various strategies that are available in literature while keeping Indian context in backdrop. We then propose our findings and conclusion by mapping the current challenges of the Indian e-tailers, the various strategies those can be adopted by them and we are suggesting a framework, specially, for Small and Medium Enterprises (SMEs) in E-Commerce business and it is not viable for them to have their own managed infrastructure and setup (Grace, 2011). We have also presented key managerial insights for logistics network in India that would enable e-tailers to realize benefits from online business.

Concepts and Definitions

Electronic commerce or e-commerce refers to a wide range of online business activities for products and services. It also pertains to "any form of business transaction in which the parties interact electronically rather than by physical exchanges or direct physical contact."

A more complete definition is: E-commerce is the use of electronic communications and digital information processing technology in business transactions to create, transform, and redefine relationships for value creation between or among organizations, and between organizations and individuals.

- **Different Types of E-Commerce Players:** The major different types of e-commerce are: business-to-business (B2B); business to- consumer (B2C); business-to-government (B2G); consumer-to-consumer (C2C); and mobile commerce (m-commerce).

E-Commerce Growth in India

For developing countries like India, e-commerce offers considerable opportunity. E-Commerce in India is still in growing stage, but even the most-pessimistic projections indicate a boom. It is believed that low cost of personal computers, a growing installed base for Internet use, and an increasingly competitive Internet Service Provider (ISP) market will help fuel e-commerce growth in Asia's second most populous nation (Bimschleger, 2014). The first e-commerce site in India was rediff.com. It was one of the most trafficked portals for both Indian and nonresidents Indians. It provided a wealth of Indian-related business news a reach engine, E-Commerce and web solution services. The past 2 years have seen a rise in the number of companies enabling e-commerce technologies and the internet in India. Major Indian portal sites have also shifted towards e-commerce instead of depending on advertising revenues. The web communities built around these portal sites with content have been effectively targeted to sell everything from event and mouse tickets the grocery and computers. The major in this services being Rediff.com and the net and India plaza with started a shopping section after in spite of RBI regulation low internet usage e-commerce sites have popped up everywhere hawking things like groceries, bakery items, gifts, books, audio and video cassettes, computer etc. none of the major players have been deterred by the low PC penetration and credit card (Bardwell, 2012).

Future of E-Commerce in India

India is developing rapidly and if development is to be measured, how can we ignore the role of e commerce in it. The internet user base in India might still be a mere 100 million which is much less when compared to its penetration in the US or UK but it's surely expanding at an alarming rate. The number of new entrants in this sphere is escalating daily and with growth rate reaching its zenith it can be presumed that in years to come, customary retailers will feel the need to switch to online business (Tang, 2006). Insights into increasing demand for broadband services, rising standards of living, availability of wider product ranges, reduced prices and busy lifestyles reveal this fact more prominently thereby giving way to online deals on gift vouchers. Going by the statistics, the E commerce market in India was worth about $2.5 billion in 2009. It rose to $8.5 billion by 2011 thus depicting a definite surge in the last two years. According to a statement released by the Internet and Mobile Association of India (IAMAI), these figures would reach up to $12 billion by 2012! To understand this scenario, we can divide E-commerce into three broad categories which include physical services, physical goods and virtual goods. Another category that is gradually making its mark is the local commerce (couponing, yellow pages, classifieds etc.) which offers significant overlaps with E-commerce. The 1st category of physical services is definitely the major contributor which includes travel ticketing, jobs, matrimonial and event management websites with travel sites accounting for 75% of all E-commerce industries! It provides attractive deals too (Lim et.al., 2010).

The 2nd category of physical goods is the one currently gaining considerable attention, thanks to the hype created by new startups/stores being launched daily. Leaders in this division are Flipkart, Infibeam, Homeshop18, Indiatimes, Naaptol, Letsbuy etc. each of which offers everything from mobile phones to pet food.

The 3rd and final category of virtual goods and gift vouchers like online music, software's, movies, games, Taj Hotel gift vouchers, Reebok gift vouchers, Pizza Hut gift vouchers etc. have been relatively lagging behind in India as compared to Europe and America, primarily due to piracy concerns and the social perspective of Indians. But the scenario is expected to change with the digital downloads segment expected to grow in the Indian E-Commerce market due to the explosion of mobile devices and the services available over the Internet at special discounts. Certain unique attributes of the E-commerce industry in India such as cash on delivery mode of payment and direct imports that lower costs considerably are probably going to bring about a speedy growth in this industry in years to come (Morris, 2012).

According to the latest research by Forrester, a leading global research and advisory firm, the e-commerce market in India is set to grow the fastest within the Asia-Pacific Region at a CAGR of over 57% between 2012-16. The report, titled "Asia Pacific Online Retail Forecast, 2011 To 2016," has been issued by Forrester Research Inc. Analyst Zia Daniell Wigder, with Steven Noble, Vikram Sehgal and Lily Varon.

E-commerce in India to explode in 2012, Indian e-shoppers will have a good time getting great deals and services online. A recent pan-India report released by Com Score Inc reveals that online shopping in India has touched a growth rate of 18 per cent and is only likely to grow further. E-commerce can become an integral part of sales strategy while it is one of the cheapest medium to reach out the new markets, if implemented successfully, it offer a smart way of expansion and doing e-commerce attribute to the successful implementation to carefully understanding the products and services, customers and the business process, easy -to-use system to extend the business on the web.

The e-commerce platforms maximize its reach to the potential customers and provide them with a convenient, satisfying and secure shopping experience.

Segments That Recorded Growth

Online channels are playing an important role of connecting with consumers of unexplored markets. The journey of online spending that started with an increasing number of buyers of travel and holiday plans in the last decade has now extended to an increase in spends on household appliances and luxury products. While segments like apparel and luxury products have registered unprecedented growth in 2011, jewelry, electronic appliances and hardware products have shown promising growth trends as well. "Indian consumers are showing greater appetite to transact online, fueling the e-commerce boom," said Anuj Kumar, CEO, Affle.

The report also found that coupon sites are rapidly gaining popularity, with 16.5 per cent of the Indian online population visiting the category in November 2011 – 27.2 million online users in India aged 15 and older accessed the retail category from a home or work computer, an increase of 18 per cent from the previous year, as consumers continue to turn to the web to shop for and purchase items and retailers continue to increase their online visibility through active marketing campaigns.

Increase in shoppers of the coupon sites indicate that pricing is playing the role of catalyst in bringing more and more shoppers online. Many of these shoppers have shown affinity towards affordable online goods, which was priced lesser than the market price. Some of the largest retail subcategories revealed that coupons category was the largest with 7.6 million visitors as consumers rapidly adopt daily deal sites. Consumer electronics ranked next with 7.1 million visitors, growing at 12 per cent over the previous year, while 5.8 million online users visited comparison shopping sites, an increase of 25 per cent from the previous year.

STUDY RATIONALE

With increase in broadband internet connection and 3G penetrations coupled with changing socio-economic status - going online is a new way of shopping for urban Indians. Indian retail E-Commerce market is witnessing a lot of momentum with a $600 Million business in 2011; it is expected to touch $9 Billion by 2016 and $70 Billion by 2020 at an estimated CAGR of 61% (Wikipedia). This opens up a new era for distribution channel, as for any retail E-Commerce business "logistics" is paramount, with enormous opportunities and challenges. The existing players in this business are yet to make any profit (or ROI: please check as profit is normally termed as operational profit), currently, they are focusing on improving quality of service, earning customer's trust and increasing customer base etc. while attracting investor owing to huge growth potential. Moreover, the lack of proper infrastructure discourages smaller players to enter or survive in this business. Clearly at this juncture, Indian marketplace lacks the technological and logistic infrastructure for high-rising e-commerce transactional volume.

One of the important factors that are aiding E-Commerce growth is logistics. Indian online retail industry has been scaling up by better co-ordination among channel partners, improving shipment delivery time at lower possible cost over last few years. Still there are issues of wrong delivery, unaccepted shipment pick-ups, product unavailability leading to promise to deliver, etc. To overcome logistical issues, retailers and brands selling online have started working with multiple service providers, according to a report by Forrester. The report, titled "Trends in Indian E-Commerce market" released during August 2012 says that serving all parts of the country effectively can be quite daunting for e-tailers and hence they work with multiple partners. Following the lead from Flipkart, E-Commerce players as well as start-ups are realizing the need to reduce logistics spend and at the same time increase customer delight. However, the increase in volumes of e-tail shipments has made all logistics companies sit up and take notice of this opportunity.

Following questions are raised in our research:

- Challenges faced by e-tailers in India and Changing face of E-Commerce business
- Strategies for E-Commerce business
- Strategies for Indian E-Commerce business

Although a wide variety of literature has been developed around small-scale retailers, the majority of studies have discussed problems they faced arising from their own inefficiency. Additionally, most of the literature has been related to developed countries such as UK, Scotland, Japan, USA and Norway. Little has been found in reference to developing countries and specifically to Indian context, where this scale of retailers captures a big portion of the family spending in fast moving consumers' goods. Also, little effort has been devoted to learn about local storekeepers that are actually conducting successful business. Our research tried to cover this gap in the literature, considering the importance of this kind of trade in less development countries.

India's Prospects in E-Commerce Field

- **Opportunity for Retailers:** A retailer can save his existence by linking his business with the on-line distribution. By doing so, they can make available much additional information about various things to the consumers, meet electronic orders and be in touch with the consumers all the time. Therefore, E-Commerce is a good opportunity.
- **Opportunity for Whole Salers/Distributer:** In the world of E-Commerce the existence of the wholesalers is at the greatest risk because the producer can easily ignore them and sell their goods to the retailers and the consumers. In such a situation those wholesalers can take advantage of E-Commerce who are capable of establishing contractors with reputed producers and linking their business with the on- line.
- **Opportunity for Producers:** Producers can take advantages of e-commerce by linking themselves with on-line, by giving better information about their products to the other links in the business chain and by a having a brand identity.
- **Opportunity for People:** As more people are getting linked with E-commerce, the demand for centre providing internet facility or cyber cafe is also increasing. Hence, the people who wish to take advantage of it can establish cyber and have their benefits.

Essential Factors for Growth of E-Commerce in India

- **Customer Convenience:** By providing Cash on delivery payment option service to customers.
    - **Replacement Guarantee:** Should offer 30-day replacement guarantee to their customers.
    - **Reach:** Enabling mobile-capable sites and supporting M-Commerce services.
    - **Location Based Services:** Since customers these days are always on the move, promoting the right product at the right time and location becomes an integral aspect
    - **Multiple Payment Option:** standard credit cards, debit cards and bank payments option should be there.
    - **Right Content:** Getting the right content and targeting customers with crisp and relevant information is of utmost importance to users on the move.
    - **Price Comparison:** Providers offering instant price comparison are highly popular amongst the price conscious customers.
    - **Shipment Option:** Low cost shipment should be there. The convenience of collecting orders post work while returning home should be there.
    - **Logistical Challenges:** In India, the geographical spread throws logistical challenges. The kind of products being offered by providers should determine the logistics planning.
    - **Legal Challenges:** There should be legal requirement of generating invoices for online transactions.
    - **Quick Service:** Timely service provided by the company.
    - **Terms and Condition:** T & C should be clear and realistic.
    - **Quality:** The product quality should be same as shown on the portal.
    - **Customer Care Centre:** A dedicated 24/7 customer care centre should be there.

RESEARCH METHODOLOGY

We performed qualitative and descriptive research based on secondary sources and extensive literature review. The supply chain that can be used for various types of E-Commerce models have been explained and attempt has been made towards identifying the factors affecting the E-Commerce sector. The present study undertakes a thorough review of basic and contemporary literature available and identified the issues which are affecting the supply chain of delivery by the E-Commerce companies (Grossbart et. Al., 1990).

Author has collected Literature, including research papers from peer-reviewed journals, conference proceedings, white papers and presentations from the industry. Papers were collected applying a structured search, using phrases such as "E-Commerce delivery models", "E-Commerce supply chain". The author has referred various International Journals like Supply Chain Management: An International Journal, International Journal of Operations and Production Management, International Journal of Physical Distribution and Logistics Management, Journal of Agribusiness in Developing and Emerging Economies, International Food and Agribusiness Management Review, IUP Journal of Supply Chain Management etc. The literature has been divided into various themes according to the delivery models and further investigation has been attempted to identify various factors affecting the supply chain (Lucas, 2013).

To validate the findings, interview and focus discussion groups were conducted in two groups where first group were told the findings of the study and the second group were not informed of the study. The conclusion from these discussions were compiled and compared with the findings from the above discussed literature survey.

Table 1 describes the companies who publically available data was studied.

The approach adopted by the author is described in the Table 2:

FINDINGS

We present our study in the below sub-sections.

Challenges Faced by E-Tailers in India

While logistics is the aiding factor in growth of Indian E-Commerce business, it is the differentiation factor too (both in terms of cost and service). There are many challenges faced by E-Commerce retailers

Table 1. List of e-commerce companies for study

Segment	Companies
Multiple products (B2C)	Amazon, Flipkart, Ebay, Rediff Shopping, Homeshop18, Tradeus, Indiaplaza, Yepme, OnlineBuy99.com, Shopclues, Jabong, Junglee, Seventymm, Infibeam
Fashion & Lifestyle, Jewellary, Home Decor	Inkfruit, Globus, Zovi, BagsKart, Violetbag, Myntra, Fabfurnish, UrbanLadder, Yebhi, Firstcry, MyBabyCart, Fernsnpetals, IndianGiftsPortal, Caratlane
Gifts	Zoomin, Snapfish, Picsquare
Electronics	Ezone, Letsbuy, LootSpot, Next, WatchKart, Chroma

Table 2. Research approach

Steps	Descriptions
Step 1	Identify top E-Commerce companies based on revenue size and presence in India
Step 2	Identify the logistics challenges faced by them by reading articles and other materials available in public domain. Looked for supply chain related post/comments by leading magazines, top executives comments/interviews and solution providers' press release.
Step 3	Identify logistics in India and understand the services provided by them
Step 4	Talk to industry experts from companies like- BigBasket.com, Flipkart. Talk to industry experts from JDA who work with clients on solving their problems
Step 5	Read the journal articles where logistics challenges of E-Commerce companies are discussed and solved. Identify different approaches adopted by the companies
Step 6	Map the various approaches to the challenges of e-Commerce companies in India
Step 7	Present the study

Figure 1. Challenges for E-Commerce logistics partners

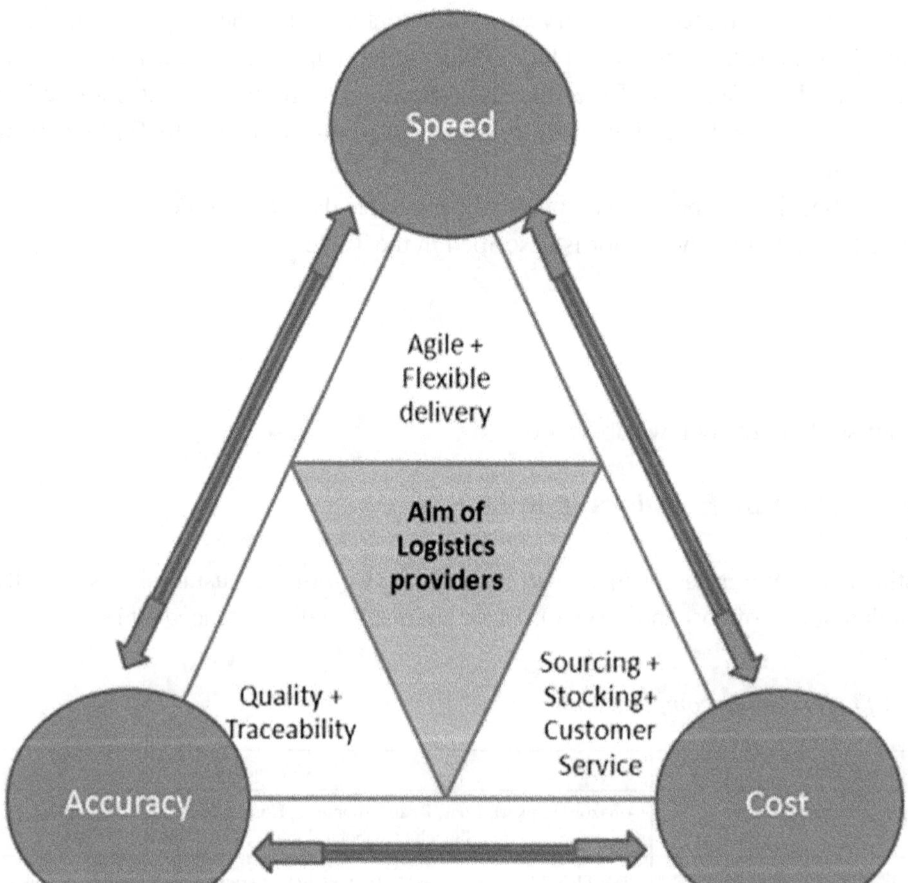

today. It is evolving field with no well-known strategy to manage the E-Commerce business. Companies are making their own way through this. Unlike warehouse shipments, where logistics partners have to deal with large Pallets, the E-Commerce logistics partners need to look at smaller shipments and be able to provide door to door delivery.

Three main challenges faced by E-Commerce logistics partners are:

- **Speed:** E-Commerce players have to be agile and flexible to deliver goods from point to point. Speed can help them to command better price than its peers in the market. Customers prefer to get the items delivered at its door steps in minimum possible time. This impacts the inventory policy, channel co-ordination, shipment mode etc.
- **Maintain Accuracy:** Maintain accuracy is one of the major challenges of the e-tailers. It's important to know the inventory accuracy, its can damage companies' reputation if they deliver something which is not available in the warehouse. Traceability of the product in the entire supply chain-warehouse, inbound and outbound shipments, is another factor which e-tailers are concerned. E-tailers want to reach a perfect level where they can track each item from point of origin to final destination.
- **Reduce Cost:** E-tailers want to achieve the entire things we discussed above but at reduced cost. In E-Commerce business costs of goods is a major competitive factor and at the same time provide better customer service. Companies are looking to for sourcing and stocking decisions that will help to reduce cost and increase customer service.

Question today is how do keep cost effective while maintain volume and deliver at incredible speed. In this paper, our focus is small and Medium Retail E-Commerce enterprises that cannot afford to own warehouses in every city. We will be talking about both Inter-cities as well as intra city delivery.

Top 3 challenges in point to point delivery:

- Speed at which goods need to be delivered point to point.
- Maintain volume as well as accuracy.
- Reduce cost.

Top 3 challenges in Distribution:

- Accurate Information flow.
- Inventory accuracy.
- Ship the product quickly.

Retailer's perspective:

- E-Commerce Retailers look at city-wise and state-wise to see if it makes sense in terms of volume-wise and cost-wise to enter into the market.
- Then retailers would want to meet their own commitment like-same day shipping.
- Have minimal touch-point in the system.
- Avoid loss, damage to the product.

Changing Face of E-Commerce Business

As indicated in Table 3, Indian e-commerce companies (like its global peers) are looking to provide products at lowest cost and increase the availability of the products. Keys factors that define the service factors of e-tailers are: Order Fulfilment time, Home Delivery, Cash on Delivery, Return policy and Reverse Logistics.

One of the most important trends of the last year has been the drive for retailers to get closer to their customers. E-retailers want to be able to provide near-instant gratification for shoppers, meaning that same -day delivery services are on the rise. Given that the major e-retailers have displayed a willingness to build owned operations, as opposed to outsourcing them. What are the options for SMEs which cannot own operations? What are the options available for them? Answers to these questions depend on the nature of business of the e-tailers. We have answered these questions in the sections below.

Strategies for E-Commerce Business

Bases on our qualitative analysis of the existing literature available, we have come up with the list of strategies which are relevant for E-Commerce business, listed in Table 4.

Table 3. Key performance indicators

Product Range	Service	Cost
Price Availability	Order fulfil time Home delivery Cash on delivery Returns policy, Reverse Logistics	Manage the cost

Table 4. E-Commerce Strategies

Logistics postponement	This is done to maintain a full line of anticipatory inventory at one or a few strategic locations. This means to postpone changes in inventory location downstream in the supply chain to the latest possible point.
Dematerialization	Companies also should try to replace physical flows with information flows. With information flows substituted for physical flows, companies can avoid stockouts without loading up on inventory, delivery can occur almost instantaneously, and the marginal cost of delivery is negligible. Information goods such as software and music are natural candidates for that strategy, which we call dematerialization.
Resource exchange	Company will have many warehouses; challenge is to know which warehouse will serve which order. This can be achieved using area pincode. Since small/mid size companies cannot own multiple warehouse, the importance of Partnership comes in (discussed next)
Partnership	Partnership with value added partners and can have multiple partners to serve maximum areas. For example, partnership with BlueDart to reach metros and Indian Post to reach to small town and villages. There can be partnership at national level and different partners for last mile delivery.
Clicks-and-Mortar Model	Last mile delivery is more expensive. In this case, product is delivered to the nearest store and customers handle the last mile. Product bundling can be used to reduce cost.
Product bundling	Product bundling is offering several products as one combined product. Unbundling can be done at the last warehouse/store and then delivered as multiple orders.
Leveraged shipments	Cost of delivery is high if order size is small. A simple measure called Delivery Value Density (DVD) can help determine whether it is economical to deliver goods to neighbourhood area in one trip.

Strategies for Indian E-Commerce Business

In this section we analyse the above discussed strategies for Indian E-Commerce business. We look at the various strategies and how can we use them for Indian environment. The business strategies are described in Table 5.

Products

Table 6 shows two types of products in the table. For fast moving goods, customer service becomes very important. Customers will not wait for the delivery. Generally, the profit margin is low, so the retailers have to place products as close to customers so that it is delivered on time and with minimum cost.

For slow moving goods, cost becomes deciding factor. Shoppers generally arm themselves with some research on the cost before placing the order. Its ok if the warehouse is placed away from the customer but inform the customer about time of the delivery.

Internet Distribution Model: Strategic Tie-Up With Manufacturer/Retailer

Described in Table 7 are owned versus managed type of inventory management. Advantage of owned inventory is retailers can ship immediately: The faster the orders are turned around, the more impressed

Table 5. Business strategies

Classification	Types
Products	Fast / Slow moving
Model	Owned/Dropped shipping
Delivery Size	Tiny/Small/Medium/Large orders
Delivery Mode	Pick-up/Home Delivery Free /Charge

Table 6. Strategies for products

Fast Moving Products	Slow Moving Products
Leveraged Shipping	Logistic postponement

Table 7. Strategies for distribution model

Owned Inventory	Managed Inventory
Leveraged Shipping	Resource Exchange

the customers are, and the better chances of getting him back the customer next time. Challenge is that inventory can sit on retailers' shelves, tying up capital.

Managed inventory or Drop shipping makes it amazingly easy to get started selling online. Retailers don't need to invest heavily in inventory, yet they can still offer thousands of items to their customers. Syncing inventory is difficult and leads to out-of-stock items often and also the margins are very low.

Delivery Size: Tiny/Small/Medium/Large Order Base

The above definition may change from retailer to retailer, what is important is that retailers need to perform benefit analysis before choosing one and also need to evaluate the initial decision at regular interval and the average order base may change or the cost to serve may change. If a retailer wants to cover entire India, then best partner to service small order base would be post offices. Strategies for delivery size are described in Table 8.

Delivery Mode

Retailers can choose to deliver at store at no cost and can charge for home delivery. For this, e-tailers need to have partnership with stores in every city. Options can be given to the shoppers at the time of placing orders where they are offered cash discounts to take a delivery from a store. Players like Chroma and Reliance Digitals, can adopt such strategies. Delivery modes are described in Table 9.

CONCLUSION

Though e-Commerce has been there for long time but it's still a mystery for most of the retailers. Retailers are still experimenting with techniques to integrate e-commerce business models with their fulfilment strategies with logistics being one of the important aspects. There are many challenges faced by E-Commerce retailers today. It is evolving field with no well-known strategy to manage the E-Commerce business. Companies are making their own way through this. Unlike warehouse shipments, where logis-

Table 8. Strategies For Delivery Size

Small/Medium order base	Large order base
Leveraged Shipping	Direct to home

Table 9. Strategies For Delivery Mode

Classification	Types
Delivery	Store pick-up vs Home Delivery
Charge based	Free vs Charged home delivery

tics partners have to deal with large Pallets, the E-Commerce logistics partners need to look at smaller shipments and be able to provide door to door delivery.

Owned: Inventory and Fulfilment Hassles

- **Benefits:** You can provide excellent customer service: You will have all the records at your fingertips to trace the order and make a correction. In the online book wars, Amazon.com has invested a great deal of money building five regional warehouses and buying a share in same-day Manhattan courier firm Kozmo.com to enable them to provide excellent customer service. As a result, they will be very hard to beat, though early on, they don't show a profit because of the huge initial investment.
- **Challenges:** You must have an efficient fulfilment system. One of the reasons that brick-and-mortar stores are slow on the uptake when it comes to online business, is that supplying retail stores is done with pallet-size logistical system. But Internet retail requires an entirely different kind of fulfilment system. Internet retail is essentially mail order, with shipments going out in parcel sizes to end users. Few brick-and-mortar retailers have a humming mail order business to draw from, and are starting from scratch with an entirely different kind of fulfilment system. An inefficient fulfilment system can lose for you the advantages in good customer service that holding the inventory gained for you.

Drop Shipping

Drop shipping is a retail method in which retailers don't keep products in stock. Instead, they partner with a wholesale supplier that stocks its own inventory - retailers transfer customer orders and shipment details to them, and they ship the goods directly to the customer. Most customers don't know is a retailer is doing drop shipping, since "private label shipping" lets retailers ship from the wholesaler with a return address and invoice customized to retailer E-Commerce store.

- **Benefits:** You Don't Need Buckets of Money: You don't need to invest heavily in inventory, yet you can still offer thousands of items to your customers.
- **Convenience and Efficiency:** Successfully launching and growing an E-Commerce business takes a lot of work, especially if you have limited resources. Not having to worry about fulfilment is incredibly convenient and frees up your time to concentrate on marketing, customer service, and operations.
- **Mobility:** With all the physical fulfilment issues handled, you're free to operate your business anywhere you can get an internet connection.
- **It's a Trusted Model:** You might be thinking that this sounds like some sketchy, fly-by-night model – but it's not. Plenty of Shopify online stores, even major retailers like Sears, use drop shipping to offer a wider selection of products to their customers without having to deal with increased inventory hassles.

Challenges:

1. **Loads of Competition and Awful Margins:** Products that can be drop shipped will spawn a lot of competition. Usually this will lead to cutthroat pricing and diminishing profit margins, making it hard to build a viable business.
    a. **Solution:** To be successful, you typically can't compete on price. Instead, you'll need to offer value in a different way, usually through top-notch product education, service or selection.
2. Syncing inventory is difficult and leads to out-of-stock items.
    a. **Solution:** The best way to mitigate this problem is to work with multiple suppliers with overlapping product lines. It's inherently dangerous to rely on a single supplier. Having two suppliers doubles the likelihood that an item will be in stock and available for shipment. Eventually, you'll sell a customer an out-of-stock item. Instead of cancelling the order, give the customer an upgraded product for free! You might not make much – if any – money on the order, but you'll likely build a loyal brand advocate.
3. It's hard to sell products that you never see.
    a. **Solution:** In today's world, it's possible to become an expert in just about everything through information online. Selling products from manufacturers with detailed websites will allow you to become intimately familiar with a product line without ever having touched a physical item. And when you do need to answer specific question about a product, a quick call to your supplier or manufacturer will give you the answer you need.
4. Involving a third party will result in more fulfilment errors, mistakes, and logistical problems.
    a. **Solution:** Even the best drop shippers make occasional mistakes, and mediocre ones make a lot of them. Suppliers are fairly good about paying to remedy problems, but when they're not, you need to be willing to spend what's necessary to resolve the issue for your customer. One of the costs of drop shipping convenience is the expense of remedying logistical problems. If you accept it as cost of doing business – and always make sure to put your customer first – it shouldn't be a long-term issue.

Fulfilment House

A fulfilment house, the offspring of the direct marketing industry, will handle some or all of the aspects of getting the product to your customer. They will maintain inventory, order new product, assemble, pick, pull, pack, and ship, all according to your specifications and with your labels. They will also handle the order taking, the Internet shopping cart, and provide an ordering and customer service call centre if you need one. In other words, you can run an entirely virtual business, outsourcing everything to the fulfilment house, if you like. Of course, they take their pound of flesh. I think this works best for proprietary products, or products with a higher than average margin.

Benefits

- **Simplify:** Typically, distribution centres have multiple processes and equipment types to handle different types of items -- fast-movers versus slow-movers, large items versus small. To be most efficient, all items need to be handled well by one process and one type of equipment, and re-slotting should be continuous and automatic without adding labour.

- **Increase Sortation With Fewer Touches**: Fulfilment operations should not only be fast and efficient in the DC -- they should increase speed and efficiency of the downstream distribution process. For example, e-commerce fulfilment operations should be able to pelletize orders with delivery truck routes in mind, and orders should "picked to plan-o-gram" of destination stores -- without additional capital expense, labour content or cycle time.
- **Fully Integrate Quality Control Function:** A fulfilment system should be able to eliminate in-line error, and with it the need for a separate QC function.
- **No Walking, No Waiting:** The modern distribution centre should offer infinite pick face density with zero operator walking.
- **Just-in-Time Capacity:** E-commerce operators need to be nimble. They must easily handle wide seasonal peak-to-mean throughput variation, and be able to quickly adapt to unpredictable market dynamics.

Challenges

Key Areas:

- **Speed:** Speed in reaching to the customer, be able to provide 24-hours/48-hours shipping options.
- **Accuracy:** Accuracy in sorting and delivering the exact product ordered by customer.
- **Network Design:** To meet all the customers across the country, also help in improving last mile delivery.
- **Automation:** Automate the fulfilment centre as much as possible.
- **Assortment:** Able to handle multiple types of assortment.
- **Reverse Logistics:** Be able to handle reverse logistics.

Figure 2. Challenges with fulfillment house

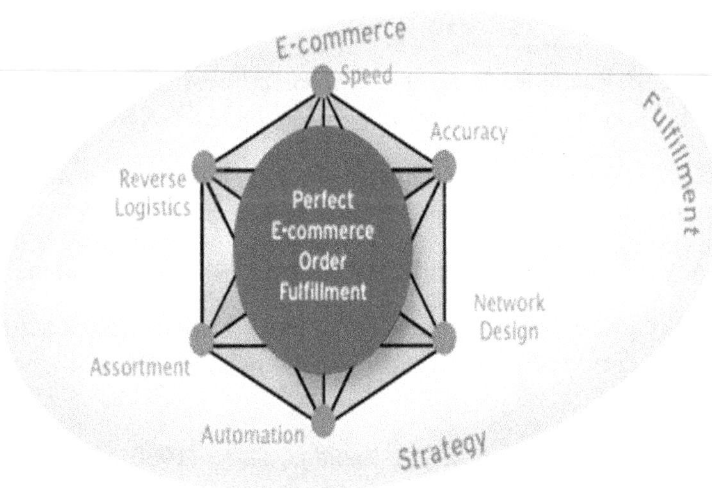

FUTURE RESEARCH DIRECTION

The future of E-Commerce is difficult to predict. There are various segments that would grow in the future like: Travel and Tourism, electronic appliances, hardware products and apparel. There are also some essential factors which will significantly contribute to the boom of the E-Commerce industry in India i.e. replacement guarantee, M-Commerce services, location based services, multiple payment option, right content, shipment option, legal requirement of generating invoices for online transactions, quick Service, T & C should be clear and realistic, the product quality should be same as shown on the portal, dedicated 24/7 customer care center should be there.

Future research should be conducted based on each of the above discussed E-Commerce segments. As E-Commerce industry in India is move to mature stage, there will be need to understand each of these growth segments.

REFERENCES

Banker. (n.d.). *ARC's WMS Global Market Research Study*. Forbes.com.

Bardwell, C. (2012). *Redefining the Shopper Experience With Omnichannel Retailing*. IDC Retail Insights.

Bimschleger, C. (2014). *How to Compete with Amazon in an Omnichannel World. RIS News: Business/ Technology Insights for Retail* Supermarket Executives.

Birchall & Rigby. (2008). Oil Costs Force P&G to Rethink Supply Network. *Financial Times*.

Bose, N. (2014). *E-tailers growth ensnared in India's logistics jungle*. Reuters.com.

Carroll, D., & Guzmán, I. (2014). *The New Omni-Channel Approach to Serving Customers*. Accenture.com.

Customer Desires Vs. Retailer Capabilities: Minding The Omni-Channel Commerce Gap. (2014). Forrester Consulting.

Gauri, D. K., Talukdar, D., & Ratchford, B. (2008). *Empirical Investigation of the Impact of Loss Leader Promotion on Store and Category Performance in Grocery Industry*. Syracuse University.

Genin, P., Lamouri, S., & Thomas, A. (2007). Improving the robustness of a supply chain tactical plan. *Supply Chain Forum: An International Journal, 8*(2), 24-35.

Gera. (n.d.). *The Six Key Pillars for Building An Everyday Bank*. Accenture.com.

Griffitt, W. (1970). Environmental Effects on Interpersonal Affective Behavior: Ambient Temperature and Attraction. *Journal of Personality and Social Psychology, 15*(3), 240–244. doi:10.1037/h0029432 PMID:5485416

Grossbart, S., Hampton, R., Rammohan, B., & Lapidus, R. S. (1990). Environmental Dispositions and Customer Response to Store Atmospherics. *Journal of Business Research, 21*(3), 225–241. doi:10.1016/0148-2963(90)90030-H

Hui, M. K. (1997). The Impact of Music on Consumers Reactions to Waiting for Services. *Journal of Retailing*, *73*(1), 87–104. doi:10.1016/S0022-4359(97)90016-6

Hui, M. K., & Bateson, J. E. G. (1991, Sept.). Perceived Control and the Effects of Crowding and Consumer Choice on the Service Experiences. *The Journal of Consumer Research*, *25*, 175–186.

Hult, G., Neese, W. T., & Bashaw, R. E. (1997). Faculty Perceptions of Marketing Journals. *Journal of Marketing Education*, *19*(1), 37–52. doi:10.1177/027347539701900105

Ian, P. H. L., & Grace, L. B. (2011). *Customer satisfaction towards retailers*. ICA, ICA NÄRA and Coop Forum.

Janardhan, S. (2013). *Unified View of Customer: It's All About Customer Experience*. TCS.com

Lewis, J. (2014). *Greatest challenge – The omni channel customer experience*. ijgolding.com.

Lim, Bassamboo, Chopra, & Daskin. (2010). *Flexibility and Fragility: Use of Chaining Strategies in the Presence of Disruption Risks*. Northwestern University research report.

Lucas, L. (2013). Diageo Overhauls Its Supply Chain. *Financial Times*.

Mitroff, I. I., & Alpaslan, M. C. (2003). Preparing for evil. *Harvard Business Review*, *81*(4), 109–115. PMID:12687925

Morris, M. (2012). *Online supply models: Who's doing what?* IGD Supply Chain Analysis.

Omnichannel Retail 2014 - Intelligence report. (2014, July). L2 Research.

Oracle. (n.d.). *The Store: The Intersection Of All Channels*. Retail TouchPoints E-Book.

Pfohl, H., Kohler, H., & Thomas, D. (2010). State of the art in supply chain risk management research: Empirical and conceptual findings and a roadmap for the implementation in practice. *Logistics Research.*, *2*(1), 33–44. doi:10.1007/s12159-010-0023-8

Schaeffer. (n.d.). *How to Succeed in Omni-Channel Retailing*. crmsearch.com.

Sodhi, M. S., & Tang, C. S. (2006). Managing Supply Chain Risk. New York: Springer.

Taleb, N. N. (2007). *The Black Swan: The Impact of the Highly Improbable*. New York: Random House.

Tang, C. S. (2006). Robust Strategies for Mitigating Supply Chain Disruptions. *International Journal of Logistics Research and Applications*, *9*(1), 33–45. doi:10.1080/13675560500405584

Terry, J. (2010). *Donofrio*. RIS News –RS&S Advanced Planning and Optimization Series.

The omni-channel opportunity for retailers: What's the story? (n.d.). *The Guardian*.

Zsidisin, G. A., & Ritchie, B. (2009). *Supply Chain Risk: A Handbook of Assessment, Management, and Performance*. New York: Springer. doi:10.1007/978-0-387-79934-6

KEY TERMS AND DEFINITIONS

5G: is the coming fifth-generation wireless broadband technology based on the IEEE 802.11ac standard. 5G will provide better speeds and coverage than the current 4G. 5G operates with a 5Ghz signal and is set to offer speeds of up to 1 Gb/s for tens of connections or tens of Mb/s for tens of thousands of connections.

Assortment: Assortment is the number of SKUs within a category. It is also called depth.

Backup Stock: Backup stock is the buffer stock or the safety stock which retailer holds to guard against stockouts, when there is a mismatch between supply and demand.

Category: The category is the basic unit of analysis for making merchandising decision.

Category Captain: Category Captain is the retailer preferred vendor, who advises the retailer on a certain category of merchandise offered by them.

Fad Merchandise: Fad merchandise is the merchandise items that generate a high level of sale for a short period of time.

Footfall: Footfall is the count of shoppers entering in to a retail store on a given day.

Gross Margin Return on Floor (GMROF): Gross margin or profit returned per floor space usually measure in gross margin per square foot.

Gross Margin: A way to measure gross profit calculated as the difference between selling price and cost price.

Gross Margin Return on Inventory Investment (GMROII): Gross Margin $ returned for every $ invested in inventory (and inventory costs).

Hypermarket: According to the Webster dictionary (1993) a hyper market is a superstore which combines a supermarket and a department store (where usually are sold products like apparel, furniture, appliances, electronics, and additionally select other lines of products such as paint, hardware, toiletries, cosmetics, photographic equipment, jewellery, toys, and sporting goods), being the result a very large retail facility which carries an enormous range of products under one roof, including full lines of groceries and general merchandise.

Impulse Buying: Any unplanned buying is called as Impulse Buying. An individual might not require a particular product but picks it up out of mere emotions and feelings.

Markdown: The difference between the original retail price and the reduced price.

Markup: The amount of money added to the wholesale price to obtain the retail price.

Millennials: (also known as the Millennial Generation or Generation Y) are the demographic cohort following Generation X. There are no precise dates when the generation starts and ends. Researchers and commentators use birth years ranging from the early 1980s to the early 2000s.

On Shelf Availability: One of important metric every retailer's performance is measured is using On Shelf Availability (OSA). OSA is defined as availability of product for sale to a shopper, in the place he expects it and at the time he wants to buy it. It is impacted by a host of different factors, all along the supply chain.

Out Of Stock (OOS): Also known as Stockout. It is a situation where the retailer does not physically possess a particular product category, on its shelf, to sell to the customer. It can be estimated from store inventory data.

Point of Purchase (POP): POP refers to all materials and physical setup in a retailer, in and around where the product is displayed.

Point of Sale (POS): POS refers to materials, brochures, signs at point of sale, or can refer to point of sale or cash register.

Point of Sale Activation (POSA): POSA is a process by which software becomes activated, useable, at the point of purchase.

Private Label: Private Label brands are the retailers store brands which are developed by retailers and available for sale at only that specific retailer.

Softlines: Softlines is the retail store department or the product line which primarily consists of merchandise such as clothing, footwear, jewelry, linens and towels.

Space Management: Management of selling space, based on consumer demand and shopping habit in order to achieve enhanced business results.

Stock Keeping Unit: A stock keeping unit (SKU) is the smallest unit available for keeping inventory control. In soft goods retailer, for instance, a SKU usually means size, color, and style. For example, a pair of boys' size 10, navy blue color, boot-cut Levis is one SKU. In some cases, a buyer is responsible for several classifications.

Supermarket: According to the Webster International dictionary (1993), a Supermarket is a self-service store or independent retail market offering a wide variety of food and household merchandise, organized into departments. It is larger in size and has a wider selection than a traditional grocery store and it is smaller than a hypermarket or superstore.

Variety: Variety is the number of different merchandising categories within a store or department. It is also called breadth.

Visual Merchandising: Visual merchandising is the art of implementing effective design ideas to increase in-store traffic and sales volume.

Section 3
Dynamics of Retail Management

Chapter 8
Retail Management and Electronic Retailing

Kijpokin Kasemsap
Suan Sunandha Rajabhat University, Thailand

ABSTRACT

This chapter presents the overview of retail management; retail management and technology; the aspects of Electronic Retailing (e-tailing); e-tailing and Electronic Commerce (e-commerce); the perspectives on online consumer behavior; and the advanced issues of e-tailing in retail environments. Retail management focuses on the processes that go into ensuring consumers can obtain the products they want from their chosen retail store. Effective retail management helps company distributes the finished products created by the business to consumers in order to determine and satisfy what buyers want and require. E-tailing is a powerful marketing technique for the right product with the right message to the right person. The chapter argues that effective retail management and e-tailing applications generate business revenue, build brand awareness, and pave the way for broader distribution in retail environments.

INTRODUCTION

Regarding retail management, the ability to apply the retail marketing mix elements and retail brand strategy concerning specific target-market conditions and a wider global marketing strategy, is functionally important in retail settings (Kasemsap, 2015a). Effective retail marketing strategies and brand management help organizations develop a competitive retail marketing review, target consumer behaviors, integrate the marketing plan into retail design, and deploy the branding strategies in the global retail industry (Kasemsap, 2016a). In order to maintain competitive advantage, retailers are required to continuously come up with the innovative offerings and systems (Lewrick, Omar, Williams, Tjandra, & Lee, 2015).

Retailing is the commercial transaction in which a buyer intends to consume the product or service through individual, family, or household use (Kasemsap, 2017a). The strength of retail organization lies in its capability of aligning demand and supply (Brajesh, 2016). Retail business involves the process of selling consumer goods or services to customers through multiple channels of distribution to earn a profit (Gencer, 2017). Martínez-Ruiz et al. (2016) indicated that to create and maintain the retail image,

DOI: 10.4018/978-1-5225-3056-5.ch008

retailers must follow the ongoing process in which all components need to be considered, including target-market characteristics, retail positioning, marketing communications, merchandise assortment, customer services, price levels, store location, and physical facilities.

The Internet is a global communication medium (Jiang & Balasubramanian, 2014) and is used as an online channel of product distribution in retail environments (Madlberger, 2009) toward gaining e-service quality and e-satisfaction (Bressolles, Durrieu, & Senecal, 2014). In the digital age, various types of products can be delivered to customers via Electronic Retailing (e-tailing) (Rose & Samouel, 2009). Modern businesses perform many transactions in an electronic environment and offer many advantages for both retailers and consumers (Adapa, 2013). E-tailing becomes a well-accepted way to purchase a wide variety of products and services (Amin & Amin, 2013) toward improving customer satisfaction (Shobeiri, Mazaheri, & Laroche, 2015).

Both globalization and competitiveness in the retail industry enhance the retail companies to reach the advanced technology in store management, product information, and customer services (Rajagopal, 2009). Online and off-line retailers fulfill a wide range of the retail functions that are beneficial to manufacturers as well as to individual consumers (Madlberger, 2005). E-tailing helps retailers conduct business online with virtual storefronts, and helps reach both local and global customers who are disadvantaged by geographical barriers (Chugh & Grandhi, 2012). Acknowledging the content that consumers perceive a retailer's website service is necessary to improve the marketing development and to ensure that e-service delivery processes are effective in global marketing (O'Cass & Carlson, 2012).

This chapter is based on a literature review of retail management and e-tailing. The extensive literature of retail management and e-tailing provides a contribution to practitioners and researchers by explaining the important issues of retail management and e-tailing in retail environments.

BACKGROUND

Regarding the magnitude of employees, value creation, and physical appearance, the retail industry is one of the largest industries in global economy (Berman & Evans, 2010). Retailing is the final stage of the supply chain (Lowson, 2001) managed by brand owners together with the retail organizations (Sen, 2008) and the sourcing networks. Networks in retailing are comprised by the brand owner, the varieties of single- and multi-brand stores, chains and departments stores, technology and service providers, ownership structures and local level supply chain facilities (Tambo, 2014). Multichannel retailing can offer a wide range of synergies for retailers when their distribution channels accommodate the consumer's preferences and their buying behavior (Madlberger, 2009). Consumer buying behavior is the process by which individuals search for, select, purchase, use, and dispose of products and services, in satisfaction of their requirements (Kasemsap, 2016b).

González-Benito et al. (2014) stated that retailers establish the store-brand strategies, leading to greater success and higher congruence with the retailer's positioning. The changing logistics networks of grocery retail companies over the last few decades are a result of striving toward the higher operational efficiency (Sternbeck & Kuhn, 2014). The main objective in retailing is to increase the impulse temptation to enhance sales (Kacen, Hess, & Walker, 2012). The development of supply chain-related operational practices is an important part of ensuring the right product mix at store level (Rajaram, 2001) concerning the cost of service, stocking, transportation, and transshipment (Jüttner, Christopher, & Baker, 2007).

Many virtual shopping modes can be recognized as online shopping, electronic shopping, Internet shopping, electronic shopping, and website-based shopping (Clemes, Gan, & Zhang, 2014). Electronic marketplaces have the potential to change how customers buy the products (Jiang & Balasubramanian, 2014). E-tailers should bring confidence among the online customers by the prompt delivery of products (Shukla & Vyas, 2016). In the digital age, consumers know the product promotions through companies' websites and e-mail campaigns (Audrain-Pontevia, N'Goala, & Poncin, 2013). The website-based commercial transaction channels continue to grow, such that approximately 45 percent of the Internet users in the United States and Europe purchase products online (Kollmann, Kuckertz, & Kayser, 2012).

IMPORTANT ISSUES OF RETAIL MANAGEMENT AND ELECTRONIC RETAILING

This section provides the overview of retail management; retail management and technology; the aspects of e-tailing; e-tailing and electronic commerce (e-commerce); the perspectives on online consumer behavior; and the advanced issues of e-tailing in retail environments.

Overview of Retail Management

While retail is extremely diverse, but retailers across the globe share many priorities by balancing the availability of the inventory, controlling the costs, and promoting customer service in order to maintain the retail strategy (Smriti, 2016). Retailers generally restrict their deployment to one of three strategies including metropolitan, large retail areas, or market size variety with specialty retailers favoring large retail areas of urban markets (Joseph & Kuby, 2016). When retailers increase the number of convenience stores, cutting supply chain costs remain the ultimate challenge for the distribution of convenience store chain (Pratapwar, 2016).

Retailers have a large number of techniques at their disposal to assist them in their location planning, but the use made of them is varied, regardless of their intrinsic merits (Hernandez, Bennison, & Cornelius, 1998). The reasons for this issue can lie in the managerial and organizational contexts in which the marketing techniques are applied (Hernandez et al., 1998). Knowing both consumers' shopping paths and consumer behavior is an essential part of successful retailing (Skogster & Uotila, 2010). Creating superior customer experience in today's retailing environments has become one of the central objectives in providing customer service (Saurav, 2016). Understanding how customer loyalty and the supply chain are connected via the effective supply chain networks functionally offers an opportunity for cost reductions and sales growth in global supply chain (Kasemsap, 2016c).

Retailers have to balance their efforts to enhance a store's attractiveness (Kurata & Nam, 2014) by ensuring a high level of sales environment surveillance without interfering with the consumers' shopping experience (Bonfanti, 2014). Consumers' shopping experience is linked to their perceptions of the store's social and environmental responsibility and moral values (Pecoraro & Uusitalo, 2014). The management of stock at store level emphasizes the issues of budgeting, pricing, and categorization for the continuous adaptation to customer preferences and store attractiveness (Teller & Reutterer, 2008). Stocking out by down pricing is common at store level (Nair & Kloss, 2006).

Promotions, special marketing incentives, and innovative pricing are accepted in various retail segments (Kurata & Yue, 2008). The changes in the import prices have large effects on both consumer prices and import volumes when the changes in retail market structure are taken into account (Raff & Schmitt, 2012). Price is important when it comes to the store choice, and if retailers consider different sustainability measures they can have a positive impact on the store choice (Hampl & Loock, 2013).

Due to the pervasiveness of impulse buying, retailing has focused considerable efforts on facilitating consumers' purchasing behavior (Roberts & Manolis, 2012). Retailers are interested in the impulse buying phenomenon because they can increase the consumers' impulsive tendencies (Pentecost & Andrews, 2010). In the context of non-food, semi-durable, life-style-oriented and branded consumer goods, international chains tend to gain a dominant position over the multi-brand single stores (Levy & Weitz, 2009).

In recent years, the global economic crisis has put the fashion retail companies in front of a magnitude of challenges not seen before, in terms of both decreased profits and price pressure (Guercini & Milanesi, 2016). Fashion retail is recognized for its strong capabilities in product innovation, while having the potential to improve the governance of technology-based process innovation (Tambo, 2015). Product innovation is the development and market introduction of the new, redesigned, and improved product or service (Kasemsap, 2016d). Fashion retailers are continuously looking for new ways to attract shoppers to their stores and increase purchases after they walk through the door (Castaldo & Grosso, 2016). Fashion retailers are delighted when shoppers feel a sudden impulse to buy new jackets, while browsing at a shopping mall in their shopping cart while standing in the checkout line (Amos, Holmes, & Keneson, 2014).

Retail Management and Technology

Technology plays a crucial role in the retail sector (Joshi, 2009). IT is considered as a driving force in the retail sector's innovation activities (Tambo, 2014), enhances the creation of new service brand experiences (Cho & Menor, 2010), and improves the just-in-time (JIT)-oriented delivery systems in the e-tailing shopping environment (Kotzab, Schnedlitz, & Neumayer, 2003). However, many retailers are not technology-savvy, ignoring this reality, which can threaten their profitability and survival in retail environments (Sánchez-Pérez, Estrella-Ramón, Segovia-López, & Marín-Carrillo, 2014).

In all areas of retailing, retail information systems play an important role in the effective information sharing among supply chain members (Yumurtacı & Oflaç, 2016). Retail information systems can encourage the processes of information integration and information sharing toward enhancing entrepreneurial success, increasing business growth and gaining customer satisfaction in global supply chain (Kasemsap, 2017b). Customer satisfaction is a measure of how a retailer's total product performs regarding customer's expectations (Gupta, 2016).

As consumers take advantage of self-service technologies as part of their shopping experience, store employees can benefit from access to the advanced digital tools beyond point-of-sale (POS) technologies in order to increase work effectiveness (Lewis & Loker, 2015). Pop-up store is a temporary retail outlet, which sells the short lines of products or unique products (Borusiak, 2014). Pop-up stores remain open only for a brief period and get their name by the analogy with the pop-up windows that appear on computer screens, while working on the Internet (de Lassus & Freire, 2014). Pop-up store retailers make use of technological tools (e.g., tablets and smartphones), thus enhancing a positive impact on customer satisfaction (Pantano, Iazzolino, & Migliano, 2013).

The item-level radio frequency identification (RFID)-enabled store management system helps improve the retail business (Choi, Cheung, Yang, & Yang, 2015). As real-time information is effectively made through RFID systems, administration and planning processes of supply chain can be significantly improved (Kasemsap, 2017c). RFID solutions can be utilized to reduce the operating costs through decreasing labor costs, enhancing automation, improving the tracing procedure, and preventing the material loss (Kasemsap, 2017d).

Aspects of Electronic Retailing

The Internet is an important tool for commercial transactions (Hsiao, 2009). The Internet commerce involves the sales and purchases of products and services over the Internet (Keeney, 1999). The growing interest in understanding what factors can affect the consumers' decisions to make purchase online is stimulated by the growth of online sales (Shih, 2004). The important factors (e.g., convenience, peer influence, the reduced price of products sold online, and the Internet experience) affect the consumers' decision to buy through the Internet (Chang, Cheung, & Lai, 2005).

The well-developed website facilitates the virtual interactions between companies and consumers, thus leading to the opportunities of product flow, where consumers are engaged with their virtual interactions with computer (Hoffman & Novak, 2009). Virtual interactions can vary from simple transactional e-mails to the conversations with product experts and recommended selections based on the previous purchases from a wide variety of websites (Smith, 2017). In addition, virtual interactions involve the purchase recommendation, grievance handling, and payment mechanisms (O'Cass & Carlson, 2012).

Electronic Retailing and Electronic Commerce

The increased applications of smartphones and tablets, along with advanced security features offered by the online retailers, add the strength to the e-commerce industry (Prashar, Vijay, & Parsad, 2015). An e-shop is the virtual equivalent of buying products or services at a brick-and-mortar retail store (Kumar, Sikdar, & Alam, 2016). As types of e-tailing click-only and click-and-mortar business models have raised instead of brick-and-mortar model and they have begun to spread across the globe (Ghorbani & Yarimoglu, 2014).

Regarding e-tailing, researchers have examined how to impulse buyers to take advantage of the behavior which has assisted brick-and-mortar retailers flourish for decades (Park, Kim, Funches, & Foxx, 2012). The emergence of e-commerce encourages the trend of moving from brick-and-mortar to click-and-mortar for companies (Dennis, Fenech, & Merrilees, 2004). Previous studies on consumers' online shopping behavior have identified a number of decision factors that consumers consider important in their agreement of online shopping (Clemes et al., 2014). The Internet shoppers and non-Internet shoppers can be distinguished by the demographic, psychographic, attitudinal, and experiential characteristics (Sin & Tse, 2002).

Virtual stores provide great efficiency in the retail value chain and their existence has paved the way for the diffusion of e-commerce (Chen & Tan, 2004). E-commerce is one of the most recognized patterns of electronic technology applied to modern business (Kasemsap, 2015b) as the online payment can be completed with greater efficiency (Kasemsap, 2016e). Through e-commerce, organizations can easily calculate and evaluate sales effectiveness, customer effectiveness, marketing campaigns, product mix, and customer engagement in global marketplace (Kasemsap, 2016f).

Many online researchers and practitioners would like to know how web browsing can stimulate the online customers to purchase products they might not buy otherwise (Park et al., 2012). Customers demonstrating higher levels of enjoyment have a more positive perception of online store environments

(Childers, Carr, Peck, & Carson, 2001). With e-commerce on the Internet, products can be globally sold through the websites of the product producers, and the customers' requirements can be collected in no time for product improvements (Huang, Chen, & Ho, 2013).

Perspectives on Online Consumer Behavior

Acknowledging the decision process of online shopping and the behaviors of online consumers is crucial for practitioners to compete in the virtual marketplace (Constantinides, 2004). Lohse et al. (2000) suggested that an improved understanding online consumer behavior is essential as it may help companies to clarify their online retail strategies for website design, online advertising, segmenting markets and product variety. Recognizing the decision factors that affect the online consumers' behaviors is crucial as the information can help improve the design of e-shopping websites, facilitate the development of online transactions, and encourage many consumers to purchase online (Chang et al., 2005).

Online consumer typologies have used general segmentation bases, such as online shopping attitudes, motivations (Hill, Beatty, & Walsh, 2013), online shopping patterns (Rohm & Swaminathan, 2004), e-store attribute performance (Ganesh, Reynolds, Luckett, & Pomirleanu, 2010), psychographic characteristics (Barnes, Bauer, Neumann, & Huber, 2007), and shopping orientations (Gehrt, Rajan, Shainesh, Czerwinski, & O'Brien, 2012). Consumers who have a favorable attitude toward a website are likely to purchase through website (Ha & Stoel, 2009).

Consumers browsing online take pleasure in seeking the product information regardless of whether they make a purchase (Smith & Sivakumar, 2004). Web browsing is recognized as an important part of the shopping experience (Park et al., 2012). While browsing the websites, consumers may encounter a special offer, a different color, and a desirable design, which can enhance a purchase (Rowley, 2001). Online buyers are more likely to enjoy browsing websites with a wide selection because they tend to be the seekers of variety (Lim & Dubinsky, 2004). Many online purchases derive from web browsing and price promotions (Earl & Potts, 2000).

Shergill and Chen (2005) stated that website design, website reliability, website customer service, and website security are the four main factors that affect on the consumers' perceptions of online shopping. Websites have online information that can assist customers when they search for products (Clemes et al., 2014). Once consumer makes an evaluation that the retailer's website experience is perceived to be innovative, the consumer will be more likely to evaluate the website to deliver the high-quality e-service (O'Cass & Carlson, 2012). The design characteristics of a web page may impact on the consumers' online buying decisions (Shergill & Chen, 2005). The content and design of websites are the important considerations when online retailers design the high-quality websites (Wolfinbarger & Gilly, 2003).

Scarpi et al. (2014) found the relationship between shopping motivations and shopping channels (i.e., online and offline shopping). It would be useful to test the moderating effects of consumers' personal characteristics (i.e., culture and online shopping expertise) and situational variables (i.e., perceived risk and time pressure) on the relationship between e-service quality and e-satisfaction in order to have a better understanding of consumers' online shopping experience (Michaud-Trevinal & Stenger, 2014). Perceived risk is a key element in the consumers' Internet shopping decision-making process (Liebermann & Stashevsky, 2002). Considering the online consumers' perceived risk can help managers improve their business strategies (Comegys, Hannula, & Vaisanen, 2006).

Advanced Issues of Electronic Retailing in Retail Environments

In the e-tailing context, retail consumers develop the perceptions of trust based on their website experiences, such as the ability for the website to deliver the innovative content, the security features, and the efficient facilitation of purchases (Chen & Dibbs, 2010), as well as the website delivering affective reactions that engender consumers' trust in the website (Hwang & Kim, 2007). Website attributes (e.g., information content, entertainment, usability, and transaction capability) can affect the consumer's intention to buy at the website and revisit the website in the future (Hausman & Siekpe, 2009).

In recognizing the horizontal competition between two suppliers, since their marketing positions are similar, and sharing information is unsuitable, these two suppliers would derive their optimal decisions of price and lead time combinations with application of maximization of their profits regarding their own capacity constraints and cost concerns along with the offer submitted by the opponent. Concerning the vertical competition between suppliers and e-tailers, the e-tailers are accepted to be small-scale, one which is less powerful than the suppliers in bargaining for prices, so the suppliers set the wholesale prices and promise the lead times to the e-tailers (Huang et al., 2013).

Being perceived as delivering an innovative e-service experience provides the e-tailers the opportunities to distinctively position its e-service in an effective manner, thus differentiating the e-tailers from their competitors toward competitive advantage in global marketing (O'Cass & Carlson, 2012). E-tailers have two contradictory objectives: on the one hand, they must provide smart shoppers with day-to-day sales promotions to increase revenues in the short run; on the other hand, they face difficulties in making these smart shoppers loyal (Audrain-Pontevia et al., 2013). Many customers have a tendency to invest the considerable time in seeking the online promotion-related information in order to achieve the price savings. Customer loyalty is difficult to achieve, although competition online demands that companies retain their online buyers (Reichheld & Schefter, 2000).

E-tailers are able to offer a higher level of choice, which means a wider range of product categories and a greater variety of products within any given category (Ward & Lee, 2000). Griffis et al. (2012) stated that referral management for e-tailers is a strategically important activity, as referrals offer a highly cost-effective method of customer acquisition. E-tailers can offer customers different services and can provide customers in comparing alternative product features and in selecting proper commodities to save their time surfing on the Internet and shopping at retail stores (Turban, King, Viehland, & Lee, 2006). E-tailers should utilize social media to allow consumers to gain the social rewards of making an impulse purchase (Amos et al., 2014).

E-tailers need to develop the pricing strategies with emotional excitement for web browsers on the shopping websites (Mazaheri, Richard, & Laroche, 2010). E-tailers effectively perform as followers who can only decide the retail prices based on the suppliers' offers. While determining on a wholesale price and its equivalent delivery time, suppliers should take into account the effect of such a decision on the e-tailers' retail price, since it may affect the market demand, and the e-tailers should recognize the retail prices (Huang et al., 2013).

FUTURE RESEARCH DIRECTIONS

The classification of the extensive literature in the domains of retail management and e-tailing will provide the potential opportunities for future research. Now, the retail industries are establishing the network marketing by online shopping, through the websites and other technology, electronic payments, and delivery through the courier and other services. E-tailing is a powerful marketing technique for the right product with the right message to the right person. Green retailing is the use of eco-friendly products, processes, and services in order to prevent the environmental degradation and create the sustainable environment for people to live. Green retailing is the process of developing products and promoting them to satisfy the customers who prefer the products of good quality, performance, and convenience at affordable cost and which do not have a detrimental impact on the environment. An examination of linkages among retail management, e-tailing, and green retailing in retail environments would seem to be viable for future research efforts.

CONCLUSION

This chapter provided the overview of retail management; retail management and technology; the aspects of e-tailing; e-tailing and e-commerce; the perspectives on online consumer behavior; and the advanced issues of e-tailing in retail environments. Retail management is an integrated part of the supply chain management. Retail management focuses on the processes that go into ensuring consumers can obtain the products they want from their chosen retail store. Effective retail management helps company distributes the finished products created by the business to consumers in order to determine and satisfy what buyers want and require.

Consumers will buy a product or service through an e-tailing campaign because they perceive its value or because it makes them look better or feel better about themselves. The e-tailing campaign is a low-overhead operation without the network of wholesalers and retailers between the seller and the consumer. An e-tailing campaign may be the only place where it is available immediately. If the product solves a difficult problem or offers an important improvement, consumers who buy from the electronic retailer can have the product in their hands sooner.

For consumers who are pressed for time and do not enjoy shopping, an e-tailing product may take on added value because the buying transaction can be completed without hassle, quickly and at hours when traditional retailing is unavailable. Consumers who see or hear an e-tailing campaign get access to products that may never show up in a retail store because the developer lacked the resources to take in the retail industry. Effective retail management and e-tailing applications generate business revenue, build brand awareness, and pave the way for broader distribution in retail environments.

REFERENCES

Adapa, S. (2013). Electronic retailing of prepared food in Australia. In K. Tarnay, S. Imre, & L. Xu (Eds.), *Research and development in e-business through service-oriented solutions* (pp. 280–292). Hershey, PA: IGI Global. doi:10.4018/978-1-4666-4181-5.ch014

Amin, B. Z., & Amin, P. (2013). A conceptual framework to understanding online consumer buying behavior. *International Journal of Online Marketing*, *3*(1), 47–63. doi:10.4018/ijom.2013010104

Amos, C., Holmes, G. R., & Keneson, W. C. (2014). A meta-analysis of consumer impulse buying. *Journal of Retailing and Consumer Services*, *21*(2), 86–97. doi:10.1016/j.jretconser.2013.11.004

Audrain-Pontevia, A. F., N'Goala, G., & Poncin, I. (2013). A good deal online: The impacts of acquisition and transaction value on e-satisfaction and e-loyalty. *Journal of Retailing and Consumer Services*, *20*(5), 445–452. doi:10.1016/j.jretconser.2013.04.002

Barnes, S. J., Bauer, H. H., Neumann, M. M., & Huber, F. (2007). Segmenting cyberspace: A customer typology for the Internet. *European Journal of Marketing*, *41*(1/2), 71–93. doi:10.1108/03090560710718120

Berman, B., & Evans, J. R. (2010). *Retail management: A strategic Approach*. Upper Saddle River, NJ: Prentice Hall.

Bonfanti, A. (2014). A dilemma for retailers: How to make store surveillance secure and appealing to shoppers. In F. Musso & E. Druica (Eds.), *Handbook of research on retailer-consumer relationship development* (pp. 297–317). Hershey, PA: IGI Global. doi:10.4018/978-1-4666-6074-8.ch016

Borusiak, B. (2014). The mechanisms for the emergence and evolution of retail formats. In F. Musso & E. Druica (Eds.), *Handbook of research on retailer-consumer relationship development* (pp. 108–126). Hershey, PA: IGI Global. doi:10.4018/978-1-4666-6074-8.ch007

Brajesh, S. (2016). Big data analytics in retail supply chain. In N. Kamath & S. Saurav (Eds.), *Handbook of research on strategic supply chain management in the retail industry* (pp. 269–289). Hershey, PA: IGI Global. doi:10.4018/978-1-4666-9894-9.ch015

Bressolles, G., Durrieu, F., & Senecal, S. (2014). A consumer typology based on e-service quality and e-satisfaction. *Journal of Retailing and Consumer Services*, *21*(6), 889–896. doi:10.1016/j.jretconser.2014.07.004

Castaldo, S., & Grosso, M. (2016). CRM in fashion retail: Building store loyalty through store trust. In A. Vecchi & C. Buckley (Eds.), *Handbook of research on global fashion management and merchandising* (pp. 509–531). Hershey, PA: IGI Global. doi:10.4018/978-1-5225-0110-7.ch021

Chang, M. K., Cheung, W., & Lai, V. S. (2005). Literature derived reference models for the adoption of online shopping. *Information & Management*, *42*(4), 543–559. doi:10.1016/S0378-7206(04)00051-5

Chen, J., & Dibbs, S. (2010). Consumer trust in the online retail context: Exploring the antecedents and consequences. *Psychology and Marketing*, *27*(4), 323–346. doi:10.1002/mar.20334

Chen, L., & Tan, J. (2004). Key determinants of consumer acceptance of virtual stores: Some empirical evidence. In J. Gupta & S. Sharma (Eds.), *Intelligent enterprises of the 21st century* (pp. 45–66). Hershey, PA: IGI Global. doi:10.4018/978-1-59140-160-5.ch004

Childers, T., Carr, C. L., Peck, J., & Carson, S. (2001). Hedonic and utilitarian motivations for online retail shopping behaviour. *Journal of Retailing*, *77*(4), 511–535. doi:10.1016/S0022-4359(01)00056-2

Cho, Y., & Menor, L. (2010). Toward a provider-based view on the design and delivery of quality e-service encounters. *Journal of Service Research*, *13*(1), 83–95. doi:10.1177/1094670509350490

Choi, S. H., Cheung, H. H., Yang, B., & Yang, Y. X. (2015). Item-level RFID for retail business improvement. In I. Lee (Ed.), *RFID technology integration for business performance improvement* (pp. 1–26). Hershey, PA: IGI Global. doi:10.4018/978-1-4666-6308-4.ch001

Chugh, R., & Grandhi, S. (2012). E-tailing: A snapshot of Australia's top 25 retailers. In K. Mohammed Rezaul (Ed.), *Strategic and pragmatic e-business: Implications for future business practices* (pp. 297–313). Hershey, PA: IGI Global. doi:10.4018/978-1-4666-1619-6.ch013

Clemes, M. D., Gan, C., & Zhang, J. (2014). An empirical analysis of online shopping adoption in Beijing, China. *Journal of Retailing and Consumer Services*, *21*(3), 364–375. doi:10.1016/j.jretconser.2013.08.003

Comegys, C., Hannula, M., & Vaisanen, J. (2006). Longitudinal comparison of Finnish and US online shopping behaviour among university students: The five-stage buying decision process. *Journal of Targeting, Measurement and Analysis for Marketing*, *14*(4), 336–356. doi:10.1057/palgrave.jt.5740193

Constantinides, E. (2004). Influencing the online consumer's behavior: The Web experience. *Internet Research*, *14*(2), 111–126. doi:10.1108/10662240410530835

de Lassus, C., & Freire, N. D. (2014). Access to the luxury brand myth in pop-up stores: A netnographic and semiotic analysis. *Journal of Retailing and Consumer Services*, *21*(1), 61–68. doi:10.1016/j.jretconser.2013.08.005

Dennis, C., Fenech, T., & Merrilees, B. (2004). *E-retailing*. London, UK: Routledge.

Earl, P. E., & Potts, J. (2000). Latent demand and the browsing shopper. *Managerial and Decision Economics*, *21*(3/4), 111–122. doi:10.1002/mde.976

Ganesh, J., Reynolds, K. E., Luckett, M. G., & Pomirleanu, N. (2010). Online shopper motivations, and e-store attributes: An examination of online patronage behavior and shopper typologies. *Journal of Retailing*, *86*(1), 106–115. doi:10.1016/j.jretai.2010.01.003

Gehrt, K. C., Rajan, M. N., Shainesh, G., Czerwinski, D., & O'Brien, M. (2012). Emergence of online shopping in India: Shopping orientation segments. *International Journal of Retail & Distribution Management*, *40*(10), 742–758. doi:10.1108/09590551211263164

Gencer, Y. G. (2017). Supply chain management in retailing business. In U. Akkucuk (Ed.), *Ethics and sustainability in global supply chain management* (pp. 197–210). Hershey, PA: IGI Global. doi:10.4018/978-1-5225-2036-8.ch011

Ghorbani, A., & Yarimoglu, E. K. (2014). E-service marketing. In A. Ghorbani (Ed.), *Marketing in the cyber era: Strategies and emerging trends* (pp. 1–8). Hershey, PA: IGI Global. doi:10.4018/978-1-4666-4864-7.ch001

González-Benito, Ó., Martos-Partal, M., & Fustinoni-Venturini, M. (2014). Retailers' price positioning and the motivational profiling of store-brand shoppers: The case of Spain. *Psychology and Marketing*, *31*(2), 115–125. doi:10.1002/mar.20680

Griffis, S. E., Rao, S., Goldsby, T. J., Voorhees, C. M., & Iyengar, D. (2012). Linking order fulfillment performance to referrals in online retailing: An empirical analysis. *Journal of Business Logistics*, *33*(4), 279–294. doi:10.1111/jbl.12002

Guercini, S., & Milanesi, M. (2016). Store openings and sourcing strategies in the internationalization of fashion industrial retailers. In A. Vecchi & C. Buckley (Eds.), *Handbook of research on global fashion management and merchandising* (pp. 374–397). Hershey, PA: IGI Global. doi:10.4018/978-1-5225-0110-7.ch015

Gupta, A. (2016). Customer service: A key differentiator in retailing. In N. Kamath & S. Saurav (Eds.), *Handbook of research on strategic supply chain management in the retail industry* (pp. 75–86). Hershey, PA: IGI Global. doi:10.4018/978-1-4666-9894-9.ch005

Ha, S., & Stoel, L. (2009). Consumer e-shopping acceptance: Antecedents in a technology acceptance model. *Journal of Business Research*, *62*(5), 565–571. doi:10.1016/j.jbusres.2008.06.016

Hampl, N., & Loock, M. (2013). Sustainable development in retailing: What is the impact on store choice? *Business Strategy and the Environment*, *22*(3), 202–216. doi:10.1002/bse.1748

Hausman, A., & Siekpe, J. (2009). The effect of web interface features on consumer online purchase intentions. *Journal of Business Research*, *62*(1), 5–13. doi:10.1016/j.jbusres.2008.01.018

Hernandez, T., Bennison, D., & Cornelius, S. (1998). The organisational context of retail locational planning. *GeoJournal*, *45*(4), 299–308. doi:10.1023/A:1006989131869

Hill, W. W., Beatty, S. E., & Walsh, G. (2013). A segmentation of adolescent online users and shoppers. *Journal of Services Marketing*, *27*(5), 347–360. doi:10.1108/JSM-10-2011-0157

Hoffman, D., & Novak, T. (2009). Flow online: Lessons learned and future prospects. *Journal of Interactive Marketing*, *23*(1), 23–34. doi:10.1016/j.intmar.2008.10.003

Hsiao, M. H. (2009). Shopping mode choice: Physical store shopping versus e-shopping. *Transportation Research Part E, Logistics and Transportation Review*, *45*(1), 86–95. doi:10.1016/j.tre.2008.06.002

Huang, Y. S., Chen, S. H., & Ho, J. W. (2013). A study on pricing and delivery strategy for e-retailing systems. *Transportation Research Part E, Logistics and Transportation Review*, *59*, 71–84. doi:10.1016/j.tre.2013.09.002

Hwang, Y., & Kim, D. (2007). Customer self-service systems: The effects of perceived web quality with service contents on enjoyment, anxiety, and e-trust. *Decision Support Systems*, *43*(3), 746–760. doi:10.1016/j.dss.2006.12.008

Jiang, P., & Balasubramanian, S. K. (2014). An empirical comparison of market efficiency: Electronic marketplaces vs. traditional retail formats. *Electronic Commerce Research and Applications*, *13*(2), 98–109. doi:10.1016/j.elerap.2013.11.003

Joseph, L., & Kuby, M. (2016). The location types of US retailers. *International Journal of Applied Geospatial Research*, *7*(4), 1–22. doi:10.4018/IJAGR.2016100101

Joshi, G. (2009). *Information technology for retail*. Oxford, UK: Oxford University Press.

Jüttner, U., Christopher, M., & Baker, S. (2007). Demand chain management: Integrating marketing and supply chain management. *Industrial Marketing Management*, *36*(3), 377–392. doi:10.1016/j.indmarman.2005.10.003

Kacen, J. J., Hess, J. D., & Walker, D. (2012). Spontaneous selection: The influence of product and retailing factors on consumer impulse purchases. *Journal of Retailing and Consumer Services*, *19*(6), 578–588. doi:10.1016/j.jretconser.2012.07.003

Kasemsap, K. (2015a). The roles of corporate marketing strategies and brand management in the global retail industry. In E. Pantano (Ed.), *Successful technological integration for competitive advantage in retail settings* (pp. 310–339). Hershey, PA: IGI Global. doi:10.4018/978-1-4666-8297-9.ch014

Kasemsap, K. (2015b). The role of electronic commerce in the global business environments. In F. Cipolla-Ficarra (Ed.), *Handbook of research on interactive information quality in expanding social network communications* (pp. 304–324). Hershey, PA: IGI Global. doi:10.4018/978-1-4666-7377-9.ch019

Kasemsap, K. (2016a). Retail marketing strategies and brand management: A global retail industry perspective. *International Journal of Social and Organizational Dynamics in IT*, *5*(2), 66–78. doi:10.4018/IJSODIT.2016070106

Kasemsap, K. (2016b). Reviewing the role of store brands in the global retail industry. In M. Gómez-Suárez & M. Martínez-Ruiz (Eds.), *Handbook of research on strategic retailing of private label products in a recovering economy* (pp. 28–53). Hershey, PA: IGI Global. doi:10.4018/978-1-5225-0220-3.ch002

Kasemsap, K. (2016c). Encouraging supply chain networks and customer loyalty in global supply chain. In N. Kamath & S. Saurav (Eds.), *Handbook of research on strategic supply chain management in the retail industry* (pp. 87–112). Hershey, PA: IGI Global. doi:10.4018/978-1-4666-9894-9.ch006

Kasemsap, K. (2016d). Creating product innovation strategies through knowledge management in global business. In A. Goel & P. Singhal (Eds.), *Product innovation through knowledge management and social media strategies* (pp. 330–357). Hershey, PA: IGI Global. doi:10.4018/978-1-4666-9607-5.ch015

Kasemsap, K. (2016e). Advocating electronic business and electronic commerce in the global marketplace. In S. Dixit & A. Sinha (Eds.), *E-retailing challenges and opportunities in the global marketplace* (pp. 1–24). Hershey, PA: IGI Global. doi:10.4018/978-1-4666-9921-2.ch001

Kasemsap, K. (2016f). Implementing electronic commerce in global marketing. In I. Lee (Ed.), *Encyclopedia of e-commerce development, implementation, and management* (pp. 591–602). Hershey, PA: IGI Global. doi:10.4018/978-1-4666-9787-4.ch043

Kasemsap, K. (2017a). Mastering fashion supply chain management and new product development in the digital age. In A. Vecchi (Ed.), *Advanced fashion technology and operations management* (pp. 65–91). Hershey, PA: IGI Global. doi:10.4018/978-1-5225-1865-5.ch003

Kasemsap, K. (2017b). Advocating information system, information integration, and information sharing in global supply chain. In G. Jamil, A. Soares, & C. Pessoa (Eds.), *Handbook of research on information management for effective logistics and supply chains* (pp. 107–130). Hershey, PA: IGI Global. doi:10.4018/978-1-5225-0973-8.ch006

Kasemsap, K. (2017c). Radio frequency identification and mobile ad-hoc network: Theories and applications. In S. Bhattacharyya, N. Das, D. Bhattacharjee, & A. Mukherjee (Eds.), *Handbook of research on recent developments in intelligent communication application* (pp. 63–95). Hershey, PA: IGI Global. doi:10.4018/978-1-5225-1785-6.ch003

Kasemsap, K. (2017d). The role of radio frequency identification in modern libraries. In I. Management Association (Ed.), Identity theft: Breakthroughs in research and practice (pp. 174–200). Hershey, PA: IGI Global. doi:10.4018/978-1-5225-0808-3.ch009

Keeney, R. L. (1999). The value of Internet commerce to the customer. *Management Science, 45*(4), 533–542. doi:10.1287/mnsc.45.4.533

Kollmann, T., Kuckertz, A., & Kayser, I. (2012). Cannibalization or synergy? Consumers' channel selection in online-offline multichannel systems. *Journal of Retailing and Consumer Services, 19*(2), 186–194. doi:10.1016/j.jretconser.2011.11.008

Kotzab, H., Schnedlitz, P., & Neumayer, K. (2003). Contemporary IT-assisted retail management. In L. Joia (Ed.), *IT-based management: Challenges and solutions* (pp. 175–203). Hershey, PA: IGI Global. doi:10.4018/978-1-59140-033-2.ch011

Kumar, A., Sikdar, P., & Alam, M. M. (2016). E-retail adoption in emerging markets: Applicability of an integrated trust and technology acceptance model. *International Journal of E-Business Research, 12*(3), 44–67. doi:10.4018/IJEBR.2016070104

Kurata, H., & Nam, S. (2014). Freshness management in the retail business. In J. Wang (Ed.), *Encyclopedia of business analytics and optimization* (pp. 960–977). Hershey, PA: IGI Global. doi:10.4018/978-1-4666-5202-6.ch089

Kurata, H., & Yue, X. (2008). Trade promotion mode choice and information sharing in fashion retail supply chains. *International Journal of Production Economics, 114*(2), 507–519. doi:10.1016/j.ijpe.2007.05.021

Levy, M., & Weitz, B. (2009). *Retailing management.* New York, NY: McGraw–Hill.

Lewis, T. L., & Loker, S. (2015). Adoption of emerging in-store technology interfaces for the apparel retail employee. In E. Pantano (Ed.), *Successful technological integration for competitive advantage in retail settings* (pp. 119–143). Hershey, PA: IGI Global. doi:10.4018/978-1-4666-8297-9.ch006

Lewrick, M., Omar, M., Williams, R. Jr, Tjandra, N. C., & Lee, Z. (2015). Radical and incremental innovation effectiveness in relation to market orientation in the retail industry: Triggers, drivers, and supporters. In E. Pantano (Ed.), *Successful technological integration for competitive advantage in retail settings* (pp. 239–268). Hershey, PA: IGI Global. doi:10.4018/978-1-4666-8297-9.ch011

Liebermann, Y., & Stashevsky, S. (2002). Perceived risks as barriers to Internet and e-commerce usage. *Qualitative Market Research*, *5*(4), 291–300. doi:10.1108/13522750210443245

Lim, H., & Dubinsky, A. J. (2004). Consumers perceptions of e-shopping characteristics: An expectancy-value approach. *Journal of Services Marketing*, *18*(7), 500–513. doi:10.1108/08876040410561839

Lohse, G., Bellman, S., & Johnson, E. J. (2000). Consumer buying behavior on the Internet: Findings from panel data. *Journal of Interactive Marketing*, *14*(1), 15–29. doi:10.1002/(SICI)1520-6653(200024)14:1<15::AID-DIR2>3.0.CO;2-C

Lowson, R. (2001). Analysing the effectiveness of European retail sourcing strategies. *European Management Journal*, *19*(5), 543–551. doi:10.1016/S0263-2373(01)00068-8

Madlberger, M. (2005). Applications of Internet-based marketing instruments by multichannel retailers: A web site analysis in the U.S. and the UK. In S. Krishnamurthy (Ed.), *Contemporary research in e-marketing* (Vol. 2, pp. 284–303). Hershey, PA: IGI Global. doi:10.4018/978-1-59140-824-6.ch011

Madlberger, M. (2009). Exogenous and endogenous antecedents of online shopping in a multichannel environment: Evidence from a catalog retailer in the German-speaking world. In Y. Wan (Ed.), *Comparison-shopping services and agent designs* (pp. 196–216). Hershey, PA: IGI Global. doi:10.4018/978-1-59904-978-6.ch013

Martínez-Ruiz, M. P., González-González, I., Jiménez-Zarco, A. I., & Izquierdo-Yusta, A. (2016). Private labels at the service of retailers' image and competitive positioning: The case of Tesco. In M. Gómez-Suárez & M. Martínez-Ruiz (Eds.), *Handbook of research on strategic retailing of private label products in a recovering economy* (pp. 104–125). Hershey, PA: IGI Global. doi:10.4018/978-1-5225-0220-3.ch005

Mazaheri, E., Richard, M. O., & Laroche, M. (2010). Investigating the moderating impact of hedonism on online consumer behavior. *Journal of Global Academy of Marketing Science*, *20*(2), 123–134. doi:10.1080/12297119.2010.9730185

Michaud-Trevinal, A., & Stenger, T. (2014). Toward a conceptualization of the online shopping experience. *Journal of Retailing and Consumer Services*, *21*(3), 314–326. doi:10.1016/j.jretconser.2014.02.009

Nair, A., & Kloss, D. J. (2006). An examination of the impact of coordinating supply chain policies and price markdowns on short lifecycle product retail performance. *International Journal of Production Economics*, *102*(2), 379–392. doi:10.1016/j.ijpe.2005.04.009

O'Cass, A., & Carlson, J. (2012). An e-retailing assessment of perceived website-service innovativeness: Implications for website quality evaluations, trust, loyalty and word of mouth. *Australasian Marketing Journal*, *20*(1), 28–36. doi:10.1016/j.ausmj.2011.10.012

Pantano, E., Iazzolino, G., & Migliano, G. (2013). Obsolescence risk in advanced technologies for retailing: A management perspective. *Journal of Retailing and Consumer Services, 20*(2), 225–233. doi:10.1016/j.jretconser.2013.01.002

Park, E. J., Kim, E. Y., Funches, V. M., & Foxx, W. (2012). Apparel product attributes, web browsing, an de-impulse buying on shopping websites. *Journal of Business Research, 65*(11), 1583–1589. doi:10.1016/j.jbusres.2011.02.043

Pecoraro, M., & Uusitalo, O. (2014). Exploring the everyday retail experience: The discourses of style and design. *Journal of Consumer Behaviour, 13*(6), 429–441. doi:10.1002/cb.1492

Pentecost, R., & Andrews, L. (2010). Fashion retailing and the bottom line: The effects of generational cohorts, gender, fashion fanship, attitudes, and impulse buying on fashion expenditure. *Journal of Retailing and Consumer Services, 17*(1), 43–52. doi:10.1016/j.jretconser.2009.09.003

Prashar, S., Vijay, T. S., & Parsad, C. (2015). Antecedents to online shopping: Factors influencing the selection of web portal. *International Journal of E-Business Research, 11*(1), 35–55. doi:10.4018/ijebr.2015010103

Pratapwar, S. S. (2016). Supply chain hub and spoke model for convenience stores. In N. Kamath & S. Saurav (Eds.), *Handbook of research on strategic supply chain management in the retail industry* (pp. 39–54). Hershey, PA: IGI Global. doi:10.4018/978-1-4666-9894-9.ch003

Raff, H., & Schmitt, N. (2012). Imports and the structure of retail markets. *The Canadian Journal of Economics. Revue Canadienne dEconomique, 45*(4), 1431–1455. doi:10.1111/j.1540-5982.2012.01743.x

Rajagopal, D. (2009). Technology and retailing and firms: Challenges ahead. In D. Rajagopal (Ed.), *Information communication technologies and globalization of retailing applications* (pp. 335–344). Hershey, PA: IGI Global. doi:10.4018/978-1-60566-248-0.ch015

Rajaram, K. (2001). Assortment planning in fashion retailing: Methodology, application and analysis. *European Journal of Operational Research, 129*(1), 186–208. doi:10.1016/S0377-2217(99)00406-3

Reichheld, F. F., & Schefter, P. (2000). E-loyalty: Your secret weapon on the web. *Harvard Business Review, 78*(4), 105–113.

Roberts, J. A., & Manolis, C. (2012). Cooking up a recipe for self-control: The three ingredients of self-control and its impact on impulse buying. *Journal of Marketing Theory and Practice, 20*(2), 173–188. doi:10.2753/MTP1069-6679200204

Rohm, A. J., & Swaminathan, V. (2004). A typology of online shoppers based on shopping motivations. *Journal of Business Research, 57*(7), 748–757. doi:10.1016/S0148-2963(02)00351-X

Rose, S., & Samouel, P. (2009). Internal psychological versus external market-driven determinants of the amount of consumer information search amongst experienced online shoppers. *Journal of Marketing Management, 25*(1/2), 171–190. doi:10.1362/026725709X410089

Rowley, J. (2001). Window shopping and browsing opportunities in cyberspace. *Journal of Consumer Behaviour, 1*(4), 369–378. doi:10.1002/cb.81

Sánchez-Pérez, M., Estrella-Ramón, A., Segovia-López, C., & Marín-Carrillo, M. B. (2014). Multichannel retailing and consumer behaviour: Strategy design and implementation. *International Journal of Applied Behavioral Economics, 3*(4), 17–39. doi:10.4018/ijabe.2014100102

Saurav, S. (2016). Customer experience impacting retail management: Study of customer centricity strategy by retailers. In N. Kamath & S. Saurav (Eds.), *Handbook of research on strategic supply chain management in the retail industry* (pp. 130–150). Hershey, PA: IGI Global. doi:10.4018/978-1-4666-9894-9.ch008

Scarpi, D., Pizzi, G., & Visentin, M. (2014). Shopping for fun or shopping to buy: Is it different online and offline? *Journal of Retailing and Consumer Services, 21*(3), 258–267. doi:10.1016/j.jretconser.2014.02.007

Sen, A. (2008). The US fashion industry: A supply chain review. *International Journal of Production Economics, 114*(2), 571–593. doi:10.1016/j.ijpe.2007.05.022

Shergill, G. S., & Chen, Z. (2005). Web-based shopping: Consumers' attitude towards online shopping in New Zealand. *Journal of Electronic Commerce Research, 6*(2), 78–92.

Shih, H. P. (2004). An empirical study on predicting user acceptance of e-shopping on the Web. *Information & Management, 41*(3), 351–368. doi:10.1016/S0378-7206(03)00079-X

Shobeiri, S., Mazaheri, E., & Laroche, M. (2015). Shopping online for goods vs. services: Where do experiential features help more? *International Journal of Consumer Studies, 39*(2), 172–179. doi:10.1111/ijcs.12165

Shukla, P., & Vyas, P. (2016). An epigrammatic view of e-retailing in India: Prospects and retrospects. In S. Dixit & A. Sinha (Eds.), *E-retailing challenges and opportunities in the global marketplace* (pp. 121–131). Hershey, PA: IGI Global. doi:10.4018/978-1-4666-9921-2.ch006

Sin, L., & Tse, A. (2002). Profiling Internet shoppers in Hong Kong: Demographic, psychographic, attitudinal and experiential factors. *Journal of International Consumer Marketing, 15*(1), 7–29. doi:10.1300/J046v15n01_02

Skogster, P., & Uotila, V. (2010). Collecting consumer behavior data with WLAN. In J. Wang (Ed.), *Innovations in supply chain management for information systems: Novel approaches* (pp. 125–141). Hershey, PA: IGI Global. doi:10.4018/978-1-60566-974-8.ch004

Smith, A. D. (2017). Exploring the inherent growth of e-tailing via e-personalization and technological innovations. *International Journal of Innovation in the Digital Economy, 8*(1), 19–46. doi:10.4018/IJIDE.2017010102

Smith, D. N., & Sivakumar, K. (2004). Flow and Internet shopping behavior: A conceptual model and research propositions. *Journal of Business Research, 57*(10), 1199–1208. doi:10.1016/S0148-2963(02)00330-2

Smriti, K. (2016). Retail supply chain management trends: Past, present and future. In N. Kamath & S. Saurav (Eds.), *Handbook of research on strategic supply chain management in the retail industry* (pp. 1–18). Hershey, PA: IGI Global. doi:10.4018/978-1-4666-9894-9.ch001

Sternbeck, M. G., & Kuhn, H. (2014). An integrative approach to determine store delivery patterns in grocery retailing. *Transportation Research Part E, Logistics and Transportation Review*, *70*, 205–224. doi:10.1016/j.tre.2014.06.007

Tambo, T. (2014). Collaboration on technological innovation in Danish fashion chains: A network perspective. *Journal of Retailing and Consumer Services*, *21*(5), 827–835. doi:10.1016/j.jretconser.2014.02.016

Tambo, T. (2015). Fashion retail innovation: About context, antecedents, and outcome in technological change projects. In E. Pantano (Ed.), *Successful technological integration for competitive advantage in retail settings* (pp. 269–294). Hershey, PA: IGI Global. doi:10.4018/978-1-4666-8297-9.ch012

Teller, C., & Reutterer, T. (2008). The evolving concept of retail attractiveness: What makes retail agglomerations attractive when customers shop at them? *Journal of Retailing and Consumer Services*, *15*(3), 127–143. doi:10.1016/j.jretconser.2007.03.003

Turban, E., King, D., Viehland, D., & Lee, J. (2006). *Electronic commerce: A managerial perspective*. Upper Saddle River, NJ: Prentice Hall.

Ward, M. R., & Lee, M. J. (2000). Internet shopping consumer search and product branding. *Journal of Product and Brand Management*, *9*(1), 6–20. doi:10.1108/10610420010316302

Wolfinbarger, M., & Gilly, M. C. (2003). eTailQ: Dimensionalizing, measuring and predicting etail quality. *Journal of Retailing*, *79*(3), 183–198. doi:10.1016/S0022-4359(03)00034-4

Yumurtacı, I. Ö., & Oflaç, B. S. (2016). Supply chain management practices in retail: The trends and future perspective. In B. Christiansen (Ed.), *Handbook of research on global supply chain management* (pp. 366–378). Hershey, PA: IGI Global. doi:10.4018/978-1-4666-9639-6.ch021

ADDITIONAL READING

Balakrishnan, A., Sundaresan, S., & Zhang, B. (2014). Browse-and-switch: Retail-online competition under value uncertainty. *Production and Operations Management*, *23*(7), 1129–1145. doi:10.1111/poms.12165

Bassi, M., Pagnozzi, M., & Piccolo, S. (2015). Product differentiation by competing vertical hierarchies. *Journal of Economics & Management Strategy*, *24*(4), 904–933. doi:10.1111/jems.12115

Bhattacharya, M., & Wamba, S. F. (2015). A conceptual framework of RFID adoption in retail using TOE framework. *International Journal of Technology Diffusion*, *6*(1), 1–32. doi:10.4018/IJTD.2015010101

Brea-Solís, H., Casadesus-Masanell, R., & Grifell-Tatjé, E. (2015). Business model evaluation: Quantifying Walmart's sources of advantage. *Strategic Entrepreneurship Journal*, *9*(1), 12–33. doi:10.1002/sej.1190

Breiter, A., & Huchzermeier, A. (2015). Promotion planning and supply chain contracting in a high–low pricing environment. *Production and Operations Management*, *24*(2), 219–236. doi:10.1111/poms.12250

Calienes, E., Carmel-Gilfilen, C., & Portillo, M. (2016). Inside the mind of the millennial shopper: Designing retail spaces for a new generation. *Journal of Interior Design*, *41*(4), 47–67. doi:10.1111/joid.12085

Carranza, J. E., Clark, R., & Houde, J. F. (2015). Price controls and market structure: Evidence from gasoline retail markets. *The Journal of Industrial Economics*, *63*(1), 152–198. doi:10.1111/joie.12071

Chkanikova, O., & Mont, O. (2015). Corporate supply chain responsibility: Drivers and barriers for sustainable food retailing. *Corporate Social Responsibility and Environmental Management*, *22*(2), 65–82. doi:10.1002/csr.1316

Chuang, H. H. C., Oliva, R., & Liu, S. (2016). On-shelf availability, retail performance, and external audits: A field experiment. *Production and Operations Management*, *25*(5), 935–951. doi:10.1111/poms.12519

David, A., & Adida, E. (2015). Competition and coordination in a two-channel supply chain. *Production and Operations Management*, *24*(8), 1358–1370. doi:10.1111/poms.12327

Evanschitzky, H., Iyer, G. R., Pillai, K. G., Kenning, P., & Schütte, R. (2015). Consumer trial, continuous use, and economic benefits of a retail service innovation: The case of the personal shopping assistant. *Journal of Product Innovation Management*, *32*(3), 459–475. doi:10.1111/jpim.12241

Huang, Q., & Gamble, J. (2015). Social expectations, gender and job satisfaction: Front-line employees in China's retail sector. *Human Resource Management Journal*, *25*(3), 331–347. doi:10.1111/1748-8583.12066

Jin, Y., Williams, B. D., Tokar, T., & Waller, M. A. (2015). Forecasting with temporally aggregated demand signals in a retail supply chain. *Journal of Business Logistics*, *36*(2), 199–211. doi:10.1111/jbl.12091

Kesavan, S., & Kushwaha, T. (2014). Differences in retail inventory investment behavior during macroeconomic shocks: Role of service level. *Production and Operations Management*, *23*(12), 2118–2136. doi:10.1111/poms.12048

Lewis, M. S. (2015). Odd prices at retail gasoline stations: Focal point pricing and tacit collusion. *Journal of Economics & Management Strategy*, *24*(3), 664–685. doi:10.1111/jems.12103

Li, J., Chan, T. Y., & Lewis, M. (2016). What happens when manufacturers perform the retailing functions? *Production and Operations Management*, *25*(8), 1391–1403. doi:10.1111/poms.12549

Li, T., Sethi, S. P., & He, X. (2015). Dynamic pricing, production, and channel coordination with stochastic learning. *Production and Operations Management*, *24*(6), 857–882. doi:10.1111/poms.12320

Liao, P. C. (2014). Input prices as signals of costs to a downstream rival and customer. *The Japanese Economic Review*, *65*(3), 414–430. doi:10.1111/jere.12020

Litz, R. A., & Pollack, J. M. (2015). Interfirm rivalry between small hardware stores and "big box" retailers: Market commonality and product mix similarity as antecedents to competitive response. *Journal of Small Business Management, 53*(2), 436–449. doi:10.1111/jsbm.12071

Liu, G., & Ko, W. W. (2014). Charity retailing in the United Kingdom: A managerial capabilities perspective. *Journal of Small Business Management, 52*(3), 390–406. doi:10.1111/jsbm.12040

Mani, V., Kesavan, S., & Swaminathan, J. M. (2015). Estimating the impact of understaffing on sales and profitability in retail stores. *Production and Operations Management, 24*(2), 201–218. doi:10.1111/poms.12237

Moatti, V., Ren, C. R., Anand, J., & Dussauge, P. (2015). Disentangling the performance effects of efficiency and bargaining power in horizontal growth strategies: An empirical investigation in the global retail industry. *Strategic Management Journal, 36*(5), 745–757. doi:10.1002/smj.2244

Mohr, A., Fastoso, F., Wang, C., & Shirodkar, V. (2014). Testing the regional performance of multinational enterprises in the retail sector: The moderating effects of timing, speed and experience. *British Journal of Management, 25*(Suppl. 1), S100–S115. doi:10.1111/1467-8551.12013

Narteh, B., & Kuada, J. (2014). Customer satisfaction with retail banking services in Ghana. *Thunderbird International Business Review, 56*(4), 353–371. doi:10.1002/tie.21626

Newing, A., Clarke, G. P., & Clarke, M. (2015). Developing and applying a disaggregated retail location model with extended retail demand estimations. *Geographical Analysis, 47*(3), 219–239. doi:10.1111/gean.12052

Paul, J., Sankaranarayanan, K. G., & Mekoth, N. (2016). Consumer satisfaction in retail stores: Theory and implications. *International Journal of Consumer Studies, 40*(6), 635–642. doi:10.1111/ijcs.12279

Peinkofer, S. T., Esper, T. L., Smith, R. J., & Williams, B. D. (2015). Assessing the impact of price promotions on consumer response to online stockouts. *Journal of Business Logistics, 36*(3), 260–272. doi:10.1111/jbl.12095

Qin, F., Rao, U. S., Gurnani, H., & Bollapragada, R. (2014). Role of random capacity risk and the retailer in decentralized supply chains with competing suppliers. *Decision Sciences, 45*(2), 255–279. doi:10.1111/deci.12067

Sousa, R., Amorim, M., Rabinovich, E., & Sodero, A. C. (2015). Customer use of virtual channels in multichannel services: Does type of activity matter? *Decision Sciences, 46*(3), 623–657. doi:10.1111/deci.12142

Stolze, H. J., Mollenkopf, D. A., & Flint, D. J. (2016). What is the right supply chain for your shopper? Exploring the shopper service ecosystem. *Journal of Business Logistics, 37*(2), 185–197. doi:10.1111/jbl.12122 van der Borgh, M., & Schepers, J. J. L. (2014). Do retailers really profit from ambidextrous managers? The impact of frontline mechanisms on new and existing product selling performance. *Journal of Product Innovation Management*, *31*(4), 710–727. doi:10.1111/jpim.12158

Verghese, K., Lewis, H., Lockrey, S., & Williams, H. (2015). Packaging's role in minimizing food loss and waste across the supply chain. *Packaging Technology and Science: An International Journal*, *28*(7), 603–620. doi:10.1002/pts.2127

Wan, X., Huang, X., & Dong, Y. (2016). The moderating role of product categories in the relationship between online fulfillment, procurement, and consumer repurchase intention: A hierarchical analysis. *Journal of Supply Chain Management*, *52*(4), 63–76. doi:10.1111/jscm.12114

Yoon, S., & Oh, J. C. (2016). A cross-national validation of a new retail customer equity model. *International Journal of Consumer Studies*, *40*(6), 652–664. doi:10.1111/ijcs.12289

Zhang, L., & Wei, Y. D. (2015). Foreign hypermarket retailers in China: Spatial penetration, local embeddedness, and structural paradox. *Geographical Review*, *105*(4), 528–550. doi:10.1111/j.1931-0846.2015.12090.x

KEY TERMS AND DEFINITIONS

Consumer Behavior: The study of how, where, when, and why people buy, utilize, and get rid of products or services.

Electronic Commerce: The type of business model, that enables a company or an individual to conduct business over an electronic network, typically the Internet.

Electronic Retailing: The sale of products and services through the Internet.

Marketing: The management process through which products and services move from concept to the customer.

Marketing Strategy: An organization's strategy that combines all of its marketing goals into one comprehensive plan.

Retail: The sale of products or commodities in small quantities directly to consumers.

Retail Management: The process of promoting greater sales and customer satisfaction by gaining a better understanding of the consumers of products and services produced by a company.

Retailing: The commercial transaction in which a buyer intends to consume the products or services.

Chapter 9
Enhancing Closed-Loop Supply Chain in Global Supply Chain

Kijpokin Kasemsap
Suan Sunandha Rajabhat University, Thailand

ABSTRACT

This chapter explains the overview of Closed-Loop Supply Chain (CLSC); CLSC activities and reverse logistics outsourcing in global supply chain; and the applications of CLSC in global supply chain. CLSC, the integration of the forward and reverse supply chains, is an emerging area of interest as firms seek to reduce the costs of product returns, increase profits through value recovery, and meet more rigorous environmental standards. In CLSC, the original manufacturer will take the used product and remake it. CLSC deals with the uncertainty in the timing, location, quantity, and quality of returned products. CLSC integrates the returns of end-of-life products from end-users to retailers, manufacturers, and suppliers for refurbishment, remanufacturing, and recycling. The chapter argues that enhancing CLSC has the potential to reach strategic goals toward sustainability in global supply chain.

INTRODUCTION

Supply chain management (SCM) is the management of material and information flow in a supply chain to provide the highest degree of customer satisfaction at the lowest possible cost (Kasemsap, 2016a), and involves the entire network of entities, directly or indirectly interlinked and interdependent in serving the same customer (Kasemsap, 2017a). Environmental, social, and economic concerns significantly motivate the operation of closed-loop supply chain (CLSC) in many industries (Keyvanshokooh, Ryan, & Kabir, 2016) toward sustainable development (He, 2015). CLSC essentially combines the traditional supply chain (i.e., forward logistics) with reverse logistics, considering the item after it is served its original purpose.

Once the item has been manufactured, shipped, and distributed through a reseller, the manufacturer works to encourage the item's return once it is no longer functional or needed. The successful global retailing requires both strategic and tactical initiatives regarding retail marketing strategies and brand management (Kasemsap, 2016b). Concerning reverse logistics, the items can either be repaired and re-

DOI: 10.4018/978-1-5225-3056-5.ch009

sold, or they can be itemized for the reuse in future products. CLSC is the important perspective related to the design, control, and operation of the supply chain system to maximize the value creation (Thiell, Zuluaga, Montañez, & van Hoof, 2011) over the product life cycle with the recovery of supply chain value (Gaur, Amini, & Rao, 2017) concerning product returns (Govindan, Soleimani, & Kannan, 2015).

Manufacturers are establishing economically viable production and distribution systems that enable the remanufacturing of used products in parallel with the manufacturing of new units. Remanufactured products are typically upgraded to the quality standards of new products, so that they can be sold in new product markets. CLSC is the significant business model for supply chain companies due to the capability of value recovery, environmental sustainability, and special importance given by customers to CLSC practices toward creating business growth (Das & Posinasetti, 2015). Environmental sustainability is important because it ensures people have water and resources, and adopting its practices protects the environment and human health (Kasemsap, 2017b).

Products first flow outbound to a customer (i.e., forward logistics); those same products then flow back inbound, often in an altered condition (i.e., reverse logistics) (Jayaraman, Guide, & Srivastava, 1999). As it is environmentally sustainable, CLSC is one of the most significant strategies in the future (Blumberg, 2004) and aims at generating profit for business enterprises (Basiri, Shemshadi, & Tarokh, 2013) through integrating forward and reverse logistics (Guide & van Wassenhove, 2009), regarding production planning, inventory control, and distribution planning (Poles, 2012) in order to recapture the additional supply chain values (Guide & van Wassenhove, 2006).

The configuration of both forward logistics and reverse logistics has a strong effect on each other (Ghezavati & Nia, 2015). The increasing need for remanufacturing due to resources shortage, environmental deterioration, and new regulations, requires companies to organize their supply chain activities in order to take advantage of integrating forward logistics and reverse logistics (Ramezani, Kimiagari, & Karimi, 2014). Regarding reverse logistics, the manufacturer retrieves the used products from the market where they are dispersed among customers (Liao & Li, 2016). In the CLSC, reverse logistics involves the after-sale operations for the reuse, refurbishing, remanufacturing, and recycling of the end-of-life products (Govindan & Popiuc, 2014).

This chapter is based on a literature review of CLSC. The extensive literature of CLSC provides a contribution to practitioners and researchers by explaining the advanced issues of CLSC in global supply chain.

BACKGROUND

Nowadays, CLSC management is a major approach to implementing sustainable operations (Sahamie, Stindt, & Nuss, 2013). Analyzing carbon emissions is critical for successfully managing sustainable production and consumption (He, Xiong, & Lin, 2016) toward sustainability (Kasemsap, 2016c). The preventive shift to a sustainable supply chain has positive business impacts including risk management, realizing gains through more efficient operations, creating sustainable products, and improving sustainability in global supply chain (Kasemsap, 2017c). Government legislation and consumer awareness on carbon emissions have required industries to seek the alternative ways to reorganize their supply chains (Xu, Pokharel, Elomri, & Mutlu, 2017).

Green supply chain management (GSCM) addresses the industrial ecosystems through various CLSC practices at the product life cycle phases (Sarkis, 2003). GSCM strategies help companies maximize the improvement of Lean Production in operations management (Kasemsap, 2016d). Lean Production implementation dimensions are important to the manufacturing organizations trying to realize manufacturing excellence for competing in the highly dynamic global marketplace (Kasemsap, 2014). The benefits of applying Lean Production include the lower levels of inventory, greater levels of stock turnover, less space required, fewer defects and rework, fewer machine and process breakdowns, higher efficiencies, improved delivery performance, faster development, greater customer satisfaction, improved employee involvement, and higher profits (Kasemsap, 2016e).

GSCM practices can manifest themselves from the process of selecting raw material to final consumption based on the aspects of reduction, reuse, recycling, and recovery (Kasemsap, 2016f). Firms that engage in the industrial symbiosis are acknowledged to belong to an industrial ecosystem (Ashton, 2008). Many supply chain companies spend large amount of money on reverse logistics, which deal with transporting and handling many returned products. Intending to reduce the needs for raw materials and energy in production, recovered products are good for customers, business, and supply chain (Corum, 2016).

The comprehensive evaluation of the CLSC technologies requires the quantitative tools that optimize the managerial decisions at both strategic and tactical levels (Banasik, Kanellopoulos, Claassen, Bloemhof-Ruwaard, & van der Vorst, 2017). The strategic design of CLSC is dealt with supply chain operations, covering procurement, production, storage, distribution, take-back, reprocessing, reuse, and recycling (Golara, Mousavi, Tarokh, & Hosseinzadeh, 2012). Lee et al. (2013) indicated that many supply chain companies need a viable business model that will facilitate them to address the environmental concerns (Wang & Hsu, 2012) and realize the reasonable returns from the returned products or overall supply chain (Guide, Harrison, & van Wassenhove, 2003). The quality of returned products may greatly vary, depending on their previous usage (Hahler & Fleischmann, 2013).

In the reverse logistics, used products obtained from consumers are supplied to a reconditioning facility where those are stored, remanufactured and then shipped for retail sale (Giri & Sharma, 2015). Since CLSC deals with material flows in supply chain, it comprises at least three activities (i.e., purchasing, transportation, and refurbishing) (Özceylan, Paksoy, & Bektas, 2014). A novel mixed integer programming (MIP) model is proposed to guarantee the optimal values of transportation amounts of assembled components and disassembled end-products in the CLSC, while determining the location of facilities (Özceylan, 2016). In addition, the total supply chain profit significantly increases with the increase in the refurbishing activity regarding CLSC (Pazhani & Ravindran, 2014).

ADVANCED ISSUES OF CLOSED-LOOP SUPPLY CHAIN

This section provides the overview of CLSC; CLSC activities and reverse logistics outsourcing in global supply chain; and the applications of CLSC in global supply chain.

Overview of Closed-Loop Supply Chain

Many manufacturers, and their retail customers, are still sitting on the fence, waiting to determine if all the talk about omnichannel distribution is only a fad or if it is something they need to get serious about. The consumer-goods sector is curiously slow to react, even though these are the companies most directly impacted by the rising consumer demand for the same-day delivery, which requires a much more flexible and responsive supply chain.

In CLSC, manufacturer produces a product with an appropriate quality acceptable to customers, and sells it through a retailer in the marketplace (Maiti & Giri, 2015). A third-party provider collects the used products from consumers and sends them back to the manufacturer (Maiti & Giri, 2015). Supply chain provider needs to deliver new or refurbished products to a group of clients under a fixed cyclic schedule (Genc & de Giovanni, 2017), and collects back a random portion of the used products in the delivery cycle for refurbishment (Huynh, So, & Gurnani, 2016). Collected products are evaluated based on product demand and product process (Shakourloo, Kazemi, & Javad, 2016).

In CLSC, the competitive factors are the retail prices of new products and incentives paid to consumers for taking back the used products (Fallah, Eskandari, & Pishvaee, 2015). The return rate of used items depends on the minimum acceptable quality level of product returns (Moshtagh & Taleizadeh, 2017) and the period of product life cycle (Jeihoonian, Zanjani, & Gendreau, 2016). Examples of CLSC include consumer returns, leasing options, and end-of-use returns with remanufacturing (Souza, 2013). The remanufacturing of end-of-life products is important in CLSC (Wei, Govindan, Li, & Zhao, 2015) because manufacturers consider a choice of whether to recover the value in their end-of-life products through remanufacturing (Ferguson & Toktay, 2006).

Management of CLSC is much more complicated than the traditional forward supply chains because the product returns are more uncertain than demands in terms of quantity, quality, and timing (Guide, Jayaraman, Srivastava, & Benton, 2000), and the valuation and setting inventory holding cost for returns are not straightforward (Teunter, van der Laan, & Inderfurth, 2000). The acquisition process of used products faces the high volatility and results in both the uncertain quantity and quality of the recycled products (He, 2017). Uncertain returns are incorporated into the model by determining a satisfactory safety stock level (Kim, Glock, & Kwon, 2014) to buffer the inventory of the used and repairable containers (Cobb, 2016).

Traditional supply chains, which only consist of forward supply chains, are failing short in addressing the raising concerns around environmental protection, and are not effective for reducing the utilization of raw materials as they do not include the activities for recycling the used products (Wang & Hsu, 2010). New product development (NPD) is the process of developing a new product for the marketplace (Kasemsap, 2016g). Forward supply chain activities include NPD, product design and engineering, procurement and production, marketing, sales, distribution, and after-sale service, while reverse supply chain activities refer to those needed to close the loop, such as product acquisition, reverse logistics, disposal, testing, sorting, refurbishing, recovery, recycling, re-marketing, and re-selling (Guide & van Wassenhove, 2009).

The operational decision of interest in matching supply with demand is the quantity of new product to order (Ketzenberg, van der Laan, & Teunter, 2006). The necessary condition for the firms to close the loop is that producing with used components is less costly than manufacturing with new materials (Savaskan, Bhattacharya, & van Wassenhove, 2004). Forward supply chain contains an array of activities resulting in the conversion of raw materials to finished products, and managers are trying to improve the performances of forward supply chain in various areas, such as demand management, procurement, and order fulfillment (Ma & Wang, 2014), whereas reverse supply chain is planned by the supply chain for the possible recovery and disposal of the products in a timely and effective manner (Das & Posinasetti, 2015).

Regarding CLSC, new materials are needed to replace materials which are not recovered by the supply chain system (Özceylan et al., 2014). End users or customers are the source of input materials (Jayaraman et al., 1999). In the reverse supply chain, the flow of used products is such that they are sent from customers back to the collection centers to organize sorting or disassembling for the processes of recovery, reuse, and disposal (Paksoy, Bektas, & Özceylan, 2011). Many CLSC network systems that collect and reprocess end of life products require the disassembly operations (Altekin & Akkan, 2012). Regarding CLSC, manufacturers prefer collecting the used products by themselves (de Giovanni & Zaccour, 2013).

The forward/reverse logistics network design is the strategic supply chain issue (Jindal & Sangwan, 2013) due to its effects on the efficiency and responsiveness of the supply chain (Zohal & Soleimani, 2016). Cost parameters of the supply chain and the demand fluctuations lead to the uncertainty nature of the supply chain (Ma, Yao, Jin, Ren, & Lv, 2016), which can be handled through using a stochastic-possibilistic programming approach (Zhalechian, Tavakkoli-Moghaddam, Zahiri, & Mohammadi, 2016).

Research on integrated products and the CLSC design has focused on the competition and coordination of manufacturers and supply chain partners (Aydin, Kwong, & Ji, 2016). The design of CLSC system should integrate the strategic decisions that minimize the total costs of CLSC (Keskin, Uster, & Cetinkaya, 2010). The total costs of CLSC include fixed location, fixed ordering, inventory holding, transportation, reprocessing costs, and returned products (Al-Salem, Diabat, Dalalah, & Alrefaei, 2016).

Closed-Loop Supply Chain Activities and Reverse Logistics Outsourcing in Global Supply Chain

Outsourcing is the contracting or subcontracting of non-core activities to free up cash, personnel, time, and facilities for activities in which a company holds competitive advantage (Kasemsap, 2016h). The trend in the outsourcing of raw materials, unfinished/semi-finished parts, and final products has been enforcing companies to give more attention to the outsourcing operations and their related decisions (Aissaoui, Haouari, & Hassini, 2007). Many supply chain organizations working on the concept of SCM are responsible for the environmental and social performance of their product and services suppliers (Guarnieri, Sobreiro, Nagano, & Serrano, 2015).

Nowadays, carriers and logistics intermediary perform more roles than what people think they do, because network connection and the ambition to remain competitive make them to take up value-added services (Kasemsap, 2017d). The third-party reverse logistics providers should be the specialists in managing the reverse flow of returned products and provide the value-added services, such as remanufacturing and refurbishing (Rogers & Tibben-Lembke, 1998). Supplier selection, including reverse logistics providers, is recognized as a key operational task for developing the sustainable supply chain (Guarnieri et al., 2015). The infrastructure for reverse logistics management can be managed through the third-party relationship, such as the reverse logistics providers and the municipal organizations (Bai & Sarkis, 2013).

Outsourcing is a popular business strategy and requires the close attention to the contract selection process (Almeida, 2007). Logistics outsourcing can be viewed as motivation to pursue environmental sustainability goals, because the third-party reverse logistics providers can assume the role in SCM toward sustainability (Colicchia, Marchet, Melacin, & Perotti, 2013). When outsourcing is convenient, a manufacturer always chooses a retailer if the outsourcees show equal performance (de Giovanni & Zaccour, 2014). When companies outsource capabilities, they can obtain various benefits, such as improved production efficiency, enhanced product quality, increased process responsiveness, and enlarged product variety (McCarthy, Silvestre, & Kietzmann, 2013).

When outsourcing the product collection, manufacturers significantly needs in order to design the adequate incentives to encourage other supply chain players to achieve the better supply chain results

(Ferguson & Toktay, 2006). For instance, ReCellular utilizes a variety of sources to collect the used phones from cellular airtime providers and third-party collectors (Guide, Jayaraman, & Linton, 2003). Kodak offers customers and retailers some economic incentives to return their cameras because components can be used to produce the new products (Savaskan et al., 2004). Interface Inc., the world's largest provider of commercial carpet tile, leases carpets instead of selling them; the ownership of off-lease products gives Interface Inc. an incentive to recover the residual value of these products (Agrawal & Tokay, 2009). Pitney-Bowes remanufactures off-lease products by offering a trade-in program (Ferguson & Toktay, 2006). Xerox obtains part of its returns from trade-ins, which has resulted in the cost savings of several hundred million dollars per year (Ray, Boyaci, & Aras, 2005). The manufacturer's decision to manage the return process with other supply chain players depends on various factors (Hammond & Beullens, 2007), such as the suitable incentive establishment.

Due to governmental legislation and customer awareness concerning environmental protection (Soleimani & Kannan, 2015), companies cannot ignore the environmental issues (Govindan, Rajendran, Sarkis, & Murugesan, 2013). Various aspects of outsourcing have to be considered by the decision maker concerning outsource activities, such as the cost of the contract and performance of the service (Almeida, 2007). The decision for outsourcing includes obtaining modern technologies, accessing local knowledge, and acquiring government assistance (McCarthy et al., 2013).

Applications of Closed-Loop Supply Chain in Global Supply Chain

There is an increasing awareness of environment problems and the need for sustainable development in academia and business (Kumar & Rahman, 2014). CLSC gains the increasing attention concerning the strict environment legislations (Talaei, Moghaddam, Pishvaee, Bozorgi-Amiri, & Gholamnejad, 2016) and the awareness of resource shortage (Hong, Xu, Du, & Wang, 2015). CLSC can be organized from a business perspective where supply chain organizations seek to maximize the value recovery (Guide & van Wassenhove, 2006) through using effective planning strategy (Nuss, Sahamie, & Stindt, 2015). An enterprise needs to apply the CLSC-related recycling strategy to achieve a better economic effectiveness if the carbon emission regulation is applied (Chen, Wang, Wang, & Chen, 2017).

Recently, the increased attention to the product recovery practices has extended the scope of traditional SCM by emphasizing the operations of collection and remanufacturing (Akçalı, Çetinkaya, & Üster, 2009). Product recovery is an important option for many industries to gain the economic benefits while protecting the environment (Kadambala, Subramanian, Tiwari, Abdulrahman, & Liu, 2017). Choosing the right CLSC configuration is crucial to the product recovery strategies (de Giovanni & Zaccour, 2014), and supply chain companies must consider in the decision-making processes toward product recovery (Rubio & Corominas, 2008).

Strategic success factors (e.g., product design, customer services, and CLSC business models) can modify CLSC processes (Schenkel, Krikke, Caniëls, & van der Laan, 2015) toward increasing business profit (Atasu, Sarvary, & van Wassenhove, 2008) and customer satisfaction. Customer satisfaction is the degree of satisfaction provided by the products or services of a company as measured by the number of repeat customers (Kasemsap, 2017e). By utilizing the processes of reduction, reuse, and remanufacturing, CLSC can reduce waste toward gaining environmental sustainability (Meade, Sarkis, & Presley, 2007). Fahimnia et al. (2013) stated that CLSC practice addresses resource depletion but adds to environmental footprint by its additional steps. The strategic-level decisions relate to the amounts of products flowing on the forward supply chains and reverse supply chains (Özceylan et al., 2014). The tactical-level decisions concern balancing the disassembly lines in the reverse supply chain (Özceylan et al., 2014). An integrated management of both lot-streaming policy and recovery decision is a critical managerial issue in CLSC (Kim, Goyal, & Kim, 2013).

Tabolt et al. (2007) highlighted the relevance of CLSC for business and government. Yang et al. (2009) developed the CLSC network model, including raw material suppliers, manufacturers, retailers, consumers, and recovery centers, in order to optimize the equilibrium state. In a common pattern of CLSC, a manufacturer collects used products and appropriates the benefits (de Giovanni & Zaccour, 2014). Amin and Zhang (2013) investigated the CLSC network including multiple plants, collection centers, demand markets, and products. An essential issue of designing the CLSC network is the determination of number and locations of facilities in each layer of CLSC network (Zarandi, Sisakht, & Davari, 2011). Shi et al. (2011) developed the CLSC system model to determine the quantities of the new and remanufactured products, the prices of products acquired, and the setting price toward gaining an overall maximization of profit in global supply chain.

Robotis et al. (2005) indicated that by adding value by remanufacturing and making the used products more attractive to customers, resellers can increase their profits. Through remanufacturing process, resellers can procure the reduced quantities, and eliminate some of their suppliers that may be providing items whose quality is lower than those of other suppliers in supply chains (Robotis et al., 2005). Recycling of used products and bringing them back to the market provides not only the environmental and customer advantages to original equipment manufacturers (OEMs), but also reducing their production cost (Lee, Gen, & Rhee, 2009). Rezapour et al. (2015) indicated that a large number of brand-owning corporations have focused on remanufacturing activities to produce more reasonably priced products (e.g., Dell, General Motors, Hewlett-Packard, Kodak, and Xerox). Financial gains and environmental improvements reported by these companies have substantially increased the interests in the remanufacturing initiatives (Rezapour et al., 2015).

Many factors affect the performance and effectiveness of CLSC, such as the design of the recycled product, the design of recycle process in terms of CLSC structure and contract design, the effectiveness recovery rate, and the yield of the CLSC (He, 2015). Because they are closer to consumers, retailers are able to achieve a higher return rate than manufacturers (de Giovanni & Zaccour, 2014). Similarly, third-party service providers can exploit their specialized skills to effectively perform the CLSC operations (de Giovanni & Zaccour, 2014). Chuang et al. (2014) investigated three different collection schemes (i.e., manufacturer collection, retailer collection, and third-party collection) for the high-tech product. If the retailer's collection cost is sufficiently high, then the reverse channel structure with manufacturer collecting is optimal to the manufacturer under economies of scale in collection cost (Chuang et al., 2014).

Economic viability is a significant factor for the environmentally sustainable behavior (Bhattacharjee & Cruz, 2015) and CLSC-related strategic policies (Guide & van Wassenhove, 2009), involving supplier, manufacturer, retailer, and collector for recognizing both product demand and product return rates (Chung, Wee, & Yang, 2008). At the retailer, used containers are collected and returned to the supplier (Kim & Glock, 2014). The supplier inspects the returned containers, and either repairs and reuses or disposes them. If reusable packaging material is not returned, the supplier needs to purchase the new packaging material, which increases the cost of operating supply chain (Kim & Glock, 2014).

The accurate forecasting of product returns is important for procurement decisions, production planning, and inventory and disposal management in the remanufacturing operations (Clottey, Benton, & Srivastava, 2012). Procurement is the execution of buying products and services in modern supply chain and various operations (Kasemsap, 2017f). The individual in charge of production planning adjusts the workforce and process flow to obtain the regular utilization of organizational resources with minimal downtime, minimal bottlenecks, and a level of output consistent with all the resources being put into the manufacturing processes (Kasemsap, 2017g).

Practitioners and academicians are paying an increasing interest to CLSC, aiming to collect and recycle the used products, with the objective of linking both environmental issues and business opportunities (Guide & van Wassenhowe, 2009). In order to gain the successful remanufacturing operations toward green supply chain, the important parameters are required: market demand for remanufactured products, technology to remanufacture, stable product technology, standard interchangeable parts, and a lower remanufacture cost than the price of a new product (Lund, 1998). Companies create the different strategies to encourage customers to buy the remanufactured products (Hashemi, Chen, & Fang, 2014). Green consumers and consumers, who consider remanufactured products green, typically recognize remanufactured products more attractive in green supply chain (Abbey, Meloy, Guide, & Atalay, 2015).

Tracking the position of packaging material in a supply chain is an important measure to increase return flows and to improve their predictability (Kim & Glock, 2014). Some best practices illustrate that radio frequency identification (RFID) systems may be a suitable tool to improve the visibility of assets in the supply chain and to prevent losses, and that RFID may reduce the amount of supply chain activity that is required for managing the flow of materials in the supply chain (Kim & Glock, 2014). RFID solutions can be utilized to reduce the operating costs through decreasing labor costs, enhancing automation, improving tracking, and preventing the loss of materials (Kasemsap, 2015). RFID makes supply chain more precise and improves the reliability of the supply chain in an effective manner (Kasemsap, 2017h). Hellstrom (2009) presented two case studies conducted at IKEA and Arla Foods and indicated that both companies are able to reduce the loss of containers through implementing RFID systems in supply chain.

FUTURE RESEARCH DIRECTIONS

The classification of the extensive literature in the domains of CLSC will provide the potential opportunities for future research. CLSC process effectively delivers an energy-efficient product made from recycled content that is less expensive, with the potential to show the greater cost savings in global supply chain. Practitioners and researchers should acknowledge the applicability of a more multidisciplinary approach toward research activities in implementing CLSC in terms of sustainable business-related variables (e.g., green operations, green distribution, green procurement, green design, and green marketing). Promoting sustainable consumption is equally important to limit negative environmental and social externalities as well as to provide markets for sustainable products (Kasemsap, 2017i). Effective waste management method reduces the consumption of natural resources and lowers the ultimate needs for waste disposal (Kasemsap, 2017j). Considering the associations among CLSC, sustainable consumption, and waste management in global supply chain should be further studied.

CONCLUSION

This chapter indicated the overview of CLSC; CLSC activities and reverse logistics outsourcing in global supply chain; and the applications of CLSC in global supply chain. Dealing with both forward and reverse chain simultaneously, CLSC plays the important role as an enabler for sustainability. In a reverse-flow supply chain, the product is collected after consumer use and recycled. What makes this system unique is that the discarded product is processed by other companies and used for something different. This makes it easier for the original manufacturer, because it does not have to remake the product. CLSC is similar to a reverse-flow supply chain, albeit with a more hands-on approach. In a closed-loop system, the original manufacturer will take the used product and remake it.

CLSC activities (e.g., remanufacturing, recycling, dismantling for spare parts, and reverse logistics) help many companies tap into the new revenue streams by finding secondary markets for their products, all while reducing their overall carbon footprint. CLSC deals with the uncertainty in the timing, location, quantity, and quality of returned products. CLSC integrates the returns of end-of-life products from end-users to retailers, manufacturers, and suppliers for refurbishment, remanufacturing, and recycling. Enhancing CLSC has the potential to reach strategic goals toward sustainability in global supply chain.

REFERENCES

Abbey, J. D., Meloy, M. G., Guide, V. D. R. Jr, & Atalay, S. (2015). Remanufactured products in closed-loop supply chains for consumer goods. *Production and Operations Management*, *24*(3), 488–503. doi:10.1111/poms.12238

Agrawal, V., & Tokay, L. B. (2009). Interdisciplinarity in closed-loop supply chain management research. In F. Ferguson & G. Souza (Eds.), *Closed-loop supply chains: New developments to improve the sustainability of business practices* (pp. 197–214). Boca Raton, FL: CRC Press.

Aissaoui, N., Haouari, M., & Hassini, E. (2007). Supplier selection and order lot sizing modeling: A review. *Computers & Operations Research*, *34*(12), 3516–3540. doi:10.1016/j.cor.2006.01.016

Akçalı, E., Çetinkaya, S., & Üster, H. (2009). Network design for reverse and closed-loop supply chains: An annotated bibliography of models and solution approaches. *Networks*, *53*(3), 231–248. doi:10.1002/net.20267

Al-Salem, M., Diabat, A., Dalalah, D., & Alrefaei, M. (2016). A closed-loop supply chain management problem: Reformulation and piecewise linearization. *Journal of Manufacturing Systems*, *40*, 1–8. doi:10.1016/j.jmsy.2016.04.001

Almeida, A. T. (2007). Multicriteria decision model for outsourcing contracts selection based on utility function and ELECTRE method. *Computers & Operations Research*, *34*(12), 3569–3574. doi:10.1016/j.cor.2006.01.003

Altekin, F. T., & Akkan, C. (2012). Task-failure-driven rebalancing of disassembly lines. *International Journal of Production Research*, *50*(18), 4955–4976. doi:10.1080/00207543.2011.616915

Amin, S. H., & Zhang, G. (2013). A multi-objective facility location model for closed-loop supply chain network under uncertain demand and return. *Applied Mathematical Modelling*, *37*(6), 4165–4176. doi:10.1016/j.apm.2012.09.039

Ashton, W. (2008). Understanding the organization of industrial ecosystems. *Journal of Industrial Ecology*, *12*(1), 34–51. doi:10.1111/j.1530-9290.2008.00002.x

Atasu, A., Sarvary, M., & van Wassenhove, L. N. (2008). Remanufacturing as a marketing strategy. *Management Science*, *54*(10), 1731–1746. doi:10.1287/mnsc.1080.0893

Aydin, R., Kwong, C. K., & Ji, P. (2016). Coordination of the closed-loop supply chain for product line design with consideration of remanufactured products. *Journal of Cleaner Production*, *114*, 286–298. doi:10.1016/j.jclepro.2015.05.116

Bai, C., & Sarkis, J. (2013). Flexibility in reverse logistics: A framework and evaluation approach. *Journal of Cleaner Production*, *47*(1), 306–316. doi:10.1016/j.jclepro.2013.01.005

Banasik, A., Kanellopoulos, A., Claassen, G. D. H., Bloemhof-Ruwaard, J. M., & van der Vorst, J. G. A. J. (2017). Closing loops in agricultural supply chains using multi-objective optimization: A case study of an industrial mushroom supply chain. *International Journal of Production Economics*, *183*, 409–420. doi:10.1016/j.ijpe.2016.08.012

Basiri, A. H., Shemshadi, A., & Tarokh, M. J. (2013). A closed-loop logistics model for green supply chain management. In Z. Luo (Ed.), *Technological solutions for modern logistics and supply chain management* (pp. 318–333). Hershey, PA: IGI Global. doi:10.4018/978-1-4666-2773-4.ch019

Bhattacharjee, S., & Cruz, J. (2015). Economic sustainability of closed loop supply chains: A holistic model for decision and policy analysis. *Decision Support Systems*, *77*, 67–86. doi:10.1016/j.dss.2015.05.011

Blumberg, D. F. (2004). *Introduction to management of reverse logistics and closed loop supply chain processes*. Boca Raton, FL: CRC Press.

Chen, Y. W., Wang, L. C., Wang, A., & Chen, T. L. (2017). A particle swarm approach for optimizing a multi-stage closed loop supply chain for the solar cell industry. *Robotics and Computer-integrated Manufacturing*, *43*, 111–123. doi:10.1016/j.rcim.2015.10.006

Chuang, C., Wang, C., & Zhao, Y. (2014). Closed-loop supply chain models for a high-tech product under alternative reverse channel and collection cost structures. *International Journal of Production Economics*, *156*, 108–123. doi:10.1016/j.ijpe.2014.05.008

Chung, S. L., Wee, H. M., & Yang, P. C. (2008). Optimal policy for a closed-loop supply chain inventory system with remanufacturing. *Mathematical and Computer Modelling*, *48*(5/6), 867–881. doi:10.1016/j.mcm.2007.11.014

Clottey, T., Benton, W. C. Jr, & Srivastava, R. (2012). Forecasting product returns for remanufacturing operations. *Decision Sciences*, *43*(4), 589–614. doi:10.1111/j.1540-5915.2012.00362.x

Cobb, B. R. (2016). Inventory control for returnable transport items in a closed-loop supply chain. *Transportation Research Part E, Logistics and Transportation Review*, *86*, 53–68. doi:10.1016/j.tre.2015.12.010

Colicchia, C., Marchet, G., Melacin, M., & Perotti, S. (2013). Building environmental sustainability: Empirical evidence from logistics service providers. *Journal of Cleaner Production*, *59*, 197–209. doi:10.1016/j.jclepro.2013.06.057

Corum, A. (2016). Remanufacturing, an added value product recovery strategy. In U. Akkucuk (Ed.), *Handbook of research on waste management techniques for sustainability* (pp. 347–367). Hershey, PA: IGI Global. doi:10.4018/978-1-4666-9723-2.ch018

Das, K., & Posinasetti, N. R. (2015). Addressing environmental concerns in closed loop supply chain design and planning. *International Journal of Production Economics*, *163*, 34–47. doi:10.1016/j.ijpe.2015.02.012

de Giovanni, P., & Zaccour, G. (2013). Cost-revenue sharing in a closed loop supply chain. *Annals of the International Society of Dynamic Games*, *12*, 395–421. doi:10.1007/978-0-8176-8355-9_20

de Giovanni, P., & Zaccour, G. (2014). A two-period game of a closed-loop supply chain. *European Journal of Operational Research*, *232*(1), 22–40. doi:10.1016/j.ejor.2013.06.032

Fahimnia, B., Sarkis, J., Dehghanian, F., Banihashemi, N., & Rahman, S. (2013). The impact of carbon pricing on a closed-loop supply chain: An Australian case study. *Journal of Cleaner Production*, *59*, 210–225. doi:10.1016/j.jclepro.2013.06.056

Fallah, H., Eskandari, H., & Pishvaee, M. S. (2015). Competitive closed-loop supply chain network design under uncertainty. *Journal of Manufacturing Systems*, *37*, 649–661. doi:10.1016/j.jmsy.2015.01.005

Ferguson, M. E., & Toktay, L. B. (2006). The effect of competition on recovery strategies. *Production and Operations Management*, *15*(3), 351–368. doi:10.1111/j.1937-5956.2006.tb00250.x

Gaur, J., Amini, M., & Rao, A. K. (2017). Closed-loop supply chain configuration for new and reconditioned products: An integrated optimization model. *Omega*, *66*, 212–223. doi:10.1016/j.omega.2015.11.008

Genc, T. S., & de Giovanni, P. (2017). Trade-in and save: A two-period closed-loop supply chain game with price and technology dependent returns. *International Journal of Production Economics*, *183*, 514–527. doi:10.1016/j.ijpe.2016.07.012

Ghezavati, V., & Nia, N. S. (2015). Development of an optimization model for product returns using genetic algorithms and simulated annealing. *Soft Computing*, *19*(11), 3055–3069. doi:10.1007/s00500-014-1465-8

Giri, B. C., & Sharma, S. (2015). Optimizing a closed-loop supply chain with manufacturing defects and quality dependent return rate. *Journal of Manufacturing Systems*, *35*, 92–111. doi:10.1016/j.jmsy.2014.11.014

Golara, S., Mousavi, N., Tarokh, M. J., & Hosseinzadeh, M. (2012). Closed-loop supply chain network design with recovery of glass containers. *International Journal of Strategic Decision Sciences*, *3*(4), 1–26. doi:10.4018/jsds.2012100101

Govindan, K., & Popiuc, M. N. (2014). Reverse supply chain coordination by revenue sharing contract: A case for the personal computers industry. *European Journal of Operational Research*, *233*(2), 326–336. doi:10.1016/j.ejor.2013.03.023

Govindan, K., Rajendran, S., Sarkis, J., & Murugesan, P. (2013). Multi criteria decision making approaches for green supplier evaluation and selection: A literature review. *Journal of Cleaner Production*, *98*, 66–83. doi:10.1016/j.jclepro.2013.06.046

Govindan, K., Soleimani, H., & Kannan, D. (2015). Reverse logistics and closed-loop supply chain: A comprehensive review to explore the future. *European Journal of Operational Research*, *240*(3), 603–626. doi:10.1016/j.ejor.2014.07.012

Guarnieri, P., Sobreiro, V. A., Nagano, M. S., & Serrano, A. L. M. (2015). The challenge of selecting and evaluating third-party reverse logistics providers in a multicriteria perspective: A Brazilian case. *Journal of Cleaner Production*, *96*, 209–219. doi:10.1016/j.jclepro.2014.05.040

Guide, V. D. R. Jr, Harrison, T. P., & van Wassenhove, L. N. (2003). The challenge of closed-loop supply chains. *Interfaces*, *33*(6), 3–6. doi:10.1287/inte.33.6.3.25182

Guide, V. D. R. Jr, Jayaraman, V., & Linton, J. D. (2003). Building contingency planning for closed-loop supply chains with product recovery. *Journal of Operations Management*, *21*(3), 259–279. doi:10.1016/S0272-6963(02)00110-9

Guide, V. D. R. Jr, Jayaraman, V., Srivastava, R., & Benton, W. C. (2000). Supply chain management for recoverable manufacturing systems. *Interfaces*, *30*(3), 125–142. doi:10.1287/inte.30.3.125.11656

Guide, V. D. R. Jr, & van Wassenhove, L. N. (2006). Closed-loop supply chains: An introduction to the feature issue (Part 1). *Production and Operations Management*, *15*(3), 345–350. doi:10.1111/j.1937-5956.2006.tb00249.x

Guide, V. D. R. Jr, & van Wassenhove, L. N. (2009). The evolution of closed-loop supply chain research. *Operations Research*, *57*(1), 10–18. doi:10.1287/opre.1080.0628

Hahler, S., & Fleischmann, M. (2013). The value of acquisition price differentiation in reverse logistics. *Journal of Business Economics*, *83*(1), 1–28. doi:10.1007/s11573-012-0641-5

Hammond, D., & Beullens, P. (2007). Closed-loop supply chain network equilibrium under legislation. *European Journal of Operational Research*, *183*(2), 895–908. doi:10.1016/j.ejor.2006.10.033

Hashemi, V., Chen, M., & Fang, L. (2014). Process planning for closed-loop aerospace manufacturing supply chain and environmental impact reduction. *Computers & Industrial Engineering*, *75*(9), 87–95. doi:10.1016/j.cie.2014.06.005

He, R., Xiong, Y., & Lin, Z. (2016). Carbon emissions in a dual channel closed loop supply chain: The impact of consumer free riding behavior. *Journal of Cleaner Production*, *134*, 384–394. doi:10.1016/j.jclepro.2016.02.142

He, Y. (2015). Acquisition pricing and remanufacturing decisions in a closed-loop supply chain. *International Journal of Production Economics*, *163*, 48–60. doi:10.1016/j.ijpe.2015.02.002

He, Y. (2017). Supply risk sharing in a closed-loop supply chain. *International Journal of Production Economics*, *183*, 39–52. doi:10.1016/j.ijpe.2016.10.012

Hellstrom, D. (2009). The cost and process of implementing RFID technology to manage and control returnable transport items. *International Journal of Logistics: Research and Applications*, *12*(1), 1–21. doi:10.1080/13675560802168526

Hong, X., Xu, L., Du, P., & Wang, W. (2015). Joint advertising, pricing and collection decisions in a closed-loop supply chain. *International Journal of Production Economics*, *167*, 12–22. doi:10.1016/j.ijpe.2015.05.001

Huynh, C. H., So, K. C., & Gurnani, H. (2016). Managing a closed-loop supply system with random returns and a cyclic delivery schedule. *European Journal of Operational Research, 255*(3), 787–796. doi:10.1016/j.ejor.2016.05.035

Jayaraman, V., Guide, V. D. R. Jr, & Srivastava, R. (1999). A closed-loop logistics model for remanufacturing. *The Journal of the Operational Research Society, 50*(5), 497–508. doi:10.1057/palgrave.jors.2600716

Jeihoonian, M., Zanjani, M. K., & Gendreau, M. (2016). Accelerating Benders decomposition for closed-loop supply chain network design: Case of used durable products with different quality levels. *European Journal of Operational Research, 251*(3), 830–845. doi:10.1016/j.ejor.2015.12.052

Jindal, A., & Sangwan, K. S. (2013). *An integrated fuzzy multi-criteria evaluation of sustainable reverse logistics network models.* Paper presented at the 2013 IEEE International Conference on Fuzzy Systems (FUZZ-IEEE 2013), Hyderabad, India. doi:10.1109/FUZZ-IEEE.2013.6622469

Kadambala, D. K., Subramanian, N., Tiwari, M. K., Abdulrahman, M., & Liu, C. (2017). Closed loop supply chain networks: Designs for energy and time value efficiency. *International Journal of Production Economics, 183*, 382–393. doi:10.1016/j.ijpe.2016.02.004

Kasemsap, K. (2014). The role of Lean Production on organizational performance. In V. Modrák & P. Semančo (Eds.), *Handbook of research on design and management of Lean Production systems* (pp. 358–388). Hershey, PA: IGI Global. doi:10.4018/978-1-4666-5039-8.ch017

Kasemsap, K. (2015). The role of radio frequency identification in modern libraries. In S. Thanuskodi (Ed.), *Handbook of research on inventive digital tools for collection management and development in modern libraries* (pp. 361–385). Hershey, PA: IGI Global. doi:10.4018/978-1-4666-8178-1.ch021

Kasemsap, K. (2016a). Fostering supply chain management in global business. In B. Christiansen (Ed.), *Handbook of research on global supply chain management* (pp. 45–71). Hershey, PA: IGI Global. doi:10.4018/978-1-4666-9639-6.ch003

Kasemsap, K. (2016b). Retail marketing strategies and brand management: A global retail industry perspective. *International Journal of Social and Organizational Dynamics in IT, 5*(2), 66–78. doi:10.4018/IJSODIT.2016070106

Kasemsap, K. (2016c). Multifaceted applications of green supply chain management. In A. Jean-Vasile (Ed.), *Food science, production, and engineering in contemporary economies* (pp. 327–354). Hershey, PA: IGI Global. doi:10.4018/978-1-5225-0341-5.ch014

Kasemsap, K. (2016d). The roles of lean and green supply chain management strategies in the global business environments. In S. Joshi & R. Joshi (Eds.), *Designing and implementing global supply chain management* (pp. 152–173). Hershey, PA: IGI Global. doi:10.4018/978-1-4666-9720-1.ch008

Kasemsap, K. (2016e). Applying Lean Production and Six Sigma in global operations. In U. Akkucuk (Ed.), *Handbook of research on waste management techniques for sustainability* (pp. 44–74). Hershey, PA: IGI Global. doi:10.4018/978-1-4666-9723-2.ch003

Kasemsap, K. (2016f). Multifaceted applications of green supply chain management. In A. Jean-Vasile (Ed.), *Food science, production, and engineering in contemporary economies* (pp. 327–354). Hershey, PA: IGI Global. doi:10.4018/978-1-5225-0341-5.ch014

Kasemsap, K. (2016g). Creating product innovation strategies through knowledge management in global business. In A. Goel & P. Singhal (Eds.), *Product innovation through knowledge management and social media strategies* (pp. 330–357). Hershey, PA: IGI Global. doi:10.4018/978-1-4666-9607-5.ch015

Kasemsap, K. (2016h). The role of strategic outsourcing in global business. In G. Alor-Hernández, C. Sánchez-Ramírez, & J. García-Alcaraz (Eds.), *Handbook of research on managerial strategies for achieving optimal performance in industrial processes* (pp. 325–357). Hershey, PA: IGI Global. doi:10.4018/978-1-5225-0130-5.ch016

Kasemsap, K. (2017a). Mastering fashion supply chain management and new product development in the digital age. In A. Vecchi (Ed.), *Advanced fashion technology and operations management* (pp. 65–91). Hershey, PA: IGI Global. doi:10.4018/978-1-5225-1865-5.ch003

Kasemsap, K. (2017b). Sustainability, environmental sustainability, and sustainable tourism: Advanced issues and implications. In N. Ray (Ed.), *Business infrastructure for sustainability in developing economies* (pp. 1–24). Hershey, PA: IGI Global. doi:10.4018/978-1-5225-2041-2.ch001

Kasemsap, K. (2017c). Advocating sustainable supply chain management and sustainability in global supply chain. In M. Khan, M. Hussain, & M. Ajmal (Eds.), *Green supply chain management for sustainable business practice* (pp. 234–271). Hershey, PA: IGI Global. doi:10.4018/978-1-5225-0635-5.ch009

Kasemsap, K. (2017d). The roles of logistics service providers and supply chain integration in global supply chain. In L. Saglietto & C. Cezanne (Eds.), *Global intermediation and logistics service providers* (pp. 265–285). Hershey, PA: IGI Global. doi:10.4018/978-1-5225-2133-4.ch014

Kasemsap, K. (2017e). Mastering customer service, customer experience, and customer orientation in the hospitality and tourism industry. In P. Vasant & K. M. (Eds.), Handbook of research on holistic optimization techniques in the hospitality, tourism, and travel industry (pp. 115–140). Hershey, PA: IGI Global. doi:10.4018/978-1-5225-1054-3.ch005

Kasemsap, K. (2017f). Mastering electronic procurement, green public procurement, and public procurement for innovation. In R. Shakya (Ed.), *Digital governance and e-government principles applied to public procurement* (pp. 29–55). Hershey, PA: IGI Global. doi:10.4018/978-1-5225-2203-4.ch002

Kasemsap, K. (2017g). Production planning: Advanced issues and implications. In U. Akkucuk (Ed.), *Ethics and sustainability in global supply chain management* (pp. 50–72). Hershey, PA: IGI Global. doi:10.4018/978-1-5225-2036-8.ch003

Kasemsap, K. (2017h). Radio frequency identification and mobile ad-hoc network: Theories and applications. In S. Bhattacharyya, N. Das, D. Bhattacharjee, & A. Mukherjee (Eds.), *Handbook of research on recent developments in intelligent communication application* (pp. 63–95). Hershey, PA: IGI Global. doi:10.4018/978-1-5225-1785-6.ch003

Kasemsap, K. (2017i). Mastering consumer attitude and sustainable consumption in the digital age. In N. Suki (Ed.), *Handbook of research on leveraging consumer psychology for effective customer engagement* (pp. 16–41). Hershey, PA: IGI Global. doi:10.4018/978-1-5225-0746-8.ch002

Kasemsap, K. (2017j). Environmental management and waste management: Principles and applications. In U. Akkucuk (Ed.), *Ethics and sustainability in global supply chain management* (pp. 26–49). Hershey, PA: IGI Global. doi:10.4018/978-1-5225-2036-8.ch002

Keskin, B. B., Uster, H., & Cetinkaya, S. (2010). Integration of strategic and tactical decisions for vendor selection under capacity constraints. *Computers & Operations Research, 37*(12), 2182–2191. doi:10.1016/j.cor.2010.03.008

Ketzenberg, M. E., van der Laan, E., & Teunter, R. H. (2006). Value of information in closed loop supply chains. *Production and Operations Management, 15*(3), 393–406. doi:10.1111/j.1937-5956.2006.tb00253.x

Keyvanshokooh, E., Ryan, S. M., & Kabir, E. (2016). Hybrid robust and stochastic optimization for closed-loop supply chain network design using accelerated Benders decomposition. *European Journal of Operational Research, 249*(1), 76–92. doi:10.1016/j.ejor.2015.08.028

Kim, T., & Glock, C. H. (2014). On the use of RFID in the management of reusable containers in closed-loop supply chains under stochastic container return quantities. *Transportation Research Part E, Logistics and Transportation Review, 64*, 12–27. doi:10.1016/j.tre.2014.01.011

Kim, T., Glock, C. H., & Kwon, Y. (2014). A closed-loop supply chain for deteriorating products under stochastic container return times. *Omega, 43*, 30–40. doi:10.1016/j.omega.2013.06.002

Kim, T., Goyal, S. K., & Kim, C. H. (2013). Lot-streaming policy for forward-reverse logistics with recovery capacity investment. *International Journal of Advanced Manufacturing Technology, 68*(1), 509–522. doi:10.1007/s00170-013-4748-9

Kumar, A., & Rahman, S. (2014). RFID-enabled process reengineering of closed-loop supply chains in the healthcare industry of Singapore. *Journal of Cleaner Production, 85*, 382–394. doi:10.1016/j.jclepro.2014.04.037

Lee, H., Zhang, T., Boile, M., Theofanis, S., & Choo, S. (2013). Designing an integrated logistics network in a supply chain system. *KSCE Journal of Civil Engineering, 17*(4), 806–814. doi:10.1007/s12205-013-0087-5

Lee, J. E., Gen, M., & Rhee, K. G. (2009). Network model and optimization of reverse logistics by hybrid genetic algorithm. *Computers & Industrial Engineering, 56*(3), 951–964. doi:10.1016/j.cie.2008.09.021

Liao, B., & Li, B. (2016). Warranty as an effective strategy for remanufactured product. *International Journal of Information Systems and Supply Chain Management, 9*(3), 83–98. doi:10.4018/IJISSCM.2016070105

Lund, R. (1998). *Remanufacturing: An American resource.* Paper presented at the 5th International Congress for Environmentally Conscious Design and Manufacturing, Rochester, NY.

Ma, J., & Wang, H. (2014). Complexity analysis of dynamic noncooperative game models for closed-loop supply chain with product recovery. *Applied Mathematical Modelling*, *38*(23), 5562–5572. doi:10.1016/j.apm.2014.02.027

Ma, R., Yao, L., Jin, M., Ren, P., & Lv, Z. (2016). Robust environmental closed-loop supply chain design under uncertainty. *Chaos, Solitons, and Fractals*, *89*, 195–202. doi:10.1016/j.chaos.2015.10.028

Maiti, T., & Giri, B. C. (2015). A closed loop supply chain under retail price and product quality dependent demand. *Journal of Manufacturing Systems*, *37*, 624–637. doi:10.1016/j.jmsy.2014.09.009

McCarthy, I. P., Silvestre, B. S., & Kietzmann, J. H. (2013). Understanding outsourcing contexts through information asymmetry and capability fit. *Production Planning & Control: The Management of Operations*, *24*(4/5), 277–283. doi:10.1080/09537287.2011.648765

Meade, L., Sarkis, J., & Presley, A. (2007). The theory and practice of reverse logistics. *International Journal of Logistics Systems and Management*, *3*(1), 56–84. doi:10.1504/IJLSM.2007.012070

Moshtagh, M. S., & Taleizadeh, A. A. (2017). Stochastic integrated manufacturing and remanufacturing model with shortage, rework and quality based return rate in a closed loop supply chain. *Journal of Cleaner Production*, *141*, 1548–1573. doi:10.1016/j.jclepro.2016.09.173

Nuss, C., Sahamie, R., & Stindt, D. (2015). The reverse supply chain planning matrix: A classification scheme for planning problems in reverse logistics. *International Journal of Management Reviews*, *17*(4), 413–436. doi:10.1111/ijmr.12046

Özceylan, E. (2016). Simultaneous optimization of closed- and open-loop supply chain networks with common components. *Journal of Manufacturing Systems*, *41*, 143–156. doi:10.1016/j.jmsy.2016.08.008

Özceylan, E., Paksoy, T., & Bektas, T. (2014). Modeling and optimizing the integrated problem of closed-loop supply chain network design and disassembly line balancing. *Transportation Research Part E, Logistics and Transportation Review*, *61*, 142–164. doi:10.1016/j.tre.2013.11.001

Paksoy, T., Bektas, T., & Özceylan, E. (2011). Operational and environmental performance measures in a multi-product closed-loop supply chain. *Transportation Research Part E, Logistics and Transportation Review*, *47*(4), 532–546. doi:10.1016/j.tre.2010.12.001

Pazhani, S., & Ravindran, A. R. (2014). Design of closed loop supply chain networks. *International Journal of Business Analytics*, *1*(1), 43–66. doi:10.4018/ijban.2014010104

Poles, R. (2012). Modeling closed loop supply chain systems. In Z. Luo (Ed.), *Advanced analytics for green and sustainable economic development: Supply chain models and financial technologies* (pp. 157–186). Hershey, PA: IGI Global. doi:10.4018/978-1-61350-156-6.ch010

Ramezani, M., Kimiagari, A. M., & Karimi, B. (2014). Closed-loop supply chain network design: A financial approach. *Applied Mathematical Modelling*, *38*(15/16), 4099–4119. doi:10.1016/j.apm.2014.02.004

Ray, S., Boyaci, T., & Aras, N. (2005). Optimal prices and trade-in rebates for durable, remanufacturable products. *Manufacturing and Services Operations Management*, *7*(3), 208–228. doi:10.1287/msom.1050.0080

Rezapour, S., Farahani, R. Z., Fahimnia, B., Govindan, K., & Mansouri, Y. (2015). Competitive closed-loop supply chain network design with price-dependent demands. *Journal of Cleaner Production*, *93*, 251–272. doi:10.1016/j.jclepro.2014.12.095

Robotis, A., Bhattacharya, S., & van Wassenhove, L. N. (2005). The effect of remanufacturing on procurement decisions for resellers in secondary markets. *European Journal of Operational Research*, *163*(3), 688–705. doi:10.1016/j.ejor.2004.01.013

Rogers, D. S., & Tibben-Lembke, R. S. (1998). *Going backwards: Reverse logistics trends and practices*. Pittsburgh, PA: Reverse Logistics Executive Council.

Rubio, S., & Corominas, A. (2008). Optimal manufacturing-remanufacturing policies in a lean production environment. *Computers & Industrial Engineering*, *55*(1), 234–242. doi:10.1016/j.cie.2007.12.009

Sahamie, R., Stindt, D., & Nuss, C. (2013). Transdisciplinary research in sustainable operations: An application to closed-loop supply chains. *Business Strategy and the Environment*, *22*(4), 245–268. doi:10.1002/bse.1771

Sarkis, J. (2003). A strategic decision framework for green supply chain management. *Journal of Cleaner Production*, *11*(4), 397–409. doi:10.1016/S0959-6526(02)00062-8

Savaskan, R. C., Bhattacharya, S., & van Wassenhove, L. N. (2004). Closed loop supply chain models with product remanufacturing. *Management Science*, *50*(2), 239–252. doi:10.1287/mnsc.1030.0186

Schenkel, M., Krikke, H., Caniëls, M. C. J., & van der Laan, E. (2015). Creating integral value for stakeholders in closed loop supply chains. *Journal of Purchasing and Supply Management*, *21*(3), 155–166. doi:10.1016/j.pursup.2015.04.003

Shakourloo, A., Kazemi, A., & Javad, M. O. M. (2016). A new model for more effective supplier selection and remanufacturing process in a closed-loop supply chain. *Applied Mathematical Modelling*, *40*(23/24), 9914–9931. doi:10.1016/j.apm.2016.06.039

Shi, J., Zhang, G., & Sha, J. (2011). Optimal production and pricing policy for a closed loop system. *Resources, Conservation and Recycling*, *55*(6), 639–647. doi:10.1016/j.resconrec.2010.05.016

Soleimani, H., & Kannan, G. (2015). A hybrid particle swarm optimization and genetic algorithm for closed-loop supply chain network design in large-scale networks. *Applied Mathematical Modelling*, *39*(14), 3990–4012. doi:10.1016/j.apm.2014.12.016

Souza, G. C. (2013). Closed-loop supply chains: A critical review, and future research. *Decision Sciences*, *44*(1), 7–38. doi:10.1111/j.1540-5915.2012.00394.x

Tabolt, S., Lefebvre, E., & Lefebvre, L. A. (2007). Closed-loop supply chain activities and derived benefits in manufacturing SMEs. *Journal of Manufacturing Technology Management*, *18*(6), 627–658. doi:10.1108/17410380710763831

Talaei, M., Moghaddam, B. F., Pishvaee, M. S., Bozorgi-Amiri, A., & Gholamnejad, S. (2016). A robust fuzzy optimization model for carbon-efficient closed-loop supply chain network design problem: A numerical illustration in electronics industry. *Journal of Cleaner Production, 113*, 662–673. doi:10.1016/j.jclepro.2015.10.074

Teunter, R., van der Laan, E., & Inderfurth, K. (2000). How to set the holding cost rates in average inventory models with reverse logistics. *Omega, 28*(4), 409–415. doi:10.1016/S0305-0483(99)00070-5

Thiell, M., Zuluaga, J. P., Montañez, J. P., & van Hoof, B. (2011). Green logistics: Global practices and their implementation in emerging markets. In Z. Luo (Ed.), *Green finance and sustainability: Environmentally-aware business models and technologies* (pp. 334–357). Hershey, PA: IGI Global. doi:10.4018/978-1-60960-531-5.ch018

Wang, H. F., & Hsu, H. W. (2010). A closed-loop logistic model with a spanning-tree based genetic algorithm. *Computers & Operations Research, 37*(2), 376–389. doi:10.1016/j.cor.2009.06.001

Wang, H. F., & Hsu, H. W. (2012). A possibilistic approach to the modeling and resolution of uncertain closed-loop logistics. *Fuzzy Optimization and Decision Making, 11*(2), 177–208. doi:10.1007/s10700-012-9120-2

Wei, J., Govindan, K., Li, Y., & Zhao, J. (2015). Pricing and collecting decisions in a closed-loop supply chain with symmetric and asymmetric information. *Computers & Operations Research, 54*, 257–265. doi:10.1016/j.cor.2013.11.021

Xu, Z., Pokharel, S., Elomri, A., & Mutlu, F. (2017). Emission policies and their analysis for the design of hybrid and dedicated closed-loop supply chains. *Journal of Cleaner Production, 142*, 4152–4168. doi:10.1016/j.jclepro.2016.09.192

Yang, G., Wang, Z., & Li, X. (2009). The optimization of the closed-loop supply chain network. *Transportation Research Part E, Logistics and Transportation Review, 45*(1), 16–28. doi:10.1016/j.tre.2008.02.007

Zarandi, M. H. F., Sisakht, A., & Davari, S. (2011). Design of a closed-loop supply chain (CLSC) model using an interactive fuzzy goal programming. *International Journal of Advanced Manufacturing Technology, 56*(5), 809–821. doi:10.1007/s00170-011-3212-y

Zhalechian, M., Tavakkoli-Moghaddam, R., Zahiri, B., & Mohammadi, M. (2016). Sustainable design of a closed-loop location-routing-inventory supply chain network under mixed uncertainty. *Transportation Research Part E, Logistics and Transportation Review, 89*, 182–214. doi:10.1016/j.tre.2016.02.011

Zohal, M., & Soleimani, H. (2016). Developing an ant colony approach for green closed-loop supply chain network design: A case study in gold industry. *Journal of Cleaner Production, 133*, 314–337. doi:10.1016/j.jclepro.2016.05.091

ADDITIONAL READING

Abdallah, T., Diabat, A., & Simchi-Levi, D. (2012). Sustainable supply chain design: A closed-loop formulation and sensitivity analysis. *Production Planning and Control*, *23*(2/3), 120–133. doi:10.1080/09537287.2011.591622

Aguezzoul, A. (2014). Third-party logistics selection problem: A literature review on criteria and methods. *Omega*, *49*, 69–78. doi:10.1016/j.omega.2014.05.009

Amin, S. H., & Baki, F. (2017). A facility location model for global closed-loop supply chain network design. *Applied Mathematical Modelling*, *41*, 316–330. doi:10.1016/j.apm.2016.08.030

Aydinliyim, T., & Murthy, N. N. (2016). Managing engineering design for competitive sourcing in closed-loop supply chains. *Decision Sciences*, *47*(2), 257–297. doi:10.1111/deci.12164

Battini, D., Bogataj, M., & Choudhary, A. (2017). Closed loop supply chain (CLSC): Economics, modelling, management and control. *International Journal of Production Economics*, *183*, 319–321. doi:10.1016/j.ijpe.2016.11.020

Bazan, E., Jaber, M. Y., & Zanoni, S. (2017). Carbon emissions and energy effects on a two-level manufacturer-retailer closed-loop supply chain model with remanufacturing subject to different coordination mechanisms. *International Journal of Production Economics*, *183*, 394–408. doi:10.1016/j.ijpe.2016.07.009

Besiou, M., & van Wassenhove, L. N. (2016). Closed-loop supply chains for photovoltaic panels: A case-based approach. *Journal of Industrial Ecology*, *20*(4), 929–937. doi:10.1111/jiec.12297

Dutta, P., Das, D., Schultmann, F., & Fröhling, M. (2016). Design and planning of a closed-loop supply chain with three way recovery and buy-back offer. *Journal of Cleaner Production*, *135*, 604–619. doi:10.1016/j.jclepro.2016.06.108

Ghayebloo, S., Tarok, M. J., Abedzadeh, M., & Diallo, C. (2013). Multi-level programming approach to a closed-loop supply chain network design. *International Journal of Strategic Decision Sciences*, *4*(4), 55–71. doi:10.4018/ijsds.2013100104

Govindan, K., & Soleimani, H. (2017). A review of reverse logistics and closed-loop supply chains: A Journal of Cleaner Production focus. *Journal of Cleaner Production*, *142*, 371–384. doi:10.1016/j.jclepro.2016.03.126

Hasani, A., Zegordi, S. H., & Nikbakhsh, E. (2012). Robust closed-loop supply chain network design for perishable goods in agile manufacturing under uncertainty. *International Journal of Production Research*, *50*(16), 4649–4669. doi:10.1080/00207543.2011.625051

Huang, Y., & Wang, Z. (2017). Closed-loop supply chain models with product take-back and hybrid remanufacturing under technology licensing. *Journal of Cleaner Production*, *142*, 3917–3927. doi:10.1016/j.jclepro.2016.10.065

Iassinovskaia, G., Limbourg, S., & Riane, F. (2017). The inventory-routing problem of returnable transport items with time windows and simultaneous pickup and delivery in closed-loop supply chains. *International Journal of Production Economics*, *183*, 570–582. doi:10.1016/j.ijpe.2016.06.024

Jeihoonian, M., Zanjani, M. K., & Gendreau, M. (2017). Closed-loop supply chain network design under uncertain quality status: Case of durable products. *International Journal of Production Economics*, *183*, 470–486. doi:10.1016/j.ijpe.2016.07.023

John, S. T., & Sridharan, R. (2013). Modelling and analysis of network design for a closed-loop supply chain. *International Journal of Logistics Systems and Management*, *14*(3), 329–352. doi:10.1504/IJLSM.2013.052064

Karamouzian, A., Jalali Naini, S. G. H., & Mazdeh, M. M. (2014). Management of returned products to a remanufacturing facility considering arrival uncertainty and priority processing. *International Journal of Operational Research*, *20*(3), 331–340. doi:10.1504/IJOR.2014.062454

Kenne, J. P., Dejax, P., & Gharbi, A. (2012). Production planning of a hybrid manufacturing: Remanufacturing system under uncertainty within a closed-loop supply chain. *International Journal of Production Economics*, *135*(1), 81–93. doi:10.1016/j.ijpe.2010.10.026

Krapp, M., Nebel, J., & Sahamie, H. (2013). Forecasting product returns in closed-loop supply chains. *International Journal of Physical Distribution & Logistics Management*, *43*(8), 614–637. doi:10.1108/IJPDLM-03-2012-0078

Lundin, J. F. (2012). Redesigning a closed-loop supply chain exposed to risks. *International Journal of Production Economics*, *140*(2), 596–603. doi:10.1016/j.ijpe.2011.01.010

Maiti, T., & Giri, B. C. (2017). Two-way product recovery in a closed-loop supply chain with variable markup under price and quality dependent demand. *International Journal of Production Economics*, *183*, 259–272. doi:10.1016/j.ijpe.2016.09.025

Miao, Z., Fu, K., Xia, Z., & Wang, Y. (2017). Models for closed-loop supply chain with trade-ins. *Omega*, *66*, 308–326. doi:10.1016/j.omega.2015.11.001

Mitra, S. (2012). Inventory management in a two-echelon closed-loop supply chain with correlated demands and returns. *Computers & Industrial Engineering*, *62*(4), 870–879. doi:10.1016/j.cie.2011.12.008

Olugu, E. U., & Wong, K. Y. (2012). An expert fuzzy rule-based system for closed-loop supply chain performance assessment in the automotive industry. *Expert Systems with Applications*, *39*(1), 375–384. doi:10.1016/j.eswa.2011.07.026

Özceylan, E., & Paksoy, T. (2013). A mixed integer programming model for a closed-loop supply-chain network. *International Journal of Production Research*, *51*(3), 718–734. doi:10.1080/00207543.2012.661090

Park, S. K., & Berger-Walliser, G. (2015). A firm-driven approach to global governance and sustainability. *American Business Law Journal*, *52*(2), 255–315. doi:10.1111/ablj.12046

Qiang, Q., Ke, K., Anderson, T., & Dong, J. (2013). The closed-loop supply chain network with competition, distribution channel investment, and uncertainties. *Omega*, *41*(2), 186–194. doi:10.1016/j.omega.2011.08.011

Reimann, M. (2016). Accurate response with refurbished consumer returns. *Decision Sciences*, *47*(1), 31–59. doi:10.1111/deci.12150

Soleimani, H., Seyyed-Esfahani, M., & Kannan, G. (2013). Incorporating risk measures in closed-loop supply chain network design. *International Journal of Production Research*, *52*(6), 1843–1867. doi:10.1080/00207543.2013.849823

Srinivasan, R., & Swink, M. (2015). Leveraging supply chain integration through planning comprehensiveness: An organizational information processing theory perspective. *Decision Sciences*, *46*(5), 823–861. doi:10.1111/deci.12166

Subulan, K., Tasan, A. S., & Baykasoglu, A. (2015). Designing an environmentally conscious tire closed-loop supply chain network with multiple recovery options using interactive fuzzy goal programming. *Applied Mathematical Modelling*, *39*(9), 2661–2702. doi:10.1016/j.apm.2014.11.004

Wang, W., Zhang, Y., Li, Y., Zhao, X., & Cheng, M. (2017). Closed-loop supply chains under reward-penalty mechanism: Retailer collection and asymmetric information. *Journal of Cleaner Production*, *142*, 3938–3955. doi:10.1016/j.jclepro.2016.10.063

Wang, Z., Soleimani, H., Kannan, D., & Xu, L. (2016). Advanced cross-entropy in closed-loop supply chain planning. *Journal of Cleaner Production*, *135*, 201–213. doi:10.1016/j.jclepro.2016.04.006

Xie, J., Liang, L., Liu, L., & Ieromonachou, P. (2017). Coordination contracts of dual-channel with cooperation advertising in closed-loop supply chains. *International Journal of Production Economics*, *183*, 528–538. doi:10.1016/j.ijpe.2016.07.026

Yadegari, E., Ekhtiari, M., Zandieh, M., & Alem-Tabriz, A. (2014). An artificial immune algorithm for a closed-loop supply chain network design problem with different delivery paths. *International Journal of Strategic Decision Sciences*, *5*(3), 27–46. doi:10.4018/ijsds.2014070102

Yi, P., Huang, M., Guo, L., & Shi, T. (2016). Dual recycling channel decision in retailer oriented closed-loop supply chain for construction machinery remanufacturing. *Journal of Cleaner Production*, *137*, 1393–1405. doi:10.1016/j.jclepro.2016.07.104

Yoo, S. H., & Kim, B. C. (2016). Joint pricing of new and refurbished items: A comparison of closed-loop supply chain models. *International Journal of Production Economics*, *182*, 132–143. doi:10.1016/j.ijpe.2016.07.017

Zeballos, L. J., Gomes, M. I., Barbosa-Povoa, A. P., & Novais, A. Q. (2012). Addressing the uncertain quality and quantity of returns in closed-loop supply chains. *Computers & Chemical Engineering*, *47*, 237–247. doi:10.1016/j.compchemeng.2012.06.034

Zhou, L., Naim, M. M., & Disney, S. M. (2017). The impact of product returns and remanufacturing uncertainties on the dynamic performance of a multi-echelon closed-loop supply chain. *International Journal of Production Economics*, *183*, 487–502. doi:10.1016/j.ijpe.2016.07.021

KEY TERMS AND DEFINITIONS

Distribution: The process of getting products to consumers.

Forward Logistics: The process of moving products from factories to consumers.

Logistics: The management of how resources are acquired, stored, and transported to their final destination.

Outsourcing: The practice used by different companies to reduce costs by transferring portions of work to outside suppliers rather than completing it internally.

Procurement: The process of buying products and services.

Production Planning: The process that ensures materials, equipment, and employees are available to meet production goals for a business.

Retailer: A person, shop, or business that sells products to the public.

Reverse Logistics: The process of moving products from their final destination for the purpose of capturing value, or proper disposal.

Supply Chain: The system of organizations, people, technologies, activities, information, and resources involved in moving product or service from supplier to customer.

Chapter 10
Predicting Online Returns

Kumari Smriti
IIMB, India

ABSTRACT

The E-commerce industry is growing year on year in double digits. But customers today are not only buying more through their computers, they are also returning more. The volume of these returns is such that it just can't be ignored. E-tailers today are following many practices to handle these returns but the 'predictability' factor is still missing from their approaches. This paper tries to fulfill that void. The framework suggested in this paper will help the E-tailers to predict the probability of a particular item being returned by a particular shopper. The idea is that if the E-tailer will know the probability of return during any transaction he/she would certainly be better equipped to handle the situation.

INTRODUCTION

This is the era in which shopping paradigm has seen the biggest shift in the way people approach shopping itself. Today the most avid of shoppers spend more time browsing at online shops rather than window shopping at a brick and mortar store. So what is that has caused this shift? Among other things, the lenient return policies from the 'E-tailers', has been the enabler for such a dramatic shift. These return policies have strengthened the bond of trust between the retailer and the consumers. The initial users of online purchasing were skeptics of buying items without seeing, feeling, touching, or trying them out or trying them on. But with almost no hassle return policies, the buyers are more open to experimenting with their purchases online. After all they know that if the product does not meet their standard of quality they won't be forced to pay for them. These reassured users have boosted the online sales of products many folds. However, the excerpts from different studies, that will be discussed later, show that it is not only the online sales that have grown but also the numbers of 'Returns'. And of late, handling these 'Returns' has become the biggest pain for online stores. The trends look to bloat these numbers in coming years and eventually hit the gross margins more badly.

Online retailing has soured over the last decade as it offers many benefits to the consumers. Unfortunately, the rate of returns of online products is alarming highly, which then eats into the profit of ecommerce retailer, who already operate on very thin margins. According to Invesp inforgraphic on online

DOI: 10.4018/978-1-5225-3056-5.ch010

return rates statistics group, at least 30% of all products ordered online are returned compared to only 8.89% bought in brick-and-mortar shops. Around 49% of retailers offer free return shipping.

Customers love return policies, both in stores and online. Now e-Retailers use this information and provide easy return policies, as a tool to compete with physical stores (Che, 1996). They have been able to do see successfully. Simply discarding return policy is no more an option. On the other hand these policies eat into the profit of the companies. Companies need a balancing act between providing returns, and yet keeping the rate low. The first step towards finding the right strategy will be for the company to be able to predict the returning behavior its customer (Cassill, 1998).

This paper does exactly that. In this paper the author suggests a model to predict returns of products among customers with high return rate.

BACKGROUND

It has been just two decades since the first secure online retail transaction (by NetMarket or Internet Shopping Network) occurred in 1994, and the online shopping industry has exploded. However, the debate between which one is better and preferred by consumers hasn't been put to an end. Online shopping has certainly seen a growing trend, but it doesn't seem like it will replace regular offline shopping anytime soon. So what are the criteria under which a user decides the Place of his/her purchase, whether it is going to be online or at a physical store? These are convenience, variety, immediacy, quality, the experience, discounts and offers, personalized attention and recommendation from sales staff, and of course pricing, to mention a few (Abbasi, et. al. 2010).

Let's look at these in detail to see how shopper behavior is affected by these considerations, or by perceptions of these. On convenience scale, online may be a tad bit better placed than the physical store, although it may seem cumbersome to people who do not use or haven't been using technology (Agarwal, 2014). Online provides access to products with just a click of a few buttons, which can be done on the move, and at anytime of the day (Chen, 2009). On Variety front, online surpasses the offline stores by a huge margin. Most of the online retail stores act like aggregators storing only bare minimum inventory at their warehouse, if any at all, and sourcing others from the manufacturers or sellers as when there is a requirement. The lack of need to store products translates into exponentially higher storage of products (Aguilar, 2010). Thus the user gets to see different products from multiple companies all at the same place. Discounts and Offers are based on real time, and cannot be fairly compared. The offline stores beat online ones comprehensively when it comes to immediacy needs of people, the product sold at an offline store is ready for use as soon as the customer pays for it (Zhang et. al., 2010). Offline stores also provide recommended buying, especially for high valued items and items related to display of wealth, prosperity or lifestyle. E.g. while buying dresses, drapes, paintings etc people prefer to get another person's opinion on what is 'in'. Sometimes it is difficult to describe what is it that you are looking for, and recommendation from sales staff is one key to finding the right item (Anderson, 2009). Next, points for quality of product ideally should have been same for both online and offline stores, as the source of supply for both of them is the same, but is not. At least the perception of Quality is definitely not the same. The reason is the experience of being able to see, touch, feel, and try the products, before having to commit to pay, techniques to gauge quality of a product is definitely much higher in Offline stores (Yu, 2008). To combat the quality perceptions many different retailers have resorted to offer offline experiences, such as opening up retail stores, or simply giving the customer an option to ask for trial from the comfort of their home, however, these have their own costs. However, one of the initial things e-tailers started to do to offset these quality perceptions was to allow users to exchange faulty products. And this has been one of the biggest, if not the biggest, reasons to driving traffic towards online store (Abbasi, 2012).

A couple of years ago people were wondering if the on-line retail would dominate traditional retail to a point that the latter dies out. We now have the answer; it is very unlikely. Immediate delivery and the power to verify the product before having to pay for it are definitely always going to keep the traditional stores alive. So to combat the latter of the two disadvantages, online stores started their biggest trick, allowing the users to return the products when it does not meet their expected quality or description.

"As much as one third of all Internet sales get returned." – Kurt Salmon, Retail consultancy 2013.
"Returns are expected to jump by 15% in the year 2014 when compared to the same in last year." – United Parcel Services Inc., Dec' 2013.

It is obvious that Return processes are a cost for a company, and hence affects the profit margins. But that is not it. The problem is actually even bigger than that. Return is also a cost for the customer (Asdecker, 2015). The customer has to initiate the process. Now even though e-commerce allows people to Return products which do not meet your standards, as combative measure to the points mentioned above, anyone who has ever tried returning products will tell you that Return policies are not as smooth as or as convenient as they sound. A typical process involves the customer initiating the process, the retailer verifying the claim and then one needs to be present at their homes or when they come to take the product, the return product then gets processed which takes a few days and then a few more days for the process to refund the money (Autry, 2005). And if any of these processes are mishandled for any reason, it will lead to unhappy customer, and a few occurrences will directly impact 'Brand Loyalty'. Ease of return is one of the criteria for online purchase and if it is not what a shopper gets, he/she may refrain from buying from this retailer, there is no dearth of online retailers today. These dissatisfied consumers may also generate bad publicity (Autry et. al., 2007). We also know that an angry customer is more likely to give bad reviews than a happy customer is to give a good review. Hence a few bad experiences can eclipse many better ones. In today's era, all you need is a tweet or a post that has a cascading effect and drastically impact Brand Image of the online store. So overall, it is not just about that 'extra' cost (that the E-tailer is going to bear on reverse logistics), but it may also harm the E-tailer's 'Brand Image' causing them their loyal customers (Bandyopadhyay et. al., 2010).

But then – 'bigger the problem, larger the benefits if that problem gets tackled' (Williams, 2002). Hence, the objective of this paper is to realize the potential behind studying these Return patterns and carving out an effective way for the 'E-tailers' to first predict the returns accurately, to enable them to take corrective measures. This paper will also introduce a framework to guide the 'E-tailers' to take both short term and long term actions to handle the returns effectively. The following excerpts from 'clear returns' make this framework the necessity of the hour –

- Fewer than 10% of products cause 50% of returns.
- 1% of your customers cause up to 10% of your returns costs.

Based on the numbers above we can say that source of the problem is fairly low and identifiable, and the benefits far reaching.

UNDERSTANDING RETURNS

Looking at the buying behavior of a shopper while he shops in a brick and mortar store, the steps involved are:

- Shopper walks into a store
- Browses the product
- Analyses the product
- Tries the product
- Buys the product
- Sometimes, in case of any issues later he/she comes back to the store and 'Returns' the product.

Now let's compare this whole buying behavior with that of an online shopper:

- Shopper logs onto a store site
- Browses the product
- Analyses the product
- Sometimes, compares the product with other similar ones
- Buys the product
- Sometimes, in case of any issues later he/she comes online and 'Returns' the product.

Now the noticeable difference between the two processes is simply that the latter misses 'trying the product' step. So how is this step important for the shopper? Well, they have tried the product in a physical store – he/she is confirmed about the product properties (size/color/material); he/she does not have to visualize how good or bad it will look after wearing; almost zero chance of wrong/late delivery of the product. Given all this, the chances of returns are less (though not zero) in a brick and mortar store (Bechwati et. al. 2005).

However, an online shopper is not lucky enough to 'try the product'. Hence he/she has to speculate on a few things, visualize the product and then buy it with certain expectations (King, 2009). Understandably so, if the E-tailer is not able to meet any of his/her expectation, the product gets returned. The reasons for such a miss can be varied, minor or major, but at end of the day the customer has been promised a return, and they are well within their rights to ask for one (Bhattacharyya, et. al., 2011). Not surprisingly then the online stores have a higher return rates than a physical store. The statistics show us that every third item sold online, gets returned. Let us try and understand these reasons. For ease of understanding we have divided into primarily two categories:

1. Controllable:
    a. Poor Quality of Products
    b. Slow shipping / late deliveries
    c. Fulfillment errors
    d. Product misinterpretation
2. Uncontrollable:
    a. Wrong size ordered
    b. Change of mind
    c. Intentional return

Currently, Etailers are putting a lot of efforts on reducing the fulfillment errors and providing better details about the products so that they can reduce the first kind of 'Returns', the controllable kind (Bjorner, et. al., 2004). However, E-tailers seem to have no clue when Return happens just because the shopper 'changed his mind' or say 'shopper ordered more product sizes to try all and keep one' kind of situations.

A study done in 4 European countries (reference Figure 1), depicts that almost half of the online returns, happen due to incorrect sizes

Free Returns option cannot be taken away from the online shoppers, completely or even selectively. This acts as one of the important reason why people are shopping more at online than stores; this is the online businesses competitive advantage over physical stores. Figure 2 shows some of the metric why shoppers prefer Returns.

Solutions and Recommendations to Tackle Returns

In order to optimize the entire returns process the following framework is recommended for e-tailers. The framework essentially consists of two prong approach namely (1) short term actions (2) long term actions.

For each and every occurrence of return, both short and long terms actions would be taken. As the name suggests the short term action would try to prevent the returns to happen in the first place and still if it happens, a smoother transaction would be suggested. And then taking some cues from these short term actions, the framework will devise a strategy to handle the returns in more effective way in future (Bjorner, et. al., 2004).

Figure 1. Reasons of returns of online sale

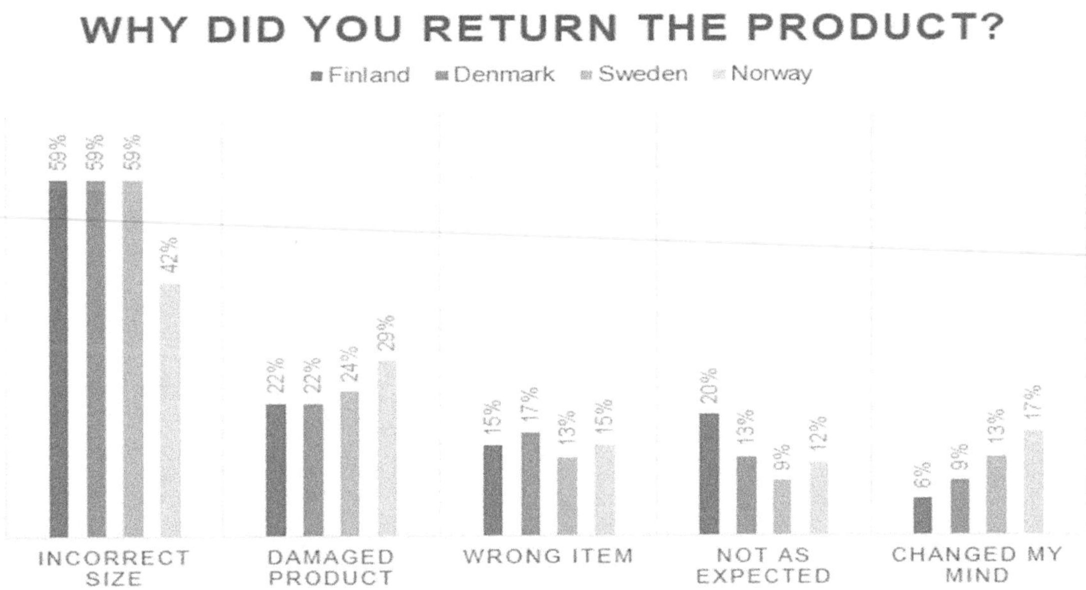

Figure 2. Returns option is important for competitive advantage

Short-Term Actions

The short term action is directed to immediate respond to a "return transaction" that the customer has initiated online.

As shown in the diagram above, the inputs to this work flow will be the Return details provided by the customer. While returning the item, user will be prompted to provide a reason of his/her return and each reason will be mapped to a 'reason code'. Based on this 'reason code' both Short term and Long term actions would be triggered (Bower, et. al., 2012). In short term action, each reason code will be mapped to a corrective action (responses). So based on the reason selected by the customer, the system will generate a response to, at first, avoid the return from happening. And even after this, if the customer

Figure 3: Short-Term action plan of return management

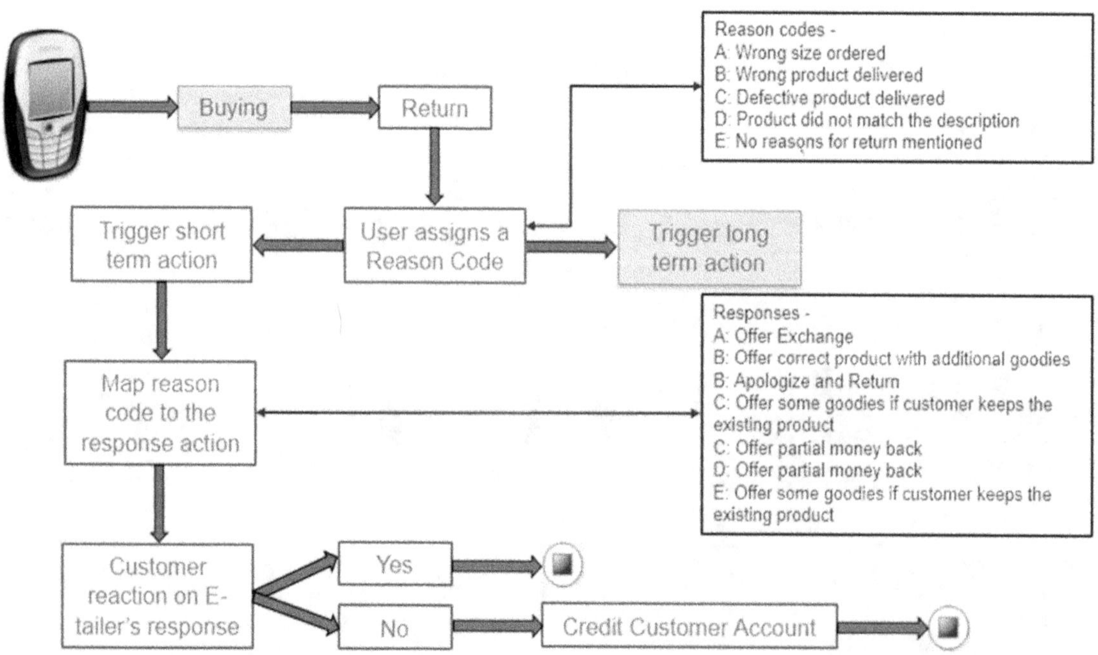

insists for the return then without probing any further, the system will credit customer's account with e-tailer back (in terms of gift vouchers, refunds etc.).

Such reason codes and their responses can be configured based on the e-tailer's preferences. E.g. a luxury e-tailer for whom the brand image is paramount, he/she can have 'defective product' in say a non-negotiable category and if it occurs, he can offer some additional benefits to the customer, along with the returns. On the other hand a furniture maker might offer bigger goodies for the customer to avoid the returns since for him/her the reverse logistics cost would be high (Browne, et. al. 2008).

Long Term Actions

- As the part of the long term action plan, the recommended process will be a two pronged solution. The first is that for product level recommendation and the second one for customer level recommendations.

Under the product level assessment, the process involved is as follows:

- Tracking of data for returns based on pre-agreed, pre-defined attributes. Examples of such attributes can be frequency of return, reason for return, monetary value of return, timeframe when returns occur, etc.
- Once the background analytics are collated and entered into a centralized database, the actual data is assigned to the respective attributes and scores based on (1) threshold levels. Weightage for these attributes are generated. The score referred to as the "return index" would hence be calculated for each product across a given period of time.

Using a set of pre-determined, pre-configured "Return Attributes", scores are assigned systemically. This approach includes assigning weightage and threshold at each attribute level in order to cater to the importance as per product type. For example see Table 2.

The attributes are e-retailer specific and can be customized as per the e-retailers' preference or business priorities. A typical example of such would be a business priority where maximum weightage is on "margin earning", etc.

Table 1. Example of data used for return tracking

Transaction Data: Product X	
Sales Period	01 – Jan -2016 to 31-Dec-2016
Total Gross Sales	100
Total Returns	20
Breakup of Returns	
6. Price	12
7. Product Feature	6
8. Perception	4
9. Quality	0
10. Total	20

Table 2. Example of defect score calculation

Defect Score Calculation				
Attributes	**Weight**	**Threshold**	**Actual**	**Score**
1. Price	40%	5%	60%	2
2. Product Features	10%	10%	30%	2
3. Perception	5%	20%	20%	1
4. Quality	15%	5%	0%	0
5. Total Returns	30%	10%	20%	2
Aggregate	100%			7
Defect Score				70%
Defect Rating				High

Scoring and rating methodology is defined as follows (see Table 3).

Based on the above approach, at the end of such assignment of scores, each product will have a "defect rating" associated with it.

In lines with the approach adopted for Product, similarly unique return attributes are recommended to be part of the "Customer" transaction tracking mechanism. At the end of the Customer Returns Score, a rating would be assigned to each customer.

The Product and Customer rating would be used in multiple scenarios, which are:

- **Product Ranging:** A product with rating of High and Medium would be thoroughly reviewed and subsequently decided to not range a highly returnable product.
- **Live Customer Transaction:** Where the returns model will be activated as soon as a customer places a product with "high" returns rating in the shopping cart. The centralized engine would be expected to trigger a search for historical data for the product, review reasons for return and display "Avoidance action" for providing additional information or features that would make the product less prone to be returned. "Avoidance action" in this reference would be derived from a database of historical data which would hold "returns reason code" that are associated with "pre-ventive action".

Table 3.Scoring and rating methodology

Scoring Methodology	
Threshold > Actual	Score = 0
Threshold = Actual	Score = 1
Threshold < Actual	Score = 2
Rating Methodology	
0% < Defect Score <30%	Rating = Low
31% < Defect Score <70%	Rating = Medium
71% < Defect Score <100%	Rating = High

- For example, when a customer selects a product Y, which has a "return rating = High" and the top 3 reasons for returns are (1) Price (2) Size (3) features, then for such a product selected as a part of the checkout basket would immediately trigger (1) price guarantee (2) past selected sizes for the customer (3) detailed description of features for the customers' awareness
- **Preventive Tracking:** A backend search engine would pro-actively track returns for all recent purchases and update scores and ratings for products and customers, which will be used for exceptional reporting and tracking for any short-term spikes in returns. Based on such information, proactive steps can be taken by the category / product owners to avoid up-coming returns.
- For example, a sudden surge in returns for product Z indicates a batch of defective products over a span of 3 days. Unless tracked, such returns could continue un-checked over a period of few weeks until alerted by supply chain, which would not otherwise be able to see such trends.

FUTURE RESEARCH DIRECTIONS

Impact of this methodology has not been studied. The future study can focus on each area within retail vertical to understand the impact. Its important to study each segment and the impact the towards gaining customer loyalty and reduced basket abandonment rates. Retail sub-segments those that can be included for separate and in-depth study are: Grocery/Foods, Drugs, Fast Moving Consumer Goods (FMCG), Foods, Apparel, Specialized segments like Books/CDs, Auto parts, Home Furnishing. Since the nature of business of each of these businesses are different there would be change in the impact on their returns as well.

CONCLUSION

Today's e-tailers have acknowledged the growing threat of eroding business value due to unconstrained returns from customers, hence, the ability to "prevent" is a priority for most e-tailers. The practice of ad-hoc reactive measures to pacify a customer by often yielding to their demands to return products will have to change, but so as to not cause the loss of comfort or flexibility of buying for the users. Being able to predict, the possibility of a product causing or a customer seeking, 'returns' would give a lot of power and control back to the business owners. However, the benefits of predicting return are not limited to just protecting margins and supply chain costs, but the predictability of 'returns' would induce positive behavior (transaction closure), as compared to disruptive actions (non-controllable 'returns'), make the process of return seamless and smooth, and prevent bad experiences for both the customers, sellers and the platform providers. Thus, predictability of 'returns' would open up a whole new opportunity for the e-tailers, this can be a step forward towards gaining customer loyalty and reduced basket abandonment rates.

The ease of shopping online without physical boundaries has no doubt expanded all possible horizons of retailer however the necessary evils that come along are yet to be tamed.

REFERENCES

Abbasi, A., Albrecht, C., Vance, A., & Hansen, J. (2012). Meta Fraud: A Meta-Learning Framework for Detecting Financial Fraud. *MIS Quarterly, 36*(4), 1293–A12.

Abbasi, A., Zhang, Z., Zimbra, D., Chen, H., Nunamaker, J., & Jay, F. (2010). Detecting Fake Websites: The Contribution of Statistical Learning Theory. *MIS Quarterly, 34*(3), 435–461.

Agarwal, R., & Dhar, V. (2014). Editorial—Big Data, Data Science, and Analytics: The Opportunity and Challenge for IS Research. *Information Systems Research, 25*(3), 443–448.

Aguilar, F. X., & Cai, Z. (2010). Conjoint effect of environmental labelling, disclosure of forest of origin andprice on consumer preferences for wood products in the US and UK. *Ecological Economics, 70*(2), 308–316.

Anderson, E. T., Hansen, K., & Simester, D. (2009). The option value of returns: Theory and empirical evidence. *Marketing Science, 28*(3), 405–423.

Asdecker, B. (2015). *Statistiken Retouren Deutschland – Definition.* Retrieved from http://www.retourenforschung.de/

Autry, C. W. (2005). Formalization of reverse logistics programs: A strategy for managing liberalized returns. *Industrial Marketing Management, 34*(7), 749–757.

Autry, C. W., Hill, D. J., & O'Brien, M. (2007). Attitude toward the customer: A study of product returns episodes. *Journal of Managerial Issues*, 315–339.

Bandyopadhyay, S., & Paul, A. A. (2010). Equilibrium returns policies in the presence of supplier competition. *Marketing Science, 29*(5), 846–857.

Bechwati, N. N., & Siegal, W. S. (2005). The Impact of the Prechoice Process on Product Returns. *Journal of Marketing Research, 42*(3), 358–367.

Bhattacharyya, S., Jha, S., Tharakunnel, K., & Westland, J. C. (2011). Data mining for credit card fraud: A comparative study. *Decision Support Systems, 50*(3), 602–613.

Bjorner, T. B., Hansen, L. G., & Russell, C. S. (2004). Environmental labelling and consumers' choice—an empirical analysis of the effect of the Nordic Swan. *Journal of Environmental Economics and Management, 47*(3), 411–434.

Bjorner, T. B., Hansen, L. G. a., & Russell, C. S. (2004). Environmental labelling and consumers' choice—an empirical analysis of the effect of the Nordic Swan. *Journal of Environmental Economics and Management, 47*(3), 411–434.

Bower, A. B., & Maxham, J. G., III. (2012). Return shipping policies of online retailers: Normative assumptions and the long-term consequences of fee and free returns. *Journal of Marketing, 76*(5), 110–124.

Browne, M., Rizet, C., Leonardi, J., & Allen, J. (2008). Analysing energy use in supply chains: the case of fruits and vegetables and furniture. *Proceedings of the Logistics Research Network Conference,* 1–6.

Cassill, N. L. (1998). Do customer returns enhance product and shopping experience satisfaction? *The International Review of Retail, Distribution and Consumer Research, 8*(1), 1–13.

Che, Y.-K. (1996). Customer return policies for experience goods. *The Journal of Industrial Economics, 44*(1), 17–24. doi:10.2307/2950557

Chen, J., & Bell, P. C. (2009). The impact of customer returns on pricing and order decisions. *European Journal of Operational Research, 195*(1), 280–295.

Choi, T.-M., Yu, Y., & Au, K.-F. (2011). A hybrid SARIMA wavelet transform method for sales forecasting. *Decision Support Systems, 51*(1), 130–140.

Clottey, T., Benton, W. C., & Srivastava, R. (2012). Forecasting product returns for remanufacturing operations. *Decision Sciences, 43*(4), 589–614.

Cohen, J. (1992). A power primer. *Psychological Bulletin, 112*(1), 155.

De, P., Hu, Y., & Rahman, M. S. (2012). An Empirical Investigation of the Effects of Product-Oriented Web Technologies on Product Returns. Working Paper.

D'Souza, C., Taghian, M., & Lamb, P. (2006). An empirical study on the influence of environmental labels on consumers. *Corporate Communications: An International Journal, 11*(2), 162–173

Dissanayake, D., & Singh, M. (2008). Managing returns in e-business. *Journal of Internet Commerce, 6*(2), 35–49.

Harris, L. C. (2010). Fraudulent consumer returns: Exploiting retailers' return policies. *European Journal of Marketing, 44*(6), 730–747.

Heiman, A., McWilliams, B., Zhao, J., & Zilberman, D. (2002). Valuation and management of money-back guarantee options. *Journal of Retailing, 78*(3), 193–205.

Heiman, A., McWilliams, B., & Zilberman, D. (2001). Demonstrations and money-back guarantees: market mechanisms to reduce uncertainty. *Journal of Business Research, 54*(1), 71–84.

Ketzenberg, M. E., & Zuidwijk, R. A. (2009). Optimal pricing, ordering, and return policies for consumer goods. *Production and Operations Management, 18*(3), 344–360.

King, D. E. (2009). Dlibml: A machine learning toolkit. *Journal of Machine Learning Research*, (10), 1755–1758.

King, T., & Dennis, C. (2006). Unethical consumers: Shopping behaviour using the qualitative analysis of theory of planned behaviour and accompanied (de) shopping. *Qualitative Market Research: An International Journal, 9*(3), 282–296.

LaRose, R. (2001). On the Negative Effects of E-Commerce: A Socio cognitive Exploration of Unregulated On-line Buying. *Journal of Computer-Mediated Communication, 6*(3), 1–37.

Petersen, J. A., & Kumar, V. (2009). Are product returns a necessary evil? Antecedents and consequences. *Journal of Marketing, 73*(3), 35–51.

Rigby, D. (2014). *Online Shopping Isn't as Profitable as You Think*. Retrieved from https://hbr.org/2014/08/online-shopping-isnt-as-profitable-as-you-think/

Sahoo, N., Singh, P. V., & Mukhopadhyay, T. (2012). A Hidden Markov Model for Collaborative Filtering. *MIS Quarterly, 36*(4), 1329–1356.

Wachter, K., Vitell, S. J., Shelton, R. K., & Park, K. (2012). Exploring consumer orientation toward returns: unethical dimensions. *Business Ethics: A European Review, 21*(1), 115–128.

Walsh, G., Möhring, M., Koot, C., & Schaarschmidt, M. (2014). Preventive product returns management systems - A review and model. *Proceedings of the European Conference on Information Systems*, 1–12.

Weber, C., Hendrickson, C., Jaramillo, P., Matthews, S., Nagengast, A., & Nealer, R. (2008). *Life cycle comparison of traditional retail and e-commerce logistics for electronic products: A case study of buy.com*. Green Design Institute, Carnegie Mellon University.

Williams, E., & Tagami, T. (2002). Energy Use in Sales and Distribution via E-Commerce and Conventional Retail: A Case Study of the Japanese Book Sector. *Journal of Industrial Ecology, 6*(2), 99–114.

Yan, R. (2009). Product categories, returns policy and pricing strategy for e-marketers. *Journal of Product & Brand Management, 18*(6), 452–460.

Yu, C.-C., & Wang, C.-S. (2008). A hybrid mining approach for optimizing returns policies in e-retailing. *Expert Systems with Applications, 35*(4), 1575–1582.

Zhang, D., Zhou, X., Leung, S. C., & Zheng, J. (2010). Vertical bagging decision trees model for credit scoring. *Expert Systems with Applications, 37*(12), 7838–7843.

KEY TERMS AND DEFINITIONS

Action Alley: The sales area of a store located immediately after entering.

Ad Slick: Ad slicks refer to the final, camera-ready advertisement. It gets its name from the glossy paper on which it is printed.

Anchor Store: A major retail store used to drive business to smaller retailers that physically surround it. These larger department stores or grocery stores are generally part of a retail chain and are the prominent business in a shopping mall.

Basket Abandonment Rates: The abandonment rate is the ratio of the number of abandoned shopping carts to the number of initiated transactions or to the number of completed transactions. The typical shopping cart abandonment rate for online retailers varies between 60% and 80%, with an average of 67.91%.

Big Box Stores: Large stand-alone store with varying market niches.

Brick and Click: This term refers to retailers that integrate their brick and mortar store with their ecommerce site. These retailers bring the best of both worlds into their business. Most brick and click companies even offer seamless web-to-store services such as in-store pick ups and returns.

Cash Flow: The movement of money in and out of a business and the resulting availability of cash.

Category Killer: A large retail chain store that is dominant in its product category. This type of store generally offers an extensive selection of merchandise at prices so low that smaller stores cannot compete.

Chain Store: One of a number of retail stores under the same ownership and dealing in the same merchandise.

Click and Collect: This is a service in which retailers enable shoppers to buy items online and pick them up in their physical stores. Modern consumers love stores that offer click-and-collect because it makes their life a lot easier. They can buy something from the comfort of their home, and just pick up the item whenever it's convenient for them, instead of paying for shipping or waiting for the mail to arrive.

Clienteling: This is a technique used by retail associates to deepen their relationship with each customer. Clienteling involves relationship-building activities such as using CRM software to collect and track customer data, providing personalized shopping experiences, and following up with shoppers in a relevant and timely way.

Comp Sales: Comparable-store sales are a measurement of productivity in revenue used to compare sales of retail stores that have been open for a year or more. Historical sales data allows retailers to compare this year's sales in their store to the same period last year.

Coupon: A promotional tool in the form of a document that can be redeemed for a discount when purchasing goods or services. Coupons feature specific savings amount or other special offer to persuade consumers to purchase specific goods or services or to purchase from specific retailers.

CRM: Customer Relationship Management: Customer relationship management (CRM) is a business strategy designed to reduce costs and increase profitability by strengthening customer loyalty.

Cross Merchandising: This refers to the practice of displaying or putting together products from different categories to drive add-on sales. Picture this: You're at the grocery store browsing the liquor section when you see a pack of lemons tacked to the tequila shelf. This is cross merchandising in action. Groceries know that people often take lemons with their tequila shots, so they strategically placed the two items together.

Drones: Drones are generally defined as unmanned aircraft. They come in all shapes, sizes and prices; from $100 toys the size of a baseball to multi-million dollar military machines the size of a vehicle.

Drop Shipping: This refers to an arrangement between a retailer and a manufacturer/distributor, in which the former transfer customer orders to the latter, who then ships the merchandise directly to the consumer. In other words, the retailer doesn't keep products in stock. Instead, it sends orders and shipment information to the manufacturer/distributor and they will be the ones who will ship to the consumer.

Fast-Moving Consumer Goods (FMCG): or consumer packaged goods (CPG) are products that are sold quickly and at relatively low cost. Examples include non-durable goods such as soft drinks, toiletries, over-the-counter drugs, processed foods and many other consumables.

High Speed Retail: Born out of people's need for faster services and less wait time, high speed retail is all about making the customer's shopping experience go by much quicker. Examples of High Speed Retail can include drive-thru grocery stores, pop-up stores, mobile businesses such as food trucks, or any retailer that implements urgent promotions or limited-time sales.

Integrated Supply Chain: This is a network of businesses and contractors that work and coordinate closely together to manufacture, transport, distribute, and sell retail goods. Unlike a regular supply chain which is more of a linear process that follows a product from one phase to the next, an Integrated Supply Chain is more collaborative and can entail joint product development, shared information, and common systems.

Inventory: Inventory is the merchandise a retail store has on hand. The term also refers to the act of counting, itemizing and recording in-stock merchandise or supplies.

Last Mile Delivery: Last mile is a term used in supply chain management and transportation planning to describe the movement of people and goods from a transportation hub to a final destination in the area. The term "last mile" was originally used in the telecommunications field but has since been applied to supply chain management. Transporting goods via freight rail networks and container ships is often the most efficient and cost-effective manner of shipping. However, when goods arrive at a high-capacity freight station or port, they must then be transported to their final destination. This last leg of the supply chain is often less efficient, comprising up to 28% of the total cost to move goods. This has become known as the "last mile problem."

Omni-Channel Retailing: Omni-channel means establishing a presence on several channels and platforms (i.e. brick-and-mortar, mobile, online, catalog etc) and enabling customers to transact, interact, and engage across these channels simultaneously or even interchangeably. It's important to note that omni-channel goes beyond simply being on multiple channels or platforms. Just because you have a website, a mobile app, and a physical store doesn't necessarily mean that you're an omni-channel retailer. In order to truly be one, you must fuse all those channels together so they give customers a seamless experience.

Plan-O-Gram: Visual description, diagram or drawing of a store's layout that includes placement of particular products and product categories.

Private Label: Products that are generally manufactured or provided by one company under another company's brand.

SKU: The stock keeping unit (SKU) is a number assigned to a product by a retailer to identify the price, product options and manufacturer.

Social Commerce: S-Commerce refers to retail models or ecommerce practices that incorporate social media, user-generated content, or social interaction. Do note that the role of social networks like Facebook or Twitter in S-Commerce isn't necessarily to serve as platforms for buying and selling; rather, they're meant to assist the process and help drive sales.

Softlines: A store department or product line primarily consisting of merchandise such as clothing, footwear, jewelry, linens and towels.

Chapter 11
Building an Effective Customer Loyalty Program

Kumari Smriti
IIMB, India

ABSTRACT

Customer loyalty schemes is a practice, employed by retailers, to reward their loyal customers. It entails giving incentives such as loyalty cards, reward points, etc. These also serve as a repository of information about a customer which helps in targeted marketing. This chapter analyses some of the successful customer loyalty programs by companies, discusses some of the reasons of failures of such program and looks at what industry experts have to say in this regard. We then collate all this information to suggests a process to identify and choose the right customer loyalty programs for a company.

INTRODUCTION

Customer loyalty schemes are an effective way for retailers to improve their customer-retention levels. There is a high cost involved in bringing in new customers compared to retaining existing ones. So increasing the customer retention can significantly boost a company`s profits. And yet most companies lack a strong customer loyalty program. Customers now-a-days can easily switch to a new supplier. To build a loyal clientele, keeping the customer satisfied is not always enough. The fact that customers are satisfied does not stop them from moving to a competitor who offers them something extra. To increase loyalty, retailers need to recognize and reward their best customers. A loyalty scheme can be used to incentivize and delight the most valued customers. That in turn can do wonders for the company`s profitability.

Retail is the earliest industry to adopt the practice of rewarding their customer through loyalty incentives. They brought in different card systems such as loyalty cards, reward cards, points and advantage cards. These cards often have barcodes which aid in further identifying the buying behavior of the customers. Some companies even promote membership programs to reward customers with consistent buying patterns.

As the average customers are becoming smarter and aware, it is becoming difficult to cater to all their demands. Customers expect value for money, at all costs. They expect a hassle free experience

DOI: 10.4018/978-1-5225-3056-5.ch011

from sales and customer service. Moreover, they want to be appreciated for their loyalty. Hence, loyalty programs should be designed keeping these smart customers in mind. These programs keep the competition at bay and act as motivators for customers to continue using the same service or product. Customer loyalty programs also provides database for further customer relationship management. The whole point of rewarding a customer with better prices or services is to encourage them to repeat their behavior. If rightly executed, a customer loyalty program can dramatically increase profitability.

A BRIEF OVERVIEW

Broadly, the chapter has been categorized under the following subjects:

- **Overview:** This section describes what a customer loyalty program is in the context of the current retail landscape. It also attempts to understand how important it is for retailers to build a strong customer loyalty program in this day and age. The research methodology used in this study has also been explained in this chapter.
- **Analysis of Some Successful Customer Loyalty Programs:** Some of the most successful customer loyalty programs across the retail industry have been explored into and analyzed in this section. The way these customer loyalty programs operate and the primary reason for the success of these programs are also discussed in some detail.
- **Why Some Programs Fail:** The reasons why some loyalty programs have failed have been discussed in this section. Some of the surveys done by industry experts elucidating the reasons behind the failure are also cited in this section.
- **What the Experts Say:** In this section, the viewpoint of industry experts have been summarized in the backdrop of the success or failure of these varied loyalty programs.
- **How to Build a Successful Customer Loyalty Program:** This section describes various suggestions to build a strong and rewarding customer loyalty program, based on the expert opinion, literature, and on the premise of having already understood what works for customers and what does not. All these suggestions have been categorically identified and listed out.

Research Methodology

Research was based on the following aspects - an extensive web-based research on current customer loyalty programs, analysis of customer`s sentiment through social media data, and analysis of interviews of industry leaders on loyalty programs of leading retail organizations.

ANALYSIS OF SOME SUCCESSFUL CUSTOMER LOYALTY PROGRAMS

Starbucks

Name of the Loyalty Program: My Starbucks Rewards

The My Starbucks Reward program offers a wide variety of hard and soft actions users can be rewarded for. Customers in the program can earn "Stars" by paying with their registered cards, participating in product promotions, and completing incentivized actions. When Stars are earned, they are stored in a customer's user profile until they are redeemed for drinks, food items, and more. Customers are also offered the chance to move up to Green and Gold levels of the program after they earn a certain amount of stars, with each level opening the door for more customer benefits. Customers can earn Stars for online and offline actions, like engaging with the brand's mobile application, buying coffee in grocery stores, and even engaging with the brand through their various social channels and public promotions (Clark 2012). The more a customer interacts with Starbucks, the more Stars they earn, and the bigger the opportunity for reward becomes.

- **The Winning Stroke:** Starbucks is truly paving the way for enterprise brands focusing on customer loyalty by rewarding customers for actions that other brands would not care for. Starbucks is truly generous, fun, and unique in their approach, which makes their loyalty program one of the most popular programs in existence. They have created a loyalty program that is centered around their users, and each piece of the experience is easy for consumers to understand (Gordon 2010).

BLOOMINGDALES

Name of the Loyalty Program: Loyallist

Bloomingdales started their Loyallist program to reward customers for in-store purchases, but this program has grown to reward users for every single dollar they spend. Whether customers purchase goods in-store, online, or at their outlets, they are rewarded with Loyallist points no matter how they pay (cash, credit, store card, and so on). Double, triple, and even quadruple points are offered at different times throughout the year. When a loyalty program member reaches 5,000 points, they receive a $25 Bloomingdale's gift card, regardless of their status in the program.

- **The Winning Stroke:** The Loyallist program is winning because it delivers well on the main goal of all loyalty programs. When members spend money, they are rewarded by points that they can use like money, which incentivizes future purchases for happy shoppers. It is simple and straight forward. Bloomingdale has also invested in a variety of applications that allow customers to access their cards and balances wherever they are, making purchasing with their program easier, thus more effective in building loyalty for their brand (Lehman 2013).

WALGREENS

Name of the Loyalty Program: Balance Rewards

The Walgreens brand is moving back to its health-focused beginnings, and part of their "health first" initiative can be seen through their Balance Rewards loyalty program. With the Balance Rewards program, members can earn points by taking care of themselves through filling prescriptions, receiving immunizations, logging points for walking and/or running, tracking weight loss, or participating in physical activities. When points are earned, they can be redeemed in increments for in-store gift cards up to $50.

- **The Winning Stroke:** Health is the most important thing people can invest in, and Walgreens is inspiring their loyalty program members to invest in their well-being first. When brands think beyond how loyal actions will help only their brand, customers are placed first and begin to give back to the brand by engaging at higher rates, becoming brand advocates, and completing incentivized actions. The type of loyalty Balance Rewards is fostering is truly reciprocal, which means that the more the brand wins, the more its customers win (Peppers & Rogers Group. 2009).

NEIMAN MARCUS

Name of the Loyalty Program: InCircle

Neiman Marcus' InCircle loyalty program offers everything that one would expect from a high-end retailer's loyalty program. Members can earn points for money spent in the store and online, and for every 10,000 points earned, they receive a $100 gift card. On top of this standard pay and redeem model, InCircle members can earn double points on certain days throughout the year, free shipping, sweepstakes entries, and more. The more points members earn, the higher they move up in the "circles" of InCircle, and with each step up, they are offered a wider variety of awesome rewards.

- **The Winning Stroke:** This program caters to shoppers who want a full store experience, rather than just great clothes. Because program members can redeem their points for a variety of goods (like free delivery for online purchases, alterations, dining, and more), the program is incredibly beneficial to the "full store" shopper. Neiman Marcus knows that their most loyal members are shoppers who take advantage of many of their services, and they crafted their program to reach this group specifically.

GILT

Name of the Loyalty Program: Gilt Insider

The Gilt Insider is an online-only loyalty program. Despite their online shopping-only capabilities, Gilt has made some fantastic strides in attracting an audience through their loyalty program. Program members can earn points for numerous activities on the Gilt.com website, including visiting the site, purchasing goods, and connecting with the brand through its various social channels. Members can redeem their points for a variety of goods, including percent-off discounts, early access to sales, free shipping, and more. Gilt has truly defined the customer actions that are most important to the brand, and incentivize accordingly in order to drive engagement (Priebatsch 2011).

- **The Winning Stroke:** Gilt has taken the traditional retail model and flipped it on its head, yielding some pretty incredible results for the brand. They have intensely studied their customer behavior patterns in order to create incentives that match the actions customers are already taking. This type of customer direction is the marketing of the future, and Gilt is already leaps and bounds ahead of its competitors.

BEST BUY

Name of the Loyalty Program: Reward Zone

Best Buy's Reward Zone is loyalty innovation at its finest. It is no surprise that times have changed for this brand, and the Reward Zone program was created to keep old customers excited about the brand's changes, and to and engage new, tech-savvy customers who aren't interested in browsing the CD section of the stores. With Reward Zone, program members can earn one point for every dollar spent, and receive a $5 gift card for every 250 points spent. If a customer spends more than $2,500 a year in the program, they are moved to the Reward Zone Premier Silver level which offers deeper discounts on money spent in-store and online, discounted shipping and delivery.

- **The Winning Stroke:** Best Buy has been in the tech business since 1966, and they have seen tremendous shifts in the technology space over the years. Through Reward Zone, Best Buy is keeping its customer base engaged by offering rewards for new actions customers are taking, like engaging with their brand through their iPhone and Android apps. Best Buy has spent some serious marketing resources on making their apps' user experience relevant and sleek, and it's paying off big time.

MACY'S

Name of the Loyalty Program: Star Rewards

Macy's is a traditional retailer, and they have taken a traditional approach to their Star Rewards program. All program members automatically receive exclusive in-store coupons through the mail that offer serious discounts when redeemed. On top of savings through coupons, members can earn points for purchases that can be redeemed for gift cards starting at $10. A final bonus is that points program members earn never expire. For a lifelong Macy's shopper, this card is as good as gold.

- **The Winning Stroke:** Macy's is a veteran in the retail space, and their card speaks to the customers who have stuck by their side throughout the years. They dug into framing their target audience before setting up the Star Rewards program that fits their needs, which has boosted loyalty from their most important consumer group.

WHY SOME PROGRAMS FAIL

Loyalty programs cannot be run by just marketing. The most effective loyalty programs leverage cross-functional teams with representatives from stores, finance, merchandising, leadership, and marketing. Customers cite unclear value propositions, lackluster program benefits, and irrelevant offers as reasons they do not like loyalty rewards programs. Irrelevant marketing communications or blasting loyalty members with irrelevant messaging remains common, and is a top factor in reducing program effectiveness and contributing to member abandonment. Lack of personalized, relevant, timely, and contextual communications, as well as not using customer preferences, purchase history, and digital footprint behaviors, results in failure to turn customer insights into marketing actions.

According to a recent research 81% of loyalty members do not know the benefits of their programs, or how and when they will receive rewards. Research cites this as a top reason why consumers are not loyal to the brand. A loyalty survey done by Maritz Loyalty Marketing reported that the majority of consumers abandon loyalty rewards programs because they grow tired of waiting for the points to accumulate. 70% of the consumers cited the length of time it takes to accrue points as the reason behind this abandonment. It takes six to nine months of spending on average to accumulate enough points to redeem them for rewards. The study also found that individuals who earn more than $125,000 annually are willing to increase their expenditure to accumulate points, but that they are very selective and will drop an existing rewards program for a new better program (Tate 2013).

The top technological challenge issue is to integrate data effectively. Retailers often complain of a lack of integration across channels, for example, consumers sign up for loyalty programs online or via email, however, the store loyalty cards or POS systems are not updated. Achieving a unified, cross-channel loyalty program requires a central customer system of record (likely being a CRM application) with real-time integration or synchronization to related applications.

Retail executives use a loyalty program solely as a method to retain customers. However, in an environment where retailers may likely have more former customers than current ones, it is surprising lapsed customers are not being tracked (Yadav 2012). A lack of attention to such customers, creates two significant problems. First, it eliminates the ability to create programs designed to reengage former customers who may be willing to comeback given their "free agent" status. Second, it does not allow marketing analytics to create models based on lapsed customer date to predict when current customers may leave so that they may be targeted with retention related treatments. These two reasons alone provide enough business value to give old customers a new look and to monitor existing customers for signs of impending attrition.

WHAT THE EXPERTS SAY

Kim Gordon (2010), writing for Entrepreneur.com, suggested that for effective loyalty programs:

- **Do Not Abandon Service:** The best customers want personalized service and support that is accessible instantly – often by phone.
- **Make Communication a Two-Way Street:** Use a variety of media to engage consumers in dialogue about the program, the brand, and their experiences.
- **Avoid Loyalty Turnoffs:** Ensure an appropriate tone and frequency of communications, and maintain an open and welcoming program that enables all participants to achieve and redeem rewards.
- **Treat Customers as Individuals:** They want retailers to learn their buying preferences and offer rewards they truly value.

Don Peppers (2009) offered similar propositions based on his years of consulting experience:

- **Insight:** Never waste an opportunity to gain additional customer insight; build information about a customer's individual needs to serve as a platform for increasing interactions.
- **Modularity:** Create a "plug-and-play" system that allows easy addition or subtraction of vendors, partners, and other relationships.
- **Openness:** Consider providing prizes that do not necessarily need to be redeemed from the company – reward the customer without setting explicit limitations about prizes being confined by store products or services.
- **Simplicity:** Avoid setting too many restrictions (such as black-out dates or specific products as rewards) to ensure that any customer who achieves the reward can actually use it.
- **Relationships:** Do not manage the program around products, brands, and stores, but rather around individual customers. Segment the program's participants to understand their particular motivations – this will allow for further improvements in the program and in the company's business.

Peppers stresses that the insight a company gains from consumer participation in their loyalty program is perhaps the greatest gain for the company, rather than any monetary benefits. Seth Priebtasch and Rob McFeeley (2011) echoed Gordon's and Peppers's suggestions in a recent Huffington Post article (McFeeley 2011) on "engineering successful customer loyalty programs." Their suggestions focused on more specific business strategies:

- **Provide Transactional Rewards with few or no Obstacles:** "Whenever the consumer is asked to complete an additional action beyond the transaction in order to gain credit in a loyalty program, a distance is placed between the positive emotion elicited by the reward and the action of purchasing an item or experience."
- **Reward Customers for Finding New Patrons:** "Turn customers into advocates for business by incentivizing them to spread the word about the deal with their friends." v Advertise the program effectively: Use social media, trained sales representatives, and traditional signage to "develop strong relationships with the customers and inform them of new offerings."
- **Provide Meaningful Rewards Options:** "Make an effort to allow customers in the loyalty program to choose how to apply their rewards," while also providing "a set of logical steps toward some clearly defined goal."

HOW TO BUILD A SUCCESSFUL CUSTOMER LOYALTY PROGRAM

Set the Target Audience

Before beginning the reward programs, it is important to get a good understanding of the target audience (Kelley 2006). The key to the success of any loyalty program lies in the detailed knowledge of customers including their demographics, current preference trends, their competitor knowledge and their motivational factors. It is also vital to know what they 'need' as opposed to what they 'want'. From direct surveys to casual customer interactions through social media engagement, there are numerous ways in which this information can be obtained.

Clear Definition of the Loyalty Program

Loose, subjective rules that require impromptu decisions as to who qualifies for the loyalty program and what benefits they receive can create more problems than profits. By defining the program before launching it, the customer appreciation will increase, which will ultimately help improve the brand identity and awareness.

Here are three key elements to consider for the program:

- Set the goals on creating deeper relationships with customers, better reviews, and greater exposure for the brand.
- Consider tiers for the program based upon how much customers spend, the number of prospects they refer, or the length of time they've been loyal.
- Focus on customer benefit over company sales.

Make Customers Feel Important

Not every industry or customer-type has the same motivation for choosing to remain loyal to a business. While customer loyalty programs can help strengthen a brand and build awareness, focusing on rewards that offer the most value for customers is far more important than mass-produced gifts stamped with logos on them. By focusing on making customers feel special, a far more positive impact is created on the bottom line than creating rewards that seem to be merely an incentive to buy more. For example, when operating a family restaurant, creating a "Wall of Fame" with loyal customers' names or pictures could work wonders. Or, in a hi-tech corporation, creating a program whereby the best customers get access to advance releases of the products/services before they are rolled out to the general market. While these specific forms of appreciation may not be right for a particular business, the same principles apply. Elevating customers to a celebrity-status or providing them a competitive advantage increases the chances that these customers will return the favor by bragging about this business to their circle of friends and colleagues, which helps create better visibility and likability for the brand.

Incorporate Reward Grades

Move customers up the spend bands. By grading rewards (for example, offering extra points for exceeding a specified spend threshold in a time period), customers can be moved up from one spend level to the next. A good example of this is how The Continuity Company (a provider of best customer marketing program) skews its rewards in its Best Customer Marketing programs (also known as 'continuity programs') to encourage lower-spending customers to move up through the spend segments. In one of the examples, the top spending band's contribution to sales increased by 41%, the next band down increased its contribution to sales by 45% and the lowest spend band decreased its contribution to sales by 7% (because customers from the lower spend segments had increased their average weekly spend and moved into higher spend segments).

Reward Better Customers Rather Than Concentrating on the Bad Ones

It can be more profitable to lose bad customers than to gain new ones. 'Cherry pickers' (customers who buy only discounted lines and nothing else) cost money, as does any low-spending customer. They cost more money to service than they generate. Designing a loyalty program that rewards better customers without rewarding this segment at all gives these less-desirable customers less reason to stay. In fact, the Syracuse, NY-based Green Hills Supermarket has observed that only around 30% of customers actually generate enough profit to cover the cost of servicing them. In Philip Kotler's version of a Pareto Principle chart, the top 20% of customers generate 80% of the profits, while the bottom 30% of customers eat up 50% of the profits that the others produce.

Create Diverse Loyalty Programs

Once there is clarity on what motivates customers into investing their savings in any product or service, it is time to formulate different reward programs. It is also important to arrive at diverse loyalty programs with rewards that are both perceptible (free house-hold or personal products and cash rewards) and intangible like points, free classes, workshops and so on, or even bumper rewards like trips. Issuing individual identification reward cards will work wonders to improve participation. The idea is not just to attract the attention of customers but also to build a strong and unique bond with them that will stand the test of time.

Increase the Customer Lifetime Value of Loyal Customers

Allocate loyalty reinvestment to the most profitable customers: Southwest Airlines' loyalty program has been a hallmark of its brand, and the 2010 revamping of the program appears to have maintained its customer appeal, while better correlating its spend to profitability. While most airlines attach rewards to miles flown, Southwest offers rewards based on ticket price. Their loyalty rewards spend remains similar to that of other loyalty-focused airlines (i.e., 8 to 9 percent of revenue passenger miles), but the program is better positioned to drive profitability (Kolowich 2015).

Increase Customer Lifetime Value (CLV) Customer Lifetime Value (CLV) is increasingly being recognized as one of the most important measures of the worth of a customer. It takes into account not only the customer's value now but the expected value over their projected lifetime as a customer. It is arguably the best way a marketer can demonstrate unequivocally that a program is working: the CLV of targeted customers will rise. Being able to identify customers through a loyalty program means being able to monitor long-term customer lifetime value, and being able to identify the demographic, socio-graphic, and even purchase profiles that define the most profitable customers - and that knowledge helps in targeting and developing more of them (Thomson 2014).

Appease the Tech Savvy Customers

While not all customers will be digitally savvy, chances are many are, and it's increasingly important that the growing mobile loyalty trend is catered to. There are many apps that small businesses can tap into for free or for a fee. If a business already uses a mobile payment platform, many of these are now integrating loyalty programs into their offerings. Explore the options and look for services that offer social media integration – making it easy for customers to share the awesomeness with their friends and even earn points for likes, shares and online reviews (Starvish 2011).

Provide Special Distinction for Loyalty Customers

Treat the loyalty members royally. Segment them out in emails and direct marketing efforts and communicate with them often. Share news of upcoming loyalty incentives or events and don't forget birthdays – offer something unique to members or opt-in email subscribers during their birthday month. Second only in importance to ease-of-use is the team's ability to make the loyal customers feel special. When creating a loyalty program, train the people who have the most interaction with the customers. This includes any staff, from salespeople, to servers, and any customer service staff who may have a direct interaction with the customer base. If the customers have questions about the loyalty program, provide them with quick answers and service. The frontline team should be able to handle these scenarios without passing the customers on to multiple people.

Develop an Easy to Use Loyalty Program

Ease of use for the customers and employees is critical. Think about the ideal customers for the program. What's the easiest way for them to join? Is it to fill out a paper form that ships with a product, or to complete a form online? Once they become a member of the program, can they access the benefits with a loyalty card, or are they provided with a special log in to the system where they can access the rewards when they want to? Whatever be the methods, remember to make it easy for the customers.

Develop a Strong Marketing Ploy

When creating the marketing for the program, take a multiple "touch" approach. First, market the program to customers for awareness and incentive, followed by additional marketing when they join the program with new information about the business so they know of all of the great products/services offered that they can take advantage of as a member. In a typical sales cycle, it is imperative to "touch" a customer multiple times before they make a buying decision. When provided with a specific reward, it is far more likely to catch their attention and get them to take action quicker. This will reduce the marketing spend, generate additional sales, and create ambassadors for the business who use word of mouth and social media to spread the good news about the business.

Build Real Customer Relationships Based on Relevance

Building relationships is crucially important but not always as straightforward as it might seem. It has been said that relationship marketing is powerful in theory but troubled in practice - an unpalatable concept but probably one with which many marketers could identify. Building a relationship with customers can lead to improved behavioral loyalty and thus to increased bottom-line profits. Examine the human elements of a long-lasting relationship; several elements can be found, all of which can be approximated by careful collection and analysis of loyalty program data. The key element, trust, can be built up by always excelling at customer service and problem correction, and by providing consistently good products and services that suit the customer's unique needs. Surprise and delight can be achieved by delivering personal offers for the most profitable loyalty program members, such as birthday discount shopping days.

Intelligent Response to Competitive Challenges

A good loyalty program's ability to tie purchases to individual customers allows quick and accurate identification of customers who defect when new competition opens nearby. They can then be enticed back with customer-specific special offers or even direct contact. In his book, Loyalty Marketing: The Second Act, Brian Woolf describes how one fairly small, older store had to face up to a competitor opening a much bigger store on the same parking lot. In anticipation, the small store was extensively remodeled, causing considerable disruption. Over the period of remodeling (a matter of several weeks) turnover dropped by 40%. However, a loyalty program enabled management to identify regular shoppers and mail them a letter thanking them for their patience and enclosing some special offers. All but 183 customers returned to the store. The store management team then sent handwritten invitations and a US$10 gift certificate to those 183 customers. All but three returned. After the new competitor opened, the smaller store's whole customer database was mailed an offer containing US$5-off coupons for US$50 orders in each of the following twelve weeks. Any customer using all twelve received an extra US$10 certificate. The result was that sales actually rose by between 6% and 7% over the months following the new opening. The competitor's store (which was approximately twice the size) achieved less than half the sales of the remodeled store. This shows the power of knowing who the customers are.

Improving Product Range and Stock Selection

Knowing what best customers buy frequently helps choose which lines to stock and which lines to expand on. The owner of a small suburban supermarket in the UK had some twelve months' notice that a large national supermarket was opening right over the road from him. He realized that without major changes he would not survive. What he did was simple but clever. The suburb in which he was situated was mixed, having mainly low-cost housing but also a very exclusive area. Many of his customers were low earners who bought their basic requirements every day or two from him - in essence, what they could carry home in a couple of bags. He knew that they would migrate to the lower prices and bigger ranges of the big chain. However, a considerable number of the more wealthy people would call in on their way home from work to pick up bread and milk and a few odds and ends. He started noting what they bought, and what they never bought. Over the months, he stopped ordering products that they never bought, and increased his range of things that they did buy. Over the year, his store slowly changed from a small supermarket to a very big delicatessen. His wealthy customers told their friends and the composition of his customer base changed from mainly low earners to mainly high earners. When the supermarket opened over the road, his low earners did migrate, but he hardly noticed the difference.

Reduce Promotional and Advertising Costs

When having a loyalty program - and the detailed data that comes with it - advertising can be targeted instead of untargeted, and significant savings can be made. There is no need to send out thousands of flyers that will be thrown away unread, or take pages of newspaper space that is irrelevant to many of the readers. Better still, the response from such targeted advertising can be measured accurately because the audience is known, and each offer can carry a unique identifier that ties the offer to both the customer and the moment of redemption. The cost-saving advantage of targeting can be astonishing. In one instance reported by the DMA a few years ago, a company mailed an offer to 450,000 of its 'better' customers. The mailing generated US$22 in revenue for each US$1 spent. On analyzing the response data, it was found that 97% of sales came from 13% of the ZIP codes. Imagine the difference that that made to the profitability of future mailings.

Develop a Master Offer

The companies that boast the highest levels of fiercely loyal customers have built that loyalty not on card programs or gimmicks, but on a solid, dependable, core offering that appeals to their customers. These companies have focused intently on what they know appeals to the type of customers they want to attract, and have determinedly concentrated on delivering what is expected every time. For example, the North American retailer Nordstrom is well known for the extreme loyalty of its customers. It built this loyalty by understanding what its customers wanted and then empowering its employees to deliver those needs consistently. The data from a good loyalty program will help improve this core offering by tailoring and molding it more closely to the customers' needs and desires.

Influence Customer Satisfaction Levels

Clearly, satisfaction is important; indeed essential. But, taken in isolation, the level of satisfaction is not a good measure of loyalty. Many auto manufacturers claim satisfaction levels higher than 90%, yet few have repurchase levels of even half that. The situation is stacked against the business: if customer satisfaction levels are low, there will be very little loyalty. However, customer satisfaction levels can be quite high without a corresponding level of loyalty. Customers have come to expect satisfaction as part and parcel of the general deal, and the fact that they are satisfied doesn't prevent them from defecting in droves to a competitor who offers something extra. The point is that, while high levels of customer satisfaction are needed in order to develop loyal customers, the measure of customer satisfaction is not a good measure of the level of loyalty. The two are not measuring the same thing.

Judge the Marketplace's Influence on Customer Loyalty

The marketplace is a key factor in the development of loyalty. The elements most closely involved are: ease of switching, and inertia. If the number of competing suppliers is high and little effort is required to switch, switching is likely. Conversely, the more time and effort invested in the relationship, the more unlikely switching becomes. The level and quality of competition has a significant effect on how easy it is for a customer to switch from any one particular supplier. When competitors are offering very similar products at similar prices, with similar levels of service, some means of useful differentiation has to be found in order to give customers a reason to be loyal. But inertia is the opposite: most banks enjoy a high level of inertia loyalty simply because it's often so difficult and time-consuming to change to a new bank and transfer direct debits and standing orders.

Promoting the Brand to Build Customer Loyalty

Every business must develop and deliver a consistently branded experience for its customers. The essence of the brand should be apparent in every interaction a customer has with the company, enabling customers to form an emotional attachment with the brand. This includes: training and enabling front-line employees who interact with customers; developing high-impact marketing campaigns; defining the brand's "promise"; and segmenting customers on the basis of value. The loyalty program provides a truly multi-channel vehicle through which to communicate this brand experience, and through which the consumer can become more attached to the company and its brand.

Rapid Market Penetration With a Coalition Program

Partnership in a coalition loyalty program is often thought of (quite rightly) as a quick method of entry into the field of customer loyalty - however, there are disadvantages that must be weighed up first, such as the ownership and usage of loyalty program and customer-specific data, and potential competition of other program partners in future markets to expand into. Successful coalition programs have a major partner in several of the key consumer sectors in order to quickly capture a significant proportion of consumers' spend. Ideally, this would be a major grocer, fuel retailer, bank or credit card, department store, and mobile telecoms provider. Proportions as high 50% - 60% of the target market can be enrolled very quickly. This means that not only is the data collected more representative of the target market but that the share of each consumer's wallet is also maximized. Most importantly, new partners joining the program after it becomes established will automatically gain the same degree of market penetration as the existing partners, and co-marketing activities with the program's operator will usually raise consumer awareness rapidly.

Build a Successful CRM (Customer Relationship Management)

The loyalty of customers stems from building relationships with them, and those relationships have to be managed. This is where CRM comes in. Whether the relationships are so finely tuned as to be one-to-one relationships, or whether they are in bigger segments or groups, the principles of management are similar. Over the past decade CRM has come to be regarded by many marketers as being synonymous with huge, costly IT systems. But many of the big companies have now passed through that stage, and are focusing more on explaining to both employees and customers the benefits of the system, and streamlining the laborious processes of data collection. CRM's reputation is improving - it is making a come-back. Some of the key faults that can cause CRM projects to fail or prevent delivery of the expected ROI are a reliance on technology as a global 'cure-all' and down-playing the importance of management level buy-in. But having the correct focus and commitment can significantly improve a CRM initiative's performance. According to IBM's research, CRM should be run at the corporate level or with a cross-functional perspective - and when this is the case, there is a 25-60% greater chance of success.

Create an Effective Customer Database

There's a myth that says most companies have enough data about their customers to conduct successful marketing campaigns. But, in fact, some of the largest firms in the world have not assembled the personal identities and key contact information of their largest customers into a single database. Instead, the information resides in the minds, drawers, or handheld PDAs of their sales representatives. Rarely is it warehoused as it should be. The amount of junk mail the average consumer gets today proves the point: despite talk of CRM, it hasn't improved relationships between consumers and their suppliers. The problem is that properly implementing a customer database is far more difficult than ever imagined. A customer loyalty program's unifying effect on data, if the data structure is properly planned based on clearly set-out business objectives, forms the basis of relationship-based campaigns that start with "Fred, we see you've moved - here's a map of your local stores to get you started" instead of mailers that start with "Dear Occupier".

Reduce Technical Problems

Avoiding technological problems with loyalty platforms. When setting out to find a ready-made or partly-customized loyalty platform, there are hundreds of points to consider before making a final choice. In 2005 a survey of the capabilities of over 30 loyalty program platforms was conducted by UK-based MJA Associates, finding that many of the solutions examined were merely "points engines" that could increment and decrement the points in a member's account but were limited in the functionality required to manage bonussing, lifestyle data collection, surveys, partner management and other fundamental operations. Most of the loyalty solution software platforms examined were lacking in many areas - particularly in terms of bonussing, partner management, survey functionality, and contact center information screens. Of the hundreds of factors, these are just a few of the most important: Application and member number tracking; Archiving of program data; Audit logs; Awards redemption processing; Bonussing functions and flexibility; Card management; Different currencies and languages; Events management; Interactive Voice Response features; Fees management; Kits and cards processes; Location hierarchy; Member services provisions for call handling; Member management, transaction and attributes recording; Partner management; Points expiration; Point types; Reporting; Security; Development kits and APIs; Statementing; Surveys; Tiering; and Financial transactions and points management. It's important that the chosen system has the necessary features, not only for today but for the future development of the loyalty program.

Designing an Effective Customer Loyalty Program: Model

Based on the discussion presented above, a customer loyalty royalty model is proposed as part of the study. The proposed model, shown in figure 1 below, incorporates superior customer value, effective supply chain management and operational alignment – these are called as Loyalty program levers. All the points discussed in this section above discuss how each of these levers is important for the very existence of a retail business.

Three levers are:

1. Superior customer value.
2. Effective supply chain management.
3. Operational alignment.

Figure 1. Customer loyalty program: model

These levers will act along with the retailers' strategies and the goals. These goals can be described as:

1. Focus areas.
2. Analytics and Insight solutions.
3. Strategic action.
4. Business goals.

CONCLUSION

Loyalty programs have become a mainstay of customer engagement in both the physical retail and online shopping spaces. Loyalty programs allow you to collect information on your customer's behaviors, with the tradeoff of presenting them with more relevant information that increase per customer revenue. In creating a program, factors that can enhance your program to make it stand out must be considered.

Customer loyalty, in itself, is a very complex and even controversial topic. It can be defined either solely by purchase behavior or by adding an attitudinal approach. This chapter included a positive attitude to the definition, as true loyalty cannot be perceived without the involvement of emotions. Customer loyalty programs are a means of practicing customer relationship management with the aim of long-term, profitable relationships. However, loyalty programs have many other objectives and sub-objectives that all aim to achieve in those long-term relationships.

The actual benefits of loyalty programs are hard to measure as they typically involve behavioral changes. In different research, the effects of loyalty programs were not straightforward, and if at all some effects were found, they prevail only in certain conditions. Loyalty programs face challenges that relate to differentiation from competitors in terms of appeal to customers. Although customer information possesses a lot of benefits, the different applications are not fully harnessed and therefore place great challenges for the future. Customers are seen to be polygamous in their loyalty, which means loyalty towards many stores. Therefore, the challenge for retailers is to activate customers and attract them to focus purchases to only one store. In addition, a demographic change in fragmentation of segments has created new challenges for targeting and for the whole design of the loyalty program strategy.

Loyalty programs could be studied from the customer view if they meet the goals set by the company. As satisfaction and store attributes seem to be one of the key determinants behind customers' store decisions, a study on the antecedents of those factors are assumed to provide practical results. The shift is towards improving the whole customer experience, and in the context of retailers, focus on service might bring some sort of competitive advantage.

Customers can be fickle with their loyalty. A single negative incident can ruin a long-standing relationship because there are viable alternatives in today's competitive market. Yet there is also an acceptance of such situations by consumers, which implies that, in spite of past disappointments, consumers are willing to keep building relationships. So, while every business must risk offending customers with imperfect transactions, they can still build meaningful relationships. Loyalty programs attempt to reward customers (and businesses) for sustaining such a relationship by providing clear incentives for patronage. In fact, successful loyalty programs can even accelerate the frequency of customer visits and volume of purchases, strengthening the connection.

To sum up, customer loyalty programs can enhance the creation of loyalty and thereby increase sales. Benefits such as bonuses and discounts make the customers concentrate their purchases to the store where the membership is held. Soft benefits that a customer loyalty program provides are more suitable in creating true loyalty, or attitudinal loyalty, as it could be called. Offering the customers soft benefits could be a key determinant of creating loyalty. It is easy for competing companies to offer price-related benefits while offers that reach beyond the monetary terms can help the company to find their competitive advantage. Also, soft benefits can create an emotional space for the customers that are sometimes valued more than the monetary benefits they receive. In this perspective, soft benefits could enhance the creation of monogamous loyalty and affective commitment. Besides the methods that loyalty programs use in order to create loyalty, the considerable issue that creates loyalty is the specific store and the staff, which does not have anything to do with customer loyalty programs. Many customers expressed the importance of competent staff, high-quality products, as well as an appealing store. Customer loyalty is therefore generated from customers' overall satisfaction and from affective commitment, which derives from the interaction with the retailer and the repeated product and service usage. Conclusively, customer loyalty programs can be used as a complement to create loyalty among customers. Customer loyalty programs alone cannot create loyalty. A company needs to have good products, functional store, and service that are the basis of why customers choose to re-patronize a certain retailer. Retailers, these days, are rightly discovering the positive impact of a customer loyalty program through the usage of a potent combination of cutting-edge technology and personalized service.

REFERENCES

Alexander, P. (2007). *Use Data to Build Customer Loyalty*. Entrepreneur.com.

Clark. (2012). *The Loyalty Guide*. The wisemarketer.com.

Donnelly. (2010). *How to Start a Customer Rewards Program*. Inc.com.

Gordon, K. T. (2010). *Customer Loyalty Brings Long-Term Sales*. Entrepreneur.com

Hennig-Thurau, T., Gwinner, K. P., & Gremler, D. D. (2002). Understanding relationship marketing outcomes: An integration of relational benefits and relationship quality. *Journal of Service Research*, *4*(3), 230–247. doi:10.1177/1094670502004003006

Kelley. (2006). *Using Loyalty Programs to Attract Consumers to Value-Added Businesses*. Extension.psu.edu.

Kolowich, L. (2015). *Customer Loyalty Programs That Actually Add Value*. Marketingdonut.co.uk.

Lehman, T. (2013). *Creating a Loyalty Program*. Newnorth.com.

Loyalty Program Development Making Loyalty Programs Mean More. (n.d.). Newsnorth.com.

Mei-Lien, L. L., & Green, L. (2011). *A mediating influence on customer loyalty: The role of perceived value*. Aabri.com.

Nideau & Singer. (2014). *The Secret To Creating Loyalty Programs That Actually Work*. Businessinsider.com.

Odonnell Company. (2014). *The benefits of a customer loyalty program*. Odonnellco.com.

Peppers & Rogers Group. (2009). *Circumstances and Customers Have Changed: Has Your Loyalty Program Kept Pace?* Oracle.com

Priebatsch, S., & McFeeley, R. (2011). *Engineering Successful Customer Loyalty Programs*. Huffingtonpost.com.

Read, B. (2009). *Top Tips To Build and Keep Customer Loyalty With CRM*. Tmcnet.com.

5. Reasons why Loyalty Programs is the best way of Customer Marketing. (2015). Cloudbiz.eu.

Schaeffer, C. (n.d.). *How to Create a Customer Loyalty Program That Works*. Crmsearch.com.

Sibiraj, P. R. (2015). *Benefits of customer loyalty programs*. Lightrains.com.

Starvish, M. (2011). *Customer Loyalty Programs That Work*. Hbswk.hbs.edu.

Tate, A. (2013). *Bigdoor blog- Top 10 Retail Loyalty Programs*. Bigdoor.com.

15. Things Good Loyalty Programs Do To Create Business Growth. (2013). Drivingretention.com.

Thomson, G. (2014). *How To Create Effective B2B Loyalty Programmes*. Customerstrategynetwork.com.

Timm, P. R. (2007). *Technology and Customer Service: Profitable Relationship Building*. Searchcrm.techtarget.com.

Yadav, R. (2012). *Next Generation Loyalty Management Systems: Trends, Challenges, and Recommendation*. Capgemini.com.

KEY TERMS AND DEFINITIONS

Advertising: Advertising refers to calling the public's attention to a business for the purpose of selling products or services through the use of various platforms such as media, print, or broadcast notices.

Coalition Program: Coalition Program is a loyalty card system that offers incentives to customers of two or more businesses in return for allowing those businesses to collect user data.

Customer Lifetime Value: Customer Lifetime Value is the total profit that a business anticipates from having an enduring commercial relationship with a customer over time.

Customer Loyalty: Customer Loyalty is the likelihood of previous customers to continue to buy from a specific retailer.

Customer Relationship Management: Customer relationship management refers to practices, strategies, and technologies that businesses use to manage and analyze customer interactions and data throughout the customer lifecycle.

Marketplace: Marketplace is a medium that allows buyers and sellers of a specific good or service to interact in order to facilitate an exchange.

Product Range: Product Range is the complete portfolio of products that a company manufactures and/or markets.

Promotion: Promotion refers to raising customer awareness of a product or brand, generating sales, and creating brand loyalty.

Chapter 12
Classification Essay of SCRM Research

Arij Lahmar
University of Sfax, Tunisia

François Galasso
University of Toulouse – Mines Albi, France

Jacques Lamothe
University of Toulouse – Mines Albi, France

Habib Chabchoub
University of Sfax, Tunisia

ABSTRACT

This article investigates the current developments in research and practices in the domain of Supply Chain Risk Management (SCRM) through a systematic and typological approach in order to improve the understanding of SCRM field. This field has created a strong scientific and professional polemic, resulting in an exponential growth of published research work, reports and article. However, it has been discussed that SCRM lacks typological approach by several authors underlining this fact through their frameworks. In response, this review examines various perceptions, notions, definitions, drivers and sources of Supply Chain Risk (SCR), in order to identify major SCRM frameworks. This analysis is required in order to identify the main issues that needed to be addressed in the field of SCRM. Thus, the objective of this paper is to classify these frameworks so as to identify news issues, opportunities and directions for further study and researches.

INTRODUCTION

The world is changing fast and businesses are getting more global everyday. The modern enterprises increasingly are moving away from their non-core businesses and rely on other partners for success of their business. Historically, the enterprises have spent less than a third of their budgets on purchased

DOI: 10.4018/978-1-5225-3056-5.ch012

goods and services, as they relied on internal processes. Today, many of these enterprises spend most of their budget on purchased goods and services.

No enterprise, big or small, can ignore partnerships in order to be competitive in the current global scenario. This is in large part because of the advantages enterprises have found in strategies such as globalization, outsourcing, supply-base rationalization, just-in-time deliveries, and lean inventories. In addition, many companies have consolidated operations both internally and externally to achieve economies of scale.

While globalization and extended supply chains partnerships offer many benefits in efficiency and effectiveness, they also bring in lot of challenges and risks. Such partnerships make supply chains more brittle and can increase risks of supply-chain disruption. There are many events that has occurred in the past that has created the need to identify and mitigate such risks. The succession of economic, industrial and social crises and natural disasters, global logistics organizations have become aware of the criticality of risk management. It has become essential to achieve a complete control of internal and external risks within the supply chain (SC) (Zsidisin 2007). Indeed, the volume of published frameworks in this field has largely grown exponentially during the last 30 years. Considering this rapid development (Kouvelis 2002), it has been argued that this nascent field lacks of works which emphasize the variety of research being accomplished in this area.

Several authors underlined this fact through their frameworks and highlighted the need for an updated, systematic and narrowed re-examination of published frameworks. Others researchers did also provide different typological reviews. But not all of them are particularly different: some embrace the same typologies but under different terminologies, while others focus only in some variants of SCRM concepts. They have been employed separately, creating the need for systematic and typological framework (Singhal 2011). This is needed for discovering and understanding all previous knowledge required for developing new research works (Boote 2005). In light of these considerations, the central purpose of this article is to identify the conceptual content of SCRM, through a systematic and typological approach, as this allows conclusions to be drawn on literature review. Such an objective is not only limited to the analysis of literature review itself, but also intend to provide a new taxonomy of this field, which may offer a way to define it.

To achieve this objective, this paper is organized as follow: Study Position section reflects the effort made with the conventional SCRM literature review in order to identify its main research areas and current issues; next section describes the research methodology adopted in this article; then the author presents the developed classification of different concepts, methods and approaches. This classification is used to highlight the similarities and differences in order to better define the limits of this concept and underline the different perspectives adopted. In the next section, author discusses the findings, with an emphasis on SCRM future research orientations.

STUDY POSITION

The SCRM has been the subject of various trends. The responses to this problem involve two disciplines: the risk management and the supply chain management (SCM). (Boote, D., Bailey 2005) point out that managers seek to create an effective and efficient SC to ensure a competitive advantage. For this reason, they need to find a balance between costs, efficiency, effectiveness, resource use and therefore, risk management has become a reality for businesses to succeed. (Christopher and Peck 2004) highlight that the SCRM mission is to preserve the natural function of SCM which is the creation of value through the SC. This highlights the link between risk management and SC in order to ensure the sustainability and survival of organizations and businesses. This link is particularly important in a time in which the relationships and interactions tend to be complicated in terms of number of partners involved, internationalization of locations and exposure to environmental, financial and political instability.

Tang, C.S presents an important framework that would enable practitioners to engage researchers to work on this important area. He introduces keywords and concepts along with several case studies and a review of academic literature. His objective was to create awareness of this important and not yet well understood subject. Moreover, he detailed existing strategies in order to stimulate practitioners to develop approaches for identifying, assessing, mitigating, and responding to different types of SCR. Nevertheless, recent studies have revealed a lack of implementation of SCRM.

Then, many publications attempt to clarify the definition of relevant terms in the area of applied risk management and security. The literature emphasizes this fact by presenting specific case of studies and researches in this context such as in the aerospace industry.

Hence it seems that SCRM had through the time, evolved from an intra-organizational focus on risk response to become focused in inter-organizational level including resilience and agility of SC. Even if this concept has known a large diffusion among academics and professionals, it reveals different perception in its uses and its applications. This was highlighted by the broad definitions, perceptions and interpretations that have been presented in published research areas. Some authors discuss that SCRM needs more theoretical frameworks along with an empirical complement focus. But this statement has a problem because in reality, managing SCR has not a direct link with the outcomes of the research about how companies do to manage SCR and why they do it in a chosen way. But this cannot lead to neglect the need for in depth studies on the SCRM and its hidden perspectives. These studies require some theoretical framework to conceptualize SCRM without a misleading oversimplification of SCRM complexity.

It is observed that the literature has treated different issues, approaches and orientations but is still missing more conceptual framework and reviews to offer a global approach and an answer for the identified research gap. The section 3 aims to define a methodology in order to deal with the numerous published materials and provide a comprehensive classification framework.

RESEARCH METHODOLOGY

Selection Process

A literature review is a necessary step in building knowledge and theoretical developments of any research field. The objective of this study is to support the identification of the conceptual content of SCRM field by following a clear process. As the SCRM is a multidisciplinary discipline, this study is limited to research journal articles. A combination of referential and critical analysis on this topic is relevant to this study. Indeed, this method is a recognized way and interprets the structure of a research field and its evolution.

Scopus and Emerald databases are used to find articles. The choice of these databases can be explained by the amount of referenced documents they cover, but they also provide information on the cited references. Then, we retrieved information for all papers published in the selected database. Then, a Java program (CiteSpace© and Gephi software©) are used to scan these documents and store the resulting data fields such as authors, publishing sources and years. Then, in a second step, we analyzed the reviews of the literature, according to four criteria: research questions, search process, data extraction and data presentation and results. Here, we included only the articles in which SCR is present as either an element or the main purpose of the article. Papers which do not cover the predefined search criteria (i.e. research question, research process, data retrieval, and presentation of data and results) were excluded. The global process is depicted in Figure 1.

Classification Framework

Understanding SCRM theoretical and methodological base, associated with SC and empirical attributes, is the starting point in order to develop an advanced level of understanding and effectiveness of SCRM implementation. Section 2 underlined the lack of a clear conceptual framework of the concepts underlying SCRM. Even the typologies developed only enumerate various perceptions and perspectives adopted by different researchers. So, based on these considerations, a taxonomy has been developed in order to analyze and to try to bring together the extracted frameworks.

In the aim of summarizing many years of SCRM research and find a common theme, the taxonomy developed, in this article, is based on particular characteristics of the different researchers' perspectives, and the degree of dependencies between frameworks. This typology consists of five categories:

Figure 1. Identification process for article selection

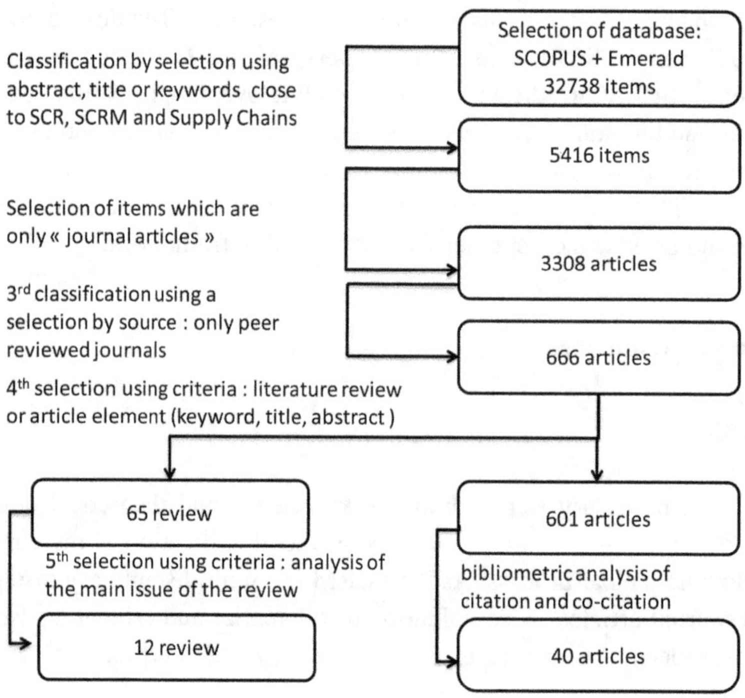

1. **Typology by Definition:** From a conceptual perspective, the first dimension aims at analyzing the variety of terms definition;
2. **Typological Approach:** This second dimension provides an analysis of SCR dimensions and typologies presented in SCRM literature;
3. **Demographic Data:** This category combines the industrial sector and the characteristics of the SC (analytical unit and structural characteristics);
4. **Research Positioning:** This represents the researcher's route to address research objectives. Although there may be a debate on which methodology is the most appropriate and whether the model provide a better understanding than others approaches;
5. **SCRM Features:** It could be viewed as a summary of majors' topics and issues in the SCRM from different authors' perspectives.

These 5 dimensions along with articles were analyzed, integrated into a global classification framework and subdivided. The summary of this classification framework is presented in figure 2 in which the criteria are linked.

RESULTS AND ANALYSIS

This section details the results obtained through the application of the classification framework to a sample of 40 state-of-the-art articles. This section details the results over each criterion as the whole detailed taxonomy is depicted in Figure 3 including all the subcategories.

Figure 2. Classification framework

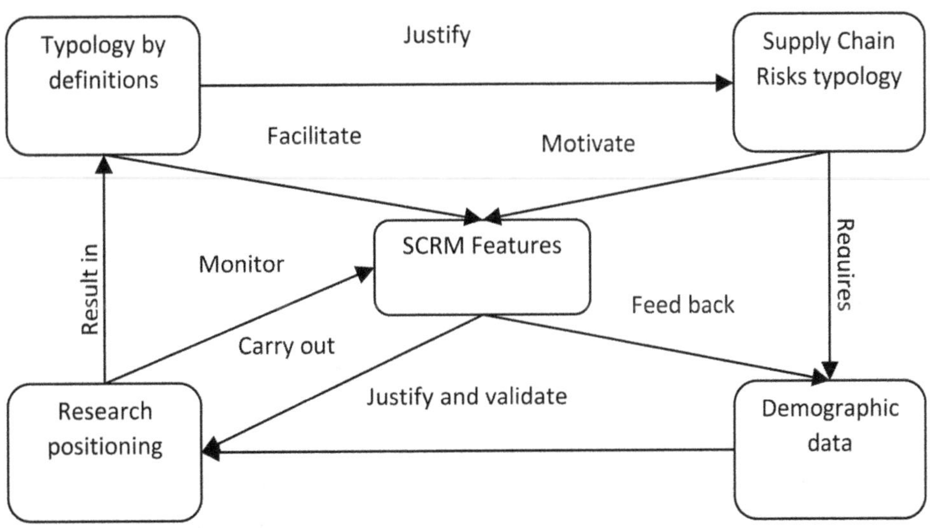

Figure 3. SCRM research frameworks

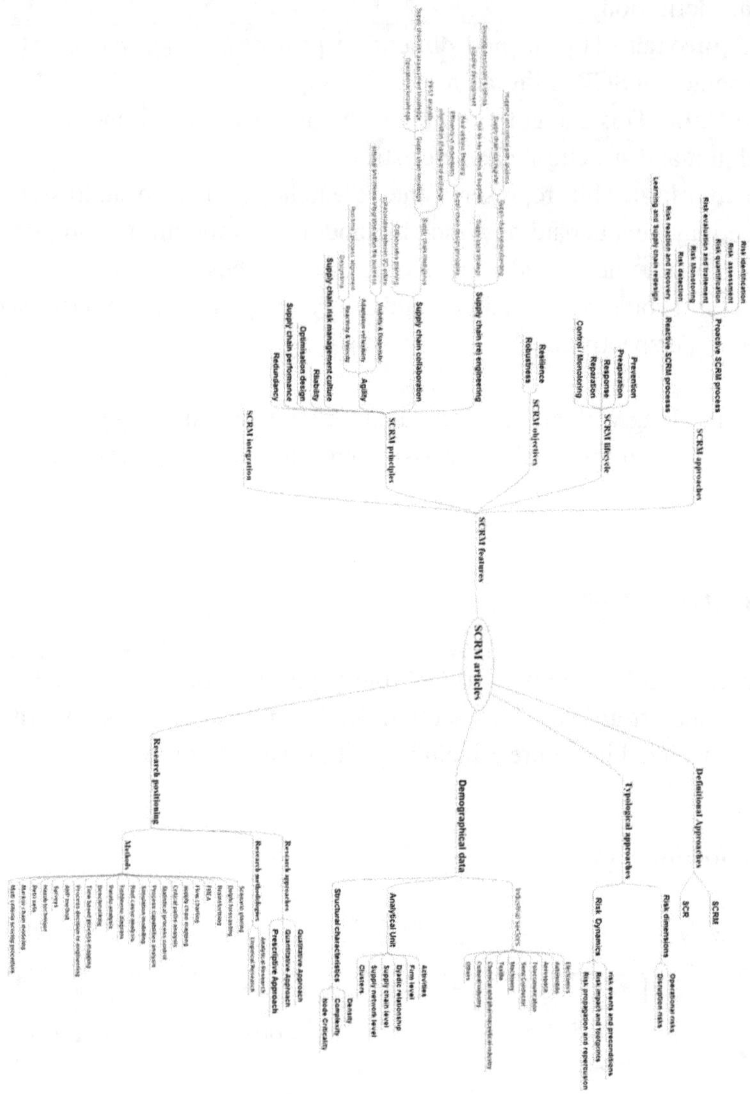

Typology by Definition

An important number of researchers take a broader view of SCRM. In most case, the definition was either used or modified. This underlines the absence of common conceptual framework relating to SCRM and SCR. (Tang 2006) has explained this fact by the maturity level of SCRM. According to (Burgess, Singh, Koroglu 2006), most researchers adopt a standard definition in a mature field. And in case of SCRM area, this domain is not yet in a maturity stage. Therefore, it is expected in coming years that developed definitions will be proposed, until a common conceptual framework is reached.

Typological Approaches

Efforts to classify and analyze typologies of SCR have been made. For instance, a typology of SCR is required to identify mitigation strategies and the probability of increasing another type of risk. Two criteria are adopted:

1. **Risk Dimensions:** Following the framework suggested by Tang a categorization of SCR, into disruption risks and operational risks, was followed. The operational risks are inherent from interactions between SC entities and arising from SC processes. Disruption risks arise from interactions between a SC and the environment. This classification allows answering two questions: who and how manage SCR.
2. **Risk Dynamics:** Risk dynamic deals with the question of how SCR can be evaluated through the time. Three components of SCR dynamics have been identified by the research, which are: risk event and preconditions, risk footprints and impacts, and risks propagation and repercussion. These three components are related to SC design characteristics and causes four possible scenarios:
    a. A low level of risk, related to one isolated node within a SC;
    b. A medium level of risk, related to one interconnected node within a SC;
    c. A high level of risk, related to one isolated node within a SC;
    d. an extreme level of risk, related to one interconnected node within a SC.

Considering these four hypothesis, it seems difficult to determine exactly the total risks aggregated at the whole SC level, even if evaluations are done node by node.

Therefore, SCRM approach should taking into consideration the dependencies and correlation between SC entities and the risk propagation through the entire SC.

Demographic Data

In order to address the different aspects of supply chains analysis and characteristics, this dimension include the three following subcategories:

Industrial Sector

Industrial sector analysis provides an insight to supply chain opportunities, risks and menaces, through knowing the weaknesses and strengths of every industrial sector. Indeed, the analysis of sector represents an intermediate entity between the whole economic system and each supply chain. SCRM should be specific to industrial sector characteristics. Researchers have revealed the question of SCRM for various industrial sectors, asking "what are the commonalities and differences among different sectors regarding SCR issues? How develop specific SCRM strategies for specific industrial sectors?

In response, two cases are distinguished: (1) the product or service is realized in response to a primary requirement (for instance: a plane used for civil transportation); (2) pathways exist in which the product or service could respond to a secondary requirement (for instance: the same plane used for military purpose).

An appropriate approach for SCRM can be assessed only by analyzing a situation considering that it is related to one of these two clusters.

Figure 4. Possible sceanarios of SCR propagation

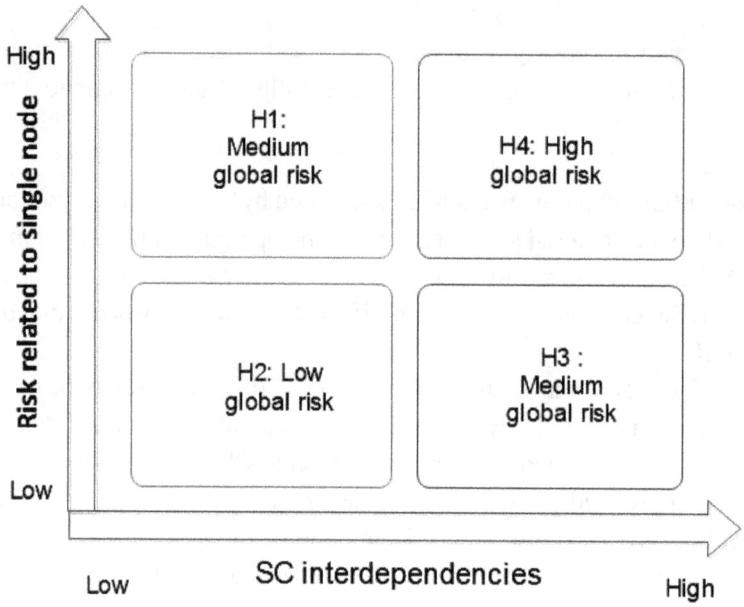

Unit of Analysis

The published papers were first categorized into four levels according to the structure of the unit of analysis from a single activity to a network of organizations. The results of classification highlight the fact that SCRM is treated from dyadic relationships rather than supply network perspective. This can be explained by the historical development of supply chain management and the strategies adopted in this field. Hence it seems SCRM was altered from a process view to a system or "network" view. The determination of supply chain structure impacts the choice of strategies and approaches of SCRM.

Structural Characteristic

The relationship between supply chain entities is considered as a potential source of risks and it should be incorporated in risk management process. Supply chain structure and configuration has a major impact on risk management assessment.

Despite this insight, a few of articles has treated the impact of supply chain entities structure and the dependencies on SCRM.

Research Positioning

The fourth important element in SCRM literature is the research positioning, which represent the researchers' choice and path leading to research objectives. This element was categorized into two sub categories. The first subcategory classified articles into quantitative, qualitative and prescriptive approach. And the second subcategory encloses two groups: empirical and analytical methodologies. Articles whose research methodology or approach is theoretical, conceptual, literature reviews, simulations or

Figure 5. Relationship between supply chain characteristics and SCR

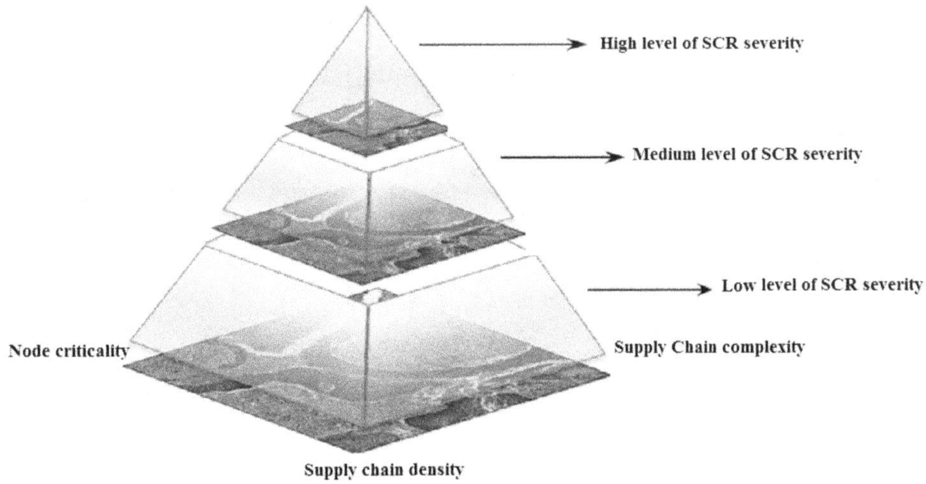

theoretical modeling were considered as conceptual research methodology. Surveys, case studies and experimental research were considered as empirical research methodology.

The conceptual methodology is used to present, describe and analyze fundamental issues and concepts. It may be viewed as an analysis of the research problem using theory. In the field of SCRM, most of papers present a conceptual methodology. For example, a research by Ritchie presents a review of qualitative models for managing operational risks. In the same orientation, another research by (Vanany 2009), present a conceptual approach to understand the impact of enablers' dynamics on mitigation strategies. Although that conceptual methodology is needed in order to understand theoretical issues of SCRM, empirical approach is required to validate the hypothesis made in this first methodology. Empirical methodology seeks and uses data (case study, surveys, experimental research, etc.) to answer theoretical questions.

SCRM Features

SCRM Lifecycle

Lifecycles are used to describe the system states through the time. Three main lifecycle phases are formation (focus on how develop and organize a system), operation (or execution, used to maintain system function and to cope with possible problems and issues) and finally the reconfiguration or the cessation (adapt the system to meet the changes or destroy it). The lifecycle is needed to recognize the impact of different choice on the system continuity and also to provide a management control. And as control and strategies evaluation are critical for SCRM, a new methodology of lifecycle is developed and adjusted for SCR. Figure 6 illustrates the supply chain risk lifecycle diagram (SCRLC).

Figure 6. SCR lifecycle

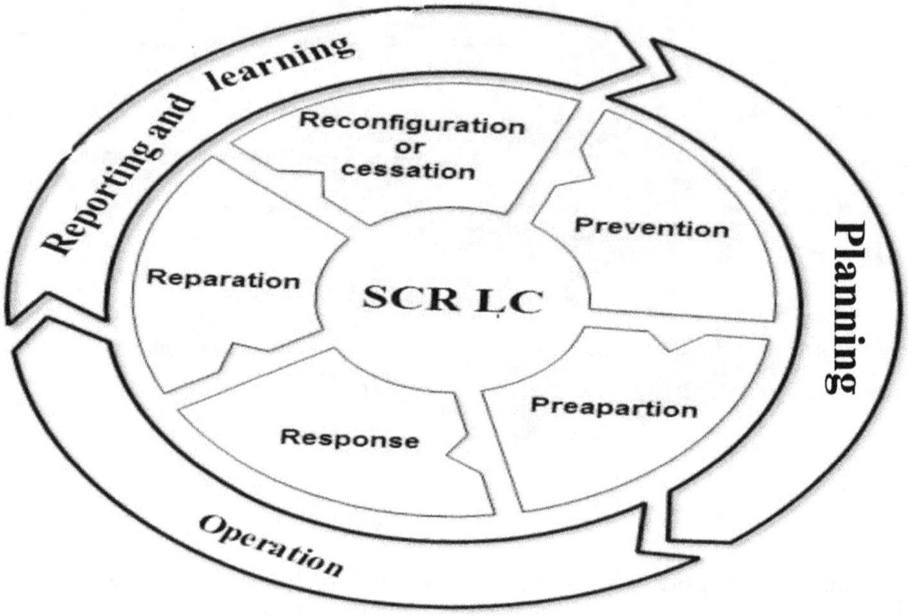

SCRM Approaches

According to (Paulsson 2005) the SCRM is a collaborative and structured approach to risk management, integrated into the planning and control of the supply chain to manage the risks that could jeopardize the attainment objectives of the supply chain. In another aspect, this definition highlights two fundamental factors in SCRM, which are: the reduction of vulnerabilities of the supply chain (objective approach), and the collective character of this approach. According to (Ritchie 1993), this is the body of any approach and methodology for managing risk in the supply chain. Others researchers and academics added some additional steps in this process or even they break the four main phases in sub-steps to facilitate the understanding of the methodology and also to facilitate it implementation. Yang suggest a five step methodology for SCRM including the selection of Risk Management Strategies.

In the same context, (Mitroff 2003) present the strategies developed for stimulating practitioners to develop a holistic approach for identifying, assessing, mitigating, and responding to different types of SCRs. Two considerations are underlined in this article: first the impact of mitigation strategies on supply chain networks and second the consideration of balance between cost and risk level in the selective process for the appropriate supply chain risk mitigation strategies.

The four step methodology presented is used in the proactive approach of SCRM. According to (Sodhi 2012) and (Pfohl 2010), the methodology aforesaid is the essence to manage risks in advance of their occurrence. But, with the diversity of supply chain risk and with the impossibility to predict and identify all risks in the supply chain and their probabilities of occurrence, the need for the reactive approach was pointed out.

(Zsidisin 2009) illustrate an orientation toward preventive approach comparing to the reactive approach. Pfohl express that SCRM was oriented towards reactive approach to avoid the possible consequences of perturbations and to improve the capacity of logistics organizations to resist disturbance and reduce vulnerabilities. But currently, an orientation towards preventive approach has been noticed. And this can be explained by the objectives of logistics networks which aim to create added value and competitive advantage. And this can be reached through better compromise risk - benefit. (Sodhi 2012) have highlighted the reality that companies do not afford the investment and cost of prevention plans and strategies of all SCRs that probably would never be materialized. For this reason, the authors suggest a kind of integration of these two approaches in order to ensure a better risk management in the supply chain.

SCRM Objectives

The focus of risk analysis is the maintaining of supply chain operations and continuity. And in order to fulfill their mission, supply chain need to be resilient or robust. These two notions were the central debate between researchers and tend to be very used indiscriminately and without the precise understanding of their meaning. (Christopher 2004) state that robustness is the ability of a system to cope with perturbation during his function. However, resilience refers to system ability to renew their performance at the original or to new level after a perturbation. In others words, supply chain robustness can be defined as the ability to resist and resilience as the ability to adapt.

SCRM Principles

Recent concerns began with the definition of basic principles and pillars needed to assist SCRM objectives. (Christopher 2004) state that resilience implies agility, collaboration and risk management culture. (Shefi 2005) highlight that flexibility is perhaps one of the more prominent proponent of the resilience, stating that instead of relying solely on supply chain redundancy, a well-managed firm should develop resilience, by building flexibility that can be used to “bounce back” from disruptions. In another perspective, (Tang 2011) recommend, in his article, nine different robust strategies for mitigating supply chain disruptions.

Between SCRM objectives and their basis, a distinction needs to be made: (1) Flexibility: the planned and/or scheduled adaptation to expected changing circumstances; (2) Agility: the unplanned and/or unscheduled adaptation to unforeseen and unexpected changing circumstances; (3) Robustness: the ability to withstand and endure changing circumstances without adaptation; (4) Resilience: the ability to survive changing circumstances despite suffering severe impact.

SCRM Integration

The SCRM need a structured and coordinated approach between supply chain entities, to reduce risk through a systematic identification approach, assessment and quantification of potential disruptions. It aims to control the degree of exposure to risk while reducing the impact on the supply chain. And this requires an integrated and structured approach. It achieves the difficulty of apprehension of the complexity and the strong interaction of the supply chain and sustainability of the approach, in line with the strategies. Moreover, the success of such an approach requires the development of a culture and conscience, which must be shared among the actors of the supply chain. This integrated approach allows achieving levels of maturation coordinated through the alignment of strategies and process integration. It then serves learning practices SCRM and a guide for future risks.

Figure 7. SCRM Objectives and principles

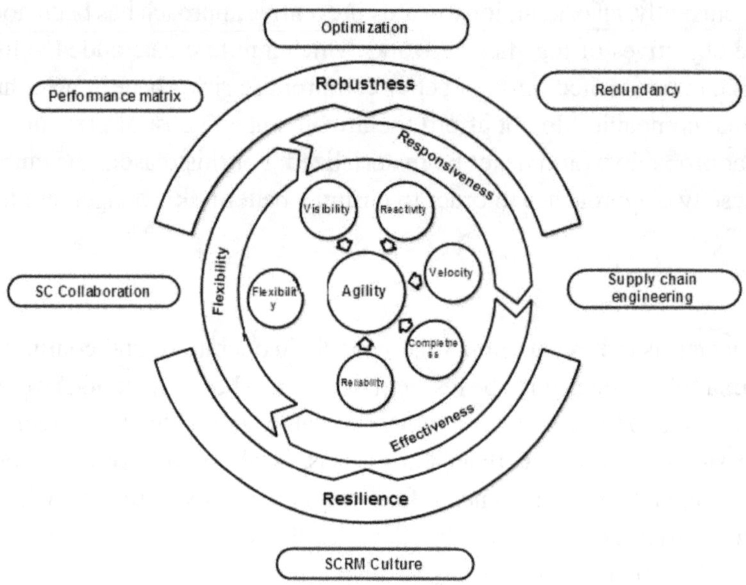

CONCLUSION

The typology developed is designed to offer a clear understanding from conceptual issues, through theoretical and methodological matters, up to covering the implementation issues of SCRM.

In order to study the various perspectives and to capture a range of views, authors adopted a conservative approach in order to avoid imposing particular perceptions of constructs. The reviews revealed some issues concerning SCRM research:

1. The lack of exploratory research (Thun 2011) and quantitative studies involving modeling and simulation tool. In addition, the limited research on supply chain risks decision strategies;
2. The lack of research on the supply chain risks interconnections;
3. The unbalance marked on the supply chain risk life cycle. We remark a common focus in the pre-disruption view of SCR life;
4. The lack of scientific research for the development of a knowledge database in the field of SCRM.

FUTURE RESEARCH DIRECTION

These issues may arise from different causes which we can enumerate: The complexity of supply chain management in combination with the instability of turbulent environment. Then, the infancy of SCRM research topic which is even today still in the development stage. Moreover, they highlight the importance of developing more research and investigation in this field.

In this perspective, a set of recommendations need to be taken into consideration in the future studies, such as:

1. Developing a better understanding of the supply chain management and its missions and how it's have been affected by risks, would have the potential effect in the supply chain decision strategy (Genin 2007);
2. Further development of theoretical and practical supply chain risk management, especially if the research agenda focuses on the following three areas (definition, process and methodology);
3. SCRM need to understand how companies' do, in reality, to manage supply chain risk and why they do it in a chosen way. And, based on research into the two previous topics, improved theory and models of supply chain risk management can be developed;
4. Finally, the integration of three sets of literature: complexity theory literature, process literature and performance theory literature that will be validated by the theoretical and empirical research.

REFERENCES

Asbjørnslett, B. E. (2009). Assessing the vulnerability of supply chains. In Supply Chain Risk. Springer US. doi:10.1007/978-0-387-79934-6_2

Boote, D., & Bailey, P. (2005). Scholars before researchers on the centrality of the literature review in research preparation. *Educational Research*, *34*(6), 3–15. doi:10.3102/0013189X034006003

Burgess, K., Singh, P. J., & Koroglu, R. (2006). Supply chain management: A structured literature review and implications for future research. *International Journal of Operations & Production Management*, *26*(7), 703–729. doi:10.1108/01443570610672202

Ceryno, P. S., Scavarda, L. F., Klingebiel, K., & Yüzgülec, G. (2012). Supply Chain Risk Management: A Content Analysis Approach. *International Journal of Industrial Engineering and Management.*, *4*(3), 141–150.

Cheng, S. K., & Kam, B. H. (2008). A conceptual framework for analysing risk in supply networks. *Journal of Enterprise Information Management*, *21*(4), 345–360. doi:10.1108/17410390810888642

Chopra, S., & Sodhi, M. S. (2004). Managing risk to avoid supply-chain breakdown. *MIT Sloan Management Review.*, *46*(1), 53–61.

Christopher, M., & Peck, H. (2004). Building the Resilient Supply Chain. *Int. J. Logistics Management.*, *15*(2), 1–14. doi:10.1108/09574090410700275

Craighead, C. W., Blackhurst, J., Rungtusanatham, M. J., & Handfield, R. B. (2007). The severity of supply chain disruptions: Design characteristics and mitigation capabilities. *Decision Sciences*, *38*(1), 131–156. doi:10.1111/j.1540-5915.2007.00151.x

Craighead, C. W., Blackhurst, J., Rungtusanatham, M. J., & Handfield, R. B. (2007). The severity of supply chain disruptions: Design characteristics and mitigation capabilities. *Decision Sciences*, *38*(1), 131–156. doi:10.1111/j.1540-5915.2007.00151.x

Dani, S., Ghadge, A., & Kalawsky, R. (2012). Supply chain risk management: Present and future scope. *International Journal of Logistics Management.*, *23*(3), 313–339. doi:10.1108/09574091211289200

Faisal, M. N., Banwet, D. K., & Shankar, R. (2006). Mapping supply chains on risk and customer sensitivity dimensions. *Industrial Management & Data Systems, 106*(6), 878–895. doi:10.1108/02635570610671533

Finch, P. (2004). Supply chain risk management. *Supply Chain Management: An International Journal, 9*(2), 183–196. doi:10.1108/13598540410527079

Genin, P., Lamouri, S., & Thomas, A. (2007). Improving the robustness of a supply chain tactical plan. *Supply Chain Forum: An International Journal, 8*(2), 24-35.

Greening, P., & Rutherford, C. (2011). Disruptions and supply networks: A multi-level, multi-theoretical relational perspective. *Int. J. of Logistics Management., 22*(1), 104–126. doi:10.1108/09574091111127570

Harland, C., Brenchley, R., & Walker, H. (2003). Risk in supply networks. *Journal of Purchasing and Supply Management, 9*(2), 51–62. doi:10.1016/S1478-4092(03)00004-9

Harland, C., Brenchley, R., & Walker, H. (2003). Risk in supply networks. *Journal of Purchasing and Supply Management, 9*(2), 51–62. doi:10.1016/S1478-4092(03)00004-9

Jüttner, U. (2005). Supply chain risk management: Understanding the business requirements from a practitioner perspective. *Int. J. of Logistics Management., 16*(1), 120–141. doi:10.1108/09574090510617385

Juttner, U., Peck, H., & Christopher, M. (2003). Supply Chain Risk Management: Outlining an Agenda for Future Research. *International Journal of Logistics: Research and Applications., 6*(4), 199–213. doi:10.1080/13675560310001627016

Kleindorfer, P. R., & Saad, G. H. (2005). Managing disruption risks in supply chains. *Production and Operations Management, 14*(1), 53–68. doi:10.1111/j.1937-5956.2005.tb00009.x

Kouvelis, P., & Milner, J. M. (2002). Supply chain capacity and outsourcing decisions: The dynamic interplay of demand and supply uncertainty. *IIE Transactions, 34*(8), 717–728. doi:10.1080/07408170208928907

Marques, G., Gourc, D., Lamothe, J., & Thierry, C. (2010). Collaboration and risk management support in uncertain supply chain context. In *International Conference on Information Systems, Logistics and Supply Chain (ILS 2010)*. Facultés Universitaires Catholiques de Mons.

Martin, K. A., Moritz, S. E., & Hall, C. R. (1999). A literature review and applied model. *The Sport Psychologist, 13*(3), 245–268. doi:10.1123/tsp.13.3.245

Mitroff, I. I., & Alpaslan, M. C. (2003). Preparing for evil. *Harvard Business Review, 81*(4), 109–115. PMID:12687925

Mitroff, I. I., & Alpaslan, M. C. (2003). Preparing for evil. *Harvard Business Review, 81*(4), 109–115. PMID:12687925

Norrman, A., & Lindroth, R. (2004). Categorization of supply chain risk and risk management. In C. Brindley (Ed.), *Supply Chain Risk* (pp. 14–27). Ashgate Publishing.

Papadakis, I. S. (2006). Financial performance of supply chains after disruptions: An event study. *Supply Chain Management: An International Journal, 11*(1), 25–33. doi:10.1108/13598540610642448

Paulsson, U. (2005). *Developing a Supply Chain Flow Risk Model.* Final paper to the NOFOMA 2005 Conference, Copenhagen, Denmark.

Pfohl, H., Kohler, H., & Thomas, D. (2010). State of the art in supply chain risk management research: Empirical and conceptual findings and a roadmap for the implementation in practice. *Logistics Research.*, *2*(1), 33–44. doi:10.1007/s12159-010-0023-8

Ritchie, B., & Brindley, C. (2007). An emergent framework for supply chain risk management and performance measurement. *The Journal of the Operational Research Society*, *58*(11), 1398–1411. doi:10.1057/palgrave.jors.2602412

Ritchie, R. L., & Marshall, D. V. (1993). *Business Risk Management.* London: Chapman & Hall.

Shefi, Y., & Rice, J. B. (2005). A Supply Chain View of the Resilient Enterprise. *MIT Sloan Management Review*, *47*(1), 41–48.

Singhal, P., Agarwal, G., & Lal Mittal, M. (2011). Supply Chain Risk Management: Review, classification and future research directions. I. J. *Bus. Sci. App. Man.*, *6*, 15–42.

Sodhi, M. S., Son, B. G., & Tang, C. S. (2012). Researchers perspectives on supply chain risk management. *Production and Operations Management*, *21*(1), 1–13. doi:10.1111/j.1937-5956.2011.01251.x

Tang, C. S. (2006). Perspectives in supply chain risk management. *International Journal of Production Economics*, *103*(2), 451–488. doi:10.1016/j.ijpe.2005.12.006

Tang, O., & Nurmaya Musa, S. (2011). Identifying risk issues and research advancements in supply chain risk management. I.J.P. *E (Norwalk, Conn.)*, *133*(1), 25–34.

Thun, J. H., & Hoenig, D. (2011). An empirical analysis of supply chain risk management in the German automotive industry. I.J.P. *E (Norwalk, Conn.)*, *131*(1), 242–249.

Vanany, I., Zailani, S., & Pujawan, N. (2009). Supply chain risk management: Literature review and future research. *International Journal of Information Systems and Supply Chain Management*, *2*(1), 16–33. doi:10.4018/jisscm.2009010102

Wacker, J. G. (1998). A definition of theory: Research guidelines for different theory building for different theory-building research methods in operations management. *Journal of Operations Management*, *16*(4), 361–385. doi:10.1016/S0272-6963(98)00019-9

Yang, Z., Aydin, G., Babich, V., & Beil, D. R. (2009). Supply disruptions, asymmetric information, and a backup production option. *Management Science*, *55*(2), 192–209. doi:10.1287/mnsc.1080.0943

Zsidisin, G. A. (2003). A Grounded Definition of Supply Risk. *J. Pur. & Sup. Man.*, *9*(5-6), 217–224. doi:10.1016/j.pursup.2003.07.002

Zsidisin, G. A., & Ritchie, B. (2009). Supply Chain Risk Management-Developments, Issues and Challenges. In G. A. Zsidisin & B. Ritchie (Eds.), *Supply Chain Risk: A Handbook of Assessment, Management, and Performance* (pp. 1–12). New York: Springer. doi:10.1007/978-0-387-79934-6_1

ADDITIONAL READING

Castillo, C. (2004, July). Disaster Preparedness and Business Continuity Planning at Boeing: An Integrated Model. *Journal of Facilities Management*, *3*(1), 5–26.

Finch, P. (2004). Supply Chain Risk Management. *Supply Chain Management: An International Journal*, *9*(2), 183–196. doi:10.1108/13598540410527079

Giunipero, L. C., & Eltantawy, R. A. (2004). Securing the Upstream Supply Chain: A Risk Management Approach. *International Journal of Physical Distribution & Logistics Management*, *34*(9), 698–713. doi:10.1108/09600030410567478

Norrman, A., & Jansson, U. (2004). Ericssons Proactive Supply Chain Risk Management Approach After a Serious Sub-supplier Accident. *International Journal of Physical Distribution & Logistics Management*, *34*(5), 434–456. doi:10.1108/09600030410545463

Pitt, M., & Goyal, S. (2004). Business Continuity Planning as a Facilities Management Tool. *Facilities*, *22*(3/4), 87–99. doi:10.1108/02632770410527824

Ritchie, B., & Brindley, C. (2007). Supply Chain Risk Management and Performance: A Guiding Framework for Future Development. *International Journal of Operations & Production Management*, *27*(3), 303–322. doi:10.1108/01443570710725563

Wu, T., Huang, S., Blackhurst, J., Zhang, X., & Wang, S. (2013). Supply chain risk management: An agent-based simulation to study the impact of retail stockouts. *IEEE Transactions on Engineering Management*, *60*(4), 676–686. doi:10.1109/TEM.2012.2190986

Yang, B., & Yang, Y. (2010). Postponement in supply chain risk management: A complexity perspective. *International Journal of Production Research*, *48*(7), 1901–1912. doi:10.1080/00207540902791850

Yu, Y., Xiong, W., & Cao, Y. (2015). A conceptual model of Supply Chain Risk Mitigation: The role of supply chain integration and organizational risk propensity. *Journal of Coastal Research*, *73*, 95–98. doi:10.2112/SI73-017.1

Zsidisin, G., Ragatz, G. L., & Melnyk, S. A. (2005). An institutional theory perspective of business continuity planning for purchasing and supply management. *International Journal of Production Research*, *43*(16), 3401–3420. doi:10.1080/00207540500095613

Zsidisin, G. A., Panelli, A., & Upton, R. (2000). Purchasing Organization Involvement in Risk Assessments, Contingency Plans, and Risk Management: An Exploratory Study. *Supply Chain Management*, *5*(4), 187–198. doi:10.1108/13598540010347307

KEY TERMS AND DEFINITIONS

Activity-Based Cost Accounting (ABC): A cost accounting system that accumulates costs based on activities performed and then uses cost drivers to allocate these costs to products or other bases, such as customers, markets, or projects. It is an attempt to allocate overhead costs on a more realistic basis than direct labor or machine hours.

Activity-Based Management (ABM): The use of activity-based costing information about cost pools and drivers, activity analysis, and business processes to identify business strategies; improve product design, manufacturing, and distribution; and remove waste from operations.

Agreements: An agreement should clearly state what you are buying and its cost. Delivery terms and responsibility, Installation related issues, if applicable, an acceptance provision detailing how and when the buyer will accept the products, warranty issues, and your remedial actions should be clearly spelled out in the agreement. Arbitration and conflict resolution mechanisms should also be included in the contract because even the best written agreements are subject to misinterpretation.

Capacity Management: The function of establishing, measuring, monitoring, and adjusting limits or levels of capacity in order to execute all manufacturing schedules; i.e., the production plan, master production schedule, material requirements plan, and dispatch list. Capacity management is executed at four levels: resource requirements planning, rough-cut capacity planning, capacity requirements planning, and input/output control.

Capacity Strategy: One of the strategic choices that a firm must make as part of its manufacturing strategy. There are three commonly recognized capacity strategies: lead, lag, and tracking. A lead capacity strategy adds capacity in anticipation of increasing demand. A lag strategy does not add capacity until the firm is operating at or beyond full capacity. A tracking strategy adds capacity in small amounts to attempt to respond to changing demand in the marketplace.

Channel Management: The management of firms or individuals that participate in the flow of goods and services from the raw material supplier and producer to the final user or customer.

Continuous Improvement: A never-ending effort to expose and eliminate root causes of problems; small step improvement as opposed to big step improvement.

Contract Management: Contract management is a strategic management discipline employed by both buyers and sellers whose objectives are to manage customer and supplier expectations and relationships, control risk and cost, and contribute to organizational profitability/success. For successful service contract administration, the buyer needs to have a realistic degree of control over the supplier's performance. Crucial to success in this area is the timely availability of accurate data including the contractor's plan of performance and the contractor's actual progress.

Cost System Design: An intelligent cost system design is one that is simple while still providing managers with information they need to make decisions. As most manufacturing processes were labor intensive at the turn of the century, a majority of cost management systems relied on direct labor to assign indirect costs to products and services. Indirect or overhead costs are costs that are associated with or caused by two or more operating activities jointly but are not traceable to each of them individually. Direct costs, on the other hand, are specifically traceable to or caused by a specific project or production operation.

Customer Relationship Management (CRM): A marketing philosophy based on putting the customer first. It involves the collection and analysis of information designed for sales and marketing decision support to understand and support existing and potential customer needs. It includes account management, catalog and order entry, payment processing, credits and adjustments, and other functions.

Customer/Order Fulfillment Process: A series of customers' interactions with an organization through the order filling process, including product/service design, production and delivery, and order status reporting.

Distribution Channel Design: The planned channels of inventory disbursement from one or more sources to field warehouses and ultimately to the customer. There are several levels in the distribution network structure.

Forecast Error: The difference between actual demand and forecast demand, stated as an absolute value or as a percentage. E.g., average forecast error, forecast accuracy, mean absolute deviation, tracking signal. There are three ways to accommodate forecasting errors: One is to try to reduce the error through better forecasting. The second is to build more visibility and flexibility into the supply chain. And the third is to reduce the lead time over which forecasts are required.

Inbound Logistics: Following the receipt of materials, parts or resale products from external suppliers, the subsequent storage, handling, and transportation requirements to facilitate either manufacturing or market distribution constitute inbound logistics.

Information Sharing: A strategic partnering relationship between suppliers and buyers is characterized by a willingness to be open, and to share forecasted demand and cost data as well as the benefits resulting from the information sharing. Both parties in the relationship generally follow a continuous improvement philosophy towards total cost of material acquisition and ownership along with quality and service. Cost, quality and schedule information that is confidential is shared both ways between firms during the early and ongoing stages of design and during the production life-cycle of the supplying relationship.

Insource vs Outsource: The act of deciding whether to produce an item internally or buy it from an outside supplier. Factors to consider in the decision include costs, capacity availability, proprietary and/or specialized knowledge, quality considerations, skill requirements, volume, and timing.

Inventory Positioning: Inventory positioning refers to the selective location of various items in the product line in plant, regional, or field warehouses. Inventory positioning has a bearing on facility location decision, and therefore, must be considered in the logistics strategy.

Lead Times/Cycle Times: 1) A span of time required to perform a process (or series of operations). 2) In a logistics context, the time between recognition of the need for an order and the receipt of goods. Individual components of lead time can include order preparation time, queue time, processing time, move or transportation time, and receiving and inspection time.

Lean Manufacturing: A philosophy of production that emphasizes the minimization of the amount of all the resources (including time) used in the various activities of the enterprise. It involves identifying and eliminating non-value-adding activities in design, production, supply chain management, and dealing with the customers. Lean producers employ teams of multi-skilled workers at all levels of the organization and use highly flexible, increasingly automated machines to produce volumes of products in potentially enormous variety. It contains a set of principles and practices to reduce cost through the relentless removal of waste and through the simplification of all manufacturing and support processes.

Section 4

Field Applications

Chapter 13
Perishable Goods Supply Cold Chain Management in India

Anju Bharti
Maharaja Agrasen Institute of Management Studies, India

Arun Mittal
Birla Institute of Technology, India

ABSTRACT

India has seen a phenomenal growth and occupies the top three positions in production from last decades in production of horticulture produce, dairy and meat products over the last decade. But at present, India's share in global farm trade is still very small even with such large production volumes. This is mainly caused due to lack of cold chain infrastructure which includes both storage and transportation facilities. The cold chain industry in India is still at a nascent stage and despite large production of perishables, the cold chain potential still remain untapped due to high share of single commodity cold storage, high initial investment (for refrigerator units and land), lack of enabling infrastructure like power & roads, lack of awareness for handling perishable produce and lapse of service either by the storage provider or the transporter leading to poor quality produce. Cold chain systems are crucial to the growth of global trade in perishable products and to the worldwide availability of food and health supplies.

INTRODUCTION

India has seen a phenomenal growth and occupies the top three positions in production from last decades in production of horticulture produce, dairy and meat products over the last decade. But at present, India's share in global farm trade is still very small even with such large production volumes. India is also one of the world's largest consumers of food. According to Top Markets Report, 2015, on Cold Chain by International Trade Administration, it is the third largest producer of agriculture. India is one of the largest producers of milk in the world with the largest livestock population. India is the second largest producer of fruits and vegetables in the world with production of 81.3 million MT and 162.2 million MT respectively but its share in global export of fruits and vegetables is around 1.4% only. Approximately,

DOI: 10.4018/978-1-5225-3056-5.ch013

18% of fruits and vegetables get wasted in the country. This is mainly caused due to lack of cold chain infrastructure which includes both storage and transportation facilities.

Food processing methods refers to value addition to agricultural or horticultural produce. The food processing sector is composed of two segments:

1. Primary food processing sector (62% in value, packaged fruits and vegetables, milk, etc.) and
2. Value added food processing sector (38% in value, processed fruits and vegetables, juices, jam & jelly etc.).

Specifically in India, around 40% of produce gets wasted due to inadequate cold chain infrastructure, and one third of losses incur during storage and transit as it has less than half the capacity to meet its current cold chain needs(www.coolingindia.in, 2016).

Now, the Indian agriculture sector is on the threshold of a major shift from traditional farming to horticulture, meat and poultry and dairy products, all of which fall under perishables. As the consumption habit is changing drastically, the demand for fresh and processed fruits and vegetables is also increasing with urban population. It is expected that Indian cold chain industry will attract more overseas partners to learn more about the market to position themselves to take full advantage of emerging opportunities. Cold chains are primarily for fruits and vegetables, meat and marine products, dairy products, ice creams and confectionery, which are perishable. The markets for cold chain have been sub-divided into a number of sectors. These are, for example, agriculture, horticulture, fisheries aquaculture, dairy, processed food for ready-to-eat together with the packaging companies, retailers, wholesalers, etc.

There is an arising increase in demand, diversification and value addition which are the dominating factor in the Indian agriculture today. The emergence of an organised retail food sector coupled with changes in FDI laws has created fresh opportunities in domestic perishables and food industry which includes the cold chain sector. The Indian government needs to focus more on food preservation so the cold storage sector may undergo a major breakthrough. The government is giving full support and has introduced various incentives and policy changes in order to eliminate production wastage and decide on fair price for harvest, increase PPP and improve the country's rural infrastructure. It is expected that Indian cool chain industry will attract more overseas partners to learn more about the market to position them to take full advantage of emerging opportunities (www.itln.in, 2014).

The success totally relies upon effective management of the 'cold chain', a term used to describe the series of interdependent operations in the production, distribution, storage and retailing of chilled and frozen foods. Control of the cold chain is vital to preserve the safety and quality of refrigerated foods and comply with legislative directives and industry 'codes of practice' (EU Commission).

REQUIREMENTS OF COLD CHAIN

Cold chain for perishable foods is becoming increasingly important. As, a study done by the United Nations Environment Program conveyed that over half of the food produced globally is lost, wasted or discarded as a result of inefficiency in the human-managed food chain. Now a day, proper temperature monitoring and management throughout the cold chain is no longer a luxury but have become a necessity. Even relatively a small variation in temperature can significantly impact the shelf life of fresh produce and its value. The cold chain requires the monitoring of temperature monitoring throughout the cold chain providing the ability to act on changes in temperature in real-time. It enables documented delivery quality which in turn provides increased customer satisfaction.

It has become a responsibility of manufacturer to maintain the quality of goods and to ensure their preservation by maintaining the correct temperature inside the vehicles so as to follow the cold chain system and its guidelines. It is, therefore, essential to track goods accurately in real time to monitor the temperature at all times.

The world has seen the impact of poor food preservation and global food supply which is undoubtedly far greater than the observed food losses alone. It is noteworthy that the loss of hundreds of millions of tonnes of foodstuffs exerts an additional effect on global warming due to wasting of the scarce or non-renewable resources required to produce and transport them. The costs of the cold chain, both economic and environmental, can often be more than offset by the economic and environmental benefits due to reduced post-harvest losses.

Table 1 shows the range of temperature of the food product storage:

The sector of cold storage is undergoing a massive transformation, with the government focusing on food preservation. A lot of stress is being laid on energy efficiency as the cold stores are energy intensive. With the advent of newer materials / equipments, every part of a cold chain rendering itself for improvement. As a result, all of them are witnessing changes like the type of construction, insulation, refrigeration equipment, and other type of controls.

Cold chain systems are very important to the growth of global trade in perishable products providing worldwide availability of food and health supplies. Each year, billions of tons of fresh food products and millions of dollars' worth are lost due to poor cold chain systems in developing markets. The World Economic Forum lists food crisis as fourth on its top global risks of highest concern for the next 10 years. Though globally, billions of dollars are spent on improving agricultural processes to create higher food yields. But the fact is that nearly half of all food never gets consumed by the consumer and this fact was totally getting ignored.

By controlling parameters of temperature, humidity and atmospheric composition, along with utilizing proper handling procedures, cold chain service providers can increase the product life of fresh foods for days, weeks or even months. The cold chain management system allows fresh products to hold their value longer while increasing their transportability and provide better opportunities expanding horizon of market reach.

Table 1. Predicted loss of fresh food storage in developing countries

Food Product Storage	At Optimum Cold Temperature	Optimum Temperature + 10° C	Optimum Temperature +20°C	Optimum Temperature + 30°C
Fresh Fish	10 days at 0° C	4-5 days at10°C	1-2 days at 20°C	A few hours at 30° C
Milk	2 Weeks at0°C	7 days at 10°C	2-3 days at 20°C	A few hours at 30° C
Fresh Green Vegetables	1Month at 0°C	2 weeks at 10°C	1 week at 20°C	Less than 2 days at 30° C
Potatoes	5-10 months at 4-12° C	Less than 2 months at 22°C	Less than 1 month at 32° C	Less than 2 weeks at 42° C
Mangoes	2-3 weeks at 13° C	1 week at 23°C	4 days at 33° C	2 days at 43° C
Apples	3-6 months a - 1°C	2 months at 10°c	1 month at 20°C	A few weeks at 30° C

Adapted from Kitinoja (2013)

Table 2. Temperature requirement of selected fresh food

Fresh Food	Temperature Requirement (°C)
Fresh fish (in ice), crustaceans and shellfish (excluding live ones)	+2
Meat and cooked meats pre-packaged for consumer use	+3
Cooked meats other than those which have been salted, smoked, dried or sterilized	+6
Butter and edible fats, including cream to be used for butter making	−14
Deep frozen foods	−18
Fishery products	−18

Source: Alexandria Engineering Journal, Volume 55, Issue 2, June 2016, Pages 1359–1365

LITERATURE REVIEW

All food company and supermarket is committing itself to provide better products. To provide good quality fresh food products, the logistics part has to be considered (Hsiao et al., 2008).The quality and safety of the fresh foods is largely influenced by the logistics (Smith, 2006). However, the researches and studies on fresh food logistics are few (Liu et al., 1999).Many perspectives can be adapted to discuss the fresh food logistics, however, the literature study indicates that analyzing the problem via the perspective of cost and effectiveness is main (Liu et al., 1999, Joshi et al., 2009; Boronico et al., 1995; Manning et al., 2006; Beardsell et al., 1999; Kelepouris et al., 2007; Henderson, 1994; Manikas et al., 2009; Manning et al., 2006).

The cost of the fresh food logistics is viewed as one of the key elements (Kelepouris et al., 2007; Henderson, 1994; Fearne et al., 1999). Hsiao et al. (2008) claim that the fresh food logistics cost is decided based on several factors, e.g. transportation, warehousing, value-added activities, and inventory management. But they also view the asset specificity, core closeness, and supply chain complexity is the determinant issues (Hsiao et al., 2008).

Logistics effectiveness is very important in maintaining cold chain. Manikas et al. (2009) point out in their survey that the bottleneck of the fresh food logistics in England is the unimproved efficiency, which results in low utilization of the facilities and space. Logistics effectiveness not only influences the quality of the fresh food, but also determines the safety of fresh food, especially in the process of primary production (Manning et al., 2006).

According to the definition proposed by Smith (2006), perishable products are: live plants, fresh or chilled vegetables, fresh mushrooms, fresh fruits, fresh cut flowers, and concentrated citrus juice. Marsden et al (1998) consider the definition of fresh food includes a wide range-- the products that need to be kept in a refrigerator can be called fresh or perishable food, such as fruits, vegetables, meats, and fish. The fresh food in this paper refers to the perishable food that should be stored in fridge, including dairy products, meats, fish, vegetables, and concentrated citrus juice. In addition, fresh food, fresh products, perishable food, and perishable products refer to the same thing in this paper.

According to Smith (2006), fresh products require much more in the logistics conditions. Many details should be considered in the fresh foods logistics procedure, such as the air quality, the temperature, the humidity, the room pressure, and even the lighting level. For example, lighting directly affects the quality of the fresh products, while the bacterial growth will be out of control without appropriate temperature and humidity.

Manikas et al (2009) discussed that automatic machines are invented to improve the efficiency of the fresh foods logistics as the general efficiency is not high. Since, the products types of the fresh foods are various and hard to be controlled by machines, so a large part of the logistics process, especially the picking process, is handled manually.

As there is no specific guideline for the foods storage so the standards in different countries can vary, though the storage environment is very important for maintaining the quality of fresh food (Smith, 2006). Manikas et al. (2009) believe that it is quite demanding to reach the storage requirements of the agricultural perishable foods, because the requirements for the storage of those products are rare and so its facilities. Most of the regional distribution centers or supermarkets still lack those facilities. But merely purchasing the facilities is not enough for satisfactory food logistics. Smith (2006) states that in order to keep the environment suitable for fresh food storage, the facilities that are used in fresh food logistics should be easy to clean or it will cost a lot to remove the bacteria and dust.

Hsiao (2008) explains that logistics outsourcing is a good choice for many supermarkets or food companies which are involved in the fresh food business. It means the fresh food logistics can be handled by an external logistics company or shipper. Hsiao et al. (2008) also argue that the decision making process for conducting outsourcing logistics is very important. Items like asset specificity, uncertainties measurement, core closeness, supply chain complexity, and logistics strategies are suggested to be evaluated in the decision making process.

Liu et al. (1999) pointed out that their survey report that the relationship between a third party logistics or outsourcing logistics company and the fresh food company should be defined clearly. But they also believed that companies should not rely too much on one or more distributors.

Rathore et al (2010) compared that the amount of food wasted in India is equivalent to annual food consumption in UK. The study done by ASSOCHAM (2013), claimed that India producers are losing Rs. 2.13 lakh crore due to supply chain loss in of fruits and vegetables.

Viswanadham (2007) mentioned that waste of food is due to lack of adequate infrastructure of processing, cold storage and transportation in India. It has resulted in loss of fresh vegetables ranged from 20 to 50% (Verma and Singh, 2004).

As reported by Capellán-Pérez (2014), there is a need of continuous power supply for overall maintenance of cold chain. Cold storage are purposely for preserving the quality of raw food. In developing countries, there is enormous shortfall in power generation and also lack of technical know-how to explore environmental friendly energy, fossil fuel is highly explored as alternative means of energy. This convectional fuel source has been widely reported as global emission of carbon dioxide which is a major contributor to global warming. Full-size table.

PROBLEMS AND VULNERABILITIES

There are various challenges faced by manufacturers and distributors of frozen products that how they will be able to maintain the cold chain of refrigerated zones within distribution centers and equipments like refrigerated docks and multi-temperature trailers.

The frozen food product's safety is a priority for every reputable distributor as it's often taken for granted by customers. Maintaining the cold chain from farm to fork is challenging. All these food products must be loaded correctly to prevent cross-contamination with raw product and damage by heavier items at the bottom of a stack. And, they must be stored at the correct temperatures (frozen, refrigerated or dry) in the truck to maintain quality and safety. During the harsh summer season, the 'reefers' (truck refrigeration units) have to work extra-hard to maintain temperature so that perishable products could retain its chillness throughout the multi-stop delivery process. Although, food distribution companies must adhere to government rules and regulations calling for greater food protection scrutiny.

In India, the production volumes of most of the fruits and vegetables are uneven. The fruits and vegetables need cold storages during the peak months of the years. However, there is a lack of cold storages. The report from Emerson food wastage and cold storage cites studies that have pegged the value of fruits, vegetables and grains wastage in India at INR 440 billion annually. From which the fruits and vegetables account for the largest portion of that wastage. The wastage is valued at INR 133 billion which is eighteen per cent of India's fruit and vegetable production go waste annually, according to data from the Central Institute of Post-Harvest Engineering and Technology (CIPHET).

The recent data published by the Ministry of Food Processing Industries is estimated at Rs 92,651 crore for loss of perishables due the wastage of agricultural produce at the national level (Naqvi Ghufran,2016). India's major agricultural goods is almost three times as high as the new budget for the agriculture sector. Though, there were food shortage issues and the constant rising food inflation, there was heavy harvest and post-harvest loss of perishables, which shown 44% increase from Rs 24,909 crore in 2015-16 to Rs 35,984 crore in 2016-17.

Further, effective cold chains and cold stores need latest technology and the major problem here is the cost of that technology. Similarly some of the fruits and vegetables are expected to be cheaper (oranges, papaya, tomatoes, onion, potato) in price as compare to the others (apples, plums, litchi, peas etc.). The cold storage cost (carrying cost) sometimes is too high that it is not commercially feasible for farmers or middlemen supply them through an effective cold chain. It results in perishablility of the goods and finally in the hike of their price in the consumer market.

Table 3. Central Institute of Post-Harvest Engineering and Technology (CIPHET),Ludhiana,2016

Commodity/Crop	Losses During Transportation(%)	Losses During Farm Operations(Includin gTransportation loss(%)	Losses During Storage (%)	Overall Total Loss(%)	Monetary Value of Loss(in Rs. Crores)
Milk	0.02	0.71	0.21	0.92	4409
Meat	0.00	1.99	0.72	2.71	1235
Marine Fish	0.91	9.61	0.91	10.52	4315
Inland Fish	0.17	4.18	1.05	5.23	3766
Egg	0.36	4.88	2.31	7.19	1320
Poultry Meat	0.66	2.76	4.00	6.74	3942
Cereals				4.65-5.99	20698
Pulses				6.36-8.41	3877
Oilseeds				3.08-9.96	8278
Fruits &Veg				4.58-15.88	40811

COLD CHAIN MANAGEMENT SYSTEM

Following are different ways of managing cold chain system (Aung MM et al, 2012):

- Quality Management System
- Risk Assessment Process
- Temperature Monitoring System
- Handling frozen food products

Although, cold chain is composed of various stages though it can also be seen as a single entity since a breakdown in temperature control in any of the stage can impact the final quality of the product. In a cold chain, the shelf life, quality, and safety of perishable food throughout the supply chain is greatly impacted by environmental factors especially temperature (Aung MM et al, 2012).

For storage and distribution of perishable food, the proper temperature condition is needed as they are time and temperature sensitive in nature and are of higher value and more vulnerable to temperature disturbances. Cold chains are very common in the food as well as in pharmaceutical industries and also some chemical shipments. It is required in order to retain high quality and good nutritional value. So, to maintain the quality, there should be increasing concerns for supply chain through quality control and monitoring of goods during the cold chain. In this sector, there is a presence of commercial systems which can monitor containers, refrigerated chambers and trucks, but they typically measure only a single or very limited number of points as they do not give complete information about the cargo. The quality can degrade depending on time and environmental conditions, it is beneficial to know and act appropriate planning when the quality and safety problems arise. As soon as the current quality status is known, the shelf life and price is adjusted dynamically and decision support to management and competitive advantages could be achieved. The fresh food highly demands proper temperature control in the whole logistics process. Therefore, to control food safety efficiently in the cold chain process, and to improve the quality monitoring and management system of cold chain logistics process, become concerns of government and enterprises.

Due to the development of telecommunication, information technology and information system, there is the rise of wireless sensing technologies which is being used in cold supply chain. Such technology like Radio Frequency Identification (RFID) and wireless sensors provides a feasible way to enhance the safety and quality of food cold chain. Integrating RFID systems with condition-monitoring systems will enhance existing track and trace applications, not only the location and movement history, but also the condition of perishable products.

Management of Cold Chain

Cold chain management refers to maintaining the proper temperature of the products through all the handoffs in the cold chain until it reaches the ultimate consumer (Aung MM et al, 2012). The aim of cold chain management is to preserve quality of perishables and deliver them to market in safe and good condition.

Quality and Safety of Frozen Foods

The process of frozen food involves reducing food temperatures to below ambient temperatures, but above –1°C. Reducing the food temperatures results in retarding many of the microbial, physical, chemical and biochemical reactions associated with food spoilage and deterioration. This is found to be effective short-term preservation of food materials. The growth of microorganism occurs slowly at chilled temperatures (generally between 0°C and +5°C) and food spoilage and deterioration reactions are inhibited to such an extent that food safety and quality is preserved for extended periods (EU commission).

Frozen foods are perishable and they deteriorate progressively throughout their life. The growth and activity of microorganisms, which may be present in the food ingredients or may be introduced when the food is handled or processed, may cause deterioration. Safe and high quality chilled foods require minimal contamination during manufacture (including cross-contamination), rapid chilling and low temperatures during storage, handling, distribution, retail display and consumer storage.

Freezing preserves the storage life of foods by making them more inert and slowing down the detrimental reactions that promote food spoilage and limit quality shelf life (EU Commision). There are major attractions with the freshness, quality, safety and convenience of frozen foods. In frozen food industry, there is an increased sophistication which has led to many breakthroughs in frozen food technology, but diligent controls are needed at all times. This technology ensures microbiological safety, extended quality shelf life, temperature control, and the retention of nutrients.

Quality and Safety Food and Agriculture Organisation (FAO) stated that managing food safety and quality is also the responsibility of governments, industry and the consumers (FAO, 2003). Quality defined by ISO is 'the totality of features and characteristics of a product that bear on its ability to satisfy stated or implied need' (Reeuwijk LP, 1998). Also, quality can be defined as 'conformance to requirement', 'fitness for use' or, more appropriately for foodstuffs, 'fitness for consumption'. Thus, quality can be described as the requirements necessary to satisfy the needs and expectations of the consumer (Ho SKM, 1994) (Peri C, 2006).

However, food quality is very general, implying many expectations which can be different from consumer to consumer. Quality includes attributes that influence a product's value to the consumer. The class of quality attributes is following:

Sensors can either be simply associated directly with the items or produce of interest or attached to a Returnable Transport Item (RTI) that is being used to transport the goods (Bowman et al, 2009). There is a problem to know the quality of the product inside containers or refrigerated rooms in cold chain without visual inspection. Therefore, quality evaluation can be considered based on the environmental factors which have direct impact on the quality of the products during their storage and distribution. The role of wireless sensors plays a very important role in this kind of sensory evaluation.

Table 4. Classes of food quality attributes (scholar.waset.org, 2012)

External	Internal	Hidden
Appearance (Sight)	Odour	Wholesomeness
Feel (touch)	Taste	Nutritive Value of Product
Defects	Textures	Safety

TEMPERATURE MONITORING

Temperature monitoring is very important component of cold supply chain. Throughout the food supply chain, many kinds of products have to be handled under controlled environmental quantities, such as temperature, humidity, vibrations and light exposure. The temperature is one of the major concerns among all these parameters due to its huge variety of effects. As the rise in temperature in frozen food may lead to microbial growth which will deteriorate the quality and may increase the risk of food poisoning(Carullo et al,2008). Therefore, perishable food products must be continuously monitored for safety and quality concerns throughout the whole supply chain to avoid the breakdown in temperature control which will impact on the final quality of the product (SARDI, 2006).

The International Institute of Refrigeration (IIR) indicated that about 300 million tonnes of produce were wasted annually through deficient refrigeration worldwide (Flores and Gormley, 2000).Therefore, the key to managing the cold chain is to monitor and maintain the product temperature in each stage of the supply chain. Temperature control in cold chain preserves both sensory and nutritional qualities. Most of the mechanisms of quality loss are determined by storage temperature and are accelerated with time spent above the recommended value. They are also promoted by temperature fluctuations (George M, 2000).

RISK ASSESSMENT PROCESS

In cold supply chain logistics, various risks are involved regarding the maintenance of quality of food. There are a number of common elements that will exist in logistics routes like

1. The type of cartons/packaging being used.
2. The type of routes to be used like by road, sea or the air as it does has an impact on products in cold van.
3. The way the products are being handled(i.e hand-offs and human elements)
4. The location and the time of year in the world where the products are going to be shipped
5. The size and the quantity of products to be shipped
6. The type of tools applied for monitoring the shipment like USB, RFID etc.
7. The procedures for storing and collection of data applied for the products to be shipped.

Risk Assessment

The risk must be identified from the past experience which mostly occurs during transportation, product handling etc. We must focus on the potential risk generating events which are commonly encountered in this sector (Peter D. Norton, 2013):

1. The point where we have human intervention in handling products
2. The point where we have product handoff point
3. When high value products are being sent on a high route
4. Transfer of products from one country to another
5. Storing the outsourced data
6. To check the carton packet before receiving at the end point.

Risk Mitigation

Various strategies must be included (Peter D. Norton, 2013):

1. We must review the supply chain to assess the scope of risk that may exist
2. Impact of assessment of the risks which can be evolved
3. Documenting the strategies to be implemented
4. Defining risk mitigation strategies

Risk management tools support enterprises to plan, implement and optimise the cold chain. Risk management ensures the integrity of the cold chain.

Food enterprises have to translate food safety requirements of new government regulations, recommendations, guidelines, customer (retailer) requirements as well as requirements of audit standards etc. into enterprise-internal specific product and process criteria.

Risk Management Methods

Strategies must be developed to avoid failures like the deterioration in the quality of perishables in any steps of cold supply chain (Schmitz Thomas, 2006). Like,

1. For maintenance of quality of perishables, temperature controlled vans should be used.
2. To correctly assess the quality of perishables through strong monitoring and to minimize the losses.
3. There should be use of approved carriers only to maintain the standard
4. Packaging must be according to the need for protecting the products
5. Placements of monitoring devices inside the shipping boxes to avoid business risk

A comprehensive risk assessment of the transportation logistics process must be continued to identify and implement adequate solutions and improvements to assure a successful shipment of the perishables satisfying consumer needs.

HANDLING FROZEN FOOD PRODUCTS

The rapid growth of sales reflects consumer satisfaction in the high quality of products, its availability throughout the year, and general convenience in product use. It is actually the preferences and appreciation by the consumer that the product values and that's why frozen foods are sold and new products are being introduced for enhancing sales.

Proper care is to be taken to maintain the quality of frozen foods which depends fundamentally on the quality of raw materials used and product manufacture. It can be at risk if failed to maintain product temperature at a suitable low level in any part of the cold chain, including storage, transport, distribution, and display in retail stores, or by faulty inventory control at all levels that would allow product to be retained for unduly long periods in the cold chain. It must be handled with utmost care to avoid operational failures which may lead to customer dissatisfaction and harm to the entire industry, not only those who may be at fault (www.cold.org.gr,2008). As the freezing process does not actually kill harmful bacteria and other organisms that were present in the food before freezing but, while frozen, bacteria populations do not continue to grow, although they will resume doing so once your food is thawed (www.foodsafety.com.au,2012).

STORAGE PERIOD

As various types of frozen foods have different stabilities in frozen storage so they develop abnormal flavors and decolorize accordingly. It has also been noticed that different lots of the same type of frozen food may have different stabilities, depending on many factors including the quality of raw material and product ingredients, processing, and packaging materials. According to the need storage life can be extended significantly as storage temperatures become colder.

TIME AND TEMPERATURE TOLERANCE (TTT)

The quality of the frozen food depends upon the integrated effects of time and temperature that affect their color, flavor and texture. The degree to which individual products tolerate the time & temperature effects is called the Time-Temperature Tolerance (TTT). Regulations or company quality-assurance standards must specify and control both the time and temperature factors to guarantee product quality.

There is an utmost importance of maintaining the frozen food quality in all segments of the frozen food industry to prevent conditions as it could lead to product deterioration in any part of the cold chain and would cause consumer dissatisfaction.

HANDLING

There can be a serious contributing factor to quality loss in frozen foods if exposed to elevated temperatures. Though, very short periods of exposure may not be serious, unless often repeated, but prolonged exposure may cause severe damage. However, for some particularly sensitive products, even a short exposure to temperatures warmer than 10-15 °F will result in marked loss in quality which will only become apparent after further storage. In cold supply chain, temperature fluctuations should be avoided because they will cause migration of moisture from the product or within the package causing formation of ice crystals and partial dehydration of the product. In general, the product temperature is more important than the air temperature. A change in air temperature for a short period may not affect the product temperature significantly (www.cold.org.gr, 2008).

There are parameters to maintain the temperature within the van while in transit. The Refrigeration equipment used in transportation of frozen foods has been designed in such a way so that it removes heat that may leak into the load compartment of the container. It should be noted that the refrigeration capacity does not provide for removal of much heat from the load. Therefore, if products are loaded with the temperature warmer than 0 °F (-18 °C), there is little or no opportunity for the product temperature to be reduced to the desired level during transit.

OPPORTUNITY

The cold chain management for perishables is envisaging a rapid growth in Indian market. The entry of the New Economic Policy of 1991 have ushered a huge prospect in the Indian market. Liberalization policy has transformed the protected economy into one of a land of opportunities for investors. According to the WTO commitments, globalization intends to integrate the Indian economy with the world economy (Bose SK and Chatterjee J, 2008).

The cold chain is required not only for the raw material but also for the frozen and ready to eat food. Avoiding spoilage and wastage of perishable products can certainly enhance the economy in direct or indirect ways. The market possesses enormous opportunities for the cold chain sector due to massive demand from consumer as their food eating habits are changing. The time has come for bridging gaps in appropriate infrastructure development, adoption of energy efficient technologies, moving from mass storage to direct access storage and use of latest equipments for the cold chain management. The cold supply chain can provide opportunity to various service providers, infrastructure designers, refrigerated vehicle manufacturers, alternate energy experts, shipping and international trade companies, temperature controlling equipment providers etc. (www.asiacoldchainshow.com, 2015).

CONCLUSION

The cold chain industry in India is still at a nascent stage and despite large production of perishables, the cold chain potential still remain untapped due to high share of single commodity cold storage, high initial investment (for refrigerator units and land), lack of enabling infrastructure like power & roads, lack of awareness for handling perishable produce and lapse of service either by the storage provider or the transporter leading to poor quality produce. However, increasing urbanization and growth of organized retail, food servicing and food processing sector are boosting the growth of cold chain industry in India. The trend is shifting towards establishing multipurpose cold storages and providing end to end services to control parameters throughout the value chain.

REFERENCES

Adekomaya, O., Jamiru, T., Sadiku, R., & Huan, Z. (2016, June). Sustaining the shelf life of fresh food in cold chain – A burden on the environment. *Alexandria Engineering Journal*, *55*(2), 1359–1365. doi:10.1016/j.aej.2016.03.024

Aung, M. (2012). Quality Monitoring and Dynamic Pricing in Cold Chain Management. *Mechatronic and Manufacturing Engineering*, *6*(2).

Bishara, R. H. (2006). Cold chain management – an essential component of the global pharmaceutical supply chain. *American Pharmaceutical Review*. Available at: www.americanpharmaceuticalreview.com/life_science/Bishara_APR.pdf

Bose, S.K., & Joydeep, C. (2008). *Challenges faced by the Indian tinplate packaging industry: An analysis*. Retrieved from file:///C:/Users/Anju%20Bharti/Desktop/paper%20for%20IGI/5_Bose_Chatterjee.pdf

Bowman, Ng, Harrison, López, & Illic. (2009). *Sensor based condition monitoring*. Building Radio Frequency Identification for the Global Environment (Bridge) Euro RFID Project.

Capellán-Pérez, M., Mediavilla, M., de Castro, C., Carpintero, Ó., & Miguel, L. J. (2014). Fossil fuel depletion and socio-economic scenarios: An integrated approach. *Energy*, *77*, 641–666. doi:10.1016/j.energy.2014.09.063

Carullo, A., Corbellini, S., Parvis, M. L., & Vallan, A. (2008). A measuring system for the assurance of the cold-chain integrity. *Proceedings of the IEEE International Instrumentation and Measurement Technology Conference*, 1598-1602. doi:10.1109/IMTC.2008.4547298

Cold Chain sea of opportunities for emerging markets. (2015). Retrieved from http://www.asiacoldchain-show.com/2015/03/13/cold-chain-sea-of-opportunities-for-emerging-markets/

FAO. (2003). *FAO's strategy for a food chain approach to food safety and quality: a framework document for the development of future strategic direction*. Retrieved from http://www.fao.org/DOCREP/MEETING/006/Y8350e.HTM

Flores, S. E., & Tunner, D. (2008, July). RFID technologies for cold chain applications. *International Institute of Refrigeration Bulletin*, 4-9.

George, M., & Gormley, R. (2000). *Managing the cold chain for quality and safety*. Retrieved from http://www.teagasc.ie/ashtown/research/preparedfoods/managing_the_c old_chain.pdf

Ghufran, N. (2016). *Food loss! A Big Challenge for Modi Government, Agro & Food Processing*. Retrieved from http://agronfoodprocessing.com/food-loss-a-big-challenge-for-modi-government/

Ho, S. K. M. (1994). Is the ISO 9000 series for Total Quality Management? *International Journal (Toronto, Ont.)*, *11*(9), 74–89.

Indian Cold Chain – An Emerging Industry. (2016). Retrieved from http://www.coolingindia.in/blog/post/id/13496/indian-cold-chain--an-emerging-industry

ITLN. (2014). *India on fast track to shape perishables logistics trends*. Retrieved from http://www.itln.in/india-on-fast-track-to-shape-perishables-logistics-trends/

Joshi, R., Banwet, D. K., & Shankar, R. (2009). Indian cold chain: Modeling the Inhibitors. *British Food Journal*, *111*(11), 1260–1283. doi:10.1108/00070700911001077

Kelepouris, T., Pramatari, K., & Doukidis, G. (2007). RFID-enabled traceability in the food supply chain. *Industrial Management & Data Systems*, *107*(2), 183–200. doi:10.1108/02635570710723804

Kovacs, G. (2008). Corporate environmental responsibility in the supply chain. *Journal of Cleaner Production*, *16*(15), 1571–1578. doi:10.1016/j.jclepro.2008.04.013

Lisa, K. (2013). *Table 1: Predicted loss of fresh food storage in developing countries – Use of cold chains for reducing food losses in developing countries* (PEF White Paper No. 13-03). The Postharvest Education Foundation (PEF).

Liu, H., & Wang, I.P. (1999). Co-ordination of international channel relationships: four case studies in the food industry in China. *Journal of Business & Industrial Marketing, 14*(2), 130-150.

Manikas, I., & Terry, L. A. (2009). A case study assessment of the operational performance of a multiple fresh produce distribution centre in the UK. *British Food Journal, 111*(5), 421–435. doi:10.1108/00070700910957276

Manning, L., Baines, R. N., & Chadd, S. A. (2006). Quality assurance models in the food supply chain. *British Food Journal, 108*(2), 91–104. doi:10.1108/00070700610644915

Maxwell, D., Sheate, W., & Vorst, R. V. D. (2006). Functional and systems aspects of the sustainable product and service development approach for industry. *Journal of Cleaner Production, 14*(17), 399–416. doi:10.1016/j.jclepro.2006.01.028

Peri, C. (2006). The universe of food quality. *Food Quality and Preference, 17*(1-2), 3–8. doi:10.1016/j.foodqual.2005.03.002

Rathore, J. (2010). Cold chain infrastructure for frozen food- a weak link in Indian retail sector. *The IUP Journal of Supply Chain Management, 7*(1-2), 90-103.

Salin, V., & Nayga, R.M. (2002). A cold chain network for food exports to developing countries. *International Journal of Physical Distribution & Logistics Management, 33*(10), 918-933.

SARDI. (2006). *Maintaining the cold chain: air freight of perishables.* South Australian Research and Development Institute. Retrieved from http://www.australianairfreight.com/vac/pdfs/airfreight_perish.pdf

Smith, D. (2006). Design and management concepts for high care food processing. *British Food Journal, 108*(1), 54–60. doi:10.1108/00070700610637634

Thomas. (2006). *Using risk management tools to manage the integrity of the cold chain.* Cold Chain-Management, 2nd International Workshop, Bonn, Germany. Retrieved from http://ccm.ytally.com/fileadmin/user_upload/downloads/12_SCHMITZ.PDF

Van Reeuwijk, L. P. (n.d.). *Guidelines for quality management in soil and plant laboratories.* Rome Publication #M-90. Retrieved from http://www.fao.org/docrep/w7295e/w7295e00.HTM

Verma, A., & Singh, K. (2004). An economic analysis of post harvest losses in fresh vegetables. *Indian Journal of Agricultural Marketing, 18*(1), 134–139.

Viswanadham, N. (2007). *Can India be food basket for the world?* Working Paper Series, IBS, Hyderabad. Retrieved from http://www.cccindia.co/corecentre/Database/Docs/Docfiles/Can_india_be.pdf

KEY TERMS AND DEFINITIONS

Cold Chain: A cold chain is a temperature-controlled supply chain. An unbroken cold chain is an uninterrupted series of refrigerated production, storage and distribution activities, along with associated equipment and logistics, which maintain a desired low-temperature range.

Cross Contamination: The process by which bacteria or other microorganisms are unintentionally transferred from one substance or object to another, with harmful effect. 'Cross-contamination between raw and cooked food is the cause of most infection'.

Frozen Food: Food preserved by a freezing process and stored in a freezer before cooking. Freezing food preserves it from the time it is prepared to the time it is eaten. Freezing food slows down decomposition by turning residual moisture into ice, inhibiting the growth of most bacterial species.

Non-Renewable Resource: A non renewable resource is a resource of economic value that cannot be readily replaced by natural means on a level equal to its consumption. Most fossil fuels, such as oil, natural gas and coal are considered non renewable resources in that their use is not sustainable because their formation takes billions of years.

Perishables: A perishable is also a type of food with a limited shelf life if it's not refrigerated. Since perishing is dying, anything perishable could die or is likely to die. Perishable foods are those likely to spoil, decay or become unsafe to consume if not kept refrigerated at 40 F° (4.4 °C) or below or frozen at 0 F° (-17.8 °C) or below. Examples of foods that must be kept refrigerated for safety include meat, poultry, fish, dairy products, and all cooked leftovers. Refrigeration slows bacterial growth and freezing stops it. There are two completely different families of bacteria that can be on food: pathogenic bacteria, the kind that cause food borne illness, and spoilage bacteria, the kind of bacteria that cause foods to deteriorate and develop unpleasant odors, tastes, and textures.

RFID: RFID (radio frequency identification) is a technology that incorporates the use of electromagnetic or electrostatic coupling in the radio frequency (RF) portion of the electromagnetic spectrum to uniquely identify an object, animal, or person. RFID is a technology similar in theory to bar codes.

Sensor: A device which detects or measures a physical property and records, indicates, or otherwise responds to it.

Chapter 14
Wastage and Cold Chain Infrastructure Relationship in Indian Food Supply Chain:
A Study From Farm to Retail

Saurav Negi
University of Petroleum and Energy Studies, India

Neeraj Anand
University of Petroleum and Energy Studies, India

ABSTRACT

India, the world's second-largest producer and one of the centers of origin of Fruits and Vegetables is also one of the biggest food wasters in the world. The challenge of feeding India's billion plus people is not really about agriculture and food production but getting the quality food to the concerned people in a right time. The biggest contributors to this waste are lack of temperature controlled transport and inadequate quality of cold storage facilities for both Farmers and Food sellers i.e. retailers. What India lacks, and needs, is a well-developed, world-class cold chain infrastructure. Without it, India's problems are vast and likely to grow. In this chapter, the authors tries to outlines the extent of Fruits and Vegetables waste in India (at various stages from farm to retail) and its ramifications on food production and safety. Authors also highlighted the challenges faced by cold chain sector in India and a roadmap for improvements. As Indian economy is based on agriculture, development of Cold Chain infrastructure from farm to retail points will play a crucial role.

INTRODUCTION

Fruit and Vegetables is a very growing sector and constitute of around 90% of horticultural produce in India. Production of horticultural crops in India has increased as compared to the situation a couple of decades ago. Several factors like globalization, Increasing urbanization, Nuclear families, working women, disposable income, changing lifestyles, and rise of organized retails are gearing up the Indian

DOI: 10.4018/978-1-5225-3056-5.ch014

fruits and vegetables supply chains for a better future. Supply chain plays a very vital role in this sector. This area becomes even more important because of perishability and very short shelf life. Supply Chain Management not only helps to cut costs, but also adds to maintain and improve the quality of produce delivered, which are perishable in nature.

India the second-largest producer of Fruits and Vegetables is also one of the biggest food wasters in the world-wasting INR 2 Lakh crore per annum worth of Fruits and Vegetables every year (ASSOCHAM, 2013).

The challenge of feeding India's billion plus people is not really about agriculture production but getting the proper food to the individuals. The biggest contributors to waste are the lack of cold chain facilities, required infrastructure and temperature controlled transportation system which is hindering the overall growth of this sector and making the supply chain inefficient.

What India lacks, and needs, is a well-established cold chain facilities and infrastructure. Without it, India's problems are vast and likely to grow. The most prone food category to a lack of cold chain infrastructure is Fruits and Vegetables where annual wastage is estimated to be around 35-40% of the total production. Various studies on Fruits and Vegetables supply chain found Poor Cold chain system as a major problem in the Supply chain of F&V which are resulting in various inefficiencies and leads to losses sand wastage across the chain.

From various studies on post-harvest losses in India, it is evident that the amount of food wasted in a year in India is equivalent to annual food consumption in some countries like UK (Rathore, Sharma, & Saxena, 2010) and the total production of the Great Britain (Khan, 2005). Controlling the level of waste is beyond the capabilities and scope of individual farmers. The problem is widespread and proper controlled temperature to maintain and sustain the quality to increase the shelf life of the produce and makes them easily available to the customer in a quality manner is a major concern. The weak and ill equipped cold chain infrastructure (Rathore, Sharma, & Saxena, 2010), improper marketing systems and facilities (Gauraha & Thakur, 2008; Singh, Kushwaha, & Verma, 2008) of the country has become the major impediments in the growth of the sector.

This chapter outlines the extent of Fruits and Vegetables waste in India and highlights where wastage occurs across the supply chain stages starting from farm to retail and its ramifications on food production and safety. The present study undertakes a thorough review of basic and contemporary literature available to explain the present status of post-harvest losses and cold chain infrastructure. It focuses on Fruits and Vegetables since India wastes more of this item than any other food product. In this chapter authors also highlighted the challenges faced by the cold chain sector in India and a roadmap for improvements, including greater use of proven technologies.

BACKGROUND

This section discusses the current Scenerio of Fruits and Vegetables production in India and its worldwide status. It has been seen that India is among the world's largest food producer and serving the food consumer all across the globe.

Cold chain system has gained an importance to the growth of international trade in perishable food items and to the global availability of food supplies. Each year, billions of tons of fresh food items with millions of dollars' worth are lost due to poor cold chain system in developing market (International Trade Administration, 2013). As per the list of World Economic Forum, food crises is the fourth top global risks of highest concern for the next 10 years (World Economic Forum, 2016). Globally, billions of dollars are spent on improving agricultural processes to create higher food produces, but the fact is that nearly half of all food produce never reaches to the consumer's plate (World Economic Forum, 2013).

Global losses in the food sector total more than $750 billion annually (FAO, 2013). These losses are majorly the outcome of lack of proper facilities, inadequate food safety handling procedures and lack of training for those human resources working in the cold chain sector.

The Current State of Fruits and Vegetables Production and Wastage in India

During 2014, India's contribution in the world production of F&V was 13.6% and 14% respectively (NHB, 2014). India is the second largest food producer in the world, after China and one of the centers of origin of F&V with the total production of 91.44 million metric tonnes of Fruits and 166.60 million metric tonnes of vegetables till the year end 2016 (NHB, 2016). The production of F&V in India has been shown in Figure 1 from the year 1991-2016 which has increased from 28.63 million metric tonnes to 91.44 million metric tonnes in fruits and 58.53 million metric tonnes to 166.60 million metric tonnes in vegetables from the year 1991-2016.

Despite high production and an existing distribution network, India finds it difficult to feed its own people. The main reason for that is high amount of food wastage due to ill-equipped and weak cold chain infrastructure of the country. Because of lack of cold chain infrastructure, poor post harvesting technology, inadequate storage and transportation and lack of food processing industry, about 20 -30 percent

Figure 1. Fruits and vegetables production in India
Source: Indian Horticulture Database, NHB, 2016

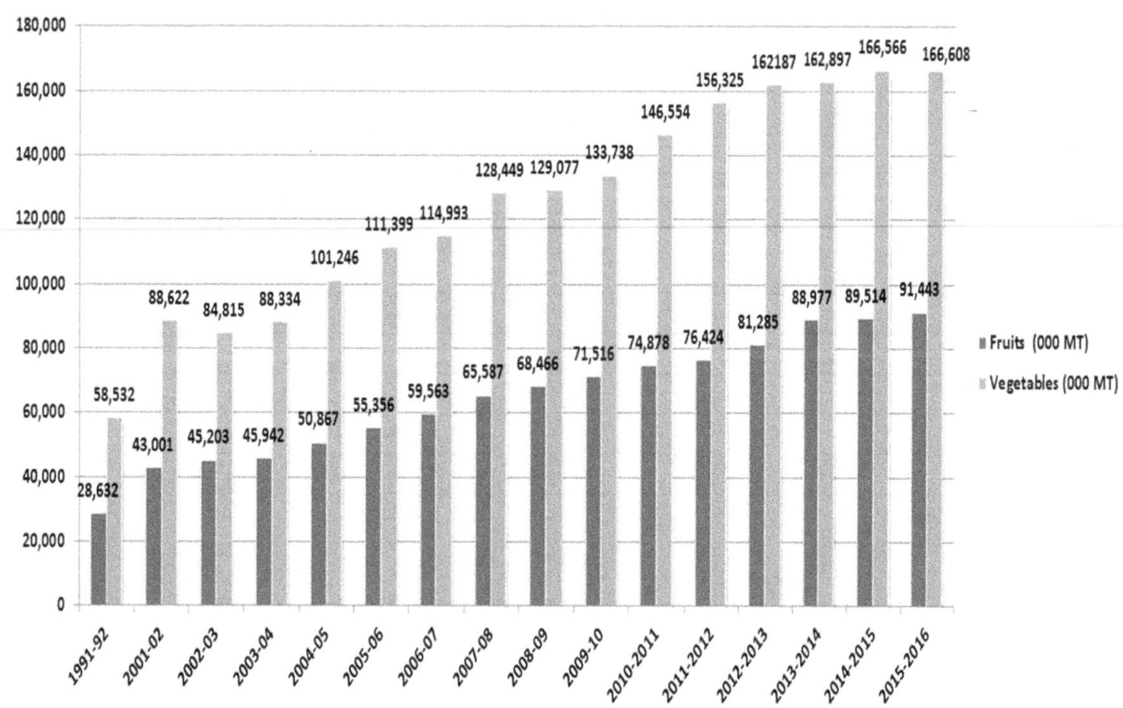

of all foods produced in India (Rs. 500 b) gets wasted annually (Mishra & Anjani, 2010; Viswanadham, 2007; Jain, 2007).

There are many studies pertaining to quality and quantity losses during and post-harvest (Negi and Anand, 2016a; Turan, 2008; Murthy, Gajanana, Sudha and Dakshinamoorthy 2009; Troger, 2007; Ozcan, 2007; Karabulut et al., 2005; Kumar et al., 2004; Lawande, 2004; Reddy, 2004; Singh, Banerjee, Singh, Pandey, Sudhakar, & Rai, 2004; Tatlidil, Kiral, Gunes, Demir, Erdemir, and Fidan 2003; Klein and Lurie, 1991; Ozcan and Baklaya, 1995; Ozcan, Balkaya and Ceyhan (1997; Dokuzoguz, 1997; Gunduz, 1997; Kaynas, Celikel, Türkes and Surmeli 1988). It has been reported that a huge amount of fresh produce is wasted in various operational stages of the F&V Supply Chain (Murthy, Gajanana, Sudha and Dakshinamoorthy 2009). According to the calculation of (ASSOCHAM, 2013) India, the producers have to forgo every year Rs. 2.13 lakh crore due to losses in the supply chain of fruits and vegetables.

The Fruits and Vegetables loss among major producing states in India has been shown in Table 1.

According to CIPHET, Ludhiana, the post-harvest losses of major agricultural produces at national level was of the order of Rs 44,143 crore per annum at 2009 wholesale prices and most of the wastage is happening in fruits and vegetables of about 5.8-18% worth value of Rs 7,437 crore in fruits and Rs 5,872 crore in vegetables (GOI, 2012) due to the lack of cold chain facilities and infrastructure. Poor cold chain infrastructure not only affects the quality of fresh produce but also affects the prices due to the non-availability of products and lack of supply due to losses and wastage.

Negi & Anand (2014) discusses that supply chain of Fruits and Vegetables in India is highly inefficient which is leading to huge losses and wastages and less income to the stakeholders in return. Apart from the loss of revenue to the farmers, it leads to increased additional costs in the supply chain which ultimately enforces the final consumers to pay high charges from his pocket.

Table 1. Fruits and vegetables losses among the major producing state

State	Total Loss (Rs. Crore)
Maharashtra	10100
Andhra Pradesh	5633
Tamil Nadu	8170
Gujarat	11398
Karnataka	7415
Uttar Pradesh	10312
Bihar	10744
Madhya Pradesh	5332
West Bengal	13657
All India	**212552**

Source: ASSOCHAM India

COLD CHAIN: PRESENT STATUS

A cold chain protects a wide variety of food produce to get deteriorate in the whole supply chain by providing temperature controlled facility. It is a logistic system that provides a series of controlled temperature storage and transport conditions from the point of origin to the point of consumption, i.e. from farm to fork. It saves fresh produce from degradation, humidity, improper expose to temperature and keeps them frozen, fresh and chilled (Saurav and Potti 2016; Bishara, 2006). Fresh foods, like vegetables, fruits, dairy, confectionary items, meat and poultry requires continuous and uninterrupted temperature controlled atmosphere known as cold chain due to their perishable nature. By controlling proper temperature throughout the chain can improve the shelf life of the products for days, weeks and even for months (for some products) and minimize the chances of losses. The basic concept of cold chain is depicted in Figure 2.

The basic difference between the supply chain of non-perishable items and the temperature controlled supply chain i.e. cold chain is the possibility of degradation in quality and value of the product, which start from the farms to the customer (Joshi et al., 2009). The basic difference between supply chain of non-perishables and cold chain is shown in the Table 2.

Figure 2. A cold chain
Source: Sapra, and Joshi (2011)

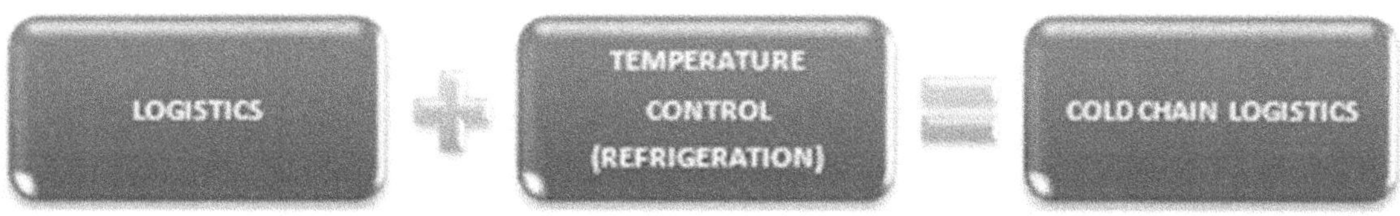

Table 2. Difference between supply chain of non-perishables and cold chain

Supply Chain of Non Perishable	Cold Chain.
Includes temperature-insensitive products like nuts, bolts, m/s and equipments.	Includes temperature-sensitive items like plant and animal-based product
Produce information regarding transaction (order, shipment, payment) and location (warehouse, traffic, inventory)	Cold chain includes "condition" and "time" along with transaction and location.
Can bear being stuck in traffic jam.	Require keeping the refrigeration system in a running state, which devours more cost.
Less transportation cost as ordinary trucks, vehicles are used.	Refrigerated vehicles are mandatory for transportation.
Different products can be loaded based on the space available	Different temperature is required for different products, e.g. milk is to be kept at 48C to 108C, whereas ice-cream requires- 18 degree Celsius.
No degradation in value while in transport.	Continuous degradation in value right from the producer till final consumption.
Stops as the product reaches customer.	Includes customer practices related to temperature sensitivity.

Source: Rohit Joshi, Devinder Kumar Banwet, Ravi Shankar, (2009)

The cold chain starts at farm level and covers up to the consumer level in a temperature controlled practices and behavior. Cold chain infrastructure generally consists of grading, sorting, packing, storage, processing and transportation facilities. A typical cold chain infrastructure is shown in Figure 3.

It contains Precooling system at farms to keep the produce fresh and refrigrated vehicles and containers for the effective and efficient movement of Fruits and Vegetables from the point of origin, i.e Farm to the point of consumption, i.e Fork. It also requires cold storage facilities to store the fresh produce in a temeprature controlled warehouse to maintain the quality of Fruits and Vegetables so they couldnot get deteriorated. The cold supply chain pertaining to Fruits and Vegetables is complex as compared to other supply chain due to the perishable nature of the produce, high fluctuations in demand and prices, increasing consumer concerns for food safety & quality (Vorst & Beulens, 2002), and the most important is its dependence on climate conditions (Salin, 1998).

Stakeholders in Cold Chain

Some of the Stakeholders like User Industries, Authorities and Associations, Cold chain Infrastructure sector and Intermediaries using cold chain in India are as follows:

User Industries

- *Fruit and Vegetable Businesses*
- *Food Processing Businesses*
- *Horticulture*
- *Livestock Producers*
- *Seafood Companies*
- *Pharmaceutical companies*
- *Hotels and Restaurants*
- *Large format retailers and wholesalers*
- *Small Retailers*
- *Laboratories/ Healthcare Centers*
- *Medical Equipment Manufacturers*
- *Oil refineries and chemical industries*
- *CRO's (Contract Research Organisations)*

Figure 3. The Cold supply chain infrastructure
Source: Sapra & Joshi (2011)

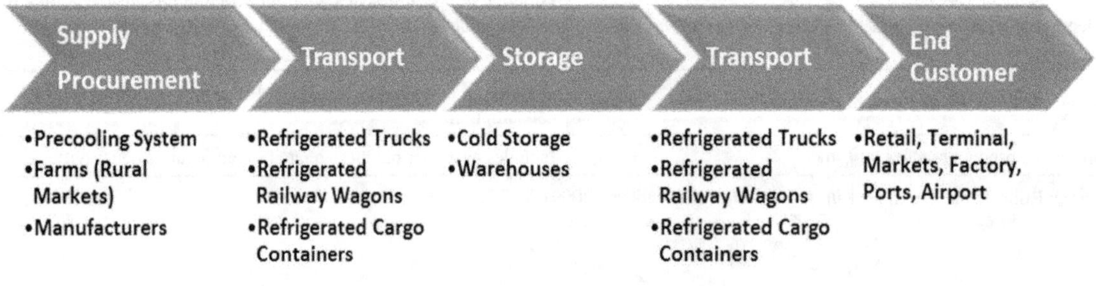

Authorities and Associations

- *Government Agencies (Planning Commission, Customs, etc.)*
- *DCGI (Drugs Controller General of India)*
- *CDSCO (Central Drug Standard Control Organization)*
- *IARW (International Association of Refrigerated Warehouses)*
- *Global Cold Chain Alliances*
- *Academic and Research Institutions*
- *Growers Association of Fruits and Vegetables*

Infrastructure

- *Warehouse/Cold Storage Owners*
- *Refrigeration and Cold Chain Equipment*
- *Technology Suppliers*
- *Refrigeration Solution Providers*
- *Specialized Equipment Providers*
- *ICD's (Inland Containers Depots)*
- *Sea/Air Ports*
- *Transport Vehicles*
- *Security*

Intermediaries

- *Logistics Service Provider*
- *Cold Logistics Players (Shipping Lines, Transporters, Container Companies) Warehousing Agents*
- *Supply Chain Solution Providers*
- *Packaging Service Providers*
- *Banks and Financial Institution*
- *Consultants From the Relevant Spheres Who Are Interested in Knowledge Building.*

Others

- *Power/Electricity*
- *Shelf Life*
- *Temperature*
- *Humidity*
- *Distance*
- *Seasonal Changes*
- *Roads Connectivity*

CHALLENGES

The trend for fresh fruits and vegetables is gaining acceptance in India and is growing at a steady rate. This increasing trend has raised various issues associated with quality, safety and availability of these fresh produce. To make the fresh produce available and achieve the quality and safety it requires proper cold chain management. The Cold chain industry in India is estimated to be presently worth over Rs.13, 000 crores (US$2.6 Billion) per annum (Narula, 2011) with various opportunities in the F&V segment in terms of trade and value addition. Despite the huge opportunities, the cold chain industry is at a nascent stage with various challenges discussed below.

India stores only two percent of its horticulture products in temperature-controlled conditions, while China stores 15 percent and Europe and North America stores 85 percent of their products in such conditions. Adequate cold storage facilities are available for just about 10 percent of India's horticulture production. Of the total annual production, 30-40 percent is wasted before consumption. During the peak production period, the gap between the demand and supply of cold storage capacity is approx. 25 million tonnes (ONICRA, 2012). Although cold storage capacity of over 30 million tonnes has been created in the country, the concept of cold-chain is still in its infancy in India. Considering the fact that India is producing about 240 million tonnes of Fruits and Vegetables every year, the development of cold-chain networks assumes high priority. Owing to the tremendous pressure on improving supply chain and reducing losses during produce handling and movement, the need for creation of a cold chain network is crucial for perishable food commodities. The cold chain sector involved in the business of Fruits and Vegetables have wide opportunities as India is the largest and second largest producer of many F&V such as Mango, Guava, Banana, Papaya, Okra, Potato, Onion, Tomato, Cabbage etc. in world production (NHB, 2016).

Regionally, the existing cold storage capacity is concentrated in terms of both number and capacity in the northern region. Uttar Pradesh and West Bengal contain over 65 percent of the cold storage units in the country and the rest are spread across India. The Region wise Number and Capacity of Cold Storages in India has been shown in Table 3.

The existing cold storage facilities are available only in the wholesale market or nearer to that market. The local market or regional market does not have the cold storage facility where the major fresh produce is sold by the farmer. Cold storage in India has been largely adopted for long-term storage of potatoes, onions and high value crops like apples, grapes and flowers. 75 percent of the cold storage capacity is used to store potatoes, while only 23 percent fall in the multi-product category (ONICRA, 2012).

The major challenges which are found from the various literatures in the cold supply chain are Lack of cold storage and warehousing facilities (Veena *et al.*, 2011; Bhardwaj & Palaparthy, 2008; Dharni & Sharma, 2008), Inadequate capacities to serve the needs (Narula, 2011), Inadequate usage/improper management of cold storage (Bhardwaj & Palaparthy, 2008); Halder & Pati, 2011), Irregular supply of

Table 3. Region wise number and capacity of cold storages in India (2011)

	Central	East/North East	North	South	West	All India
Number	430 (7.0%)	975 (15.8%)	2895 (47.0%)	866 (14.1%)	990 (16.1%)	6156 (100%)
Capacity (Million MT)	1.71 (6.0%)	7.82 (27.3%)	14.95 (52.1%)	1.95 (6.8%)	2.25 (7.9%)	28.68 (100%)

Source: ONICRA (2012)

power or shortage of power to run cold chain (Kapoor, 2009; Shukla D., 2010), Poor post-harvest cold chain technology (Kapoor, 2009), lack of temperature controlled vehicle for the movement of goods (Negi & Anand, 2015a) and non-availability of cold chain infrastructure in traditional retail supply chain of F&V (Negi and Anand 2016b).

Maheshwar & Chanakwa (2006) also highlighted various gaps in cold chain such as poor infrastructure, unavailability of cold storage in close proximity to farms, insufficient cold storage capacity, poor transportation infrastructure etc. Because of these bottlenecks in cold supply chain this sector is suffering from maximum inefficiency and decreases the returns of F&V which affect the income of the farmers and their livelihood. It plays a very vital role and is the backbone for the supply chain of F&V industry but due to the bottlenecks it becomes a very weak link and one of the main reasons for Supply chain losses in food. Negi & Anand (2015b) in his study on cold chain also highlighted that the cold chain infrastructure from farm to retail stage in India has emerged as one of the weakest link in the supply chain of fruits and vegetables sector resulting to losses.

Around 95% of the cold storages are in private hands and because of high charges, an average Indian farmer is not able to avail the facilities of cold storage (Dharni & Sharma, 2008). There is a lack of ownership within the chain and all the players are concerned with their own revenue maximization with limited attention towards the overall profit of the chain. This lack of a holistic view of a supply chain is leading to the post-harvest waste (Shukla & Jharkharia, 2013).

The magnitude of losses is also depends on the infrastructure such as road connectivity and network (Kader & Rolle, 2004). In India most of the northern and eastern region is covered with hilly terrain areas and are the major sources of Fruits and Vegetables but losses and wastage is also one of the major problems of fresh supply chain in hilly areas (Negi and Anand 2015c). The road connectivity for cold chain and network infrastructure in such areas are very poor which takes a long time to take the fresh fruits and vegetables product to the market and deteriorate the quality and condition of the produce which results in wastage. Modi *et al.* (2009) highlighted that the villages, farms and the markets in the Uttarakhand state (Hilly region) are not well connected as well as there are lack of cold chain facilities and the farmers had to somehow bring their harvests to the nearby road for transportation, which increased the wastage of their produce. On its way to market, a lack of proper cold chain facilities results in greater wastage of the fresh produce. Prompt measures are required by the government and other stakeholders in India to improve the state of cold chains and to reduce the huge losses of fruits and vegetables and large amount of money. A lot is yet to happen in the industry with respect to development of technology, Government plans, and strategy before it can transform the lives of farmers and the growth of Indian economy.

According to ASSOCHAM (2013) in his study "Opportunities in Cold Chain: Emerging Trends and Market Challenges-2013", during the period of 2009-2017, the cold chain industry in India is expected to grow at a CAGR of around 25.8 per cent to reach INR 64 billion. The National Horticulture Board (NHB) recommends that investments worth INR 550.74 billion in new cold storage capacity are needed by 2015–16 to keep up with the increasing production of fruits and vegetables.

If the projected growth in Fruits and Vegetables production becomes a reality and cold chain industry investments are not made, the current food waste scenario will only become worse. Despite initiatives by the Government of India and investments by private players to develop efficient cold chain infrastructure, the cold storage industry continues to face a lot of challenges. Further enhancement in the cold storage capacity for Fruits and Vegetable would be very beneficial to both the farmer and the consumer as it minimizes wastages and provides fresher and off-seasonal food items to the consumers.

NEED GAPS

- Lack of backward and forward linkages to supplement cold chain (High VDC- Variable Distribution Cost).
- Needs to study the potential risks and the return on investment (RoI) with reference to Cold Chain Infrastructure like Coolers, warehouses, refrigerated trucks, carriers, shopping malls and others.
- High cost of power: Agricultural sector is offered subsidized power tariffs by the Government of India; Cold chain industry is instead subjected to industrial power tariffs.
- Lack of knowhow and trained manpower.
- 104 million metric tons Perishable produce is transported between cities each year. Only 4 million metric tons moves via reefer mode.
- Lack of Optimization Practice/Technique in reefer transport
- Lack of two-way cargo movement/ back haulage.
- Poor timely deliveries and inefficient utilization of fleets.
- Reefer location tracking challenges (Technology effectiveness and low penetration)
- Third-party logistics:
    - Manual- handling reduces the product quality and life.
    - Lack of 3 Party solution providers for small players. Geographical and service range expanding on project basis from big players. Logistics providers with air conditioned trucks, automatic handling equipment and trained manpower will provide end-to-end support.
    - Lack of end-to-end solutions. One can also adapt state-of-the-art techniques such as cross docking that will reduce the transit times and inventory.
- **FP Industry:** The Central government allows 100% FDI in this sector to promote food processing and increase the shelf life of the product.
- Discontinuous Energy Supply for hours (Backup power is very expensive)
- Education and awareness. Low acceptance due to high costs.

Further the identified challenges in cold chain infrastructure pertaining to Fruits and Vegetables supply chain in India may be graphically represented as shown in Figure 4.

ROADMAP FOR IMPROVEMENTS

India can take further its economic growth by embarking upon strategies and measures to improve its cold chain infrastructural facilities which will reduce the losses and wastage in food and also helps to develop the Indian economy. Prevalent and yielding practices from the developed countries may be adopted and replicated for the betterment of this sector. On the basis of studies, the following measures are suggested to enhance the agribusiness of Fruits and Vegetables sector, curb huge amount of losses and wastage and improve the livelihood of farmers, rural areas and Indian economy as a whole.

Figure 4. Challenges in cold chain in India
Source: Negi and Anand (2015), Cold Chain in India

What we require is an integrated cold chain infrastructure covering major production areas, processing units and distribution centers which will call for the following:

- Strong fleet of refrigerated transport vehicles to connect the farm level storage facilities, the processing units and the various distribution centers.
- At retail outlets, display cabinets for marketing of frozen food products are to be provided.
- Need to augment cold storage facilities and container handling facilities at major ports as also an air cargo complex for targeting the global market.
- Infrastructure should be improved in terms of connectivity to farms, grading and packaging facilities etc.
- Cold chain facilities can be developed at the central areas of major Fruits and Vegetables production belt by Government, NGOs or any private firm.
- The adoption of various proven technology solutions can help bring down operating costs and improve quality of Fruits and Vegetables by increasing the shelf life.
- Multipurpose cold storage facilities can be designed to store a range of commodities such as fruit, vegetables, dry fruits, spices, pulses and milk throughout the year. These facilities may have separate chambers that operate at various temperatures and are simultaneously maintained. This makes them more cost and space efficient and delivers higher profitability. This method helps to increase shelf life while ensuring the quality and freshness of the produce.
- Concerned government ministries and authorities like Ministry of Food Processing, National Horticulture Board and NCCD should encourage entrepreneurship in agribusiness by providing subsidies, grants, and assisting (providing technical support) in setting up of cold chain infrastructure/facilities and processing units.
- Strong fleet of refrigerated transport vehicles to connect the farm level storage facilities, the processing units and the various distribution centers.

- Losses due to poor storage and transportation can be minimized by use of Refrigerated Containers which can be used to supplement the existing conventional cold storages.
- Developing efficient and effective cold chain infrastructure has to be the concerted effort of the entire stakeholder present in the supply chain of Fruits and Vegetables sector. There has to be structural changes at different levels of the supply chain-Farmers, Local Intermediaries, Wholesale, Retailers and Consumers. The government, private, public-private partnership, cooperative societies, technology providers, educational institutions dealing in agricultural studies and NGOs can play a very important role in improving the cold chain situations.

TOP PLAYERS IN INDIA

Some of the Top players in India pertaining to cold chain are discussed in this section. Same are as follows:

Snowman Frozen Foods

- A joint venture between Gateway Distiparks, Mitsubishi Corp and Nichirei Logistics Group. Nichirei of Japan is the fourth largest in this business in the world.
- Income $10.2 million in 2010.

Fresh and Healthy Enterprises

- A subsidiary of the state-owned Container Corporation of India (CONCOR), which deals in transporting containers via rail.
- India's largest CA store with capacity of 12,000 MT at Rai in Sonepat, Haryana.

Coldstar Logistics

- Incubated by Tuscan Ventures, a $ 50 million venture capital fund in 2010.
- 3 existing and 9 WIP warehouses across India.

RK Foodland

- A 35 year old 3pl company with pan-India presence.
- Clients include Domino's, Abbott, GSK, and Cadbury.

GATI RedSun

- A leading cold chain company for perishable goods and frozen items.
- The Hyderabad-based Gati recently bought a majority stake in the company. Gati plans to scale up operations in cold chain logistics.

Adani Agrifresh

- A logistics venture formed by the Gujarat-based $ 6 Billion Adani Group.
- Has invested $ 40 Million in setting up 3 CA stores in HP.
- Promotes FARMPIK Brand in North India.

IMPLICATION AND DIRECTION FOR FUTURE RESEARCH

The study has highlighted the cold chain infrastructure and its relationship with losses and wastages of F&Vs. In this chapter, major factors pertaining to cold chain infrastructures are also determined which are leading to losses and wastage in the F&V supply chain. The measures that have been adopted in various cases to minimize the losses and wastage are also discussed. The study will be helpful to the various stakeholders involved in the supply chain of F&V like Farmers, Retailers, Transporters, Local traders, Commission Agents, Cold storage providers etc. to identify and map the factors leading to losses and wastage due to the lack of cold chain infrastructure, and to also adopt appropriate suggested measures to offset the risk of losses and wastage. Prompt measures are required by the Government, related authorities and regulatory bodies in India to improve the situation of cold chain and to mark down the existing losses.

This study will be helpful for the researcher to further empirically test and validate the challenges pertaining to cold chain infrastructure in various regions of the country. A similar research can be carried out with the help of identified challenges with reference to other industries which are associated with cold chain. Researches can also be carried out to overcome the issues pertaining to Cold chain infrastructure like "Return on Investment (ROI) models for establishing a cold chain infrastructure". It can be carried out separately for hilly as well as plain areas.

CONCLUSION

The Fruits and Vegetables sector is seen as an emerging and fast growing business sector in India. With the present food wastage, food shortage, food security and safety are issues taking on growing prominence in India. Considering the current levels of Fruits and Vegetables wasted, cold chain facilities will play an important role in feeding the country populations.

The study and research conducted on the supply chain of F&V in India suggest that there is a dearth of cold chain infrastructure and it becomes a weak link in the supply chain of fruits and vegetables. Cold chain which is known as a backbone for the F&V supply chain is suffering from various bottlenecks which results in the losses of huge quantity and money. These losses and efficiency can be improved by providing proper cold chain facilities such as cold storage, processing facilities, and refrigerated transportation system to the farmers in the local or regional markets and by attracting large number of private Agri business players to set up infrastructural facilities. To develop a world-class cold chain infrastructure, the government and industry bodies need to join hands to adopt better and more efficient technologies to prolong the shelf life of food products and to bring commensurate economic returns to the farmers. This will not only ensure year-round availability of perishable food products and reasonable prices to the consumers but also equitable distribution to other parts of the country.

REFERENCES

ASSOCHAM. (2013a). *Horticulture Sector in India- State level experience*. New Delhi: The Associated Chambes of Commerce and Industry of India.

ASSOCHAM. (2013b). *Opportunities in Cold Chain: Emerging Trends and Market Challenges-2013*. New Delhi: ASSOCHAM Publication.

Bhardwaj, S., & Palaparthy, I. (2008). Factors Influencing Indian Supply Chains of of Fruits and Vegetables: A Literature Review. *The Icfai University Journal of Supply Chain Management*, *V*(3), 59–68.

Bishara, R. H. (2006). *Cold chain management – an essential component of the global pharmaceutical supply chain*. Retrieved from American Pharmaceutical Review: www.americanpharmaceuticalreview.com/life_science/Bishara_APR.pdf

Dharni, K., & Sharma, S. (2008). Food Processing in India: Opportunities and Constraints. *The Icfai University Journal of Agricultural Economics*, *V*(3), 30–38.

Dokuzoguz, M. (1997). *Developments on Storage of Horticultural Products in Turkey*. First Symposium of Storage and Marketing in Horticultural Products, Yalova, Turkey. (in Turkish)

Gauraha, A., & Thakur, B. (2008). Comparative economic analysis of post-harvest losses in vegetables and foodgrains crops in Chhattisgarh. *Indian Journal of Agricultural Economics*, *63*(3), 376.

GOI. (2012). *Annual Report- Ministry of Food Processing Industries*. New Delhi: Government of India.

Gunduz, M. (1997). Market Structure, Storage, Marketing Systems and Foreign Trade Relations in Horticulture Products. *First Symposium of Storage and Marketing in Horticultural Products*, 9-14. (in Turkish)

Halder, P., & Pati, S. (2011). A Need For Paradigm Shift to Improve Supply Chain Management of Fruits & Vegetables in India. *Asian Journal of Agriculture and Rural Development*, *1*(1), 1–20.

Jain, N. (2007). *International Conference on Agribusiness and Food Industry in Developing Countries: Opportunities and Challenges*. Retrieved February 19, 2013, from IIM Lucknow: http://www.iiml.ac.in/events/Program.html

Kader, A., & Rolle, R. (2004). *In the role of post harvest management in assuring the quality and safety of horticultural produce*. Rome: FAO Food and Agricultural Organizations of the United Nations.

Kapoor, P. (2009, July 28). *Doctoc-International Summit on Food Processing and Agribusiness.* Retrieved January 22, 2014, from Docstoc.com: http://www.docstoc.com/docs/127265667/ENTREPRENEURIAL-OPPORTUNITIES-IN-THE-AGRI-BUSINESS

Karabulut, O. A., Kuruoglu, G., Ilhan, K., & Arslan, U. (2005). Using of Heat Treatments against Post-harvest Diseases, J. Ondokuz Mayıs Univ. [in Turkish]. *Facul. Agric., 20*(1), 94–101.

Kaynas, K., Celikel, F. G., Türkes, N., & Surmeli, N. (1988). *Studies on Maturity Physiology of Storage Facilities and of Some Tomato Varieties Grown in Yalova and Iznik Regions. In Vegetable Breeding in Open Research Project Report* (pp. 415–423). Ataturk Horticulture Research Institute. (in Turkish)

Khan, A. (2005, September 5). *The domestic food market: is India ready for food processing?* Retrieved January 26, 2014, from India Development Foundation: http://www.idfresearch.org/pdf/dommarket.pdf

Klein, J. D., & Lurie, S. (1991). Postharvest Heat Treatment and Fruit Quality. *Postharvest News Inf., 2*, 15–19.

Kumar, S., Pal, S., & Joshi, P. K. (2004). Vegetable Sector in India: An Overview. Impact of Vegetable Research in India, National Centre for Agrıcultural Economics and Policy Research, ICAR.

Lawande, K. E. (2004). Status of Onion and Garlic Research in India. Impact of Vegetable Research in India, National Centre for Agrıcultural Economics and Polıcy Research, ICAR.

Maheshwar, C., & Chanakwa, T. S. (2006). Postharvest losses due to gaps in cold chain in India-A solution. *ISHS Acta Horticulturae 712: IV International Conference on Managing Quality in Chains - The Integrated View on Fruits and Vegetables Quality.* Retrieved January 26, 2014, from Acta Horticulturae: http://www.actahort.org/books/712/712_100.htm

Mishra, P. K., & Anjani, S. (2010). *Supply Chain Management of Agricultural Commodities through Electronic Spot Exchanges.* Retrieved from http://ssrn.com/abstract=1728686

Modi, P., Mishra, D., Gulati, H., & Murugesan, K. (2009). Uttarakhand state cooperative federation: Can it help the horticulture farmers? *Vision—The Journal of Business Perspective, 13*(2), 53-61.

Murthy, D. S., Gajanana, T. M., Sudha, M., & Dakshinamoorthy, V. (2009). Marketing and Post harvest losses in fruits: Its implications on Availability and economy. *Indian Journal of Agricultural Economics, 64*(2), 259–275.

Narula, S. A. (2011). Reinventing cold chain industry in India: Need of the hour: Interview with Mr Sanjay Aggarwal. *Journal of Agribusiness in Developing and Emerging Economies, 1*(2), jadee.2011.52401baa.001. doi:10.1108/jadee.2011.52401baa.001

Negi, S., & Anand, N. (2016a). Factors Leading to Losses and Wastage in the Supply Chain of Fruits and Vegetables Sector in India. *Energy Infrastructure and Transportation Challenges and Way Forward-Conference Proceedings, International Conference on Management of Infrastructure* (pp. I 89 - I 105). Dehradun.

Negi, S., & Anand, N. (2016b). An Overview of Fruits and Vegetable's Retail Supply Chain Models in India. In N. Kamath, & S. Saurav (Eds.), Handbook of research on strategic supply chain management in the retail industry (pp. 170-187). Hershey, PA: Business Science Reference, IGI Global.

Negi, S., & Anand, N. (2015a). Issues and challenges in the supply chain of fruits & vegetables sector in India: A Review. *International Journal of Managing Value and Supply Chains*, *6*(2), 47–62. doi:10.5121/ijmvsc.2015.6205

Negi, S., & Anand, N. (2015b). Cold Chain: A Weak Link in the Fruits and Vegetables Supply Chain in India. *The IUP Journal of Supply Chain Management*, 48-62.

Negi, S., & Anand, N. (2015c). Supply Chain of Fruits & Vegetables' Agribusiness in Uttarakhand (India): Major Issues and Challenges. *Journal of Supply Chain Management Systems*, *4*(1 & 2), 43–57.

Negi, S., & Anand, N. (2014, December). Supply Chain Efficiency: An Insight from Fruits and Vegetables Sector in India. *Journal of Operations and Supply Chain Management*, *7*(2), 154–167. doi:10.12660/joscmv7n2p154-167

NHB. (2014). *Horticulture Statistics at a glance.* Retrieved February 21, 2017, from National Horticulture Board: http://nhb.gov.in/PDFViwer.aspx?enc=3ZOO8K5CzcdC/Yq6HcdIxC0U1kZZenFuNVXacDLxz28=

NHB. (2016). *3rd Advance Estimate of Area and Production of Horticulture Crops (2015-2016).* Retrieved March 21, 2017, from National Horticulture Board: http://nhb.gov.in/PDFViwer.aspx?enc=3ZOO8K5CzcdC/Yq6HcdIxC0U1kZZenFuNVXacDLxz28=

ONICRA. (2012). *Indian Cold Chain Industry.* Retrieved January 25, 2015, from ONICRA: http://www.onicra.com/images/pdf/publications/coldchainindustryreportjune2014.pdf

Ozcan, M. (2007). *Affects on Quality and Durability of Harvest and Post-Harvest Practices in Horticultural Products.* Retrieved September 18, 2013, from http://www.carsambaziraatodasi.com/ab1_1.asp

Ozcan, M., & Balkaya, A. (1995). Causes of Harvest and Post-Harvest Losses on Fruits and Vegetables Product Grown in Amasya Province. *J. Ondokuz Mayıs Univ.* [in Turkish]. *Facul Agric.*, *10*(1), 51–61.

Ozcan, M., Balkaya, A., & Ceyhan, V. (1997). Analysis of Vegetable Marketing Activities in the Black Sea region. *First Symposium of Storage and Marketing in Horticultural Products*, 229-234s. (in Turkish)

Rathore, J., Sharma, A., & Saxena, K. (2010). Cold Chain Infrastructure for Frozen Food:A Weak Link in Indian Retail Sector. *The IUP Journal of Supply Chain Management*, *7*(1-2), 90–103.

Reddy, P. P. (2004). Vegetable Research in India-An IIHR Perspective. Impact of Vegetable Research in India, National Centre for Agricultural Economics and Policy Research, ICAR.

Salin, V., & Nayga, R. M. Jr. (2003). A cold chain network for food exports to developing countries. *International Journal of Physical Distribution & Logistics Management*, *33*(10), 918–933. doi:10.1108/09600030310508717

Sapra, R., & Joshi, S. (2011, Nov-Dec). *Cold Chain Logistics Sector Analysis Nov-Dec.* Retrieved February 4, 2014, from Business Design: http://www.businessdesign.co.in/webfiles/Project/312313092332Cold%20Chain%20Logistics_Jan.2011.pdf

Saurav, S., & Potti, R. (2016). Cold Chain Logistics in India: A Study. In A. Dwivedi (Ed.), Innovative Solutions for Implementing Global Supply Chains in Emerging Markets (pp. 159-172). IGI Global. doi:10.4018/978-1-4666-9795-9.ch011

Shukla, D. (2010). *UNCTAD.* Retrieved January 22, 2014, from http://unctad.org/sections/wcmu/docs/ettcp05_en.pdf

Shukla, M., & Jharkharia, S. (2013). Agri-fresh produce supply chain management: A state-of-the-artliterature review. *International Journal of Operations & Production Management, 33*(2), 114–158. doi:10.1108/01443571311295608

Singh, B., Banerjee, M. K., Singh, K. P., Pandey, P. K., Sudhakar, P., & Rai, M. (2004). *AICRP on Vegetables in India: Evolution andAchievements Impact of Vegetable Research in India.* New Delhi: National Centre for Agrıcultural Economics and Polıcy Research,ICAR.

Singh, R., Kushwaha, R., & Verma, S. K. (2008). An economic appraisal of post-harvest losses in vegetable in Uttar Pradesh. *Indian Journal of Agricultural Economics, 63*(3), 378.

Tatlidil, F., Kiral, T., Gunes, A., Demir, K., Erdemir, G., & Fidan, H. (2003). *Economic Analysis of Crop losses during Pre-Harvest and Harvest Periods in Tomato Production in the Ayaşand Nallıhan Districts of Ankara Province.* Academic Press.

Troger, K., Hensel, O., & Burkert, A. (2007). Conservation of Onion and Tomato in Niger - Assessment of Post-Harvest Losses and Drying Methods. In *Conference on International Agricultural Research for Development.* University of Kassel-Witzenhausen and University of Gottingen.

Turan. (2008). *Post-harvest Practices on Fruits.* Author.

Veena, Babu, K. N., & Venkatesha, H. R. (2011). Supply Chain: A Differentiator in Marketing Fresh Produce. *The IUP Journal of Supply Chain Management, 8*(1), 23-36.

Viswanadham, N. (2007). *Can India be the food basket for the world?* Working Paper series, IBS, Hyderabad. Retrieved from http://www.cccindia.co/corecentre/Database/Docs/DocFiles/Can_India_be.pdf

Vorst, J. V., & Beulens, A. (2002). Identifying sources of uncertainty to generate supply chain redesign strategies. *International Journal of Physical Distribution & Logistics Management, 32*(6), 409–430. doi:10.1108/09600030210437951

World Economic Forum. (2016). *The Global Risks 2016* (11th ed.). Geneva: World Economic Forum.

World Economic Forum. (2013). *Outlook on the Logistics and Supply Chain Industry 2013.* Geneva: World Economic Forum.

ADDITIONAL READING

Aneesh, M., & Arnav, S. (2011). Cold chain: Finally warming up to India. *Infrastructure Today*, 22-25.

Blanco, A. M., Masini, G., Petracci, N., & Bandoni, J. A. (2005). Operations management of a packaging plant in the fruit industry. *Journal of Food Engineering*, *70*(3), 299–307. doi:10.1016/j.jfoodeng.2004.05.075

Bogataj, M., Bogataj, L., & Vodopivec, R. (2005). Stability of perishable goods in cold logistic chains. *International Journal of Production Economics*, *93/94*, 345–356. doi:10.1016/j.ijpe.2004.06.032

Bourlakis, C., & Bourlakis, M. (2005). Information technology safeguards, logistics asset specificity and fourth-party logistics network creation in the food retail chain. *Journal of Business and Industrial Marketing*, *20*(2), 88–98. doi:10.1108/08858620510583687

Bourlakis, M. A., & Weightman, P. W. (Eds.). (2008). *Food supply chain management*. John Wiley & Sons.

Derens, E., Palagos, B., & Guilpart, J. (2006). The cold chain of chilled products under supervision in France. In *13th World Congress of Food Science & Technology 2006* (pp. 823-823). doi:10.1051/IUFoST:20060823

Donk, D. P. V., Akkerman, R., & Vaart, T. V. (2008). Opportunities and realities of supply chain integration: The case of food manufacturers. *British Food Journal*, *110*(2), 218–235. doi:10.1108/00070700810849925

Donselaar, K., Woensel, T., Broekmeulen, R., & Fransoo, J. (2006). Inventory control of perishables in supermarkets. *International Journal of Production Economics*, *104*(2), 462–472. doi:10.1016/j.ijpe.2004.10.019

Emond, J. P. (2008). The cold chain. *RFID-Technology and applications*, 144-156.

Fearne, A., & Hughes, D. (2000). Success factors in the fresh produce supply chain: Insights from the UK. *British Food Journal*, *102*(10), 760–772.

Fearne, A., Barrow, S., & Schulenberg, D. (2006). Implanting the benefits of buyer-supplier collaboration in the soft fruit sector. *Supply Chain Management: An International Journal*, *11*(1), 3–5. doi:10.1108/13598540610642402

Fernie, J., & Sparks, L. (2014). *Logistics and retail management: emerging issues and new challenges in the retail supply chain*. Kogan Page Publishers.

Goldman, A., Ramaswami, S., & Krider, R. E. (2002). Barriers to the advancement of modern food retail formats: Theory and measurement. *Journal of Retailing*, *78*(4), 281–295. doi:10.1016/S0022-4359(02)00098-2

Hahn, K. H., Hwant, H., & Shinn, S. W. (2004). A returns policy for distribution channel coordination of perishable items. *European Journal of Operational Research*, *152*(3), 770–780. doi:10.1016/S0377-2217(02)00753-1

Heap, R. D. (2006). Cold chain performance issues now and in the future. *Bulletin of the IIR, 4.*

Hingley, M. K. (2005). Power imbalanced relationships: Cases from UK fresh food supply. *International Journal of Retail & Distribution Management*, *33*(8), 551–569. doi:10.1108/09590550510608368

International Trade Administration. (2016). Retrieved March 30, 2017, from 2016 Top Markets Report Cold Chain: http://trade.gov/topmarkets/pdf/Cold_Chain_Executive_Summary.pdf

Jedermann, R., Ruiz-Garcia, L., & Lang, W. (2009). Spatial temperature profiling by semi-passive RFID loggers for perishable food transportation. *Computers and Electronics in Agriculture*, *65*(2), 145–154. doi:10.1016/j.compag.2008.08.006

Joshi, R., Banwet, D. K., & Shankar, R. (2009). Indian cold chain: Modeling the inhibitors. *British Food Journal*, *111*(11), 1260–1283. doi:10.1108/00070700911001077

Kuo, J. C., & Chen, M. C. (2010). Developing an advanced multi-temperature joint distribution system for the food cold chain. *Food Control*, *21*(4), 559–566. doi:10.1016/j.foodcont.2009.08.007

Kittipanya-ngam, P., Shi, Y., & Gregory, M. J. (2011). Exploring geographical dispersion in Thailand-based food supply chain (FSC). *Benchmarking: An International Journal*, *18*(6), 802–833. doi:10.1108/14635771111180716

Likar, K., & Jevšnik, M. (2006). Cold chain maintaining in food trade. *Food Control*, *17*(2), 108–113. doi:10.1016/j.foodcont.2004.09.009

Mahajan, R., Garg, S., & Sharma, P. B. (2016). Food Cold Chain Management: An Indian Perspective. In A. Dwivedi, Innovative Solutions for Implementing Global Supply Chains in Emerging Markets (pp. 187-202). IGI Global.

Mahajan, R., Garg, S., & Sharma, P. B. (2011). Indian frozen peas market: A case study on FPIL. *International Journal of Globalisation and Small Business*, *4*(2), 154–169. doi:10.1504/IJGSB.2011.042250

Marsden, T., Banks, J., & Bristow, G. (2000). Food supply chain approaches: Exploring their role in rural development. *Sociologia Ruralis*, *40*(4), 424–438. doi:10.1111/1467-9523.00158

Mingfei, L., & Ting, Y. (2011, July). The cold chain logistics performance evaluation on sideline products based on data envelopment analysis. In *Product Innovation Management (ICPIM), 2011 6th International Conference on* (pp. 371-374). IEEE. doi:10.1109/ICPIM.2011.5983679

Ovca, A., & Jevšnik, M. (2009). Maintaining a cold chain from purchase to the home and at home: Consumer opinions. *Food Control*, *20*(2), 167–172. doi:10.1016/j.foodcont.2008.03.010

Punt, H., & Huysamer, M. (2005). Supply chain technology and assessment—temperature variances in a 12 m integral reefer container carrying plums under a dual temperature shipping regime. *Acta Horticulturae*, *687*(687), 289–296. doi:10.17660/ActaHortic.2005.687.35

Ren, Y., Hu, Q., & Huang, X. (2011, August). Researching on benefit assignment of logistics system in cold chain for food. In *Emergency Management and Management Sciences (ICEMMS), 2011 2nd IEEE International Conference on* (pp. 513-515). IEEE.

Ruiz García, L., & Lunadei, L. (2010). *Monitoring cold chain logistics by means of RFID*. In-Tech. doi:10.5772/8006

Viator, C. L., Fang, W. Y., Hadley, J. L., Aiew, W., Salin, V., & Nayga, R. (2001), *Infrastructure Needs Assessment for Distribution of Frozen Processed Potato Products in Southeast Asian Countries*, Final report on Cooperative Agreement No. 5599-109, prepared for US Department of Agriculture, Foreign Agriculture Service, available at: http://agecon.tamu.edu/faculty/salin/research/aptapg.html

Xiaohong, X. U., Lan, H., & Wang, R. (2010, January). Identification of critical control points of the food cold chain logistic process. In *Logistics Systems and Intelligent Management, 2010 International Conference on* (Vol. 1, pp. 164-168). IEEE. doi:10.1109/ICLSIM.2010.5461444

KEY TERMS AND DEFINITIONS

Cold Chain: A cold chain is a temperature-controlled supply chain. An unbroken cold chain is an uninterrupted series of storage and distribution activities which maintain a given temperature range. It is used to help extend and ensure the shelf life of products such as fresh agricultural produce, seafood, frozen food.

Cold Storage: It refers to a form of refrigerated storage.

Food Loss and Wastage: Food loss and food waste refer to the decrease of food in subsequent stages of the food supply chain intended for human consumption.

Horticulture: Horticulture is the branch of agriculture that deals with the art, science, technology, and business of growing plants. It includes the cultivation of medicinal plants, fruits, vegetables, nuts, seeds, herbs, sprouts, mushrooms, algae, flowers, seaweeds and non-food crops such as grass and ornamental trees and plants.

Infrastructure: The basic physical and organizational structures and facilities (e.g. buildings, roads, and power supplies) needed for the operation of a society or enterprise.

Local Intermediaries: Firm or person (such as a broker or consultant) who acts as a mediator on a link between parties to a business deal, investment decision, negotiation, etc.

Metric Ton (MT): Equal to 1000 kilogram. Also called tonne.

NGO: A non-governmental organization (NGO) is a not-for-profit organization that is independent from states and international governmental organizations.

Post-Harvest: In agriculture, postharvest handling is the stage of crop production immediately following harvest, including cooling, cleaning, sorting and packing.

Reefer Trucks: A refrigerator truck is a van or truck designed to carry perishable freight at specific temperatures. Like refrigerator cars, refrigerated trucks differ from simple insulated and ventilated vans (commonly used for transporting fruit), neither of which are fitted with cooling apparatus. It can be ice-cooled, equipped with any one of a variety of mechanical refrigeration systems powered by small displacement diesel engines, or utilize carbon dioxide (either as dry ice or in liquid form) as a cooling agent.

Refrigerated Container: A refrigerated container or reefer is an intermodal container (shipping container) used in intermodal freight transport that is refrigerated for the transportation of temperature sensitive cargo.

Shelf Life: The length of time a product may be stored without becoming unsuitable for use or consumption.

Supply Chain: The sequence of processes involved in the production and distribution of a commodity from the point of origin to the point of consumption.

Chapter 15
Supply Chain Management in Pharmaceutical Industry:
Opportunities and Challenges for Retailers

Snehil Saurav
BL Kapoor Hospital, India

ABSTRACT

In this research paper, author has studied top pharmaceutical companies around the globe and their relationship with pharmacies. Based on the analysis author has identified current challenges their supply chain is facing and how IT can help them to make their supply chain more responsive and reliable. IT framework which can address the supply chain challenges has also been proposed here. Second part of the paper deals with how retailers can help the industry to overcome these challenges. Pharma companies need to partner with pharmacies for a win-win situation and this partnership can address most of the challenges being faced by the industry. This partnership will help in various ways like getting accurate information across the entire chain at any point and at any location, Instant access to real-time demand by the end user, visibility of all handovers in the supply chain and helps in setting-up seamless collaboration between all parties.

INTRODUCTION

The pharmaceutical industry is responsible for the development, production and marketing of medications. Thus, its immense importance as a global sector is evident. The total level of pharmaceutical revenue worldwide had reached nearly one trillion U.S. dollars. North America is responsible for the largest portion, generating more than 40 percent of these revenues. This is mostly due to the leading role of the U.S. pharmaceutical industry. But as in many other industries, the Chinese pharmaceutical sector shows the highest growth rates over the last years.

Still, the leading pharmaceutical companies come from the United States and Europe. Based on prescription sales, NYC-based Pfizer is the world's second largest pharmaceutical company. In 2013, the company generated some 45 billion U.S. dollars in pure pharmaceutical sales, while total revenue

DOI: 10.4018/978-1-5225-3056-5.ch015

stood at nearly 52 billion U.S. dollars. Other top global players from the United States are Johnson & Johnson, Merck and AbbVie. Novartis and Roche from Switzerland, GlaxoSmithKline and AstraZeneca from the United Kingdom, and French Sanofi are the European big five.

Branded, patented medicines by far make up the largest share of pharmaceutical revenues. Humira, an anti-inflammatory drug, generated nearly 10 billion U.S. dollars of revenue worldwide. Oncologics continue to be the leading therapeutic class based on revenue. In 2013, cancer drugs made around 67 billion U.S. dollars of revenue globally. Other major therapy classes were pain drugs, antihypertensives and antidiabetics.

More than any other industry, the pharmaceutical sector is highly dependent on its research and development segment. Pharmaceutical companies invest 20 percent and more of their revenues in R&D measures. The United States is a traditional stronghold of pharmaceutical innovation. Most new substances introduced to the market trace their origin to the United States. Because of the steadily loss of patent protection, the invention of new drugs is of vital importance for the pharmaceutical industry. Revenue losses due to patent expiry often are very significant, as it can be seen with Pfizer's Lipitor.

The pharmaceutical and biotech industry is under severe pressure. Research & Development (R&D) costs are spiralling, development timelines are growing, payer pushback is increasing and consumers are becoming increasingly knowledgeable about care options. The industry is responding driving time out of development, becoming smarter about stopping projects early in the development cycle, and increasing efficiency through rationalization or outsourcing of non-core activities.

As scientific advances enable the industry to move from a 'one-size-fits-all' approach to care, to one of segmentation, personalization and wellness, so the supply chain will need to evolve. The supply chain of the future will be built around flexibility, responsiveness and reliability shifting the supply paradigm from a stock-based model to an order-based model. In this research we highlight and prioritizes the top 10 global health pharmaceutical supply chain challenges and how supply chain help the companies to address some of its immediate concerns.

The largest U.S. companies on the global market are Johnson & Johnson, Pfizer and Merck &Co. Johnson & Johnson generated around 75 billion U.S. dollars of revenue in 2014 and in the same year Japan's pharmaceutical revenue came to about 70.5 billion euros in total. The North American pharmaceutical market was still the world's largest regional market. Japan held 10.8 percent of global pharmaceutical market revenue. This share increased down to some eight percent in 2015.

An IMS report indicated that Biologics (a majority of which would be temperature-sensitive products) would constitute about 19–20% of the total pharmaceutical sales by 2017. Current indications state that Biologics are growing by 18%, compared to the 3–5% growth in pharmaceutical sales overall.

The Indian pharmaceuticals market is the third largest in terms of volume and thirteenth largest in terms of value, as per a report by Equity Master. India is the largest provider of generic drugs globally with the Indian generics accounting for 20 per cent of global exports in terms of volume. The Indian pharma industry, which is expected to grow over 15 per cent per annum between 2015 and 2020, will outperform the global pharma industry, which is set to grow at an annual rate of 5 per cent between the same period. The market is expected to grow to US$ 55 billion by 2020, thereby emerging as the sixth largest pharmaceutical market globally by absolute size, as stated by Mr Arun Singh, Indian Ambassador to the US. Branded generics dominate the pharmaceuticals market, constituting nearly 80 per cent of the market share (in terms of revenues).

India has also maintained its lead over China in pharmaceutical exports with a year-on-year growth of 11.44 per cent to US$ 12.91 billion in FY 2015-16, according to data from the Ministry of Commerce and Industry. Imports of pharmaceutical products rose marginally by 0.80 per cent year-on-year to US$ 1,641.15 million. Overall drug approvals given by the US Food and Drug Administration (USFDA) to Indian companies have nearly doubled to 201 in FY 2015-16 from 109 in FY 2014-15. The country accounts for around 30 per cent (by volume) and about 10 per cent (value) in the US$ 70-80 billion US generics market. The Indian pharmaceuticals market increased at a CAGR of 17.46 per cent in 2015 from US$ 6 billion in 2005 and is expected to expand at a CAGR of 15.92 per cent to US$ 55 billion by 2020. By 2020, India is likely to be among the top three pharmaceutical markets by incremental growth and sixth largest market globally in absolute size.

Coming to Pharmacy stores in India, their biggest challenge is lack of visibility into the stocks of the CFA (Carrying & Forwarding Agent) which leads to the non-availability of products in the store. This results in sales loss for the pharmacy stores. The sales force and the CFA plays an important role in demand generation processes for the pharma companies. That's the reason this chapter is being included in this book. The stores complete the Supply Chain process along with the CFAs which helps in demand fulfilment. Pharma companies all over the world and so India too, focusses a lot on the improvement and training of the sales force which can bring competitive advantage over others in the market place.

BACKGROUND

Branded, patented medicines by far make up the largest share of pharmaceutical revenues. Humira, an anti-inflammatory drug, generated nearly 10 billion U.S. dollars of revenue worldwide. Oncologic continue to be the leading therapeutic based on revenue. In 2013, cancer drugs made around 67 billion

Figure 1. A typical pharmaceutical supply chain

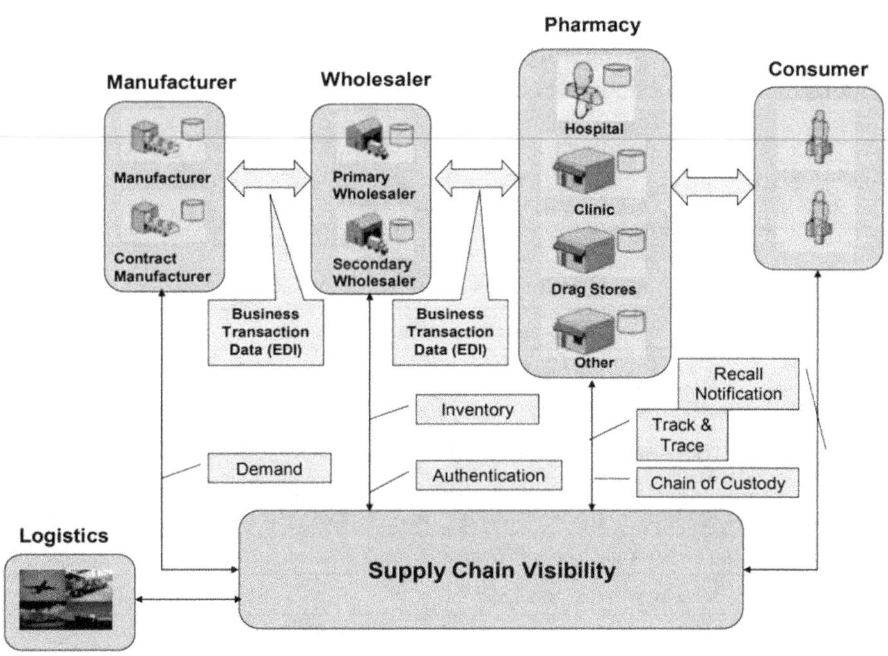

U.S. dollars of revenue globally. Other major therapy classes were pain drugs, antihypertensive and antidiabetics. Still, the leading pharmaceutical companies come from the United States and Europe

Based on prescription sales, NYC-based Pfizer is the world's second largest pharmaceutical company. In 2013, the company generated some 45 billion U.S. dollars in pure pharmaceutical sales, while total revenue stood at nearly 52 billion U.S. dollars. Other top global players from the United States are Johnson & Johnson, Merck and AbbVie. Novartis and Roche from Switzerland, GlaxoSmithKline and AstraZeneca from the United Kingdom, and French Sanofi are the European big five.

The efficiency in the Supply Chain system has been brought in by many pharmaceutical companies over the years with focus on process engineering, process re-engineering and process improvement, primarily driving customer oriented financial metric as these metric directly impact the financial parameters of the companies (Anon 2002). It is about time to integrate Supply Chain and the demand generation process with a holistic customer focused approach in search of excellence and its important for every player in the pharma industry.

The pharmaceutical industry is a complex process, operations and organizations fraught with conflicting objectives and numerous intractable constraints (Ballance,1992). A highly regulated environment coupled with the life altering nature of the products characterizes the pharmaceutical industry as a uniquely difficult system involved in the discovery, development and manufacture of drugs and medications (Bhagwat 1995). Pharmaceutical industry is one of the ten industries identified for detailed investigation under Phase I of the SC2020 project. The pharmaceutical industry makes a large contribution to the national GDP and extremely critical to the well-being of any nation.

This paper aims at proposing an information technology framework on the supply chain for pharmaceutical industry. The paper adopts the exploratory study as research method, involving a producer of generic drugs and its main distributor. Data was collected by semi-structured interviews. In pharmaceutical supply chain, sharing information boosted by information technology translates into greater flexibility and reliability, lower costs, obtained through more reliable forecasting, and lower inventory requirements. Second part of the paper aims at how the supply chain can be made effective and efficient at the pharmacy store side.

In Table 1 we list the set of steps we followed to arrive at our findings.

Table 2 contains the list of public listed companies which we considered for our research.

Table 1. Analytical steps

	Steps
Step 1	Reach to case studies available on the public domain like Novartis, Pfizer, Merck, AstraZeneca case studies
Step 2	Visited websites of some top companies operating in multiple countries
Step 3	Browsed through the websites of top supply chain magazines.
Step 4	Read through their Annual reports, Earnings call and other company reports of global companies.
Step 5	Looked for supply chain related post/comments by leading magazines, top executives comments/interviews and solution providers' press release.
Step 6	Interview supply chain analytics experts and pharma industry experts both from industry and academia.
Step 7	Analyse these qualitative data and Propose a framework for IT practice
Step 8	Analyze qualitative data for pharmacy retail practice

Table 2. List of companies

Company	Country	Revenue (U$ Million)
Johnson & Johnson	United States	70,074
Bayer AG	Germany	51,428.3
Novartis AG	Switzerland	50,359
Roche Holding Ltd.	Switzerland	50,004.1
Pfizer Inc.	United States	48,851
Merck & Co., Inc.	United States	39,498
Sanofi SA	France	38,702.3
GlaxoSmithKline plc	United Kingdom	36,568.2
AstraZeneca plc	United Kingdom	24,708
AbbVie Inc	United States	22,859
Abbott Laboratories	United States	20,405
Eli Lilly and Co	United States	19,958.7
Teva Pharmaceutical Industries Limited	Israel	19,652
Boehringer Ingelheim GmbH	Germany	17,676.5
Bristol-Myers Squibb Co	United States	16,560
Takeda Pharmaceutical Co Ltd	Japan	16,191.4
Novo Nordisk A/S	Denmark	16,063.4
Allergan plc	Ireland	15,071
Mylan NV	United Kingdom	9,429.3
Celgene Corporation	United States	9,256
DAIICHI SANKYO COMPANY, LIMITED	Japan	8,373.1
Aspen Pharmacare Holdings Limited	South Africa	3,158.4
Dr.Reddy's Laboratories Ltd	India	2,458
Aurobindo Pharma Ltd	India	1,983.1
Cipla Ltd	India	1,856.3
Cadila Healthcare Ltd	India	1,415.5
Glenmark Pharmaceuticals	India	1,084.7

Author has also considered privately held companies and gone through the various materials available online. Author has extended his study to represent the information technology (IT) factors which are crucial for success of integrated and efficient supply chain management. Author has designed a framework to represent IT success factors for implementing a successful supply chain strategy at Pharma companies. The focus is on being more agile and that the same time has high availability.

Indian Pharma Companies

Authors have referred to Indian pharmaceutical companies for the study. The Indian pharmaceuticals market is the third largest in terms of volume and thirteenth largest in terms of value, as per a report by

Equity Master. India is the largest provider of generic drugs globally with the Indian generics accounting for 20 per cent of global exports in terms of volume. The Indian pharma industry, which is expected to grow over 15 per cent per annum between 2015 and 2020, will outperform the global pharma industry, which is set to grow at an annual rate of 5 per cent between the same period! The market is expected to grow to US$ 55 billion by 2020, thereby emerging as the sixth largest pharmaceutical market globally by absolute size, as stated by Mr Arun Singh, Indian Ambassador to the US.

By 2020, India is likely to be among the top three pharmaceutical markets by incremental growth and sixth largest market globally in absolute size. The Indian pharmaceutical market size is expected to grow to US$ 100 billion by 2025, driven by increasing consumer spending, rapid urbanization, and raising healthcare insurance among others.

MAIN FOCUS OF THE CHAPTER

Pharmaceutical Supply Chain Challenges

Pharmaceutical companies have to operate internationally and can not restrict themselves to a particular region because of the nature of the competition. Executives working in the pharmaceutical industry for past several years have realized the need to work globally either to source the raw material or for manufacturing plants for keeping the cost lower and the same time sell products to address the growing markets globally (Booth 1999). To manage and control the supply chains in the current global scenario, executives face more complex supply chain challenges. Authors have reviewed various research documents, advisory council reports and interviews of the experts.

Authors find that the companies are now moving from a supplier–buyer mentality supply chain to a more intelligent supply networks that can provide information "on-demand." In the "On-demand" supply network, collaboration occurs during the entire supply chain from the raw-material supplier to the distribution company that delivers the final product safely to the end user through retail pharmacies (Zigiaris 2000). This change in model in being necessitated because of the challenges being faced by the

Figure 2.Indian pharmaceutical companies market share

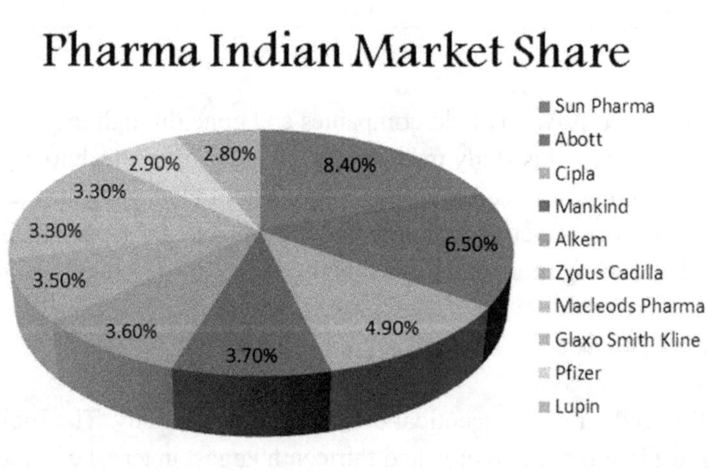

industry. In next few paragraphs presented are the challenges being faced by the pharmaceutical supply chain in general and pharmacy store business in particular (Ahmad 2009).

Role of Pharmacy Stores in Pharmaceutical Supply Chain

In order to understand the challenges faced by the Pharmacy store and propose solutions, lets understand the role played by pharmacy stores in the pharmaceutical supply chain. Author has analyzed the information from some of the companies mentioned in list 2 and the local pharmacy stores/chains and referenced secondary articles. Author's understanding is presented in this section.

- Demand Visibility by providing Inventory requirement to the pharma companies is the most important role. Pharma companies depend on these retailers to sell their products. How to reduce the inventory level but still be able to meet the demand is a concern of these stores? Is possible to reduce inventory? Pharma companies and also their distributors/wholesalers have no visibility to the inventory status (Biotto 2012).
- Better manage inventory to reduce the wastage and make it available to the buyers in best of the condition and sell it before the medicines expire is the second most important role of the pharmacy stores (Bishara 2006).
- Real-time inventory tracking and trace for controlled drugs is also required from the pharmacy.
- Visibility to sample drugs is required. Currently, there is no system to manage the sample drugs.
- Visibility to price change is a problem and pharma companies depend on the stores for the information (Castillo-Villar 2012).
- Expired date tracking
- Regulation and Compliance Visibility
- Current practice can not eliminate the Bullwhip effect. A mechanism to provide visibility of demand is needed by the wholesalers up to manufacturers to reduce BullWhip effect.

Pharmacy Stores Challenges and Opportunities

There are many challenges unique to pharmacy store supply chain management. Facing the prospect of managing a chain of pharmacies can seem to be a daunting task anytime. One of the challenges faced by pharmacy stores supply chain management involves drug ordering for multiple locations (Caswell 200). Even though these stores buy in bulk, how much inventory to order can be a big challenge. Thus, wherever possible, pharmacy chain management wants to order for all stores in the entire chain or purchasing groups at one time. But, each store is different and has its own set of unique needs and requirements. The stores need to be clustered in order to manage them well but still supply chain management is faced with a very challenging task.

There is a shortage of qualified pharmacy personnel in the developing countries like India where demand is increasing at a rapid pace (Deisingh 2005). Thus, the management of the chain has to work hard to properly allocate its human resources throughout the stores included in the chain. Understanding and following government regulations and compliance is a complex task in itself. sticky and complex issue for pharmaceutical supply. There can be many legal requirements to be adept at understanding and ensuring compliance with the applicable statutes and regulations in all of the jurisdictions where the pharmacy chain operates an outlet or store (Flach 2000).

Key issues associated with this supply chain are summarized based on literature review as follows:

- Multiple categories of medicines
- Statutory requirements for track and trace capabilities (e-Pedigree)
- Highly regulated environment requiring extensive data collection and information exchange to ensure chain of custody and monitoring of various controls
- Management of product expiry – for safety, error prevention, reassignment, safe disposal
- Cold chain required for temperature controlled product movement
- Globalization and outsourcing
- Complex demand patterns
    - Predictable pattern for mid-life cycle products
    - Highly unpredictable for new introductions
    - Low volume high mix spread over a large area needing quick response for
- Controlled products (prescription drugs – branded or generics) requiring a high level of constant management
- Varying regulations across global markets
- Drug recall management
- Elimination of counterfeits
- Deal with data accuracy and related problems
- Highly inefficient order management
- Lack of process standardization in purchasing, inventory management, etc (Zhang 2007).
- Lack of collaboration across players

SOLUTIONS AND RECOMMENDATIONS

Recommendations and findings have been put under various headers in this section.

Supply Chain Challenges in Pharmaceutical Industry

From our study top 10 challenges that have come up are listed in Table 3.

Pharma companies require capabilities more than a traditional ERP system can provide. Companies need intelligence in the system along with the complete view of the production and movement of goods from start to finish. Intelligence will also provide with suggestions and also connect different/disparate systems of its suppliers, partners, and logistics providers. Need for a collaborative system that is equipped with reliable information throughout the supply chain will rise sooner or later.

Opportunities Available in the Industry

From the other studies that we have read, we see following opportunities that the companies are looking forward to:

- Accurate information across the entire chain at any point and at any location
- Instant access to real-time updates and alerts if issues are detected

Table 3. Top 10 challenges

	List of challenges
1.	Lack of coordination
2.	Inventory management
3.	Absent demand information
4.	Human resource dependency
5.	Order management
6.	Shortage avoidance
7.	Expiration
8.	Warehouse management
9.	Temperature control
10.	Shipment visibility

- Visibility of all handovers in the supply chain
- Traceability back to source of all materials
- Seamless collaboration between all parties the

Generally, we see that there is a disruption in the market and then the companies struggle to respond to the disruption. These disruptions are unforeseen but in the pharma industry case, everyone knew of the disruptions that has come due to the patent expiration of the blockbuster drugs. Still we find many of the pharma companies not yet ready to respond. The generic companies who were ready waiting to take the benefit are ahead in race compared to their big size competitors. To respond — to cut costs and become more agile — industry leaders rationalize their sourcing and distribution, and add operational efficiencies. Although they are reluctant to make these moves at first, companies soon discover that seemingly modest shifts in supply chain strategy can transform their industry and dramatically boost performance. Haltingly at first, and then in a great wave of activity, the prevailing practices of the industry change. It happened to automobiles and chemicals in the 1980s and 1990s and to consumer packaged goods in the 1990s and 2000s. Now it's the turn of pharmaceutical companies.

IT Framework to Support Supply Chain

To address the challenges identified in the previous section, the pharma industries IT strategy must be based on identified pillars of benefits. These pillars will act as the main areas of interest around which the IT strategy would be centered.

Figure 3 shows a typical IT system landscape. Channel here is to use combine the above IT System Landscape with the pillars of functionality and address the challenges mentioned in the Table 3. We have identified eight technology-enabled measures of functionality from our analysis. Using these, pharmaceutical companies can expand the data they collect and improve their approach to managing and analyzing these data to get more out of their supply chain. The 8 approaches are:

Figure 3. Revenue growth of India Pharma companies

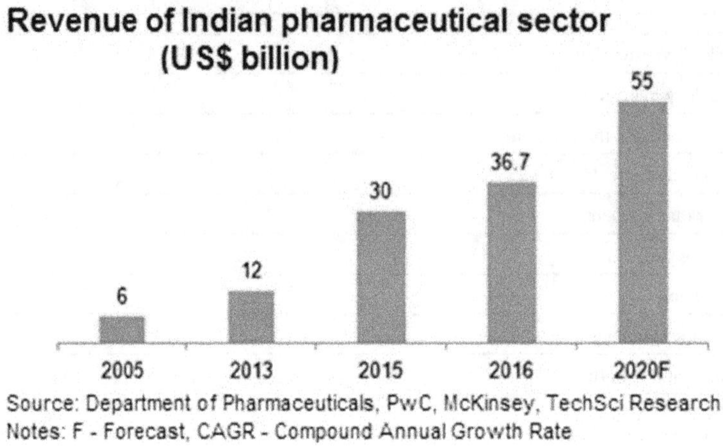

1. **Integrate All Data:** In order to get the maximum benefit from technology trends, it is imperative to manage and integrate data generated throughout the pharmaceutical supply chain.
2. **Collaborate Internally and Externally:** The main objective of collaboration is to encourage the networking between the participants in all the stages, from research, development, commercialization to delivery. This will enable to share and increase knowledge.
3. **Employ IT-Enabled Portfolio-Decision Support:** The more information you have, the better decision you can make. Data-driven decisions can be made is you have the right information and you

Figure 4.A typical IT system landscape

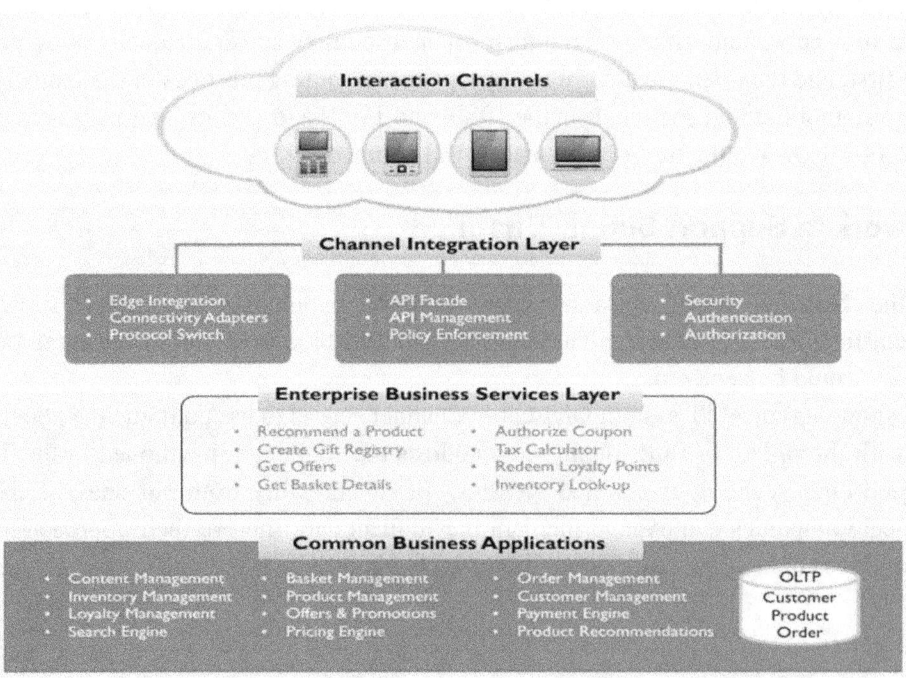

analyze that information. Technologies like visual dashboards might help in the decision making process for current and future projects, forecasting, etc.

4. **Leverage New Discovery Technologies:** Pharmaceutical industry is benefited by using cutting-edge tools. For example, "technologies that produce a lot of data quickly, for example, next-generation sequencing, which, within 18 to 24 months, will make it possible to sequence an entire human genome at a cost of roughly $100.
5. **Deploy Sensors and Devices:** Companies should take advantage from current technologies like smartphones, which can be used as instrumentation devices, to collect a big amount of data, and use it for further research.
6. **Raise Clinical-Trial Efficiency:** The information collected by devices such those mentioned above, "will enable improvements in clinical-trial design and outcomes as well as greater efficiency"
7. **Improve Safety and Risk Management:** Companies can collect information, regarding safety of the drugs they produce, from relatively new channels, like websites where customers might be complaining about the effectiveness of a particular drug.
8. **Sharpen Focus on Real-World Evidence:** To expand their data beyond clinical trials, some leading pharmaceutical companies are creating proprietary data networks to gather, analyze, share, and respond to real-world outcomes and claims data.

Based on the study, essential aspects of the IT framework are listed in the figure 5.

IT Strategy has to be strategic in nature. There are 4 phases of a Pharma business where IT strategy can complement the business strategy. These are:

Figure 5. IT design approach

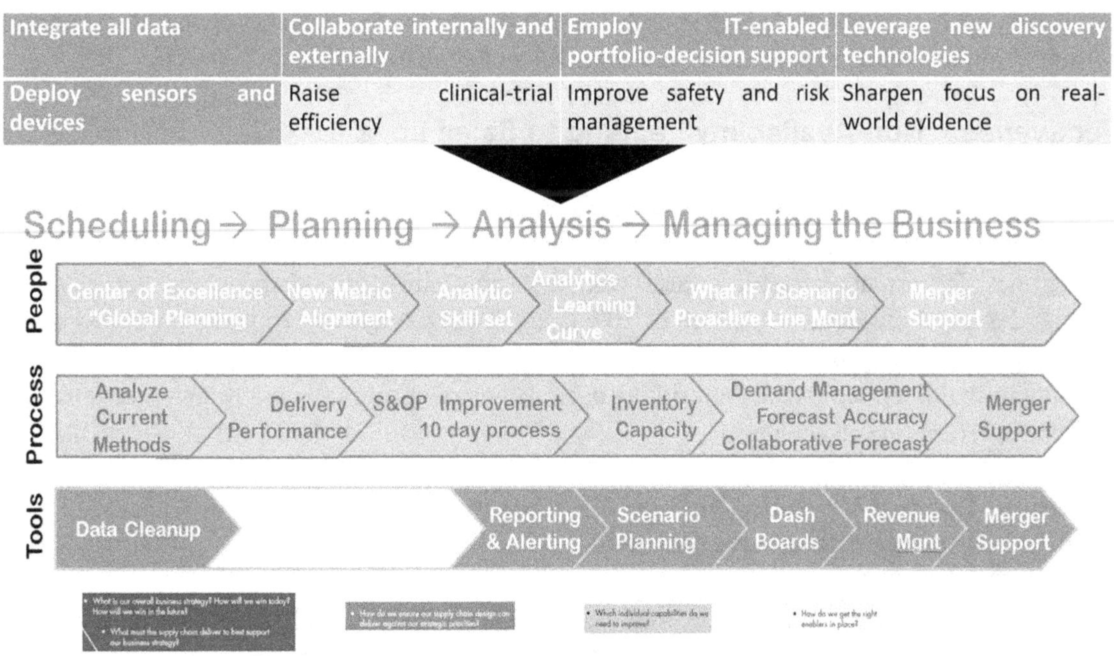

- **Scheduling:** This is based on overall business strategy and the key questions asked here are: How will we win today? What must the IT deliver to support the next gen supply chain strategy?
- **Planning:** Make sure supply chain design can deliver against the company's strategic priorities.
- **Analysis:** This phase is about analyzing the current state and be able to company with strategy to move to a better "to-be" state.
- **Managing the Business:** Get the right enablers in the place which will support the business growth targets.

Probably the single most important driver in the pharmaceutical industry is the time-to-market. Companies secure very significant returns in the early life of a successful drug, before any competition. The competition-free life is shortening, typically from 5 to 1–2 years. Pharma companies have been looking for IT strategy to shorten their time to market with different capabilities. The advancements made in data analytics field is helping them to uncover the result faster than ever before. The strategy discussed here and the IT capabilities will help the pharma companies to meet their immediate challenges.

Pharmacy Store Role in Supply Chain

Effectiveness of the distribution supply chain between the CFA and the stores results in making products available to the end consumer, this results in decreased in loss of sales over the retail counter. Efficiency of the distribution supply chain between the CFA and the stores results in making products available to the end consumer, which results in reduction of excess inventory levels in the channel and a month-end 'skew' in stockists' inventories.

With new product introduction driven growth on the wane, effective channel management can be a strategic differentiator for the Pharma companies in times to come. Channel management is the key to growing the classic brands but what is less understood is the positive impact it has on the ethical portfolio by virtue of improved trade hygiene and focused efforts of ethical sales reps".

Effectiveness: Non-Availability Leading to Sales Loss

Loss of sales due to non-availability of products at the retailer's end is a reality in the current pharma distribution setup. However, the incidence and quantum of this loss differs across geographies and product categories. The extent of sales loss varies from 0-1% in Metros (across product categories) to up to 5% in tier 2 & rural geographies (as high as 20% in small OTX brands). The variation in loss of sales across geographies and product categories can be attributed to supply chain aspects such as the reach of the supply chain, service levels, the working capital constraints of stockists, awareness of customers and financial returns to stakeholders.

Efficiency: Lack of Visibility of Post CFA Supply Chain Leading to Excess Inventories

One of the key operational reasons for excess inventories in the channel is the lack of visibility of pharma companies into stock holding and stock movement in the post CFA supply chain. In the current state, visibility of the post-CFA supply chain is limited, and is traditionally through the visits of the sales force to stockists/retailers as well as through the monthly stock and sale statements of stockists. As a consequence of this opacity in the chain, pharma companies rely on primary sales to stockists as a metric for measurement of performance. Driven by sales targets on primary sales, the sales force may resort to pushing stocks to distributors at month end, which may result in a month end skew in stockist inventories. Where there are variances in demand and primary sales is not aligned to secondary sales, there is an inventory pile-up at stockists.

Some Implications of Gaps in Distribution Effectiveness and Efficiency

- **Faster Decline of Heritage OTX Brands:** While the findings of the survey indicate a volume sales loss in the range of up to 5% in OTX brands (up to 20% in small OTX brands), primarily in tier 2 and rural markets, if companies are unable to arrest this loss of sales (compounded over 10 years), it would mean a revenue loss of 30% to 50%. For heritage OTX brands that typically encounter a prescription shift to new molecules, this kind of de-growth will mean faster erosion of brand equity and hasten their decline. Loss of sales could be significantly higher for relatively smaller OTX brands, resulting in their wiped out from the market.

'On the contrary, if companies are able to plug the gap in availability of these categories, it would mean a volume growth of 3%–5% every year, which could almost double the size of a heritage brand over 10 years. The delta between the two cases is 100% to 200%, which emphasizes the benefits of ensuring availability.

- **Increased Pressure of High Growth on Existing Prescription Products**: Large pharmaceutical companies typically set targets in correlation with the growth of the pharma market. In the absence of growth of OTX brands, and with new product (molecule) launches ceasing to be a key growth driver after the implementation of the product patent regime, pressure on achieving growth in prescription (Rx) products will be significantly higher.
- **Adverse Impact on the Growth of Existing Prescription Brands Due to Conflict of Resource Allocation:** To manage the pressure of high growth, companies could consider two options. They can either neglect heritage OTX brands and invest fully in prescription products, which would indirectly contribute to the faster erosion of heritage brands, or invest the effort of their sales representatives in managing the availability of OTX brands, and thereby detract from their focus on prescription brands. This could lead to a potential conflict of resource allocation leading to sub-optimal performance in both.
- **Month End Sales Skew:** Lack of visibility of stock holding and movements in the post CFA supply chain leads to companies relying on primary sales for setting objectives. If aggressive primary sales targets in prescription and OTX categories do not match the actual demand in the market, it results in month end sales push to stockists.

Way Forward

For the issues of distribution effectiveness and efficiency identified, the key levers to address the root causes are:

- Increase visibility of the channel
- Release working capital at the stockist
- Ensure generated efficiencies are passed down the channel up to retailers

FUTURE RESEARCH DIRECTIONS

As a follow-up of the research presented in this paper, a potential initiative for improving visibility to inventory based on Kanban practices can be the topic to research upon. Close co-operations between pharmacy stores with manufacturers without impacting the relationships and at the same time avoid sharing of data violation will be the topic to research next.

CONCLUSION

Earlier times when world's largest and biggest pharma companies ruled the world with their top patent generating high profit. The supply chain was seen as a tool where the focus was on security of supply. IT systems were used for integration of different departments and provide visibility in the supply chain. Currently when most of the world's well known drug patents have expired or going to expire, there is a sudden push by the drug manufacturing companies to revisit the components of their supply chains and identifying ways of extracting additional benefits from them. The focus is on value that their IT strategy can bring in to their "value chain" - no longer called as supply chain. The focus has gone beyong integration and visibility benefits. We have see atleast 8 new areas where the companies are putting or has to put in coming years. The 8 approaches which are described in the earlier sections are: Integrate all data, collaborate internally and externally, Employ IT-enabled portfolio-decision support, Leverage new discovery technologies, deploy sensors and devices, raise clinical-trial efficiency, improve safety and risk management and Sharpen focus on real-world evidence.

The pharmaceutical distribution and retailing plays a very important role in the overall pharmaceutical industry supply chain. It is one of the most complex and and at the same time less understood aspects of the pharmaceuticals business. This industry has a unique channel characterized by high degree of fragmentation. In India, industry has over 60,000 stockists, semi-stockists and 600,000 retailers, unorganized independent units with inadequate information infrastructure. Our focus has been to understand how the visibility in the channel can be increased beyond the CFA stock points. Effective and efficient channel management is not only a tactical necessity but can be a strategic enabler for growth and pharmaceutical industries are looking into complete channel to improve their overall supply chain score and make it their competitive strength.

REFERENCES

Ahmad, N., Awan, M., Raouf, A., & Sparks, L. (2009). Development of a service quality scale for pharmaceutical supply chains. *International Journal of Pharmaceutical and Healthcare Marketing*, *3*(1), 26–45. doi:10.1108/17506120910948494

Anon, . (2002). Summary of the executive session on emergency preparedness and the pharmaceutical supply chain. *American Journal of Health-System Pharmacy*, *59*(3), 247–253. PMID:11862636

Bailey, K., & Francis, M. (2008). Managing information flows for improved value chain performance. *International Journal of Production Economics*, *111*(1), 2–12. doi:10.1016/j.ijpe.2006.11.017

Ballance, R., Pogany, J., & Forstner, H. (1992). *The world's pharmaceutical industries*. London, UK: Edward Elgar.

Barratt, M., & Oke, A. (2007). Antecedents of supply chain visibility in retail supply chains: A resource-based theory perspective. *Journal of Operations Management*, *25*(6), 1217–1233. doi:10.1016/j.jom.2007.01.003

Bhagwat, Y., & Griggs, F. T. (1995). Analysis of riskiness of pharmaceutical industry firms. *Journal of Research in Pharmaceutical Economics*, *6*(1), 65–76. doi:10.1300/J063v06n01_05

Biotto, M., De Toni, A., & Nonino, F. (2012). Knowledge and cultural diffusion along the supply chain as drivers of product quality improvement. *International Journal of Logistics Management*, *2*(2), 212–237. doi:10.1108/09574091211265369

Bishara, R. (2006). Cold Chain Management-An Essential Component of the Global Pharmaceutical Supply Chain. *American Pharmaceutical Review*, *1*, 105–109.

Booth, R. (1999). *The global supply chain*. FT healthcare management report. London: Financial Times Business Ltd.

Castillo-Villar, K. K., Smith, N. R., & Simonton, J. L. (2012). A model for supply chain design considering the cost of quality. *Applied Mathematical Modelling*, *36*(12), 5920–5935. doi:10.1016/j.apm.2012.01.046

Caswell, J. A. (2000). Analyzing quality and quality assurance (Including labeling) for GMOS. *Agbioforum Journal*, *3*, 225–230.

Deisingh, A. K. (2005). Pharmaceutical counterfeiting. *Analyst (London)*, *130*(3), 271–279. doi:10.1039/b407759h PMID:15724152

Flach, A. (2000). Topically Applied Nonsteroidal Anti-inflammatory Drugs and Corneal Problems: An Interim Review and Comment. *Ophthalmology*, *107*(7), 1224–1226. doi:10.1016/S0161-6420(00)00223-2 PMID:10889089

Fontanella. (2007). *The Supply Chain Management Market Sizing Report, 2006-2011*. AMR Research.

Ford, E. W., & Scanlon, D. P. (2007). Promise and problems with supply chain management approaches to health care purchasing. *Health Care Management Review*, *32*(3), 192–202. doi:10.1097/01.HMR.0000281623.35987.cf PMID:17666990

Lamming, R., Caldwell, N., Phillips, W., & Harrison, D. (2005). Sharing Sensitive Information in Supply Relationships: The Flaws in One-way Open-book Negotiation and the Need for Transparency. *European Management Journal*, *23*(5), 554–563. doi:10.1016/j.emj.2005.09.010

Lyles, M. A., Flynn, B. B., & Frohlich, M. (2008). All Supply Chains Dont Flow Through: Understanding Supply Chain Issues in Product Recalls. *Management and Organization Review*, *4*(02), 167–182. doi:10.1111/j.1740-8784.2008.00106.x

Maruchecka, A., Greisb, N., Menac, C., & Cai, L. (2011). Product safety and security in the global supply chain: Issues, challenges and research opportunities. *Journal of Operations Management*, *29*(7-8), 707–720. doi:10.1016/j.jom.2011.06.007

Mathews, A. W., & Burton, T. M. (2008, March 7). German firm recalls Heparin with China link; Batches had ingredient from different source than Baxter's product. *Wall Street Journal*, p. B4.

McFarlane, D., & Sheffi, Y. (2003). The impact of automatic identification on supply chain operations. *The International Journal of Logistics Management*, *3*(1), 1–17. doi:10.1108/09574090310806503

Oberholzer-Gee, F., & Inamdar, S. N. (2004). Mercks recall of Rofecoxib—A strategic perspective. *The New England Journal of Medicine*, *351*(21), 2147–2149. doi:10.1056/NEJMp048284 PMID:15548771

Patterson, K. A., Grimm, C. M., & Corsi, T. M. (2003). Adopting new technologies for supply chain management. *Transportation Research Part E, Logistics and Transportation Review*, *3*(2), 95–121. doi:10.1016/S1366-5545(02)00041-8

Paulraj, A., Lado, A. A., & Chen, I. J. (2008). Inter-organizational communication as a relational competency: Antecedents and performance outcomes in collaborative buyer-supplier relationships. *Journal of Operations Management*, *26*(1), 45–64. doi:10.1016/j.jom.2007.04.001

Rose, D. F. (2003). *Introduction to e-Supply Chain Management: Engaging Technology to Build Market-Winning Business Partnerships. St.* Lucie Press.

Schoenthaler, R. (2003). Creating real-time supply chain visibility - Even in aftermarket sales and service, transparency is crucial. *Electronic Business*, *29*, 12–12.

Shah, N. (2004). Pharmaceutical supply chains: Key issues and strategies for optimization. *Computers & Chemical Engineering*, *4*(6-7), 929–941. doi:10.1016/j.compchemeng.2003.09.022

Starbird, S. A. (2001). Penalties, rewards, and inspection: Provisions for quality in supply chain contracts. *Journal of Operations Research*, *52*(1), 109–115. doi:10.1057/palgrave.jors.2601048

Walters, D., & Jones, P. (2001). Value and value chains in healthcare: A quality management perspective. *The TQM Magazine*, *13*(5), 319–333. doi:10.1108/EUM0000000005858

Walters, D., & Lancaster, G. (2008). Implementing value strategy through the value chain. *Management Decision*, *38*(3), 160–178. doi:10.1108/EUM0000000005344

Wei, H. S., & Wang, E. T. G. (2007). Creating Strategic Value from Supply Chain Visibility - the Dynamic Capabilities View. *Proc. 40th Hawaii Int. Conf. System Sci.*, 7. doi:10.1109/HICSS.2007.157

Yao, Kurata, & Mukhopadhyay. (2008). Incentives to reliable order fulfillment for an Internet drop-shipping supply chain. *Int. J. Production Economics, 113*, 324-334.

Zhang, C., & Zhang, C. (2007). Design and simulation of demand information sharing in a supply chain. *Simulation Modelling Practice and Theory*, *15*(1), 32–46. doi:10.1016/j.simpat.2006.09.011

KEY TERMS AND DEFINITIONS

Backsourcing: The process of bringing outsourced operations such as Information technology, back in in-house. This commonly occurs after an outsourcing contract has either expired or has been terminated. Also known as Insourcing.

Bill of Lading (BOL): A contract prepared by the carrier containing a detailed list of information relating to a shipment of goods (ie. item, quantity, value, date, port, cosigner, etc), which obligates the carrier to transport the goods to said destination based on which seller can claim consideration and buyer can take delivery of goods.

Cross Dock/Cross Docking (XDK): A practice in logistics of unloading materials from an incoming semi-trailer truck or rail car and loading these materials directly into outbound trucks, trailers, or rail cars, with little or no storage in between. This practice eliminates overhead expenses associated with storage.

Cumulative Lead Time: The total amount of time required to make a part assuming there are no components for its assembly in stock.

Cycle Time: The amount of time that transpires from the time a task (or series of tasks) is initiated to the time a task is completed. For example, from the time a shipping order is printed to the time it is loaded on the truck and the system is updated.

Freight Forwarder: A firm specializing in the supply of transportation services. By buying large volumes of land, sea, air, and pipeline transportation at low rates, freight forwarders are able to offer attractive rates to small businesses who products they combine into large shipments.

Integrated Logistics: A comprehensive, system-wide view of the entire supply chain as a single process, from raw materials supply through finished goods distribution. All functions that make up the supply chain are managed as a single entity, rather than managing individual functions separately.

Just in Time (JIT): A technique for optimizing the manufacturing process and improving inventory control by ensuring goods arrive just in time for the next step in the process. Just in time principles eliminate excess inventory, and rely on frequent small deliveries when required to reduce storage and holding costs.

Key Performance Indicator (KPI): A performance measure which helps gauge the level of success in a supply chain. Some common logistics KPIs are delivery time, production cycle time, % order fill rate, etc.

Lead Time: The total time that elapses between an order's placement and its receipt. Lead time includes the time required for order transmittal, processing, preparation, and transit.

Locator System: A locator system is a part of a warehouse management system (WMS), and is utilized by warehouses to increase the efficiency in inventory tracking. Locator systems often utilize barcode technology to identify each item's exact location.

Material Handling: The processes warehouses utilize to move, store and handle materials between procurement and shipping. Material handling includes short-distance movement of goods within a storage area, including the use of rolling bins, conveyors, forklifts, and other equipment.

Obsolete Inventory: Inventory that has had no usage for a set period of time, ranging from weeks to years depending on the industry. Obsolete inventory is also known as dead inventory.

Order Cycle: The time and process involved from the placement of an order to the receipt of the shipment.

Order Management: The planning, directing, monitoring, and controlling of processes related to customer orders, manufacturing orders, and purchase orders. Order management includes order entry, picking, packing, shipping, and billing.

Order Processing: Involves transfer and checking data from the time the order is accepted, until the invoice reaches the customer.

Safety Stock: Stock used to ensure the availability of products in the case of deviations in supply or demand.

Total Average Inventory: The average normal use stock, combined with both the average lead stock, and safety stock.

Vendor-Managed Inventory: The control of inventory at a 3PL warehouse by client or vendor.

Chapter 16
Developing Sustainable Retail Food Value Chain for India: A Challenge for the Next Century

Rupali Das
Malla Reddy Dental College for Women, India

ABSTRACT

Ever increasing population, rising prosperity supported by ongoing urbanization has accelerated the demand for food in India. At the same time, area under agriculture is decreasing and food production is coming under pressure owing to limitations on resources and other environmental considerations. In the coming decades, doing more with less will be a key priority for all those involved in food production. In this chapter, we will also look at the challenges and opportunities available for the food supply chain management. This chapter sets out the premise that the food industry, throughout the value chain, has a tremendous opportunity, as well as an obligation, to meet the needs of new, more sophisticated and more demanding consumers while satisfying shareholders' demands for returns—and in doing so creating a sustainable food supply for the new millennium.

INTRODUCTION

The world is at the start of a new agricultural era, in which boosting yields and reducing harvest losses will be essential to feeding the world's growing populations. Emerging markets—and in particular the most advanced developing economies—are at the forefront of this movement. In recent years Brazil, Russia, India and China, among others, have had a major influence on changing global food production and consumption patterns. They have also been some of the world's most successful food producers over the last two decades. As their influence on global food markets rises, it is worth investigating these countries' success factors in the field of agricultural production. Food and groceries retail in India is the largest segment of the Rs.25.3 trillion retail market accounting for 69% of the overall market. However, the market penetration of organized food retail is just 2%, providing a huge opportunity. In comparison, the penetration of consumer durables is 27%, apparel and footwear 18% each, and jewelry 14%.

DOI: 10.4018/978-1-5225-3056-5.ch016

Food Retailers in India

Accumulated losses at India's top 10 food retailers, who account for about 40% of the organized retail sector's revenue, stood at Rs. 13,000 crore in 2013-14 on revenue of around Rs. 23,500 crore (source: Crisil Ratings). The report does not include profitable retailers like Future Value Retail Ltd (Future Value) and Avenue Supermarts Ltd, which operates DMart retail chain. By 2016-17, their losses would have peaked to Rs. 17,000 crore as revenue increases to Rs.32,000-35,000 crore over the next three years to fiscal 2017. After that, as the twin benefits of size and an optimized operating model kick in, at least half of the retailers analyzed will break-even. But the paradox is, to recover the monies, they will have to continue expanding. That's because of wafer-thin net margins of 2% to 2.5% in the business. No other retail vertical (such as apparel, consumer durables and footwear) has witnessed hemorrhaging of this magnitude. The losses were because retail businesses were still in their gestation period and in the process of carrying out large-scale expansions.

With the new government not appearing keen to open up multi-brand retail to foreign direct investment, what will also keep these retailers going is the backing of intrepid promoters ready to add skin to the game because they see immense potential in India. As of March 2014, CRISIL estimates these retailers have invested about Rs. 19,000 crores in opening new stores and funding losses through direct equity infusions, and loans from banks and promoters. These investments are likely to continue and will help multiply revenue. To stem losses, retailers have taken several initiatives, but these will yield results only gradually (Ruben 2007).

Rural Retail in India

The rural market offers a vast untapped potential; it should also be recognized that it is not that easy to operate in rural market because of several problems. Today, the extreme challenge for the rural marketer is to reach out to the most remote rural destinations and increase rural incomes (Nizamuddin 2013). About 750 million Indians reside in about 6 lakhs villages and even the powerful marketers like HLL and ITC have recently been able to cover only about 2 to 2.5 lakhs villages while about 1 to 1.5 lakhs villages have been connected through Project Shakti and E-Chaupal initiatives. Rural marketing is thus a time consuming affair and requires considerable investments in terms of evolving appropriate strategies with a view to tackle the problems (Bhateja 2012). A lot need to be done for expanding distribution coverage and the daunting task ahead is to overcome challenges like infrastructure, market organization and staff, etc. (Ross 2011).

Food Value Chain

While farmers are often focused on the production side of their businesses, they also have to know exactly how they will sell what they produce and how it will get to market (Raghunath 2007). If they don't manage these supply chain facilities and services themselves, they must obtain them in some way. A chain of food business facilities and services from field to fork is called a Food Value Chain. That's because triple-bottom-line consumer and business values are pivotal in any food value chain (Melville 2004). The figure below shows the different players and the stage in a food value chain.

Food Value Chain and Food Supply Chain

"Food supply chain" is the generic and mainstream term for the sum of the many food production, manufacturing, and marketing links from farm to table. Those links include equipment dealers, seed suppliers, food processors, distributors, and even government regulators. The term Food Value Chain is a permutation of the food supply chain concept that has emerged recently. In food supply chains, farmers typically anonymous, interchangeable parts; that is, an apple is an apple is an apple, and it doesn't matter where it comes from or how it was grown, as long as it's big and red! In food value chains, the farmer (and where and how they raise their food etc.) is a core product quality. People, places, and practices matter (Kumar 2009). Therefore, everyone in the chain — from the seed supplier to the produce broker — becomes interested and invested in making sure the chain produces sustainable farm businesses along the way (Betts 2009). It follows that the term Food Value Chain comes from "values-based food supply chain," which is a way of describing how changes in consumer and community values are driving changes in food supply chains. The Food Value Chain, therefore, represents an important set of considerations and to be called as a successful food value chain, all of the partners must get benefited from it.

STUDY RATIONALE

The Indian retail sector is on a roll. All major Indian retail companies are on an expansionist mode. Even non-retailing companies have or are planning to make major investments in retailing and / or supply chain. In this chapter, we focus on the movement of retail industry in the food sector in India. Instead of only analyzing the retail opportunities in the Indian context, this study makes a case for corporate participation in the entire food supply chain. A new modernized framework model of the food supply chain is proposed and entry of both domestic as well as international players is recommended keeping

Figure 1. Food value chain

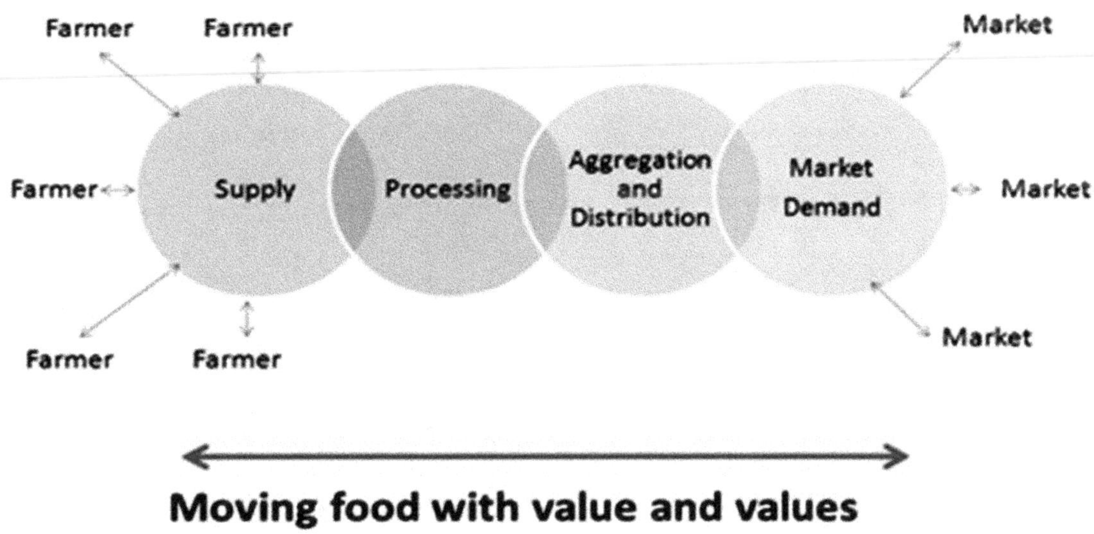

in consideration the current regulatory regime (Ganjyal 2010). Figure below describes a typical food supply chain.

India – World's Leading Producer of Fresh fruits and Vegetables, Pulses, Rice and Wheat. Yet Malnutrition is a common phenomenon in India. 60% of children in India are underweight and malnourished and as a total 21% of the total population is malnourished. According to World Bank, productivity losses in India due to stunted growth, iodine deficiencies and iron deficiencies are equal to almost 3% of GDP. Growth in Agricultural Productivity has increased from 40% to 500% in the past 40 years, yet the availability of food remains a problem for many households in India. This research was conducted to assess the agricultural successes of the high-growth Indian market. This report also offers a number of best-practice solutions from other high growth regions of the world like Russia, Brazil and China. The hope is that, by examining these markets' agricultural practices, some consensus might emerge about how best to co-operate on a global level to secure food supplies over the coming decades.

This chapter addresses following objectives:

- The study the evolving food supply chain in Indian scenario and the challenges faced by the industry
- To study the best practices from food value chain of other high growth regions
- Propose a framework for developing a sustainable food value chain in India

METHODOLOGY

Analysis is presented based on secondary data sources. The study is divided into 3 parts: Indian Food Supply Chain Scenario, Food Supply Chain scenario from other high growth regions which includes: Brazil, China and Russia (Sarkar 2010). The process followed for the research included scanning more

Figure 2. Defining food supply chain

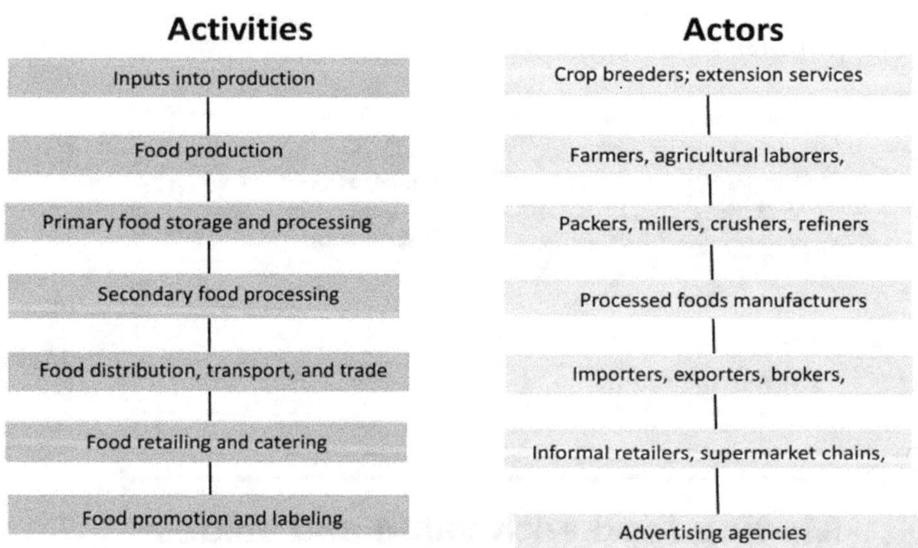

than 100 blogs, company websites, research journals and industry reports. The top 10 food and grocery retailers in India were studies which included: Aditya Birla Retail Ltd, Bharti Retail Ltd, Heritage Foods (India) Ltd, HyperCITY Retail (India) Ltd, Max Hypermarket India Pvt. Ltd, METRO Cash & Carry India Pvt. Ltd, Reliance Fresh Ltd, Spencer's Retail Ltd, Trent Hypermarket Ltd and Wal-Mart India Pvt. Ltd. These companies account for 40% of the organized retail in India (Selani 2014). Various articles, company executives' interviews and industry reports available in the public domain have been referred. This chapter also includes study of various case studies available for Indian context, derived the challenges for all the partners included as part of the value chain. Case studies of global companies have been covered to understand the global trend and used this for benchmarking Indian industry. The steps we followed are listed in the table II below.

We present our analysis in the sections to follow under the three major themes:

- Challenges faced for implementing food value chain
- Indian food value chain versus the global standard on the "4-Pillar Benchmarking" framework.
- Present a Sustainable Food Value Chain for the Indian scenario.

Benchmarking model is presented in "4-pillar Benchmarking model". Our benchmarking study uses a four-phased approach: planning, data collection, data analysis and reporting, and adaptations of study findings. As shown in the figure above, food value chain has four main processes: Supply, Processing, Aggregation & Distribution and Market Demand. As part of the study, top factors within each of the processes would be identified and the current state of food value chain in India would be ranked on each of these factors. The factors and ratings would be captured as shown in the table below.

Based on ratings of Best in class companies and Indian industry on 4-pillar Benchmarking model is presented under section two of the findings.

In the final section of the Findings, the focus has been to develop a Sustainable Food Value Chain for Indian scenario. The various dependent factors which include internal as well as external factors were studied. Various sustainable models have also been studied like those for Logistics, Retail, etc.

Table 1. Analytical steps undertaken for the study

Step 1	Identify top 10 industries in organized food retail in India and also the companies operating in rural market like ITC and HLL. Read through their company reports and analysts reports.
Step 2	Look for blogs and reports of agriculture revolution in other growth economies like Brazil, Russia and China.
Step 3	Looked for supply chain related post/comments by leading magazines, top executives comments/interviews and solution providers' press release.
Step 4	Data collection- Data about retailers cold chain capabilities, its challenges and future strategies
Step 5	Focus study on global companies. Above steps repeated for global companies as well.
Step 6	Present benchmarking study on "4-Pillar" Benchmarking framework. 4 pillars are Supply, Processing, Aggregation & Distribution and Market Demand.
Step 7	Based on the information gathered from all the sources and analyzing the information, a framework for sustainable food value chain is being presented for the Indian scenario.

Figure 3: Food value chain

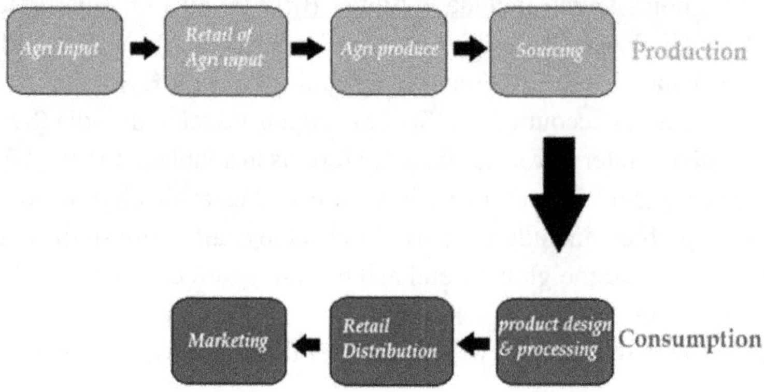

FINDINGS

Findings from the study have been presented under different headers below:

Food Value Chain in India

The conditions at this major wholesale market, which has changed little in decades, reflect one of the biggest threats to food security in India, especially as the pace of urbanization requires more food to be brought to cities. With India's farm-to-fork networks still dominated by politically influential traditional traders and small shops, the country has struggled to modernize its food supply chain and attract large-scale investment into cold-storage, refrigerated trucks and other modern logistics. As a result, much of India's agricultural output rots – or seriously degrades – before reaching consumers, even as hunger and malnutrition remain.

Table 2. Benchmarking Factors

Processes	Factors	Ratings
Supply	Factor 1 Factor 2 Factor 3	**Level 1**: Transactional **Level 2**: Commercial **Level 3**: Proactive **Level 4:** Strategic **Level 5**: Class leading
Processing	Factor 1 Factor 2 Factor 3	
Aggregation & Distribution	Factor 1 Factor 2 Factor 3	
Market Demand	Factor 1 Factor 2 Factor 3	

Challenges

- **Poor Infrastructure:** India has the second longest Road Network in the world. But less than 2% of the entire road length is covered by National Highways. This 2% of the road handles 40% of the Cargo. We can't expect the same vehicles to run in other smaller roads and we need to depend on other modes of transportation. Normal distance travelled by an Indian Truck is 250-300 km/day as against an International norm of 600-800 km/day. Also most of the roads in India can support only 16.2 tons as against an International norm of 36 tons. Railway network is not very suitable for transit of Food items. In India, only 6% of the logistics is organized.
- **Sales Channel:** There is a need to reach out to producers in the value chain. The process is not efficient and this space is filled with politically influential people which increases the cost in the value chain but the benefit is not passed on to the producers.
- **Absence of Adequate Warehouses:** Two types of Warehousing are required for Food Produces. One is a sheltered Warehouse to store Food Grains like Rice, wheat and Cereals. The other one is Cold Storage Facility to store Fruits and Vegetables. Many of the warehouses have inadequate capacity. The crop production has gone up significantly over the years, but the warehouses have not increased. Cold Storage Facility is important for storing Fruits, Vegetables and Milk. The existing Cold Storage Facilities can store 21.7 mn tons food produce, but the requirement is more than 31 mn tons.
- **Food Safety:** There is also a worry about the content of the food, its origin, freshness, and safety.
- **Judicious Use of Scarce Resources:** Further complicating the global food supply chain is the resource intensity of food production. Water and energy are two scarce resources in heavy demand in the production and distribution of food.
  - **Water:** Water is a scarce commodity in many parts of the world where the population is growing the fastest. Climate change is also impacting water supply in some areas of the world. At the same time, pumping, treating, and moving large volumes of water require a great deal of energy.
  - **Energy:** Modern farms use large amounts of energy to plant, fertilize, irrigate, and harvest crops. In many cases, traditional fossil fuels are used to provide this energy, and a change to more sustainable energy resources will be required. Finally, commodities such as corn are now consumed as a source of energy as well as of food production and are therefore, more expensive. The result is a dramatic rise in the cost of food worldwide.
- **Food Sustainability:** Modern farming techniques, such as genetic modification, are being debated and are often perceived as negative. Buying local and the organic food movement are growing trends that have taken hold with the modern consumer.

Areas of Opportunities

- **Encouraging 3PL (Third Party Logistics) Players:** 3PL are Service Providers who take care of End to End Delivery. The concept of single Logistics Service Provider (LSP) is at an infant level. Government must encourage 3PL players by easing the norms. A single logistics service means that there will be no loss of Food produces in between due to the presence of various players.
- **Warehouse With Private-Public Partnership:** Government must encourage Private firms to set up Warehouses. There have been few cases of Private Public Partnership in this sector.

Table 3. Indian food value chain analysis

Process	Factors	Indian Scenario	Level
Supply	Land Ownership & Credit Availability	India has the second largest agricultural land in the world. Credits are available from bank at marginal rate.	Level 4
	Seeds, Fertilizers & Machinery	India has setup institutions like IFFCO, drought management systems, kisan call center, etc.	Level 2
	Dependency on external factors	Dependency on monsoon, over-pumping of water, overexploited forest land, etc. is a major challenge.	Level 1
Processing	Machinery availability	Machinery owned by private companies is a boost to the sector.	Level 3
	Regulatory Environment	Regulatory environment has all the mechanism but effective implementation is the key to success.	Level 3
	R&D	There are many government funded institutes but output of the quality of research is no way helping. NGOs and private companies are helping the sector.	Level 3
Aggregation & Distribution	Infrastructure	Poor Infrastructure	Level 2
	Storage	Many of the warehouses have inadequate capacity.	Level 2
	Logistics & Supply Chain	The concept of single Logistics Service Provider (LSP) is at an infant level.	Level 1
Market Demand	Volatility	Food prices and availability	Level 3
	Complexity	Food security for all.	Level 3
	Scrutiny	Food safety and health and wellness are major concern.	Level 2

Global Best Practices vs. Indian Scenario

Based on the study, presented in the table below are the factors that impact each of the processes of a food value chain. Process column captures the four main processes of a value chain as discussed earlier in the study rationale section. The top factors have been identified as part of the study and listed under the factors column in the table. The third column highlights the current Indian state under each of the factors and based on this, the level has been calculated and put up in the fourth column.

Listed below are some of the observations about the food value chain in India:

- **Supply:** India has the second largest agricultural land in the world, only the United States has more agricultural land than India. Take the case of China. India has more arable land than China. This, despite the fact its total area is only a little over 34 percent that of China. However, China produces more rice and wheat than India does. Institutions like Indian Farmers Fertilizers Cooperative

Limited (IFFCO) are setup to provide farmers with all the required material but such programs and schemes do not reach to all the farmers. Agriculture and allied sectors like forestry and fisheries accounted for 13.7% of the GDP (Gross Domestic Product) in 2013, about 50% of the total workforce. The economic contribution of agriculture to India's GDP is steadily declining with the country's broad-based economic growth. Still, agriculture is demographically the broadest economic sector and plays a significant role in the overall socio-economic fabric of India.

- **Processing:** In India, the food sector has emerged as a high-growth and high-profit sector due to its immense potential for value addition, particularly within the food processing industry. Accounting for about 32 per cent of the country's total food market, the food processing industry is one of the largest industries in India and is ranked fifth in terms of production, consumption, export and expected growth. The total food production in India is likely to double in the next 10 years with the country's domestic food market estimated to reach US$ 258 billion by 2015. The Government of India has been instrumental in the growth and development of the food processing industry. The government through the Ministry of Food Processing Industries (MoFPI) is making all efforts to encourage investments in the business. It has approved proposals for joint ventures (JV), foreign collaborations, industrial licences and 100 per cent export oriented units.
- **Aggregation and Distribution:** Factors have been studied and captured above in section one of the findings.
- **Market Demand:** Food security, food prices, and food safety summarize the multitude of concerns consumers have about food. Continuing headlines about the global food shortage, skyrocketing food prices, massive food riots, genetically modified foods, and global food recalls illustrate just some of the issues. Compounding the problems, consumers cannot change their consumption habits drastically enough to offset the world's growing population; the increasing demand for high-value, resource-intensive foods by the burgeoning middle class in emerging markets; the use of food ingredients for alternative energy; or the climate changes that are causing water shortages and low crop yields.

Based on the current level of each factor, presented in the figure below is the "4-pillar Benchmarking model" developed by the author. The model highlights the current state and the reader can gauge the areas of improvement in the sector. The study is intended for the stakeholders to analyze the current situation and contribute to improve the situation.

A Framework for Sustainable Food Value Chain

Based on the various stakeholders, the drivers for the growth of the food value chain in India and Impact parameters, author has suggested a model that can help the sector to benchmark itself and also to derive the benefits from the drivers. The framework shown in the figure below is intended for all those associated directly or indirectly in the food value chain in India to understand the impact parameters and use the drivers to move from current to higher state which would also help in the overall development of all those who work in this sector, most importantly the farmers.

The five stages of a food value chain are identified as: Underdeveloped (Stage I), Emerging (Stage II), Developing (Stage III), Advancing (Stage IV) and Leading (Stage V).The framework talks about how the Indian food value chain from move from the current stage of Emerging to Advancing and finally reach Leading stage.

Figure 4. Benchmarking

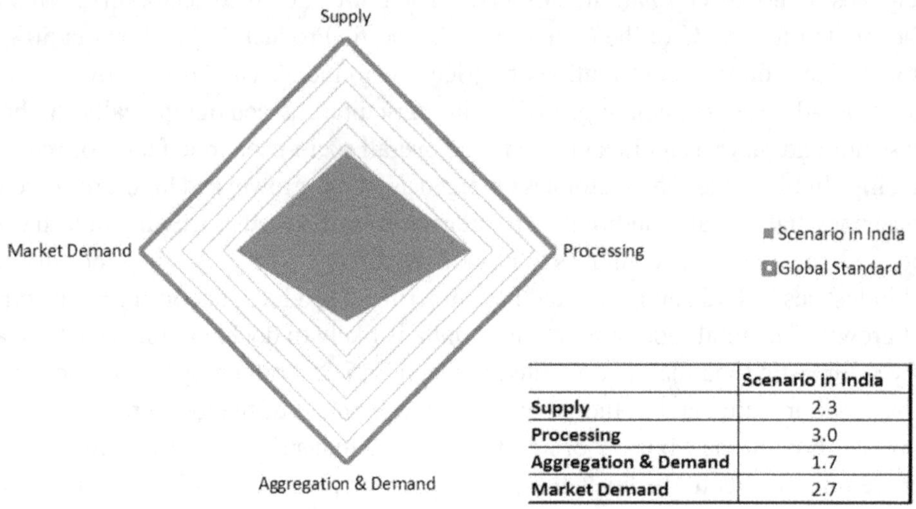

	Scenario in India
Supply	2.3
Processing	3.0
Aggregation & Demand	1.7
Market Demand	2.7

First, the value chain needs to define the role of each of the processes discussed earlier:

- **Supply:** Research & Development, Farming and Trading, micro finance, sourcing hubs, seeds, pesticides, fertilizers and laboratory sourcing. Best practices of these areas should reach to the supply point.
- **Processing:** Value add processing, manufacturing, marketing and sales.

Figure 5. Proposed framework for the food value chain

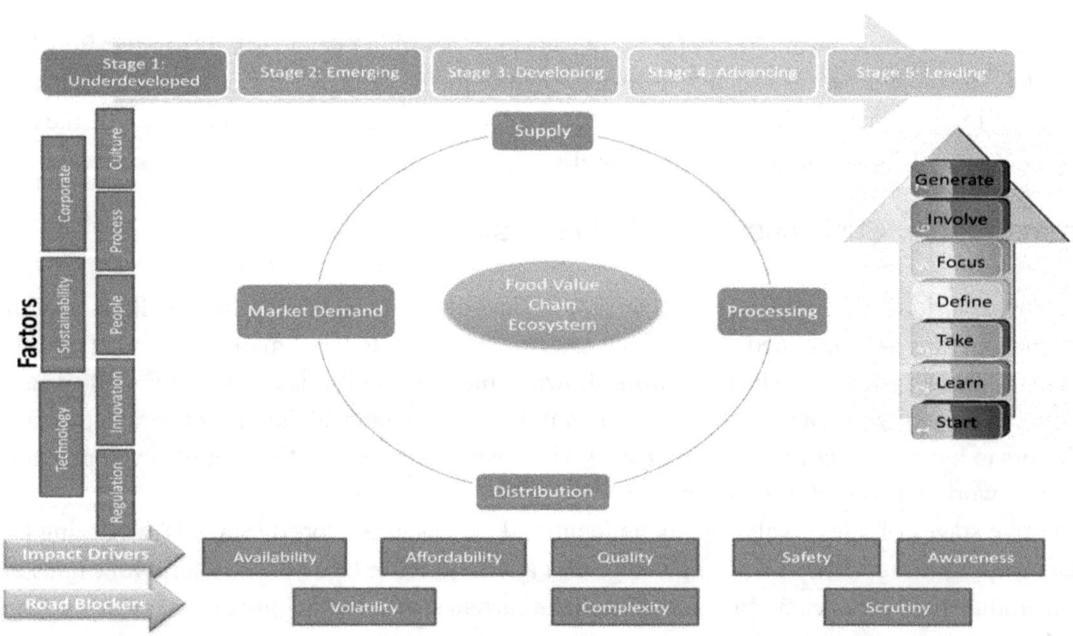

- **Aggregation & Distribution:** Distribution, warehousing, packaging, food parks and cold chains.
- **Market Demand:** Value proposition, brand & positioning, segmentation, delivery and service.

Factors such as volatility in the demand, complexity in the chain and scrutiny by the regulatory bodies act as road blocks for the development of food value chain (Zhang 2011). But these would remain same and the framework suggest to work along with these factors.

Following factors impact the value chain: Availability of source, Affordability of the product by the masses, Quality of the processed food delivered, Safety of the food and creating awareness about the benefits of the products delivered.

Proposed here is a 7 steps design that can take a stage 1 to the stage 5. These are:

- **Start:** Start to build a culture that puts the benefit of value chain at the center and aligns objectives, targets, rewards and recognition with customer demand.
- **Learn:** Learn to be adaptive—use detailed customer insight to test, learn and act quickly, accelerating the process with prototypes.
- **Take:** Take a realistic look at your propositions (solutions, not products)—what will it take to deliver what customers want at a price they want to pay and still make money?
- **Define:** Define your target customers and their needs.
- **Focus:** Focus on some key levers and build momentum throughout the organization.
- **Involve:** Involve distributors and, together, build stronger partnerships.
- **Generate:** Generate customer engagement across their life cycle — this is vital to building loyalty.

CONCLUSION

India is all set to become the food supplier of the world. It has the cultivable land, all the seasons for production of all varieties of fruits and vegetables, well developed agribusiness system that works in its own way. The business system is tuned to food habits (cooking at home) and convenience (kirana stores) of rural and urban folks of the previous generation. Factors such as rapid growth in the economy, the technological innovations in home appliances such as refrigerators microwave ovens, rise of families with dual incomes and the changing food habits of the population all point to the increasing need for healthy processed food. The supply chain sector is very weak with no process owner and this can spell disaster. The food supply chain needs the attention of the academics, the industry and the Government.

Agri-food Value Chains are designed to increase competitive advantage through collaboration in a venture that links producers, processors, marketers, food service companies, retailers and supporting groups such as shippers, research groups and suppliers. A Value Chain can be defined as a strategic partnership among inter-dependent businesses that collaborate to progressively create value for the final consumer resulting in a collective competitive advantage (Terpend 2008). The basic characteristic of a Value Chain is market-focused collaboration; different business enterprises working together to produce and market products and services effectively and efficiently. Value Chains allow businesses to respond to the marketplace by linking production, processing and marketing activities to market demands.

While change in emerging markets is dramatic, there is also a worry about the content of the food, its origin, freshness, and safety. These consumers are increasingly concerned about the sustainability of food production and its impact on the environment. Modern farming techniques, such as genetic modification, are being debated and are often perceived as negative.

Product distribution and sales channels are also changing. Retailers are increasing the number of convenience stores in strategic locations that cater to the "grab and go" consumer (e.g., gas stations, public transport stations). To supply these small shops, which maintain little inventory, the underlying distribution network must be able to match supply and demand with the rapid replenishment of stock. The food and beverage sector is also participating in the growing popularity of online shopping. To offset the costs of home delivery, companies will need to establish a network of convenient pickup points and closely collaborate with logistics partners. Water and energy are two scarce resources in heavy demand in the production and distribution of food.

This study sets out the premise that the food industry, throughout the value chain, has a tremendous opportunity, as well as an obligation, to meet the needs of new, more sophisticated and more demanding consumers while satisfying shareholders' demands for returns—and in doing so creating a sustainable food supply for the new millennium.

FUTURE RESEARCH DIRECTIONS

The application of information technology (IT) is no longer limited to transportation or the weather while studying the impact on Supply Chain. It plays a significant role in other sectors including the food supply chain and brings value to the whole process. The successful employment of IT in the food supply chain can greatly improve product safety and quality and the same time positively impact the food shortage problem. The application of IT in the food sector is mostly seen developed countries, although the developing countries are adopting the principles and methods at a slower pace. Future research should focus on the role of IT developments in the food supply chain integration and monitoring as technology improves and at the same time new technologies are being widely adopted by the food technology industry. Research can be focused to review the components of IT followed by supply chain management, traceability, food processing and packaging, and the application of nanotechnology in food processing and packaging. Such research will greatly help to address the food shortage and wastage problems in a big country like India.

REFERENCES

Aramyan, L. H., Ondersteijn, C., Kooten, O., & Lansink, A. O. (2006). Performance indicators in agri-food production chains. In C. J. Ondersteijn, J. H. Wijnands, R. B. Huirne, & O. Kooten (Eds.), *Quantifying the agri-food supply chain* (pp. 47–64). Dordrecht: Springer. doi:10.1007/1-4020-4693-6_5

Ashenbaum, B., Maltz, A., Ellram, L., & Barratt, M. A. (2009). Organizational alignment and supply chain governance structure: Introduction and construct validation. *The International Journal of Logistics Management*, *20*(2), 169–186. doi:10.1108/09574090910981279

Barney, J. B. (1990). The debate between traditional management theory and organizational economics: Substantive differences or intergroup conflict? *Academy of Management Review*, *15*(3), 382–393. doi:10.2307/258014

Betts, T., & Tadisina, S. K. (2009, May). Supply chain agility, collaboration, and performance: how do they relate? *Proceedings of Annual Conference of the Production and Operations Management Society*, 20.

Bueren, A., Schierholz, R., Kolbe, L., & Brenner, W. (2004, January). Customer knowledge management - improving performance of customer relationship management with knowledge management. *Proceedings of the Hawaii International Conference on System Sciences*, 28. doi:10.1109/HICSS.2004.1265416

FAIDA Revisited Realizing the potential. (2004). McKinsey report.

Fawcett, S. E., Ogden, J. A., Magnan, G. M., & Cooper, M. B. (2006). Organizational commitment and governance for supply chain success. *International Journal of Physical Distribution & Logistics Management, 36*(1), 22–35. doi:10.1108/09600030610642913

Feeding a Billion: Role of the Food Processing Industry. (2013). AT Kearney.

Flynn, B. B., Huo, B., & Zhao, X. (2010). The impact of supply chain integration on performance: A contingency and configuration approach. *Journal of Operations Management*, *28*(1), 58–71. doi:10.1016/j.jom.2009.06.001

Food & FMCG Supply Chain. (n.d.). Retrieved from www.futuresupplychains.com

Ganjyal, G., & Hanna, M. (2002). A review on residence time distribution (RTD) in food extruders and study on the potential of neural networks in RTD modeling. *Journal of Food Science*, *67*(6), 1996–2002. doi:10.1111/j.1365-2621.2002.tb09491.x

Ghiassi, M., & Spera, C. (2003). Defining the internet-based supply chain system for mass customized markets. *Computers & Industrial Engineering*, *45*(1), 17–41. doi:10.1016/S0360-8352(03)00017-2

Ghosh, A., & Fedorowicz, J. (2008). The role of trust in supply chain governance. *Business Process Management Journal*, *14*(4), 453–470. doi:10.1108/14637150810888019

Gunasekaran, A., & Ngai, E. W. T. (2004). Information systems in supply chain integration and management. *European Journal of Operational Research*, *159*(2), 269–295. doi:10.1016/j.ejor.2003.08.016

Gunasekaran, A., & Ngai, E. W. T. (2012). Decision support systems for logistics and supply chain management. *Decision Support Systems*, *52*(4), 777–778. doi:10.1016/j.dss.2011.11.012

Gyau, A., & Spiller, A. (2008). The impact of supply chain governance structures on the inter-firm relationship performance in agribusiness. *Agricultural Economics*, *54*(4), 176–185.

Henderson, E. J., & Cool, K. O. (2010). Experience and learning in wine supply chain negotiations. *Supply Chain Forum an International Journal*, *11*(1), 42–55.

Hsu, C.-C., Kannan, V. R., Tan, K.-C., & Leong, G. K. (2008). Information sharing, buyer-supplier relationships, and firm performance: A multi-region analysis. *International Journal of Physical Distribution & Logistics Management*, *38*(4), 296–310. doi:10.1108/09600030810875391

Humphreys, P. K., Lai, M. K., & Sculli, D. (2001). An inter-organizational information system for supply chain management. *International Journal of Production Economics*, *70*(3), 245–255. doi:10.1016/S0925-5273(00)00070-0

India: Issues and Priorities for Agriculture. (2012). Retrieved from http://www.worldbank.org/en/news/feature/2012/05/17/india-agriculture-issues-priorities

India's Sleeping Giant. (1997). Food. *The McKinsey Quarterly.*

Iyer, K. N. S., Germain, R., & Claycomb, C. (2009). B2B e-commerce supply chain integration and performance: A contingency fit perspective on the role of environment. *Information & Management*, *46*(6), 313–322. doi:10.1016/j.im.2009.06.002

Jain, K., & Dubey, A. (2005). Supply chain collaboration: a governance perspective. *Supply Chain Forum: An International Journal in Supply Chain, 6*(2),50-57.

Kazmin. (2014). *India tackles supply chain to cut food waste*. FT.com.

Khan. (2013). Marketing Revolution in Rural India: Emerging Trends and Strategies. *Journal of Business Administration and Education.*

Kumar, N., Sarkar, B. C., & Sharma, H. K. (2010). Development and characterization of extruded product using carrot pomace and rice flour. *Int J Food Eng*, *6*(3), 1–24. doi:10.2202/1556-3758.1824

Melville, N., Kraemer, K., & Gurbaxani, V. (2004). Review: information technology and organizational performance: an integrative model of it business value. *Management Information Systems Quarterly*, *28*(2), 283–322.

Ramesh, P., Singh, M., & Rao, A. S. (2005, February 25). Organic farming: Its relevance to the Indian context. *Current Science*, *88*(4), 563.

Retail scenario in India: Unlimited opportunity. (2003). McKinsey-CII report.

Ross, D. F. (2011). Introduction to supply chain management technologies (2nd ed.). Boca Raton, FL: CRC Press.

Ruben, R., Boselie, D., & Lu, H. (2007). Vegetables procurement by Asian supermarkets: A transaction cost approach. *Supply Chain Management: An International Journal*, *12*(1), 60–68. doi:10.1108/13598540710724365

Selani, M. M., Brazaca, S. G., Dos Santos Dias, C. T., Ratnayake, W. S., Flores, R. A., & Bianchini, A. (2014). Characterisation and potential application of pineapple pomace in an extruded product for fibre enhancement. *Food Chemistry*, *163*, 23–30. doi:10.1016/j.foodchem.2014.04.076 PMID:24912691

Terpend, R., Tyler, B. B., Krause, D. R., & Handfield, R. B. (2008). Buyer-supplier relationships: Derived value over two decades. *Journal of Supply Chain Management*, *44*(2), 28–55. doi:10.1111/j.1745-493X.2008.00053.x

The Agriculture and Food Value Chain. (2013). KPMG Report.

The great Indian retail revolution. (2004). Rediff.com.

Value Chains in Agriculture. (2015). *Food and Agri-Products Sectors*. Government of Canada.

Zhang, X., van Donk, D. P., & van der Vaart, T. (2011). Does ICT influence supply chain management and performance? a review of survey-based research. *International Journal of Operations & Production Management*, *31*(11), 1215–1247. doi:10.1108/01443571111178501

KEY TERMS AND DEFINITIONS

Aeration: When air is trapped in a mixture.

Antioxidant: A substance that stops fat in food going rancid.

Ambient Temperature: Normal room temperature (20-25ºC).

Antibacterial: Substance that will usually destroy bacteria.

Blast Chill: To cool food quickly by blasting it with cold air.

Blast Freeezing: Quickly freezing that makes small ice crystals which do less damage to the food than slow freezing.

Caramelisation: Process of changing the colour of sugar from white to brown when heated.

Consumer: A person who buys or uses products and services.

Cook-Chill: Food that has been cooked, fast chilled and then stored at low temperature.

Cross Contamination: The transfer of harmful bacteria from one area to another.

Danger Zone: The temperature range (5 to 63ºC) in which bacteria grow.

Date Marking: Of manufactured foods. Best before is the date up until the food will remain in peak condition. Perishable foods have a Use By date up to which the food can be kept if stored appropriately.

Due Diligence: In food preparation this means that the company has set up systems to help avoid contamination of food products.

Flavour Enhancers: Tasteless substances used to enhance the taste of savoury foods.

Foams: A mixture of gas and liquid is called a foam, e.g. air whisked into egg white creates a foam.

Food Additive: A substance added to a food product to improve its quality.

Food Spoilage: Caused by the natural decay of food or by contamination by micro organisms.

HACCP: Hazard analysis and critical control point.

Higher Level Making Skills: Food preparation and cooking skills which require care, precision and understanding and which can be carried out to a high standard.

High-Risk Food: Food which is an ideal medium for the growth of bacteria or micro-organisms.

Market Research: The study of consumers' needs, preferences and lifestyles.

Modified Atmospheric Packaging (MAP): Used to extend the shelf life of food. The packs are gas flashed to reduce the amount of oxygen and replace it with carbon dioxide or nitrogen.

Nutritional Analysis: Using resources to find out the nutritional content of a product.

Nutritional Content: The type and quantity of nutrients which the product supplies.

Nutritional Labelling: The information relating to nutrients and energy in the food which is stated on packaging.

Product Analysis: Examining a food product to find out the ingredients, packaging characteristics and properties.

Product Specification: A list of features/characteristics/properties which a food product must meet.

Profiling Test: Sensory evaluation test to identify individual specific characteristics of product.

Quality Assurance: A guarantee by retailers and manufacturers that products are safe and of a good quality.

Quality Control: Steps taken to check a product at various stages of making to ensure a consistent and high quality outcome is achieved.

Scaling Up: Multiplying up proportionally. Increasing a recipe for bulk production, keeping the ratio and proportions the same.

Sensory Analysis: Identifying the sensory characteristics of products, i.e. taste, texture, appearance, mouth-feel, colour.

Sensory Evaluation: Using the range of senses to assess a food product – appearance, smell, taste.

Sensory Qualities: The look, smell, taste, feel and sound of food products.

Shelf Life: The length of time a food product can be kept and be safe to eat.

Shortening: When fat coats the flour particles preventing absorption of water resulting in a crumbly mixture.

Textured Vegetable Protein: Protein produced from soya beans. It is either extruded or formed into chunks. Used as an alternative protein and as a meat extender.

Tolerance Levels: The amount of difference allowed when making.

Ultra Heat Treatment (UHT): The high temperature, short time sterilization of milk known as long life milk.

Vacuum Packaging: A method of preserving food by removing air.

Vegans: People who eat no products of animal origin.

Vegetarians: Those who for a variety of reasons, choose not to eat meat.

Viscosity: The thickness of a liquid or a mixture, such as a sauce.

Compilation of References

Things Good Loyalty Programs Do To Create Business Growth. (2013). Drivingretention.com.

Reasons why Loyalty Programs is the best way of Customer Marketing. (2015). Cloudbiz.eu.

Abbasi, A., Albrecht, C., Vance, A., & Hansen, J. (2012). Meta Fraud: A Meta-Learning Framework for Detecting Financial Fraud. *MIS Quarterly, 36*(4), 1293–A12.

Abbasi, A., Zhang, Z., Zimbra, D., Chen, H., Nunamaker, J., & Jay, F. (2010). Detecting Fake Websites: The Contribution of Statistical Learning Theory. *MIS Quarterly, 34*(3), 435–461.

Abbey, J. D., Meloy, M. G., Guide, V. D. R. Jr, & Atalay, S. (2015). Remanufactured products in closed-loop supply chains for consumer goods. *Production and Operations Management, 24*(3), 488–503. doi:10.1111/poms.12238

Adams, A. A. (2007). Regulating CCTV. In *Ethicomp 2007: Proceedings of the Ninth International Conference*. Tokyo: Meiji University.

Adams, A. A., Murata, K., & Orito, Y. (2010). The Development of Japanese Data Protection. *Policy and Internet, 2*(2), 95–126.

Adams, A. A., Murata, K., & Orito, Y. (2012). Tender Electronic Eyes. *Case Studies on CCTV Deployment in Japan.*

Adapa, S. (2013). Electronic retailing of prepared food in Australia. In K. Tarnay, S. Imre, & L. Xu (Eds.), *Research and development in e-business through service-oriented solutions* (pp. 280–292). Hershey, PA: IGI Global. doi:10.4018/978-1-4666-4181-5.ch014

Adekomaya, O., Jamiru, T., Sadiku, R., & Huan, Z. (2016, June). Sustaining the shelf life of fresh food in cold chain – A burden on the environment. *Alexandria Engineering Journal, 55*(2), 1359–1365. doi:10.1016/j.aej.2016.03.024

Adrian, M. (2011, January). Big Data: It's going mainstream, and it's your next opportunity. *Teradata Magazine, Q1*(5), 38–42.

Agarwal, R., & Dhar, V. (2014). Editorial—Big Data, Data Science, and Analytics: The Opportunity and Challenge for IS Research. *Information Systems Research, 25*(3), 443–448.

Agrawal, D., Bernstein, P., & Bertino, E. (2011). Challenges and Opportunities with big data 2011-1. *Proceedings of the VLDB Endowment* (pp. 1–16). Retrieved from http://dl.acm.org/citation.cfm?id=2367572

Agrawal, V., & Tokay, L. B. (2009). Interdisciplinarity in closed-loop supply chain management research. In F. Ferguson & G. Souza (Eds.), *Closed-loop supply chains: New developments to improve the sustainability of business practices* (pp. 197–214). Boca Raton, FL: CRC Press.

Aguilar, F. X., & Cai, Z. (2010). Conjoint effect of environmental labelling, disclosure of forest of origin andprice on consumer preferences for wood products in the US and UK. *Ecological Economics, 70*(2), 308–316.

Ahmad, N., Awan, M., Raouf, A., & Sparks, L. (2009). Development of a service quality scale for pharmaceutical supply chains. *International Journal of Pharmaceutical and Healthcare Marketing*, *3*(1), 26–45. doi:10.1108/17506120910948494

Ailawadi, K. L., & Farris, P. W. (2017). Managing multi- and omni-channel distribution: Metrics and research directions. *Journal of Retailing*, *93*(1), 120–135. doi:10.1016/j.jretai.2016.12.003

Aissaoui, N., Haouari, M., & Hassini, E. (2007). Supplier selection and order lot sizing modeling: A review. *Computers & Operations Research*, *34*(12), 3516–3540. doi:10.1016/j.cor.2006.01.016

Akçalı, E., Çetinkaya, S., & Üster, H. (2009). Network design for reverse and closed-loop supply chains: An annotated bibliography of models and solution approaches. *Networks*, *53*(3), 231–248. doi:10.1002/net.20267

Akroush, M. N., & Al-Debei, M. M. (2015). An integrated model of factors affecting consumer attitudes towards online shopping. *Business Process Management Journal*, *21*(6), 1353–1376. doi:10.1108/BPMJ-02-2015-0022

Alexander, P. (2007). *Use Data to Build Customer Loyalty*. Entrepreneur.com.

Ali, M. M., Babai, M. Z., Boylan, J. E., & Syntetos, A. A. (2017). Supply chain forecasting when information is not shared. *European Journal of Operational Research*, *260*(3), 984–994. doi:10.1016/j.ejor.2016.11.046

Almeida, A. T. (2007). Multicriteria decision model for outsourcing contracts selection based on utility function and ELECTRE method. *Computers & Operations Research*, *34*(12), 3569–3574. doi:10.1016/j.cor.2006.01.003

Al-Salem, M., Diabat, A., Dalalah, D., & Alrefaei, M. (2016). A closed-loop supply chain management problem: Reformulation and piecewise linearization. *Journal of Manufacturing Systems*, *40*, 1–8. doi:10.1016/j.jmsy.2016.04.001

Altekin, F. T., & Akkan, C. (2012). Task-failure-driven rebalancing of disassembly lines. *International Journal of Production Research*, *50*(18), 4955–4976. doi:10.1080/00207543.2011.616915

Amin, B. Z., & Amin, P. (2013). A conceptual framework to understanding online consumer buying behavior. *International Journal of Online Marketing*, *3*(1), 47–63. doi:10.4018/ijom.2013010104

Amin, S. H., & Zhang, G. (2013). A multi-objective facility location model for closed-loop supply chain network under uncertain demand and return. *Applied Mathematical Modelling*, *37*(6), 4165–4176. doi:10.1016/j.apm.2012.09.039

Amos, C., Holmes, G. R., & Keneson, W. C. (2014). A meta-analysis of consumer impulse buying. *Journal of Retailing and Consumer Services*, *21*(2), 86–97. doi:10.1016/j.jretconser.2013.11.004

Anderson, E. T., Hansen, K., & Simester, D. (2009). The option value of returns: Theory and empirical evidence. *Marketing Science, 28*(3), 405–423.

Annesley, J., Colombo, A., Orwell, J., & Velastin, S. A. 2007. A Profile of MPEG-7 for Visual Surveillance. *Proceedings Fourth IEEE Advanced Video and Signal-Based Surveillance (AVSS)*, 482-487. doi:10.1109/AVSS.2007.4425358

Anon, . (2002). Summary of the executive session on emergency preparedness and the pharmaceutical supply chain. *American Journal of Health-System Pharmacy*, *59*(3), 247–253. PMID:11862636

Aramyan, L. H., Ondersteijn, C., Kooten, O., & Lansink, A. O. (2006). Performance indicators in agri-food production chains. In C. J. Ondersteijn, J. H. Wijnands, R. B. Huirne, & O. Kooten (Eds.), *Quantifying the agri-food supply chain* (pp. 47–64). Dordrecht: Springer. doi:10.1007/1-4020-4693-6_5

Arnold, S. E. (1992). Information manufacturing: The road to database quality. *Database*, *15*(5), 32–39.

Asbjørnslett, B. E. (2009). Assessing the vulnerability of supply chains. In Supply Chain Risk. Springer US. doi:10.1007/978-0-387-79934-6_2

Asdecker, B. (2015). *Statistiken Retouren Deutschland – Definition.* Retrieved from http://www.retourenforschung.de/

Ashenbaum, B., Maltz, A., Ellram, L., & Barratt, M. A. (2009). Organizational alignment and supply chain governance structure: Introduction and construct validation. *The International Journal of Logistics Management, 20*(2), 169–186. doi:10.1108/09574090910981279

Ashton, W. (2008). Understanding the organization of industrial ecosystems. *Journal of Industrial Ecology, 12*(1), 34–51. doi:10.1111/j.1530-9290.2008.00002.x

ASSOCHAM. (2013a). *Horticulture Sector in India- State level experience.* New Delhi: The Associated Chambes of Commerce and Industry of India.

ASSOCHAM. (2013b). *Opportunities in Cold Chain: Emerging Trends and Market Challenges-2013.* New Delhi: ASSOCHAM Publication.

Atasu, A., Sarvary, M., & van Wassenhove, L. N. (2008). Remanufacturing as a marketing strategy. *Management Science, 54*(10), 1731–1746. doi:10.1287/mnsc.1080.0893

Audrain-Pontevia, A. F., N'Goala, G., & Poncin, I. (2013). A good deal online: The impacts of acquisition and transaction value on e-satisfaction and e-loyalty. *Journal of Retailing and Consumer Services, 20*(5), 445–452. doi:10.1016/j.jretconser.2013.04.002

Aung, M. (2012). Quality Monitoring and Dynamic Pricing in Cold Chain Management. *Mechatronic and Manufacturing Engineering, 6*(2).

Autry, C. W. (2005). Formalization of reverse logistics programs: A strategy for managing liberalized returns. *Industrial Marketing Management, 34*(7), 749–757.

Autry, C. W., Hill, D. J., & O'Brien, M. (2007). Attitude toward the customer: A study of product returns episodes. *Journal of Managerial Issues*, 315–339.

Aydin, R., Kwong, C. K., & Ji, P. (2016). Coordination of the closed-loop supply chain for product line design with consideration of remanufactured products. *Journal of Cleaner Production, 114*, 286–298. doi:10.1016/j.jclepro.2015.05.116

Baesens, A. (2014). *Analytics in a big data world: The essential guide to data science and its applications.* Hoboken, NJ: John Wiley & Sons.

Bai, C., & Sarkis, J. (2013). Flexibility in reverse logistics: A framework and evaluation approach. *Journal of Cleaner Production, 47*(1), 306–316. doi:10.1016/j.jclepro.2013.01.005

Bailey, K., & Francis, M. (2008). Managing information flows for improved value chain performance. *International Journal of Production Economics, 111*(1), 2–12. doi:10.1016/j.ijpe.2006.11.017

Baker, Grewal, & Parasuraman. (1994). The Influence of Store Environment on Quality Inferences and Store Image. *Journal of Academy of Marketing Science, 22*(4), 328-39.

Balfour, A., Farquhar, B., & Langmann, G. (1998). The consumer needs in global electronic commerce. *Electronic Markets, 8*(2), 9–12. doi:10.1080/10196789800000017

Ballance, R., Pogany, J., & Forstner, H. (1992). *The world's pharmaceutical industries.* London, UK: Edward Elgar.

Ballou, D. P., & Pazer, H. L. (1985). Modeling data and process quality in multi-input, multi-output information systems. *Management Science*, *31*(2), 150–162. doi:10.1287/mnsc.31.2.150

Ballou, D. P., Wang, R., & Pacer, H. (1998). Modeling information manufacturing systems to determine information product quality. *Management Science*, *44*(4), 462–484. doi:10.1287/mnsc.44.4.462

Banasik, A., Kanellopoulos, A., Claassen, G. D. H., Bloemhof-Ruwaard, J. M., & van der Vorst, J. G. A. J. (2017). Closing loops in agricultural supply chains using multi-objective optimization: A case study of an industrial mushroom supply chain. *International Journal of Production Economics*, *183*, 409–420. doi:10.1016/j.ijpe.2016.08.012

Bandyopadhyay, S., & Paul, A. A. (2010). Equilibrium returns policies in the presence of supplier competition. *Marketing Science, 29*(5), 846–857.

Banker. (n.d.). *ARC's WMS global market research study*. Forbes.com.

Banker. (n.d.). *ARC's WMS Global Market Research Study*. Forbes.com.

Bardwell. (n.d.). Redefining the Shopper Experience With Omnichannel Retailing. *IDC Retail Insights.*

Bardwell, C. (2012). *Redefining the Shopper Experience With Omnichannel Retailing*. IDC Retail Insights.

Barnes, C. (2016). Omni-channel retail-challenges and opportunities for packaging innovation. In P. Burgess (Ed.), Integrating the packaging and product experience in food and beverages: a road-map to consumer satisfaction. Duxford: Woodhead Publishing. doi:10.1016/B978-0-08-100356-5.00004-8

Barnes, S. J., Bauer, H. H., Neumann, M. M., & Huber, F. (2007). Segmenting cyberspace: A customer typology for the Internet. *European Journal of Marketing*, *41*(1/2), 71–93. doi:10.1108/03090560710718120

Barney, J. B. (1990). The debate between traditional management theory and organizational economics: Substantive differences or intergroup conflict? *Academy of Management Review*, *15*(3), 382–393. doi:10.2307/258014

Baroudi, J. J., & Orlikowski, W. J. (1988). A short-form measure of user information satisfaction: A psychometric evaluation and notes on use. *Journal of Management Information Systems*, *4*(4), 44–59. doi:10.1080/07421222.1988.11517807

Barratt, M., & Oke, A. (2007). Antecedents of supply chain visibility in retail supply chains: A resource-based theory perspective. *Journal of Operations Management*, *25*(6), 1217–1233. doi:10.1016/j.jom.2007.01.003

Basiri, A. H., Shemshadi, A., & Tarokh, M. J. (2013). A closed-loop logistics model for green supply chain management. In Z. Luo (Ed.), *Technological solutions for modern logistics and supply chain management* (pp. 318–333). Hershey, PA: IGI Global. doi:10.4018/978-1-4666-2773-4.ch019

Battani, C., Cappelli, C., Francians, C., & Maurino, A. (2009). Methodologies for data quality assessment and improvement. *Association for Computing Machinery Computing Surveys*, *41*(3), 1–52.

Bazzani, L., Cristani, M., Perina, M., & Murino, V. (2012). Multiple-Shot Person ReIdentification by Chromatic and Epitomic Analyses. *Pattern Recognition Letters*, *33*(7), 898–903. doi:10.1016/j.patrec.2011.11.016

BBC. (2003). *Pensioner Freed After FBI Bungle*. Retrieved from news.bbc.co.uk/2/hi/uk_news/england/2799791.stm

Bechwati, N. N., & Siegal, W. S. (2005). The Impact of the Prechoice Process on Product Returns. *Journal of Marketing Research, 42*(3), 358–367.

Beck, N., & Rygl, D. (2015). Categorization of multiple channel retailing in multi-, cross-, and omni-channel retailing for retailers and retailing. *Journal of Retailing and Consumer Services*, *27*, 170–178. doi:10.1016/j.jretconser.2015.08.001

Bellenger, D. N., & Korgaonkar, P. (1980). Profiling the Recreational Shopper. *Journal of Retailing*, *56*(3), 77–92.

Belu, M. G., & Marinoiu, A. M. (2014). A new distribution strategy: The omnichannel strategy. *The Romanian Economic Journal, 17*(52), 117–133.

Ben Shitrit, H., Berclaz, J., Fleuret, F., & Fua, P. (2011). Tracking Multiple People under Global Appearance Constraints. *Computer Vision (ICCV), 2011 IEEE International Conference on*, 137-144.

Berger, A. M. (2000). *Privacy Mode for Acquisition Cameras and Camcorders.* U.S. Patent 6,067,399.

Berman, B., & Evans, J. R. (2010). *Retail management: A strategic Approach.* Upper Saddle River, NJ: Prentice Hall.

Berman, B., & Thelen, S. (2004). A guide to developing and managing a well-integrated multi-channel retail strategy. *International Journal of Retail & Distribution Management, 32*(3), 147–156. doi:10.1108/09590550410524939

Betts, T., & Tadisina, S. K. (2009, May). Supply chain agility, collaboration, and performance: how do they relate? *Proceedings of Annual Conference of the Production and Operations Management Society*, 20.

Beulke, D. (2011). *Big Data Impacts Data Management: The 5 Vs of Big Data.* Retrieved from http://davebeulke.com/big-data-impacts-data-management-the-five-vs-of-big-data/

Bhagwat, Y., & Griggs, F. T. (1995). Analysis of riskiness of pharmaceutical industry firms. *Journal of Research in Pharmaceutical Economics, 6*(1), 65–76. doi:10.1300/J063v06n01_05

Bhardwaj, S., & Palaparthy, I. (2008). Factors Influencing Indian Supply Chains of of Fruits and Vegetables: A Literature Review. *The Icfai University Journal of Supply Chain Management, V*(3), 59–68.

Bhattacharjee, S., & Cruz, J. (2015). Economic sustainability of closed loop supply chains: A holistic model for decision and policy analysis. *Decision Support Systems, 77*, 67–86. doi:10.1016/j.dss.2015.05.011

Bhattacharyya, S., Jha, S., Tharakunnel, K., & Westland, J. C. (2011). Data mining for credit card fraud: A comparative study. *Decision Support Systems, 50*(3), 602–613.

Bhattacherjee, A. (2012). Social Science Research: principles, methods, and practices. Open Access Textbooks.

Bimschleger. (2014). *How to Compete with Amazon in an Omnichannel World.* RIS News: Business/Technology Insights for Retail, Supermarket Executives.

Bimschleger, C. (2014). *How to Compete with Amazon in an Omnichannel World. RIS News: Business/Technology Insights for Retail* Supermarket Executives.

Biotto, M., De Toni, A., & Nonino, F. (2012). Knowledge and cultural diffusion along the supply chain as drivers of product quality improvement. *International Journal of Logistics Management, 2*(2), 212–237. doi:10.1108/09574091211265369

Birchall & Rigby. (2008). Oil Costs Force P&G to Rethink Supply Network. *Financial Times.*

Birchall, J., & Rigby, E. (2008). Oil Costs Force P&G to Rethink Supply Network. *Financial Times.*

Bishara, R. H. (2006). Cold chain management – an essential component of the global pharmaceutical supply chain. *American Pharmaceutical Review*. Available at: www.americanpharmaceuticalreview.com/life_science/Bishara_APR.pdf

Bishara, R. H. (2006). *Cold chain management – an essential component of the global pharmaceutical supply chain.* Retrieved from American Pharmaceutical Review: www.americanpharmaceuticalreview.com/life_science/Bishara_APR.pdf

Bishara, R. (2006). Cold Chain Management-An Essential Component of the Global Pharmaceutical Supply Chain. *American Pharmaceutical Review, 1*, 105–109.

Bitner, M. J. (1992, April). Servicescapes: The Impact of Physical Surroundings on Customer and Employees. *Journal of Marketing, 56*, 57–71. doi:10.2307/1252042

Bjorner, T. B., Hansen, L. G. a., & Russell, C. S. (2004). Environmental labelling and consumers' choice—an empirical analysis of the effect of the Nordic Swan. *Journal of Environmental Economics and Management, 47*(3), 411–434.

Bjorner, T. B., Hansen, L. G., & Russell, C. S. (2004). Environmental labelling and consumers' choice—an empirical analysis of the effect of the Nordic Swan. *Journal of Environmental Economics and Management, 47*(3), 411–434.

Blake, R., & Mangiameli, P. (2011). The effects and interactions of data quality and problem complexity on classification. *Association for Computing Machinery Journal of Data and Information Quality, 2*(2), 1–28. doi:10.1145/1891879.1891881

Blumberg, D. F. (2004). *Introduction to management of reverse logistics and closed loop supply chain processes*. Boca Raton, FL: CRC Press.

Bonfanti, A. (2014). A dilemma for retailers: How to make store surveillance secure and appealing to shoppers. In F. Musso & E. Druica (Eds.), *Handbook of research on retailer-consumer relationship development* (pp. 297–317). Hershey, PA: IGI Global. doi:10.4018/978-1-4666-6074-8.ch016

Boote, D., & Bailey, P. (2005). Scholars before researchers on the centrality of the literature review in research preparation. *Educational Research, 34*(6), 3–15. doi:10.3102/0013189X034006003

Booth, R. (1999). *The global supply chain*. FT healthcare management report. London: Financial Times Business Ltd.

Borusiak, B. (2014). The mechanisms for the emergence and evolution of retail formats. In F. Musso & E. Druica (Eds.), *Handbook of research on retailer-consumer relationship development* (pp. 108–126). Hershey, PA: IGI Global. doi:10.4018/978-1-4666-6074-8.ch007

Bose, N. (2014). *E-tailers growth ensnared in India's logistics jungle*. Reuters.com.

Bose, S.K., & Joydeep, C. (2008). *Challenges faced by the Indian tinplate packaging industry: An analysis*. Retrieved from file:///C:/Users/Anju%20Bharti/Desktop/paper%20for%20IGI/5_Bose_Chatterjee.pdf

Bower, A. B., & Maxham, J. G., III. (2012). Return shipping policies of online retailers: Normative assumptions and the long-term consequences of fee and free returns. *Journal of Marketing, 76*(5), 110–124.

Bowman, Ng, Harrison, López, & Illic. (2009). *Sensor based condition monitoring*. Building Radio Frequency Identification for the Global Environment (Bridge) Euro RFID Project.

boyd, d., & Crawford, K. (2012). Critical questions for big data. *Information, Communication & Society, 15*(5), 662-679. doi:10.1080/1369118X.2012.678878

Brajesh, S. (2016). Big data analytics in retail supply chain. In N. Kamath & S. Saurav (Eds.), *Handbook of research on strategic supply chain management in the retail industry* (pp. 269–289). Hershey, PA: IGI Global. doi:10.4018/978-1-4666-9894-9.ch015

Braun, V., & Clarke, V. (2006). Using thematic analysis in psychology. *Qualitative Research in Psychology, 3*(2), 77–101. doi:10.1191/1478088706qp063oa

Bressolles, G., Durrieu, F., & Senecal, S. (2014). A consumer typology based on e-service quality and e-satisfaction. *Journal of Retailing and Consumer Services, 21*(6), 889–896. doi:10.1016/j.jretconser.2014.07.004

Brown, S., & Reid, R. (1955). Psychological Aspects of Shopping: A Supplement to the New Consumer. *Chicago Tribune*.

Browne, M., Rizet, C., Leonardi, J., & Allen, J. (2008). Analysing energy use in supply chains: the case of fruits and vegetables and furniture. *Proceedings of the Logistics Research Network Conference*, 1–6.

Brown, I., & Russell, J. (2007). Radio frequency identification technology: An exploratory study on adoption in the South African retail sector. *Inter. J.Informat.Manage.*, *27*(4), 250–265. doi:10.1016/j.ijinfomgt.2007.02.007

Brown, J. R., & Dant, R. P. (2008). Scientific Method and Retailing Research: A Retrospective. *Journal of Retailing*, *84*(1), 1–13. doi:10.1016/j.jretai.2008.03.001

Brynjolfsson, E., Hu, Y. J., & Rahman, M. S. (2013). Competing in the age of omnichannel retailing. *MIT Sloan Management Review*, *54*(4), 22–29.

Bueren, A., Schierholz, R., Kolbe, L., & Brenner, W. (2004, January). Customer knowledge management - improving performance of customer relationship management with knowledge management. *Proceedings of the Hawaii International Conference on System Sciences*, 28. doi:10.1109/HICSS.2004.1265416

Burgess, K., Singh, P. J., & Koroglu, R. (2006). Supply chain management: A structured literature review and implications for future research. *International Journal of Operations & Production Management*, *26*(7), 703–729. doi:10.1108/01443570610672202

Burke, R. R. (1997). Do you see what I see? The future of virtual shopping. *Journal of the Academy of Marketing Science*, *25*(4), 352–360. doi:10.1177/0092070397254007

Camm, J., Cochran, J., Fry, M., Ohlmann, J., & Anderson, D. (2014). A Categorization of Analytical Methods and Models. In *Essentials of Business Analytics* (pp. 5–7). Cengage Learning.

Capellán-Pérez, M., Mediavilla, M., de Castro, C., Carpintero, Ó., & Miguel, L. J. (2014). Fossil fuel depletion and socio-economic scenarios: An integrated approach. *Energy*, *77*, 641–666. doi:10.1016/j.energy.2014.09.063

Carman, J. M. (1990). Consumer perceptions of service quality: An assessment of the SERVQUAL dimensions. *Journal of Retailing*, *66*(1), 33–35.

Carroll & Guzmán. (n.d.). *The New Omni-Channel Approach to Serving Customers*. accenture.com.

Carroll, D., & Guzmán, I. (2014). *The New Omni-Channel Approach to Serving Customers*. Accenture.com.

Carullo, A., Corbellini, S., Parvis, M. L., & Vallan, A. (2008). A measuring system for the assurance of the cold-chain integrity. *Proceedings of the IEEE International Instrumentation and Measurement Technology Conference*, 1598-1602. doi:10.1109/IMTC.2008.4547298

Cassill, N. L. (1998). Do customer returns enhance product and shopping experience satisfaction? *The International Review of Retail, Distribution and Consumer Research*, *8*(1), 1–13.

Castaldo, S., & Grosso, M. (2016). CRM in fashion retail: Building store loyalty through store trust. In A. Vecchi & C. Buckley (Eds.), *Handbook of research on global fashion management and merchandising* (pp. 509–531). Hershey, PA: IGI Global. doi:10.4018/978-1-5225-0110-7.ch021

Castillo-Villar, K. K., Smith, N. R., & Simonton, J. L. (2012). A model for supply chain design considering the cost of quality. *Applied Mathematical Modelling*, *36*(12), 5920–5935. doi:10.1016/j.apm.2012.01.046

Caswell, J. A. (2000). Analyzing quality and quality assurance (Including labeling) for GMOS. *Agbioforum Journal*, *3*, 225–230.

Ceryno, P. S., Scavarda, L. F., Klingebiel, K., & Yüzgülec, G. (2012). Supply Chain Risk Management: A Content Analysis Approach. *International Journal of Industrial Engineering and Management.*, *4*(3), 141–150.

Cezar, J., Jacques, S., & Musse, S. R. (2010). Crowd Analysis Using Computer Vision Techniques. *IEEE Signal Processing Magazine*, *27*, 66–77.

Chang, M. K., Cheung, W., & Lai, V. S. (2005). Literature derived reference models for the adoption of online shopping. *Information & Management*, *42*(4), 543–559. doi:10.1016/S0378-7206(04)00051-5

Charman, A. J., Petersen, L. M., Piper, L. E., Liedeman, R., & Legg, T. (2015). Small area census approach to measure the township informal economy in South Africa. *Journal of Mixed Methods Research*, 1–23.

Chebat, J.-C., Gelinas-Chebat, C., & Filiatrault, P. (1993). Interactive Effects of Musical and Visual Cues on Time Perception: An Application to Waiting Lines in Banks. *Perceptual and Motor Skills*, *77*(3), 995–1020. doi:10.2466/pms.1993.77.3.995 PMID:8284188

Chen, C. L., & Zhang, C. Y. (2014). Data-intensive applications, challenges, techniques and technologies: A survey on big data. *Information Sciences*, 1–34. doi:10.1016/j.ins.2014.01.015

Chen, J., & Bell, P. C. (2009). The impact of customer returns on pricing and order decisions. *European Journal of Operational Research, 195*(1), 280–295.

Cheng, S. K., & Kam, B. H. (2008). A conceptual framework for analysing risk in supply networks. *Journal of Enterprise Information Management*, *21*(4), 345–360. doi:10.1108/17410390810888642

Chen, H., Chiang, R., & Storey, V. (2012). Business Intelligence and analytics: From big data to Big Impact. *Management Information Systems Quarterly*, *36*(4), 1165–1188.

Chen, J., & Dibbs, S. (2010). Consumer trust in the online retail context: Exploring the antecedents and consequences. *Psychology and Marketing*, *27*(4), 323–346. doi:10.1002/mar.20334

Chen, L., & Tan, J. (2004). Key determinants of consumer acceptance of virtual stores: Some empirical evidence. In J. Gupta & S. Sharma (Eds.), *Intelligent enterprises of the 21st century* (pp. 45–66). Hershey, PA: IGI Global. doi:10.4018/978-1-59140-160-5.ch004

Chen, Y. W., Wang, L. C., Wang, A., & Chen, T. L. (2017). A particle swarm approach for optimizing a multi-stage closed loop supply chain for the solar cell industry. *Robotics and Computer-integrated Manufacturing*, *43*, 111–123. doi:10.1016/j.rcim.2015.10.006

Che, Y.-K. (1996). Customer return policies for experience goods. *The Journal of Industrial Economics*, *44*(1), 17–24. doi:10.2307/2950557

Childers, T., Carr, C. L., Peck, J., & Carson, S. (2001). Hedonic and utilitarian motivations for online retail shopping behaviour. *Journal of Retailing*, *77*(4), 511–535. doi:10.1016/S0022-4359(01)00056-2

Cho, D. W., Lee, Y. H., Ahn, S. H., & Hwang, M. K. (2012). A framework for measuring the performance of service supply chain management. *Computers & Industrial Engineering*, *62*(3), 801–818. doi:10.1016/j.cie.2011.11.014

Choi, T.-M., Yu, Y., & Au, K.-F. (2011). A hybrid SARIMA wavelet transform method for sales forecasting. *Decision Support Systems, 51*(1), 130–140.

Choi, S. H., Cheung, H. H., Yang, B., & Yang, Y. X. (2015). Item-level RFID for retail business improvement. In I. Lee (Ed.), *RFID technology integration for business performance improvement* (pp. 1–26). Hershey, PA: IGI Global. doi:10.4018/978-1-4666-6308-4.ch001

Chopra & Sodhi. (2004). *Managing Risk to Avoid Supply-Chain Breakdown*. Retrieved from www.sloanreview.mit.edu

Chopra, S., & Sodhi, M. S. (2004). Managing risk to avoid supply-chain breakdown. *MIT Sloan Management Review.*, *46*(1), 53–61.

Cho, Y., & Menor, L. (2010). Toward a provider-based view on the design and delivery of quality e-service encounters. *Journal of Service Research*, *13*(1), 83–95. doi:10.1177/1094670509350490

Christopher, M., & Peck, H. (2004). Building the Resilient Supply Chain. *Int. J. Logistics Management.*, *15*(2), 1–14. doi:10.1108/09574090410700275

Chuang, C., Wang, C., & Zhao, Y. (2014). Closed-loop supply chain models for a high-tech product under alternative reverse channel and collection cost structures. *International Journal of Production Economics*, *156*, 108–123. doi:10.1016/j.ijpe.2014.05.008

Chugh, R., & Grandhi, S. (2012). E-tailing: A snapshot of Australia's top 25 retailers. In K. Mohammed Rezaul (Ed.), *Strategic and pragmatic e-business: Implications for future business practices* (pp. 297–313). Hershey, PA: IGI Global. doi:10.4018/978-1-4666-1619-6.ch013

Chung, S. L., Wee, H. M., & Yang, P. C. (2008). Optimal policy for a closed-loop supply chain inventory system with remanufacturing. *Mathematical and Computer Modelling*, *48*(5/6), 867–881. doi:10.1016/j.mcm.2007.11.014

Clark. (2012). *The Loyalty Guide*. The wisemarketer.com.

Clemes, M. D., Gan, C., & Zhang, J. (2014). An empirical analysis of online shopping adoption in Beijing, China. *Journal of Retailing and Consumer Services*, *21*(3), 364–375. doi:10.1016/j.jretconser.2013.08.003

Clottey, T., Benton, W. C., & Srivastava, R. (2012). Forecasting product returns for remanufacturing operations. *Decision Sciences*, *43*(4), 589–614.

Clottey, T., Benton, W. C. Jr, & Srivastava, R. (2012). Forecasting product returns for remanufacturing operations. *Decision Sciences*, *43*(4), 589–614. doi:10.1111/j.1540-5915.2012.00362.x

Cobb, B. R. (2016). Inventory control for returnable transport items in a closed-loop supply chain. *Transportation Research Part E, Logistics and Transportation Review*, *86*, 53–68. doi:10.1016/j.tre.2015.12.010

Coetzer, B., van der Merwe, J., & Josephs, B. (2011). *Information Management and Video Analytics: The Future of Intelligent Video Surveillance*. InTech. Retrieved from http://tinyurl.com/78flxuy

Cohen, J. (1992). A power primer. *Psychological Bulletin*, *112*(1), 155.

Cold Chain sea of opportunities for emerging markets. (2015). Retrieved from http://www.asiacoldchainshow.com/2015/03/13/cold-chain-sea-of-opportunities-for-emerging-markets/

Colicchia, C., Marchet, G., Melacin, M., & Perotti, S. (2013). Building environmental sustainability: Empirical evidence from logistics service providers. *Journal of Cleaner Production*, *59*, 197–209. doi:10.1016/j.jclepro.2013.06.057

Comegys, C., Hannula, M., & Vaisanen, J. (2006). Longitudinal comparison of Finnish and US online shopping behaviour among university students: The five-stage buying decision process. *Journal of Targeting, Measurement and Analysis for Marketing*, *14*(4), 336–356. doi:10.1057/palgrave.jt.5740193

Constantinides, E. (2004). Influencing the online consumer's behavior: The Web experience. *Internet Research*, *14*(2), 111–126. doi:10.1108/10662240410530835

Cooke, J. A. (2013). Three trends to watch in 2013, Perspective. *Supply Chain Quarterly*, *1*, 11.

Cooper, A. (2012). What is Analytics? Definition and Essential Characteristics. *CETIS Analytics Series, 1*(5), 1–10.

Corum, A. (2016). Remanufacturing, an added value product recovery strategy. In U. Akkucuk (Ed.), *Handbook of research on waste management techniques for sustainability* (pp. 347–367). Hershey, PA: IGI Global. doi:10.4018/978-1-4666-9723-2.ch018

Coudert, F., Gemo, M., Beslay, L., & Andritsos, F. (2011). Pervasive Monitoring: Appreciating Citizen's Surveillance as Digital Evidence in Legal Proceedings. *Imaging for Crime Detection and Prevention 2011 (ICDP 2011), 4th International Conference on*, 1-6.

Cox, J., & Dale, B. G. (2001). Service quality and e-commerce: An exploratory analysis. *Managing Service Quality, 11*(2), 121–131. doi:10.1108/09604520110387257

Craighead, C. W., Blackhurst, J., Rungtusanatham, M. J., & Handfield, R. B. (2007). The severity of supply chain disruptions: Design characteristics and mitigation capabilities. *Decision Sciences, 38*(1), 131–156. doi:10.1111/j.1540-5915.2007.00151.x

Crosby, P. (1995). *Philip Crosby's Reflections on Quality*. McGraw-Hill.

Cullen, C. W. (1990). *Shopping as Entertainment: Implications for the Shopping Centre Manager*. University of Stirling: Institute for Retail Studies.

Customer Desires Vs. Retailer Capabilities: Minding The Omni-Channel Commerce Gap. (2014). Forrester Consulting.

Cuzzocrea, A., Song, I., & Davis, K. (2011). Analytics over large-scale multidimensional data: the big data revolution! In *Proceedings of the ACM 14th international workshop on Data Warehousing and OLAP* (pp. 101–103). New York: ACM. doi:10.1145/2064676.2064695

D'Souza, C., Taghian, M., & Lamb, P. (2006). An empirical study on the influence of environmental labels on consumers. *Corporate Communications: An International Journal, 11*(2), 162–173

Dani, S., Ghadge, A., & Kalawsky, R. (2012). Supply chain risk management: Present and future scope. *International Journal of Logistics Management., 23*(3), 313–339. doi:10.1108/09574091211289200

Darden, W. R., & Babin, B. J. (1994, Feb.). Exploring the Concept of Affective Quality: Expanding the Concept of Retail Personality. *Journal of Business Research, 29*, 101–110. doi:10.1016/0148-2963(94)90014-0

Das, K., & Posinasetti, N. R. (2015). Addressing environmental concerns in closed loop supply chain design and planning. *International Journal of Production Economics, 163*, 34–47. doi:10.1016/j.ijpe.2015.02.012

Davenport, T., & Dyche, J. (2013). *Big data in Big Companies* (White paper). Retrieved from http://swqlab.fov.unimb.si/moodle/pluginfile.php/9774/course/section/534/Big-Data-in-BigCompanies.pdf

Davenport, T. (2013). Analytics 3.0. *Harvard Business Review, 91*(12), 64–72.

Davenport, T. H. (1998). Putting the enterprise into the enterprise system. *Harvard Business Review, 76*(4). PMID:10181586

Davenport, T. H., Barth, P., & Bean, R. (2012). How 'Big Data' Is Different. *MIT Sloan Management Review, 54*(1), 43–46.

Davenport, T. H., Harris, J. G., & Morison, R. (2010). *Analytics at work – smart decisions, better results*. Boston: Harvard Business Press.

Davenport, T. H., & Prusiks, L. (2000). *Working knowledge: how organizations manage what they know*. Boston: Harvard Business Press.

Davenport, T., Barth, P., & Bean, R. (2012). How "big data" is different. *MIT Sloan Management Review, 54*(1), 22–24.

Davenport, T., & Patil, D. (2012). Data Scientist: The sexiest job of the 21 st century. *Harvard Business Review*, *90*(10), 70–76. PMID:23074866

De Carvalho, J., & Campomar, M. C. (2014). Multichannel at retail and omni-channel: Challenges for marketing and logistics. *Business & Management Review*, *4*(3), 103–113.

de Giovanni, P., & Zaccour, G. (2013). Cost-revenue sharing in a closed loop supply chain. *Annals of the International Society of Dynamic Games*, *12*, 395–421. doi:10.1007/978-0-8176-8355-9_20

de Giovanni, P., & Zaccour, G. (2014). A two-period game of a closed-loop supply chain. *European Journal of Operational Research*, *232*(1), 22–40. doi:10.1016/j.ejor.2013.06.032

de Lassus, C., & Freire, N. D. (2014). Access to the luxury brand myth in pop-up stores: A netnographic and semiotic analysis. *Journal of Retailing and Consumer Services*, *21*(1), 61–68. doi:10.1016/j.jretconser.2013.08.005

de Waart, D., & Kemper, S. (2004). 5 steps to service supply chain excellence. *Supply Chain Management Review*, *8*(1), 28–35.

De, P., Hu, Y., & Rahman, M. S. (2012). An Empirical Investigation of the Effects of Product-Oriented Web Technologies on Product Returns. Working Paper.

Dee, H. M., & Velastin, S. A. (2008). How Close Are We To Solving the Problem of Automated Visual Surveillance? A Review of Real-World Surveillance, Scientific Progress and Evaluative Mechanisms. *Machine Vision and Applications*, *19*(5-6), 329–343. doi:10.1007/s00138-007-0077-z

Dee, H., & Hogg, D. (2004). Detecting Inexplicable Behaviour. In *Proceedings of the British Machine Vision Conference*. The British Machine Vision Association.

Dee, H., & Hogg, D. (2006). Navigational Strategies and Surveillance. In *Proceedings of the IEEE International Workshop on Visual Surveillance (ECCV-VS)*. IEEE Computer Society Press.

Deisingh, A. K. (2005). Pharmaceutical counterfeiting. *Analyst (London)*, *130*(3), 271–279. doi:10.1039/b407759h PMID:15724152

Delen, D., & Demirkan, H. (2013). Data, information and analytics as services. *Decision Support Systems*, *55*(1), 359–363. doi:10.1016/j.dss.2012.05.044

Deloitte & MHI. (2014). *The 2014 MHI Annual Industry Report – Innovation the driven supply chain*. Charlotte, NC: MHI.

Deloitte & MHI. (2016). *The 2016 MHI Annual Industry Report – Accelerating change: How innovation is driving digital, always-on Supply Chains*. MHI.

Deming, W. E. (2000). The New Economics for Industry, Government, Education (2nd ed.). MIT Press.

Dennis, C., Fenech, T., & Merrilees, B. (2004). *E-retailing*. London, UK: Routledge.

Devlin, B., Rogers, S., & Myers, J. (2012). *Big data comes of age* (whitepaper). Retrieved from http://www-03.ibm.com/systems/hu/resources/big_data_comes_of_age.pdf

Dharni, K., & Sharma, S. (2008). Food Processing in India: Opportunities and Constraints. *The Icfai University Journal of Agricultural Economics*, *V*(3), 30–38.

Dick, A. R., & Brooks, M. J. (2003). Issues in Automated Visual Surveillance. Academic Press.

Dietrich, B., Plachy, E. C., & Norton, M. F. (2014). *Analytics across the enterprise: How IBM realize business value from big data and analytics*. Boston: IBM Press Books.

Dissanayake, D., & Singh, M. (2008). Managing returns in e-business. *Journal of Internet Commerce, 6*(2), 35–49.

Dokuzoguz, M. (1997). *Developments on Storage of Horticultural Products in Turkey*. First Symposium of Storage and Marketing in Horticultural Products, Yalova, Turkey. (in Turkish)

Dollár, P., Wojek, C., Schiele, B., & Perona, P. (2012). *Pedestrian Detection: An Evaluation of the State of the Art. Pattern Analysis and Machine Intelligence, 34*(4), 743–761.

Doll, W. J., & Torkzadeh, G. (1988). The measurement of end-user computing satisfaction. *Management Information Systems Quarterly, 12*(June), 259–274. doi:10.2307/248851

Donald, C. (2005). How Many Monitors Should a CCTV Operator View? In *CCTV Image* (p. 355). London: STL Publishing.

Donnelly. (2010). *How to Start a Customer Rewards Program*. Inc.com.

Donovan, R. J., Rossiter, J. R., Marcoolyn, G., & Nesdale, A. (1994). Store Atmosphere and Purchasing Behavior. *Journal of Retailing, 70*(3), 283–294. doi:10.1016/0022-4359(94)90037-X

Donthu, N., & Garcia, A. (1999, May). The Internet Shopper. *Journal of Advertising Research*, 52–58.

Dorman, A. J. (2013). *Omni-channel retail and the new age consumer: an empirical analysis of direct-to- consumer channel interaction in the retail industry*. CMC Senior Theses. Paper 590. Retrieved March 29, 2017, from http://scholarship.claremont.edu/cmc_theses/590

Dufaux, F., & Ebrahimi, T. (2008). Scrambling for Privacy Protection in Video Surveillance Systems. *IEEE Transactions on Circuits and Systems for Video Technology, 18*(8), 1168–1174. doi:10.1109/TCSVT.2008.928225

Duffy, J. A. M., & Ketchand, A. A. (1998). Examining the role of service quality in overall service satisfaction. *Journal of Managerial Issues, 10*(2), 240–255.

Dutta, D., & Bose, I. (2015). Managing a Big Data project: The case of Ramco Cements Limited. *International Journal of Production Economics, 165*, 293–306. doi:10.1016/j.ijpe.2014.12.032

Earl, P. E., & Potts, J. (2000). Latent demand and the browsing shopper. *Managerial and Decision Economics, 21*(3/4), 111–122. doi:10.1002/mde.976

Ellram, L. M., Tate, W. L., & Billington, C. (2004). Understanding and Managing the Services Supply Chain. *Journal of Supply Chain Management, 40*(4), 17–32. doi:10.1111/j.1745-493X.2004.tb00176.x

Emery, J. C. (1969). *Organizational planning and control systems: Theory and management*. New York: Macmillan.

Eroglu, S., & Harrell, G. D. (1986). Retail Crowding: Theoretical and Strategic Implications. *Journal of Retailing, 62*(4), 346–363.

Evans, M., Boyle, J. N., & Ferryman, J. (2012). Vehicle Classification using Evolutionary Forests. *Proceedings International Conference on Pattern Recognition Applications and Methods*, 387-393.

Fahimnia, B., Sarkis, J., Dehghanian, F., Banihashemi, N., & Rahman, S. (2013). The impact of carbon pricing on a closed-loop supply chain: An Australian case study. *Journal of Cleaner Production, 59*, 210–225. doi:10.1016/j.jclepro.2013.06.056

FAIDA Revisited Realizing the potential. (2004). McKinsey report.

Fairchild, A. M. (2014). Extending the network: Defining product delivery partnering preferences for omni-channel commerce. *Procedia Technology, 16*, 447–451. doi:10.1016/j.protcy.2014.10.111

Faisal, M. N., Banwet, D. K., & Shankar, R. (2006). Mapping supply chains on risk and customer sensitivity dimensions. *Industrial Management & Data Systems*, *106*(6), 878–895. doi:10.1108/02635570610671533

Falk, J. (2014). *Physical mobile interaction in omni-channel retailing using the customers' smartphone to interact with smart objects in a store* (Student paper). Linköpings universitet. Retrieved March 30, 2017, from http://www.diva-portal.org/smash/get/diva2:728289/FULLTEXT01.pdf

Fallah, H., Eskandari, H., & Pishvaee, M. S. (2015). Competitive closed-loop supply chain network design under uncertainty. *Journal of Manufacturing Systems*, *37*, 649–661. doi:10.1016/j.jmsy.2015.01.005

Fan, W., & Bifet, A. (2013). Mining big data: Current status, and forecast to the future. *ACM SIGKDD Explorations Newsletter*, *14*(2), 1–5. doi:10.1145/2481244.2481246

FAO. (2003). *FAO's strategy for a food chain approach to food safety and quality: a framework document for the development of future strategic direction.* Retrieved from http://www.fao.org/DOCREP/MEETING/006/Y8350e.HTM

Fawcett, S. E., Ogden, J. A., Magnan, G. M., & Cooper, M. B. (2006). Organizational commitment and governance for supply chain success. *International Journal of Physical Distribution & Logistics Management*, *36*(1), 22–35. doi:10.1108/09600030610642913

Feeding a Billion: Role of the Food Processing Industry. (2013). AT Kearney.

Ferguson, M. E., & Toktay, L. B. (2006). The effect of competition on recovery strategies. *Production and Operations Management*, *15*(3), 351–368. doi:10.1111/j.1937-5956.2006.tb00250.x

Finch, P. (2004). Supply chain risk management. *Supply Chain Management: An International Journal*, *9*(2), 183–196. doi:10.1108/13598540410527079

Fisher, D., DeLine, R., Czerwinski, M., & Drucker, S. (2012). Interactions with big data analytics. *Interaction*, *19*(3), 50–59. doi:10.1145/2168931.2168943

Fitzgerald, M. (2015). Gone fishing -- for data. *MIT Sloan Management Review*, *56*(3), 7–7.

Flach, A. (2000). Topically Applied Nonsteroidal Anti-inflammatory Drugs and Corneal Problems: An Interim Review and Comment. *Ophthalmology*, *107*(7), 1224–1226. doi:10.1016/S0161-6420(00)00223-2 PMID:10889089

Flores, S. E., & Tunner, D. (2008, July). RFID technologies for cold chain applications. *International Institute of Refrigeration Bulletin*, 4-9.

Flynn, B. B., Huo, B., & Zhao, X. (2010). The impact of supply chain integration on performance: A contingency and configuration approach. *Journal of Operations Management*, *28*(1), 58–71. doi:10.1016/j.jom.2009.06.001

Fontanella. (2007). *The Supply Chain Management Market Sizing Report, 2006-2011*. AMR Research.

Food & FMCG Supply Chain. (n.d.). Retrieved from www.futuresupplychains.com

Ford, E. W., & Scanlon, D. P. (2007). Promise and problems with supply chain management approaches to health care purchasing. *Health Care Management Review*, *32*(3), 192–202. doi:10.1097/01.HMR.0000281623.35987.cf PMID:17666990

Forrester Consulting. (2014). *Customer Desires Vs. Retailer Capabilities: Minding The Omni-Channel Commerce Gap*. Author.

Foxall, G. R., & Greenley, G. E. (1999). Consumers Emotional Responses to Service Environments. *Journal of Business Research*, *46*(2), 149–158. doi:10.1016/S0148-2963(98)00018-6

Ganesh, J., Reynolds, K. E., Luckett, M. G., & Pomirleanu, N. (2010). Online shopper motivations, and e-store attributes: An examination of online patronage behavior and shopper typologies. *Journal of Retailing*, *86*(1), 106–115. doi:10.1016/j.jretai.2010.01.003

Ganjyal, G., & Hanna, M. (2002). A review on residence time distribution (RTD) in food extruders and study on the potential of neural networks in RTD modeling. *Journal of Food Science*, *67*(6), 1996–2002. doi:10.1111/j.1365-2621.2002.tb09491.x

Gardner, M. P., & Siomkos, G. J. (1985). Toward a Methodology for Assessing the Effects of In-Store Atmospherics. In R. Lutz (Ed.), *Advances in Consumer Research*. Chicago, IL: Association for Consumer Research.

Gauraha, A., & Thakur, B. (2008). Comparative economic analysis of post-harvest losses in vegetables and foodgrains crops in Chhattisgarh. *Indian Journal of Agricultural Economics*, *63*(3), 376.

Gauri, D. K., Talukdar, D., & Ratchford, B. (2008). *Empirical Investigation of the Impact of Loss Leader Promotion on Store and Category Performance in Grocery Industry*. Syracuse University.

Gaur, J., Amini, M., & Rao, A. K. (2017). Closed-loop supply chain configuration for new and reconditioned products: An integrated optimization model. *Omega*, *66*, 212–223. doi:10.1016/j.omega.2015.11.008

Gehrt, K. C., Rajan, M. N., Shainesh, G., Czerwinski, D., & O'Brien, M. (2012). Emergence of online shopping in India: Shopping orientation segments. *International Journal of Retail & Distribution Management*, *40*(10), 742–758. doi:10.1108/09590551211263164

Gencer, Y. G. (2017). Supply chain management in retailing business. In U. Akkucuk (Ed.), *Ethics and sustainability in global supply chain management* (pp. 197–210). Hershey, PA: IGI Global. doi:10.4018/978-1-5225-2036-8.ch011

Genc, T. S., & de Giovanni, P. (2017). Trade-in and save: A two-period closed-loop supply chain game with price and technology dependent returns. *International Journal of Production Economics*, *183*, 514–527. doi:10.1016/j.ijpe.2016.07.012

Genin, P., Lamouri, S., & Thomas, A. (2007). Improving the robustness of a supply chain tactical plan. *Supply Chain Forum: An International Journal, 8*(2), 24-35.

Gentry, J. W., & Burns, A. C. (1977-78). How 'Important' Are Evaluative Criteria in Shopping Center Patronage. *Journal of Retailing*, *4*(Winter), 73–85.

George, M., & Gormley, R. (2000). *Managing the cold chain for quality and safety*. Retrieved from http://www.teagasc.ie/ashtown/research/preparedfoods/managing_the_c old_chain.pdf

Gera. (n.d.). *The Six Key Pillars for Building An Everyday Bank*. Accenture.com.

Ghezavati, V., & Nia, N. S. (2015). Development of an optimization model for product returns using genetic algorithms and simulated annealing. *Soft Computing*, *19*(11), 3055–3069. doi:10.1007/s00500-014-1465-8

Ghiassi, M., & Spera, C. (2003). Defining the internet-based supply chain system for mass customized markets. *Computers & Industrial Engineering*, *45*(1), 17–41. doi:10.1016/S0360-8352(03)00017-2

Ghorbani, A., & Yarimoglu, E. K. (2014). E-service marketing. In A. Ghorbani (Ed.), *Marketing in the cyber era: Strategies and emerging trends* (pp. 1–8). Hershey, PA: IGI Global. doi:10.4018/978-1-4666-4864-7.ch001

Ghosh, A., & Fedorowicz, J. (2008). The role of trust in supply chain governance. *Business Process Management Journal*, *14*(4), 453–470. doi:10.1108/14637150810888019

Ghufran, N. (2016). *Food loss! A Big Challenge for Modi Government, Agro & Food Processing*. Retrieved from http://agronfoodprocessing.com/food-loss-a-big-challenge-for-modi-government/

Gillett, P. L. (1973, July). A Profile of In-home Shoppers. *Journal of Marketing, 34*, 40–45.

Giri, B. C., & Sharma, S. (2015). Optimizing a closed-loop supply chain with manufacturing defects and quality dependent return rate. *Journal of Manufacturing Systems, 35*, 92–111. doi:10.1016/j.jmsy.2014.11.014

GOI. (2012). *Annual Report- Ministry of Food Processing Industries*. New Delhi: Government of India.

Gol, A. (2008). Issues and challenges of retail business. *Journal of Retail Management, 6*, 23.

Golara, S., Mousavi, N., Tarokh, M. J., & Hosseinzadeh, M. (2012). Closed-loop supply chain network design with recovery of glass containers. *International Journal of Strategic Decision Sciences, 3*(4), 1–26. doi:10.4018/jsds.2012100101

Gong, S., Loy, C. C., & Xiang, T. (2011). *Security and Surveillance*. Springer. doi:10.1007/978-0-85729-997-0_23

González-Benito, Ó., Martos-Partal, M., & Fustinoni-Venturini, M. (2014). Retailers' price positioning and the motivational profiling of store-brand shoppers: The case of Spain. *Psychology and Marketing, 31*(2), 115–125. doi:10.1002/mar.20680

Goold, B. J. (2002). Privacy Rights and Public Spaces: CCTV and the Problem of the Unobservable Observer. *Criminal Justice Ethics, 21*(1), 21–27. doi:10.1080/0731129X.2002.9992113

Gordon, K. T. (2010). *Customer Loyalty Brings Long-Term Sales*. Entrepreneur.com

Govindan, K., & Popiuc, M. N. (2014). Reverse supply chain coordination by revenue sharing contract: A case for the personal computers industry. *European Journal of Operational Research, 233*(2), 326–336. doi:10.1016/j.ejor.2013.03.023

Govindan, K., Rajendran, S., Sarkis, J., & Murugesan, P. (2013). Multi criteria decision making approaches for green supplier evaluation and selection: A literature review. *Journal of Cleaner Production, 98*, 66–83. doi:10.1016/j.jclepro.2013.06.046

Govindan, K., Soleimani, H., & Kannan, D. (2015). Reverse logistics and closed-loop supply chain: A comprehensive review to explore the future. *European Journal of Operational Research, 240*(3), 603–626. doi:10.1016/j.ejor.2014.07.012

Govindarajan, A., Sinha, A., & Uichanco, J. (2017). *Inventory optimization for fulfillment integration in omnichannel retailing*. Ross School of Business Working Paper, Working Paper No. 1341, February 2017. Retrieved March 30, 2017, from https://deepblue.lib.umich.edu/bitstream/handle/2027.42/136157/1341_Govindarajan.pdf?sequence=1&isAllowed=y

Gray, R. (2000, March 2). E-tail must deliver on Web promises. *Marketing*, 37-8.

Greening, P., & Rutherford, C. (2011). Disruptions and supply networks: A multi-level, multi-theoretical relational perspective. *Int. J. of Logistics Management., 22*(1), 104–126. doi:10.1108/09574091111127570

Grewal, D., & Baker, J. (1994). Do Retail Environmental Factors Affect Consumers Price Acceptability? An Empirical Examination. *International Journal of Research in Marketing, 11*(2), 107–115. doi:10.1016/0167-8116(94)90022-1

Griff, D. A., & Palmer, J. (1999, Jan.). Leveraging the Web for corporate success. *Business Horizons, 42*, 3–10. doi:10.1016/S0007-6813(99)80043-3

Griffis, S. E., Rao, S., Goldsby, T. J., Voorhees, C. M., & Iyengar, D. (2012). Linking order fulfillment performance to referrals in online retailing: An empirical analysis. *Journal of Business Logistics, 33*(4), 279–294. doi:10.1111/jbl.12002

Griffith, D. A., & Krampf, R. A. (1998). An examination of the Web-based strategies of the top 100 US retailers. *Journal of Marketing Theory and Practice, 6*(3), 12–23. doi:10.1080/10696679.1998.11501801

Griffitt, W. (1970). Environmental Effects on Interpersonal Affective Behavior: Ambient Temperature and Attraction. *Journal of Personality and Social Psychology, 15*(3), 240–244. doi:10.1037/h0029432 PMID:5485416

Grossbart, S., Hampton, R., Rammohan, B., & Lapidus, R. S. (1990). Environmental Dispositions and Customer Response to Store Atmospherics. *Journal of Business Research*, *21*(3), 225–241. doi:10.1016/0148-2963(90)90030-H

Guarnieri, P., Sobreiro, V. A., Nagano, M. S., & Serrano, A. L. M. (2015). The challenge of selecting and evaluating third-party reverse logistics providers in a multicriteria perspective: A Brazilian case. *Journal of Cleaner Production*, *96*, 209–219. doi:10.1016/j.jclepro.2014.05.040

Guercini, S., & Milanesi, M. (2016). Store openings and sourcing strategies in the internationalization of fashion industrial retailers. In A. Vecchi & C. Buckley (Eds.), *Handbook of research on global fashion management and merchandising* (pp. 374–397). Hershey, PA: IGI Global. doi:10.4018/978-1-5225-0110-7.ch015

Guide, V. D. R. Jr, Harrison, T. P., & van Wassenhove, L. N. (2003). The challenge of closed-loop supply chains. *Interfaces*, *33*(6), 3–6. doi:10.1287/inte.33.6.3.25182

Guide, V. D. R. Jr, Jayaraman, V., & Linton, J. D. (2003). Building contingency planning for closed-loop supply chains with product recovery. *Journal of Operations Management*, *21*(3), 259–279. doi:10.1016/S0272-6963(02)00110-9

Guide, V. D. R. Jr, Jayaraman, V., Srivastava, R., & Benton, W. C. (2000). Supply chain management for recoverable manufacturing systems. *Interfaces*, *30*(3), 125–142. doi:10.1287/inte.30.3.125.11656

Guide, V. D. R. Jr, & van Wassenhove, L. N. (2006). Closed-loop supply chains: An introduction to the feature issue (Part 1). *Production and Operations Management*, *15*(3), 345–350. doi:10.1111/j.1937-5956.2006.tb00249.x

Guide, V. D. R. Jr, & van Wassenhove, L. N. (2009). The evolution of closed-loop supply chain research. *Operations Research*, *57*(1), 10–18. doi:10.1287/opre.1080.0628

Gulnaz, B. P., & Gokulakannan, P. (2016). Omnichannel retailing. In S. Dixit & A. Sinha (Eds.), *E-Retailing Challenges and Opportunities in the Global Marketplace* (pp. 244–255). Hershey, PA: IGI Global.

Gunasekaran, A., & Ngai, E. W. T. (2004). Information systems in supply chain integration and management. *European Journal of Operational Research*, *159*(2), 269–295. doi:10.1016/j.ejor.2003.08.016

Gunasekaran, A., & Ngai, E. W. T. (2012). Decision support systems for logistics and supply chain management. *Decision Support Systems*, *52*(4), 777–778. doi:10.1016/j.dss.2011.11.012

Gunduz, M. (1997). Market Structure, Storage, Marketing Systems and Foreign Trade Relations in Horticulture Products. *First Symposium of Storage and Marketing in Horticultural Products*, 9-14. (in Turkish)

Gupta, A. (2016). Customer service: A key differentiator in retailing. In N. Kamath & S. Saurav (Eds.), *Handbook of research on strategic supply chain management in the retail industry* (pp. 75–86). Hershey, PA: IGI Global. doi:10.4018/978-1-4666-9894-9.ch005

Gyau, A., & Spiller, A. (2008). The impact of supply chain governance structures on the inter-firm relationship performance in agribusiness. *Agricultural Economics*, *54*(4), 176–185.

Hahler, S., & Fleischmann, M. (2013). The value of acquisition price differentiation in reverse logistics. *Journal of Business Economics*, *83*(1), 1–28. doi:10.1007/s11573-012-0641-5

Halder, P., & Pati, S. (2011). A Need For Paradigm Shift to Improve Supply Chain Management of Fruits & Vegetables in India. *Asian Journal of Agriculture and Rural Development*, *1*(1), 1–20.

Hammond, D., & Beullens, P. (2007). Closed-loop supply chain network equilibrium under legislation. *European Journal of Operational Research*, *183*(2), 895–908. doi:10.1016/j.ejor.2006.10.033

Hampl, N., & Loock, M. (2013). Sustainable development in retailing: What is the impact on store choice? *Business Strategy and the Environment*, *22*(3), 202–216. doi:10.1002/bse.1748

Hardoon, D. R., & Shmueli, G. (2013). *Getting started with business analytics: insightful decision-making*. CRC Press.

Harland, C., Brenchley, R., & Walker, H. (2003). Risk in supply networks. *Journal of Purchasing and Supply Management*, *9*(2), 51–62. doi:10.1016/S1478-4092(03)00004-9

Harris, L. C. (2010). Fraudulent consumer returns: Exploiting retailers' return policies. *European Journal of Marketing*, *44*(6), 730–747.

Ha, S., & Stoel, L. (2009). Consumer e-shopping acceptance: Antecedents in a technology acceptance model. *Journal of Business Research*, *62*(5), 565–571. doi:10.1016/j.jbusres.2008.06.016

Ha, S., & Stoel, L. (2012). Online apparel retailing: Roles of e-shopping quality and experiential e-shopping motives. *Journal of Service Management*, *23*(2), 197–215. doi:10.1108/09564231211226114

Hashemi, V., Chen, M., & Fang, L. (2014). Process planning for closed-loop aerospace manufacturing supply chain and environmental impact reduction. *Computers & Industrial Engineering*, *75*(9), 87–95. doi:10.1016/j.cie.2014.06.005

Hassani, H., & Silva, E. S. (2015). Forecasting with big data: A review. *Annals of Data Science*, *2*(1), 5–19. doi:10.1007/s40745-015-0029-9

Haug, A., & Arlbjorn, J. S. (2011). Barriers to master data quality. *Journal of Enterprise Information Management*, *24*(3), 288–303. doi:10.1108/17410391111122862

Hauge, A., Arlbjorn, J. S., & Pedersen, A. (2009). A classification model of ERP system data quality. *Industrial Management & Data Systems*, *109*(8), 1053–1068. doi:10.1108/02635570910991292

Hausman, A., & Siekpe, J. (2009). The effect of web interface features on consumer online purchase intentions. *Journal of Business Research*, *62*(1), 5–13. doi:10.1016/j.jbusres.2008.01.018

HBR. (2012, Oct.). Getting Control of Big Data. *Harvard Business Review*.

Heiman, A., McWilliams, B., & Zilberman, D. (2001). Demonstrations and money-back guarantees: market mechanisms to reduce uncertainty. *Journal of Business Research*, *54*(1), 71–84.

Heiman, A., McWilliams, B., Zhao, J., & Zilberman, D. (2002). Valuation and management of money-back guarantee options. *Journal of Retailing*, *78*(3), 193–205.

Helbing, D., & Molnar, P. (1995). Social Force Model for Pedestrian Dynamics. *Physical Review E: Statistical Physics, Plasmas, Fluids, and Related Interdisciplinary Topics*, 51. PMID:9963139

Hellstrom, D. (2009). The cost and process of implementing RFID technology to manage and control returnable transport items. *International Journal of Logistics: Research and Applications*, *12*(1), 1–21. doi:10.1080/13675560802168526

He, M., Xie, J., Wu, X., Hu, Q., & Dai, Y. (2016). Capability Coordination in Automobile Logistics Service Supply Chain Based on Reliability. *Procedia Engineering*, *137*, 325–333. doi:10.1016/j.proeng.2016.01.265

Hempel, L., & Töpfer, E. (2004). *CCTV in Europe* (Final Report). Tech. rept. Urban Eye Project: HPSE-CT2001-00094.

Henderson, E. J., & Cool, K. O. (2010). Experience and learning in wine supply chain negotiations. *Supply Chain Forum an International Journal*, *11*(1), 42–55.

Hennig-Thurau, T., Gwinner, K. P., & Gremler, D. D. (2002). Understanding relationship marketing outcomes: An integration of relational benefits and relationship quality. *Journal of Service Research*, *4*(3), 230–247. doi:10.1177/1094670502004003006

He, R., Xiong, Y., & Lin, Z. (2016). Carbon emissions in a dual channel closed loop supply chain: The impact of consumer free riding behavior. *Journal of Cleaner Production*, *134*, 384–394. doi:10.1016/j.jclepro.2016.02.142

Hernandez, T., Bennison, D., & Cornelius, S. (1998). The organisational context of retail locational planning. *GeoJournal*, *45*(4), 299–308. doi:10.1023/A:1006989131869

He, Y. (2015). Acquisition pricing and remanufacturing decisions in a closed-loop supply chain. *International Journal of Production Economics*, *163*, 48–60. doi:10.1016/j.ijpe.2015.02.002

He, Y. (2017). Supply risk sharing in a closed-loop supply chain. *International Journal of Production Economics*, *183*, 39–52. doi:10.1016/j.ijpe.2016.10.012

Hill, W. W., Beatty, S. E., & Walsh, G. (2013). A segmentation of adolescent online users and shoppers. *Journal of Services Marketing*, *27*(5), 347–360. doi:10.1108/JSM-10-2011-0157

Hoffman, D., & Novak, T. (2009). Flow online: Lessons learned and future prospects. *Journal of Interactive Marketing*, *23*(1), 23–34. doi:10.1016/j.intmar.2008.10.003

Hong, X., Xu, L., Du, P., & Wang, W. (2015). Joint advertising, pricing and collection decisions in a closed-loop supply chain. *International Journal of Production Economics*, *167*, 12–22. doi:10.1016/j.ijpe.2015.05.001

Ho, S. K. M. (1994). Is the ISO 9000 series for Total Quality Management? *International Journal (Toronto, Ont.)*, *11*(9), 74–89.

Hsiao, M. H. (2009). Shopping mode choice: Physical store shopping versus e-shopping. *Transportation Research Part E, Logistics and Transportation Review*, *45*(1), 86–95. doi:10.1016/j.tre.2008.06.002

Hsu, C.-C., Kannan, V. R., Tan, K.-C., & Leong, G. K. (2008). Information sharing, buyer-supplier relationships, and firm performance: A multi-region analysis. *International Journal of Physical Distribution & Logistics Management*, *38*(4), 296–310. doi:10.1108/09600030810875391

Huang, Y. S., Chen, S. H., & Ho, J. W. (2013). A study on pricing and delivery strategy for e-retailing systems. *Transportation Research Part E, Logistics and Transportation Review*, *59*, 71–84. doi:10.1016/j.tre.2013.09.002

Hübner, A., Holzapfel, A., & Kuhn, H. (2016). Distribution systems in omni-channel retailing. *Business Research*, *9*(2), 255–296. doi:10.1007/s40685-016-0034-7

Huh, Y. U., Keller, F. R., Redman, T. C., & Watkins, A. R. (1990). Data quality. *Information and Software Technology*, *32*(8), 559–565. doi:10.1016/0950-5849(90)90146-I

Hui, M. K. (1997). The Impact of Music on Consumers Reactions to Waiting for Services. *Journal of Retailing*, *73*(1), 87–104. doi:10.1016/S0022-4359(97)90016-6

Hui, M. K., & Bateson, J. E. G. (1991, Sept.). Perceived Control and the Effects of Crowding and Consumer Choice on the Service Experiences. *The Journal of Consumer Research*, *25*, 175–186.

Hult, G., Neese, W. T., & Bashaw, R. E. (1997). Faculty Perceptions of Marketing Journals. *Journal of Marketing Education*, *19*(1), 37–52. doi:10.1177/027347539701900105

Humphreys, P. K., Lai, M. K., & Sculli, D. (2001). An inter-organizational information system for supply chain management. *International Journal of Production Economics*, *70*(3), 245–255. doi:10.1016/S0925-5273(00)00070-0

Hu, W., Tan, T., Wang, L., & Maybank, S. (2004). A Survey on Visual Surveillance of Object Motions and Behaviour. *IEEE Transactions on Systems, Man, and Cybernetics*, *34*(3), 334–252. doi:10.1109/TSMCC.2004.829274 PMID:15369076

Huynh, C. H., So, K. C., & Gurnani, H. (2016). Managing a closed-loop supply system with random returns and a cyclic delivery schedule. *European Journal of Operational Research*, *255*(3), 787–796. doi:10.1016/j.ejor.2016.05.035

Hwang, Y., & Kim, D. (2007). Customer self-service systems: The effects of perceived web quality with service contents on enjoyment, anxiety, and e-trust. *Decision Support Systems*, *43*(3), 746–760. doi:10.1016/j.dss.2006.12.008

Ian, P. H. L., & Grace, L. B. (2011). *Customer satisfaction towards retailers*. ICA, ICA NÄRA and Coop Forum.

IBM. (2015). *The Four V's of Big Data*. Retrieved from http://www.ibmbigdatahub.com/infographic/four-vs-big-data

Immonen, A., Paakkonen, P., & Ovaska, E. (2015, October 16). paracone, P., & vasa, E (2015). Evaluating the quality of social media data in big data architecture. *IEEE Access*, *3*, 2028–2043. doi:10.1109/ACCESS.2015.2490723

Independent Police Complaints Commission (UK). (2007). *Stockwell One: Investigation into the shooting of Jean Charles de Menezes at Stockwell underground station on 22 July 2005*. Author.

India: Issues and Priorities for Agriculture. (2012). Retrieved from http://www.worldbank.org/en/news/feature/2012/05/17/india-agriculture-issues-priorities

India's Sleeping Giant. (1997). Food. *The McKinsey Quarterly*.

Indian Cold Chain – An Emerging Industry. (2016). Retrieved from http://www.coolingindia.in/blog/post/id/13496/indian-cold-chain--an-emerging-industry

Introna, L. D., & Wood, D. (2004). Picturing Algorithmic Surveillance: The Politics of Facial Recognition Systems. *Surveillance & Society*, *2*(2/3), 177–198.

Ishfaq, R., Defee, C. C., Gibson, B. J., & Raja, U. (2016). Realignment of the physical distribution process in omni-channel fulfillment. *International Journal of Physical Distribution & Logistics Management*, *46*(6/7), 543–561. doi:10.1108/IJPDLM-02-2015-0032

ITLN. (2014). *India on fast track to shape perishables logistics trends*. Retrieved from http://www.itln.in/india-on-fast-track-to-shape-perishables-logistics-trends/

Iyer, K. N. S., Germain, R., & Claycomb, C. (2009). B2B e-commerce supply chain integration and performance: A contingency fit perspective on the role of environment. *Information & Management*, *46*(6), 313–322. doi:10.1016/j.im.2009.06.002

Jacobs, A. (2009). The pathologies of big data. *Communications of the ACM*, *52*(8), 36–44. doi:10.1145/1536616.1536632

Jain, K., & Dubey, A. (2005). Supply chain collaboration: a governance perspective. *Supply Chain Forum: An International Journal in Supply Chain, 6*(2),50-57.

Jain, N. (2007). *International Conference on Agribusiness and Food Industry in Developing Countries: Opportunities and Challenges*. Retrieved February 19, 2013, from IIM Lucknow: http://www.iiml.ac.in/events/Program.html

Janardhan, S. (2008). *Unified View of Customer: It's All About Customer Experience*. TCS.com.

Janardhan, S. (2013). *Unified View of Customer: It's All About Customer Experience*. TCS.com

Jayaraman, V., Guide, V. D. R. Jr, & Srivastava, R. (1999). A closed-loop logistics model for remanufacturing. *The Journal of the Operational Research Society*, *50*(5), 497–508. doi:10.1057/palgrave.jors.2600716

Jeihoonian, M., Zanjani, M. K., & Gendreau, M. (2016). Accelerating Benders decomposition for closed-loop supply chain network design: Case of used durable products with different quality levels. *European Journal of Operational Research, 251*(3), 830–845. doi:10.1016/j.ejor.2015.12.052

Jia, K., & Gong, S. (2008). Generalized Face Super-Resolution. *IEEE Transactions on Image Processing, 17*(6), 873–886. doi:10.1109/TIP.2008.922421 PMID:18482883

Jiang, L. A., Yang, Z., & Jun, M. (2013). Measuring consumer perceptions of online shopping convenience. *Journal of Service Management, 24*(2), 191–214. doi:10.1108/09564231311323962

Jiang, P., & Balasubramanian, S. K. (2014). An empirical comparison of market efficiency: Electronic marketplaces vs. traditional retail formats. *Electronic Commerce Research and Applications, 13*(2), 98–109. doi:10.1016/j.elerap.2013.11.003

Jindal, A., & Sangwan, K. S. (2013). *An integrated fuzzy multi-criteria evaluation of sustainable reverse logistics network models*. Paper presented at the 2013 IEEE International Conference on Fuzzy Systems (FUZZ-IEEE 2013), Hyderabad, India. doi:10.1109/FUZZ-IEEE.2013.6622469

Johnston, R. (1995). The determinants of service quality: Satisfiers and dissatisfiers. *International Journal of Service Industry Management, 8*(5), 53–71. doi:10.1108/09564239510101536

Jones-Farmer, L. A., Ezell, J. D., & Hazen, B. T. (2013). *Applying control chart methods to enhance data quality*. Technimetrics.

Joseph, L., & Kuby, M. (2016). The location types of US retailers. *International Journal of Applied Geospatial Research, 7*(4), 1–22. doi:10.4018/IJAGR.2016100101

Joshi, G. (2009). *Information technology for retail*. Oxford, UK: Oxford University Press.

Joshi, R., Banwet, D. K., & Shankar, R. (2009). Indian cold chain: Modeling the Inhibitors. *British Food Journal, 111*(11), 1260–1283. doi:10.1108/00070700911001077

Juaneda-Ayensa, E., Mosquera, A., & Murillo, Y. S. (2016). Omnichannel customer behavior: Key drivers of technology acceptance and use and their effects on purchase intention. *Frontiers in Psychology, 7*, 1–11. doi:10.3389/fpsyg.2016.01117 PMID:27516749

Juran, J. M., & Godfrey, A. B. (1999). *Juran's Quality Handbook* (5th ed.). McGraw-Hill.

Jüttner, U. (2005). Supply chain risk management: Understanding the business requirements from a practitioner perspective. *Int. J. of Logistics Management., 16*(1), 120–141. doi:10.1108/09574090510617385

Jüttner, U., Christopher, M., & Baker, S. (2007). Demand chain management: Integrating marketing and supply chain management. *Industrial Marketing Management, 36*(3), 377–392. doi:10.1016/j.indmarman.2005.10.003

Juttner, U., Peck, H., & Christopher, M. (2003). Supply Chain Risk Management: Outlining an Agenda for Future Research. *International Journal of Logistics: Research and Applications., 6*(4), 199–213. doi:10.1080/13675560310001627016

Kacen, J. J., Hess, J. D., & Walker, D. (2012). Spontaneous selection: The influence of product and retailing factors on consumer impulse purchases. *Journal of Retailing and Consumer Services, 19*(6), 578–588. doi:10.1016/j.jretconser.2012.07.003

Kadambala, D. K., Subramanian, N., Tiwari, M. K., Abdulrahman, M., & Liu, C. (2017). Closed loop supply chain networks: Designs for energy and time value efficiency. *International Journal of Production Economics, 183*, 382–393. doi:10.1016/j.ijpe.2016.02.004

Kader, A., & Rolle, R. (2004). *In the role of post harvest management in assuring the quality and safety of horticultural produce*. Rome: FAO Food and Agricultural Organizations of the United Nations.

Kahan, B. K., Strong, D. M., & Wang, R. Y. (2002). Information quality benchmarks: Product and service performance. *Communications of the ACM*, *45*(4), 184–192. doi:10.1145/505248.506007

Kaisler, S., Armour, F., Espinosa, J. A., & Money, W. (2013). Big data: Issues and Challenges Moving Forward. In *2013 46th Hawaii International Conference on System Sciences* (pp. 995–1004). Maui, HI: IEEE. doi:10.1109/HICSS.2013.645

Kapoor, P. (2009, July 28). *Doctoc-International Summit on Food Processing and Agribusiness.* Retrieved January 22, 2014, from Docstoc.com: http://www.docstoc.com/docs/127265667/ENTREPRENEURIAL-OPPORTUNITIES-IN-THE-AGRI-BUSINESS

Karabulut, O. A., Kuruoglu, G., Ilhan, K., & Arslan, U. (2005). Using of Heat Treatments against Postharvest Diseases, J. Ondokuz Mayıs Univ. [in Turkish]. *Facul. Agric.*, *20*(1), 94–101.

Kasemsap, K. (2017d). The role of radio frequency identification in modern libraries. In I. Management Association (Ed.), Identity theft: Breakthroughs in research and practice (pp. 174–200). Hershey, PA: IGI Global. doi:10.4018/978-1-5225-0808-3.ch009

Kasemsap, K. (2017e). Mastering customer service, customer experience, and customer orientation in the hospitality and tourism industry. In P. Vasant & K. M. (Eds.), Handbook of research on holistic optimization techniques in the hospitality, tourism, and travel industry (pp. 115–140). Hershey, PA: IGI Global. doi:10.4018/978-1-5225-1054-3.ch005

Kasemsap, K. (2014). The role of Lean Production on organizational performance. In V. Modrák & P. Semančo (Eds.), *Handbook of research on design and management of Lean Production systems* (pp. 358–388). Hershey, PA: IGI Global. doi:10.4018/978-1-4666-5039-8.ch017

Kasemsap, K. (2015). The role of radio frequency identification in modern libraries. In S. Thanuskodi (Ed.), *Handbook of research on inventive digital tools for collection management and development in modern libraries* (pp. 361–385). Hershey, PA: IGI Global. doi:10.4018/978-1-4666-8178-1.ch021

Kasemsap, K. (2015a). The roles of corporate marketing strategies and brand management in the global retail industry. In E. Pantano (Ed.), *Successful technological integration for competitive advantage in retail settings* (pp. 310–339). Hershey, PA: IGI Global. doi:10.4018/978-1-4666-8297-9.ch014

Kasemsap, K. (2015b). The role of electronic commerce in the global business environments. In F. Cipolla-Ficarra (Ed.), *Handbook of research on interactive information quality in expanding social network communications* (pp. 304–324). Hershey, PA: IGI Global. doi:10.4018/978-1-4666-7377-9.ch019

Kasemsap, K. (2016a). Fostering supply chain management in global business. In B. Christiansen (Ed.), *Handbook of research on global supply chain management* (pp. 45–71). Hershey, PA: IGI Global. doi:10.4018/978-1-4666-9639-6.ch003

Kasemsap, K. (2016a). Retail marketing strategies and brand management: A global retail industry perspective. *International Journal of Social and Organizational Dynamics in IT*, *5*(2), 66–78. doi:10.4018/IJSODIT.2016070106

Kasemsap, K. (2016b). Reviewing the role of store brands in the global retail industry. In M. Gómez-Suárez & M. Martínez-Ruiz (Eds.), *Handbook of research on strategic retailing of private label products in a recovering economy* (pp. 28–53). Hershey, PA: IGI Global. doi:10.4018/978-1-5225-0220-3.ch002

Kasemsap, K. (2016c). Encouraging supply chain networks and customer loyalty in global supply chain. In N. Kamath & S. Saurav (Eds.), *Handbook of research on strategic supply chain management in the retail industry* (pp. 87–112). Hershey, PA: IGI Global. doi:10.4018/978-1-4666-9894-9.ch006

Kasemsap, K. (2016c). Multifaceted applications of green supply chain management. In A. Jean-Vasile (Ed.), *Food science, production, and engineering in contemporary economies* (pp. 327–354). Hershey, PA: IGI Global. doi:10.4018/978-1-5225-0341-5.ch014

Kasemsap, K. (2016d). Creating product innovation strategies through knowledge management in global business. In A. Goel & P. Singhal (Eds.), *Product innovation through knowledge management and social media strategies* (pp. 330–357). Hershey, PA: IGI Global. doi:10.4018/978-1-4666-9607-5.ch015

Kasemsap, K. (2016d). The roles of lean and green supply chain management strategies in the global business environments. In S. Joshi & R. Joshi (Eds.), *Designing and implementing global supply chain management* (pp. 152–173). Hershey, PA: IGI Global. doi:10.4018/978-1-4666-9720-1.ch008

Kasemsap, K. (2016e). Advocating electronic business and electronic commerce in the global marketplace. In S. Dixit & A. Sinha (Eds.), *E-retailing challenges and opportunities in the global marketplace* (pp. 1–24). Hershey, PA: IGI Global. doi:10.4018/978-1-4666-9921-2.ch001

Kasemsap, K. (2016e). Applying Lean Production and Six Sigma in global operations. In U. Akkucuk (Ed.), *Handbook of research on waste management techniques for sustainability* (pp. 44–74). Hershey, PA: IGI Global. doi:10.4018/978-1-4666-9723-2.ch003

Kasemsap, K. (2016f). Implementing electronic commerce in global marketing. In I. Lee (Ed.), *Encyclopedia of e-commerce development, implementation, and management* (pp. 591–602). Hershey, PA: IGI Global. doi:10.4018/978-1-4666-9787-4.ch043

Kasemsap, K. (2016h). The role of strategic outsourcing in global business. In G. Alor-Hernández, C. Sánchez-Ramírez, & J. García-Alcaraz (Eds.), *Handbook of research on managerial strategies for achieving optimal performance in industrial processes* (pp. 325–357). Hershey, PA: IGI Global. doi:10.4018/978-1-5225-0130-5.ch016

Kasemsap, K. (2017a). Mastering fashion supply chain management and new product development in the digital age. In A. Vecchi (Ed.), *Advanced fashion technology and operations management* (pp. 65–91). Hershey, PA: IGI Global. doi:10.4018/978-1-5225-1865-5.ch003

Kasemsap, K. (2017b). Advocating information system, information integration, and information sharing in global supply chain. In G. Jamil, A. Soares, & C. Pessoa (Eds.), *Handbook of research on information management for effective logistics and supply chains* (pp. 107–130). Hershey, PA: IGI Global. doi:10.4018/978-1-5225-0973-8.ch006

Kasemsap, K. (2017b). Sustainability, environmental sustainability, and sustainable tourism: Advanced issues and implications. In N. Ray (Ed.), *Business infrastructure for sustainability in developing economies* (pp. 1–24). Hershey, PA: IGI Global. doi:10.4018/978-1-5225-2041-2.ch001

Kasemsap, K. (2017c). Advocating sustainable supply chain management and sustainability in global supply chain. In M. Khan, M. Hussain, & M. Ajmal (Eds.), *Green supply chain management for sustainable business practice* (pp. 234–271). Hershey, PA: IGI Global. doi:10.4018/978-1-5225-0635-5.ch009

Kasemsap, K. (2017c). Radio frequency identification and mobile ad-hoc network: Theories and applications. In S. Bhattacharyya, N. Das, D. Bhattacharjee, & A. Mukherjee (Eds.), *Handbook of research on recent developments in intelligent communication application* (pp. 63–95). Hershey, PA: IGI Global. doi:10.4018/978-1-5225-1785-6.ch003

Kasemsap, K. (2017d). The roles of logistics service providers and supply chain integration in global supply chain. In L. Saglietto & C. Cezanne (Eds.), *Global intermediation and logistics service providers* (pp. 265–285). Hershey, PA: IGI Global. doi:10.4018/978-1-5225-2133-4.ch014

Kasemsap, K. (2017f). Mastering electronic procurement, green public procurement, and public procurement for innovation. In R. Shakya (Ed.), *Digital governance and e-government principles applied to public procurement* (pp. 29–55). Hershey, PA: IGI Global. doi:10.4018/978-1-5225-2203-4.ch002

Kasemsap, K. (2017g). Production planning: Advanced issues and implications. In U. Akkucuk (Ed.), *Ethics and sustainability in global supply chain management* (pp. 50–72). Hershey, PA: IGI Global. doi:10.4018/978-1-5225-2036-8.ch003

Kasemsap, K. (2017i). Mastering consumer attitude and sustainable consumption in the digital age. In N. Suki (Ed.), *Handbook of research on leveraging consumer psychology for effective customer engagement* (pp. 16–41). Hershey, PA: IGI Global. doi:10.4018/978-1-5225-0746-8.ch002

Kasemsap, K. (2017j). Environmental management and waste management: Principles and applications. In U. Akkucuk (Ed.), *Ethics and sustainability in global supply chain management* (pp. 26–49). Hershey, PA: IGI Global. doi:10.4018/978-1-5225-2036-8.ch002

Kaynas, K., Celikel, F. G., Türkes, N., & Surmeli, N. (1988). *Studies on Maturity Physiology of Storage Facilities and of Some Tomato Varieties Grown in Yalova and Iznik Regions. In Vegetable Breeding in Open Research Project Report* (pp. 415–423). Ataturk Horticulture Research Institute. (in Turkish)

Kazmin. (2014). *India tackles supply chain to cut food waste.* FT.com.

Kearns. (2013). *Supply chain 2.0.* Academic Press.

Keeney, R. L. (1999). The value of Internet commerce to the customer. *Management Science, 45*(4), 533–542. doi:10.1287/mnsc.45.4.533

Kelepouris, T., Pramatari, K., & Doukidis, G. (2007). RFID-enabled traceability in the food supply chain. *Industrial Management & Data Systems, 107*(2), 183–200. doi:10.1108/02635570710723804

Kelley. (2006). *Using Loyalty Programs to Attract Consumers to Value-Added Businesses.* Extension.psu.edu.

Kemperman, A., van Delft, L., & Borgers, A. (2015). Omni-channel fashion shopping. In E. Pantano (Ed.), *Successful Technological Integration for Competitive Advantage in Retail Settings* (pp. 144–167). Hershey, PA: IGI Global. doi:10.4018/978-1-4666-8297-9.ch007

Keskin, B. B., Uster, H., & Cetinkaya, S. (2010). Integration of strategic and tactical decisions for vendor selection under capacity constraints. *Computers & Operations Research, 37*(12), 2182–2191. doi:10.1016/j.cor.2010.03.008

Ketzenberg, M. E., & Zuidwijk, R. A. (2009). Optimal pricing, ordering, and return policies for consumer goods. *Production and Operations Management, 18*(3), 344–360.

Ketzenberg, M. E., van der Laan, E., & Teunter, R. H. (2006). Value of information in closed loop supply chains. *Production and Operations Management, 15*(3), 393–406. doi:10.1111/j.1937-5956.2006.tb00253.x

Keyvanshokooh, E., Ryan, S. M., & Kabir, E. (2016). Hybrid robust and stochastic optimization for closed-loop supply chain network design using accelerated Benders decomposition. *European Journal of Operational Research, 249*(1), 76–92. doi:10.1016/j.ejor.2015.08.028

Khan, A. (2005, September 5). *The domestic food market: is India ready for food processing?* Retrieved January 26, 2014, from India Development Foundation: http://www.idfresearch.org/pdf/dommarket.pdf

Khan. (2013). Marketing Revolution in Rural India: Emerging Trends and Strategies. *Journal of Business Administration and Education.*

Kim, T., & Glock, C. H. (2014). On the use of RFID in the management of reusable containers in closed-loop supply chains under stochastic container return quantities. *Transportation Research Part E, Logistics and Transportation Review*, *64*, 12–27. doi:10.1016/j.tre.2014.01.011

Kim, T., Glock, C. H., & Kwon, Y. (2014). A closed-loop supply chain for deteriorating products under stochastic container return times. *Omega*, *43*, 30–40. doi:10.1016/j.omega.2013.06.002

Kim, T., Goyal, S. K., & Kim, C. H. (2013). Lot-streaming policy for forward-reverse logistics with recovery capacity investment. *International Journal of Advanced Manufacturing Technology*, *68*(1), 509–522. doi:10.1007/s00170-013-4748-9

King, T., & Dennis, C. (2006). Unethical consumers: Shopping behaviour using the qualitative analysis of theory of planned behaviour and accompanied (de) shopping. *Qualitative Market Research: An International Journal*, *9*(3), 282–296.

King, D. E. (2009). Dlibml: A machine learning toolkit. *Journal of Machine Learning Research*, (10), 1755–1758.

Kleindorfer, P. R., & Saad, G. H. (2005). Managing disruption risks in supply chains. *Production and Operations Management*, *14*(1), 53–68. doi:10.1111/j.1937-5956.2005.tb00009.x

Klein, J. D., & Lurie, S. (1991). Postharvest Heat Treatment and Fruit Quality. *Postharvest News Inf.*, *2*, 15–19.

Kline, B., & Wagner, J. (1994). Information Sources and Retail Buyer Decision-Making: The Effect of Product Specific Buying Experience. *Journal of Retailing*, *70*(1), 75–88. doi:10.1016/0022-4359(94)90030-2

Ko, T. (2011). *Video Surveillance*. InTech. Retrieved from http://tinyurl.com/8hlveuk

Kollmann, T., Kuckertz, A., & Kayser, I. (2012). Cannibalization or synergy? Consumers' channel selection in online-offline multichannel systems. *Journal of Retailing and Consumer Services*, *19*(2), 186–194. doi:10.1016/j.jretconser.2011.11.008

Kolowich, L. (2015). *Customer Loyalty Programs That Actually Add Value*. Marketingdonut.co.uk.

Kotzab, H., Schnedlitz, P., & Neumayer, K. (2003). Contemporary IT-assisted retail management. In L. Joia (Ed.), *IT-based management: Challenges and solutions* (pp. 175–203). Hershey, PA: IGI Global. doi:10.4018/978-1-59140-033-2.ch011

Kouvelis, P., & Milner, J. M. (2002). Supply chain capacity and outsourcing decisions: The dynamic interplay of demand and supply uncertainty. *IIE Transactions*, *34*(8), 717–728. doi:10.1080/07408170208928907

Kovacs, G. (2008). Corporate environmental responsibility in the supply chain. *Journal of Cleaner Production*, *16*(15), 1571–1578. doi:10.1016/j.jclepro.2008.04.013

Kumar, R., & Hu, M. (2015, Sept.). Is your supply chain ready for the omni-channel revolution? *Supply Chain Management Review*, 76-78. Retrieved March 29, 2017, from https://www.atkearney.com/documents/10192/6464222/SCMR1509_OpAdvantage2.pdf/705bfa25-814b-4991-9853-66cf7648d0b2

Kumar, S., & Deshmukh, S. (2005). *Business intelligence: delivering business value through supply chain analytics.* Infosys White Paper. Retrieved from http://www.bcubeglobal.com/wp-content/uploads/supply-chain-analytics.pdf

Kumar, S., Pal, S., & Joshi, P. K. (2004). Vegetable Sector in India: An Overview. Impact of Vegetable Research in India, National Centre for Agrıcultural Economics and Policy Research, ICAR.

Kumar, A., & Rahman, S. (2014). RFID-enabled process reengineering of closed-loop supply chains in the healthcare industry of Singapore. *Journal of Cleaner Production*, *85*, 382–394. doi:10.1016/j.jclepro.2014.04.037

Kumar, A., Sikdar, P., & Alam, M. M. (2016). E-retail adoption in emerging markets: Applicability of an integrated trust and technology acceptance model. *International Journal of E-Business Research*, *12*(3), 44–67. doi:10.4018/IJEBR.2016070104

Kumar, N., Sarkar, B. C., & Sharma, H. K. (2010). Development and characterization of extruded product using carrot pomace and rice flour. *Int J Food Eng*, *6*(3), 1–24. doi:10.2202/1556-3758.1824

Kurata, H., & Nam, S. (2014). Freshness management in the retail business. In J. Wang (Ed.), *Encyclopedia of business analytics and optimization* (pp. 960–977). Hershey, PA: IGI Global. doi:10.4018/978-1-4666-5202-6.ch089

Kurata, H., & Yue, X. (2008). Trade promotion mode choice and information sharing in fashion retail supply chains. *International Journal of Production Economics*, *114*(2), 507–519. doi:10.1016/j.ijpe.2007.05.021

Kwon, O., Lee, N., & Shin, B. (2014). Data quality management, data usage experience and acquisition intention of big data analytics. *Inter. J. Informat. Manage.*, *34*(3), 387–394. doi:10.1016/j.ijinfomgt.2014.02.002

Lamming, R., Caldwell, N., Phillips, W., & Harrison, D. (2005). Sharing Sensitive Information in Supply Relationships: The Flaws in One-way Open-book Negotiation and the Need for Transparency. *European Management Journal*, *23*(5), 554–563. doi:10.1016/j.emj.2005.09.010

Laney, D. (2001). *3D data management: controlling data volume, velocity, and variety*. Retrieved from http://www.blogs.gartner.com/doug-laney/files/2012/01/ad949-3D-Data-Management-Controlling-Data-Volume-Velocityand-Variety.pdf

LaRose, R. (2001). On the Negative Effects of E-Commerce: A Socio cognitive Exploration of Unregulated On-line Buying. *Journal of Computer-Mediated Communication, 6*(3), 1–37.

Lawande, K. E. (2004). Status of Onion and Garlic Research in India. Impact of Vegetable Research in India, National Centre for Agricultural Economics and Policy Research, ICAR.

Lazaris, C., & Vrechopoulos, A. (2014). From multi-channel to "omnichannel" retailing: review of the literature and calls for research. *2nd International Conference on Contemporary Marketing Issues,* 1-6.

Lee, H., Zhang, T., Boile, M., Theofanis, S., & Choo, S. (2013). Designing an integrated logistics network in a supply chain system. *KSCE Journal of Civil Engineering*, *17*(4), 806–814. doi:10.1007/s12205-013-0087-5

Lee, J. E., Gen, M., & Rhee, K. G. (2009). Network model and optimization of reverse logistics by hybrid genetic algorithm. *Computers & Industrial Engineering*, *56*(3), 951–964. doi:10.1016/j.cie.2008.09.021

Lee, S.-W., Park, J., & Lee, S.-W. (2006). Low Resolution Face Recognition Based on Support Vector Data Description. *Pattern Recognition*, *39*(9), 1809–1812. doi:10.1016/j.patcog.2006.04.033

Lee, Y. W., Pipino, L., Strong, D. M., & Wang, R. Y. (2004). Process-embedded data integrity. *Journal of Database Management*, *15*(1), 87–103. doi:10.4018/jdm.2004010104

Lee, Y. W., Strong, D. M., Kahn, B. K., & Wang, R. Y. (2002). AIMQ: A methodology for information quality assessment. *Information & Management*, *40*(2), 133–146. doi:10.1016/S0378-7206(02)00043-5

Lehman, T. (2013). *Creating a Loyalty Program*. Newnorth.com.

Levy, M., & Weitz, B. (2009). *Retailing management*. New York, NY: McGraw–Hill.

Levy, M., & Weitz, B. A. (1998). *Retailing Management* (3rd ed.). Chicago: Irwin McGraw-Hill.

Lewis, J. (2014). *Greatest challenge – The omni channel customer experience*. ijgolding.com.

Lewis. (2014). *Greatest challenge – The omni channel customer experience*. ijgolding.com.

Lewis, T. L., & Loker, S. (2015). Adoption of emerging in-store technology interfaces for the apparel retail employee. In E. Pantano (Ed.), *Successful technological integration for competitive advantage in retail settings* (pp. 119–143). Hershey, PA: IGI Global. doi:10.4018/978-1-4666-8297-9.ch006

Lewrick, M., Omar, M., Williams, R. Jr, Tjandra, N. C., & Lee, Z. (2015). Radical and incremental innovation effectiveness in relation to market orientation in the retail industry: Triggers, drivers, and supporters. In E. Pantano (Ed.), *Successful technological integration for competitive advantage in retail settings* (pp. 239–268). Hershey, PA: IGI Global. doi:10.4018/978-1-4666-8297-9.ch011

Liao, B., & Li, B. (2016). Warranty as an effective strategy for remanufactured product. *International Journal of Information Systems and Supply Chain Management, 9*(3), 83–98. doi:10.4018/IJISSCM.2016070105

Liebermann, Y., & Stashevsky, S. (2002). Perceived risks as barriers to Internet and e-commerce usage. *Qualitative Market Research, 5*(4), 291–300. doi:10.1108/13522750210443245

Lim, Bassamboo, Chopra, & Daskin. (2010). *Flexibility and Fragility: Use of Chaining Strategies in the Presence of Disruption Risks.* Northwestern University research report.

Lim, M., Bassamboo, A., Chopra, S., & Daskin, M. S. (2010). *Flexibility and Fragility: Use of Chaining Strategies in the Presence of Disruption Risks.* Northwestern University research report.

Lima, A. F. S. (2015). *Omni-channel retail strategies: an outlook to portuguese business transformation.* Dissertation Proposal Master in Management. Retrieved March 10, 2017, from https://repositorio-aberto.up.pt/bitstream/10216/79958/2/36198.pdf

Lim, H., & Dubinsky, A. J. (2004). Consumers perceptions of e-shopping characteristics: An expectancy-value approach. *Journal of Services Marketing, 18*(7), 500–513. doi:10.1108/08876040410561839

Lisa, K. (2013). *Table 1: Predicted loss of fresh food storage in developing countries – Use of cold chains for reducing food losses in developing countries* (PEF White Paper No. 13-03). The Postharvest Education Foundation (PEF).

Liu, H., & Wang, I.P. (1999). Co-ordination of international channel relationships: four case studies in the food industry in China. *Journal of Business & Industrial Marketing, 14*(2), 130-150.

Lohse, G., Bellman, S., & Johnson, E. J. (2000). Consumer buying behavior on the Internet: Findings from panel data. *Journal of Interactive Marketing, 14*(1), 15–29. doi:10.1002/(SICI)1520-6653(200024)14:1<15::AID-DIR2>3.0.CO;2-C

Lowson, R. (2001). Analysing the effectiveness of European retail sourcing strategies. *European Management Journal, 19*(5), 543–551. doi:10.1016/S0263-2373(01)00068-8

Loyalty Program Development Making Loyalty Programs Mean More. (n.d.). Newsnorth.com.

Lucas, L. (2013). Diageo Overhauls Its Supply Chain. *Financial Times.*

Luedi, A. F. (1997). Personalize or perish. *Electronic Markets, 7*(3), 22–25. doi:10.1080/10196789700000032

Lund, R. (1998). *Remanufacturing: An American resource.* Paper presented at the 5th International Congress for Environmentally Conscious Design and Manufacturing, Rochester, NY.

Lyles, M. A., Flynn, B. B., & Frohlich, M. (2008). All Supply Chains Dont Flow Through: Understanding Supply Chain Issues in Product Recalls. *Management and Organization Review, 4*(02), 167–182. doi:10.1111/j.1740-8784.2008.00106.x

Madden, S. (2012). From databases to big data. *IEEE Internet Computing, 16*(3), 4–6. doi:10.1109/MIC.2012.50

Madlberger, M. (2005). Applications of Internet-based marketing instruments by multichannel retailers: A web site analysis in the U.S. and the UK. In S. Krishnamurthy (Ed.), *Contemporary research in e-marketing* (Vol. 2, pp. 284–303). Hershey, PA: IGI Global. doi:10.4018/978-1-59140-824-6.ch011

Madlberger, M. (2009). Exogenous and endogenous antecedents of online shopping in a multichannel environment: Evidence from a catalog retailer in the German-speaking world. In Y. Wan (Ed.), *Comparison-shopping services and agent designs* (pp. 196–216). Hershey, PA: IGI Global. doi:10.4018/978-1-59904-978-6.ch013

Madsen, M. (2013). *The Challenges of big data & Approaches to Data Quality (White paper).* Rogue River. Retrieved from http://fm.sap.com/data/UPLOAD/files/The_Challenges_of_Big_Data_&_Approaches_to_Data_Quality.pdf

Maheshwar, C., & Chanakwa, T. S. (2006). Postharvest losses due to gaps in cold chain in India-A solution. *ISHS Acta Horticulturae 712: IV International Conference on Managing Quality in Chains - The Integrated View on Fruits and Vegetables Quality.* Retrieved January 26, 2014, from Acta Horticulturae: http://www.actahort.org/books/712/712_100.htm

Maiti, T., & Giri, B. C. (2015). A closed loop supply chain under retail price and product quality dependent demand. *Journal of Manufacturing Systems, 37*, 624–637. doi:10.1016/j.jmsy.2014.09.009

Ma, J., & Wang, H. (2014). Complexity analysis of dynamic noncooperative game models for closed-loop supply chain with product recovery. *Applied Mathematical Modelling, 38*(23), 5562–5572. doi:10.1016/j.apm.2014.02.027

Malhotra, N. K. (1983). A Threshold Model of Store Choice. *Journal of Retailing, 59*(2), 3–21.

Manikas, I., & Terry, L. A. (2009). A case study assessment of the operational performance of a multiple fresh produce distribution centre in the UK. *British Food Journal, 111*(5), 421–435. doi:10.1108/00070700910957276

Manning, L., Baines, R. N., & Chadd, S. A. (2006). Quality assurance models in the food supply chain. *British Food Journal, 108*(2), 91–104. doi:10.1108/00070700610644915

Manyika, J., Chui, M., Brown, B., Bughin, J., Dobbs, R., Roxburgh, C., & Byers, A. (2011). Big data: The next frontier for innovation, competition, and productivity. Academic Press.

Manyika, J., Chui, M., Brown, B., Bughin, J., Dobbs, R., Roxburgh, C., & Byers, A. H. (2011). *Big data: The next frontier for innovation, competition, and productivity.* Retrieved from http://www.mckinsey.com/business-functions/business-technology/our-insights/big-data-the-next-frontier-for-innovation

Ma, R., Yao, L., Jin, M., Ren, P., & Lv, Z. (2016). Robust environmental closed-loop supply chain design under uncertainty. *Chaos, Solitons, and Fractals, 89*, 195–202. doi:10.1016/j.chaos.2015.10.028

March, S. T., & Hevner, A. R. (2007). Integrated decision support systems: A data warehousing perspective. *Decision Support Systems, 43*(3), 1031–1043. doi:10.1016/j.dss.2005.05.029

MarketResearch.com. (2011). *Global Video Surveillance Market, Applications and Management Services Forecasts (2010-2015).* Retrieved from www.marketresearch.com/MarketsandMarkets-v3719/GlobalVideo-Surveillance-Applications-Management-6083117/

Marques, G., Gourc, D., Lamothe, J., & Thierry, C. (2010). Collaboration and risk management support in uncertain supply chain context. In *International Conference on Information Systems, Logistics and Supply Chain (ILS 2010).* Facultés Universitaires Catholiques de Mons.

Martínez-Ruiz, M. P., González-González, I., Jiménez-Zarco, A. I., & Izquierdo-Yusta, A. (2016). Private labels at the service of retailers' image and competitive positioning: The case of Tesco. In M. Gómez-Suárez & M. Martínez-Ruiz (Eds.), *Handbook of research on strategic retailing of private label products in a recovering economy* (pp. 104–125). Hershey, PA: IGI Global. doi:10.4018/978-1-5225-0220-3.ch005

Martin, K. A., Moritz, S. E., & Hall, C. R. (1999). A literature review and applied model. *The Sport Psychologist*, *13*(3), 245–268. doi:10.1123/tsp.13.3.245

Maruchecka, A., Greisb, N., Menac, C., & Cai, L. (2011). Product safety and security in the global supply chain: Issues, challenges and research opportunities. *Journal of Operations Management*, *29*(7-8), 707–720. doi:10.1016/j.jom.2011.06.007

Mathews, A. W., & Burton, T. M. (2008, March 7). German firm recalls Heparin with China link; Batches had ingredient from different source than Baxter's product. *Wall Street Journal*, p. B4.

Maxwell, D., Sheate, W., & Vorst, R. V. D. (2006). Functional and systems aspects of the sustainable product and service development approach for industry. *Journal of Cleaner Production*, *14*(17), 399–416. doi:10.1016/j.jclepro.2006.01.028

Mazaheri, E., Richard, M. O., & Laroche, M. (2010). Investigating the moderating impact of hedonism on online consumer behavior. *Journal of Global Academy of Marketing Science*, *20*(2), 123–134. doi:10.1080/12297119.2010.9730185

McAfee, A., & Brynjolfsson, E. (2012). Big data: The management revolution. *Harvard Business Review*, *90*(10), 1–9. PMID:23074865

McAfee, A., & Brynjolfsson, E. (2012). Big data: The management revolution. *Harvard Business Review*, *90*(10), 61–68. PMID:23074865

McCarthy, I. P., Silvestre, B. S., & Kietzmann, J. H. (2013). Understanding outsourcing contexts through information asymmetry and capability fit. *Production Planning & Control: The Management of Operations*, *24*(4/5), 277–283. doi:10.1080/09537287.2011.648765

McCreadie, R., Macdonald, C., & Ounis, I. (2012). MapReduce indexing strategies: Studying scalability and efficiency. *Information Processing & Management*, *48*(5), 873–888. doi:10.1016/j.ipm.2010.12.003

McFarlane, D., & Sheffi, Y. (2003). The impact of automatic identification on supply chain operations. *The International Journal of Logistics Management*, *3*(1), 1–17. doi:10.1108/09574090310806503

Meade, L., Sarkis, J., & Presley, A. (2007). The theory and practice of reverse logistics. *International Journal of Logistics Systems and Management*, *3*(1), 56–84. doi:10.1504/IJLSM.2007.012070

Mei-Lien, L. L., & Green, L. (2011). *A mediating influence on customer loyalty: The role of perceived value.* Aabri.com.

Melville, N., Kraemer, K., & Gurbaxani, V. (2004). Review: information technology and organizational performance: an integrative model of it business value. *Management Information Systems Quarterly*, *28*(2), 283–322.

Michael, K., & Miller, K. (2013). Big data: New opportunities and new challenges. *Computer*, *46*(6), 22–24. doi:10.1109/MC.2013.196

Michaud-Trevinal, A., & Stenger, T. (2014). Toward a conceptualization of the online shopping experience. *Journal of Retailing and Consumer Services*, *21*(3), 314–326. doi:10.1016/j.jretconser.2014.02.009

Miller, H. G., & Mork, P. (2013). From Data to Decisions: A Value Chain for Big Data. *IT Professional*, *15*(1), 57–59. doi:10.1109/MITP.2013.11

Milliman, R. E. (1982). Using Background Music to Affect the Behavior of Supermarket Shoppers. *Journal of Marketing*, *46*(2), 86–91. doi:10.2307/1251706

Milliman, R. E. (1986, Sept.). The Influence of Background Music on the Behavior of Restaurant Patrons. *The Journal of Consumer Research*, *13*, 286–289. doi:10.1086/209068

Mishra, P. K., & Anjani, S. (2010). *Supply Chain Management of Agricultural Commodities through Electronic Spot Exchanges*. Retrieved from http://ssrn.com/abstract=1728686

Mitchell, D. J., Kahn, B. E., & Knasko, S. C. (1995, Sept.). Theres Something in the Air: Effects of Ambient Odor on Consumer Decision Making. *The Journal of Consumer Research*, *22*, 229–238. doi:10.1086/209447

Mitroff, I. I., & Alpaslan, M. C. (2003). Preparing for evil. *Harvard Business Review*, *81*(4), 109–115. PMID:12687925

Modi, P., Mishra, D., Gulati, H., & Murugesan, K. (2009). Uttarakhand state cooperative federation: Can it help the horticulture farmers? *Vision—The Journal of Business Perspective, 13*(2), 53-61.

Mohamed, S., Ismail, O., & Hogan, O. (2012). *Data equity Unlocking the value of big data*. London: Whitepaper.

Mohanty, S., Jagadeesh, M., & Srivatsa, H. (2013). *Big data Imperatives: Enterprise "big data" Warehouse," BI'Implementations and Analytics*. Apress. doi:10.1007/978-1-4302-4873-6

Morris, M. (2012). *Online supply models: Who's doing what?* IGD Supply Chain Analysis.

Morris. (2012). *Online supply models: Who's doing what?* IGD Supply Chain Analysis.

Moschis, G. P. (1976). Shopping Orientations and Consumer Uses of Information. *Journal of Retailing*, *52*(2), 61–70, 93.

Moshtagh, M. S., & Taleizadeh, A. A. (2017). Stochastic integrated manufacturing and remanufacturing model with shortage, rework and quality based return rate in a closed loop supply chain. *Journal of Cleaner Production*, *141*, 1548–1573. doi:10.1016/j.jclepro.2016.09.173

Moussaid, M., Perozo, N., Garnier, S., Helbing, D., & Theraulaz, G. (2010). The Walking Behaviour of Pedestrian Social Groups and Its Impact on Crowd Dynamics. *PLoS ONE*, *5*(4), e10047. doi:10.1371/journal.pone.0010047 PMID:20383280

Murphy, C., Kaiser, G., Hu, L., & Wu, L. (2008). Properties of machine learning applications for use in metamorphic testing, *Proceeding of the 20th Internal Conference on Software Engineering and Knowledge Engineering (SEKE)*, 867-872.

Murthy, D. S., Gajanana, T. M., Sudha, M., & Dakshinamoorthy, V. (2009). Marketing and Post harvest losses in fruits: Its implications on Availability and economy. *Indian Journal of Agricultural Economics*, *64*(2), 259–275.

Myers, M., & Avison, D. (2002). An introduction to qualitative research in Information Systems. In *Qualitative Research in Information Systems* (pp. 3–12). London: Sage Publications. doi:10.4135/9781849209687.n1

Nair, A., & Kloss, D. J. (2006). An examination of the impact of coordinating supply chain policies and price markdowns on short lifecycle product retail performance. *International Journal of Production Economics*, *102*(2), 379–392. doi:10.1016/j.ijpe.2005.04.009

Nandita. (2014). *E-tailers growth ensnared in India's logistics jungle*. Reuters.com.

Narula, S. A. (2011). Reinventing cold chain industry in India: Need of the hour: Interview with Mr Sanjay Aggarwal. *Journal of Agribusiness in Developing and Emerging Economies*, *1*(2), jadee.2011.52401baa.001. doi:10.1108/jadee.2011.52401baa.001

Negi, S., & Anand, N. (2015b). Cold Chain: A Weak Link in the Fruits and Vegetables Supply Chain in India. *The IUP Journal of Supply Chain Management*, 48-62.

Negi, S., & Anand, N. (2016a). Factors Leading to Losses and Wastage in the Supply Chain of Fruits and Vegetables Sector in India. *Energy Infrastructure and Transportation Challenges and Way Forward-Conference Proceedings, International Conference on Management of Infrastructure* (pp. I 89 - I 105). Dehradun.

Negi, S., & Anand, N. (2016b). An Overview of Fruits and Vegetable's Retail Supply Chain Models in India. In N. Kamath, & S. Saurav (Eds.), Handbook of research on strategic supply chain management in the retail industry (pp. 170-187). Hershey, PA: Business Science Reference, IGI Global.

Negi, S., & Anand, N. (2014, December). Supply Chain Efficiency: An Insight from Fruits and Vegetables Sector in India. *Journal of Operations and Supply Chain Management*, *7*(2), 154–167. doi:10.12660/joscmv7n2p154-167

Negi, S., & Anand, N. (2015a). Issues and challenges in the supply chain of fruits & vegetables sector in India: A Review. *International Journal of Managing Value and Supply Chains*, *6*(2), 47–62. doi:10.5121/ijmvsc.2015.6205

Negi, S., & Anand, N. (2015c). Supply Chain of Fruits & Vegetables' Agribusiness in Uttarakhand (India): Major Issues and Challenges. *Journal of Supply Chain Management Systems*, *4*(1 & 2), 43–57.

Neslin, S. A., Grewal, D., Leghorn, R., Shankar, V., Teerling, M. L., Thomas, J. S., & Verhoef, P. C. (2006). Challenges and opportunities in multichannel customer management. *Journal of Service Research*, *9*(2), 95–112. doi:10.1177/1094670506293559

NHB. (2014). *Horticulture Statistics at a glance.* Retrieved February 21, 2017, from National Horticulture Board: http://nhb.gov.in/PDFViwer.aspx?enc=3ZOO8K5CzcdC/Yq6HcdIxC0U1kZZenFuNVXacDLxz28=

NHB. (2016). *3rd Advance Estimate of Area and Production of Horticulture Crops (2015-2016).* Retrieved March 21, 2017, from National Horticulture Board: http://nhb.gov.in/PDFViwer.aspx?enc=3ZOO8K5CzcdC/Yq6HcdIxC0U1kZZenFuNVXacDLxz28=

Nideau & Singer. (2014). *The Secret To Creating Loyalty Programs That Actually Work.* Businessinsider.com.

Norris, C., & Armstrong, G. (1999). *The Maximum Surveillance Society: The Rise of CCTV.* Oxford, UK: Berg.

Norrman, A., & Lindroth, R. (2004). Categorization of supply chain risk and risk management. In C. Brindley (Ed.), *Supply Chain Risk* (pp. 14–27). Ashgate Publishing.

Nuss, C., Sahamie, R., & Stindt, D. (2015). The reverse supply chain planning matrix: A classification scheme for planning problems in reverse logistics. *International Journal of Management Reviews*, *17*(4), 413–436. doi:10.1111/ijmr.12046

O'Cass, A., & Carlson, J. (2012). An e-retailing assessment of perceived website-service innovativeness: Implications for website quality evaluations, trust, loyalty and word of mouth. *Australasian Marketing Journal*, *20*(1), 28–36. doi:10.1016/j.ausmj.2011.10.012

Oberholzer-Gee, F., & Inamdar, S. N. (2004). Mercks recall of Rofecoxib—A strategic perspective. *The New England Journal of Medicine*, *351*(21), 2147–2149. doi:10.1056/NEJMp048284 PMID:15548771

Odonnell Company. (2014). *The benefits of a customer loyalty program.* Odonnellco.com.

Omnichannel Retail 2014 - Intelligence report. (2014, July). L2 Research.

ONICRA. (2012). *Indian Cold Chain Industry.* Retrieved January 25, 2015, from ONICRA: http://www.onicra.com/images/pdf/publications/coldchainindustryreportjune2014.pdf

Oracle. (n.d.). *The Store: The Intersection Of All Channels.* Retail TouchPoints E-Book.

Orrite, C., Martinez, F., Herrero, E., Ragheb, H., & Velastin, S. (2008). Independent Viewpoint Silhouette-based Human Action Modelling and Recognition. *Proc. 1st International Workshop on Machine Learning for Vision-based Motion Analysis in conjunction with the European Conference on Computer Vision (ECCV).*

Ozcan, M. (2007). *Affects on Quality and Durability of Harvest and Post-Harvest Practices in Horticultural Products.* Retrieved September 18, 2013, from http://www.carsambaziraatodasi.com/ab1_1.asp

Ozcan, M., & Balkaya, A. (1995). Causes of Harvest and Post-Harvest Losses on Fruits and Vegetables Product Grown in Amasya Province. *J. Ondokuz Mayıs Univ.* [in Turkish]. *Facul Agric., 10*(1), 51–61.

Ozcan, M., Balkaya, A., & Ceyhan, V. (1997). Analysis of Vegetable Marketing Activities in the Black Sea region. *First Symposium of Storage and Marketing in Horticultural Products*, 229-234s. (in Turkish)

Özceylan, E. (2016). Simultaneous optimization of closed- and open-loop supply chain networks with common components. *Journal of Manufacturing Systems, 41*, 143–156. doi:10.1016/j.jmsy.2016.08.008

Özceylan, E., Paksoy, T., & Bektas, T. (2014). Modeling and optimizing the integrated problem of closed-loop supply chain network design and disassembly line balancing. *Transportation Research Part E, Logistics and Transportation Review, 61*, 142–164. doi:10.1016/j.tre.2013.11.001

Paksoy, T., Bektas, T., & Özceylan, E. (2011). Operational and environmental performance measures in a multi-product closed-loop supply chain. *Transportation Research Part E, Logistics and Transportation Review, 47*(4), 532–546. doi:10.1016/j.tre.2010.12.001

Pal, K. (2016). *Supply Chain Coordination Based on Web Service, Supply Chain Management in the Big Data Era.* IGI Global.

Pantano, E., Iazzolino, G., & Migliano, G. (2013). Obsolescence risk in advanced technologies for retailing: A management perspective. *Journal of Retailing and Consumer Services, 20*(2), 225–233. doi:10.1016/j.jretconser.2013.01.002

Papadakis, I. S. (2006). Financial performance of supply chains after disruptions: An event study. *Supply Chain Management: An International Journal, 11*(1), 25–33. doi:10.1108/13598540610642448

Park, E. J., Kim, E. Y., Funches, V. M., & Foxx, W. (2012). Apparel product attributes, web browsing, an de-impulse buying on shopping websites. *Journal of Business Research, 65*(11), 1583–1589. doi:10.1016/j.jbusres.2011.02.043

Park, J.-S., & Lee, S.-W. (2008). An Example-Based Face Hallucination Method for SingleFrame, Low-Resolution Facial Images. *IEEE Transactions on Image Processing, 17*(10), 1806–1816. doi:10.1109/TIP.2008.2001394 PMID:18784029

Parssian, A. (2006). Managerial decision support with knowledge of accuracy and completeness of the relational aggregate functions. *Decision Support Systems, 42*(3), 1494–1502. doi:10.1016/j.dss.2005.12.005

Patino, L., Bremond, F., Evans, M., Shahrokni, A., & Ferryman, J. (2010). Video Activity and Reporting with Incremental Unsupervised Learning. *Proceedings Seventh IEEE Advanced Video and Signal-Based Surveillance (AVSS)*, 511-518. doi:10.1109/AVSS.2010.74

Patterson, K. A., Grimm, C. M., & Corsi, T. M. (2003). Adopting new technologies for supply chain management. *Transportation Research Part E, Logistics and Transportation Review, 3*(2), 95–121. doi:10.1016/S1366-5545(02)00041-8

Paulraj, A., Lado, A. A., & Chen, I. J. (2008). Inter-organizational communication as a relational competency: Antecedents and performance outcomes in collaborative buyer-supplier relationships. *Journal of Operations Management, 26*(1), 45–64. doi:10.1016/j.jom.2007.04.001

Paulsson, U. (2005). *Developing a Supply Chain Flow Risk Model.* Final paper to the NOFOMA 2005 Conference, Copenhagen, Denmark.

Pazhani, S., & Ravindran, A. R. (2014). Design of closed loop supply chain networks. *International Journal of Business Analytics, 1*(1), 43–66. doi:10.4018/ijban.2014010104

Pecoraro, M., & Uusitalo, O. (2014). Exploring the everyday retail experience: The discourses of style and design. *Journal of Consumer Behaviour, 13*(6), 429–441. doi:10.1002/cb.1492

Pentecost, R., & Andrews, L. (2010). Fashion retailing and the bottom line: The effects of generational cohorts, gender, fashion fanship, attitudes, and impulse buying on fashion expenditure. *Journal of Retailing and Consumer Services, 17*(1), 43–52. doi:10.1016/j.jretconser.2009.09.003

Peppers & Rogers Group. (2009). *Circumstances and Customers Have Changed: Has Your Loyalty Program Kept Pace?* Oracle.com

Peri, C. (2006). The universe of food quality. *Food Quality and Preference, 17*(1-2), 3–8. doi:10.1016/j.foodqual.2005.03.002

Petersen, J. A., & Kumar, V. (2009). Are product returns a necessary evil? Antecedents and consequences. *Journal of Marketing, 73*(3), 35–51.

Pfohl, H., Kohler, H., & Thomas, D. (2010). State of the art in supply chain risk management research: Empirical and conceptual findings and a roadmap for the implementation in practice. *Logistics Research., 2*(1), 33–44. doi:10.1007/s12159-010-0023-8

Pipino, L. L., Lee, Y. W., & Wang, R. Y. (2002). Data quality assessment. *Communications of the ACM, 45*(4), 211–218. doi:10.1145/505248.506010

Poles, R. (2012). Modeling closed loop supply chain systems. In Z. Luo (Ed.), *Advanced analytics for green and sustainable economic development: Supply chain models and financial technologies* (pp. 157–186). Hershey, PA: IGI Global. doi:10.4018/978-1-61350-156-6.ch010

Pollamarasetty, S., & Potti, R. (2016). Omni-channel retailing: enriching customers' shopping experience. In N. Kamath & S. Saurav (Eds.), *Handbook of Research on Strategic Supply Chain Management in the Retail Industry* (pp. 233–249). Hershey, PA: IGI Global. doi:10.4018/978-1-4666-9894-9.ch013

Porter, M. E. (1980). *Competitive strategy: technique for analyzing industries and competitors.* New York: Free Press.

Prashar, S., Vijay, T. S., & Parsad, C. (2015). Antecedents to online shopping: Factors influencing the selection of web portal. *International Journal of E-Business Research, 11*(1), 35–55. doi:10.4018/ijebr.2015010103

Pratapwar, S. S. (2016). Supply chain hub and spoke model for convenience stores. In N. Kamath & S. Saurav (Eds.), *Handbook of research on strategic supply chain management in the retail industry* (pp. 39–54). Hershey, PA: IGI Global. doi:10.4018/978-1-4666-9894-9.ch003

Priebatsch, S., & McFeeley, R. (2011). *Engineering Successful Customer Loyalty Programs.* Huffingtonpost.com.

Punj, G. (2012). Consumer decision making on the web: A theoritical analysis and research guidelines. *Psychology and Marketing, 29*(10), 791–803. doi:10.1002/mar.20564

Raff, H., & Schmitt, N. (2012). Imports and the structure of retail markets. *The Canadian Journal of Economics. Revue Canadienne dEconomique*, *45*(4), 1431–1455. doi:10.1111/j.1540-5982.2012.01743.x

Ragheb, H., Velastin, S., Remagnino, P., & Ellis, T. (2008). ViHASi: Virtual Human Action Silhouette Data for the Evaluation of Silhouette-Based Action Recognition Methods. *Proceedings Computer Vision and Pattern Recognition (CVPR'07)*, 1-8.

Rajagopal, D. (2009). Technology and retailing and firms: Challenges ahead. In D. Rajagopal (Ed.), *Information communication technologies and globalization of retailing applications* (pp. 335–344). Hershey, PA: IGI Global. doi:10.4018/978-1-60566-248-0.ch015

Rajakumar, M., & Sushma, M. (2013). Challenges and Opportunities of big data Analytics in Business Applications. *Inter. J.Electro. Communicat.Computer Engineer.*, *4*(6), 6–9.

Rajaram, K. (2001). Assortment planning in fashion retailing: Methodology, application and analysis. *European Journal of Operational Research*, *129*(1), 186–208. doi:10.1016/S0377-2217(99)00406-3

Ramesh, P., Singh, M., & Rao, A. S. (2005, February 25). Organic farming: Its relevance to the Indian context. *Current Science*, *88*(4), 563.

Ramezani, M., Kimiagari, A. M., & Karimi, B. (2014). Closed-loop supply chain network design: A financial approach. *Applied Mathematical Modelling*, *38*(15/16), 4099–4119. doi:10.1016/j.apm.2014.02.004

Ramish, A., Azhar, T. M., & Rasheed, H. (2017). Building a comprehensive service supply chain conceptual framework: A step ahead, based on comparative analysis of previous frameworks. *International Journal of Services and Operations Management*, *26*(1), 97–121. doi:10.1504/IJSOM.2017.080679

Ram, M. (2013). To identify the factors impacting customer satisfaction in food retail supermarkets. *International Journal of Research and Development - A Management Review*, *2*, 2319–5479.

Rathore, J. (2010). Cold chain infrastructure for frozen food- a weak link in Indian retail sector. *The IUP Journal of Supply Chain Management, 7*(1-2), 90-103.

Rathore, J., Sharma, A., & Saxena, K. (2010). Cold Chain Infrastructure for Frozen Food:A Weak Link in Indian Retail Sector. *The IUP Journal of Supply Chain Management*, *7*(1-2), 90–103.

Ray, S., Boyaci, T., & Aras, N. (2005). Optimal prices and trade-in rebates for durable, remanufacturable products. *Manufacturing and Services Operations Management*, *7*(3), 208–228. doi:10.1287/msom.1050.0080

Read, B. (2009). *Top Tips To Build and Keep Customer Loyalty With CRM*. Tmcnet.com.

Reddy, P. P. (2004). Vegetable Research in India-An IIHR Perspective. Impact of Vegetable Research in India, National Centre for Agrıcultural Economics and Polıcy Research, ICAR.

Reeves, B., & Nass, C. (2002). *The Media Equation* (2nd ed.). Stanford, CA: CSLI.

Reichheld, F. F., & Schefter, P. (2000). E-loyalty: Your secret weapon on the web. *Harvard Business Review*, *78*(4), 105–113.

Retail scenario in India: Unlimited opportunity. (2003). McKinsey-CII report.

Retail Trade Sales. (2013). Retrieved from http://www.statssa.gov.za/publications/P62421/P62421March2013.pdf

Rezapour, S., Farahani, R. Z., Fahimnia, B., Govindan, K., & Mansouri, Y. (2015). Competitive closed-loop supply chain network design with price-dependent demands. *Journal of Cleaner Production*, *93*, 251–272. doi:10.1016/j.jclepro.2014.12.095

Rigby, D. (2011b, Dec. 7). Omnichannel retail delivering on customer expectations. *Harvard Business Review*, 1-4.

Rigby, D. (2014). *Online Shopping Isn't as Profitable as You Think.* Retrieved from https://hbr.org/2014/08/online-shopping-isnt-as-profitable-as-you-think/

Rigby, D., Kris, M., Josh, C., & Suzanne, T. (2012). Omnichannel retailing: digital disruption and retailer opportunities. *Bain Retail Holiday Newsletter.* Retrieved March 29, 2017, from http://goo. gl/47MwZX

Rigby, D. (2011a). The future of shopping. *Harvard Business Review*, *89*(12), 65–76.

Ritchie, B., & Brindley, C. (2007). An emergent framework for supply chain risk management and performance measurement. *The Journal of the Operational Research Society*, *58*(11), 1398–1411. doi:10.1057/palgrave.jors.2602412

Ritchie, R. L., & Marshall, D. V. (1993). *Business Risk Management.* London: Chapman & Hall.

Roberts, J. A., & Manolis, C. (2012). Cooking up a recipe for self-control: The three ingredients of self-control and its impact on impulse buying. *Journal of Marketing Theory and Practice*, *20*(2), 173–188. doi:10.2753/MTP1069-6679200204

Robotis, A., Bhattacharya, S., & van Wassenhove, L. N. (2005). The effect of remanufacturing on procurement decisions for resellers in secondary markets. *European Journal of Operational Research*, *163*(3), 688–705. doi:10.1016/j.ejor.2004.01.013

Rogers, D. S., & Tibben-Lembke, R. S. (1998). *Going backwards: Reverse logistics trends and practices.* Pittsburgh, PA: Reverse Logistics Executive Council.

Rohm, A. J., & Swaminathan, V. (2004). A typology of online shoppers based on shopping motivations. *Journal of Business Research*, *57*(7), 748–757. doi:10.1016/S0148-2963(02)00351-X

Rose, D. F. (2003). *Introduction to e-Supply Chain Management: Engaging Technology to Build Market-Winning Business Partnerships. St.* Lucie Press.

Rose, S., & Samouel, P. (2009). Internal psychological versus external market-driven determinants of the amount of consumer information search amongst experienced online shoppers. *Journal of Marketing Management*, *25*(1/2), 171–190. doi:10.1362/026725709X410089

Ross, D. F. (2011). Introduction to supply chain management technologies (2nd ed.). Boca Raton, FL: CRC Press.

Rowell, J. (2015). Omni-channel retailing: The changing battleground. *Romanian Distribution Committee Magazine*, *6*(4), 10–17.

Rowley, J. (2001). Window shopping and browsing opportunities in cyberspace. *Journal of Consumer Behaviour*, *1*(4), 369–378. doi:10.1002/cb.81

Ruben, R., Boselie, D., & Lu, H. (2007). Vegetables procurement by Asian supermarkets: A transaction cost approach. *Supply Chain Management: An International Journal*, *12*(1), 60–68. doi:10.1108/13598540710724365

Rubio, S., & Corominas, A. (2008). Optimal manufacturing-remanufacturing policies in a lean production environment. *Computers & Industrial Engineering*, *55*(1), 234–242. doi:10.1016/j.cie.2007.12.009

Russom, P. (2011). *Big data analytics.* TDWI Best Practices Report, Fourth Quarter.

Saccani, N., Johansson, P., & Perona, M. (2007). Configuring the after-sales service supply chain: A multiple case study. *International Journal of Production Economics, 110*(1–2), 52–69. doi:10.1016/j.ijpe.2007.02.009

Sahamie, R., Stindt, D., & Nuss, C. (2013). Transdisciplinary research in sustainable operations: An application to closed-loop supply chains. *Business Strategy and the Environment, 22*(4), 245–268. doi:10.1002/bse.1771

Sahoo, N., Singh, P. V., & Mukhopadhyay, T. (2012). A Hidden Markov Model for Collaborative Filtering. *MIS Quarterly, 36*(4), 1329–1356.

Salin, V., & Nayga, R.M. (2002). A cold chain network for food exports to developing countries. *International Journal of Physical Distribution & Logistics Management, 33*(10), 918-933.

Salin, V., & Nayga, R. M. Jr. (2003). A cold chain network for food exports to developing countries. *International Journal of Physical Distribution & Logistics Management, 33*(10), 918–933. doi:10.1108/09600030310508717

Sánchez-Pérez, M., Estrella-Ramón, A., Segovia-López, C., & Marín-Carrillo, M. B. (2014). Multichannel retailing and consumer behaviour: Strategy design and implementation. *International Journal of Applied Behavioral Economics, 3*(4), 17–39. doi:10.4018/ijabe.2014100102

Sapra, R., & Joshi, S. (2011, Nov-Dec). *Cold Chain Logistics Sector Analysis Nov-Dec.* Retrieved February 4, 2014, from Business Design: http://www.businessdesign.co.in/webfiles/Project/312313092332Cold%20Chain%20Logistics_Jan.2011.pdf

SARDI. (2006). *Maintaining the cold chain: air freight of perishables.* South Australian Research and Development Institute. Retrieved from http://www.australianairfreight.com/vac/pdfs/airfreight_perish.pdf

Sarkis, J. (2003). A strategic decision framework for green supply chain management. *Journal of Cleaner Production, 11*(4), 397–409. doi:10.1016/S0959-6526(02)00062-8

Sathi, A. (2012). Big data analytics: Disruptive technologies for changing the game. MC Press Online, LLC.

Saunders, M., Lewis, P., & Thornhill, A. (2009). Research methods for business students (5th ed.). London: Pearson Education Limited.

Saurav, S., & Potti, R. (2016). Cold Chain Logistics in India: A Study. In A. Dwivedi (Ed.), Innovative Solutions for Implementing Global Supply Chains in Emerging Markets (pp. 159-172). IGI Global. doi:10.4018/978-1-4666-9795-9.ch011

Saurav, S. (2016). Customer experience impacting retail management: Study of customer centricity strategy by retailers. In N. Kamath & S. Saurav (Eds.), *Handbook of research on strategic supply chain management in the retail industry* (pp. 130–150). Hershey, PA: IGI Global. doi:10.4018/978-1-4666-9894-9.ch008

Savaskan, R. C., Bhattacharya, S., & van Wassenhove, L. N. (2004). Closed loop supply chain models with product remanufacturing. *Management Science, 50*(2), 239–252. doi:10.1287/mnsc.1030.0186

Sawant, N., & Shah, H. (2013). *Big data Application Architecture. Big data Application Architecture Q & A.* Apress. doi:10.1007/978-1-4302-6293-0

Scannapieco, M., & Catarci, T. (2002). Data quality under a computer science perspective. *Archivi and Computer*, 21-15.

Scarpi, D., Pizzi, G., & Visentin, M. (2014). Shopping for fun or shopping to buy: Is it different online and offline? *Journal of Retailing and Consumer Services, 21*(3), 258–267. doi:10.1016/j.jretconser.2014.02.007

Schaeffer, C. (n.d.). *How to Create a Customer Loyalty Program That Works.* Crmsearch.com.

Schaeffer. (n.d.). *How to Succeed in Omni-Channel Retailing*. crmsearch.com.

Schenkel, M., Krikke, H., Caniëls, M. C. J., & van der Laan, E. (2015). Creating integral value for stakeholders in closed loop supply chains. *Journal of Purchasing and Supply Management*, *21*(3), 155–166. doi:10.1016/j.pursup.2015.04.003

Schoenbachler, D. D., & Gordon, G. L. (2002). Multi-channel shopping: Understanding what drives channel choice. *Journal of Consumer Marketing*, *19*(1), 42–53. doi:10.1108/07363760210414943

Schoenthaler, R. (2003). Creating real-time supply chain visibility - Even in aftermarket sales and service, transparency is crucial. *Electronic Business*, *29*, 12–12.

Selani, M. M., Brazaca, S. G., Dos Santos Dias, C. T., Ratnayake, W. S., Flores, R. A., & Bianchini, A. (2014). Characterisation and potential application of pineapple pomace in an extruded product for fibre enhancement. *Food Chemistry*, *163*, 23–30. doi:10.1016/j.foodchem.2014.04.076 PMID:24912691

Sen, A. (2008). The US fashion industry: A supply chain review. *International Journal of Production Economics*, *114*(2), 571–593. doi:10.1016/j.ijpe.2007.05.022

Senior, A., Pankanti, A., Brown, L., Ying-Li, T., Ekin, A., Connell, J., & Lu, M. et al. (2005). Enabling Privacy through Computer Vision. *IEEE Security and Privacy*, *3*(3), 50–57. doi:10.1109/MSP.2005.65

Sepúlveda-Rojas, J. P., Rojas, F., Valdés-González, H., & San Martín, M. (2015). Forecasting Models Selection Mechanism for Supply Chain Demand Estimation. *Procedia Computer Science*, *55*, 1060–1068. doi:10.1016/j.procs.2015.07.068

Shah, N. (2004). Pharmaceutical supply chains: Key issues and strategies for optimization. *Computers & Chemical Engineering*, *4*(6-7), 929–941. doi:10.1016/j.compchemeng.2003.09.022

Shakourloo, A., Kazemi, A., & Javad, M. O. M. (2016). A new model for more effective supplier selection and remanufacturing process in a closed-loop supply chain. *Applied Mathematical Modelling*, *40*(23/24), 9914–9931. doi:10.1016/j.apm.2016.06.039

Shearer, C. (2000). The CRISP-DM model: The new blueprint for data mining. *Journal of Data Warehousing*, *5*(4), 13–22.

Shefi, Y., & Rice, J. B. (2005). A Supply Chain View of the Resilient Enterprise. *MIT Sloan Management Review*, *47*(1), 41–48.

Shergill, G. S., & Chen, Z. (2005). Web-based shopping: Consumers' attitude towards online shopping in New Zealand. *Journal of Electronic Commerce Research*, *6*(2), 78–92.

Shih, H. P. (2004). An empirical study on predicting user acceptance of e-shopping on the Web. *Information & Management*, *41*(3), 351–368. doi:10.1016/S0378-7206(03)00079-X

Shi, J., Zhang, G., & Sha, J. (2011). Optimal production and pricing policy for a closed loop system. *Resources, Conservation and Recycling*, *55*(6), 639–647. doi:10.1016/j.resconrec.2010.05.016

Shmueli, G., & Koppius, O. (2011). Predictive Analytics in Information Systems Research. *Management Information Systems Quarterly*, *35*(3), 553–572.

Shobeiri, S., Mazaheri, E., & Laroche, M. (2015). Shopping online for goods vs. services: Where do experiential features help more? *International Journal of Consumer Studies*, *39*(2), 172–179. doi:10.1111/ijcs.12165

Shukla, D. (2010). *UNCTAD*. Retrieved January 22, 2014, from http://unctad.org/sections/wcmu/docs/ettcp05_en.pdf

Shukla, M., & Jharkharia, S. (2013). Agri-fresh produce supply chain management: A state-of-the-artliterature review. *International Journal of Operations & Production Management*, *33*(2), 114–158. doi:10.1108/01443571311295608

Shukla, P., & Vyas, P. (2016). An epigrammatic view of e-retailing in India: Prospects and retrospects. In S. Dixit & A. Sinha (Eds.), *E-retailing challenges and opportunities in the global marketplace* (pp. 121–131). Hershey, PA: IGI Global. doi:10.4018/978-1-4666-9921-2.ch006

Sibiraj, P. R. (2015). *Benefits of customer loyalty programs*. Lightrains.com.

Siegel, E. (2013). *Predictive analytics: The power to predict who will click, buy, lie or die*. Hoboken, NJ: John Wiley & Sons Inc.

Singhal, P., Agarwal, G., & Lal Mittal, M. (2011). Supply Chain Risk Management: Review, classification and future research directions. I. J. *Bus. Sci. App. Man.*, *6*, 15–42.

Singh, B., Banerjee, M. K., Singh, K. P., Pandey, P. K., Sudhakar, P., & Rai, M. (2004). *AICRP on Vegetables in India: Evolution andAchievements Impact of Vegetable Research in India*. New Delhi: National Centre for Agricultural Economics and Policy Research,ICAR.

Singh, R., Kushwaha, R., & Verma, S. K. (2008). An economic appraisal of post-harvest losses in vegetable in Uttar Pradesh. *Indian Journal of Agricultural Economics*, *63*(3), 378.

Singh, S., & Singh, N. (2012). Big data analytics. *2012 International Conference on Communication, Information & Computing Technology (ICCICT)*, 1–4.

Sin, L., & Tse, A. (2002). Profiling Internet shoppers in Hong Kong: Demographic, psychographic, attitudinal and experiential factors. *Journal of International Consumer Marketing*, *15*(1), 7–29. doi:10.1300/J046v15n01_02

Skogster, P., & Uotila, V. (2010). Collecting consumer behavior data with WLAN. In J. Wang (Ed.), *Innovations in supply chain management for information systems: Novel approaches* (pp. 125–141). Hershey, PA: IGI Global. doi:10.4018/978-1-60566-974-8.ch004

Smith & Curnow. (1966, June). 'Arousal Hypothesis' and the Effects of Music on Purchasing Behavior. *Journal of Applied Psychology, 50*, 255-56.

Smith, A. D. (2017). Exploring the inherent growth of e-tailing via e-personalization and technological innovations. *International Journal of Innovation in the Digital Economy*, *8*(1), 19–46. doi:10.4018/IJIDE.2017010102

Smith, D. (2006). Design and management concepts for high care food processing. *British Food Journal*, *108*(1), 54–60. doi:10.1108/00070700610637634

Smith, D. N., & Sivakumar, K. (2004). Flow and Internet shopping behavior: A conceptual model and research propositions. *Journal of Business Research*, *57*(10), 1199–1208. doi:10.1016/S0148-2963(02)00330-2

Smriti, K. (2016). Retail supply chain management trends: Past, present and future. In N. Kamath & S. Saurav (Eds.), *Handbook of research on strategic supply chain management in the retail industry* (pp. 1–18). Hershey, PA: IGI Global. doi:10.4018/978-1-4666-9894-9.ch001

Sodhi, M. S., & Tang, C. S. (2006). Managing Supply Chain Risk. New York: Springer.

Sodhi, M. S., Son, B. G., & Tang, C. S. (2012). Researchers perspectives on supply chain risk management. *Production and Operations Management*, *21*(1), 1–13. doi:10.1111/j.1937-5956.2011.01251.x

Sodhi, M. S., & Tang, C. S. (2012). *Managing Supply Chain Risk*. Springer. doi:10.1007/978-1-4614-3238-8

Soleimani, H., & Kannan, G. (2015). A hybrid particle swarm optimization and genetic algorithm for closed-loop supply chain network design in large-scale networks. *Applied Mathematical Modelling, 39*(14), 3990–4012. doi:10.1016/j.apm.2014.12.016

Souza, G. C. (2013). Closed-loop supply chains: A critical review, and future research. *Decision Sciences, 44*(1), 7–38. doi:10.1111/j.1540-5915.2012.00394.x

Spangenberg, E. R., Crowley, A. E., & Henderson, P. W. (1996, April). Improving the Store Environment: Do Olfactory Cues Affect Evaluations and Behaviors. *Journal of Marketing, 60*, 67–80. doi:10.2307/1251931

Spiess, J., TJoens, Y., Dragnea, R., Spencer, P., & Philippart, L. (2014). Using big data to improve customer experience and business performance. *Bell Labs Technical J., 18*(4), 3–17. doi:10.1002/bltj.21642

Spindler, T., Wartmann, C., Hovestadt, L., Roth, D., Van Gool, L., & Steffen, A. (2008). Privacy in Video Surveilled Spaces. *Computers & Security, 16*(2), 199–222. doi:10.3233/JCS-2008-16205

Staflund, L., & Kersmark, M. (2015). *Omni-channel retailing: Blurring the lines between online and offline* (Dissertation). Retrieved March 29, 2017, from http://urn.kb.se/resolve?urn=urn:nbn:se:hj:diva-27392

Starbird, S. A. (2001). Penalties, rewards, and inspection: Provisions for quality in supply chain contracts. *Journal of Operations Research, 52*(1), 109–115. doi:10.1057/palgrave.jors.2601048

Starvish, M. (2011). *Customer Loyalty Programs That Work*. Hbswk.hbs.edu.

Sternbeck, M. G., & Kuhn, H. (2014). An integrative approach to determine store delivery patterns in grocery retailing. *Transportation Research Part E, Logistics and Transportation Review, 70*, 205–224. doi:10.1016/j.tre.2014.06.007

Stock, J. R. (2013). Supply chain management: A look back, a look ahead. *Supply Chain Quarterly, 2*, 22–26.

Storbacka, K., Strandvik, T., & Gro¨nroos, C. (1994). Managing customer relationships for profit: The dynamics of relationship quality. *International Journal of Service Industry Management, 5*(5), 21–38. doi:10.1108/09564239410074358

Strydom, J. (2015). David Against Goliath: Predicting The Survival Of Formal Small Businesses In Soweto. *Inter.Busin. Econ.Res. J., 14*(3), 463–476.

C. Sun, H. Talbot, S. Ourselin, & T. Adriaansen (Eds.). (2003). *Proceedings of the Seventh International Conference on Digital Image Computing: Techniques and Applications, DICTA 2003*. Sydney, Australia: CSIRO Publishing.

Svilvar, M., Charkraborty, A. & Kenora, A. (2013, Oct.). Big data analytics in marketing. *OR/MS Today*, 22-25.

Syntetos, A. A., Babai, Z., Boylan, J. E., Kolassa, S., & Nikolopoulos, K. (2016). Supply chain forecasting: Theory, practice, their gap and the future. *European Journal of Operational Research, 252*(1), 1–26. doi:10.1016/j.ejor.2015.11.010

Tabolt, S., Lefebvre, E., & Lefebvre, L. A. (2007). Closed-loop supply chain activities and derived benefits in manufacturing SMEs. *Journal of Manufacturing Technology Management, 18*(6), 627–658. doi:10.1108/17410380710763831

Talaei, M., Moghaddam, B. F., Pishvaee, M. S., Bozorgi-Amiri, A., & Gholamnejad, S. (2016). A robust fuzzy optimization model for carbon-efficient closed-loop supply chain network design problem: A numerical illustration in electronics industry. *Journal of Cleaner Production, 113*, 662–673. doi:10.1016/j.jclepro.2015.10.074

Taleb, N. N. (2007). *The Black Swan: The Impact of the Highly Improbable*. New York: Random House.

Tambo, T. (2014). Collaboration on technological innovation in Danish fashion chains: A network perspective. *Journal of Retailing and Consumer Services, 21*(5), 827–835. doi:10.1016/j.jretconser.2014.02.016

Tambo, T. (2015). Fashion retail innovation: About context, antecedents, and outcome in technological change projects. In E. Pantano (Ed.), *Successful technological integration for competitive advantage in retail settings* (pp. 269–294). Hershey, PA: IGI Global. doi:10.4018/978-1-4666-8297-9.ch012

Tambo, T. (2015). Omni-channel retail information systems. In *Encyclopedia of Information Science and Technology* (3rd ed.; pp. 874–882). IGI Global. doi:10.4018/978-1-4666-5888-2.ch083

Tang, C.S. (2012). Robust Strategies for Mitigating Supply Chain Disruptions. *International Journal of Logistics Research and Applications, 9*(1), 33-45.

Tang, C. S. (2006). Perspectives in supply chain risk management. *International Journal of Production Economics, 103*(2), 451–488. doi:10.1016/j.ijpe.2005.12.006

Tang, C. S. (2006). Robust Strategies for Mitigating Supply Chain Disruptions. *International Journal of Logistics Research and Applications, 9*(1), 33–45. doi:10.1080/13675560500405584

Tang, O., & Nurmaya Musa, S. (2011). Identifying risk issues and research advancements in supply chain risk management. I.J.P. *E (Norwalk, Conn.), 133*(1), 25–34.

Tate, A. (2013). *Bigdoor blog- Top 10 Retail Loyalty Programs.* Bigdoor.com.

Tatlidil, F., Kiral, T., Gunes, A., Demir, K., Erdemir, G., & Fidan, H. (2003). *Economic Analysis of Crop losses during Pre-Harvest and Harvest Periods in Tomato Production in the Ayaşand Nallıhan Districts of Ankara Province.* Academic Press.

Tekiner, F., & Keane, J. A. (2013). *Big Data Framework.* Paper presented at the 2013 IEEE International Conference on Systems, Man, and Cybernetics, Manchester, UK. doi:10.1109/SMC.2013.258

Teller, C., & Reutterer, T. (2008). The evolving concept of retail attractiveness: What makes retail agglomerations attractive when customers shop at them? *Journal of Retailing and Consumer Services, 15*(3), 127–143. doi:10.1016/j.jretconser.2007.03.003

Terpend, R., Tyler, B. B., Krause, D. R., & Handfield, R. B. (2008). Buyer-supplier relationships: Derived value over two decades. *Journal of Supply Chain Management, 44*(2), 28–55. doi:10.1111/j.1745-493X.2008.00053.x

Terry, J. (2010). *Donofrio.* RIS News –RS&S Advanced Planning and Optimization Series.

Teunter, R., van der Laan, E., & Inderfurth, K. (2000). How to set the holding cost rates in average inventory models with reverse logistics. *Omega, 28*(4), 409–415. doi:10.1016/S0305-0483(99)00070-5

The Agriculture and Food Value Chain. (2013). KPMG Report.

The great Indian retail revolution. (2004). Rediff.com.

The omni-channel opportunity for retailers: What's the story? (n.d.). *The Guardian.*

The omni-channel opportunity for retailers: What's the story?. (n.d.). *The Guardian.*

Thiell, M., Zuluaga, J. P., Montañez, J. P., & van Hoof, B. (2011). Green logistics: Global practices and their implementation in emerging markets. In Z. Luo (Ed.), *Green finance and sustainability: Environmentally-aware business models and technologies* (pp. 334–357). Hershey, PA: IGI Global. doi:10.4018/978-1-60960-531-5.ch018

Thomas. (2006). *Using risk management tools to manage the integrity of the cold chain.* Cold Chain-Management, 2nd International Workshop, Bonn, Germany. Retrieved from http://ccm.ytally.com/fileadmin/user_upload/downloads/12_SCHMITZ.PDF

Thomson, G. (2014). *How To Create Effective B2B Loyalty Programmes*. Customerstrategynetwork.com.

Thun, J. H., & Hoenig, D. (2011). An empirical analysis of supply chain risk management in the German automotive industry. I.J.P. *E (Norwalk, Conn.)*, *131*(1), 242–249.

Tickner, A. H., & Poulton, E. C. (1973). Monitoring up to 16 Synthetic Television Pictures Showing a Great Deal of Movement. *Ergonomics*, *16*(4), 381–401. doi:10.1080/00140137308924529 PMID:28086276

Timm, P. R. (2007). *Technology and Customer Service: Profitable Relationship Building*. Searchcrm.techtarget.com.

Troger, K., Hensel, O., & Burkert, A. (2007). Conservation of Onion and Tomato in Niger - Assessment of Post-Harvest Losses and Drying Methods. In *Conference on International Agricultural Research for Development*. University of Kassel-Witzenhausen and University of Gottingen.

Turan. (2008). *Post-harvest Practices on Fruits*. Author.

Turban, E., King, D., Viehland, D., & Lee, J. (2006). *Electronic commerce: A managerial perspective*. Upper Saddle River, NJ: Prentice Hall.

Tweed, D., & Ferryman, J. (2008). Enhancing Change Detection in Low-Quality Surveillance Video with Markov Random Fields. *Proc. 1st ACM International Workshop on Vision Networks for Behaviour Analysis (VNBA'08).*

Ularu, E., Puican, F., Apostu, A., & Velicanu, M. (2012). Perspectives on big data and big data Analytics. *Database Syst. J.*, *3*(4), 3–15.

Valera, M., Velastin, S., Ellis, A.-L., & Ferryman, J. (2011). Communication Mechanisms and Middleware for Distributed Video Surveillance. *IEEE Transactions on Circuits and Systems for Video Technology*, *21*(12), 1795–1809. doi:10.1109/TCSVT.2011.2133850

Value Chains in Agriculture. (2015). *Food and Agri-Products Sectors*. Government of Canada.

van der Laan, E., van Dalen, J., Rohrmoser, M., & Simpson, R. (2016). Demand forecasting and order planning for humanitarian logistics: An empirical assessment. *Journal of Operations Management*, *45*, 114–122. doi:10.1016/j.jom.2016.05.004

Van Reeuwijk, L. P. (n.d.). *Guidelines for quality management in soil and plant laboratories*. Rome Publication #M-90. Retrieved from http://www.fao.org/docrep/w7295e/w7295e00.HTM

Vanany, I., Zailani, S., & Pujawan, N. (2009). Supply chain risk management: Literature review and future research. *International Journal of Information Systems and Supply Chain Management*, *2*(1), 16–33. doi:10.4018/jisscm.2009010102

Veena, Babu, K. N., & Venkatesha, H. R. (2011). Supply Chain: A Differentiator in Marketing Fresh Produce. *The IUP Journal of Supply Chain Management, 8*(1), 23-36.

Verhoef, P. C., Kannan, P. K., & Inman, J. J. (2015). From multi-channel retailing to omni-channel retailing introduction to the special issue on multi-channel retailing. *Journal of Retailing*, *91*(2), 174–181. doi:10.1016/j.jretai.2015.02.005

Verma, A., & Singh, K. (2004). An economic analysis of post harvest losses in fresh vegetables. *Indian Journal of Agricultural Marketing*, *18*(1), 134–139.

Violino, B. (2015, July 31). 5 Things You Need to Know about data lakes. *CIO*, *28*(10), 17–17.

Viswanadham, N. (2007). *Can India be food basket for the world?* Working Paper Series, IBS, Hyderabad. Retrieved from http://www.cccindia.co/corecentre/Database/Docs/Docfiles/Can_india_be.pdf

Viswanadham, N. (2007). *Can India be the food basket for the world?* Working Paper series, IBS, Hyderabad. Retrieved from http://www.cccindia.co/corecentre/Database/Docs/DocFiles/Can_India_be.pdf

Vorst, J. V., & Beulens, A. (2002). Identifying sources of uncertainty to generate supply chain redesign strategies. *International Journal of Physical Distribution & Logistics Management*, *32*(6), 409–430. doi:10.1108/09600030210437951

Wachter, K., Vitell, S. J., Shelton, R. K., & Park, K. (2012). Exploring consumer orientation toward returns: unethical dimensions. *Business Ethics: A European Review*, *21*(1), 115–128.

Wacker, J. G. (1998). A definition of theory: Research guidelines for different theory building for different theory-building research methods in operations management. *Journal of Operations Management*, *16*(4), 361–385. doi:10.1016/S0272-6963(98)00019-9

Waller, M. A., & Fawcett, S. E. (2013). Data Science, Predictive Analytics, and Big Data: A Revolution That Will Transform Supply Chain Design and Management. *Journal of Business Logistics*, *34*(2), 77–84. doi:10.1111/jbl.12010

Walsh, G., Möhring, M., Koot, C., & Schaarschmidt, M. (2014). Preventive product returns management systems - A review and model. *Proceedings of the European Conference on Information Systems*, 1–12.

Walters, D., & Jones, P. (2001). Value and value chains in healthcare: A quality management perspective. *The TQM Magazine*, *13*(5), 319–333. doi:10.1108/EUM0000000005858

Walters, D., & Lancaster, G. (2008). Implementing value strategy through the value chain. *Management Decision*, *38*(3), 160–178. doi:10.1108/EUM0000000005344

Wang, H. F., & Hsu, H. W. (2010). A closed-loop logistic model with a spanning-tree based genetic algorithm. *Computers & Operations Research*, *37*(2), 376–389. doi:10.1016/j.cor.2009.06.001

Wang, H. F., & Hsu, H. W. (2012). A possibilistic approach to the modeling and resolution of uncertain closed-loop logistics. *Fuzzy Optimization and Decision Making*, *11*(2), 177–208. doi:10.1007/s10700-012-9120-2

Wang, R. Y., & Kon, H. B. (1993). Towards total data quality management (TDQM). In R. Y. Wanf (Ed.), *Information technology in action: Trends and perspectives*. Englewood Cliffs, NJ: Prentice-Hall.

Wang, R. Y., Storey, V. C., & Firth, C. P. (1995). A framework for analysis of data quality research. *IEEE Transactions on Knowledge and Data Engineering*, *7*(4), 623–640. doi:10.1109/69.404034

Wang, R. Y., & Strong, D. M. (1996). Beyond Accuracy: What data quality means to data consumers. *Journal of Management Information Systems*, *12*(4), 5–33. doi:10.1080/07421222.1996.11518099

Ward, M. R., & Lee, M. J. (2000). Internet shopping consumer search and product branding. *Journal of Product and Brand Management*, *9*(1), 6–20. doi:10.1108/10610420010316302

Watson, M., Lewis, S., Cacioppi, P., & Jayaraman, J. (2013). *Supply chain network design – applying optimization and analytics to the global supply chain*. FT Press.

Watson, H. J. (2015). Data Lakes, Data Labs, and Sandboxes. *Business Intelligence Journal*, *20*(1), 4–7.

Watts, S., Shankaranarayanan, G., & Even, A. (2009). Data quality assessment in context: A cognitive perspective. *Decision Support Systems*, *48*(1), 202–211. doi:10.1016/j.dss.2009.07.012

Weber, C., Hendrickson, C., Jaramillo, P., Matthews, S., Nagengast, A., & Nealer, R. (2008). *Life cycle comparison of traditional retail and e-commerce logistics for electronic products: A case study of buy.com*. Green Design Institute, Carnegie Mellon University.

Wei, H. S., & Wang, E. T. G. (2007). Creating Strategic Value from Supply Chain Visibility - the Dynamic Capabilities View. *Proc. 40th Hawaii Int. Conf. System Sci.*, 7. doi:10.1109/HICSS.2007.157

Wei, J., Govindan, K., Li, Y., & Zhao, J. (2015). Pricing and collecting decisions in a closed-loop supply chain with symmetric and asymmetric information. *Computers & Operations Research*, *54*, 257–265. doi:10.1016/j.cor.2013.11.021

Welsh, B. P., & Farrington, D. P. (2009). Public Area CCTV and Crime Prevention: An Update Systematic Review and Meta-Analysis. *Justice Quarterly*, *26*(4), 716–745. doi:10.1080/07418820802506206

Williams, E., & Tagami, T. (2002). Energy Use in Sales and Distribution via E-Commerce and Conventional Retail: A Case Study of the Japanese Book Sector. *Journal of Industrial Ecology*, *6*(2), 99–114.

Williamson, O. (1996). *The Mechanisms of Governance*. New York: Oxford University Press.

Wilson, H., & Daniel, E. (2007). The multi-channel challenge: A dynamic capability approach. *Industrial Marketing Management*, *36*(1), 10–20. doi:10.1016/j.indmarman.2006.06.015

Wixom, B. H., & Ross, J. W. (2017). How to Monetize Your Data, MIT Sloan Management Review. *Spring Issue*, *58*(3), 10–13.

Wolfinbarger, M., & Gilly, M. C. (2003). eTailQ: Dimensionalizing, measuring and predicting etail quality. *Journal of Retailing*, *79*(3), 183–198. doi:10.1016/S0022-4359(03)00034-4

World Economic Forum. (2013). *Outlook on the Logistics and Supply Chain Industry 2013*. Geneva: World Economic Forum.

World Economic Forum. (2016). *The Global Risks 2016* (11th ed.). Geneva: World Economic Forum.

Xu, Z., Pokharel, S., Elomri, A., & Mutlu, F. (2017). Emission policies and their analysis for the design of hybrid and dedicated closed-loop supply chains. *Journal of Cleaner Production*, *142*, 4152–4168. doi:10.1016/j.jclepro.2016.09.192

Yadav, R. (2012). *Next Generation Loyalty Management Systems: Trends, Challenges, and Recommendation*. Capgemini.com.

Yadav, R., & Kumar, T. (2015). Usage of Big Data Analytics for Customer Relationship Management. *Inter. J. Adva. Res. Computer Sci.*, *6*(2).

Yan, R. (2009). Product categories, returns policy and pricing strategy for e-marketers. *Journal of Product & Brand Management*, *18*(6), 452–460.

Yang, G., Wang, Z., & Li, X. (2009). The optimization of the closed-loop supply chain network. *Transportation Research Part E, Logistics and Transportation Review*, *45*(1), 16–28. doi:10.1016/j.tre.2008.02.007

Yang, Z., Aydin, G., Babich, V., & Beil, D. R. (2009). Supply disruptions, asymmetric information, and a backup production option. *Management Science*, *55*(2), 192–209. doi:10.1287/mnsc.1080.0943

Yao, Kurata, & Mukhopadhyay. (2008). Incentives to reliable order fulfillment for an Internet drop-shipping supply chain. *Int. J. Production Economics*, *113*, 324-334.

Yilmaz, A., Javed, O., & Shah, M. (2006). Object Tracking: A Survey. *ACM Computing Surveys*, *38*(4), 13, es. doi:10.1145/1177352.1177355

Yu, C.-C., & Wang, C.-S. (2008). A hybrid mining approach for optimizing returns policies in e-retailing. *Expert Systems with Applications, 35*(4), 1575–1582.

Yumurtacı, I. Ö., & Oflaç, B. S. (2016). Supply chain management practices in retail: The trends and future perspective. In B. Christiansen (Ed.), *Handbook of research on global supply chain management* (pp. 366–378). Hershey, PA: IGI Global. doi:10.4018/978-1-4666-9639-6.ch021

Zaidenberg, S., Boulay, B., & Bremond, F. (2012). A Generic Framework for Video Understanding Applied to Group Behaviour Recognition. *Proceedings of the IEEE Ninth International Conference on Advanced Video and Signal-Based Surveillance (AVSS 2012)*, 126-142.

Zarandi, M. H. F., Sisakht, A., & Davari, S. (2011). Design of a closed-loop supply chain (CLSC) model using an interactive fuzzy goal programming. *International Journal of Advanced Manufacturing Technology, 56*(5), 809–821. doi:10.1007/s00170-011-3212-y

Zeithaml, V. A., Berry, L. L., & Parasuraman, A. (1990). *Delivering quality service: Balancing customer perceptions and expectations*. New York: Free Press.

Zeithaml, V. A., Berry, L. L., & Parasuraman, A. (1993). The nature and determinants of customer expectations of service. *Journal of the Academy of Marketing Science, 21*(1), 1–12. doi:10.1177/0092070393211001

Zhalechian, M., Tavakkoli-Moghaddam, R., Zahiri, B., & Mohammadi, M. (2016). Sustainable design of a closed-loop location-routing-inventory supply chain network under mixed uncertainty. *Transportation Research Part E, Logistics and Transportation Review, 89*, 182–214. doi:10.1016/j.tre.2016.02.011

Zhan, B., Monekosso, D. N., Remagnino, P., Velastin, S. A., & Xu, L. Q. (2008). Crowd Analysis: A Survey. *Machine Vision and Applications, 19*(5-6), 345–357. doi:10.1007/s00138-008-0132-4

Zhang, D., Zhou, X., Leung, S. C., & Zheng, J. (2010). Vertical bagging decision trees model for credit scoring. *Expert Systems with Applications, 37*(12), 7838–7843.

Zhang, C., & Zhang, C. (2007). Design and simulation of demand information sharing in a supply chain. *Simulation Modelling Practice and Theory, 15*(1), 32–46. doi:10.1016/j.simpat.2006.09.011

Zhang, X., van Donk, D. P., & van der Vaart, T. (2011). Does ICT influence supply chain management and performance? a review of survey-based research. *International Journal of Operations & Production Management, 31*(11), 1215–1247. doi:10.1108/01443571111178501

Zohal, M., & Soleimani, H. (2016). Developing an ant colony approach for green closed-loop supply chain network design: A case study in gold industry. *Journal of Cleaner Production, 133*, 314–337. doi:10.1016/j.jclepro.2016.05.091

Zsidisin, G. A. (2003). A Grounded Definition of Supply Risk. *J. Pur. & Sup. Man., 9*(5-6), 217–224. doi:10.1016/j.pursup.2003.07.002

Zsidisin, G. A., & Ritchie, B. (2009). Supply Chain Risk Management-Developments, Issues and Challenges. In G. A. Zsidisin & B. Ritchie (Eds.), *Supply Chain Risk: A Handbook of Assessment, Management, and Performance* (pp. 1–12). New York: Springer. doi:10.1007/978-0-387-79934-6_1

Zsidisin, G. A., & Ritchie, B. (2009). *Supply Chain Risk: A Handbook of Assessment, Management, and Performance*. New York: Springer. doi:10.1007/978-0-387-79934-6

About the Contributors

Akhilesh Kumar, PhD, is currently working as an Assistant Professor in the Department of Industrial & Systems Engineering at Indian Institute of Technology, Kharagpur. Previously, he worked as a Solution Architect in Consulting Team at JDA Software, Bangalore. He received his B.Tech degree in Manufacturing Engineering from National Institute of Foundry and Forge Technology (India) and Ph.D. degree in Industrial Engineering from Wayne State University (U.S.A.) in the year 2005 and 2011, respectively. His teaching interests include non-linear programming, multivariate statistical models, generalized linear models, machine learning and data analytics. He has authored various courses, lectures and workshops on applied machine learning and data analytics at IIT Kharagpur and other premier institute. He has authored several technical papers. His publications appeared in such journals as International Journal of Production Economics, European Journal of Operational Research, Expert System with Applications, IEEE. He carried out collaborative research with multi-national companies as Ford Motor Company and Delphi Automotive LLP. He has delivered lectures on various topics in companies as TELCON, HAL, McNally Bharat. He also appeared on Marquis Who's Who in America in 2011.

Swapnil Saurav works with JDA Software as Senior Project Manager. Swapnil is an ambitious, creative, and a highly motivated individual, who has a passion for supply chain with focus on retail and manufacturing industries and an uncompromising commitment to quality and outstanding customer service. He has been invited as key note speaker at various industry forums and has a passion for teaching & developing leaders of tomorrow.

* * *

Neeraj Anand is PhD in Management. He has guided various PhD scholars working in the area of Supply chain management and general Management. He has published more than 25 research papers in internal refereed journals. Currently he is the Professor-LSCM and Associate Dean-Research at UPES, Dehradun.

Anju Bharti, PhD, works as an Senior Assistant Professor at Maharaja Agrasen Institute of Technology, Rohini, Delhi from last ten yrs. my area is in marketing, values and ethics in business, CSR, environmental studies, etc. Dr. Bharti also worked as sales executive in sales and marketing for glaxosmithkline beecham from 1996 to 2004. Awarded PhD and the topic was'Cold chain maintenance for frozen food in selected outlets of Rajasthan'. and M.Phil in 'Environment Impact Assessment'. Published many papers and articles in seminars and conferences of national and International repute.

Habib Chabchoub is a Full Professor and director of Bussiness School ISB Sfax Tunisia. He received his PhD from Laval Unives. His main research concerns the operations management and supply chain management.

Rohit Das is pursuing his MBA from MET Institute of Management, Mumbai. He is a chemical engineer by education and his interests include learning about Supply Chain Management. He loves to read and stay updated with developments happening in supply chain management areas.

Rupali Das is a practicing Periodontist from Hyderabad (India). She has done her Master of Dental Science (MDS) with a specialization in periodontics. She has over 5 years of experience and specializes in bone augmentation procedures, periodontal surgery, laser surgery and implantology. She loves to write on topics related to health.

Sourabh Deshmukh is a Senior Manager in HP Inc. He has over 20 years of work experience in consulting, operations management and analytics based solution development. Sourabh has worked across domains including Supply Chain, Customer Service & Support, Strategic Sourcing, Product Innovation. He is a Mechanical Engineer from NIT Trichy, and has Masters in Industrial Engineering from Texas A&M University, USA. Sourabh currently stays in Bangalore with his family.

François Galasso is an Associate Professor at the University of Toulouse Capitole and Associate researcher at the Industrial Engineering Department of the IMT Mines Albi-Carmaux. He received his PhD in 2007 from Institut National Polytechnique de Toulouse. His main research concerns Supply Chain Planning and Risk Management in Supply Chains.

Kedar P. Joshi is currently working as Associate Professor at T A Pai Management Institute, Maniapl. He holds Fellow (PhD) in the Operations Management Area from IIM Lucknow. His areas of research and interest are Operations Management, Supply Chain Management, Pricing and Revenue Management. He is also an Education Associate with Inchainge for the India and Middle East region. Inchainge is in the world's leading simulations and learning programs in Supply Chain Management and Supply Chain Finance. He holds Masters degree in Production Engineering from Mumbai University and Bachelors engineering in Mechanical Engineering from Shivaji University.

Kijpokin Kasemsap received his BEng degree in Mechanical Engineering from King Mongkut's University of Technology, Thonburi, his MBA degree from Ramkhamhaeng University, and his DBA degree in Human Resource Management from Suan Sunandha Rajabhat University. Dr. Kasemsap is a Special Lecturer in the Faculty of Management Sciences, Suan Sunandha Rajabhat University, based in Bangkok, Thailand. Dr. Kasemsap is a Member of the International Economics Development and Research Center (IEDRC), the International Foundation for Research and Development (IFRD), and the International Innovative Scientific and Research Organization (IISRO). Dr. Kasemsap also serves on the International Advisory Committee (IAC) for the International Association of Academicians and Researchers (INAAR). Dr. Kasemsap is the sole author of over 250 peer-reviewed international publications and book chapters on business, education, and information technology. Dr. Kasemsap is included in the TOP 100 Professionals–2016 and in the 10th edition of 2000 Outstanding Intellectuals of the 21st Century by the International Biographical Centre, Cambridge, England.

Jacques Lamothe is a Full Professor and deputy director at the Industrial Engineering Department of the IMT Mines Albi-Carmaux. He received his PhD in 1996 from Ecole Nationale Supérieure de l'Aéronautique et de l'Espace (Sup'Aero). His main research concerns the design and the control of supply chains.

Arij Lahmar is a PhD student in the field of supply chain management at the University of Sfax.

Arun Mittal, PhD, is an assistant professor at Birla Institute of Technology, Mesra Ranchi, (Deemed Univeristy), Noida Campus. He has around 10 years of experience of teaching General Management and Marketing subjects. His research areas are Retail Management, Advertising and Social Media Marketing. He has published about 15 research papers and articles in the journals of repute. He has produced 2 PhDs and currently guiding 5 PhD scholars in the areas of Social CRM, Luxury Marketing and Social Media Marketing.

Saurav Negi teaches Logistics and Supply Chain Management related subjects like Introduction to Logistics and Supply Chain, Understanding logistics, Retail Logistics at University of Petroleum and Energy Studies, Dehradun, India. He is working in the area of Fresh supply chain. His area of Interests are fresh agro supply chain, retail supply chain, cold chain, etc. He has attended various Intenational and National Conferences including conferences at IIMs and also published various research papers in international journal of repute. He also review papers for some international journals indexed with SCOPUS.

Erkan Özdemir received the Master degree and the PhD degree from the Uludağ University in Turkey. He is currently working as an Assoc. Prof. in the department of business administration at Uludağ University in Turkey. He teaches marketing management, sales management, marketing strategies courses at Uludağ University. His research interests are marketing, consumer behavior, high-tech marketing and innovation. Dr. Özdemir has written three books named as Marketing Strategies to Women Consumers, Marketing Ethics, Marketing of High-Tech Products and Services. He has many published articles in different journals. He also served as an assistant researcher at Uludağ University Technology Transfer Office Project supported by The Scientific and Technological Research Council of Turkey (TÜBİTAK) between 2014 and 2015 and has been in charge of business development and entrepreneurship department at Uludağ University Technology Transfer Office.

Kamalendu Pal is with the Department of Computer Science, School of Mathematics, Computer Science and Engineering, City, University London. Kamalendu received his BSc (Hons) degree in Physics from Calcutta University, India, Postgraduate Diploma in Computer Science from Pune, India; MSc degree in Software Systems Technology from Sheffield University, Postgraduate Diploma in Artificial Intelligence from Kingston University, MPhil degree in Computer Science from University College London, and MBA degree from University of Hull, United Kingdom. He has published dozens of research papers in international journals and conferences. His research interests include knowledge-based systems, decision support systems, computer integrated design, software engineering, and service oriented computing. He is a member of the British Computer Society, the Institution of Engineering and Technology, and the IEEE Computer Society.

Snehil Saurav is a practicing doctor with interest in retail sector. His interest lies in figuring out different ways on how healthcare benefit can be accessed by millions of people without coming to a hospital. He thinks healthcare industry can learn a lot from retail industry so that the care is provided to the remotest of people in a world where healthcare is getting expensive and far from reach of many people.

Harkirat Singh was born in Patiala in 1995. He received the B.Tech degree in Mechanical engineering from the University of Kurukshetra, Haryana India, in 2015 and currently pursuing MBA in Marketing and operations from ICFAI Business School, Hyderabad, India His main areas of research interest are Big Data Analytics, Internet of things, Intelligent video analytics.

Navneet Kumar Singh has more than 6 years of experience. He is an ambitious, creative and highly motivated individual, who has a passion for foreign language and translation study. He developed his interest in eCommerce business domain while working at Amazon. He holds MA French from the English and Foreign languages university, Hyderabad and BA HONS French from Amity University, Noida. Currently he is employed with ecommerce company in Hyderabad, India.

Kumari Smriti is a MBA graduate from IIM Lucknow, Smriti loves to write on subjects related to Marketing areas, Technologies in Business and Supply Chain Management.

Kedareshwaran Subramanian is working as an Assistant Professor in T.A. Pai Management Institute (TAPMI), Manipal in the Operations and Information Science Area. He has over ten years full-time work experience as a business school faculty. Prior to that, he was working in industry for four years in various IT roles such as programmer, business analyst & product manager. He has completed his Bachelors in Engineering in Computers and Post Graduate Diploma in Business Administration with Finance major and Systems minor. Currently he is pursuing his PhD from Manipal University and has completed his proposal defense. His areas of research and teaching include Business Intelligence & Visual Analytics, Marketing Analytics & Enterprise Resource Planning.

Mine Yılmaz is a Ph.D. candidate at Uludag University, in Bursa, Turkey. She received her MBA degree in Business Administration at Middlesex University in London, 2014. Her research interests include international marketing and online marketing. She also gives marketing, e-marketing, international marketing lectures as a guest lecturer at Uludag University, Vocational School of Social Sciences in Bursa, Turkey since 2016, January.

Index

J

K

L

M

N

O

P

Q

R

S

T

U

V

W

Stay Current on the Latest Emerging Research Developments

Become an IGI Global Reviewer for Authored Book Projects

The overall success of an authored book project is dependent on quality and timely reviews.

In this competitive age of scholarly publishing, constructive and timely feedback significantly decreases the turnaround time of manuscripts from submission to acceptance, allowing the publication and discovery of progressive research at a much more expeditious rate. Several IGI Global authored book projects are currently seeking highly qualified experts in the field to fill vacancies on their respective editorial review boards:

Applications may be sent to:
development@igi-global.com

Applicants must have a doctorate (or an equivalent degree) as well as publishing and reviewing experience. Reviewers are asked to write reviews in a timely, collegial, and constructive manner. All reviewers will begin their role on an ad-hoc basis for a period of one year, and upon successful completion of this term can be considered for full editorial review board status, with the potential for a subsequent promotion to Associate Editor.

If you have a colleague that may be interested in this opportunity, we encourage you to share this information with them.

www.ingramcontent.com/pod-product-compliance
Lightning Source LLC
LaVergne TN
LVHW062122300926
849161LV00010B/2520